Start with Science TOOLKIT

The **Start with Science TOOLKIT** is a valuable resource for teachers to have at their fingertips. It enhances an understanding of science and science teaching skills, and stimulates an appreciation of science.

The resource book, **Start with Science**, is a guide to inquiry-based science, written by Dr. Jean Shaw and Dr. Debby Chessin for the K-8 teacher. With this book, you are encouraged to:

- brainstorm about the uses of science tools,
- learn about the history of the tools,
- perform "hands-on" investigations,
- experience teamwork,
- share and reflect on students' discoveries,
- interpret data, and
- **make connections with the Benchmarks of Science Literacy and the National Science Education Standards.**

Start with Science includes eight modules using a variety of tools to learn and teach more about physical science, life science, earth science, and environmental science.

The complete **Start with Science TOOLKIT** includes not only this excellent science resource book, but also a roomy attaché with shoulder strap and hand-grip, and science tools that are correlated to the eight units in the resource book.

The **Start with Science TOOLKIT** includes the following science tools:

Hand Lens 3x/6x plastic lens

Medicine Dropper Plastic with 2 ml capacity and rubber bulb

Forceps Nickel plated

Petri Dishes two plastic dishes

Graduated Cylinder 50 ml polypropylene with easy to-read markings

Student Thermometers two with red alcohol, white vinyl backing and dual scales

Vials six 40 ml with self-sealing caps

Testing Papers Red and blue litmus filter papers

Funnel 3" plastic

Mineral Specimens Set of four: talc, calcite, quartz, and corundum

Ceramic Streak Plate

Prism and Mirrors one 1/2" right angle plastic prism and two 2 1/4" x 3 1/2" mirrors

Batteries, Bulbs, Sockets, and Wire two D-cell batteries and battery holders, 2 bulb sockets and 2 bulbs, and 25 ft wire

Magnets four donut and two bar magnets, 8 oz. iron filings

Adult Safety Goggles Impact resistant

Start with Science TOOLKIT

MK9807-087001

Retail Value	$68.00
Special College Price	$34.00

ELEMENTARY AND MIDDLE SCHOOL MATHEMATICS

TEACHING DEVELOPMENTALLY

THIRD EDITION

JOHN A. VAN DE WALLE

Virginia Commonwealth University

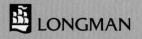 LONGMAN

An Imprint of Addison Wesley Longman, Inc.

New York • Reading, Massachusetts • Menlo Park, California • Harlow, England
Don Mills, Ontario • Sydney • Mexico City • Madrid • Amsterdam

Acquisitions Editor: Virginia L. Blanford
Development Manager: Arlene Bessenoff
Project Editor: Ellen MacElree
Design Manager and Text Designer: Wendy Ann Fredericks
Cover Designer: Kay Petronio
Art Studio: ElectraGraphics, Inc.
Electronic Production Manager: Su Levine
Desktop Administrator: Laura Leever
Senior Manufacturing Manager: Willie Lane
Electronic Page Makeup: Laura Leever
Printer and Binder: Courier Companies, Inc.
Cover Printer: The Lehigh Press, Inc.

Library of Congress Cataloging-in-Publication Data

Van de Walle, John A.
    Elementary and middle school mathematics : teaching
developmentally / John A. Van de Walle. --3rd ed.
        p.   cm.
    Rev. ed. of: Elementary school mathematics. 2nd ed. ©1994.
    Includes bibliographical references and index.
    ISBN 0-8013-1866-1
    1. Mathematics--Study and teaching (Elementary) 2. Mathmematics-
-Study and teaching (Middle school)   I. Van de Walle, John A.
Elementary school mathematics.   II. Title.
QA135.5.V34   1997
510′.71′2--dc21   97-21802
                                                               CIP

Copyright © 1998 by Addison Wesley Longman, Inc.

ISBN 0-8013-1866-1
    2345678910—CRK—009998

Contents in Brief

Contents   vi
Preface   xvii

SECTION 1
FOUNDATIONS OF TEACHING MATHEMATICS   1

1. Teaching Mathematics: Reflections and Directions   3

2. Exploring What It Means to Do Mathematics   10

3. Developing Understanding in Mathematics   22

4. Teaching Through Problem Solving   39

5. Building Assessment into Instruction   62

SECTION 2
DEVELOPMENT OF MATHEMATICAL CONCEPTS AND PROCEDURES   91

6. Developing Number Concepts and Number Sense   93

7. Developing Meanings for the Operations   117

8. Helping Children Master the Basic Facts   140

9. Whole-Number Place-Value Development   162

10. Mental Computation and Estimation   190

11. Pencil-and-Paper Computation with Whole Numbers   213

12. Developing Fraction Concepts   237

13. Computation with Fractions   260

14. Decimal and Percent Concepts and Decimal Computation   274

15. Developing Concepts of Ratio and Proportion   292

16. Developing Measurement Concepts   310

17. Geometric Thinking and Geometric Concepts   342

18. Logical Reasoning: Attribute and Pattern Activities   392

19. Exploring Concepts of Probability and Statistics   408

20. Preparing for Algebra   436

21. Functions and Variables   457

SECTION 3
ISSUES AND PERSPECTIVES   481

22. Planning for Effective Instruction   483

23. Teaching All Children Mathematics   501

24. Technology and School Mathematics   517

Appendix A   Curriculum and Evaluation Standards for School Mathematics   A-1

Appendix B   Professional Standards for Teaching Mathematics   A-8

References   R-1
    Children's Literature   R-8
Index   I-1
Blackline Masters and Materials Construction Tips   BL-1

CONTENTS

Preface   xvii

SECTION 1
FOUNDATIONS OF TEACHING MATHEMATICS   1

CHAPTER 1
TEACHING MATHEMATICS: REFLECTIONS AND DIRECTIONS   3

The Revolution in School Mathematics   3
Forces Driving the Revolution   4
    The Demands of Society   4
    The Influence of Technology   4
    The Direction of NCTM   4
The Curriculum and Evaluation Standards for School Mathematics   5
    What Are the Curriculum Standards?   5
    The Vision of the Standards   5
    The Four "Theme" Standards   5
    The Evaluation Standards   5
The Professional Standards for Teaching Mathematics   6
    Five Shifts in Classroom Environment   6
    Mathematics for All Students   7
    Teaching Standards   7
The Assessment Standards for School Mathematics   7
Teaching Mathematics   7
    An Invitation to Learn   7

REFLECTIONS ON CHAPTER 1: WRITING TO LEARN   8
FOR DISCUSSION AND EXPLORATION   8
SUGGESTED READINGS   8

CHAPTER 2
EXPLORING WHAT IT MEANS TO DO MATHEMATICS   10

Changing Perceptions and New Goals   10
    Traditional Views of School Mathematics   10
    Mathematics as a Science of Pattern and Order   11
    New Goals for Students   11
    All Mathematics Can Be Understood   12

What Does It Mean to Do Mathematics?   12
    The Verbs of Doing Mathematics   13
    An Environment for Doing Mathematics   13
An Invitation to Do Mathematics   13
    Let's Do Some Mathematics!   13
    No Answer Book   18
    Some More Explorations   18
The Teacher's Role   19

REFLECTIONS ON CHAPTER 2: WRITING TO LEARN   20
FOR DISCUSSION AND EXPLORATION   20
SUGGESTED READINGS   20

CHAPTER 3
DEVELOPING UNDERSTANDING IN MATHEMATICS   22

A Constructivist View of Learning   22
    Constructing Understanding   22
    Constructing Knowledge: Some Examples   22
    Principles of Constructivism   25
Knowledge of Mathematics   25
    Conceptual Knowledge of Mathematics   25
    Procedural Knowledge of Mathematics   26
    The Role of Procedural Knowledge   27
Understanding Mathematics   27
    Relational Versus Instrumental Understanding   27
    Benefits of Relational Understanding   29
The Role of Models in Developing Understanding   30
    Models for Mathematical Concepts   30
    Using Models in the Classroom   33
Teaching Developmentally   33
    Foundations of a Developmental Approach   33
    Strategies for Effective Teaching   34
    Reflecting on Student Activities   35

REFLECTIONS ON CHAPTER 3: WRITING TO LEARN   37
FOR DISCUSSION AND EXPLORATION   37
SUGGESTED READINGS   37

CHAPTER 4
TEACHING THROUGH PROBLEM SOLVING   39

A General Framework for Problem Solving   39
    Problems and Performance Tasks   39
    Pólya's Four Phases of Problem Solving   40

Teaching Mathematics Is a Problem-Solving
    Endeavor   41
    Understanding Your Goals   41
    Planning the Tasks   42
    Implementing Your Plan   42
    Looking Back   42
Teaching Actions Before, During, and After
    the Problem   42
    Before Actions   42
    During Actions   44
    After Actions   46
Finding Tasks and Problems   47
    Story or Word Problems   48
    A New Concept   48
    Computation   48
    Translations   48
    Manipulative Tasks   49
    Created Problems   49
    Children's Literature   50
    Open Exploration   50
    Explanations and Error Analysis   50
Teaching About Problem Solving   50
    Strategies and Processes for Problem Solving   51
    Metacognition and Problem Solving   51
    Affective Factors and Problem Solving   51
Achieving Problem-Solving Goals While Students
    Learn   52
    A Perspective on Teaching About Problem Solving   52
    Developing Problem-Solving Strategies   53
    Developing Metacognitive Habits   58
    Attending to Affective Goals   58
Assessment Reflects Goals and Values   59
REFLECTIONS ON CHAPTER 4: WRITING TO LEARN   59
FOR DISCUSSION AND EXPLORATION   60
SUGGESTED READINGS   60

CHAPTER 5
BUILDING ASSESSMENT
INTO INSTRUCTION   62

The *Assessment Standards*   62
    What Is Assessment?   62
    Six Assessment Standards   62
    Purposes of Assessment   63
What Should Be Assessed?   65
    Mathematical Power   65
    Concepts and Procedures   66
Combining Instruction and Assessment   66
    Performance Tasks   66
    Examples of Performance Tasks   67
Collecting Data from Performance Tasks   71
    Performance Indicators and Rubrics   71
    More Examples of Rubrics   72

Observation of Performance Tasks   75
Other Assessment Options   76
    Listening Requires Good Questions   76
    Writing and Journals   78
    Student Self-Assessment   80
    Tests   82
Portfolios in the Assessment Plan   83
    Portfolio Content Suggestions   83
    Portfolio Management   85
Diagnostic Interviews   85
    Reasons to Consider an Interview   85
    Planning an Interview   85
    Suggestions for Effective Interviews   86
Grading   86
    Confronting the Myth   86
    Grading Issues   87

REFLECTIONS ON CHAPTER 5: WRITING TO LEARN   88
FOR DISCUSSION AND EXPLORATION   88
SUGGESTED READINGS   89

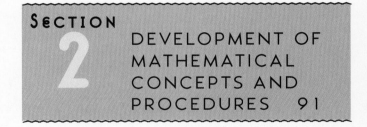

SECTION
2
DEVELOPMENT OF
MATHEMATICAL
CONCEPTS AND
PROCEDURES   91

CHAPTER 6
DEVELOPING NUMBER CONCEPTS
AND NUMBER SENSE   93

Early Number Sense   93
The Beginnings of Number Concepts   94
    Counting   94
    The Relationships of More, Less, and Same   95
    Procedural Knowledge of Numbers   97
    Numeral Writing and Recognition   97
    Oral Counting   97
    Counting Sets   98
Development of Relationships Among Numbers 1
    Through 10   99
    A Collection of Number Relationships   100
    Spatial Relationships: Patterned Set
        Recognition   100
    One and Two More, One and Two Less   101
    Anchoring Numbers to 5 and 10   103
    Part-Part-Whole Relationships   104
    Dot Card Activities   108
Relationships for Numbers 10 to 20   109
    A Pre-Place-Value Relationship with 10   109

Extending More and Less Relationships   110
Double and Near-Double Relationships   110
Number Sense and the Real World   111
Estimation and Measuring   111
More Connections   111
Graphs   112
Literature Connections   112
Anno's Counting House (Anno, 1982)   113
The Very Hungry Caterpillar (Carle, 1969)   113
Two Ways to Count to Ten (Dee, 1988)   113
Extensions to Early Mental Mathematics   114
REFLECTIONS ON CHAPTER 6: WRITING TO LEARN   115
FOR DISCUSSION AND EXPLORATION   115
SUGGESTED READINGS   115

CHAPTER 7
DEVELOPING MEANINGS
FOR THE OPERATIONS   117

Two Sources of Operation Meanings   117
Operation Meanings from Word Problems   117
Basic Meanings Developed with Models   118
Translations: Models, Words, and Symbols   118
Word Problems for Addition and Subtraction   119
Examples of Problems for Each Structure   120
Reflections on the Four Problem Types   121
Using Addition and Subtraction Word Problems in the
Classroom   121
Models for Addition and Subtraction   122
Models for Part-Part-Whole Meanings   122
Models for Comparison Meanings   124
The Order Property and the Zero Property   125
Word Problems for Multiplication and Division   126
Examples of Problems for Each Structure   126
Reflections on Multiplicative Problems   129
Notation, Language, and Remainders   129
Using Multiplication and Division Word Problems in the
Classroom   130
Models for Multiplication and Division   131
Multiplication and Division Activities   131
Useful Multiplication and Division Properties   133
Story Problems in the Upper Grades   134
Dealing with Large Numbers in Problems   134
Two-Step Problems   135
Assessment Notes   136
Literature Connections   137
How Many Snails? (Giganti, 1992)   137
More than One (Hoban, 1981)   137
Each Orange Had 8 Slices (Giganti, 1992)   137
REFLECTIONS ON CHAPTER 7: WRITING TO LEARN   138
FOR DISCUSSION AND EXPLORATION   138
SUGGESTED READINGS   138

CHAPTER 8
HELPING CHILDREN
MASTER THE BASIC FACTS   140

A Three-Step Approach to Fact Mastery   140
The Role of Number and Operation Concepts   141
Development of Efficient Strategies   141
Drill of Efficient Methods and Strategy Selection   142
Overview of the Approach   142
Strategies for Addition Facts   143
One-More-Than and Two-More-Than Facts   143
Facts with Zero   144
Doubles   145
Near Doubles   145
Make-10 Facts   147
Other Strategies and the Last Six Facts   148
Strategies for Subtraction Facts   149
Subtraction as Think-Addition   149
Subtraction Facts with Sums to 10   150
The 36 "Hard" Subtraction Facts: Sums Greater
than 10   150
Strategies for Multiplication Facts   153
Doubles   154
Fives Facts   154
Zeros and Ones   154
Nifty Nines   155
Helping Facts   156
Division Facts and "Near Facts"   157
Making It Work   157
Three Steps to Success   158
What About Timed Tests?   158
Facts No Barrier to Good Mathematics   159
Fact Remediation with Upper-Grade Students   159
REFLECTIONS ON CHAPTER 8: WRITING TO LEARN   160
FOR DISCUSSION AND EXPLORATION   160
SUGGESTED READINGS   160

CHAPTER 9
WHOLE-NUMBER PLACE-VALUE
DEVELOPMENT   162

Early Development of Place-Value Ideas   163
Number Ideas Before Place Value   163
Basic Ideas of Place Value   163
A Relational Understanding   165
Models for Place Value   165
Base 10 Models and the Ten-Makes-One
Relationship   166
Developing Place-Value Concepts and
Procedures   168
Grouping Activities   168
Oral Names for Numbers   172
Written Symbols   174

Number Sense Development   177
   Relative Magnitude   177
   Connections to Real-World Ideas   178
   Approximate Numbers and Rounding   178
   Looking Toward Computation   180
Numbers Beyond 1000   183
   Extending the Place-Value System   183
   Conceptualizing Large Numbers   184
Literature Connections   185
   Moira's Birthday (Munsch, 1987)   186
   How to Count like a Martian (St. John, 1975)   186
   The King's Commissioners (Friedman, 1994)   186
   A Million Fish . . . More or Less (McKissack, 1992)   186
Assessment Notes   186
   Ongoing Assessment   186
   Diagnosis of Place-Value Concepts   187
REFLECTIONS ON CHAPTER 9: WRITING TO LEARN   188
FOR DISCUSSION AND EXPLORATION   188
SUGGESTED READINGS   189

Estimation Exercises   205
   Calculator Activities   205
   Computer Programs   207
   Activities for the Overhead Projector   207
Estimating with Fractions, Decimals, and
   Percents   208
Literature Connections   208
   Cookies (Jaspersohn, 1993)   209
   Is a Blue Whale the Biggest Thing There Is?
   (Wells, 1993)   209
   The 329th Friend (Sharmat, 1979)   209
Assessment Notes   209
   Ongoing Assessment   209
   Occasional Interviews   210
REFLECTIONS ON CHAPTER 10: WRITING
   TO LEARN   210
FOR DISCUSSION AND EXPLORATION   211
SUGGESTED READINGS   211

CHAPTER 10
MENTAL COMPUTATION AND ESTIMATION   190

Alternative Forms of Computation   190
   Real-World Choosing   191
   Contrasts with Traditional Algorithms   192
Mental Methods in the Curriculum   192
   Learning and Selecting Methods   192
   Scope and Sequence   193
Mental Addition and Subtraction   194
   Adding and Subtracting Tens and Hundreds   194
   Higher-Decade Addition and Subtraction Facts   194
   Front-End Approaches for Addition   195
   Flexible Approaches for Subtraction   195
   Working with Nice Numbers   196
   Compatible Numbers   196
Mental Multiplication   197
   Factors with Zeros   197
   Front-End Multiplying   197
   Compensation with Eights and Nines   198
   Halve and Double   198
Mental Division   198
   Zeros in Division   199
   Working by Parts   199
   Missing-Factor Practice   199
Computational Estimation   200
   Teaching Estimation   200
   An Early Estimation Alternative   200
Computational Estimation Strategies   201
   Front-End Methods   202
   Rounding Methods   202
   Using Compatible Numbers   203

CHAPTER 11
PENCIL-AND-PAPER COMPUTATION WITH WHOLE NUMBERS   213

Pencil-and-Paper Methods in Perspective   213
   Algorithms Outside the Classroom   213
   Student-Invented Methods   214
   Guiding the Traditional Algorithms   215
   A Constructivist Alternative   215
Readiness Activities: Trading   215
Developing the Addition Algorithm   217
   Explorations and Invented Algorithms   217
   Directed Development of an Addition Algorithm   218
Developing the Subtraction Algorithm   220
   Explorations and Invented Algorithms   220
   Directed Development of a Subtraction
   Algorithm   220
Developing the Multiplication Algorithm   221
   Explorations and Invented Algorithms   221
   Directed Development of a Multiplication
   Algorithm   223
   One-Digit Multipliers   223
   Two-Digit Multipliers   223
   A Repeated Addition Development   227
Developing a Division Algorithm   228
   Explorations and Invented Algorithms   228
   Directed Development of a Division Algorithm   230
   Two-Digit Divisors   233
Assessment Notes   234
REFLECTIONS ON CHAPTER 11:
   WRITING TO LEARN   235
FOR DISCUSSION AND EXPLORATION   235
SUGGESTED READINGS   235

CHAPTER 12
DEVELOPING FRACTION CONCEPTS   237

Fractions in the Curriculum   237
Three Categories of Fraction Models   238
   Region or Area Models   238
   Length or Measurement Models   239
   Set Models   240
Developing the Concept of Fractional Parts   240
   Constructing Fractional Parts   241
   Connecting Concepts with Symbolism   243
   Exercises with Parts and Wholes   245
Fraction Number Sense   248
   Flexibility with Fractional Parts   248
   Close to Zero, One-Half, and One   249
   Thinking About Which Is More   250
   Other Methods of Comparison   252
   Estimation   252
Equivalent-Fraction Concepts   253
   Concepts Versus Rules   253
   Finding Different Names for Fractions   253
   Developing an Equivalent-Fraction Algorithm   256
Literature Connections   257
   The Doorbell Rang (Hutchins, 1986)   257
   Gator Pie (Mathews, 1979)   257
   The Man Who Counted: A Collection of Mathematical Adventures (Tahan, 1993)   257

REFLECTIONS ON CHAPTER 12: WRITING TO LEARN   257
FOR DISCUSSION AND EXPLORATION   258
SUGGESTED READINGS   258

CHAPTER 13
COMPUTATION WITH FRACTIONS   260

Number Sense and Fraction Algorithms   260
   The Danger of Rules   261
   A Number Sense Approach   261
Addition and Subtraction   261
   Informal Exploration   261
   Developing the Algorithm   263
   Mixed Numbers   264
Multiplication   265
   Informal Exploration   265
   Developing the Algorithm   265
Division   269
   Concept Exploration   269
   Developing the Algorithms   271

REFLECTIONS ON CHAPTER 13: WRITING TO LEARN   272
FOR DISCUSSION AND EXPLORATION   273
SUGGESTED READINGS   273

CHAPTER 14
DECIMAL AND PERCENT CONCEPTS AND DECIMAL COMPUTATION   274

Connecting Two Different Representational Systems   274
   Base 10 Fractions   275
   Extending the Place-Value System   276
   Making the Fraction-Decimal Connection   279
Developing Decimal Number Sense   280
   Familiar Fractions Connected to Decimals   281
   Approximation with a Nice Fraction   282
   Ordering Decimal Numbers   282
   Other Fraction-Decimal Equivalents   283
Introducing Percents   284
   A Third Operator System   284
   Realistic Percent Problems   285
Computation with Decimals   287
   The Role of Estimation   287
   Addition and Subtraction   288
   Multiplication and Division   288
Literature Connections   289
   The Phantom Tollbooth (Juster, 1961)   289
Assessment Notes   290

REFLECTIONS ON CHAPTER 14: WRITING TO LEARN   290
FOR DISCUSSION AND EXPLORATION   290
SUGGESTED READINGS   291

CHAPTER 15
DEVELOPING CONCEPTS OF RATIO AND PROPORTION   292

Proportional Reasoning   292
   Examples of Ratios in Different Contexts   293
   Proportions   294
   Proportional Reasoning and Children   294
Informal Activities to Develop Proportional Reasoning   296
   Selection of Equivalent Ratios   297
   Scaling Activities   299
   Construction and Measurement Activities   300
Solving Proportions   303
   An Informal Approach   303
   The Cross-Product Algorithm   304
   Percent Problems as Proportions   305
Literature Connections   307
   How Big? How Fast? How Hungry? (Waverly, 1990)   307
   Counting on Frank (Clement, 1991)   307
   The Borrowers (Norton, 1953)   307
Assessment Notes   307

REFLECTIONS ON CHAPTER 15: WRITING TO LEARN   308
FOR DISCUSSION AND EXPLORATION   308
SUGGESTED READINGS   308

CHAPTER 16

DEVELOPING MEASUREMENT
CONCEPTS   310

The Meaning and Process of Measuring   310
Developing Measurement Concepts and Skills   311
   A General Plan of Instruction   312
   Informal Units and Standard Units: Reasons for Using
      Each   313
   The Role of Estimation in Learning
      Measurement   313
   Helping Children with Measurement Estimates   314
   The Approximate Nature of Measurement   314
   Suggested Measurement Sequence   314
Measuring Length   315
   Comparison Activities   315
   Using Units of Length   315
   Two Units and Fractional Parts of Units   316
   Making and Using Rulers   317
Measuring Area   318
   Comparison Activities   318
   Using Units of Area   320
   Using Grids   321
Measuring Volume and Capacity   322
   Comparison Activities   322
   Using Units of Volume   323
   Making and Using Measuring Cups   323
Measuring Weight and Mass   323
   Making Comparisons   323
   Using Units of Weight or Mass   324
   Making and Using a Scale   324
Measuring Angles   325
   Comparing Angles   325
   Using Units of Angular Measure   325
   Making a Protractor   325
Introducing Standard Units   326
   Instructional Goals   326
   Important Standard Units   329
Estimating Measures   330
   Techniques of Measurement Estimation   330
   Tips for Teaching Estimation   331
   Measurement Estimation Activities   331
Developing Formulas   331
   Common Difficulties   332
   Areas of Simple Plane Shapes   333
   Volumes of Common Solid Shapes   335
Time and Clock Reading   336
   Measuring Time   336
   Clock Reading   337

Assessment Notes   338
   Focus on Ideas   338
   Standard Units   339
   Formulas   339
Literature Connections   339
   How Big Is a Foot? (Myller, 1990)   339
   Jim and the Beanstalk (Briggs, 1970)   339
   Counting on Frank (Clement, 1991)   339
   8,000 Stones (Wolkstein, 1972)   340
REFLECTIONS ON CHAPTER 16: WRITING TO LEARN   340
FOR DISCUSSION AND EXPLORATION   340
SUGGESTED READINGS   340

CHAPTER 17

GEOMETRIC THINKING
AND GEOMETRIC CONCEPTS   342

Three Exploratory Activities   342
   Reflections on the Activities   343
   Geometry Activities Are Problem-Solving
      Activities   344
   Geometry Activities and Hands-On Materials   344
Informal Geometry   344
   What Is Informal Geometry?   344
   Why Study Geometry?   345
The Development of Geometric Thinking   345
   The van Hiele Levels of Geometric Thought   345
   Characteristics of the Levels of Thought   347
   Implications for Instruction   347
Informal Geometry Activities: Level 0   349
   Exploring Shapes and Properties   349
   Constructing Shapes   352
   Geometric Problem-Solving Activities   356
   Tessellations   360
Informal Geometry Activities: Level 1   361
   Transitions to Level 1   361
   Classifying Shapes by Properties   361
   Constructing and Measuring Shapes   364
   Exploring Special Properties and Relationships   370
   Geometric Problem-Solving Activities   376
   Tessellations Revisited   377
Informal Geometry Activities: Level 2   378
   Definitions and Properties   379
   Informal Proofs   379
Informal Geometry on the Computer   383
   Computer Versions of Geometric Models   383
   Tools to Explore Relationships   384
   Logo and Informal Geometry   385
Assessment Notes   387
   What to Assess   387
   Clarifying Your Geometry Objectives   388
   Mathematical Power in Geometry   389
   Putting It All Together   389

REFLECTIONS ON CHAPTER 17: WRITING TO LEARN   390
FOR DISCUSSION AND EXPLORATION   390
SUGGESTED READINGS   390

CHAPTER 18
LOGICAL REASONING: ATTRIBUTE AND PATTERN ACTIVITIES   392

Objectives of Attribute and Pattern Activities   392
   Strategy Goals   392
   Metacognitive Goals   393
   Affective Goals   393
Attribute Materials and Activities   393
   Attribute Materials   393
   Activities with Attribute Materials   394
Repeating Patterns   399
   Using Materials in Patterning   399
   Repeating-Pattern Activities   399
   Two-Dimensional Patterns   401
Growing Patterns   401
Other Patterns to Explore   402
   The Fibonacci Sequence   402
   Numeric Patterns   403
   Patterns with the Calculator   403
Literature Connections   406
   Frog and Toad Are Friends (Lobal, 1970)   406
   Pattern (Pluckrose, 1988)   406
   Anno's Mysterious Multiplying Jar
     (Anno & Anno, 1983)   406

REFLECTIONS ON CHAPTER 18: WRITING TO LEARN   406
FOR DISCUSSION AND EXPLORATION   407
SUGGESTED READINGS   407

CHAPTER 19
EXPLORING CONCEPTS OF PROBABILITY AND STATISTICS   408

Probability and Statistics in Schools   408
Introduction to Probability   409
   Two Experiments   409
   Theoretical Versus Experimental Probability   409
   Implications for Instruction   410
Developing Probability Concepts   410
   Early Concepts of Chance   411
   Determining Probabilities for Simple Events   411
   Random Numbers and Electronic Devices   412
   Experiments with Two or More Independent
     Events   413
   Theoretical Probabilities with an Area Model   415
   Exploring Dependent Events   415
Simulations   417

Gathering and Making Sense of Data   418
Graphical Representations   419
   Bar Graphs   420
   Stem-and-Leaf Plots   422
   Continuous Data Graphs   423
   Circle Graphs   424
Descriptive Statistics   425
   Averages   425
   Box-and-Whisker Plots   425
   Understanding the Mean   427
Scatter Plots and Relationships   428
   Scatter Plots   429
   Best-Fit Lines   430
   Thinking About Functional Relationships   432
   Ideas for Investigations   432
Assessment Notes   433
   Probability   433
   Statistics   433

REFLECTIONS ON CHAPTER 19: WRITING TO LEARN   434
FOR DISCUSSION AND EXPLORATION   434
SUGGESTED READINGS   434

CHAPTER 20
PREPARING FOR ALGEBRA   436

Exploring Topics in Number Theory   436
   Primes and Factorization   437
   Patterns on a Hundreds Chart   438
   Tests for Divisibility   439
Large Numbers, Small Numbers, and Exponents   440
   Exponents   440
   Using Calculators   440
   Very Large Numbers   442
   Representation of Large Numbers:
     Scientific Notation   442
   Negative Exponents   443
   Very Small Numbers   443
Integer Concepts   444
   Intuitive Examples of Signed Quantities   444
   Mathematical Definition of Negative Numbers   445
Operations with Integers   445
   Models for the Operations   445
   A Problem-Solving Approach   446
   Addition and Subtraction   446
   Multiplication and Division   449
Rational Numbers   450
   Fractions as Indicated Division   450
   Fractions as Rational Numbers   452
Real Numbers   453
   Introducing the Concept of Roots   453
   Real Numbers   453
Literature Connections   454
   The Phantom Tollbooth (Juster, 1961)   454

In One Day (Parker, 1984) 454
Math Curse (Scieszka & Smith, 1995) 454
Assessment Notes 454

REFLECTIONS ON CHAPTER 20: WRITING TO LEARN 455
FOR DISCUSSION AND EXPLORATION 455
SUGGESTED READINGS 455

CHAPTER 21
FUNCTIONS AND VARIABLES 457

Function Concept and Representations 457
    Five Representations of a Function 458
    Developing Function Concepts in the Classroom 461
Functions from Patterns 463
    Materials, Frames, and Tables 463
    Searching for Relationships 464
Functions from the Real World 467
    Relationships Found in the Real World 467
    Proportional Situations 468
    Functions from Formulas 468
    Functions from Scatter Plot Data 470
    Graphs Without Equations 471
Variables 473
    Misunderstandings 473
    Meanings and Uses of Variables 474
    Expressions as Quantities 474
    Evaluating Expressions and Formulas 476
    Solving Equations 477
Assessment Notes 478

REFLECTIONS ON CHAPTER 21: WRITING TO LEARN 478
FOR DISCUSSION AND EXPLORATION 479
SUGGESTED READINGS 479

SECTION 3
ISSUES AND PERSPECTIVES 482

CHAPTER 22
PLANNING FOR EFFECTIVE INSTRUCTION 483

Student-Centered Lessons 483
    Three-Part Structure 483
    Written Work 484
    Minilessons 484
Teacher-Directed Lessons 485
    Two-Part Structure 485

Variations 486
Planning for Diversity 487
    Involve Students in Collaborative Activities 487
    Plan Differentiated Tasks 488
    Use Workstations 488
    Avoid Skill-Oriented Tasks 488
Cooperative Learning Groups 488
    Size and Composition 488
    Developing Productive Group Behavior 489
    Group Recording and Reporting 490
    Assessment of Group Work 490
Writing in the Mathematics Classroom 492
    Value of Writing in Mathematics 492
    Types of Writing Activities 493
    Practical Suggestions 494
Review and Practice 495
    Drill and Practice 495
    Periodic Review 496
Homework 496
    Homework Used for Conceptual Development 496
    Homework Used for Drill 497
    Using Homework in the Classroom 497
Role of the Textbook 497
    How Are Textbooks Developed? 497
    Teacher's Editions 498
    Two-Page Lesson Format 498
    Suggestions for Textbook Use 498

REFLECTIONS ON CHAPTER 22: WRITING TO LEARN 499
FOR DISCUSSION AND EXPLORATION 499
SUGGESTED READINGS 500

CHAPTER 23
TEACHING ALL CHILDREN MATHEMATICS 501

Mathematics for All Children 501
    Diversity in Today's Classroom 501
    Challenging Traditional Beliefs 502
Children with Learning Problems 502
    Categories of Disabilities 503
    Inclusion or Referral? 503
Specific Learning Disabilities 503
    A Perspective on Learning Disabilities 504
    Adaptations for Specific Learning Difficulties 504
Mental Disabilities 506
    Modifications in Instruction 507
    Modifications in Curriculum 507
Multicultural and Social Equity 507
    A Question of Access 507
    Expectations 508
    Examples of What Works 509
From Gender Bias to Gender Equity 510
    Defining the Problem of Gender Inequity 510
    Possible Causes of Gender Inequity 511

Working Toward Gender Equity: What Can
  Be Done? 512
Mathematics for the Gifted and Talented 512
  Identification of the Mathematically Gifted 513
  Acceleration or Enrichment 513
  A Model for Instruction 513
REFLECTIONS ON CHAPTER 23: WRITING TO LEARN 515
FOR DISCUSSION AND EXPLORATION 515
SUGGESTED READINGS 516

CHAPTER 24
TECHNOLOGY AND
SCHOOL MATHEMATICS 517

Technology and Mathematics Education:
  A General Perspective 517
  NCTM'S Position on the Use of Technology 517
  Technology's Threefold Impact on Mathematics
  Education 518
Calculators in the Mathematics Classroom 519
  Reasons for Using Calculators 519
  Practical Considerations Concerning Calculators 521
  Graphing Calculators 522
  When and Where to Use Calculators 523
The Computer as a Tool in Mathematics 523
  Computer Manipulatives as Tools 524
  Spreadsheets 524
  Data Graphing Software 526
  Dynamic Geometry Software 526
  Function Graphers 527
Instructional Software 527
  Drill and Practice 527
  Problem Solving 527
  Concept Instruction 528

Mathematics on the Internet 528
  Professional Information 528
  Lessons and Curriculum 529
  Databases 529
Learning Through Programming 529
  Programming to Learn Mathematics 530
  Programming and Problem-Solving Skills 530
  Problem Solving and the Logo Language 530
  A Brief Look at Logo 531
REFLECTIONS ON CHAPTER 24: WRITING TO LEARN 533
FOR DISCUSSION AND EXPLORATION 533
SUGGESTED READINGS 533

APPENDIX A
CURRICULUM AND EVALUATION
STANDARDS FOR SCHOOL
MATHEMATICS A-1

APPENDIX B
PROFESSIONAL STANDARDS
FOR TEACHING MATHEMATICS A-8

References R-1
  Children's Literature R-8
Index I-1
**Blackline Masters and Materials
 Construction Tips BL-1**

PREFACE

Children will become confident "doers" of mathematics only if mathematics makes sense to them and if they believe in their ability to make sense of it.

(TRAFTON & CLAUS, 1994, P. 21)

To help students make sense of mathematics and become confident in their ability to do so is an excellent goal for teachers and a principal goal of this book. *Elementary and Middle School Mathematics* is both a guide and an instructional resource to help you with the challenging and rewarding task of helping all children become confident "doers of mathematics."

The third edition of this book comes nearly a decade after the National Council of Teachers of Mathematics published the *Curriculum and Evaluation Standards for School Mathematics*. That seminal document began an exciting period of change and growth in mathematics education that continues today. We continue to understand more about how children learn mathematics. There is new and exciting content for children to learn. There is new technology to help make it possible. This new edition reflects the ongoing growth and change in mathematics education. It is designed to help you be the most important part of that growth—a facilitator who helps children develop confidence and understanding as they do mathematics.

What You Will Find in This Book

I have divided this book into three sections. Each plays an important role in helping you become an effective teacher. Together they serve as both a resource and a reference book for teaching mathematics.

Section 1: Foundations

The more I work with teachers, the more I find that at all grade levels, a strong understanding of the foundational ideas of mathematics education has the greatest impact on teacher effectiveness. The best teachers I know have a good sense of how children learn and how to involve them in doing mathematics. In each edition of this book, I have worked hardest at developing and revising these five chapters to make them reflective of current research and practice and to extend the implications of these ideas to the rest of the text. These are not just overview chapters that are required in an academic text. Rather, these are the most important chapters of the book. They provide foundational ideas for the teaching of mathematics at any grade level.

Section 2: Concepts and Procedures

Chapters 6 through 21 build on the foundational ideas found in the first section as each explores the specific mathematics content found in grades K to 8. Every major topic of the K–8 curriculum is addressed in depth. Each chapter provides a perspective on the mathematical content and on how children best learn that content, as well as numerous suggestions for activities to engage children in the process of doing mathematics. This book is unique in its treatment of so many topics in such a thorough manner.

Many teachers use this text as a resource book and consult it as they plan each new unit. It provides them with plenty of activities and a clear understanding of the development of content. The activities for children, each enclosed in a box and identified by a title, are integrated directly into the text. Reflecting on the activities as you read can help you think about the mathematics from the perspective of the child. Most require students to figure something out, to search for a pattern, to explain a reason for an idea—to do mathematics as problem solving. As a teacher, you are encouraged to go beyond students' answers and discuss the results of activities, requiring them to justify and explain their results or to elaborate new ideas.

The activities are also there for you. They are meant to be read along with the text, not as asides. After all, you are constructing new knowledge yourself—knowledge about teaching mathematics to children. Like your students, you must be actively engaged in *your own learning* about *children learning* mathematics. By actually doing the activities as you read through the book, you can get an idea of how children might react to or learn from each activity.

Section 3: Issues and Perspectives

That these three chapters are found at the end of the book should in no way diminish their importance. As the foundational chapters of Section 1 provide a framework for the teaching of mathematics, the ideas in this section offer perspective on overarching issues that also build on that foundation. Read these chapters, or portions of them, at any time, depending on your needs and interests.

How do you design a lesson? In Chapter 22, two general approaches are offered so that you can develop your own style and still use a constructivist approach. How do you form cooperative learning groups? Details based on expert thinking are provided. Answers or suggestions are also offered for working in a diverse classroom, drill and practice, writing in mathematics, homework, and the use of the traditional textbook.

NCTM has made it very clear that good mathematics should be accessible to all children. In Chapter 23, you will read about working with children with learning disabilities, children with mental disabilities, and gifted children. In addition, an up-to-date perspective is provided on multicultural and socioeconomic issues. Gender equity is also discussed. Though no easy answers are offered, the information is current, research-based, and thought-provoking, in keeping with the main ideas of the book.

Chapter 24 looks at the role of the calculator and the computer in teaching mathematics. Here you will find NCTM's position on the use of calculators and computers and a framework that will guide your use and selection of technology as you teach. Included are ideas for profitable use of the Internet and a look at the Logo computer programming language.

Special Features of This Text

This third edition of *Elementary and Middle School Mathematics* retains all of the features that I believe have helped make the previous two editions so successful. A few new additions have been included to make it even better. Here are 11 things to look for.

Big Ideas (New!)

A constructivist perspective calls teachers to plan activities around big ideas rather than tiny skills and concepts. To help develop an understanding of what is meant by "big ideas," each chapter in Section 2 begins with a brief overview and a listing of the big conceptual ideas related to that chapter. As you read these chapters, the Big Ideas list will help you begin to see how smaller ideas are actually developed as a part of these larger concepts.

Activities

This is both a textbook and a resource for teachers. I have included as many activities as space will allow. Most of these are clearly identified by a box and a title. Other ideas are described directly in the text or in the illustrations. Every activity found here should be considered for its potential for doing mathematics as problem solving, as described in Chapter 4. You are encouraged to use and modify activities in ways that challenge children to think and to wrestle with ideas.

Drawings

You will find no decorative or unnecessary art in this text. Every drawing is an integral part of the text information and should not be overlooked. Color is used within the illustrations to make them even more explanatory. Drawings are used whenever a picture seemed better than words or to highlight the most important ideas. I frequently tell my students to "read the pictures" as one of the fastest ways to the important information in the book.

Assessment Notes (New!)

Near the end of most chapters in Section 2, you will find a short discussion headed "Assessment Notes." These sections are designed to point to special assessment ideas that build on the general themes of the chapter on assessment, Chapter 5. It is worth noting that most activities in the book are also appropriate as performance assessments. There is no need to have a special reference book for assessment tasks.

Literature Connections (New!)

Children's literature is one of the most inviting ways to get children actively involved in doing mathematics. Many of the chapters in Section 2 contain a feature titled "Literature Connections." Generally you will find at least three children's literature titles suggested, with a brief description of how the mathematics of the chapter can be profitably built on the stories. Though certainly not a comprehensive listing of potential literature, these annotated listings provide all you need to get started using this exciting vehicle for teaching mathematics. Each work featured under this head appears in a separate reference list at the back of the book.

Computers and Calculators

Calculator activities are found in every chapter involving numbers and are identified with a small calculator icon so that you can easily find them. Special efforts have been made in this third edition to expand the use of graphing calculators for middle school activities. Computer activities are included in instances when the computer can have a unique impact on learning. Chapter 24 expands on the use of technology even further.

Writing to Learn

To help you focus on the important pedagogical ideas, a list of focusing questions are found at the end of every chapter under the heading "Reflections on Chapter *N:* Writing to Learn." These questions are designed to help you reflect on the main points of the chapter. Actually writing out the answers to these questions in your own words is one of the best ways for you to develop your understanding of each chapter's main ideas.

Explorations

Following the Writing to Learn list are a few additional questions that ask you to explore an issue, reflect on observations in a classroom, compare text ideas with those found in traditional curriculum materials, or perhaps take a position on a controversial issue. There are rarely "right" answers to these questions, but they will certainly stimulate thought and perhaps even provoke spirited conversations. Discuss these with your peer group or with teachers in the classroom.

Suggested Readings

The end of each chapter contains a bibliography of useful reading selections to augment the information found in the chapter. Usually these are taken from NCTM journals, yearbooks, and other professional resources that are targeted for the classroom teacher. New in this edition, three or four of the selections deemed most important or most useful are provided with a short annotation under the head "Highly Recommended." It would have been nice to annotate the whole list but space does not permit. (Note that all sources *cited within the text proper* appear in the References at the back of the book.)

NCTM *Standards* (New!)

This edition contains listings of standards taken directly from each of the NCTM's three *Standards* documents. In Appendix A, you will find all of the standards from the K–4 and 5–8 sections of the *Curriculum and Evaluation Standards for School Mathematics.* As in the previous editions, the tables of increased and decreased attention from these two sections are also included. Appendix B contains the six Standards for Teaching Mathematics from the *Professional Standards for Teaching Mathematics.* In Chapter 5, you will find the six Assessment Standards as well as the four Purposes of Assessment found in the *Assessment Standards for School Mathematics.*

Blackline Masters

The Blackline Masters section at the end of the book offers an extensive collection of masters and also directions for making important instructional materials. Many of these masters are unique to this book and support especially interesting activities. Suggestions for the use of these materials are found throughout the book. You are encouraged to copy these pages and duplicate them for your classroom or for activities with children. (Permission to copy these pages is granted on the copyright page.)

New in This Edition

Revisions for the third edition went far beyond the addition of the new features or a change in design. I have made a serious effort to make this text reflect the most current thinking about teaching mathematics that I thought was possible and still be a useful text with which a preservice teacher can grow. Perhaps as much as 40 percent of the text is new, and revisions have been made throughout every chapter. Though the basic structure and philosophy of the book remain the same, I have worked to improve this edition in very specific ways.

New Foundations Chapters

Section 1 parallels the first five chapters of the second edition, but I believe these chapters show significant improvement and, with respect to problem solving, a significant change.

All five chapters have been completely rewritten. Chapters 1, 2, and 5 are better organized, with a more focused purpose. Let me comment a bit more on Chapters 3 and 4.

Chapter 3, "Developing Understanding in Mathematics," is more tightly focused on the constructivist view of learning. This rewritten and reorganized chapter reflects my own professional growth as a constructivist. I have continued to learn from teachers and from many things that have been written at the teacher level about how children learn. You will find a much expanded discussion of the role that models play in learning. It is important for teachers to understand that the presence of manipulatives in no way guarantees learning. The chapter is now more readable, more focused on children, and I hope more friendly while remaining challenging.

Chapter 4, "Teaching Through Problem Solving," is completely new and unique among texts of this kind. Here I have taken to heart the first of the *Curriculum Standards,* mathematics *as* problem solving. This chapter now describes a primary approach to the teaching of all mathematics. The thesis developed is that all mathematics can be taught in a problem-solving environment. Understanding what that means can and should guide the design of lessons and interaction in the classroom. Problem solving is, then, no longer a separate strand of the curriculum but a way of learning and doing mathematics.

Changes in the Content Chapters

The most apparent change in Section 2 is the addition of Chapter 21, "Functions and Variables." This is a completely new chapter in which function concepts are developed through five modes: real contexts, language, equations, tables, and graphs. The chapter leans heavily on the use of the graphing calculator, builds on the development of functions through data and through patterns, and avoids the tedium of formalistic approaches. With the addition of this chapter and modifications to other content for the middle grades, the text now completely covers all important content in grades 6 to 8.

Other notable changes can be found in the chapters on operations, place value, and computation. However, no chapter is completely without revision. I made a serious effort to reflect on every chapter in the book. Every activity was reconsidered to be certain that it could be incorporated profitably into the problem-solving view developed in Chapter 4. Many were modified or replaced.

New Issues and Perspective

All three chapters in Section 3 are completely new. The content of these chapters was described earlier. I am proud to say that these chapters represent the most current thinking in the profession. Discussions of diversity in the classroom, writing in mathematics, and drill and practice are completely new. There is enough detail in the planning chapter to make it useful and effective for a teacher wishing to implement the ideas of this book.

In Chapter 23, "Teaching All Children Mathematics," the notion that all children can learn mathematics in much the same manner is supported by research and by examples of successful projects. New topics include multicultural issues and gender equity.

The technology chapter is designed to offer perspective on the use of calculators and computers, reflecting recent advances in these areas. It includes the most recent position statement on technology from NCTM. A new section on the Internet is designed to introduce teachers to this resource for mathematics education and teaching ideas.

Notes to the Instructor

To my knowledge, no other text offers your students as much as this one does. Most important, it develops a strong theoretical perspective of children learning mathematics—not a casual overview. That perspective is reflected throughout the book. Second, prospective teachers find the book to be a valuable resource that almost all carry into the classroom rather than sell back to the bookstore. Many classroom teachers and school principals buy the book for the same purpose. I have tried to write in a style that respects teachers as professionals without asking them to wade through educational jargon. My students tell me it is a readable and usable book.

It remains a very long book, full of more ideas and information than any other text. It is not a book to "cover" but a book to use. I have never attempted to teach the content of the entire book in a single semester and would never expect you to. In the past, I have seen the content coverage and detail as a luxury rather than a burden. You are able to pick and choose topics you like to emphasize, have some topics assigned as reading, and design a course that best suits your purposes.

With this edition, I have a different thought to add to these options. I now believe that the five chapters in Section 1 provide the core material essential to becoming an effective teacher. A possible suggestion is to spend a significant portion of your course on developing these key ideas about teaching children. Use an even smaller list of content topics than you would have before. Let the content you select be a vehicle for discussion of the general themes. Many chapters can be read without your input. Even those you do not assign will most likely be taken into the classroom for future use. By developing the foundational ideas thoroughly and placing a quality resource in your students' hands, you will, I believe, achieve even more than trying to cover every topic in the elementary or middle grades.

As I continue to talk to friends around the country who have used the previous editions, I am struck by the many different styles of methods courses that are possible. All instructors seem to find their own best way to use the book. I am hesitant, therefore, to dictate a course, but I am proud to offer this text. I wish you and your teachers much success and excitement as you explore good mathematics.

ACKNOWLEDGMENTS

Though much revised in this edition and the second, the general approach of *Elementary and Middle School Mathematics* was developed with the first edition. Substantial credit for the success of the first edition belongs to the mathematics educators who gave time and great care in offering detailed comments on the original draft manuscript. Regardless of how many subsequent editions this text may see, I will always be most sincerely indebted to John Dossey of Illinois State University, Bob Gilbert of Florida International University, Warren Crown of Rutgers University, and Steven Willoughby of the University of Arizona. Few mathematics educators of their stature would take the time and effort that they gave to this endeavor.

In preparing this third edition, I have received thoughtful input from the following educators, who offered comments on the second edition and/or on the manuscript for the third:

Rudie Alec, Wayne State University

Christine A. Browning, Western Michigan University

Lowell Gadberry, Southwestern Oklahoma State University

Anna Graeber, University of Maryland, College Park

Tom Kandl, Slippery Rock University

Beverly Kochmann, Saint Cloud State University

R. Mike Krach, Towson State University

Patricia Lamphere, Texas A&M University

Vena M. Long, University of Missouri, Kansas City

Eula Ewing Monroe, Brigham Young University

Emma M. Owens, Clemson University

James L. Overholt, California State University, Chico

Paula Raabe, National-Louis University

Sherry Renga, Eastern Washington University

Karen Cameron Scanlon, Seton Hill College

Edna O. Schack, Morehead State University

Markham B. Schack, Morehead State University

Carla Tayeh, Eastern Michigan University

Gail P. Tooker, SUNY Geneseo

Barbara Wofford, University of Tennessee, Chattanooga

Louise Yeazel, University of Wisconsin, Madison

Each of these professionals has challenged me to think through issues and rewarded me with helpful input.

Special thanks goes to Terri Okes, a fourth-grade teacher who taught from the second edition while serving as our teacher in residence and who read the manuscript for the third edition. Comments from her unique dual position of teacher and teacher educator were most helpful.

There were many people involved in the production of this book. However, very special recognition is due Ellen MacElree, the Project Editor for Longman, and Judy Kiviat, who proofread the page proofs. These two women provided an almost unbelievable attention to detail, worked untiringly for many months, kept in constant communication with me and with each other, and managed always to remain spirited, friendly, and professional. Their contribution is impossible to measure.

A Personal Note

Working on this book over the years has often been a lonely, daunting, and humbling endeavor. The extraordinary support, encouragement, and patience that my wife, Sharon, has given to me without reservation or complaint has made working on the first and subsequent editions possible. Her faith in me has helped me believe in myself. Her enduring love has made it all worthwhile. She has spent many long nights and weekends alone so that I could work on "the book." In this endeavor and throughout our lives together, she has been my strongest supporter. I have watched as she has grown in her own professional life and treasure her support of mine all the more.

With all my love, thank you, Sharon.

JOHN A. VAN DE WALLE

SECTION

1

FOUNDATIONS OF TEACHING MATHEMATICS

CHAPTER 1   TEACHING MATHEMATICS: REFLECTIONS AND DIRECTIONS

CHAPTER 2   EXPLORING WHAT IT MEANS TO DO MATHEMATICS

CHAPTER 3   DEVELOPING UNDERSTANDING IN MATHEMATICS

CHAPTER 4   TEACHING THROUGH PROBLEM SOLVING

CHAPTER 5   BUILDING ASSESSMENT INTO INSTRUCTION

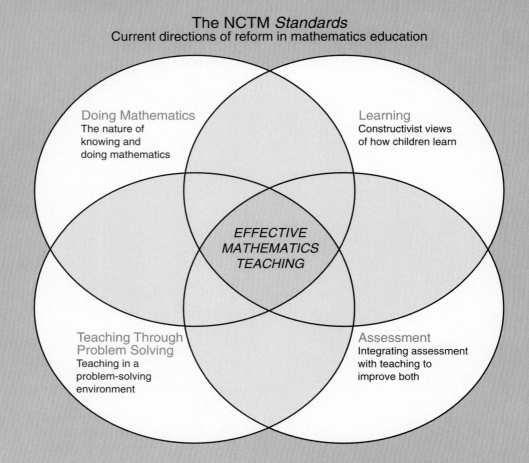

The NCTM *Standards*
Current directions of reform in mathematics education

Doing Mathematics
The nature of knowing and doing mathematics

Learning
Constructivist views of how children learn

EFFECTIVE MATHEMATICS TEACHING

Teaching Through Problem Solving
Teaching in a problem-solving environment

Assessment
Integrating assessment with teaching to improve both

As depicted in the figure, effective teaching of mathematics happens when it is firmly based on four pervasive constructs brought together in the context of the revolution in mathematics education led by the National Council of Teachers of Mathematics (NCTM).

The call for reform in mathematics education is mandated by the needs of our rapidly changing, highly technological society. This movement has been guided by three professional documents published by NCTM: the *Standards* documents on curriculum, teaching, and assessment. These documents are discussed in Chapter 1.

In Chapters 2 through 5, the key ideas of effective teaching are developed. The first requirement is to develop a vision of the discipline. In Chapter 2 we see that mathematics is more than computation, rules, and procedures. Mathematics is a science of pattern and order. An understanding of how children learn is developed in Chapter 3. The nearly unanimous view of children's learning mathematics is based on constructivist theory, which asserts that children must actively construct ideas rather than passively absorb them. General strategies or guidelines for teaching that reflect both the nature of mathematics and how children learn are developed in Chapter 4. Mathematics should be taught as a problem-solving endeavor to engage the minds of children and to develop the nature of the discipline. Finally, in Chapter 5, we see how assessment strategies must be fully integrated with instruction to promote learning and instruction in an appropriate manner.

These five chapters develop the spirit and philosophy of the rest of the book and of teaching mathematics at any grade level.

CHAPTER

TEACHING MATHEMATICS: REFLECTIONS AND DIRECTIONS

This book is about teaching mathematics or, perhaps in better words, helping children learn mathematics. So let's just start there, with *teaching mathematics*.

What kinds of images and emotions does that simple phrase bring to your mind? Consider first the mathematics part. What does the discipline of mathematics mean to you? What does mathematics mean in the elementary and middle school? Pause right now and reflect on your own ideas about the topic of mathematics. What is it? How does it make you feel? What does it mean to "do mathematics"? Where do calculators and computers fit in? What parts of the subject seem most important? Write down three or four of your strongest thoughts about mathematics. Compare your thoughts with those of others. After reading the chapter, return to what you wrote here.

Next focus on the teaching part. Someday soon you will find yourself in front of a class of students, or perhaps you are already teaching. Your goal is for children to learn mathematics. What general ideas will guide the way you will teach mathematics? Do you think your ideas about teaching mathematics are influenced by your view of what mathematics is or how well you like or understand it yourself? Do children learn mathematics differently from other topics? How can you make it interesting and enjoyable? If mathematics is not exactly your favorite subject, do you think that had anything to do with the way you were taught? How can you help children like the subject more than you do? Add your written thoughts on these questions to those about mathematics, and return to them at the end of the chapter.

These are hard questions. They do not have simple, unique answers with which everyone will agree.

THE REVOLUTION IN SCHOOL MATHEMATICS

It is reasonable to say that the United States is in the middle of a revolution in mathematics education, a revolution that is more positive, more pervasive, and more widely accepted than any change that has preceded it. From kindergarten to college, changes are occurring in what mathematics is taught and the manner in which it is taught. Though the momentum for change was building for some time before, a reasonable date for the beginning of this revolution is 1989, the year that the National Council of Teachers of Mathematics (NCTM) published the *Curriculum and Evaluation Standards for School Mathematics*. This landmark document provided standards and direction for the mathematics that should be taught in our schools. The publication of the *Curriculum Standards* has received unanimous support and praise from nearly every sector of the education, business, and political communities. It has provided the philosophy and direction for curriculum reform in virtually every state and local school district throughout the nation.

In the same year as the release of the *Curriculum Standards* by NCTM, the Mathematical Sciences Education Board (MSEB) released *Everybody Counts: A Report to the Nation on the Future of School Mathematics*. This very readable document outlined the nature of mathematics, the needs of our changing society, and the problems with our past efforts in mathematics education, and it echoed the directions for mathematics suggested by the *Curriculum Standards*. These two publications provided the most clearly articulated vision

3

of where we should be heading. Anyone wishing to understand the need for and direction of change in mathematics education that was envisioned as we entered the 1990s should begin with these two books.

And the revolution continues. As the decade nears its end, it must be admitted that the vision of the *Curriculum Standards* has not been realized. The *Curriculum Standards* generated interest and provided philosphy and direction. Yet actual change in long-held beliefs about school mathematics has been slow.

FORCES DRIVING THE REVOLUTION

A growing body of educational research has given us real insight into just how children learn about numbers, fractions, geometry, and other aspects of mathematics. This increased understanding of the learning process significantly influences teaching methods. As for the curriculum in school mathematics, two factors have provided a significant impetus for the change we are now experiencing: (1) the needs of society in a highly technological and global economy and (2) advances in technology, most specifically calculators and computers.

The Demands of Society

Years ago, school mathematics was focused almost entirely on the skills of pencil-and-paper computation. The vast majority of jobs in industry and agriculture demanded little more, and much of the mathematics required for the average job revolved around simple computational skills. Few of the nation's students were ever expected to study mathematics in college or to contribute to the research efforts of the mathematics and science community. It became fashionable (and unfortunately remains so) to proclaim one's personal incompetence in mathematics and science. For no other subject in the curriculum are Americans so quick to proclaim their inadequacies.

In a world that is increasingly complex and dominated by quantitative information in every facet of its economy, mathematical thinking has become indispensable in even the most ordinary jobs. Mathematical thinking is not the same as the computational skills of yesterday's school mathematics. It involves the ability and the habits of reasoning and solving problems. It includes having number sense—intuition about numbers, their magnitudes, their effects in operations, and their relationships to real quantities and phenomena. It implies the ability to interpret charts and graphs meaningfully and to understand basic concepts of probability and data analysis. It includes spatial sense—a familiarity with shapes and relationships among them. These are the

basic skills of today's society. Higher-order thinking skills remain entirely human. These skills of the mind are expected of everyone in the modern workplace. By contrast, facility with the computational skills of the recent past are almost never needed in the workplace, and such facility has very little to do with mathematical thinking.

The Influence of Technology

Technology pervades our everyday life, from our microwave ovens and videodisk players to supermarket scanners and "surfing the Net." Computerization is replacing nearly every mundane facet of the workplace. The calculator and the computer in particular have had a major effect on school mathematics in three significant ways.

First, the calculator and the computer have drastically reduced the importance of low-level computational skills. It remains critically important that all students master basic facts such as $12 - 7$ or 6×8. These facts assist in mental computations, estimations, and many aspects of numeric reasoning. But long and tedious computations are simply obsolete.

Second, the calculator and computer provide new instructional approaches to significant ideas. Activities have been designed with simple calculators that assist children in developing basic ideas about numbers such as place value, relationships between fractions and decimals, and the relative magnitudes of numbers. Estimation skills, mental mathematics, and even drill of basic facts can be enhanced by the calculator. Contrary to persistent beliefs held by parents and some teachers, there is, after hundreds of studies over two decades, no evidence that calculators have a negative effect on basic skills or concepts. Quite the opposite is true: The calculator is a powerful teaching tool.

Third, technology has changed what we are able to teach. This is especially obvious in the upper grades. The graphing calculator and computer software now easily perform calculations, do tedious statistical procedures, and accurately draw, measure, and manipulate all manner of geometric shapes and constructions. These technologies are readily available, opening new worlds that were never before accessible to students. For example, the graphing calculator permits students to display the graph of almost any equation, make changes in the equation, and instantly observe the results. Many graphs can be sketched and compared in minutes. Students are able to focus on relationships that the various graphs exhibit and on real applications of graphs. Functions need not be restricted to those that are easily plotted by hand.

The Direction of NCTM

The National Council of Teachers of Mathematics is a professional, nonprofit, nonfederally funded organization. It celebrated its seventy-fifth anniversary in 1995. It provides leadership for teachers through its various journals and conferences.

As noted earlier, NCTM's release of the *Curriculum and Evaluation Standards for School Mathematics* in 1989 was a benchmark event in school mathematics. In 1991, NCTM published the *Professional Standards for Teaching Mathematics*. The *Professional Standards* articulates a vision of teaching mathematics and builds on the notion found in the *Curriculum Standards* that good and significant mathematics is a vision for all children, not just a few. NCTM completed the package with the *Assessment Standards for School Mathematics* in 1995. This third book of the *Standards* trilogy shows clearly the necessity of integrating assessment with instruction and indicates the key role that assessment plays in implementing change. These three documents are described in the sections that follow and provide a framework for much of what you will learn in this book.

THE *CURRICULUM AND EVALUATION STANDARDS FOR SCHOOL MATHEMATICS*

With its virtually universal acceptance, the *Curriculum Standards* gave momentum and articulated direction to a reform movement that, for ten years before 1989, could only be described as one of minimal and isolated change. Since its publication, new curriculum objectives have been written, textbooks are changing (albeit very slowly), and teaching methods are beginning to look different.

What Are the *Curriculum Standards*?

The *Curriculum Standards* established a "vision of what it means to be mathematically literate" in today's society. Though not a curriculum for mathematics, the *Standards* provided a general philosophy for mathematics education as well as direction and focus for each specific content area and for assessment. Woven throughout are examples of appropriate learning activities that suggest the intended spirit of instruction. The full intent of the document has not by any means been completely realized, although it remains the single most important source of direction in the profession. NCTM's Commission on the Future of the *Standards* has recommended and their board of directors has accepted the development of a new *Standards* document to appear in the year 2000. The revision of the *Standards* will reflect changes that have occurred in the past decade, particularly in the area of technology and new information about the teaching and learning of mathematics.

The *Curriculum Standards* is divided into four sections: K–4, 5–8, 9–12, and Evaluation. Within each section are 13 or 14 standards or statements about a particular area of mathematics. As noted in its introduction, "A standard is a statement that can be used to judge the quality of a mathematics curriculum or methods of evaluation. Thus, standards are statements about what is valued" (NCTM, 1989, p. 2).

Each of the three grade-level sections of the *Curriculum Standards* begins with a chart that outlines suggested changes in content emphasis. Even a casual review of these charts can provide a snapshot of suggested changes from the curriculum of the 1980s. The change-in-emphasis charts for the K–4 and 5–8 sections can be found in Appendix A of this book. It would be a good idea to spend some time with this material, both now and as you consider each different content area of the elementary and middle grades curriculum. Most likely you will recognize the descriptions under the heading "Decreased Attention" as being very similar to what you recall from your own school experiences. The "Increased Attention" column indicates the general direction of the *Standards*.

Appendix A also lists the 13 standards for K–4 and for 5–8. In the actual document, each standard is accompanied by a three- or four-page amplifying discussion that is essential to understanding the full intent of the *Standards'* authors.

The Vision of the *Standards*

The *Curriculum Standards* outlines five goals for students: (1) to value mathematics, (2) to become confident in their ability to do mathematics, (3) to become mathematical problem solvers, (4) to learn to communicate mathematically, and (5) to learn to reason mathematically. These goals are aimed at the development of *mathematical power*. This refers to students' abilities to "explore, conjecture, and reason logically, as well as the ability to use a variety of mathematical methods effectively to solve nonroutine problems. . . . It includes reasoning, means of communication, and notions of context. In addition, for each individual, mathematical power involves the development of personal self confidence" (NCTM, 1989, p. 5). The concept of mathematical power is an overarching agenda referred to in each of the next three chapters.

The Four "Theme" Standards

In each of the three grade-level sections of the *Curriculum Standards*, the first four standards have the same titles:

1. Mathematics as Problem Solving
2. Mathematics as Communication
3. Mathematics as Reasoning
4. Mathematical Connections

These four standards represent pervasive themes of an appropriate mathematics curriculum; they can be applied to nearly every area and every lesson. To teach with these four standards clearly in mind is what it means to teach in a "*Standards*-oriented" manner.

Mathematics as Problem Solving

Notice the second word in this standard. Mathematics *as* problem solving means much more than learning to solve problems. Problem solving is not a separate strand or topic. According to the *Curriculum Standards,* "Problem solving should be the central focus of the mathematics curriculum. As such, it is a primary goal of all mathematics instruction and an integral part of all mathematical activity" (NCTM, 1989, p. 23). The "Mathematics as Problem Solving" standard speaks to learning and doing mathematics in a spirit of inquiry and figuring things out. It talks about being able to formulate problems and judge results. It speaks about confidence in solving problems. These processes and attitudes apply to all of mathematics. Problem solving is a way of thinking and reasoning used in the learning and the doing of mathematics.

Mathematics as Communication

The communication standards at each level point to the importance of being able to talk about, write about, describe, and explain mathematical ideas. Symbolism in mathematics, along with visual aids such as charts and graphs, should become ways of expressing mathematical ideas to others. This means that students should learn not only to interpret the language of mathematics but also to use that language themselves. Learning to communicate in mathematics makes accessible the world of mathematics beyond the classroom. It also fosters interaction and exploration of ideas in the classroom as students learn in an active, verbal environment.

Mathematics as Reasoning

To reason is as integral to mathematics as problem solving. The *Standards* tells us that reasoning should be a part of mathematical activity from kindergarten on. To observe and extend a pattern, defend a result, or decide if an answer is correct are all activities that involve logical reasoning. When reasoning is part of all mathematics, students learn that mathematics is not a collection of arbitrary rules but a system that makes sense and can be figured out.

Mathematical Connections

The theme of connections is really threefold. First, the connection standards refer to connections within and among mathematical ideas. Addition and subtraction are intimately related. Fractional parts of a whole are connected to concepts of decimals and percents.

Second, the symbols and procedures of mathematics should be clearly connected to the conceptual knowledge that the symbolism represents. Rules such as "invert the divisor and multiply" should never be learned in the absence of well-developed supporting concepts.

Third, mathematics should be connected to the real world and to other disciplines. Children should see that mathematics plays a significant role in art, science, and social studies. This suggests that mathematics should frequently be integrated with other discipline areas and also that applications of mathematics in the real world should be explored. Mathematics should be viewed as a meaningful and relevant discipline, in terms of both how it is done and how it is used.

The Evaluation Standards

The Evaluation section of the *Curriculum Standards* reflects the four basic themes while presenting one of the most significant challenges in the document. It is clear that if the mathematics curriculum is going to focus on problem solving, reasoning, communication, and connections, the assessment program must also focus on these themes. A valid assessment program should move the curriculum in mathematics away from a focus on answers and answer-getting to a focus on the things that are most important. Teachers who fail to change their assessment practices from those that served an earlier, outdated curriculum find great discrepancies between what they are testing and what they are teaching. Progress toward implementing assessment practices in concert with a *Standards*-oriented curriculum as originally envisioned in 1989 is only now beginning to happen.

THE *PROFESSIONAL STANDARDS FOR TEACHING MATHEMATICS*

Whereas the *Curriculum Standards* was aimed at content and assessment, the *Professional Standards for Teaching Mathematics* focuses on instruction and teachers. The *Professional Standards* asserts that teachers are the key agents of change in the classroom. If the revolution begun by the *Curriculum Standards* is to come to fruition, teachers must shift from a teacher-centered to a child-centered approach to instruction. Research in cognitive psychology and mathematics education suggests that students actively construct their own meanings through assimilation of new information and engaging experiences. They do not simply absorb knowledge placed before them by the teacher. The *Professional Standards* describes teaching that supports the *Curriculum Standards* and incorporates this constructivist view of learning in its suggestions for instruction.

Five Shifts in Classroom Environment

The introduction to the *Professional Standards* lists five major shifts in the environment of the mathematics classroom. The authors see these shifts as necessary to allow students to develop mathematical power. According to the document, teachers need to shift

- Toward classrooms as mathematics communities and away from classrooms as simply a collection of individuals

- Toward logic and mathematical evidence as verification and away from the teacher as the sole authority for right answers
- Toward mathematical reasoning and away from mere memorizing procedures
- Toward conjecturing, inventing, and problem solving and away from an emphasis on the mechanistic finding of answers
- Toward connecting mathematics, its ideas, and its applications and away from treating mathematics as a body of isolated concepts and procedures

Mathematics for All Students

In all three standards documents, but highlighted in the *Professional Standards,* is the phrase "mathematics for all students." Both new and experienced teachers should be keenly aware that the standards documents are not elitist ideals reserved for gifted students. NCTM (1991) has endorsed the following:

> As a professional organization and as individuals within that organization, the Board of Directors sees the comprehensive mathematics education of every child as its most compelling goal. By "every child" we mean specifically—
>
> - students who have been denied access in any way to educational opportunities as well as those who have not;
> - students who are African American, Hispanic, American Indian, and other minorities as well as those who are considered to be a part of the majority;
> - students who are female as well as those who are male; and
> - students who have not been successful in school and mathematics as well as those who have been successful. (p. 4)

The issue of *all* children is of increasing importance as more and more classrooms include students who in the past would have been relegated to special classrooms and altered curricula. No students should receive a second-level curriculum or second-best instruction. (This issue is discussed in more detail in Chapter 23.)

Teaching Standards

The first section of the *Professional Standards* contains six standards for the teaching of mathematics, arranged in four categories: providing worthwhile mathematical tasks, encouraging discourse among students and between students and teacher, providing for an environment in which learning will be enhanced, and analyzing continually both teaching and learning. Chapter 4 of this text describes teaching through problem solving—a process involving these very same ideas: selecting problems or tasks, creating an environment of mathematical discourse, and considering the infor-

mation gained from students each day in making decisions for the next day. A listing of the six teaching standards can be found in Appendix B.

THE *ASSESSMENT STANDARDS FOR SCHOOL MATHEMATICS*

The *Assessment Standards for School Mathematics* was published in 1995. This third *Standards* document completes the vision of the revolution begun in 1989 and expands the ideas found in the Evaluation section of the *Curriculum Standards.*

During the early 1990s, a flurry of professional literature urged teachers at all levels and in all disciplines to use "alternative assessment" practices, including portfolios, performance tasks, rubrics, and journals. The *Assessment Standards* makes no effort to add to that growing mound of literature. Like the other standards documents, it is not a how-to guide but a statement of philosophy and purpose, a book to provide guidance without prescription. It consists of six standards for assessment: mathematics, learning, equity, openness, inference, and coherence. Further, it describes in some detail four purposes of assessment: to monitor the progress of students, to help make instructional decisions, to evaluate students' achievement, and to evaluate programs. All are aimed at the improvement of student learning.

The inescapable message of the *Assessment Standards* is that assessment and instruction are not separate activities but are intimately intertwined in improving the learning of mathematics. Chapter 5 of this text describes the six assessment standards and discusses the four purposes. There you will find suggestions for making assessment an integral component of instruction, an absolute essential factor in being a *Standards*-oriented teacher.

TEACHING MATHEMATICS

At the outset of this chapter, you were asked to consider your thoughts about the phrase *teaching mathematics.* It is quite possible that much of what you have read about so far is different from your own school experiences with school mathematics. Or you may have read this outline of the revolution in school mathematics with a nodding familiarity. In either case, living up to the *Standards* documents is a significant yet exciting challenge.

An Invitation to Learn

As a practicing or prospective teacher facing the challenge of the *Standards* documents, you may need to confront some of your personal beliefs and ideas about what it means to *do mathematics,* how one goes about *learning mathematics,* how to *teach mathematics through problem solving,* and what it means to *assess mathematics* integrated with instruction. The next four chapters of this book help you develop these four foundational ideas for teaching developmentally, ideas at the heart of the vision of the *Standards.*

Section II of the book examines specific topics in mathematics and offers suggestions that can be incorporated into the *Standards* framework. The 16 chapters in the second section are designed not only as text material but also as an activity resource for your future or current teaching. Section III covers other topics that influence mathematics teaching across all strands and grade levels: planning and related classroom issues, reaching all children in mathematics, and the role of technology. The chapters in this last section are appropriate to be read at any time.

New directions in mathematics education have opened a world of exciting investigations in mathematics to all students. Mathematics can no longer be equated with mundane computational skills.

Teaching mathematics can be an exciting adventure. Perhaps the most exciting part is that you will grow and learn along with your students. Enjoy the journey!

REFLECTIONS ON CHAPTER 1: WRITING TO LEARN

At the end of each chapter of this book, you will find a series of questions under this same heading. The questions are designed to help you reflect on the most important ideas of the chapter. Writing (or talking aloud with a peer) is an excellent way to explore new ideas and incorporate them into your own knowledge base. The writing (or discussion) will help make the ideas your own. After you have written your responses in your own words, return to the text to compare what you have written with the book. Make changes, if necessary, or discuss differences with your instructor.

1. In the world outside of schools, what kinds of mathematics are commonly used, and how does this compare to the mathematics that was taught before 1960? What does this discrepancy say about the mathematics that should be taught in schools?

2. Of the three ways that technology has influenced mathematics in schools, which one or two do you see as the most significant? Explain your choice(s).

3. If the five goals of the *Curriculum Standards* were realized, how would that contribute to "mathematical power"? Describe briefly each of the first four thematic standards that appear in each of the three grade-level sections of the *Curriculum Standards.* Notice how similar these four themes are to the five goals.

4. This chapter outlined only a few of the ideas found in the *Professional Standards.* Among these are five shifts in the classroom environment from traditional approaches to a *Standards*-oriented approach. Examine these five shifts, and describe in a few sentences what aspects of the shifts seem most significant to you.

FOR DISCUSSION AND EXPLORATION

1. Select a textbook used at a grade level that interests you. Compare the table of contents and the general spirit of the text with the directions suggested by the change-in-emphasis tables from the *Curriculum Standards* found in Appendix A. How does the textbook stack up? If there are differences, what are some possible reasons? What are the implications for a classroom teacher using that text?

2. What proportion (percentage) of time is currently being spent in schools on pencil-and-paper computation? Make a guess for several different grade levels. How much time do you think is spent on other forms of computation (estimation, mental computation, calculators)? How much time is spent on noncomputational topics such as probability, measurement, or geometry? Compare your estimates with a textbook series, or discuss these areas with a classroom teacher or curriculum specialist.

3. How does curriculum get changed? Take one of the following roles: teacher, district supervisor, state supervisor. Select a specific change that you believe should be made in the mathematics curriculum or instruction. How could you implement that change? What factors make change slow and difficult? How do you think change happens?

SUGGESTED READINGS

At the very least, every teacher should read the introduction and appropriate grade level of the *Curriculum Standards,* the Teaching Standards section of the *Professional Standards,* and all of the *Assessment Standards.*

Highly Recommended

Cooney, T. J. (Ed.). (1990). *Teaching and learning mathematics in the 1990s.* Reston, VA: National Council of Teachers of Mathematics.

This NCTM yearbook remains current even at the end of the decade and provides insights into the spirit and direction of all three *Standards* documents even though published less than a year after the *Curriculum Standards.* Twenty-eight short chapters address perspectives on teaching and learning, the role of assessment in instruction, cultural issues, and the impact of technology.

Mathematical Sciences Education Board, National Research Council. (1989). *Everybody counts: A report to the nation on the future of mathematics education.* Washington, DC: National Academy Press.

This little booklet can easily be read in an evening yet will provide food for hours and hours of reflection. Lynn Arthur Steen, who prepared the book, provides a compelling rationale for reform in both the mathematics we teach and how it is taught. Steen's description of mathematics as the science of pattern and order is used throughout this text. Myths concerning the nature of mathematics, how it is learned, and by whom are challenged from an angle that is difficult to dispute. This is "must reading" for anyone who even remotely doubts that there is a need for reform in mathematics education in this country.

Rowan, T. E., & Morrow, L. J. (Eds.). (1993). *Implementing the K–8 curriculum and evaluation standards: Readings from the* Arithmetic Teacher. Reston, VA: National Council of Teachers of Mathematics.

In the two years that followed the publication of the *Curriculum Standards,* NCTM's publication for K–8 teachers, the *Arithmetic Teacher,* published a short article each month offering suggestions for implementing the *Standards.* Each article describes the spirit of one or more standards and suggests classroom activities. This is not only a good resource but also an excellent way to get a feel for the message of the *Curriculum Standards.* A few of the articles reprinted in the book are included in the Other Suggestions listing.

Trafton, P. R., & Claus, A. S. (1994). A changing curriculum for a changing age. In C. A. Thornton & N. S. Bley (Eds.), *Windows of opportunity: Mathematics for students with special needs* (pp. 19–39). Reston, VA: National Council of Teachers of Mathematics.

Trafton was chair of the K–4 writing group for the *Curriculum Standards* and is a leading voice in mathematics education reform. With Claus, he describes in one chapter the vision of the *Standards* and the challenges that vision presents to teachers. The chapter ends with a vignette from a second-grade classroom that vividly brings home the meaning of reform.

Other Suggestions

Campbell, P. F., & Bamberger, H. J. (1990). The vision of problem solving in the *Standards. Arithmetic Teacher, 37*(9), 14–17.

Enochs, L. G. (Ed.). (1990). NCTM Standards [Special issue]. *School Science and Mathematics, 90*(6).

Garofalo, J., & Mtewa, D. K. (1990). Mathematics as reasoning. *Arithmetic Teacher, 37*(5), 16–18.

Lindquist, M. M. (1989). It's time to change. In P. R. Trafton (Ed.), *New directions for elementary school mathematics* (pp. 1–13). Reston, VA: National Council of Teachers of Mathematics.

Lindquist, M. M. (1992). Reflections on the mathematics assessment of the National Assessment of Educational Progress. In I. Wirszup & R. Streit (Eds.), *Developments in school mathematics education around the world* (Vol. 3, pp. 163–184). Reston, VA: National Council of Teachers of Mathematics.

Mathematical Sciences Education Board, National Research Council. (1990). *Reshaping school mathematics: A philosophy and framework for curriculum.* Washington, DC: National Academy Press.

Mullis, I. V. S., Dossey, J. A., Owen, E. U., & Phillips, G. W. (1991). *The state of mathematics achievement: NAEP's 1990 assessment of the nation and the trial assessment of the states.* Washington, DC: National Center for Education Statistics.

National Council of Teachers of Mathematics: Commission on Teaching Standards for School Mathematics. (1989). *Curriculum and evaluation standards for school mathematics.* Reston, VA: Author.

National Council of Teachers of Mathematics: Commission on Teaching Standards for School Mathematics. (1991). *Professional standards for teaching mathematics.* Reston, VA: Author.

National Council of Teachers of Mathematics: Commission on Teaching Standards for School Mathematics. (1995). *Assessment standards for school mathematics.* Reston, VA: Author.

Payne, J. N. (1990). New directions in mathematics education. In J. N. Payne (Ed.), *Mathematics for the young child* (pp. 1–15). Reston, VA: National Council of Teachers of Mathematics.

Romberg, T. A. (1992). Toward a world-class curriculum in the United States. In I. Wirszup & R. Streit (Eds.), *Developments in school mathematics education around the world* (Vol. 3, pp. 223–235). Reston, VA: National Council of Teachers of Mathematics.

Steen, L. A. (1990). *Mathematics for all Americans.* In T. J. Cooney (Ed.), *Teaching and learning mathematics in the 1990s* (pp. 130–134). Reston, VA: National Council of Teachers of Mathematics.

Van de Walle, J. A. (1991). Redefining computation. *Arithmetic Teacher, 38*(5), 46–51.

Willoughby, S. S. (1990). *Mathematics education for a changing world.* Alexandria, VA: Association for Supervision and Curriculum Development.

Willoughby, S. S. (1996). *The Standards*—Some second thoughts. *Mathematics Teaching in the Middle School, 2,* 8–11.

Whitin, D. J. (1992). The dangers of implementing the *Standards:* or, When bad things happen to good ideas. *Arithmetic Teacher, 40,* 8–9.

Chapter

EXPLORING WHAT IT MEANS TO DO MATHEMATICS

According to the NCTM *Curriculum and Evaluation Standards,* "Knowing mathematics is doing mathematics." Exactly what does that mean? How would you describe what you are doing when you are doing mathematics? Stop for a moment and write a few sentences about what it means to know and do mathematics, based on your own experiences. Then put your paper aside until you have finished this chapter. As you read this and the next three chapters, you may have to confront your views about mathematics and consider some changes.

The description of mathematics you will read about here may not match your personal experiences. That's OK! It is OK to come to this point with whatever beliefs were developed in your previous mathematics experiences. However, it is not OK to accept outdated ideas about mathematics and expect to be a quality teacher. Your obligation and challenge as you read this chapter and this book is to reconceptualize your own understanding of what it means to know and do mathematics so that the children with whom you work will have an exciting and accurate vision of mathematics.

CHANGING PERCEPTIONS AND NEW GOALS

Your perception of mathematics has been profoundly influenced by the way you were taught. Most people's view of mathematics is fairly well established by about seventh grade unless an unusually influential teacher or experience intervenes.

Much change has taken place since 1989 when NCTM published the *Curriculum Standards* and set a vision for change in mathematics classrooms. There may be more materials in the rooms and more classes where children work in groups. Calculators are a bit more accepted, and schools brag about the number of computers they have. But beyond these surface features, too many classrooms are fundamentally similar to those found in the 1980s and before.

Traditional Views of School Mathematics

The Traditional Classroom

In the traditional elementary or middle school classroom, the teacher represents the source of all that is to be known in mathematics. Lessons commonly begin with a review of material covered the day before and a check of any homework that was assigned. Then the teacher explains whatever new idea is on the next page of the text. The instruction generally consists of showing the children how they are to do the assigned exercises. In primary classrooms, there may even be a hands-on activity using some form of manipulation, but the children are still following the directions of the teacher. Students work at the exercises, trying to follow what was demonstrated. If someone has difficulty, the teacher will show again how the work is to be done. There is an almost complete focus on getting answers that are then checked by the teacher to determine if they are correct. End-of-chapter tests require that the procedures practiced during the previous week or so be executed accurately. Most kids get through the day.

The curriculum has also been very slow to change. In the traditional classroom, it consists largely of computation, with countless rules presented in bite-sized chunks. Each chunk (e.g., "Invert the divisor and multiply") is explained briefly and practiced extensively.

Children's Perceptions

Children emerge from these experiences with a view that mathematics is an endless series of arbitrary rules, handed down by the teacher, who must in turn get them from some very smart source. The students' role in this exercise is largely passive: Accept what you are told, and try to master each new rule. Students see the teacher as the ultimate source of truth in the classroom. The teacher shows how to do the problems and decides if the answers are correct.

The very fact that children are neither asked nor required to understand these rules or evaluate their own answers says loudly, "You can't possibly comprehend these ideas." By the fifth or sixth grade, many children simply refuse to attempt a problem that has not first been explained: "You haven't shown us how to do this." Such helplessness is a natural consequence of the bits-and-pieces, rules-without-reasons approach to mathematics. Children accept that every problem must have a predetermined method of solution, that there is only one way to solve any problem, and that there is not even an expectation that they could solve a problem unless someone gave them the solution method ahead of time. A follow-the-rules, computation-dominated, answer-oriented view of mathematics is a gross distortion of what mathematics is really about.

This rule-driven "mathematics" cannot be very exciting for most students. Some are good at learning rules and thrive on the ensuing good grades. But these are not necessarily the best thinkers in the room. They are the best trivia masters. The traditional system rewards rule learning and offers little opportunity actually to do mathematics.

Mathematics as a Science of Pattern and Order

Mathematics is the science of pattern and order. This wonderfully simple description of mathematics is found in the thought-provoking publication *Everybody Counts* (MSEB, 1989; see also Schoenfeld, 1992). This definition and the vision of the NCTM *Standards* challenge the popular social view of mathematics as a discipline dominated by computation and rules without reasons. It can easily be argued that doing computation, such as long division, is not doing mathematics at all. Calculators can do the same thing, and calculators can only calculate—they cannot do mathematics. At the same time, the *invention* of a method for doing division is certainly mathematics. That involves a search for some order in our number system coupled with ideas about what division means.

Consider the early study of algebra. One can learn to graph the equation of a parabola by simply following rules and plotting points. Now calculators are readily available to do that as well, and with a speed and precision we could never hope to achieve. But understanding why certain forms of equations always produce parabolic graphs involves a search for patterns in the way numbers behave. Discovering what types of real-world relationships (a pendulum swing related to the length of the pendulum, for example) are represented by parabolic graphs is even more interesting and scientific—and infinitely more valuable than the ability to plot the curve if someone else provides the equation.

Even the youngest schoolchildren can and should be involved in significant searches for patterns and order. Have you ever noticed that 6 + 7 is the same as 5 + 8 and 4 + 9? What is the pattern? What are the relationships? When two odd numbers are multiplied, the result is also odd, but if the same numbers are added or subtracted, the result is even. There is a logic behind simple results such as these, an order and a pattern. And pattern is not just in numbers but in everything around us. The world is full of order and pattern: in nature, in art, in buildings, in music. Pattern and order are found in commerce, science, medicine, manufacturing, and sociology. Mathematics discovers this order and uses it in a multitude of fascinating ways, improving our lives and expanding our knowledge. School must begin to help children with this process of discovery.

New Goals for Students

In the introduction to the *Curriculum Standards,* five important educational goals are described for all students, not just those few who traditionally gravitate toward mathematics. These goals state that all students should

1. Learn to value mathematics
2. Become confident in their ability to do mathematics
3. Become mathematical problem solvers
4. Learn to communicate mathematics
5. Learn to reason mathematically

As you will see, these goals are intricately bound together in the process of doing mathematics. All can and will be addressed within a classroom reflecting a true mathematical environment.

Valuing Mathematics

"Why do I have to know this stuff?" This refrain is heard all too often by teachers of mathematics, especially in the upper grades. The mathematics of computation for the sake of computation is certainly open to criticism. But the mathematics of reasoning, problem solving, and patterns is intimately connected with the fabric of modern life. Virtually every job role in today's society requires mathematics and, more important, mathematical thinking. Today's employers are searching for the ability to solve problems that have never been encountered before. Children need to see themselves learning to reason and learning to solve problems, not just learning skills. Furthermore, whenever these are realistic and connected with real data from real-life situations, the inescapable conclusion is that this is "important stuff."

Being Confident

As the need for mathematical thinking pervades our society, the need to feel ownership of that thinking power is all-important. We are well into an era when it can no longer be fashionable to announce, "I never was any good at math." Children must, from the earliest grades and continually throughout their school experiences, be made to feel the importance of personal success in solving problems, figuring things out, and making sense of the world. It is difficult to develop confidence in your mathematical abilities if all you do in that domain is follow unfathomable rules that seem handed down from above. Only by making your own sense of things, discovering a pattern, figuring out a relationship, solving a problem, or inventing a procedure can you begin to develop a sense of "I can do mathematics!" As teachers of children, it is imperative that we provide an atmosphere in which such self-confidence can develop in every child.

Being a Mathematical Problem Solver

Problem solving has been the focus of school mathematics for more than two decades, yet we still have not made it the essence of mathematics. It remains an activity done separately from the rest of the curriculum in times set aside for the purpose. Problem solving is much more than finding answers to exercises labeled "problem solving." Problem solving and the process of searching for pattern and order are virtually synonymous. Mathematics *is* problem solving. So our task is to investigate mathematical ideas in a problem-solving environment, to help children experience mathematics the way real mathematics is actually done.

Communicating Mathematics

Mathematics is thinking, solving problems, and searching for order. The symbolism so closely associated with mathematics is only a means of recording and expressing mathematics and communicating these ideas to others. Children need to view written work in mathematics from this perspective. In the same sense, children need to learn other modes of mathematical expression, including oral and written reports, drawings, graphs, and charts. Each day should include discussion or writing about the mathematical thinking that is going on in the classroom. No better way exists for wrestling with an idea than to attempt to articulate it to

others. Mathematical expression, therefore, is part of the process and not an end in itself.

Reasoning in Mathematics

Reasoning is at the heart of the shift from memorizing rules to doing mathematics. Finding pattern and order is to make sense of things, to figure out why, to solve problems. Without reasoning, mathematics is reduced to mindless skills that seem mysterious and useless in the real world. With logic and reasoning, mathematics makes sense; it is alive and profoundly useful. Our goal as teachers is to help our students develop the habit of providing an argument or a rationale for a response as part of every answer. When reasoning is valued, children can and do learn that the reasons for their answers are at least as important as the answers themselves. No longer should we hear children say, "Do we divide in this one?" but rather, "I think we should divide here *because* . . ." The habit is best started in kindergarten, but it is never too late to learn the habit, the satisfaction, and the value of defending ideas through logical argument.

Mindless procedures are routinely carried out by computers or by people on the lowest rung of the pay scale. Virtually every productively employed person in our society needs to know how to think and to solve problems they have never encountered before.

All Mathematics Can Be Understood

A major premise of this text, also reflected in the *Standards,* is that the ideas to which children are exposed in mathematics can and should be completely understood by them. *There are no exceptions!* In general, children are capable of learning all of the mathematics we want them to learn, and they can learn it in a meaningful manner. Children must believe this, not because we tell them, but because the experiences we provide make it abundantly clear. For some the struggle to learn may take more time, but all can learn.

WHAT DOES IT MEAN TO DO MATHEMATICS?

Like mathematics, music has many branches categorized in a variety of ways (classical, jazz, rock; instrumental, vocal); it has a sparse notational system for preserving information (notes, time-signatures, clefs) and theories that describe the structure of compositions (scales, patterns). However, no matter how many of the artifacts of music one has learned, it is not the same as doing music. It is only when one performs that one knows music. Similarly, in mathematics one can learn the concepts about numbers, how to solve equations, and so on, but that is not doing mathematics. Doing mathematics involves solving problems, abstracting, inventing, proving, and so forth. (Romberg, 1992, p. 61)

Certainly it is true that the notes and scales of mathematics are important. But we will never teach real mathematics and entice students into the discipline if we do not continually immerse them in "playing the music" of mathematical explorations.

The Verbs of Doing Mathematics

Envision for a moment an elementary mathematics class where students are doing mathematics. What verbs would you use to describe the activity in this classroom? Stop for a moment and make a short list before reading further.

Many children in traditional mathematics classes tend to think of mathematics as "work" or "getting answers." They talk about "plussing" and "doing times" (multiplication). The following collection of verbs is taken from the NCTM *Curriculum Standards* document and reflects a more appropriate view of doing mathematics:

explore	represent	explain
investigate	formulate	predict
conjecture	discover	develop
solve	justify	describe
construct	verify	use

When children are engaged in the kinds of activities suggested by this list, they will necessarily be involved with the ideas under consideration. It is virtually impossible for them to be passive observers. These verbs can also be associated with the five goals for students set by the *Curriculum Standards*. Pick one and reflect on the goals. Which goal or goals would you associate with the verb you selected? For example, *discovering* is an activity that can directly affect a child's personal confidence in his or her ability to do mathematics: "If I discovered this on my own (or in my group), I must be pretty good."

A major shift is called for from an environment that focuses on getting answers to one that focuses on the thinking process itself; teaching through sense making and problem solving is very different from teaching rules to get answers.

An Environment for Doing Mathematics

Look again at the verbs of doing mathematics. They are action verbs. They require reaching out, taking risks, placing ideas out where others can see. Contrast these with the verbs that might reflect the traditional mathematics classroom: *listen, copy, memorize, drill.* These are passive activities. They require no risks and little initiative. Doing mathematics takes effort and initiative. Though thinking, reasoning, and sense making can be fun, it can nevertheless be a bit frightening to stick your neck out when no one tells you exactly what to do.

The classroom must be an environment where doing mathematics is not threatening, where every student is respected for his or her ideas. Students should feel comfortable taking risks, knowing that they will not be ridiculed. At the same time, every student must participate and be actively involved.

The teacher's role is to create this spirit of inquiry, trust, and expectation. Within that environment, students are invited to do mathematics. Problems are posed; students wrestle toward solutions. The focus is on students actively engaged in *doing mathematics* and not on teachers telling and explaining. Students work in groups, in pairs, or individually, but they are always sharing and discussing. Reasoning is celebrated as students defend their methods and justify their solutions.

Teaching through problems means trying to determine what the students know and understand and then selecting and posing tasks or problems that will help them develop the desired new knowledge (Campbell & Johnson, 1995; Lappan & Briars, 1995).

AN INVITATION TO DO MATHEMATICS

It is very possible that your past experiences doing mathematics have not been in the spirit of investigation and reasoning envisioned by the *Standards*. Before thinking about engaging in a science of pattern and order with children, it is important to do a little of that sort of science yourself. That is what we will attempt to do here.

If possible, find one or two friends to work together with you. Get some paper out to scribble ideas on. Try not to be shy about your ideas. Respect and listen to the ideas of your friends. (You can and should challenge their ideas, but don't belittle them.) Perhaps your instructor will have you do some of these or similar explorations in class. It is still a good idea to work on a few of these tasks yourself.

The text will provide hints and suggestions in a poor substitution for the interaction of a teacher. Don't read too much at once. Stop and do as much as you can until you and your group are stuck—really stuck; then read a bit more.

Let's Do Some Mathematics!

We will explore four different problems. Each is independent of the others. None requires any sophisticated mathematics, not even algebra. Don't be passive! Try your ideas out. Have fun!

······································

START AND JUMP NUMBERS:
SEARCHING FOR PATTERNS

You will need to make a list of numbers that begin with a "start number" and increase by a fixed amount we will call the "jump number." Let's use 3 as the start number and 5 as the jump number.

Write the start number at the top of your list. Next write 8, then 13, and so on, "jumping" by 5 each time until your list extends to about 130.

Your task is to examine this list of numbers and find as many patterns as you possibly can. Share your ideas with the group, and write down every pattern you agree really is a pattern.

 Get to work before reading further. Keep looking for patterns until you simply cannot think of any more.

A Few Ideas.   Here are some kinds of things you may already have thought of.

- There is at least one alternating pattern.
- Have you looked at odd and even numbers?
- What can you say about the number in the tens place?

  How did you think about the first two numbers with no tens-place digits?

  What happens when the numbers reach above 100? (There are two ways to think about that.)

- Have you tried doing any adding of numbers? Numbers in the list? Digits in the numbers?

 If you haven't tried something on this list, do that now.

Don't forget to think about what happens to your patterns after the numbers go over 100. How are you thinking about 113? One way is as 1 hundred, 1 ten, and 3 ones. But of course it could also be "eleventy-three" where the tens digit has gone from 9 to 10 to 11. How do these different perspectives affect your patterns? What would happen after 1000?

When you added the *digits* in the numbers, the sums are 3, 8, 4, 9, 5, 10, 6, 11, 7, 12, 8, . . . Did you look at every other number in this string? And what is the sum for 113? Is it 5 or is it 14? (There is no "right" answer here. But it is interesting to consider different possibilities.)

Next Steps.   Sometimes when you have discovered some patterns in mathematics, it is a good idea to make some changes and see how the changes affect the patterns. What changes might you make in this problem?

 Try some ideas now before going on.

Your changes may be even more interesting than the following suggestions. But here are some ideas that seem a bit more obvious than others:

- Change the start number but keep the jump number equal to 5. What is the same and what is different?
- Try keeping the start number the same and examine different jump numbers. You will find out that changing

jump numbers really "messes things up" a lot compared to changing the start numbers.

- If you have patterns for several different jump numbers, what can you figure out about how a jump number affects the patterns? For example, when the jump number was 5, the ones-digit pattern repeated every two numbers—it had a length of two. But when the jump number is 3, the length of the ones-digit pattern is ten! Do other jump numbers create different lengths?

- For a jump number of 3, how is the ones-digit pattern related to the circle of numbers in Figure 2.1? Are there other circles of numbers for other jump numbers?

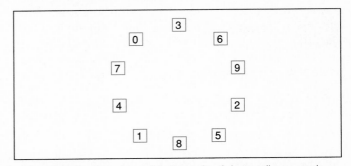

● **Figure 2.1**   For jumps of 3, this cycle of digits will occur in the ones place.

Looking Back.   You may want to explore this idea even further—or perhaps you've had enough of jump numbers. There are more ideas than have been suggested here.

A calculator can be used to make the list generation easy for young children or to work with big jump numbers, like 25 or 36. Most simple calculators have an automatic constant feature that will add the same number successively. For example, if you press 3 ⊞ 5 ⊟ and then keep pressing ⊟, you will get the first sequence of numbers you wrote. (The calculator "stores" the last operation of +5 and repeats the operation on the display for each press of ⊟. This also works for the other three operations.)

Though pattern is the main idea here, the structure of place value in terms of ones and tens pops up several times, as when you need to decide whether 113 is 11 tens and 3 ones or 1 hundred, 1 ten, and 3 ones. Adding up the digits is the same as counting how many base 10 pieces (ones, tens, and hundreds) you would need to show the number. The concept of a common divisor is waiting to be discovered in the discussion of different jump numbers and how long the sequences will be.

You might want to explore using the automatic constant feature for multiplication or division. That produces a whole new set of ideas to consider.

TWO MACHINES, ONE JOB

Ron's Recycle Shop was started when Ron bought a used paper-shredding machine. Business was good, so Ron bought a new shredding machine. The old machine could shred a truckload of paper

in 4 hours. The new machine could shred the same truckload in only 2 hours. How long will it take to shred a truckload of paper if Ron runs both shredders at the same time?

···

Get Started.   Sometimes you just have to jump in and do something. Before reading any of the ideas that follow, go ahead and work on this until you either get an answer or get stuck. If you get an answer, try to decide how you can establish that it is correct. If you get stuck, be absolutely certain you are stuck. Write down everything you know, and examine every idea you have had.

 Work before reading on.

Stuck?   Are there any assumptions made in the problem that you may be overlooking? Do the machines run simultaneously? The problem says "at the same time." Do they run just as fast when working together as when they work alone?

 If this gives you an idea, pursue it before reading more.

Have you tried to predict approximately how much time you think it should take the two machines? Just make an estimate in round numbers. For example, will it be closer to 1 hour or closer to 4 hours? What causes you to answer as you have? Can you tell if your "guestimate" makes sense or is at least in the ballpark? Checking a guess in this way sometimes leads to a new insight.

Some people draw pictures to solve problems. Others like to use something they can move or change. For example, you might draw a rectangle or a line segment to stand

for the truckload of paper, or you might get some counters (chips, plastic cubes, pennies) and make a collection that stands for the truckload.

 Go back and try some more.

Consider Solutions of Others.   Here are solutions of three elementary school teachers who worked on this problem. (The examples are adapted from Schifter & Fosnot, 1993, pp. 24–27.) You might pretend that they are in your group or in your class and you hear their discussions.

Betsy teaches sixth grade. Here is Betsy's solution:

Betsy holds up a bar of plastic cubes. "Let's say these 16 cubes are the truckload of paper. In 1 hour, the new machine shreds 8 cubes and the old machine 4 cubes." Betsy breaks off 8 cubes and then 4 cubes. "That leaves these 4 cubes. If the new machine did 8 cubes' worth in 1 hour, it can do 2 cubes' worth in 15 minutes. The old machine does half as much, or 1 cube." As she says this, she breaks off 3 more cubes. "That is 1 hour and 15 minutes, and we still have 1 cube left." Long pause. "Well, the new machine did 2 cubes in 15 minutes, so it will do this cube in $7\frac{1}{2}$ minutes. Add that onto the 1 hour and 15 minutes. The total time will be 1 hour $22\frac{1}{2}$ minutes." (See Figure 2.2.)

Cora teaches fourth grade. Cora disagrees with Betsy. Here is her proposal:

"This rectangle [see Figure 2.3] stands for the whole truckload. In 1 hour, the new machine will do half of this." The rectangle is divided in half. "In 1 hour, the old machine could do $\frac{1}{4}$ of the paper." The rectangle is divided accordingly. "So in 1 hour, the two machines have done $\frac{3}{4}$ of the truck and there is $\frac{1}{4}$ left. What is left is one-third as much as what they already did, so it should take the two machines one-third as long to do that part as it took to do the first part. One-third of an hour is 20 minutes. That means it takes 1 hour and 20 minutes to do it all."

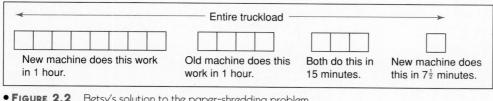

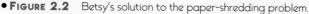

● **FIGURE 2.2**   Betsy's solution to the paper-shredding problem.

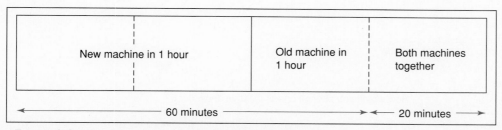

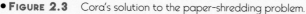

● **FIGURE 2.3**   Cora's solution to the paper-shredding problem.

Sylvia teaches third grade. She and her partner have these thoughts:

At first, we solved the problem by averaging. We decided that it would take 3 hours because that's the average. Then Deborah asked how we knew to average. We thought we had a reason, but then Deborah asked how Ron would feel if his two machines together took longer than just the new one that could do the job in only 2 hours. So we can see that 3 hours doesn't make sense. So we still don't know whether it's 1 hour and 20 minutes or 1 hour and $22\frac{1}{2}$ minutes.

At the SummerMath institute where these teachers were participants, they were not told the solution to this problem. That in itself caused some disturbance. There was no differential reaction to Betsy or Cora. But there is little value in seeing a solution from a book or from a teacher. You end up feeling that the teacher is very smart and you are not so smart. No solution is provided here either.

If you have a solution, a good thing to do is see first why you think you are correct and try to articulate that. Then see if you can find a different way to solve the problem than the way you did it the first time. (What would be the value of two different solutions with only one answer?)

WHAT CAN YOU FIND OUT ABOUT THIS?

First or second graders might be confronted with this observation:

When you make the first number 1 more and the second number 1 less, you get the same answer.

$7 + 7 = 14$ is the same as $8 + 6 = 14$

It works for 5 + 5 too:

$5 + 5 = 10$ is the same as $6 + 4 = 10$

What can you find out about this?

This proves to be an excellent exploration for young children to help them begin to see how facts are related. Your task here is to examine *what happens when you change addition to multiplication in this exploration. What can you find out about that?* ($7 \times 7 = 49$ and $8 \times 6 = 48$).

STOP *Explore until you have developed some ideas. Write down whatever ideas you discover.*

Try Using a Physical Model.   You have probably found some interesting patterns. Can you tell why these patterns work? In the case of addition, it is fairly easy to see that when you take from one number and give to the other, the total stays the same. That is not exactly the way multiplication works. One way to explore this is to make rectangles for each product and see how they change when you adjust one factor up and the other down (see Figure 2.4a).

Instead of rectangles, you may think of multiplication as equal sets. For example, 7×7 means seven sets with seven things in each. You increase the number of sets and decrease the number in each set (or the other way around; see Figure 2.4b).

STOP *Work with one or both of these approaches to see if you get any insights.*

Things to Examine.   There are a few different ways to go with this exploration. Here are a couple of suggestions. You may be pursuing something a bit different than these ideas. That is fine! The idea in this problem is to conduct your own exploration—to see what you can find out.

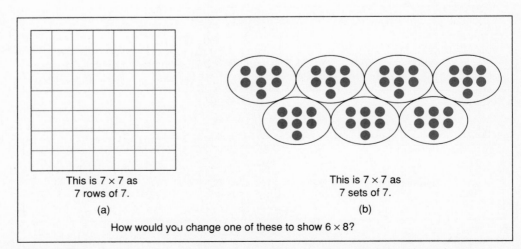

This is 7 × 7 as
7 rows of 7.
(a)

This is 7 × 7 as
7 sets of 7.
(b)

How would you change one of these to show 6 × 8?

● **FIGURE 2.4**   Two physical ways to think about multiplication that might help in the exploration.

- Have you looked at how the first two numbers are related? For example, 7×7, 5×5, 9×9 are all products with like factors. How do those results differ when the two factors are 1 apart (7×8 or 12×13)? What about when the factors differ by 2 or by 3?

- Maybe you have adjusted the factors up and down by 1. What if you go from 7×7 to 9×5? Try making adjustments by other numbers.

- Does it make any difference in the results if you use big numbers instead of small ones?

- What if *both* factors increase?

This exploration has lots of answers. What is especially nice is that only the situation is presented. The questions to answer are the ones *you* ask. When the problem is really yours and it is not clear that the teacher already knows the answer, students feel a lot more ownership and interest. Rather than "What do you want me to do?" problem ownership shifts the situation to "I think I am going to . . ." (Baker & Baker, 1990). The suggested questions offered here were presented as a list because this is a book. In a classroom, the teacher can select challenges and make suggestions when necessary. The teacher can also help students make their own conjectures and observations. Frequently, children will pursue a completely different tack than the one anticipated. Maybe your ideas here were different. Scientists explore new ideas that strike them as interesting and promising. They do not blindly follow the direction of others. Mathematics is a science.

....

THE BEST CHANCE OF PURPLE

Three students are spinning to get purple on the given spinners (either a red then blue or a blue then red; see Figure 2.5). Mary chooses to spin twice on spinner A; John chooses to spin twice on spinner B; and Susan chooses to spin first on spinner A and then on spinner B. Who has the best chance of getting a red and a blue? (Lappan & Even, 1989, p. 17)

....

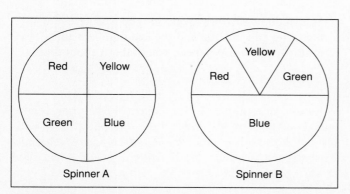

• **FIGURE 2.5**   You may spin A twice, B twice, or A then B. Which option offers you the best chance of spinning a red and a blue?

STOP   *As with the other problems, the first thing is to think about the problem and what you know and then to try something that gives you some help. Before reading the suggestions, see what you can come up with.*

Try It Out.   Sometimes it is tough to get a feel for problems that seem too abstract to think about. One thing that can be done in situations involving chance is to find a way to create the chance and see what happens. For this problem, you can easily make spinners using a freehand drawing on paper, a paper clip, and a pencil. Put your pencil point through the loop of the clip and on the center of your spinner. Now you can flip the paper clip "pointer." Try at least 20 pairs of spins for each choice, and keep track of what happens.

- For Susan's choice (A then B), would it matter if she spun B first and then A? Why or why not?

- Try to describe why you think purple is more or less likely in one of the three cases compared to the other two. It sometimes helps to talk through what you have observed to come up with a way to apply some more precise reasoning.

STOP   *Try these suggestions before reading on.*

Try Tree Diagrams.   On spinner A, the four colors each have the same chance of coming up. You could make a tree diagram for A with four branches, and all the branches would have the same chance (see Figure 2.6). On spinner B, what is the relationship between the blue region and each of the others? How could you make a tree diagram for B with each branch having the same chance?

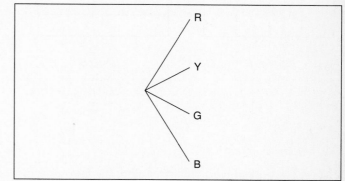

• **FIGURE 2.6**   A tree diagram for spinner A in Figure 2.5.

If you can draw a tree diagram for spinner A, how can you add to the diagram so that it represents spinning A twice in succession? Why does your tree diagram make sense? What on your diagram represents getting purple?

How could you make tree diagrams for John's and Susan's choices? Why do they make sense?

Whatever idea you come up with on paper should be tested by actually spinning the spinner or spinners.

 Tree diagrams are only one way to approach this. You may have a different way. As long as your way seems to make sense and you are getting somewhere, stick with that way. There is one more suggestion to follow, but don't read further if you have an idea to work on.

Using Grids. Suppose that you had a square that represented all the possible outcomes for spinner A and a similar square for spinner B. There are many ways to divide a square in four equal parts, but someone figured out that if you use lines going all in the same direction, you can make comparisons of the outcome of one event (one square) with the outcomes of another event (the same square or a different square). This can be done by placing one square on top of the other. Make the lines on one square go the opposite way from the lines on the other. Make a tracing of one square in Figure 2.7 and place it on the other. You end up with 24 little sections.

Why are there six subdivisions for the spinner B square? What does each of the 24 little rectangles stand for? What sections would represent purple? In any other method you have been trying, did 24 come into play when you were looking at spinner A followed by B?

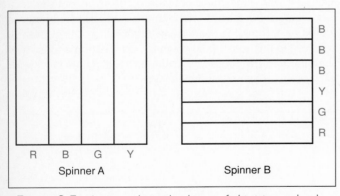

● FIGURE 2.7 A square shows the chance of obtaining each color for the spinners in Figure 2.5.

No Answer Book

If you have worked hard on any or all of the four tasks just presented, you still may not have answers or found all of the patterns and ideas that someone else found. If you really gave it some effort and took some risks in sharing whatever ideas you had, you are on the right track. The science of pattern and order sometimes takes a little time and nearly always requires effort.

No answers or solutions are given in this text. How do you feel about that? What about the "right" answers? Are your answers correct? What makes the solution to any investigation "correct"?

In the classroom, the ready availability of the answer book or the teacher's providing the solution or verifying that an answer is correct all send a clear message to children about doing mathematics. These all-too-available sources of answers convey the idea that the mathematics being done has already been done—the problems have already been solved. The students' job is to find the answers that you, the teacher, already have. "Why work or take risks when the answer will come when the teacher tells us?" In the real world of problem solving outside the classroom, there are no teachers with answers and no answer books.

If you were teaching and the problem you presented completely stumped the entire class for several days, what would you do? This is a tough question. You do not just continue to wait and expect a miracle. That would not be teaching. The more traditional choice is to break the problem into substeps and ask a series of easily answered questions in such a way that the final question answers the problem. The assumption is that the children understand the solution to the problem because they answered all the questions. However, all the students do is answer these well-structured easy questions that they are unlikely to be able to ask of themselves. It is the teacher's choice of the questions that solves the problem.

Some More Explorations

Here are four more explorations you may wish to try. For these tasks, there are no hints or discussions, only the problems. Perhaps your instructor will entertain one or more of these in class. You could try them with children in middle school. The first two could be profitably worked on in fourth or fifth grade. But the main purpose of presenting them here is to give you an opportunity to do some more mathematics and to begin to experience what that means—what it feels like.

....

FOUR CONSECUTIVE NUMBERS

Some people say that to add four consecutive numbers, you add the first and the last numbers and multiply by two. What can you find out about that?

....

Here is an example: 4, 5, 6, and 7 are four consecutive numbers. The sum is 22. Also $4 + 7 = 11$ and $11 \times 2 = 22$. The problem is taken from *Natural Learning and Mathematics* (Stoessiger & Edmunds, 1992). The authors use this task to provide a wonderful illustration of how 11- and 12-year-olds can generate ideas and make them grow. The book is highly recommended.

ACROBATS, GRANDMAS, AND IVAN

The problem is to use the information given to figure out who will win the third round of tug-of-war.

Round 1: On one side are four acrobats, each of equal strength. On the other side are five neighborhood grandmas, each of equal strength. The result is dead even.

Round 2: On one side is Ivan, a dog. Ivan is pitted against two of the grandmas and one acrobat. Again, it's a draw.

Round 3: Ivan and three of the grandmas are on one side, and the four acrobats are on the other.

Who will win the third round?

This problem was originally called "A Mathematical Tug-of-War" and is found in *Mathematics for Smarty Pants* by Marilyn Burns (1982). For a discussion of how fifth graders approached the problem, see *50 Problem-Solving Lessons: Grades 1–6* (Burns, 1996). Silver, Smith, and Nelson (1995) discuss solutions offered by eighth graders.

PIZZAS: SMALL, MEDIUM, AND LARGE

In the thousands of pizza restaurants across the United States, pizzas are sold in small, medium, and large sizes—usually measured by the diameter of the circular pie. Of course, the prices are different for the three sizes. Do you think a large pizza is usually the best buy?

The Sole D'Italia Pizzeria sells small, medium, and large pies. The small pie is nine inches in diameter, the medium pie is twelve inches in diameter, and the large pie is fifteen inches in diameter. For a plain cheese small pizza, Sole D'Italia charges $6; for a medium pizza, it charges $9; for a large pizza, it charges $12. Are these fair prices?

- *Which measures should be most closely related to the prices charged—circumference or area or radius or diameter? Why?*
- *Use your results to write a report on the fairness of Sole D'Italia's pizza prices.*

This problem (Lappan & Briars, 1995, p. 139) has a number of characteristics worth noting. First, it is contextual; it is a very realistic problem that might interest middle grade students. Second, the teacher can predict with some certainty what mathematics students will encounter in this problem (measurement and relationships in the geometry of circles). There are lots of ideas about circle measurement involved. This would be a good problem to use *before* the children have developed a collection of formulas. Students have many ways to get at the circle measures, including measuring some actual circles. Formulas are not necessary. There is also a nice opportunity to discuss rate as a type of ratio in this problem.

TRAPEZOIDS

A trapezoid is a four-sided figure with one pair of opposite sides parallel. Draw a trapezoid that has an area of 36.

If a teacher or a text gives you a formula for the area of a trapezoid, this is not a very interesting task. But there are some nice possibilities for discovering patterns and learning about area and perhaps even developing a formula that can come from this. One suggestion is to get some grid paper and draw some trapezoids. (Blackline Masters are provided at the back of the book.)

THE TEACHER'S ROLE

In the traditional view of mathematics as consisting of a fixed set of rules and procedures, "figuring it out" has very little place other than deciding what rule or procedure to use. Mathematics is commonly known as the epitome of the "well-structured discipline." Lauren Resnick (1988) makes a compelling argument that perhaps we should begin to envision mathematics as an ill-structured discipline:

> We need to take seriously, with and for young learners, the propositions that mathematical statements can have more than one interpretation, that interpretation is the responsibility of every individual using mathematical expressions, and that argument and debate about interpretations and their implications are as natural in mathematics as they are in politics or literature. Such teaching would aim to develop both capability and disposition for finding relationships among mathematical entities and between mathematical statements and situations involving quantities, relationships, and patterns. (p. 33)

Return to Romberg's analogy of learning about music (see p. 12). Classrooms must be social environments in which children learn more than just the notes—the rules and the procedures. Classrooms need to be environments where students wrestle with how the notes might be played and what ideas seem to make the best "music." In short, mathematics classrooms must be cultural environments or communities in which the music of mathematics is played and the notes and scales are learned along the way.

Being the teacher responsible for creating this environment may sound overwhelming. You may have envisioned teaching mathematics as relatively easy. Just demonstrate the rules and manage practice. The preceding pages have tried to paint a different view. Creating a classroom culture and environment in which children are doing mathematics is not easy. There is no reason to believe that you will be an expert from the start.

NCTM's *Professional Standards for Teaching Mathematics* offers important guidelines and examples of teachers making changes toward this vision of doing mathematics. As noted in Chapter 1, the first of the major shifts envisioned by the *Professional Standards* is "toward classrooms as mathematical communities" and "away from classrooms as simply a collection of individuals" (p. 3). So that you can create this mathematical community, you first need a perspective on what doing mathematics feels like. Next you need to understand how children develop mathematical ideas. That is what you will encounter in the next chapter. In Chapter 4, we will take the vision of doing mathematics and how children learn through problem solving and suggest some strategies for teaching with problems. It is an exciting venture!

A listing of each of the six standards for teaching mathematics from the first section of the *Professional Standards* is found in Appendix B. For each of these, the NCTM document includes six or seven pages of discussion and excellent examples that go well beyond the statement of the standard. This section of the *Professional Standards* document is important reading for all teachers.

REFLECTIONS ON CHAPTER 2: WRITING TO LEARN

1. Explain what is meant by "Mathematics is a science of pattern and order." Contrast this view with traditional school mathematics, which is largely a collection of rules and procedures.

2. Select the *Curriculum Standards'* goal for students that you think is most important. Explain the goal itself and why you selected it.

3. Why is doing pencil-and-paper computation not "doing mathematics"?

4. How does Lauren Resnick's idea that mathematics might be better characterized as an ill-structured discipline rather than a well-structured one compare with the notion of mathematics as a science of pattern and order?

FOR DISCUSSION AND EXPLORATION

1. What factors do today's teachers face that get in the way of implementing real doing of mathematics as described in this chapter and in books such as *Everybody Counts*? What should teachers do to deal with these factors?

2. Explore the teacher's edition of any current basal textbook series for any grade level of your interest. Pick one chapter, and identify lessons or activities that promote doing mathematics as a science of pattern and order. In general, would you say that the flavor of the chapter you selected is in the spirit of mathematics as a science of pattern and order?

3. In the *Professional Standards,* read the first vignette (pp. 11–15), in which a sixth-grade teacher of five years confronts her own realization that she needs to change. In reaction to this vignette you might

   a. Try her lesson with fifth- to seventh-grade children

   b. Design a lesson on a topic of your own choice that would serve the same purpose of getting children actively involved in real mathematics

   c. Take a lesson out of a fifth- to seventh-grade book and discuss how this teacher might now decide to teach the lesson

SUGGESTED READINGS

Highly Recommended

Lampert, M. (1990). When the problem is not the question and the solution is not the answer: Mathematical knowing and teaching. *American Educational Research Journal, 27,* 29–63.

   Magdeline Lampert is one of mathematics education's most articulate voices encouraging the shift toward classrooms as communities where children do mathematics. In this article, she clearly articulates the spirit of the traditional classroom and how it adversely affects the concept of mathematics held by children and teachers.

Schifter, D., & Fosnot, C. T. (1993). *Reconstructing mathematics education: Stories of teachers meeting the challenge of reform.* New York: Teachers College Press.

   The authors describe real teachers confronting their own concept of mathematics by doing real mathematics themselves. There are also many insights into the classrooms to which these teachers return. It is in this book that Betsy and Cora solve the paper shredder problem (the context was changed). If you feel a bit threatened by the call for change, this book can give you some company.

Stoessiger, R., & Edmunds, J. (1992). *Natural learning and mathematics.* Portsmouth, NH: Heinemann.

   A wonderfully readable book by two experienced teachers and researchers. The authors suggest that mathematics can be taught in a manner parallel to the language experience approach to reading. They have helped teachers make this change and share many insights. You will find it hard to believe the things children did with the problem of adding four consecutive numbers.

Other Suggestions

Backhouse, J., Haggarty, L., Pirie, S., & Stratton, J. (1992). *Improving the learning of mathematics.* Portsmouth, NH: Heinemann.

Baker, D., Semple, C., & Stead, T. (1990). *How big is the moon?* Portsmouth, NH: Heinemann.

Baker, J., & Baker, A. (1990). *Mathematics in process.* Portsmouth, NH: Heinemann.

Ball, D. L. (1991). Improving, not standardizing, teaching. *Arithmetic Teacher, 39*(1), 18–22.

Ball, D. L. (1991). What's all this talk about discourse? *Arithmetic Teacher, 39*(2), 44–48.

Baroody, A. J. (1993). *Problem solving, reasoning, and communicating (K–8): Helping children think mathematically.* Columbus, OH: Merrill.

Borasi, R. (1990). The invisible hand operating in mathematics instruction: Students' conceptions and expectations. In T. J. Cooney (Ed.), *Teaching and learning mathematics in the 1990s* (pp. 174–182). Reston, VA: National Council of Teachers of Mathematics.

Burns, M. (1992). *About teaching mathematics: A K–8 resource.* White Plains, NY: Cuisenaire (distributor).

Campbell, P. F. (1990). The vision of problem solving in the *Standards. Arithmetic Teacher, 37*(9), 14–17.

Cobb, P., & Merkel, B. (1989). Thinking strategies: Teaching arithmetic through problem solving. In P. R. Trafton (Ed.), *New directions for elementary school mathematics* (pp. 70–81). Reston, VA: National Council of Teachers of Mathematics.

Cobb, P., Yackel, E., Wood, T., & Wheatley, G. (1988). Creating a problem-solving atmosphere. *Arithmetic Teacher, 36*(1), 46–47.

Corwin, R. B. (1993). Doing mathematics together: Creating a mathematical culture. *Arithmetic Teacher, 40,* 338–341.

Garofalo, J. (1989). Beliefs and their influence on mathematical performance. *Mathematics Teacher, 82,* 502–505.

Garofalo, J., & Durant, K. (1991). Where did that come from? A frequent response to mathematics instruction. *School Science and Mathematics, 91,* 318–321.

Hyde, A. A., & Hyde, P. R. (1991). *Mathwise: Teaching mathematical thinking and problem solving.* Portsmouth, NH: Heinemann.

Koehler, M. S., & Prior, M. (1993). Classroom interactions: The heartbeat of the teaching/learning process. In D. T. Owens (Ed.), *Research ideas for the classroom: Middle grades mathematics* (pp. 280–298). Old Tappan, NJ: Macmillan.

Lappan, G., & Schram, P. W. (1989). Communication and reasoning: Critical dimensions of sense making in mathematics. In P. R. Trafton (Ed.), *New directions for elementary school mathematics* (pp. 14–30). Reston, VA: National Council of Teachers of Mathematics.

National Council of Teachers of Mathematics. (1990). *Reaching higher: A problem-solving approach to elementary school mathematics* [Video and teacher's guide]. Reston, VA: Author.

Schoenfeld, A. H. (1989). Problem solving in context(s). In R. I. Charles & E. A. Silver (Eds.), *The teaching and assessing of mathematical problem solving* (pp. 82–92). Reston, VA: National Council of Teachers of Mathematics.

Silver, E. A., & Smith, M. S. (1990). Teaching mathematics and thinking. *Arithmetic Teacher, 37*(8), 34–37.

Smith, S. Z., Smith, M. E., & Romberg, T. A. (1993). What the NCTM *Standards* look like in one classroom. *Educational Leadership, 50*(8), 4–7.

Whitin, D. J. (1989). The power of mathematical investigations. In P. R. Trafton (Ed.), *New directions for elementary school mathematics* (pp. 183–195). Reston, VA: National Council of Teachers of Mathematics.

Whitin, D. J., Mills, H., & O'Keefe, T. (1990). *Living and learning mathematics: Stories and strategies for supporting mathematical literacy.* Portsmouth, NH: Heinemann.

Wiske, M. S., & Levinson, C. Y. (1993). How teachers are implementing the NCTM *Standards. Educational Leadership, 50*(8), 8–12.

CHAPTER

DEVELOPING UNDERSTANDING
IN MATHEMATICS

It is a commonly accepted goal among mathematics educators that students should understand mathematics (Hiebert & Carpenter, 1992). The most widely accepted view of how children learn, a theory known as *constructivism,* suggests that children must be active participants in the development of their own understanding. Constructivism provides us with insights concerning how children learn mathematics and suggests instructional strategies that are radically different from those you have most likely experienced in the mathematics classroom.

A CONSTRUCTIVIST VIEW OF LEARNING

Though still a contemporary position, constructivism is firmly rooted in the cognitive school of psychology and the theories of Piaget dating back at least as far as 1960. Constructivism rejects the notion that children are blank slates. They do not absorb ideas as teachers present them. Rather, children are creators of their own knowledge.

Constructing Understanding

To construct or build something in the physical world requires tools, materials, and effort. How we come to understand the world around us can be viewed in an analogous manner. The tools we use to build understanding are our existing ideas, the knowledge that we already possess. The materials we act on to build understanding may be things we see, hear, or touch—elements of our physical surroundings. Sometimes the materials are our own thoughts and ideas. In building new ideas, active and reflective thought is the effort that must be supplied. If minds are not active, nothing happens.

Piaget's view of the mind was one of constantly changing structures that help us make sense of what we perceive (Brooks & Brooks, 1993; Labinowicz, 1980). When we confront something—an object in our environment, something someone says, a story we read, a thought of our own—we make a mental effort to understand it. The effort causes a change—often unnoticeable and at other times quite startling.

When the things we perceive are familiar to us or are things that we "know," we know them because they fit our previously developed understanding. Piaget referred to this mental activity as *assimilation,* fitting our experiences or perceptions into existing ideas. At other times, the things we perceive do not fit; something doesn't quite make sense. To understand this conflicting input and to relieve the *dissonance* (or *disequilibrium*), our ideas must be modified or new ideas must be created to make the current idea fit. This is the action of *accommodation,* a modification or growth of our cognitive framework that permits assimilation of the new idea (Labinowicz, 1980, 1985).

The theory of constructivism is based on the mental activities of assimilation and accommodation that Piaget described. In the terms of the constructivists, "Knowledge is not passively received either through the senses or by way of communication. Knowledge is actively built up by the (knowing) subject" (von Glasersfeld, 1990, p. 22). Active learners try to "know and understand" by trying to make ideas fit with what they already know. The building or constructing comes as existing ideas are changed, elaborated, and expanded to allow the new ideas to fit.

Constructing Knowledge: Some Examples

It is one thing to describe constructivism in theoretical terms or to say that we "actively build our own understanding." It is quite another thing to make this theory fit our own understanding of what it means to know and learn. Some examples may help.

Constructing a Relationship

Listed here is a string of numbers. Before reading further, spend a minute or so memorizing it so that you can repeat it orally or in writing.

$$2\ 5\ 8\ 1\ 1\ 1\ 4\ 1\ 7\ 2\ 0\ 2\ 3$$

How did you approach the task? Many people separate the list into smaller chunks: for example, 258–111–417–2023. Four or five chunks are easier to remember than the entire string of 13 separate numbers. If you tried this method or a similar one, how long do you think you will remember the list? An hour? A day? If you practice, especially if you say it aloud, invent a singsong cadence, and perhaps write it down 40 or 50 times, your memory would probably be improved. Most people know several number strings, such as phone numbers and Social Security numbers, that they have learned in just that way.

If you think your mastery of the number string is weak and that you will likely forget it soon, look again at the numbers. However, this time look for some kind of pattern or rule. Try it now!

In a group of adults given this memory task, one woman had the string mastered in less than 20 seconds and was quite confident that she would recall the string two or three weeks later with no practice. She pointed out that the list starts with 2, and then 3 is added to each successive number: 2, 5, 8, 11, 14, 17, 20, 23. She commented that it was because she was in a mathematics class that convinced her there must be some logic or pattern involved, so she looked for one from the outset.

What can be learned from this example? First, the idea of adding 3 each time is not visible in that string of numbers. It is a relationship of "3 more than" between certain numbers. You had to construct that relationship on the string of numbers. That relationship cannot be perceived with your senses. Though perhaps trivial for an adult, the idea of "plus

3" or "3 more than" had to be a part of your existing knowledge base. Without the plus-3 tool, you cannot create this new relationship among the numbers.

It is significant that a disposition to look for a pattern or relationship played a key role. Recall from Chapter 2 that in an atmosphere where students expect to find relationships and believe in their own abilities, they will be more likely to look for patterns and relationships.

Once the relationship of the numbers is seen using your own knowledge of plus 3, the string is very easy to recall. This has little to do with the quantity of material to be mastered. Relationships within the new material are integrated with your existing ideas of pattern, addition, number, and "3 more than." The connections provide stability. (Imagine being a child and being told this clever idea but not having the plus-3 idea with which to understand what you were being told.)

Finally, there is a positive feeling of satisfaction at having accomplished the task so easily when it seemed a bit formidable at the outset. Even if you had to be told about the pattern, by being able to integrate it into your framework of ideas, it becomes a clever, albeit not very profound, tidbit of knowledge. And it's yours!

Constructing Computation Methods

Computational procedures or algorithms are traditionally taught by showing the class how each step in the process is done, working some examples together, and then practicing until the method is well established. It is highly probable that you learned to do long division this way. The understanding that you constructed as you mastered the procedure was very limited. You knew how but very likely did not know why. Nor would you have ever invented that procedure on your own.

What happens when children are not taught the procedures but are taught instead the meanings of the operations and have been helped to develop a good understanding of place-value concepts? Consider the solution methods of two fourth-grade children who had been taught in just such a manner. Both children were from predominantly urban schools where a highly constructivist approach to mathematics had been in place for several years. They were asked to solve the following problem: "Four children had 3 bags of M&M's. They decided to open all 3 bags of candy and share the M&M's fairly. There were 52 M&M candies in each bag. How many M&M candies did each child get?" (Campbell & Johnson, 1995, pp. 35–36). Their solutions are shown in Figure 3.1 (p. 24).

Both children were able to determine the product 3×52 mentally. The two children used different cognitive tools to solve the problem of $156 \div 4$. Marlena interpreted the task as "How many sets of 4 can be made from 156?" She first used facts that were either easy or available to her: 10×4 and 4×4. These totals she subtracted from 156 until she got to 100. This seemed to cue her to use 25 fours. Marlena

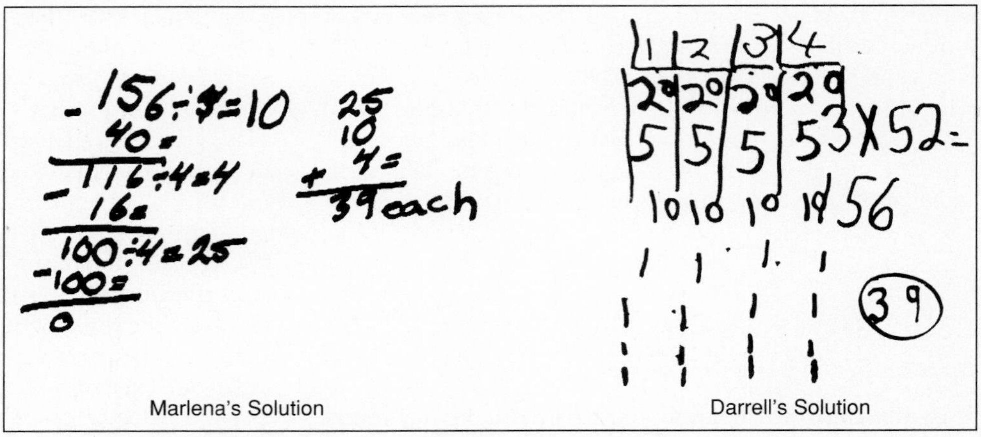

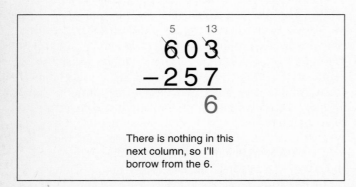

• **FIGURE 3.1**   Two fourth-grade children construct unique solutions to a computation.
Source: Campbell & Johnson (1995). Used with permission.

made no hesitation in adding the number of sets of 4 that she found in 156 and knew the answer was 39 candies for each child.

Darrell's approach was more directly related to the sharing context of the problem. He formed four columns and distributed amounts to each, accumulating the amounts mentally and orally as he wrote the numbers. Like Marlena, Darrell used numbers that were either easy or available to him; first 20 to each, then 5, then 10, and then a series of ones. He added one of the columns without hesitation (Rowan, 1995).

Neither of these division methods is the efficient procedure you learned. If computational speed and proficiency were your goal, you might be tempted to argue that the children need further instruction. But both children clearly constructed ideas about the computation that had meaning to them. They demonstrated confidence, understanding, and a belief that they could solve the problem.

In contrast to these two children, consider a third-grade child in a traditional classroom. She has made a quite common error in subtraction, as shown in Figure 3.2. The child was presented with a situation that was partly familiar and partly not. What was familiar was that the problem ap-

peared on a mathematics worksheet, it was subtraction, and the class had been doing subtraction with borrowing. This context narrowed the choices of ways to give meaning to the situation. But this problem was a little different from the child's existing ideas. She knew she should borrow from the next column, but the next column contained a 0. She could not take 1 from the 0. That part was different. The child decided that "the next column" must mean the next one that has something in it. She therefore borrowed from the 6 and ignored the 0. This child gave her own meaning to the rule "borrow from the next column."

In this example, the existing ideas that were brought to the situation were unfortunately quite limited and consisted mostly of procedural information that was not connected to a firm understanding of place value. Recall that the tools for constructing knowledge consist of existing ideas. When a difficulty arises (*disequilibrium*), a child searches through the local network of ideas (those that are immediately related to the task) and uses what is available. Few third-grade children consciously think about place-value concepts while doing routine computation. However, had the procedural knowledge of borrowing been more tightly connected to concepts of place value, it is much more likely that this child's understanding of the task would have been modified or constructed correctly.

Children rarely give random responses (Ginsburg, 1977; Labinowicz, 1985). Their answers tend to make sense in terms of their personal perspective or in terms of the knowledge they are using to give meaning to the situation. In many instances, children's existing knowledge is incomplete or inaccurate, or perhaps the knowledge we assume to be there simply is not. In such situations, as in the present example, new knowledge may be constructed inaccurately.

Developing a Formula

Gary Tsuruda is a middle school teacher who has made a significant shift in his teaching to reflect his understanding

$$\overset{5}{\cancel{6}}\,0\,\overset{13}{\cancel{3}}$$
$$-2\,5\,7$$
$$\overline{6}$$

There is nothing in this next column, so I'll borrow from the 6.

• **FIGURE 3.2**   Children sometimes invent incorrect meanings by extending poorly understood rules.

TRAPEZOID AREA

GOAL: *Find an easy way to determine the area of any trapezoid.*

Be sure that you understand the answers to each of these questions:

1. What does "area" mean?
2. What is a trapezoid?
3. How do you find the area of other polygons? Show as many different ways as you can.

Now see if your group can find an easy way to determine the area of any trapezoid.

HINTS:

1. Draw several trapezoids on dot paper and find their areas. Look for patterns.
2. Consider how you find the area of other polygons. Are any of the key ideas similar?
3. You might try cutting out trapezoids and piecing them together.
4. If you find a way to determine the area, make sure it is as easy as you can make it and that it works for *any* trapezoid.

WRITE-UP:

1. Explain your answers to the first three questions in detail. Tell how your group reached agreement on the answers.
2. Tell what you did to get your formula for the area of any trapezoid. Did you use any of the hints? How did they help you?
3. Show your formula and give an illustration of how it works.

•FIGURE 3.3 A middle school example in which students are required to construct a formula.

Source: Tsuruda (1994, p. 7). Used with permission.

of the constructivist view of learning. His classes frequently work in small groups to solve problems presented in written form. Figure 3.3 shows one example. Students are to work on developing a formula for finding the area of a trapezoid. Notice that the initial questions bring the requisite ideas needed for the task to the students' conscious level. Next they are asked to do some exploration and look for patterns. From these explorations the group must come up with a formula, test it, describe how it was developed and illustrate its use.

The task requires a lot of reflective thinking on the part of the students. They have one another to brainstorm with, and the teacher is there to listen and to provide hints, encouragement, and suggestions. Tsuruda (1994) reports that every group was able to produce a formula. "Not all the formulas looked like the typical textbook formula, but they were all correct, and more important, each formula made sense according to the way the students in that group had constructed the knowledge from the data they themselves had generated" (p. 6).

Principles of Constructivism

Constructing knowledge is an extremely active endeavor on the part of the learner (Baroody 1987; Cobb, 1988; von Glasersfeld, 1990). To construct and understand a new idea involves making connections between old ideas and new ones. "How does this fit with what I already know?" "How can I understand this in the face of my current understanding of this idea?" Mathematical ideas cannot be "poured into" a passive learner. Children must be mentally active for learning to take place. In classrooms, children must be encouraged to wrestle with new ideas, to work at fitting them into existing networks, and to challenge their own ideas and those of others. Put simply, constructing knowledge requires *reflective thought,* actively thinking about or mentally working on an idea.

Networks of ideas that presently exist in the learner's mind determine how an idea might be constructed. These integrated networks, frequently referred to as *cognitive schemas,* are both the product of constructing knowledge and the tools with which new knowledge is constructed. The more connections with the existing network of ideas, the better the new ideas are understood. As learning occurs, the networks are rearranged, added to, or otherwise modified. When there is active, reflective thought, schemas are constantly being modified or changed so that ideas fit better with what is known.

KNOWLEDGE OF MATHEMATICS

All knowledge consists of internal or mental representations of ideas that our mind has constructed. For some time now, mathematics educators have found it useful to distinguish between *conceptual knowledge* and *procedural knowledge* (Hiebert & Carpenter, 1992; Hiebert & Lefevre, 1986; Hiebert & Lindquist, 1990). *Conceptual knowledge* consists of relationships constructed internally and connected to already existing ideas. It is the type of knowledge Piaget referred to as logico-mathematical knowledge (Kamii, 1985, 1989; Labinowicz, 1985). *Procedural knowledge* of mathematics is knowledge of the rules and the procedures that one uses in carrying out routine mathematical tasks and of the symbolism that is used to represent mathematics.

Conceptual Knowledge of Mathematics

Ideas such as seven, rectangle, ones/tens/hundreds (as in place value), sum, product, equivalent, ratio, and negative are all examples of mathematical relationships or concepts.

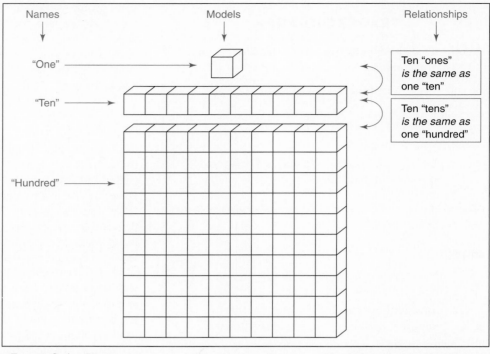

Names   Models   Relationships

"One" ⟶

"Ten" ⟶

"Hundred" ⟶

Ten "ones"
is the same as
one "ten"

Ten "tens"
is the same as
one "hundred"

● **FIGURE 3.4**   *Objects and names of objects are not the same as relationships between the objects.*

Figure 3.4 shows three blocks commonly used to represent ones, tens, and hundreds. By the middle of second grade, most children have seen pictures of these or have used the actual blocks. It is quite common for these children to be able to identify the rod as the "ten" piece and the large square block as the "hundred" piece. Does this mean that they have constructed the concept of ten and hundred? All that is known for sure is that they have learned the names for these objects, the common conventional names of the blocks. The mathematical concept of ten is that *a ten is the same as ten ones.* Ten is not a rod. The concept is the relationship between the rod and the small cube. It is not the rod or a bundle of ten sticks or any other model of a ten. This relationship called "ten" must be created by children within their own minds.

In Figure 3.5, the shape labeled A is a rectangle. But, if we call shape B "one" or a "whole," then we might refer to shape A as "one-half." The idea of "half" is the *relationship* between shapes A and B, a relationship that must be constructed in our mind. It is not in either rectangle. In fact, if we decide to call shape C the whole, shape A becomes "one-

fourth." The physical rectangle did not change in any way. The concepts of "half" and "fourth" are not in the rectangle A; we construct them in our mind. The rectangles help us "see" the relationships, but what we see are rectangles, not concepts.

Procedural Knowledge of Mathematics

Knowledge of mathematics consists of more than concepts. Concepts are represented by special words and mathematical symbols. Step-by-step procedures exist for performing tasks such as multiplying 47×68. These symbols, words, and procedures can be supported by concepts, but by themselves they are not conceptual ideas.

Symbolism includes expressions such as $(9 - 5) \times 2 = 8$, π, $<$, and $\neq$. What meaning is attached to this symbolic knowledge depends on how it is understood—what concepts and other ideas the individual connects to the symbols.

Procedures are the step-by-step routines learned to accomplish some task. "To add two three-digit numbers, first add the numbers in the right-hand column. If the answer is 10 or more, put the 1 above the second column, and write the other digit under the first column. Proceed in a similar manner for the next two columns in order." We can say that someone who can accomplish a task such as this has knowledge of that procedure. Again, the conceptual understanding that may or may not support the procedural knowledge can vary considerably from one student to the next.

Some procedures are very simple and may even be confused with conceptual knowledge. For example, seventh-grade children may be shown how to add the integers ⁻7

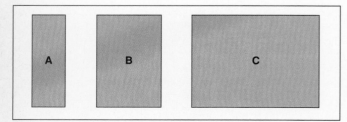

A   B   C

● **FIGURE 3.5**   *Three shapes, different relationships.*

and $^+4$ by combining 7 red "negative" checkers with 4 yellow "positive" checkers. Pairs consisting of 1 red and 1 yellow checker are removed, and the result is noted. In this example, there would be 3 red negative checkers remaining, and the students would record $^-3$ as the sum. This might be called a manipulative or physical procedure. Notice that it is conceivable that a student could master a procedure such as this with very little understanding.

The Role of Procedural Knowledge

Procedural knowledge of mathematics plays a very important role both in learning and in doing mathematics. Algorithmic procedures help us do routine tasks easily and thus free our minds to concentrate on more important tasks. Symbolism is a powerful mechanism for conveying mathematical ideas to others and for "doodling around" with an idea as we do mathematics. But even the most skillful use of a procedure will not help develop conceptual knowledge that is related to that procedure (Hiebert, 1990). Doing endless long-division exercises will not help a child understand what division means.

From the vantage of learning mathematics, the question of how procedures and conceptual ideas can be linked is much more important than the usefulness of the procedure itself (Hiebert & Carpenter, 1992). Recall the two children who used their own invented procedure to solve $156 \div 4$ (see Figure 3.1, p. 24). Clearly there was an active and useful interaction between the procedures the children invented and the ideas they were constructing about division.

It is generally accepted that procedural rules should never be learned in the absence of a concept, although, unfortunately, that happens far too often.

UNDERSTANDING MATHEMATICS

It is possible to say that we know something or we do not. In other words, knowledge is something that we either have or we don't have. Understanding is another matter. Most readers of this book would agree that they *know* division. But do you completely *understand* division? Do you know all there is to know about division? Think about what you do know about division. Do all of your adult peers have the same understanding? Did Darrell and Marlena have the same understanding of division as you have?

Schifter and Fosnot (1993) describe a third-grade class where several children are discussing the problem of sharing 90 jelly beans among four children. They decide to use base 10 models (ones and tens). They share 2 tens to each group and trade a ten for 10 ones. They next share 2 ones to each group. There is then a discussion of what to do with the 2 leftover ones and how to write down what they have done. One child suggests "$22\frac{1}{2}$" and another "22 R 2." They decide

that the best answer for any division depends on the situation and what you want to do with the leftovers.

In a more traditional class, another third grader was quite confident in her ability to do long divisions such as $24{,}682 \div 5$. When asked what the "R 2" meant when she computed $32 \div 5$, she could only identify the 2 as the remainder. Asked to demonstrate $32 \div 5$ with blocks, she began but then decided it couldn't be done. The child was at a loss to explain "R 2" in terms of the leftover counters (Schifter & Fosnot, 1993). These children all have different understandings of division. Some are very rich understandings; some are very limited. All are different.

Relational Versus Instrumental Understanding

Understanding can be described as a measure of the quality and quantity of connections that an idea has with existing ideas. Understanding depends on the existence of appropriate ideas and on the creation of new connections (Backhouse, Haggarty, Pirie, & Stratton, 1992; Davis, 1986; Hiebert & Carpenter, 1992; Janvier, 1987; Schroeder & Lester, 1989). As we just saw, it is rarely an all-or-nothing proposition.

One way that we can think about an individual's understanding is that it exists along a continuum. At one extreme is a very rich set of connections. The understood idea is associated with many other existing ideas in a meaningful network of concepts and procedures. Hiebert and Carpenter (1992) refer to "webs" of interrelated ideas. This richly connected end of the continuum of understanding will be referred to in this text as *relational understanding,* borrowing a term made popular by Richard Skemp (1978). At the other end of the continuum, ideas are completely isolated or nearly so. Understanding at this end of the continuum, where knowledge is isolated and not integrated with other ideas, will be referred to as *instrumental understanding,* again borrowing terminology from Skemp. Knowledge that is learned instrumentally is learned by rote, generally through drill and practice.

Understanding Conceptual Knowledge

As new relationships (mathematical concepts) are constructed, they are almost certainly connected to the ideas that were used to construct them. Consider the concept of "seven" as constructed by a child in the first grade. Seven for a first grader is most likely connected to the counting procedure and the construct of "more than" and is probably understood as less than 10 and more than 2. What else will this child eventually connect to the concept of seven as it now exists? Seven is 1 more than 6, it is 2 less than 9, it is the combination of 3 and 4 or 2 and 5, it is odd, it is small compared to 73 and large compared to one-tenth, it is the number of days in a week, it is "lucky," it is prime, and on and on. The web of potential ideas connected to a number can grow large and involved.

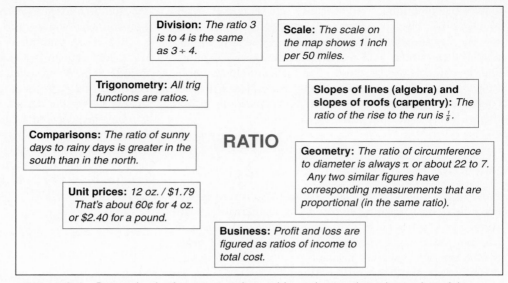

Division: *The ratio 3 is to 4 is the same as 3 ÷ 4.*

Scale: *The scale on the map shows 1 inch per 50 miles.*

Trigonometry: *All trig functions are ratios.*

Slopes of lines (algebra) and slopes of roofs (carpentry): *The ratio of the rise to the run is $\frac{1}{8}$.*

Comparisons: *The ratio of sunny days to rainy days is greater in the south than in the north.*

RATIO

Geometry: *The ratio of circumference to diameter is always π or about 22 to 7. Any two similar figures have corresponding measurements that are proportional (in the same ratio).*

Unit prices: *12 oz. / $1.79 That's about 60¢ for 4 oz. or $2.40 for a pound.*

Business: *Profit and loss are figured as ratios of income to total cost.*

● **FIGURE 3.6** *Potential web of associations that could contribute to the understanding of the concept of "ratio."*

As another example of a rich, *relational* understanding, consider the many ideas that a learner could potentially associate with the concept of "ratio" (see Figure 3.6). Unfortunately, many children learn only procedural knowledge connected with ratio, such as "given one ratio, how do you find an equivalent ratio?"

Understanding Procedural Knowledge

When talking about understanding procedural knowledge, the most important connection we want children to make is to meaningful concepts. "Rules without reasons," what Skemp was referring to when he coined the term *instrumental understanding*, should never be permitted in a mathematics classroom.

Every single mathematical procedure is potentially connected with large networks of information. In many instances, two or more different procedures are connected through a conceptual linkage. For example, to get half of a number, you can divide by 2 or multiply by 0.5. Conceptual relationships give meaning to both procedures and indicate that they are equivalent while on the surface they appear quite distinct.

Procedural knowledge is most susceptible to instrumental understanding or rote rule learning. Many of us were unfortunately taught instrumentally, taught to master rules that we learned by rote memorization with no hint of why they worked. You may know the rule "invert the divisor and multiply" but not be able to make up a simple word problem to go with $\frac{3}{4} \div \frac{1}{2}$. What does it mean to divide $\frac{3}{4}$ by $\frac{1}{2}$? On the Fourth National Assessment of Educational **Progress (NAEP), roughly 80 percent of seventh-grade students were able to express** $5\frac{1}{4}$ correctly as $\frac{21}{4}$. However, when asked whether $5\frac{1}{4}$ meant $5 + \frac{1}{4}$, $5 - \frac{1}{4}$, $5 \times \frac{1}{4}$, or $5 \div \frac{1}{4}$, fewer than half of the children chose the correct expression.

Too many children are using procedures with fractions without an understanding of the concepts behind them (Kouba et al., 1988a).

At the second- and third-grade levels, many children are able to subtract with pencil and paper but are unable to explain the meaning of the little numbers that they write when they "borrow." They also do not understand that the number written after regrouping is the same quantity as before (see Figure 3.7). These same children are able to use sticks and bundles of ten sticks to do the same subtraction (Cauley, 1988). They seem to have conceptual knowledge of place value and regrouping and also procedural knowledge of regrouping but have failed to connect the two ideas. No matter how rich or useful their understanding of place value may be, the regrouping process is left disconnected from these concepts; it is known only instrumentally.

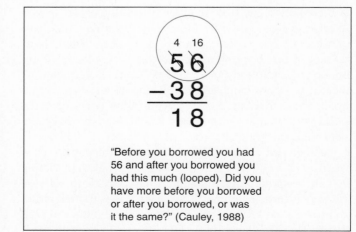

"Before you borrowed you had 56 and after you borrowed you had this much (looped). Did you have more before you borrowed or after you borrowed, or was it the same?" (Cauley, 1988)

● **FIGURE 3.7** *To the question in the figure, roughly one-third of second- and third-grade children responded "more before," another third thought "more after," and one-third knew it was the same.*

This last example illustrates that it is possible to have taught children the corresponding conceptual knowledge related to a procedure but failed in helping them connect the concepts with the procedure. Unfortunately, it is much more common to find children who simply do not possess the conceptual knowledge that supports a procedure.

Think of a mathematical procedure you are familiar with. Then decide how you would describe your understanding of that procedure. Would you describe it as relational understanding or as instrumental understanding? How has your understanding affected your growth of other related ideas?

The Individual Nature of Understanding

Because understanding is measured by the quantity and quality of the connections or associations that an individual is able to make with other already formed networks of ideas, it follows that understanding depends to a very large degree on what networks and ideas the child brings to the task of understanding. Consider the idea of ratio with its many potential connections as noted in Figure 3.6 (p. 28). Do you, for example, currently possess all of the ideas surrounding this concept of ratio? Do you think the average seventh- or eighth-grade student does? Understanding is a highly subjective aspect of knowledge. This feature of understanding should be ever-present in the mind of teachers dealing with a class of children. When you ask, "Do you understand?" be aware that children could answer this question in the affirmative and all have different degrees and types of understanding.

Benefits of Relational Understanding

To teach for relational understanding requires a lot of work and effort. Concepts and connections develop over time, not in a day. Instructional materials must be made. The classroom must be organized for group work and maximum interaction with and among the children. There are important benefits to be derived from relational understanding that make the effort not only worthwhile but also essential. Relational understanding is intrinsically rewarding, enhances memory, requires that less be remembered, helps with learning new concepts and procedures, improves problem-solving abilities, can be self-generative, and has a positive effect on attitudes and beliefs.

It Is Intrinsically Rewarding

Nearly all people, and certainly children, enjoy learning. This is especially true when new information connects with ideas already possessed. The new knowledge makes sense; it fits; it feels good. Children who learn by rote must be motivated by external means: for the sake of a test, to please a parent, from fear of failure, or to receive some reward. Such learning is distasteful. Rewards of an extra recess or a star on a chart may be effective in the short run but do nothing to encourage a love of the subject when the rewards are removed. Mathematics learned relationally is frequently just plain fun.

It Enhances Memory

Memory is a process of retrieving information. When concepts and procedures are learned relationally, there is much less chance that the information will deteriorate; connected information is simply more likely than disconnected information to be retained over time. Retrieval of the information is also easier. Connected information provides an entire web of ideas to reach for. If what you need to recall seems distant, by reflecting on ideas that are related, the desired idea is eventually found. Retrieving disconnected information is more like finding a needle in a haystack.

A large portion of instructional time in American schools is devoted to reteaching and review. If ideas were learned relationally instead of instrumentally, much less time would need to be spent on review.

There Is Less to Remember

Traditional approaches have tended to fragment mathematics into seemingly endless lists of isolated skills, concepts, rules, and symbols. The lists are so lengthy that teachers and students become overwhelmed. Constructivists, for their part, talk about teaching "big ideas" (Brooks & Brooks, 1993; Schifter & Fosnot, 1993). Big ideas are really the large networks of interrelated concepts. Ideas are learned relationally when they are integrated into a larger web of information, a big idea. Frequently, the network is so well constructed that whole chunks of information are stored and retrieved as single entities rather than isolated bits. For example, knowledge of place value subsumes rules about lining up decimal points, ordering decimal numbers, moving decimal points to the right or left in decimal/percent conversions, rounding and estimating, and a host of other ideas. Similarly, knowledge of equivalent fractions ties together rules concerning common denominators, reducing fractions, and changing between mixed numbers and whole numbers.

It Helps with Learning New Concepts and Procedures

An idea fully understood in mathematics is more easily extended to learn a new idea. Number concepts and relationships help in the mastery of basic facts, fraction knowledge and place-value knowledge come together to make decimal learning easier, and decimal concepts directly enhance an understanding of percentage concepts and procedures. Many of the ideas of elementary arithmetic become the model for understanding ideas in algebra. Reducing fractions by finding common prime factors is the same thing as canceling out common factors.

Without these connections, children will need to learn each new piece of information they encounter as a separate, unrelated idea.

It Improves Problem-Solving Abilities

Between 1973 and 1986, the NAEP gathered data on the mathematics proficiency of the nation's 9-, 13-, and 17-year-olds. A consistent trend was a significantly lower level of performance in both problem solving and concepts than in traditional computational skills (Dossey, Mullis, Lindquist, & Chambers, 1988). The results are largely a reflection of the emphasis on basic skills in the U.S. curriculum, but they also point out that skills developed in isolation are not very useful when it comes to solving problems and thinking. Problem solving requires both procedural and conceptual knowledge. Both are much more useful to the problem solver when intertwined and connected (Silver, 1986).

It Is Self-Generative

The term *organic* is used by Skemp (1978) to denote this searching and growth quality of relational understanding. Skemp notes that when knowledge or gaining knowledge is found to be pleasurable, people who have had that experience of pleasure are likely to seek or invent new ideas on their own, especially when confronted with problematic situations. "Inventions that operate on understandings can generate new understandings, suggesting a kind of snowball effect. As networks grow and become more structured, they increase the potential for invention" (Hiebert & Carpenter, 1992, p. 74).

It Improves Attitudes and Beliefs

Relational understanding has an affective effect as well as a cognitive effect. When learning relationally, the learner tends to develop a positive self-concept about his or her ability to learn and understand mathematics. There is a definite sense of "I can do this! I understand!" A sense of self-worth develops. Knowledge learned relationally is not foreign or strange. There is no reason to fear it or to be in awe of it. Mathematics then makes sense. It is not some mysterious world that only "smart people" dare enter. At the other end of the continuum, instrumental understanding has the potential of producing real mathematics anxiety. Math anxiety is a real phenomenon that involves definite fear and avoidance behavior. It is self-destructive. The more one fears and avoids mathematics, the more one is reinforced in beliefs of inadequacy.

Relational understanding also promotes a positive view about mathematics itself. Sensing the connectedness and logic of mathematics, students are more likely to gravitate toward it or to describe the discipline in positive terms. Students positively disposed to the discipline of mathematics are much more likely to pursue its study. Encouraging a much larger percentage of children to study mathematics and related fields is a serious national goal.

THE ROLE OF MODELS IN DEVELOPING UNDERSTANDING

It has become a cliché that good teachers use a "hands-on approach" to teach mathematics. Manipulatives, or physical materials to model mathematical concepts, are certainly important tools available for helping children learn mathematics. But they are not the panacea that some seem to believe. It is important that you have a good perspective on how manipulatives can help or fail to help children construct ideas.

Models for Mathematical Concepts

Before defining a model, return for a moment to the idea of a mathematical concept as a relationship, a logical idea. There are no physical examples of mathematical concepts in the physical world. The concept of "hundred," for example, is a quantity relationship that a group of 100 items has with a single item of the same type. We can talk of 100 people, 100 dollars, or 100 acts of kindness. None of those sets *is* a hundred. Hundred is only a relationship that the group has with one thing like those in the group. It is impossible to imagine "hundred" without first understanding "one."

A *model* for a mathematical concept refers to any object, picture, or drawing that represents the concept or on which the relationship for that concept can be imposed. In this sense, any group of 100 objects can represent the concept "hundred" because we can impose the 100-to-1 relationship on the group and a single element of the group. It is often said that a model "illustrates" a concept. To illustrate implies showing. That would mean that when you looked at the model, you would see an example of the concept. Technically, all that is actually seen with your eyes is the physical object. Only your mind can impose the mathematical relationship on the objects (Thompson, 1994). This brings us back to one of the main tenets of constructivism: Knowledge is actively created by the child, not passively received from the teacher, the book, or physical materials.

Examples of Models

As noted, physical materials have become enormously popular as tools for teaching mathematics. They can run the gamut from common objects such as lima beans for counters to commercially produced materials such as wooden rods or plastic geometric shapes. Figure 3.8 (p. 31) shows six common examples of models for six different concepts. Consider each of the concepts and the corresponding model. Try to separate the physical model from the relationship that you must impose on the model in order to "see" the concept.

For the examples in Figure 3.8:

• The concept of "six" is a relationship between sets that can be matched to the words *one, two, three, four, five, six.* Changing a set of counters by adding one changes the

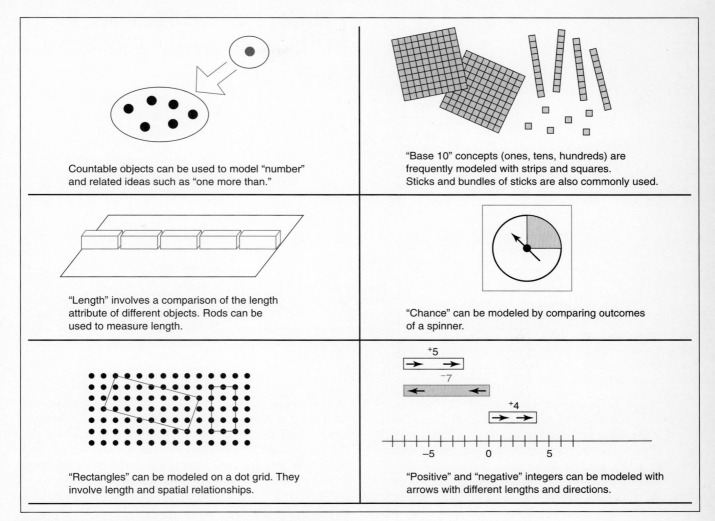

Countable objects can be used to model "number" and related ideas such as "one more than."

"Base 10" concepts (ones, tens, hundreds) are frequently modeled with strips and squares. Sticks and bundles of sticks are also commonly used.

"Length" involves a comparison of the length attribute of different objects. Rods can be used to measure length.

"Chance" can be modeled by comparing outcomes of a spinner.

"Rectangles" can be modeled on a dot grid. They involve length and spatial relationships.

"Positive" and "negative" integers can be modeled with arrows with different lengths and directions.

• **FIGURE 3.8** *Examples of models to illustrate mathematics concepts.*

relationship. The difference between the set of 6 and the set of 7 is the relationship "one more than."

- The concept of "length" could not be developed without making comparisons of the length attribute of different objects. The length measure of an object is a comparison relationship of the length of the object to the length of the unit.
- The concept of "rectangle" is a combination of spatial and length relationships. By drawing on dot paper, the relationships of the opposite sides' being of equal length and parallel and the adjacent sides' meeting at right angles can be illustrated.
- The concept of "hundred" is not in the larger square but in the relationship of that square to the strip ("ten") and to the little square ("one").
- "Chance" is a relationship between the frequency of an event's happening compared with all possible outcomes. The spinner can be used to create relative frequencies. These can be predicted by observing relationships of sectors of the spinner. Note how chance and probability are integrated with ideas of fractions and ratio.

- The concept of a "negative integer" is based on the relationship "is the opposite of." Negative quantities exist only in relation to positive quantities. Arrows on the number line are not themselves negative quantities but model the "opposite of" relationship in terms of direction and size or magnitude in terms of length.

One frequently used model for integers consists of sets of counters in two colors, perhaps red for negative quantities and yellow for positive. With the counter model, the opposite aspect of integers must be imposed on the two available colors with the idea that one color is to be understood as the opposite of the other. Even though colored counters and arrows are radically different, the same relationships can be imposed on each. Children must construct relationships in order to "see" positive and negative integers in either model.

It is important to include calculators in any list of common models. At every grade level, K–16, the calculator models a wide variety of numeric relationships by quickly and easily demonstrating the effects of these ideas. For example, if the calculator is made to count by increments of 0.01 (press ⊞ 0.01 ⊜), the relationship of one-hundredth

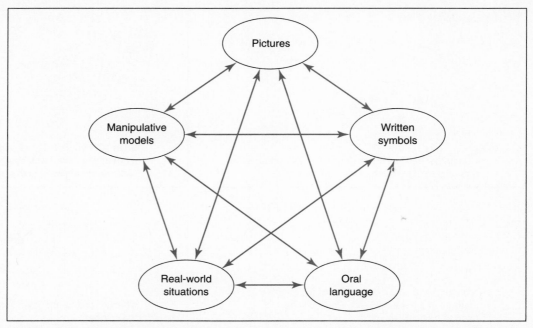

● **FIGURE 3.9**   Five different representations of mathematical ideas. Translations between and within each mode can help develop new concepts.

to one whole is illustrated. Press 3 $\boxed{+}$ 0.01. How many presses of $\boxed{=}$ are required to get from 3 to 4? Doing the required 100 presses and observing how the display changes along the way is quite impressive. Especially note what happens after 3.19, 3.29, and so on.

As a second example, how would you use the calculator to divide 348 by 26, giving both quotient and remainder, without pressing the $\boxed{\div}$ key? There are at least three solutions to this task. (Can you find one or two of them?) Solving the problem helps students develop relationships between multiplication and division.

Models and Constructing Mathematics

If you reflect for a moment on this definition of a model, you may well be perplexed. It would seem that a child would need to know the relationship before imposing it on the model. If the concept does not come *from* the model—and it does not—how does the child get it?

Mathematical concepts that children are in the process of constructing are not the well-formed ideas conceived by adults. New ideas are formulated little by little over time. As children actively reflect on their new ideas, they test them out through as many different avenues as we might provide. For example, this is where the value of student discussions and group work comes in. Talking through an idea, arguing for a viewpoint, listening to others, and describing and explaining are all mentally active ways of testing an emerging idea against reality. As this testing process goes on, the developing idea gets modified and elaborated and further integrated with existing ideas. When there is a good fit with external reality, the likelihood of a correct concept's having been formed is good.

Models can play this same role, that of a testing ground for emerging ideas. Models can be thought of as "thinker toys," "tester toys," and "talker toys."* It is difficult for students (of all ages) to talk about and test out abstract relationships using words alone. Models give learners something to think about, explore with, talk about, and reason with.

Expanding the Idea of a Model

Lesh, Post, and Behr (1987) talk about five "representations" for concepts, two of which are manipulative models and pictures (see Figure 3.9). In their research, they also consider written symbolism, oral language, and real-world situations to be representations or models of concepts. Their research has found that children who have difficulty translating a concept from one representation to another are the same children who have difficulty solving problems and understanding computations. Strengthening the ability to move between and among these representations improves the growth of children's concepts.

The five representations in Figure 3.9 are simply an expansion of the model concept. The more ways that children are given to think about and test out an emerging idea, the better chance it has of being formed correctly and integrated into a rich web of ideas—relational understanding.

---

*The term "thinker toy" is taken from Seymour Papert's popular book *Mindstorms* (1980), in which the inventor of the Logo computer language describes his vision of the computer as a powerful and flexible device that encourages learners of any age to play with ideas and work through problems. "Tester toys" and "talker toys" were suggested by Laura Domalik, a first-grade teacher.

Using Models in the Classroom

If we think of models as thinker toys or talker toys, we can identify three related uses for them in a developmental approach to teaching:

1. To help children develop new concepts or relationships
2. To help children make connections between concepts and symbols
3. To assess children's understanding

Models Help Develop New Concepts

Models help children think and reflect on new ideas. To that end, they should always be readily available for students to select and use freely. A variety of models should be available to help with an important idea. Students should be encouraged to select and use materials to help them work through a problem or explain an idea to their group.

You will undoubtedly encounter situations in which you use a model that you think clearly illustrates an idea but the child just doesn't get it. Remember that you already possess the well-formed concept so you are able to impose it on the model. The child, on the other hand, is in the process of creating the concept and is using the model to test an emerging idea. Your job is to get children to think with models; to work actively at the test-revise-test-revise process until the new concept fits with the physical model you have offered. It is not possible to show mathematics with models. You can only provide models on which mathematical relationships or concepts can be imposed. When the child's concept fits the model, he or she "sees" the concept. When it does not fit, the child cannot "see" the concept in the model in the same way that you do. His or her concept is different than the one that can correctly be imposed on the model and must undergo further construction or revision.

Models Help Connect Symbols and Concepts

Frequently teachers will say, "But when they try to do it without manipulatives, they can't." It is naive to expect children automatically to transfer newly formed ideas to symbolic procedures without some guidance. Models can serve as a link between concepts and symbols as well as a means of developing concepts.

A general approach is to have students write down what they have done with models. "Write an equation to tell what you just did." "I see how you did that problem with the blocks. How would you go about recording what you did?" When children see written mathematics as expressions or recordings of ideas that they have already developed, the written or symbolic form is more likely to make sense.

Models Provide Insights to Children's Thinking

As already noted, it is difficult to talk about and explain abstract ideas. If we want to know what concepts and understanding children have constructed, a good suggestion is to have them explain ideas with manipulative materials. This might be done in a diagnostic setting where you sit down one-on-one with a child and try to find out what he or she is thinking. It also makes good sense to conduct regular full-class assessments using materials. According to the *Curriculum Standards*, "If students' understandings are closely related to the use of physical materials, they should be allowed to use these materials to demonstrate their knowledge during assessment" (NCTM, 1989, p. 195). (Assessment is discussed in depth in Chapter 5.)

Models Can Be Used Incorrectly

Note that free use of models is very different from overly directed use. There is a natural temptation to get out the materials and "show" children how to use them. Children will blindly follow the teacher's directions, and it may even look as if they understand. It is just as possible to get students to move blocks around mindlessly as it is to teach them to "invert and multiply" mindlessly. Neither promotes thinking or aids in the development of concepts (Clements & Battista, 1990).

A natural result of overly directing the use of models is that children begin to use them as answer-getting devices rather than as thinker toys. When getting answers rather than solving problems becomes the focus of a lesson, children will gravitate to the easiest method available to get the answers. For example, if you have carefully shown and explained to children how to get an answer with a set of counters, then an imitation of that method is what they will most likely select. The activity will not be reflective if all the child is doing is getting answers by moving blocks according to your directions. When an activity is not reflective, very little real growth occurs. Very little understanding is constructed.

TEACHING DEVELOPMENTALLY

Teaching involves decision making. Decisions are made as you plan lessons. *What is the best task to propose tomorrow? Considering what happened today, what will move the children forward?* And decisions are made minute to minute in the classroom. *How should I respond? Should they struggle some more, or should I intervene? Is progress being made? How can I help Suzy move in the correct direction without defeating her?*

The ideas that have been discussed in this chapter provide a theoretical basis for making those decisions.

Foundations of a Developmental Approach

Following is a summary of the major implications of the theory that has been discussed. A teacher who keeps these ideas in mind can be said to be basing his or her instruction on a constructivist view of learning or, in the terminology of this book, a *developmental approach*.

1. *Children construct their own knowledge and understanding; we cannot transmit ideas to passive learners.* Each child comes to us with a unique but rich collection of ideas. These ideas are the tools that will be used to construct new concepts and procedures as students wrestle with ideas, discuss solutions, challenge their own and others' conjectures, explain their methods, and solve engaging problems. Ideas cannot be poured into children as if they were empty vessels.

2. *Knowledge and understanding are unique for each learner.* Each child's network of ideas is likely to be somewhat different from that of the next child. As new ideas are formed, they will be integrated into that web of ideas in a unique way as well. We should not try to make all children the same.

3. *Reflective thinking is the single most important ingredient for effective learning.* To be an effective teacher, you must provide activities that engage children in active, reflective thinking. They must stimulate children to tap into those personal networks of ideas and use them. Passive children are not learning.

4. *Effective teaching is a child-centered activity.* In a constructivist classroom, the emphasis is on learning rather than teaching. Students are given the task of learning. The role of the teacher is to engage the students by posing good problems and creating a classroom atmosphere of exploration and sense making. The source of mathematical truth is found in the reasoning carried out by the class. The teacher is not the arbiter of what is mathematically correct.

Strategies for Effective Teaching

It is a major premise of this book that the single most important question to ask about our teaching is, "How can we structure lessons to promote reflective thought?" Here are seven suggestions. Perhaps you will be able to add to the list.

1. Create a mathematical environment.
2. Pose worthwhile mathematical tasks.
3. Use cooperative learning groups.
4. Use models and calculators as thinking tools.
5. Encourage discourse and writing.
6. Require justification of student responses.
7. Listen actively.

Create a Mathematical Environment

In a mathematical environment, students feel comfortable trying out ideas, sharing insights, challenging others, seeking advice from both other students and the teacher, explaining their thinking, and taking risks. No one is permitted to be a passive observer. An environment with these features is built around expectations, respect, and a teacher

who believes that *all* children can learn. Learning takes effort, and children need to know that as a class, their task is to work at doing mathematics. The interactions of a mathematical environment require students and teachers alike to respect one another, to listen attentively, and to learn to disagree without offending.

We cannot simply tell children how to think or what habits to acquire. Processes and habits of thought are acquired over time within a community where such thinking and habits are the norm. In a community of mathematical discourse, students evaluate their own assumptions and those of others and argue about what is mathematically true (Corwin, 1996; Lampert, 1990). The goal is to let all students believe that they are the authors of mathematical ideas and logical arguments. Reasoning and mathematical argument, in this environment, are the sources of an idea's legitimacy—not the teacher. As Schoenfeld put it, "'Figuring it out' is what mathematics is all about" (1988, p. 87). The classroom environment should be a place where "figuring it out" is common practice.

In an urban school in Montgomery County, Maryland, fourth graders were observed to raise their hand during a discussion and say, "I would like to add to what Marcel just said" or "I disagree with Tawanna." All students would face the speaker and listen attentively. In the same school, second-grade students would raise their hand with the index finger pointing up to indicate "a point of interest," a polite way to disagree. In both classrooms, it was clear that teachers had spent time and effort developing this atmosphere of respect. "Creating contexts where students can safely express their own mathematical ideas is a central teaching task and a step toward developing students' mathematical power" (Smith, 1996, p. 397).

Pose Worthwhile Mathematical Tasks

In constructivist classrooms, lessons are built around problems and explorations. Problems can be of virtually any type. They may involve a computation to solve a relatively simple story problem or a completely open-ended challenge to see what ideas can be discovered in a situation. Problems may be spontaneous questions posed by the teacher. Even some games can have a "figure it out" quality that serves as a problem-solving task (Burns, 1992a, 1996; Kamii & Lewis, 1990). Standard 1 of the *Professional Standards for Teaching Mathematics* provides an entire list of criteria for good tasks.

By contrast, traditional classrooms have left problems to the end of the unit. It was thought that students must first be taught mathematics before it could be used. In the constructivist classroom, problems are used as a means of learning rather than as an application at the end of learning.

The selection of good tasks requires that you listen each day to the way students are thinking about whatever mathematics is currently being discussed. The selection of the next day's task should be made in such a way as to help children reflect on the new ideas you want students to develop (Fennema, Carpenter, Franke, & Carey, 1993). Look for explorations that embody the big ideas of the chapter. As students wrestle with these problems, the tiny skills and ideas of the traditional curriculum will emerge. In a good task, students will "bump into" the important mathematics you have in mind for them to learn (Lappan & Briars, 1995).

Use Cooperative Learning Groups

Placing children in groups of three or four to work on a problem is an extremely useful strategy for encouraging the discourse and interaction envisioned in a mathematical community. A classroom arranged in small groups has many times the amount of interaction and discussion going on as can be accomplished in a full-class setting. Frequently, a simple pairing of students is all that is necessary. In groups or pairs, children are much more willing and able to speak out, explore ideas, explain things to their group, question and learn from one another, pose arguments, and have their own ideas challenged in a friendly atmosphere of learning. Children will take risks within a small group that they would never dream of taking in front of an entire class. Groups should usually be heterogeneous in ability so that all students experience good thinking and reasoning.

While the groups are at work, the teacher has the opportunity to be an active listener to six or more different discussions. Time should always be allotted for full-class discussions so that group members can share their group's ideas and the teacher can focus attention on important ideas. (See Chapter 22 for a more detailed discussion of cooperative groups.)

Use Models and Calculators as Thinking Tools

The arguments for using models have already been thoroughly discussed. It is worth repeating that models help children explore ideas and make sense of them. Many good explorations are actually posed in terms of physical materials. For example, "Try to find different ways to make the number 437 using ones, tens, and hundreds pieces. What patterns can you find? What else do you notice about the ways you can make 437?" Here the model is the focus of the problem rather than a way of exploring a different task.

Manipulatives and calculators should always be readily available for student use as a regular part of your classroom environment. This is just as true for middle school classrooms as for the kindergarten.

Encourage Discourse and Writing

To explain an idea orally or in written form forces us to wrestle with that idea until it is really ours and we personally understand it. The more we try to explain something or argue reasonably about something, the more connections we will search for and use in our explanation or in our argument. Talking gets the talker involved.

When children are asked to respond to and critique others, they are similarly forced to attend, to assimilate what is being said into personal mental schemes. Frequently, when we get involved verbally with an idea, we find ourselves changing or modifying the idea in midstream. The reflective

thought required to make an explanation or argue a point is a true learning experience in itself (Corwin, 1996; Whitin & Wilde, 1995; Yackel, Cobb, Wood, Wheatley, & Merkel, 1990). There has long been a "writing to learn" movement in education that is slowly but surely growing in mathematics education (Azzolino, 1990; Countryman, 1992). Writing includes journals, formal essays, and reports on problem solutions or methods and is also a significant tool in assessment. Countryman states, "The writer reflects on, returns to, and builds upon what has gone before" (p. 59). Writing is an important form of interaction.

Require Justification of Student Responses

Requiring children to explain or defend their responses has a positive effect on how children view mathematics and their own mathematical abilities. Doing so also promotes confidence and self-worth. Justification of responses forces students to think reflectively. To defend or explain eliminates guessing or responses based on rote learning. Thus having children explain their answers is another excellent mechanism for getting the same benefits that were discussed under Encourage Discourse and Writing.

Requiring students to explain why, to tell how, and to detail their ideas communicates that mathematics is not mysterious or unfathomable. There is no need for the teacher to pose as the source of mathematical truth.

Listen Actively

To promote reflective thinking requires that teaching be child-centered, not teacher-centered. By placing attention on the children's thoughts instead of our own, we encourage children to do more thinking and hence to search for and strengthen more internal connections—in short, understanding. When children respond to questions or make an observation in class, an interested but nonevaluative response is a way to ask for an elaboration. "Tell me more about that, Karen" or "I see. Why do you think that?" Even a simple "Um-hmm" followed by silence is very effective, permitting the child and others to continue their thinking.

Active listening requires that we believe in children's ideas. To wait 45 seconds, a minute, or even longer for a child to find a response or formulate even a simple idea is much easier when we believe that whatever the child says reflects a unique and valuable understanding. When you believe in children, children sense it and respond accordingly.

Reflecting on Student Activities

Throughout this book, in every student textbook, and in every article you read or in-service workshop you attend, you will hear and read about suggestions for activities, problems, tasks, or explorations that someone believes are effective in helping children learn some aspect of mathematics. Selecting activities or tasks is, as Lappan and Briars (1995) contend, a

Cobb, P., Wood, T., Yackel, E., & McNeal, E. (1993). Mathematics as procedural instructions and mathematics as meaningful activity: The reality of teaching for understanding. In R. B. Davis & C. A. Maher (Eds.), *School, mathematics, and the world of reality* (pp. 119–133). Needham Heights, MA: Allyn & Bacon.

Davis, R. B. (1986). *Learning mathematics: The cognitive science approach to mathematics education.* Norwood, NJ: Ablex.

Eisenhart, J., Borko, H., Underhill, R., Brown, C., Jones, D., & Agard, P. (1993). Conceptual knowledge falls through the cracks: Complexities of learning to teach mathematics for understanding. *Journal for Research in Mathematics Education, 24*, 8–40.

Fennema, E., Carpenter, T. P., Franke, M. L., & Carey, D. A. (1993). Learning to use children's mathematics thinking: A case study. In R. B. Davis & C. A. Maher (Eds.), *School, mathematics, and the world of reality* (pp. 93–117). Needham Heights, MA: Allyn & Bacon.

Ginsburg, H. P., & Baron, J. (1993). Cognition: Young children's construction of mathematics. In R. J. Jensen (Ed.), *Research ideas for the classroom: Early childhood mathematics* (pp. 3–21). Old Tappan, NJ: Macmillan.

Greenes, C., Schulman, L., & Spungin, R. (1992). Stimulating communication in mathematics. *Arithmetic Teacher, 40*, 78–82.

Hart, L. C., Schultz, K., Najee-ullah, D., & Nash, L. (1992). The role of reflection in teaching. *Arithmetic Teacher, 40*, 40–42.

Hiebert, J. (1987). The struggle to link written symbols with understandings: An update. *Arithmetic Teacher, 36*(7), 38–44.

Hiebert, J. (1990). The role of routine procedures in the development of mathematical competence. In T. J. Cooney (Ed.), *Teaching and learning mathematics in the 1990s* (pp. 31–40). Reston, VA: National Council of Teachers of Mathematics.

Hiebert, J., & Lindquist, M. M. (1990). Developing mathematical knowledge in the young child. In J. N. Payne (Ed.), *Mathematics for the young child* (pp. 17–36). Reston, VA: National Council of Teachers of Mathematics.

Juraschek, W. (1983). Piaget and middle school mathematics. *School Science and Mathematics, 83*, 5–13.

Kamii, C. (1990). Constructivism and beginning arithmetic (K–2). In T. J. Cooney (Ed.), *Teaching and learning mathematics in the 1990s* (pp. 22–30). Reston, VA: National Council of Teachers of Mathematics.

Kloosterman, P., & Gainey, P. H. (1993). Students' thinking: Middle grades mathematics. In D. T. Owens (Ed.), *Research ideas for the classroom: Middle grades mathematics* (pp. 3–21). Old Tappan, NJ: Macmillan.

Labinowicz, E. (1985). *Learning from children: New beginnings for teaching numerical thinking.* Menlo Park, CA: AWL Supplemental.

Noddings, N. (1993). Constructivism and caring. In R. B. Davis & C. A. Maher (Eds.), *School, mathematics, and the world of reality* (pp. 35–50). Needham Heights, MA: Allyn & Bacon.

Perkins, D., & Blythe, T. (1994). Putting understanding up front. *Educational Leadership, 51*(5), 4–7.

Schifter, D. (1996). A constructivist perspective on teaching and learning mathematics. *Phi Delta Kappan, 77*, 492–499.

Schwartz, J. E. (1992). "Silent teacher" and mathematics as reasoning. *Arithmetic Teacher, 40*, 122–124.

Silver, E. A., Smith, M. S., & Nelson, B. S. (1995). The QUASAR project: Equity concerns meet mathematics education reform in the middle school. In W. G. Secada, E. Fennema, & L. B. Adajian (Eds.), *New directions for equity in mathematics education* (pp. 9–56). New York: Cambridge University Press.

Smith, J. P., III. (1996). Efficacy and teaching mathematics by telling: A challenge for reform. *Journal for Research in Mathematics Education, 27*, 387–402.

Thompson, P. W. (1994). Concrete materials and teaching for mathematical understanding. *Arithmetic Teacher, 41*, 556–558.

Whitin, D. J. (1993). Number sense and the importance of asking "Why?" In S. Brown & M. Walter (Eds.), *Problem posing: Reflections and applications* (pp. 121–129). Hillsdale, NJ: Erlbaum.

Whitin, D. J., & Wilde, S. (1995). *It's the story that counts: More children's books for mathematical learning, K–6.* Portsmouth, NH: Heinemann.

Wiske, M. S. (1994). How teaching for understanding changes the rules in the classroom. *Educational Leadership, 51*(5), 18–21.

Wood, T. (1995). An emerging practice of teaching. In P. Cobb & H. Bauersfeld (Eds.), *The emergence of mathematical meaning: Interaction in classroom cultures* (pp. 203–227). Hillsdale, NJ: Erlbaum.

CHAPTER

TEACHING THROUGH
PROBLEM SOLVING

If the creation of the conceptual networks that constitute each individual's map of reality—including her mathematical understanding—is the product of constructive and interpretive activity, then it follows that no matter how lucidly and patiently teachers explain to their students, they cannot understand for their students.

SCHIFTER & FOSNOT (1993, P. 9)

Constructivism is student-powered learning.

MARY MCPHILLIPS, FOURTH-GRADE TEACHER

A developmental or constructivist view of learning mathematics requires a significant paradigm shift in how mathematics should best be taught, a shift implicit in the quotations. In traditional programs, teachers "taught" by telling and students learned by listening. Exercises followed to determine if the students could do what had been taught. The students' responsibility was to do as they had been shown in the precise manner they had been shown.

Constructivism suggests that students *begin* learning with doing—trying to make sense of unfamiliar situations, testing new ideas and conjectures, and even posing their own questions to answer. In short, students need to be engaged in doing mathematics, in sense making, in the science of pattern and order. The problems and questions of the constructivist mathematics classroom are opportunities for students to learn, not tests to see if they can follow the example of the teacher's demonstration.

A GENERAL FRAMEWORK FOR PROBLEM SOLVING

The major pedagogical implication of the constructivist theory is that students will learn mathematics best through solving problems. How do teachers teach this way? How can teachers help students be better problem solvers? These questions provide the focus of this chapter.

Problems and Performance Tasks

The term *problem* in mathematics has a long history and has evolved in meaning. The term *performance task* is relatively new and is associated with assessment in mathematics. In this chapter and the next, you will see why there is very little real difference.

What Is a Problem?

If we are going to talk about problem solving, it would be good to have a clear understanding of what a problem is. Two definitions are offered here:

1. A problem is a doubtful or difficult question; a matter of inquiry, discussion, or thought; a question that exercises the mind (*Oxford English Dictionary*).

2. A problem is a situation or task for which

   a. The person confronting that task wants or needs to find a solution

b. The person has no readily available procedure for finding the solution

c. The person makes an attempt to find the solution (Charles & Lester, 1982, p. 5)

The Charles and Lester definition points to three important factors that might be summarized as desire, blockage, and effort. All three of these ingredients of a problem illustrate the fact that what may be a problem for one person may not be a problem for another. Mathematical knowledge available to an older student may remove the blockage component that makes the situation a real problem for a younger child. The desire and effort aspects relate to affective considerations: Do I really care enough about this problem to work on it? Both definitions point to the fact that problems are not routine exercises.

Once you accept problem solving as consisting of any activity that involves desire, blockage, and effort, the realm of tasks that present problems widens substantially. That is, problems need not consist of "word problems" in the traditional sense. ("There were 8 birds on the fence. If 3 fly away, how many will be left on the fence?") Nor is it even essential that a problem have a predetermined answer. For example, suppose that students were given a collection of 20 or 30 geometric shapes of all varieties. "Find some shapes that could go together or that are alike in some way. Tell me your reasoning." This geometry example includes the component of blockage in that the student must consider an unfamiliar set of materials, impose on them some logical classification, and then defend it. There is no "right" way to do it and no predetermined answer. The more answers a child comes up with, the more thinking and problem solving is being done.

What Is a Performance Task?

The following definition is adapted from similar definitions found primarily in the assessment literature. A *performance task* is a problem (sometimes open-ended), a project, or an investigation, always presented in a spirit of inquiry. Furthermore:

- It may be an individual, pair, or group task.
- It may involve hands-on materials or drawings or calculators.
- Justification and explanation for answers and results are the responsibility of students.
- It should include some form of report—oral or written—or a physical product.

What this definition does is translate "problem" as just described into "learning opportunity." It suggests how problems appear in classrooms. A performance task is the principal means of promoting mathematical learning.

Note that the definition does not include the term *assessment*. This is the definition of a good task to engage students in *doing mathematics*. In the next chapter, on assessment, you will see the definition repeated. Performance tasks are also the principal means of gathering information about what children know. There should be absolutely no distinction between top-quality performance *learning* tasks and performance *assessment* tasks. To fail to equate these two necessarily indicates some lack of alignment between instruction and assessment.

Pólya's Four Phases of Problem Solving

No person has had as great an effect on how mathematics educators think about problem solving as George Pólya. Schoenfeld (1987) writes, "For mathematics education and for the world of problem solving, 1945 marked a line of demarcation between two eras: problem solving before and after Pólya. Pólya's influence on the study of mathematical thinking, and on the study of productive thinking in general, has been enormous" (p. 27). It was in 1945 that Pólya published *How to Solve It,* a book that for the first time suggested that there were general strategies or *heuristics* for solving problems. Pólya's strategies are used in a four-step framework for the problem-solving process:

1. *Understand the problem.*
2. *Devise a plan or decide on an approach for attacking the problem.*
3. *Carry out the plan.*
4. *Look back at the problem, the answer, and what you have done to get there.*

Pólya's four-step approach has become the standard model for problem-solving behavior and is still found in one form or another in most mainstream mathematics textbooks from kindergarten through high school. The four stages are best understood to be an organizer for instruction and also for planning and should not be seen as a prescription for how to solve problems. We now know that listing these stages or explaining them to students does very little to help them become better problem solvers (Lester, 1994). The Pólya framework remains worth examining from the perspective of the teacher.

Understand the Problem

The first thing a problem solver should do is reflect on the task and get a firm grasp of what is known and what needs to be done. Decide what information is important and what seems unimportant. Examine the conditions that will have an impact on the meaning of the problem or the solution. Be very clear about what is being asked for in the problem. It may be helpful to reformulate some of the information, perhaps make lists of knowns and unknowns or draw pictures, charts, or diagrams. Begin to think of what similar situations you have experienced that may be like this problem or contribute to its solution.

The very act of going through this understanding phase is calming. It gets the problem solver doing something productive without having to decide what to do. Thinking about a problem is an active and involving process. The amount of time and effort spent in this first phase is a major difference between good problem solvers and poor problem solvers.

Devise a Plan

The second phase shifts the emphasis from information found *in* the problem to reflection on ideas that might be brought *to* the problem. Of course, what can be brought to the problem is unique to each problem solver. There are mathematical concepts and procedures. There are general processes or strategies. For example, could I solve a simpler problem that would help? Maybe I could draw a picture (or try a simpler version of this problem or look for a pattern). Perhaps the structure of the problem calls to mind a similar problem that has been solved successfully.

Carry Out the Plan

Carrying out the plan is partly a matter of following through with the approach selected, carefully taking each step along the way. The more sophisticated aspect of carrying out the plan is the self-monitoring of your own progress and regulation of the methods you are using: metacognitive activity. If you become blocked along the way in a solution process, some recycling of the general scheme is called for. Sometimes it may require returning to the original problem to be sure that it is understood correctly or that a key idea was not overlooked. Or it may be that the approach to the problem requires rethinking. In such cases, a search for a new way of approaching the problem is called for.

Look Back

A problem should never be considered "solved" simply because an answer has been found. Three significant looking-back activities should always be considered: (1) look at the answer, (2) look at the solution process or method, and (3) look at the problem itself.

Answer. In the real world, there is no index or teacher to verify that the answer you have reached is correct. Consequently, some effort must be made to make sure that the answer arrived at is indeed a solution. How this may be done will vary with the problem. Is the solution in the ballpark of what was expected? Could there be other answers? Is there a way to verify the answer by checking it against all of the conditions? Are there any contradictions between the answer and the conditions of the problem? Did the logic used really make sense? Were the calculations correct?

Process. The process by which a problem was solved is very much tied to making a judgment of the solution. In fact, it will be difficult for children to justify their answers without explaining how they arrived at them. Attention to method also communicates that there is rarely a single "right" method but rather lots of good methods. Could it have been solved in a different way? In an easier way? Is this approach useful in other problems? Has the method been used before? Sometimes just labeling the solution method helps make it more accessible for future problems.

Problem. Finally, be sure to consider what was learned from the problem itself. Now that the problem has been solved, are there other questions similar to or related to this problem that can be answered? If the numbers were bigger or the conditions different somehow, could you still solve the problem? Is there a general case that can be solved because of having solved this special case? What features of the problem might be changed to create a similar problem that may be solvable, interesting, challenging, or more useful?

In this chapter, the Pólya stages will provide a framework for three different aspects of teaching mathematics: for the "teacher's problem" of making instructional choices and decisions, for how mathematics is taught via problem solving, and for helping children learn how to solve problems.

TEACHING MATHEMATICS IS A PROBLEM-SOLVING ENDEAVOR

> There is no other decision that teachers make that has a greater impact on students' opportunity to learn and on their perceptions about what mathematics is than the selection or creation of the tasks with which the teacher engages the students in studying mathematics. (Lappan & Briars, 1995, p. 138)

Slow down, reread that quotation, and give it some thought. It is a powerful statement!

Teachers in traditional, mainstream classrooms tend to plan lessons based on the sequence of activities supplied by a mainstream textbook. Although textbooks have much to offer teachers as resources and general curriculum guides (see Chapter 22), a text-based approach to planning is essentially flawed. Text-based planning denies the child-centered view that is basic in a constructivist approach. It assumes that all children are essentially alike and that every activity on every preceding page has accomplished its intended purpose.

Teaching is much like solving a problem and fits well into the framework of the four phases of problem solving described by Pólya (Rowan & Bourne, 1994).

Understanding Your Goals

As a first step, be clear about what you want to accomplish: What mathematics do you want children to develop based on what you know about your students in this area of content? The mathematics and the children cannot be separated in determining your goals.

For direction as to where you want to head mathematically, stay focused on the big ideas of the curriculum (number relationships, place value, meanings of operations, fraction concepts, mental computation, etc.). Frequently these are units in your text, but often they are even larger ideas than single units. With a big-idea mentality, you can avoid the easy trap of teaching to each atomized concept and skill found in the pages of the text. As a result, you will select broader, more open-ended tasks that permit integration of a wider variety of concepts.

The other consideration is your students. Do you possibly need to do an exploratory activity for the main purpose of finding out where to begin? Based on recent lessons, what do they bring already to these big ideas and what is yet to be developed? What have you observed that suggests concepts they already possess? Where have children been having difficulty due to poorly formed ideas?

Planning the Tasks

Selecting good tasks means selecting problems, explorations, or activities that will most likely cause children to wrestle meaningfully and thoughtfully with the mathematics you identified in the understand phase of your planning. This selection process can, on the surface, be a daunting task, one that has sent many teachers back to the two-textbook-pages-per-day approach to lesson planning.

As you will see a bit later in this chapter, there are many good ways to find and create tasks, especially when basing your selection on big ideas instead of an atomized curriculum of isolated skills. The key question in considering a task or problem for your students is, "How can this problem (or activity) be used to help cause reflective thinking about the mathematics I want to develop?"

Implementing Your Plan

What you do with your students in the classroom represents the major shift in teaching—away from teacher telling and toward student-directed activity. Good planning will help you focus appropriately on the needs and strengths of individual children. When teaching by following the textbook pages, the agenda becomes getting children to do the exercises. The developmental approach keeps you focused on individual children developing integrated networks of ideas. Teaching in a problem-oriented classroom will be discussed in greater detail shortly.

Looking Back

If you are an active listener in a student-centered classroom, your children will constantly be telling you what they know and how they understand the ideas being discussed. There will be different levels of skills and different understandings. Make notes either during the lesson or as soon thereafter as is reasonable. This information supplies the data for much of the next day's planning. It helps you understand what you need to accomplish next and provides hints for which direction to go.

TEACHING ACTIONS BEFORE, DURING, AND AFTER THE PROBLEM

The shift from teacher telling to students doing does not imply that the teacher simply provides a problem or task and sits back, waiting for magic to happen. As the teacher, you are responsible for making the atmosphere work. Teaching actions in a problem-solving or mathematical environment can be separated into three parts: *before* actions (what you do to get an activity started), *during* actions (what you do while your students are working on a problem), and *after* actions (what you do to help students reflect on what they have been doing).

Before Actions

The things you do with your students before setting them to work on a problem correspond to Pólya's first phase of problem solving, understanding the problem. You want to be sure that students understand what the task involves and be sure they are thinking about the ideas that you hope they will "bump into" as they work on the problem. As you will see in the suggestions in the following sections, the task or activity influences how you might work with your students in this before phase.

Ask Questions to Clarify the Task or Problem

Consider the task of mastering the multiplication facts. Of all 100 multiplication facts, the most difficult can each be connected or related to an easier fact already learned.

> Use a fact you already know to help you solve each of these facts: 4×6, 6×8, 7×6, 3×8.

For this performance task, it is essential that students understand the idea of using a helping fact. They have most likely used helping facts in addition. You can build on this by asking, "When you were learning addition facts, how could knowing $6 + 6$ help you know $6 + 7$?" You may also need to help students understand what is meant by a fact they know—one they have mastered and know without counting.

When using a word problem, it is useful to ask a series of direct questions that can be answered just by looking at the problem.

> The local candy store purchased candy in cartons of 12 boxes per carton. The price paid for one carton was $42.50. Each box contained 8 candy bars,

which the store was going to sell individually. What was the candy store's cost for each candy bar?

"What did the candy store do? What is in a carton? What is in a box? What is the price of one carton? What does that mean when it says 'each box'?" The last question here is to identify vocabulary that may be misunderstood. It is also useful to be sure students can explain to you what the problem is asking. Rereading a problem does little good, but having students restate the problem in their own words forces them to think about what the problem is asking.

It is important to note that while you may be guiding this discussion, the students are doing the thinking. Do not explain problems. Rather, ask questions that help students focus on what they know and what they need to know.

Brainstorm

If your activity or task will present a new concept or if the problem is relatively complex, a preliminary brainstorming session may help get students on the correct track before they get too lost in doing the problem.

A second-grade teacher in an urban school was planning an initial discussion of fractions. She needed to find out just what ideas her students had before she could decide exactly what to do next. On the overhead projector, she drew a simple square with both diagonals (see Figure 4.1). "Today we are going to begin talking about fractions. I want to find out what you know. Look at the figure on the screen, and think of one thing you can say about it." She used a "think-pair-share" strategy, suggesting that after they had thought of an idea, they should talk about the ideas with a partner. This gave all students the opportunity to put their ideas into words before having to share with the full class. When she then began calling on children to share their ideas, most children were ready. All ideas were written on the overhead without comment or judgment: "There is an X." "It is a fraction." "All the triangles are equal." The full list of ideas covered the board. Acceptance of the ideas gave all students a sense of confidence and involvement.

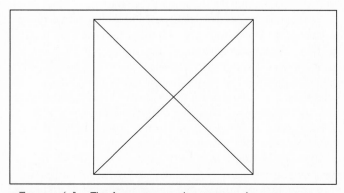

● **Figure 4.1** This figure was used to initiate a brainstorming session with second graders to find out what they knew about fractions.

When the brainstorming had fairly well exhausted ideas, the teacher focused on the comment about the triangles' all being equal. "In your groups, I want you to talk about this: Does it matter that the pieces are equal fractions?" The resulting discussion helped develop the ideas of fair shares for fractions and also connected with some ideas about symmetry the students had been working on earlier.

As a second example, consider this seventh- or eighth-grade problem designed to be an early investigation of ratio.

Shaquille O'Neal, the basketball player, is 7'0" tall. How high off the floor does he have to jump to dunk the basketball?

The teacher might ask what the class can tell from the problem and what other information the students may need to know. As students offer suggestions, they are written on the board in a list without judgment. Students should be given the opportunity to ask questions, and comments written down should be clarified so that all understand. Soon students will realize that they do not know how high above his head O'Neal can reach. If not suggested by the students, the teacher can pose the question, "Is there a way we can measure ourselves to figure out how high 'Shaq' can reach?" In this example, the brainstorming serves the purpose of steering the students to looking at arm-height ratios, since ratio was the intended content. At the same time, what ratios and how these will be used can still be worked out by the students. Since there are multiple approaches, students will be able to use ideas that make sense to them.

Establish Expectations

With many performance tasks, even a simple word problem, you may want students to focus on and think about more than just the answer to the problem.

Jimmy had 4 boxes. Each box had 6 pencils in it. How many pencils did Jimmy have?

At the second-grade level, you might be interested in connecting the solution with appropriate symbolism or encouraging written communication. You could suggest to students that they may use whatever method they wish to solve the problem, but you want to see what they did. It is difficult for young children to "explain," but they can draw pictures or tell what they did. You may also want them to write an equation or number sentence to go along with their solution. You may want them to write a full sentence that tells the answer, not just write down a number. Since none of these things are in the problem statement, you need to clarify what you want done.

Often there are many different solutions or solution paths to a problem. To get more than minimal work from students, challenge (or require) them to find different solutions or solution methods.

....

Find some ways to make $1\frac{1}{4}$ into two parts.

....

In the brainstorming on this task, students may come up with different ways to think about $1\frac{1}{4}$. For example, there are different models (sets that can be divided into fourths, paper that can be folded). Someone may mention different measurements that come in fourths such as quarts and gallons or quarters and dollars. Others may think of $1\frac{1}{4}$ as 1.25. And there are equivalent fractions. By discussing ideas before students set off to work, all students hear a variety of ideas and have a better notion of what they might try to do. You cannot predict that all of those ideas will develop in your class, but the discussion will get ideas started. You might also suggest that after students have explored one idea and found at least four different combinations for $1\frac{1}{4}$, they use a different way to think of $1\frac{1}{4}$ and try to come up with a new set of ideas. If you want students to come up with two solution methods, suggest that they look for two solution methods.

Begin with a Simple Version of the Task

Suppose that you are interested in developing some ideas about area and perimeter in the fourth or fifth grade. This is the task you plan to present (Lappan & Evan, 1989):

....

Assume that the edge of a square is 1 unit. Add squares to this shape so that it has a perimeter of 18.

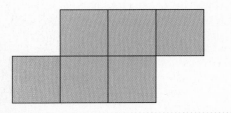

....

Instead of beginning with this problem, you might consider one of the following:

- Draw a 3-by-5 rectangle of squares on the board, and let students tell things they know about the shape. (It's a rectangle. It has squares. There are 15 squares. There are 3 rows of five.) If no one mentions the words *area* and *perimeter,* you could write those two words on the board

and ask if those words can be used in talking about this figure.

- Provide students with some square tiles or grid paper. "I want everyone to make a shape that has a perimeter of 12 units. After you make your shape, find out what its area is." After a short time, have several students share their shapes.

Each of these "warm-ups" gets the vocabulary you will need for your exploration out in the open. The second activity suggests the tiles as a possible model that students may choose to use. It has the added benefit of hinting that there are different figures with the same perimeter.

During Actions

Once the problem or activity has been discussed and you are comfortable that students understand the task, set them to work. It is a good idea for students to get in the habit of working in groups so that there is no lost time in moving from the full-class discussion to the small groups. Groups of three or four work well, but pairs of students, especially at the K–2 level, can work also. (Chapter 22 includes a detailed discussion of cooperative group work.) Your role now shifts to that of facilitator and active listener. You might sit down with a group, listen for a while, have the students explain what they are doing, or just take notes.

Help Students Plan Before They Act

Reflecting on Pólya's second phase of problem solving, students should talk with their group to decide on a plan of action. Frequently, individual students will simply ignore the group and begin working on their own. Require that each group talk about what needs to be done, how the group members will go about doing it, and when appropriate, who will do what tasks. For some tasks, students need to decide what materials or method they will use. For the area and perimeter problem described earlier: Do they need grid paper or square tiles, or do they want to just use drawings? Someone might be assigned the job of recording information while others make changes in the shape.

Students may need to negotiate how they want to approach a problem when there are differing views. By requiring that students come to some agreement before beginning, students will have a greater sense of ownership in their work. When there are strongly divergent opinions, you can help students respect each other's view by suggesting that they try one way and then the other way. They will then be able to compare approaches. If time is too short for that, help students quickly negotiate without argument.

There is no value in making an issue over planning versus carrying out. However, it is often useful to suggest that students pause and think about what they want to do before they get too far along.

Interact Appropriately

Once students are profitably engaged in working on a problem, Pólya's third stage, you will face difficult decisions about if and how you will interact with them. Should you let them stumble down the wrong path? How much direction should you provide? Do you correct errors you see?

Provide Hints and Suggestions. If a group is searching for a place to begin, a hint may be appropriate. Be careful to avoid telling students how to go about solving the problem. You might suggest that they try using a particular manipulative or draw a picture if that seems appropriate.

> In Fern's Furniture Store, Fern has priced all of her furniture at 20 percent over wholesale. In preparation for a sale, she tells her staff to cut all prices by 10 percent. Will Fern be making 10 percent profit, less than 10 percent profit, or more than 10 percent profit? Explain your answer.

Consider these hints:

- Try drawing a picture or a diagram of something that shows what 10 percent off means.
- Try drawing a picture or a diagram that shows what 20 percent more means.
- Let's try a simpler problem. Suppose that you had 8 blocks and got 25 percent more. Then you lost 25 percent of the new collection.
- Maybe you could pick a price of something and see what happens.

Encourage Testing of Ideas. Students should know that it is their responsibility to justify their own solutions and methods and that you are rarely going to tell them that what they are doing is "right" or "wrong." Use phrases such as "I see what you have done. How can you check that somehow?" and "How can we tell if that makes sense?" frequently and with good solutions at least as often as with faulty ones. It is a good idea to have students write down their explanations or draw pictures showing their reasoning. The justification of results should always be part of the solving of problems and need not wait for a discussion at the end. It is important that students see justifying their results as part of the task of solving problems—part of doing mathematics.

> Farmer Brown kept horses in his barn. One day, he watched as Luke brought in 16 horses to the barn. When Farmer Brown went into the barn and counted his horses, he found there were 23 horses in all. How many horses were in the barn to begin with?

This sounds like an addition problem. It has the action of joining and talks about "in all." Many children will add. "Now that you know how many horses were there to start, check that some way. Maybe you could work it out with counters."

Sometimes two children or two groups will come up with different solutions or answers. You might bring this to the attention of both groups. "I noticed that Megan's group and this group have different answers. You also seem to be using different methods. I wonder which group is correct."

For example, suppose that children were asked to determine the area of an irregular blob shape. Different groups may use different methods. If filling the region with squares on a grid, they may use different judgments when counting squares near the edge of the region as either in or out. The discussion is less about who is "right" than about seeing that judgments and measuring methods are different.

Suggest Extensions. Lots of good problems are simple on the surface. It is the extensions that are excellent. The area/perimeter task is a case in point. Many students will quickly come up with one or two solutions. "I see you found one way to do this. Are there any other solutions? Are any of the solutions different or more interesting than others? Which of the shapes you found with a perimeter of 18 is the largest and which the smallest? Does the perimeter always change when you add another tile?"

What can you find out about that? This general question is at the very heart of mathematics as a science of pattern and order. It asks students to look for something interesting, to generalize. For example, in the area/perimeter problem, squares can be added to a shape in three situations: If a new square touches the old shape on only one side, the perimeter increases by 2. If it touches on two sides, there is no increase. If it fits into a "U" and touches on three sides, the perimeter actually decreases by 2.

Questions that begin "What if you tried . . . ?" or "Would that same idea work for . . . ?" are also ways to suggest different extensions. For example, "Suppose you tried to find all the shapes possible with a perimeter of 18. What could you find out about the areas?"

Find a Second Method. The value of students' solving a problem in more than one way cannot be overestimated. It shifts the value system in the classroom from answers to processes and thinking. It is a good way for students to make new and different connections.

For example, consider this sixth-grade problem:

> The dress was originally priced at $90. If the sale price is 25 percent off, how much will it cost on sale?

This is an example of a straightforward problem with a single answer. Many students will solve it by multiplying by 0.25 and subtracting the result from $90. The suggestion to find another way may be all that is necessary. Others may require specific directions: "How would you do it with fractions instead of decimals?" "Draw me a diagram that explains what you did." "How could this be done in just one step?" "Think of a way that you could do this mentally without any multiplication."

Third graders will frequently solve this next problem by counting or using addition:

....

Maxine had saved up $9. The next day, she received her allowance. Now she has $12. How much allowance did she get?

....

"How would you do that on a calculator?" and "Can you write an equation that tells what you did?" are ways of encouraging children to connect 9 plus ? = 12 with 12 − 9.

Solving a problem in a second way can help students who have made an error find the mistake on their own. Perhaps a student has used a symbolic method of her own invention and has made an error in reasoning. Suggesting only that she try now to do the problem with physical models (so that you can understand what she did) may be all that is necessary to have her make a self-correction. Here are some more examples of problems that lend themselves to multiple methods:

....

Make a graph showing our favorite ice-cream flavors.

Add 37 + 48 in your head (mentally).

How many 3″ by 9″ bricks are needed to pave an 8′ by 12′ patio?

....

Use Praise Cautiously

Comments such as "Good job!" and "Super work!" roll off the tongue easily. We use these statements to help children feel good about themselves. There is evidence to suggest that we should be cautious when using expressions of praise, especially with respect to student products and solutions (Schwartz, 1996). Praise not only supports students' feelings, but it also evaluates. "Good job!" says, "Yes, you did that correctly." "Nice work" can establish an expectation for others that products must be neat or beautiful in order to have value. This can make students who do excellent mathematical science hide their efforts if they appear sloppy or poorly presented.

In place of praise that is judgmental, Schwartz suggests comments of interest and extension: "I wonder what would happen if you tried . . ." or "Please tell me how you figured

that out." Notice that these phrases express interest and value the child's thinking. They also can and should be used regardless of the validity of the responses.

After Actions

If the class has been set to work on a problem in groups, in pairs, or even independently, there is real value in allotting a significant portion of time to bring the class back together for discussion or debriefing. Here is the opportunity to value the thinking of all children and to share the wealth of ideas that will emerge from across your classroom. This is the fourth phase of Pólya's four steps to problem solving. Your first agenda is to listen without judgment to students' justifications of their answers. This will undoubtedly include their descriptions of solution methods. That is your second agenda, to see different solution methods. Finally, when it is appropriate, you want to explore extensions or generalizations of the problem. You may offer your own suggestions occasionally, but most ideas should come from your students.

Conducting the Discussion

You may want simply to list answers from all of the groups and put them on the board. Following that, you can return to one or more students to get explanations for their solutions or to explain their processes. At other times, you may choose to call on groups that you noticed earlier doing something interesting or something of special value to your agenda. This does not need to be restricted to correct solutions.

When there are different answers, the full class should be involved in the discourse concerning which answers are correct. Allow those responsible for the answers to defend them, and then open the discussion to the class. "Who has an idea about this? George, I noticed that you got a different answer than Tomeka. What do you think of her explanation?" Resist with every fiber in you the temptation to judge the correctness of an answer. Even when the class fails to come to a conclusion, rather than provide your solution, suggest that perhaps you will need to return to this later—and then be sure to do so. Later will be when students have gained some additional insights to help them.

One of your functions is to be sure that all students participate, that all listen, and that all understand what is being said. Moving along too quickly cheats those students who are not quite able to follow the faster explanations of the best children in the room. Encourage students to ask questions. "Pete, did you understand how they did that? Do you want to ask Mary a question?"

Frequently teachers will try to help a student with an explanation by inferring what the student intends and then translating for the others. "Class, do you see what Cassie is saying? What she really means is . . ." This may very well be a correct interpretation of the child's imprecise response. However, it takes over from the child the task of communication. Clear expression of ideas is an important aspect of doing mathematics. Furthermore, you may be saying things for the child that he or she did not actually intend. As an alternative, direct difficult statements back to the class. "Mandy, did you understand what Cassie was saying? Lewis, do you want to ask Cassie a question about what she just said?" Or you might have Cassie repeat the explanation one step at a time and get the class to help with needed clarification. In any event, your job is to orchestrate the discourse, not take over for the students.

When you are satisfied with the discussion around the answer and the solution, you can entertain extensions to the problem. If there are good extensions or follow-ups to a problem that interest students, you can decide to return the class to groups or begin with extension as a new exploration the following day. The value of discussing extensions and alternative directions with the full class will quickly be seen in the richness of ideas that are shared.

Discussion in a Diverse Class

For a variety of reasons, teachers are finding a wider range of academic diversity in their classrooms. The NCTM *Standards* are very clear in expressing the belief that all children can learn the mathematics of the regular curriculum. This view is supported by a number of prominent mathematics educators, including those who have worked extensively with at-risk populations (Campbell, P. F., 1996; NCTM, 1989, 1991; Silver & Stein, 1996; Trafton & Claus, 1994). Furthermore, a constructivist approach to mathematics education suggests that there is much greater value in having all children work together than to separate children into ability groups. It is preferable to have diverse or heterogeneous cooperative groups as well. When groups are reporting to the full class, traditionally slower children will have already had a chance to work with and think about good ideas by virtue of having worked in their group.

But the needs and abilities of children are different, and it requires skill and practice to conduct a large group discussion that is balanced and includes all children. Rowan and Bourne (1994) offer some excellent suggestions based on their work in an urban, multiracial, multiethnic, low-socioeconomic school district. They emphasize that the most important factor is to be clear about the purpose of group discussion—that is, to share and explore the variety of strategies, ideas, and solutions generated by the class and to learn to communicate these ideas in a rich mathematical discourse. This is quite different from the more traditional focus of checking for correct answers. When all that is important is hearing that someone got a correct answer, teachers will call on the students with their hands raised, note the correct response, and move on. Every class will have a handful of students who are always ready to respond. Other children learn to be passive or more likely do not even partici-

pate. So rule number one is that the discussion is more important than hearing an answer.

A second suggestion is to begin discussions by calling first on the children who tend to be shy or lack the ability to express themselves well. Rowan and Bourne note that the more obvious ideas are generally given at the outset of a discussion. When asked to participate early and given sufficient time to formulate their thoughts, these reticent children can more easily participate and thus be valued.

A useful technique is to ask questions that are more open-ended and do not demand a specific, easily evaluated response. Questions such as "Tell me what you were thinking," "How did your group get your answer?" "Does that seem to make sense? Why or why not?" and "Can you draw a picture to show what you did?" all afford children the opportunity to provide individual ideas without the pressure of risking being "wrong."

Make it a habit to ask for explanations to accompany *all* answers. Soon the request for an explanation will not signal an incorrect response, as children initially believe. Many incorrect answers are the result of small errors accompanied by excellent thinking. Likewise, many correct answers may not represent the correct or insightful thinking you might have guessed. A child who has given an incorrect answer is very likely to see the error and correct it during the explanation. Explanations need not be evaluated by the teacher. "Does someone have a different idea or want to comment on what Danielle just said?" Try to support children's thinking without evaluating responses. All children should hear the same teacher reactions that only the "smart kids" used to hear.

Many times a student will get stuck in the middle of an explanation. The silence can be difficult, and there is a temptation to call on someone else to "help him out" or suggest that the child get assistance from a classmate. Though well intentioned, the message this sends to the child is that he is not capable on his own. Children must learn that time will be given and that their classmates trust and believe in one another. This attitude conveys support and confidence and is usually all that is necessary to get a quality response.

There will, of course, be times when a response is simply not forthcoming. When this occurs, you might suggest that the child take some time to get his thoughts together or work out the idea with some materials, and promise to return to him later. And then be *certain* to return to hear what the child has figured out.

FINDING TASKS AND PROBLEMS

"Are there really enough problems to use this approach for everything I teach?" If you have a more traditional, how-to-get-the-answer view of school mathematics, it may seem nearly impossible to imagine teaching with a problem-solving approach for the entire curriculum. As you will see, if you focus on big ideas in the curriculum and broaden your notion of "problem" to include almost any task that involves wrestling with a new idea (desire, blockage, and effort), then the source of tasks is virtually limitless.

Every teacher should invest periodically in quality resource materials and should regularly read at least one of NCTM's journals for teachers, *Teaching Children Mathematics* or *Mathematics Teaching in the Middle School*. Resource books and journals will keep you current with the profession and provide ideas for tasks and problems. However, by broadening your concept of "problem," you should have no difficulty finding thought-provoking challenges appropriate for your students without a frenetic search for ideas. The examples that follow suggest categories of problems that occur across most grade levels and content strands.

Story or Word Problems

Story problems or word problems are appropriate at every grade level.

> **It took 3 hours and 45 minutes to drive to Grandma Smith's house. That was three times as long as it took to get to Grandma Phipps's. How long did it take to get to Grandma Phipps's?**

The purpose of such problems is to develop understanding of one of the four basic operations in a realistic context. Rather than wait until students have learned about an operation, you can begin a study of operations with problems and see what students know based on how they solve them.

A useful variation of these problems (also known as *translation problems*) is to include either extra or insufficient information. The next example has extra data.

> **George and Bernie each bought 3 bags of marbles. The marbles cost 69 cents a bag. Each bag has 25 marbles, including 5 special cat's-eye marbles. How many marbles did the boys buy?**

Such variations of translation problems are an excellent way to encourage students to pay more attention to problem information and analyze what is given and what is asked.

Almost any concept can be imbedded in some real context. Even when problems are not provided in your text, always consider what meaningful, real-world context might be used. Then create your own word problems in contexts meaningful to students.

A New Concept

Most concepts in the curriculum can be presented to students with some form of an example that may be unfamiliar to the students.

> **What are some things you can tell about the number 3.52? What happens when you add, subtract, multiply, or divide with this number? How big is it? Where would you find it on the number line? What else can you tell about 3.52?**

In this example, students at about the fourth grade can tell you what they know and help you plan what to do with decimals. Note that no suggestion was made that 3.52 is between 3 and 4 or that it is a fraction.

Computation

The computation area of the curriculum is full of rules for computing in preestablished ways. Rules tend to impede thinking rather than aid it. Before a specific procedure is taught, pose a computational task and ask students to invent methods for doing it.

> **Solve the problem $418 \div 6$ without using your calculator. You may use any other methods that make sense to you.**

This approach can be used with fractions, decimals, and whole numbers, at all grade levels. What is required is belief in students. After years of struggling to teach subtraction with regrouping in a traditional manner, one third-grade teacher decided to ask students to do it any way that made sense to them. She never returned to directed teaching after seeing the power of student ideas.

Sometimes it is helpful to put the computations in a story problem. Context seems to be helpful to a lot of children who see the example cited here as very abstract. It could easily be recast as a story about six children sharing a box of 418 pogs.

Another variation is to request a method that can be done mentally or a method that will give a good estimate.

Translations

An extremely important activity for developing understanding is translation from one external representation of an idea to another. In Chapter 3, the notion of representations was expanded to include five different representations as illus-

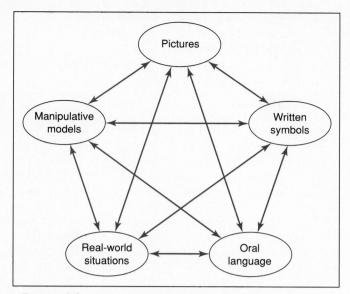

• **FIGURE 4.2** *Translations between external representations provide a rich source of profitable challenges.*

trated in Figure 4.2 (Lesh, Post, & Behr, 1987). Recall that each of the arrows represents a possible translation.

Here are three examples of translations:

1. Solve the problem (any story problem) by drawing a picture to help.
2. We just finished finding some equivalent fractions for $\frac{3}{4}$ and $\frac{1}{3}$ using our pie pieces. Now use sets of counters to show these same equivalent fractions.
3. Use any materials you wish to explain what "R 2" means in this equation: $27 \div 5 = 5$ R 2.

The first example is a translation from a real-world context to pictures. Example 2 shows that translations can be made within one of the categories of representations, in this case from one manipulative to another. Similar "within" translations can be made in each of the other four modes as well. The third example is a translation from written symbols to manipulative models.

Manipulative Tasks

Many good tasks simply require that students do something using a designated manipulative. This example is aimed at the concepts of "similarity" and "ratio" at the seventh- or eighth-grade level.

On your dot paper, draw a large and a small shape that are similar to each other. How can you show that they are similar? What can you find out about your similar shapes? Draw a third shape that is almost like your first two but is not quite similar.

By not specifying exactly how the activity should be done, you obtain a result that is a true reflection of the students' concepts.

The following example uses a similar approach for part-part-whole number concepts at the K–1 level.

Use your plastic connecting cubes to show four different ways to make 6.

Created Problems

There is much problem-solving activity in constructing problems from collected or presented data, from a story that has been read, or from an experience children may have had such as a field trip, a video, or a CD-ROM.

Make up three questions that can be answered using the information in this graph.

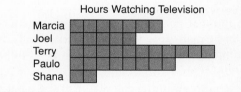

Hours Watching Television

One of the best sources of data is the students in your own class or the children in the school. Measurement units suggest gathering arm span or shoe lengths. Surveys can collect information from eye color to lunch preferences. Collected data can be part of a unit on probability or statistics. In the upper grades, it may be a discussion of ratios and making comparisons of various data between and among groups. Data from newspapers and the community can be very interesting. Consider the McDonald's claim about "billions served." How much is a billion hamburgers? How many are served in a day? What about the paper used to wrap them? These and similar ideas can be used in units on large numbers, measurements, and percentages as well as the more obvious statistics units.

Children's Literature

Children's literature can be used in numerous ways to create reflective tasks at all grade levels, and there are many excellent books to help you in this area (Bresser, 1995; Burns, 1992a; Sheffield, 1995; Welchman-Tischler, 1992; Whitin & Wilde, 1992, 1995). A very popular children's book, *The Doorbell Rang* (Hutchins, 1986), can be used with different agendas at various grade levels. The story is a sequential tale of children sharing 12 cookies. On each page, more children come to the kitchen, and the 12 cookies must be redistributed. This simple yet engaging story can lead to exploring ways to make equal parts of almost any number for children at the K–2 level. It is a springboard for multiplication and division at the 3–4 level. It can also be used to explore fraction concepts at the 4–6 level.

> How could the children share all 12 cookies if there were 9 children?

Open Exploration

The question "What can you find out about this?" can be applied to any new or emerging idea that students can explore. The significant feature of this question is that students ask their own questions, creating a sense of personal investment in the problem (Baker & Baker, 1990). Here are two examples at opposite ends of the K–8 range.

> 1. A number is called *even* if that many cubes can be made into two equal bars. If not, the number is called *odd*. What can you find out about that?
> 2. Use your graphing calculator to see what you can find out about equations that have the form $y = mX + b$. For example, $y = -2X + 4$.

Explanations and Error Analysis

A fictitious "friend that is 10 years old" or "some children in Mrs. McKinney's room" can be used to present conceptual errors or misunderstandings to children for their analysis.

> 1. A fifth grader was trying to put numbers in increasing order. This is what he did:
>
>   *3.4   3.38   3.45   3.4026*
>
>   What would you tell him?

> 2. How would you explain what multiplication means to the children in Mrs. Stevens's second-grade class?
> 3. A Martian visitor thinks that 2 + 37 is 237. What would you say to him?

The nine different ways to think about creating problem-solving tasks that you have just read about are only suggestions. The essence of a useful activity is something that makes students ponder over, figure out, reason, make sense of—in general, reflect on—the ideas you want students to develop. Some "problems" will be short questions posed spontaneously during class. Others may involve deciding on a strategy for winning a game or why an activity is done the way the book tells us. Most tasks are planned with careful thought.

In the traditional mathematics classroom, questions are asked that have already been answered through teacher telling. Problems are posed only after solutions are demonstrated for similar tasks. To answer those questions or solve those problems requires only recall, not sense making (Wood, 1995). When recall fails and without a habit of thinking and solving problems, there is no place else for the student to turn.

TEACHING ABOUT PROBLEM SOLVING

Teaching through problem solving completely blends problem solving with learning mathematics. Children are *doing* mathematics (solving problems) as they are *learning* mathematics (solving problems). A very natural reaction is to find ways to help children become better problem solvers—teach them how to solve problems. Though this can and should be done, it should be done *as we help them learn mathematics.* "Problem solving is not a distinct topic but a process that should permeate the entire program and provide the context in which concepts and skills can be learned" (NCTM, 1989, p. 23). To help students with problem-solving skills, teachers must be aware of what good problem solving consists of and integrate the development of these skills into nearly every lesson.

In addition to the knowledge of mathematical ideas, three other aspects of cognition are important for students to become good problem solvers: (1) problem-solving *strategies,* general approaches that can be used in a wide variety of problem situations; (2) *metacognitive processes,* monitoring and regulating one's own thinking and behavior; and (3) *beliefs and attitudes,* including self-confidence, willingness, and perseverance in the area of problem solving (Schoenfeld, 1992). We will examine each of these three areas, establish corresponding goals for students, and finally, make suggestions for how to help children achieve these goals as we teach.

Strategies and Processes for Problem Solving

Strategies or *heuristics* for solving problems are identifiable methods of approaching a task that are completely independent of the specific topic or subject matter.

Strategies for understanding a problem or task are the things that are desirable to do before you charge blindly into action. Stop to be sure the problem or task is understood. Sort out nonessential aspects of the problem, and identify critical information either given or yet to be searched out. Restate the problem in simple terms, and check to be sure this new personal version of the problem is the same task as the original.

Once the problem is well understood, the next step is to stop and think, "How are we going to work on this? What tools or methods or ways of working on problems might I use here?" This *strategy selection process* is one of matching a useful tool or approach to the task at hand.

It is fine to talk about selecting a strategy, but to select, you must actually have strategies from which to choose. Strategies that can be used to approach a variety of problems develop with experience over a long period of time as problems are solved and you reflect on how the problems were solved. These carrying-out strategies include such things as drawing a picture, making a chart, or trying a simpler version of the problem.

Looking-back processes coincide with the three things that you should look back at once an answer has been found. First, and most important, is the answer. Justifying the answer is as important a problem-solving process as the strategies for getting the answer. How one justifies an answer will vary with the task or problem.

Looking back also includes an examination of how the problem was solved (Could it have been done differently or more efficiently?) and of the problem itself (Can this problem be extended, modified, generalized?). These looking-back activities are essentially the things that define Pólya's fourth phase of problem solving.

Metacognition and Problem Solving

Metacognition refers to conscious monitoring (being aware of how and why you are doing something) and regulation (choosing to do something or deciding to make changes) of your own thought process. Good problem solvers monitor their thinking regularly and automatically. They are deliberate about their problem-solving actions. They recognize when they are stuck or do not fully understand and make conscious decisions to switch strategies, rethink the problem, search for related content knowledge that may help, or simply start afresh.

Poor problem solvers apparently have not learned this behavior or are unaware that it is useful. They tend to be impulsive, spending little time reflecting on a novel problem. They select a plan of attack very quickly and then stick with this initial approach, ignoring their lack of progress. Nor are poor problem solvers able to explain why they used the selected strategy or if they even believe it should work (Schoenfeld, 1992).

There seems to be a strong connection between problem-solving success and instruction that has integrated cognitive monitoring and regulatory practices with strategy instruction. As with strategies, there is evidence that metacognitive behavior can be learned (Campione, Brown, & Connell, 1989; Garofalo, 1987; Lester, 1989). Further, students who learn to monitor and regulate their own problem-solving behaviors do show improvement in problem solving.

Affective Factors and Problem Solving

How students feel about problem solving and the subject of mathematics in general has a significant effect on how they approach problems and ultimately on how well they succeed in mathematics. Put very simply, those who come to believe that they can solve problems and enjoy doing so tend to become better problem solvers. In contrast, think about a student who has the following negative ideas about mathematics:

- If you can't figure out how to do the problem right away, you must be stupid.
- Mathematics problems have only one right answer, and there is only one way to go about solving them.
- An average student like me has no chance unless the teacher tells me how to solve the problem.
- I am no good at solving problems. I must be stupid.

Obviously, students who harbor such ideas are not going to do very well. They will not persevere, they will be unwilling to try, and they will not be very receptive to a nonprescriptive approach.

Attitudes (likes, dislikes, preferences) are nearly as important as beliefs. Children who enjoy solving problems and feel satisfaction or pleasure at conquering a perplexing problem are much more likely to persevere, make second and third attempts, and even search out new problems. Negative attitudes have just the opposite effect.

GOALS FOR GOOD PROBLEM SOLVING

The discussion in the text can be summarized in this list of goals for helping students become better problem solvers.

Strategy and Process Goals

1. *Improve problem analysis skills.* To improve students' ability to analyze an unfamiliar problem, identify wanted and needed information, ignore nonessential information, and clearly state the goal of the problem or task.

2. *Develop and select strategies.* To help students develop a collection of problem-solving strategies or heuristics that are useful in a variety of problem-solving settings and to select and use a strategy or combination of strategies appropriate to the problem at hand.

3. *Justify solutions.* To improve students' ability to assess the solutions to problems in light of the information in the problem and the approaches used.

4. *Extend or generalize problems.* To help students learn to go beyond the solution to problems in light of the information in the problem and the approaches used.

Metacognitive Goal

- *Monitor and regulate actions.* To help students develop the habit and ability to monitor and regulate their thinking processes at each stage of the problem-solving process.

Affective Goals

1. *Develop confidence and belief in abilities.* To develop students' self-confidence in their ability to *do* mathematics and to confront unfamiliar tasks without being given a ready-made prescription for a solution.

2. *Improve willingness to try.* To improve students' willingness to attempt unfamiliar problems.

3. *Improve perseverance with a task.* To improve students' perseverence in their attempts at solving problems and not to be easily discouraged by initial setbacks.

4. *Foster enjoyment of mathematics.* To help students learn to enjoy and sense personal reward in the process of thinking, searching for patterns, and solving problems—to enjoy doing mathematics.

ACHIEVING PROBLEM-SOLVING GOALS WHILE STUDENTS LEARN

The goals of problem solving are extremely important. Yet, as the *Curriculum Standards* correctly indicates, there should not be a separate curriculum agenda to teach these goals. They can and should be developed as students are solving problems—doing mathematics—every day.

A Perspective on Teaching About Problem Solving

As problem solving became a major agenda of mathematics education during the 1980s and early 1990s, it evolved into a de facto strand of the mathematics curriculum. A variety of special programs were developed, and teachers were encouraged to set aside an hour or more each week that they would devote to "teaching problem solving."

Process Problems

Included in the instruction was usually an effort to help students understand George Pólya's four steps of problem solving or some variation of those steps. The predominant activity of the problem-solving strand had children solving "nonstandard" problems or *process problems*. A process problem is one that can be solved by applying a clearly identifiable heuristic or strategy to obtain a solution. *Process problems* are so named because of their teaching role of focusing students' attention on the process of solving the problem rather than on the mathematical content. The content that students are most likely going to "bump into" when doing a process problem is the strategy or strategies they use when solving the problem.

The following example of a process problem is so popular that it has become a classic in the problem-solving literature.

One day Farmer Brown was counting his pigs and chickens. He noticed that they had 60 legs and that there were 22 animals in all. How many of each kind of animal (pigs and chickens) did he have?

Two things made process problems such as the pigs-and-chickens problem so popular. First, they were not "routine." Students could not simply take the two numbers in the problem and perform an operation with them. In 1985, routine word problems were all too typically found near the end of chapters on operations, multiplication problems were at the end of multiplication chapters, and so on. Many process problems involve no computation at all, and none are solved by a simple computation. Second, students solving these problems tended to use clearly describable strategies. These could be discussed, labeled, and used in other problems. Frequently, one problem can be solved in several different ways. Solution methods for the pigs-and-chickens problem include a guess-and-check approach, drawing a picture, or creating a table or chart.

Process problems remain intuitively appealing to mathematics educators and to classroom teachers. Students do get involved in some excellent thinking as they do these problems. Adults and children who like to solve problems find them intriguing in the same way as riddles or puzzles. The first two editions of this text covered process problems extensively. It is reasonable to assume that they will still have a prominent position in mainstream textbooks, popular resource books, and local curriculum guides as we move into the twenty-first century.

Lessons from Research

Having painted that picture of process problems, why do you not find them included in this edition of this book? There are a number of reasons. First, process problems tend to halt the instruction in the regular curriculum, creating the undesirable problem-solving strand. Moreover, time lost from the agenda of the regular curriculum cannot be recovered. Second, when students learn strategies through the process problem approach, the strategies are taught by use of classes of problems that tend to be very similar in structure. Students appear to use these strategies in a prescriptive manner that is not the same as selecting strategies from those that have become familiar as Pólya intended (Schoenfeld, 1992). Third, while evidence suggests that children do learn and use strategies, it is not clear that they are actually using them anywhere but in process problems. The benefits seem mostly to come from the fact that students solving process problems were solving more problems than students in programs without process problems. This no doubt increased their self-confidence, improved their perceptions of mathematics, and enhanced their belief that they can solve problems. These very same benefits are readily achieved in any classroom in which students are engaged in problem solving and sense making as they learn mathematical concepts (Campbell, P. F., 1996; Rowan and Bourne 1994; Schifter & Fosnot, 1993; Silver, Smith, & Nelson, 1995; Silver & Stein, 1996; Wood, Cobb, Yackel, & Dillon, 1993).

Frank Lester (1994), a leading researcher in the area of problem solving, outlines some things we know from over 25 years of extensive research on solving problems:

1. Students must solve problems to improve their problem-solving ability.

2. Problem-solving ability develops slowly over a prolonged period of time.

3. Students must perceive that the teacher believes that problem solving is important.

4. Most students benefit from systematically planned problem-solving instruction.

5. Teaching students about specific strategies and about Pólya's four phases of problem solving does very little to improve their general problem-solving ability.

The conclusion is that all of the goals of problem solving previously outlined can and will be attained in mathematics classrooms that employ a problem-solving approach to the regular curriculum on a daily basis. It is important that the teacher be clearly aware of the goals of problem solving and focus attention on them regularly. Helping children learn about problem solving is an ongoing endeavor that is completely integrated with a constructivist view of learning and developmental teaching as described in this text.

Developing Problem-Solving Strategies

Once you remove yourself from the traditional teacher roles of showing and telling how to do every tiny procedure and explaining every concept, you take on the role of facilitating the science of pattern and order. The phrase "Here is how you do . . ." is replaced with "How can we figure out . . . ?" Although you maintain a leadership position, you are helping children negotiate meaning. You must be seen as an active participant in this negotiation, this sense-making discourse. As you teach, problem-solving strategies and processes are not "taught" but modeled. Students adapt these ways of approaching problems as you yourself become part of the problem-solving environment.

Understanding-the-Task Strategies

The "Before Actions" part of this chapter covered the kinds of things that can be done to help students learn to stop and understand a problem. As you daily model the process of posing a task or problem followed immediately by a discussion of what is known, needed, and asked for or expected in the task, children will begin to understand that this is part of what solving problems is about. Soon you can say, "Before we get started, what should we do first?" Let students articulate good understanding strategies such as "Tell what we know" in their own language. Eventually, you can put students in groups and present problems or tasks without having to provide such explicit guidance. Give the responsibility to the students to do the things that you have modeled.

Plan-and-Carry-Out Strategies

Problems, tasks, and activities should always be selected on the basis of the mathematics content that you want students to learn and your understanding of what your students will bring to them. There is no need to select problems for the sake of a strategy alone.

Class discussions after a problem has been solved or an activity has been explored should always involve a justification of the answers or results. That discussion will inevitably include a discussion of methods that were used. When important or especially useful strategies crop up, they should be identified, highlighted, and discussed. Labeling a strategy provides a useful means for students to talk about their methods and for you to provide hints and suggestions.

The strategies described here are the same as those that have become popular along with process problems. However, no listing of strategies should ever be considered definitive or all-inclusive. These are simply the strategies that seem most useful at the elementary and middle school levels. With each strategy are examples of content-based problems or activities where the strategy might be used.

Draw a Picture, Act It Out, Use a Model.   This will be the most widely used strategy for doing mathematics in your classroom. This is the strategy of models as "thinker toys" as described in Chapter 3. "Act it out" extends models to a real interpretation of the problem situation.

Almost any story problem with manageable numbers may profitably use this strategy.

> **The circus came to town on Wednesday. There were 8 acrobats and lots of clowns. There were 7 more clowns than acrobats. How many clowns were in the circus? (K–2)**

In this problem, students might use counters or draw a picture to help get a solution. The counters help analyze the structure of the problem.

In the next problem, models might be used a bit differently.

> **Brian is reading a book with 243 pages. So far he has read 186 pages. How many more pages does he have yet to read? (2–3)**

Here the materials might be selected if the problem were posed before students were taught how to do subtraction with pencil and paper in the traditional manner.

> **Peaches are selling at 3 pounds for $2.89. How much will 7 pounds cost? (6–8)**

This type of ratio problem frequently causes students difficulty because they can't remember how to set up the correct proportion. As you will see in Chapter 15, simple drawings can help students think through these situations, as shown in Figure 4.3.

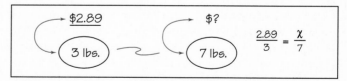

●**FIGURE 4.3**   *A drawing is used to establish a correct proportion by using the same relationship in the two cases.*

Look for a Pattern.   As mathematics is the science of pattern and order, pattern searching is in many activities. At the earliest grades, there are activities that are designed mainly for the purpose of having students begin to understand what pattern is all about. In some sense, these activities (see Chapter 18) could be called process problems. Here is an example:

> **Look at the pattern on the following strip. Use connecting cubes to copy the pattern and then extend it as far as you want. Then use another**

material (buttons, shells, or the like) to make a pattern that is the same as the one on the card. We will talk about how your two patterns are the same. (K–2)

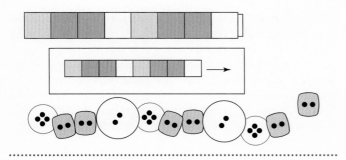

Patterns in number and in operations play a huge role in helping students learn about and master basic facts. The next example is explored in Chapter 8.

Examine the nines table for multiplication. What patterns can you find? How can these patterns help you remember the nines facts? (3–4)

Pattern continues to be a major factor into the middle and high school years. With the help of a graphing calculator, students can examine the effect of each coefficient in the quadratic equation $y = ax^2 + bx + c$. By holding two of the three coefficients fixed, they can try different examples of the third and establish a pattern that describes the effect of that coefficient on the shape of the curve.

Make a Table or Chart.   Charts of data, function tables, tables for operations, and tables involving measurement are a major form of communication within mathematics. The use of a chart is often combined with pattern searching as a means of solving problems or constructing new ideas.

Use two-color counters, and find all of the ways to make 9 in two parts. Make a chart to record the parts you find. (1–2).

In this example, the children may or may not put the data in a nice order. If not, an extension of the task is to search for a pattern and reorganize the table to show a pattern.

The next task is an example of "scaling" rates or ratios for the purpose of helping students begin to construct this difficult concept. Though used as a pedagogical device (Chapter

15), charts in this form are common in magazines and brochures.

Dad gets 23 miles per gallon of gas in his car. How far can he go on 5, 10, 15, . . . gallons of gas? Make a chart showing this information. (5–7)

Of course, not all charts are numeric tables. A tree diagram is a useful chart often used in analysis of probability situations. Figure 4.4 illustrates a tree diagram for two spins of a spinner with three unequal sections. Can you explain why there are two branches for the blue section?

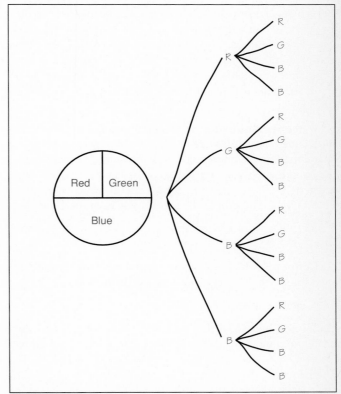

● FIGURE 4.4   *A tree diagram is a form of chart. Here one is used to account for all outcomes of a three-part spinner. Each branch has an equal chance of occurring.*

Try a Simpler Form of the Problem.   This is a powerful strategy beginning about the third or fourth grade. The general idea is to modify or simplify the quantities in a problem so that the resulting task is easier to understand and analyze. By solving the easier problem, the hope is to gain insights that can then be used to solve the original, more complex problem. One of the first places this strategy is found useful is in the analysis of real-world story problems that have quantities that are not easily modeled.

> **Tickets to the ball game sell for $4.75 each. On Saturday, 817 adults and 524 children attended. All paid the same price. The concession stand sold 1,275 boxes of popcorn, a record number. How much was taken in at the box office? (3–5)**

If students have difficulty deciding on or defending a choice of operations, a good suggestion is to substitute small numbers (e.g., $4 tickets, 8 adults, 5 children). With the smaller numbers, a picture of 13 sets with 4 in each would suggest or explain the choice of multiplication. A similar approach is useful when problems involve fractions or decimals.

The simpler-problem approach is found in computational estimation. The whole idea of using rounded numbers to get an estimate is using a simpler problem. In the last problem, a "simpler problem" could be $5 tickets and a total of 1,300 attendees. The product of $6,500 is a reasonable estimate and can be computed mentally. Solving a simpler problem in this sense is a good way to see if an exact result is "in the ballpark," using the estimate as a rough check on an answer.

Write an Equation or Open Sentence.   Like charts and tables, equations are a major communication tool in mathematics. We often translate a problematic situation into an equation because the equation is easier to work with, suggests a familiar pattern, or is a useful way to communicate an idea. The process begins as early as grade 1 and continues throughout mathematics.

> **Deron took 12 pogs to the tournament and came home with 18. How many pogs did he win? (1–2)**

If children first solve this problem with counters and then write an equation to tell what they did, some children will write $12 + 6 = 18$ and others will write $18 - 12 = 6$. The latter form is the computation form because it has the answer isolated. Had the numbers required a calculator, the computation form would be necessary. The first form, with the answer as an addend, reflects the syntax of the problem. The discussion about these two equations is a discussion of two ways to communicate one idea. Students will eventually see how the two equations are related. Writing the equation becomes an important tool for making sense of the situation. Equations can and should be written for problems at all grade levels to help clarify ideas and relationships.

> **Brian bought a lawn mower for $329 to start a summer lawn-mowing business. He averages about $27 per lawn. How many lawns will he need to cut before he has made a profit of $500? (5–8)**

This problem is a good illustration of a real situation that can be translated profitably into an equation ($P = N \times 27 - 329$), a chart, and also a graph. Students begin to see that the chart, equation, and graph are all different representations of the same real-world relationship.

Guess and Check or Try and Adjust.   The essence of this strategy is to make an educated or reasoned guess at the solution and then see how the guess fits the conditions. If there is a good fit, you may be finished, and a guess has solved the problem. If not, the check should tell you in which direction to adjust the guess. Situations where this strategy is useful generally have multiple conditions that make it difficult to compute a true solution.

> **Soda cans must hold 355 ml of liquid and also have a bit of extra "head room." You are a designer for the product manager and have the task of designing the shape of a new can for Sudzy Soda. What is the best height and diameter for the can? You want the can to use a minimum amount of aluminum, be comfortable to hold, and be easy to pour and drink from. It should also be easy to stack and place in shipping cartons and on shelves. (6–8)**

This problem combines geometry, measurement, and some real-world considerations. It could be used to motivate the development of a volume formula or a surface area formula. There is no single "correct" answer. Once formulas are established for volume and the surface of sides, top, and bottom, initial guesses can be made for height and diameter. If these formulas are put into a simple spreadsheet on a computer, successive guesses can be made and a record kept of each.

The try-and-adjust strategy is perhaps seen more frequently in a slightly less rigorous form. Consider this geometry problem:

> **I used two identical shapes to make a rectangle. What might they have been? (Baker & Baker, 1991). (3–8)**

Here there are no numeric conditions to check or to indicate how to adjust a guess. At the same time, the best way to work on this task is to *do something*. Make an attempt! Once you have done something, you can examine what you have done, and that result may tell you something more to do. In this sense, the strategy is not at all the same as the guess-and-check method that might be used to solve the soda can problem. There, each guess will move you closer to a single solution. Here, a guess is a way to generate another idea. It is a response to "What can you find out about that?" Perhaps this form of the strategy should be called "guess and explore" or "try and see what you can find out."

Work Backward from the Solution. This strategy is also very well represented in the literature around process problems. The problems designed for this strategy usually have a series of events ending with a given conclusion. The task is to find the starting point. Here is an example of a typical process problem that may have some value in the regular curriculum.

....

Terika and Wanda inherited a collection of figurines from their great-grandmother. They agreed on a plan to decide who would get which figures. Since Terika was older, she would go first and select one-fourth of the figurines for herself. Then Wanda would get to choose half of the remaining figures. That left 6 figurines that they decided to keep as "common property" until a later date. How many figurines did they inherit to begin with? (5–6)

....

As noted earlier, there is an element of challenge and intrigue in these problems that is hard for some people to resist. The criticism of this particular strategy is that in real life, these situations don't happen. The girls would know what they began with. If there is a content value, it is in the fractions and working from a part to a whole amount in terms of sets. Process problems for the work-backward strategy often involve arithmetic operations. To work through these problems backward demands wrestling with the idea of inverse operations. The content of the inverse relationship is more significant than the strategy.

Make an Organized List. This is another strategy that is easier to find in process problems than in the regular curriculum. The strategy is aimed at systematically accounting for all possible outcomes in a situation, either to find out how many possibilities there are or to be sure that all possible outcomes have been accounted for. *How many different ways are there to make 27 cents?* is a good example of an organized-list process problem. No one ever needs to know how many ways there are to make 27 cents. At the same time, it is a good problem for students who need practice working with money. Again, content outweighs strategy.

One area where organized lists are very important is in probability.

....

What is the probability of rolling a 5 or a 6 using two dice? (5–8)

....

Determining theoretical probabilities for well-defined events such as in this problem requires figuring out the number of possible outcomes. For two dice, are there 11

outcomes (the sums 2 through 12) or 36 outcomes (six possibilities for each die)?

Use Logical Reasoning. It almost seems silly to call logical reasoning a strategy when reasoning is such an integral component of doing mathematics. "Mathematics as reasoning" is the third standard at each level of the *Curriculum Standards.* Reasoning is what we expect students to do as they justify their answers, make conjectures, and apply deductive arguments.

In the same way that patterning activities are used to develop the concept of what a pattern is, logic activities, especially those using attribute materials, have long been popular in the primary grades (see Chapter 18). The following teacher-directed activity where the children are the attribute material is a good example of a logical-reasoning problem.

....

I am going to sort you children into two groups, one child at a time. All in the first group have something in common. No one in the other group has this property. After I have sorted some of you, try to predict who else will be in each group. (Children are sorted based on something visual such as "wears glasses" or "has sneakers on.") (K–3)

....

Each of the following tasks for older children involves if-then logic, the main indication of logical reasoning.

....

How much larger is 0.76×5 than 0.75×5? How can you decide without any computation? (Kulm, 1994). (6–8)

....

Cut out two identical triangles. Using only those two triangles and a ruler, how can you find the area of one triangle? (Assume that the formula for parallelograms has been developed but not the formula for triangles.) (4–6)

....

Use your graphing calculator to find the intersection of $y = 3x - 5$ and $y = -2x + 4$. What can you tell about the coordinates of this point? Explain.

....

Looking-Back Strategies

Looking-back strategies are those things that should always be done after a solution has been found: justify the answer, consider how the problem was solved, and look for possible extensions or generalizations. These will all be developed if you follow the "after actions" discussed earlier. As with the understand-the-problem strategies, students should eventually come to accept responsibility for doing these things themselves without your leading every discussion. You want to help students understand that postproblem reflection is not just something that one does in school but something that should be done whenever a problem is solved.

Developing Metacognitive Habits

We know that it is important to help students learn to monitor and control their own progress in problem solving. A simple formula that can be employed consists of three questions:

- *What* are you doing?
- *Why* are you doing it?
- *How* does it help you?

In some form or another, these are questions we want children to begin asking themselves. Though the exact form of the three questions is not significant, the idea is to be persistent with this reflective questioning as students work through problems or explorations. You can ask the questions as you sit down to listen to any group. By joining the group, you model questioning that you want the students eventually to do on their own. When you feel that students are beginning to understand the process of monitoring, each group can designate (or you can assign) a member to be the monitor. The monitor's job is to be the reflective questioner the same way you have modeled when working with the group.

Students can also be helped in developing self-monitoring habits after their problem-solving activity is over. The assistance can be provided orally, in a written format, or through self-rating forms. A 5-minute discussion after a problem is over can focus on what types of things were done in solving the problem. "What did you do that helped you understand the problem? Did you find any numbers or information you didn't need? How did you decide what to do? Did you think about your answer after you got it? How did you decide your answer was right?"

Questioning similar to this tells students that all of these things are important. If they know you are going to be asking such questions, there is an increased chance that students will think about them ahead of time. Oral discussions with the class will be most helpful with younger children for whom written formats are difficult.

An approach that can be used periodically is to have students respond to a metacognitive checklist shortly after solving a problem. For each of the statements shown in Figure 4.5, students circle one of these responses: NO (I didn't do this), MAYBE (I may have done this), or YES (I did do this).

Use the results of a checklist such as this one as a basis for class discussion. Students can talk about why they responded as they did and hear what other students were thinking about while solving the same problem. The responses also provide information that you can use to help the class or individuals improve their monitoring habits.

BEFORE

Before you began to solve the problem, what did you do?

1. I read the problem more than once.
2. I tried to find everything out about the problem that I could.
3. I asked myself, "Do I really understand what the problem is asking me?"
4. I thought about what information I needed to solve this problem.
5. I asked myself, "Have I ever worked a problem like this before?"
6. I asked myself, "Is there information in this problem I do not need?"

DURING

As you worked the problem, what did you do?

7. I kept looking back at the problem as I worked.
8. I had to stop and rethink what I was doing and why.
9. I checked my work as I went along step by step.
10. I had to start over and do it differently.
11. I asked myself, "Is what I am doing getting me closer to the answer?"

AFTER

After you finished working the problem, what did you do?

12. I checked to see if all my calculations were correct.
13. I went over my work to see if it still seemed like a good way to do the problem.
14. I looked at the problem to see if my answer made sense.
15. I thought about a different way to solve the problem.
16. I tried to see if I could tell more than what the problem asked for.

•**FIGURE 4.5**   *Suggestions for a metacognitive checklist.*

Source: Adapted from Fortunato, Hecht, Tittle, & Alvarez (1991).

Attending to Affective Goals

In Chapter 3, we noted that key elements of a mathematical environment were expectations, respect, and a belief that all children are capable. An environment built on high expectations for all students and respect for their thoughts will go a long way toward achieving the affective goals listed for problem solving. Listed here are some additional ideas to help with these goals for all students.

Build In Success

In the beginning of the year, plan problems that you are confident your students can solve. The success should clearly be your students' and not due to your careful guidance. Avoid creating a false success that depends on your showing the way at every step and curve.

Praise Efforts and Risk Taking

Students need to hear frequently that they are "good thinkers" capable of good, productive thought. When students volunteer ideas, listen carefully and actively to each idea, and give credit for the thinking and the risk that children take by venturing to speak out. Be careful to focus praise on the risk or effort and not the products of that effort, regardless of the quality of the ideas. If weak or incorrect ideas are put down or ignored, the children who ventured forth with those ideas will think twice before ever trying again. After some time, the reluctance turns into a belief that "I'm no good. I can't think of good ideas." The same negative message comes through when praise is reserved only for the "best" ideas.

Listen to All Students

Avoid ending a discussion with the first correct answer. As you make nonevaluative responses, you will find many children repeating the same idea. Were they just copying a known leader? Perhaps, but more likely they were busy thinking and did not even hear what had already been said by those who were a bit faster. If ten hands go up, ten children may have been doing good thinking. If you forget to listen to lots of children, lots of children will not hear your praise. Don't forget the suggestion made earlier to call on less secure students early in a discussion so that the most obvious ideas are not "taken" by the more aggressive students. (See "After Actions," pp. 46–47.)

Provide Special Successes for Special Children

Not all children will develop the same problem-solving abilities, but all have abilities and can contribute. This must be something you truly believe because it is difficult to fake. Students who are slower or not as strong need success also. One way to provide success for them is to involve them in groups with strong and supportive children. In group settings, all children can be made to feel the success of the group work. Slower students can also be quietly given special hints that move them toward success.

ASSESSMENT REFLECTS GOALS AND VALUES

If you believe in the goals for problem solving, these goals should be communicated to your students as part of your expectations. Children best learn of your values and beliefs by observing your excitement, interest, and commitment to solving problems with them on a daily basis. However, communication of your goals is not sufficient by itself. Nothing undermines a stated value system more quickly than a failure to assess and evaluate based on these values. Each of the goals in each of the three categories—strategies, metacognition, and affect—can and should be assessed. That means that real data should be gathered and used in your communication with students and parents concerning achievement. Much of this information can be collected in the form of observation schemes, both over time and focused within specific activities. Student self-reporting, individually and as a group, can also be used.

These methods will be discussed in detail in Chapter 5. For now it is sufficient to note that if you revert to a traditional evaluation scheme based only on answers, then it is only answers that students will see as important. For you to achieve a complete and effective approach to problem solving throughout your curriculum, the entire list of problem-solving goals must be assessed as one major way of communicating your value system.

REFLECTIONS ON CHAPTER 4: WRITING TO LEARN

1. Why is a problem for one person not necessarily a problem for another? The computational exercises that we all used to call problems are not problems at all. Why is that?

2. Explain briefly the essential features of each step of the four-step plan devised by George Pólya. In the looking-back stage, what three things do we want students to look at?

3. Describe at least two specific things that teachers might do before students begin work on a problem. Give an example where your idea is appropriate (other than the example provided in the text).

4. In the "during" teacher actions, how can you help children with each of the plan and carry-out phases of problem solving?

5. Describe the kind of information you want to discuss in the "after" portion of a lesson.

6. How do the decisions a teacher makes correspond to the four phases of problem solving?

7. Select an activity from any chapter in Section 2 of this text. How can the activity be used as a "problem" for the purpose of instruction in the sense taken in this chapter? If you were using this activity in the classroom, what suggestions from the "before" actions for teachers would you use? Explain.

8. What is the difference between teaching *through* problem solving and teaching *about* problem solving?

9. The goals for problem solving fall into three categories: strategies, metacognition, and affect. For each category, briefly tell what a teacher can do to address these goals.

10. Why must your assessment program include problem-solving goals?

FOR DISCUSSION AND EXPLORATION

1. What would you do if you posed a task or problem and no group did what you expected, and as a result the content you intended to teach was not addressed?

2. Review the affective objectives for problem solving. How do you personally stack up on these objectives? What major factors in your experiences caused these attitudes toward problem solving? If you had negative experiences in school, how can you be sure your students will not experience the same things?

3. You (or perhaps your instructor) may disagree with the position articulated in this chapter that says we do not need to teach with nonstandard or process problems. Examine a commercially available problem-solving program that is based on process problems. Three possibilities are *Problem-Solving Experiences in Mathematics* (Charles et al., 1985), *The Problem Solver: Activities for Learning Problem Solving Strategies* (Goodnow, Hoogeboom, Moretti, Stephens, & Scanlin, 1987), and *Problem of the Day* (1993). How do these programs fit your understanding of the needs of problem-solving instruction?

4. Examine a basal textbook for one grade. If possible, select a text first published in 1993 or later. How would you characterize the approach to instruction in general, compared to that developed in this chapter? What types of problems are provided? You should examine the teacher's edition of the book to obtain an accurate perspective.

SUGGESTED READINGS

Highly Recommended

Borasi, R. (1992). *Learning mathematics through inquiry.* Portsmouth, NH: Heinemann.

Borasi describes in great detail a ten-lesson "minicourse" on mathematical definitions conducted with two 16-year-old girls. It includes insights into the girls' thoughts as they change their perceptions of doing and learning mathematics as well as Borasi's unique perspectives on mathematics as a humanistic discipline and learning as meaning-making. The topics are only slightly above the middle grades level, but the discussion as a reflection of the current chapter is worth reading by all teachers of mathematics.

Burns, M. (1996). *50 problem-solving lessons: Grades 1–6.* White Plains, NY: Cuisenaire Co. of America (distributor).

The 50 lessons are all in the spirit of teaching through problem solving. The content strands include number, geometry, measurement, statistics, probability, patterns and functions, algebra, and logic. Each is described in a few pages with ample examples of children's work, all in the spirit of this master teacher of mathematics. Not only a good resource but a good model also.

National Council of Teachers of Mathematics: Commission on Teaching Standards for School Mathematics. (1991). *Professional standards for teaching mathematics.* Reston, VA: Author.

Sometimes it seems necessary to be more emphatic in recommending that teachers read the *Standards* documents. The suggestion here is to read the introduction (15 pages) and the first six Teaching Standards (pp. 19–67). Not only does this document set standards for teaching mathematics that are important, but the vignettes that accompany each standard, pictures of real teachers struggling to change, are excellent examples of teaching through problem solving.

Rowan, T. E., & Bourne, B. (1994). *Thinking like mathematicians: Putting the K–4 Standards into practice.* Portsmouth, NH: Heinemann.

A must read for any teacher in the K–5 range. Rowan and Bourne describe in 132 pages the spirit of the *Standards* as carried out by teachers in urban, multiethnic Montgomery County, Maryland, schools. The schools described were part of a project funded by the National Science Foundation to explore the effectiveness of a constructivist approach (see Campbell, P. F., 1996). The book contains practical suggestions and inspiring stories from teachers and from the classroom. Many of Rowan and Bourne's thoughts have found their way into the current chapter.

Other Suggestions

Arvold, B., Turner, P., & Cooney, T. J. (1996). Analyzing teaching and learning: The art of listening. *Mathematics Teacher, 89,* 326–329.

Baker, A., & Baker, J. (1990). *Mathematics in process.* Portsmouth, NH: Heinemann.

Baker, A., & Baker, J. (1991). *Maths in the mind: A process approach to mental strategies.* Portsmouth, NH: Heinemann.

Brown, S. L., & Walter, M. I. (1990). *The art of problem posing* (2nd ed.). Hillsdale, NJ: Erlbaum.

Buschman, L. (1995). Communicating in the language of mathematics. *Teaching Children Mathematics, 1,* 324–329.

Burns, M. (1992). *About teaching mathematics: A K–8 resource.* White Plains, NY: Cuisenaire (distributor).

Campbell, P. F. (1996). Empowering children and teachers in the elementary mathematics classrooms of urban schools. *Urban Education, 30,* 449–475.

Chambers, D. L. (1995). Improving instruction by listening to children. *Teaching Children Mathematics, 1,* 378–380.

Charles, R., & Lester, F. K. (1982). *Teaching problem solving: What, why and how.* Palo Alto, CA: Dale Seymour.

Charles, R., et al. (1985). *Problem-solving experiences in mathematics (grades 1 to 8).* Menlo Park, CA: AWL Supplemental.

Corwin, R. B. (1993). Doing mathematics together: Creating a mathematical culture. *Arithmetic Teacher, 40,* 338–341.

Cramer, K., & Karnowski, L. (1995). The importance of informal language in representing mathematical ideas. *Teaching Children Mathematics, 1,* 332–335.

Fortunato, I., Hecht, D., Tittle, C. K., & Alvarez, L. (1991). Metacognition and problem solving. *Arithmetic Teacher, 39*(4), 38–40.

Garofalo, J. (1987). Metacognition and school mathematics. *Arithmetic Teacher, 34*(9), 22–23.

Garofalo, J., & Bryant, J. (1992). Assessing reasonableness: Some observations and suggestions. *Arithmetic Teacher, 40,* 210–212.

Garofalo, J., & Lester, F. K. (1985). Metacognition, cognitive monitoring, and mathematical performance. *Journal for Research in Mathematics Education, 16,* 163–176.

Goodnow, J., Hoogeboom, S., Moretti, G., Stephens, M., & Scanlin, A. (1987). *The problem solver: Activities for learning problem solving strategies.* Palo Alto, CA: Creative Publications.

Hembre, R., & Marsh, H. (1993). Problem solving in early childhood: Building foundations. In R. J. Jensen (Ed.), *Research ideas for the classroom: Early childhood mathematics* (pp. 151–170). Old Tappan, NJ: Macmillan.

Hiebert, J., & Wearne, D. (1993). Instructional tasks, classroom discourse, and students' learning in second-grade arithmetic. *American Educational Research Journal, 30,* 393–425.

Hyde, A. A., & Hyde, P. R. (1991). *Mathwise: Teaching mathematical thinking and problem solving.* Portsmouth, NH: Heinemann.

Kersh, M. E., & McDonald, J. (1991). How do I solve thee? Let me count the ways! *Arithmetic Teacher, 39*(2), 38–41.

Kilman, M. (1993). Integrating mathematics and literature in the elementary classroom. *Arithmetic Teacher, 40,* 318–321.

Kroll, D. L., & Miller, T. (1993). Insights from research on mathematical problem solving in the middle grades. In D. T. Owens (Ed.), *Research ideas for the classroom: Middle grades mathematics* (pp. 58–77). Old Tappan, NJ: Macmillan.

Mason, J., Burton, L., & Stacey, K. (1982). *Thinking mathematically.* London: Addison-Wesley.

McNeal, B. (1995). Learning not to think in a textbook-based mathematics class. *Journal of Mathematical Behavior, 14,* 205–234.

Meyer, C., & Sallee, T. (1983). *Make it simpler: A practical guide to problem solving in mathematics.* Menlo Park, CA: AWL Supplemental.

Reys, B. J., & Long, V. M. (1995). Teacher as architect of mathematical tasks. *Teaching Children Mathematics, 1,* 296–299.

Scheibelhut, C. (1994). I do and I understand, I reflect and I improve. *Teaching Children Mathematics, 1,* 242–246.

Schifter, D., & Fosnot, C. T. (1993). *Reconstructing mathematics education: Stories of teachers meeting the challenge of reform.* New York: Teachers College Press.

Schwartz, S. L. (1996). Hidden messages in teacher talk: Praise and empowerment. *Teaching Children Mathematics, 2,* 396–401.

Sgroi, R. J. (1992). Systematizing trial and error using spreadsheets. *Arithmetic Teacher, 39*(7), 8–12.

Sigurdson, S. E., Olson, A. T., & Mason, R. (1994). Problem solving and mathematics learning. *Journal of Mathematical Behavior, 13,* 361–388.

Silver, E. A., & Stein, M. K. (1996). The QUASAR project: The "revolution of the possible" in mathematics instructional reform in urban middle schools. *Urban Education, 30,* 476–521.

Silver, E. A., Kilpatrick, J., & Schlesinger, B. (1990). *Thinking through mathematics: Fostering inquiry and communication in mathematics classrooms.* New York: College Entrance Examination Board.

Smith, J. P., III. (1996). Efficacy and teaching mathematics by telling: A challenge for reform. *Journal for Research in Mathematics Education, 27,* 387–402.

Szetela, W. (1986). The checkerboard problem extended, extended, extended, . . . *School Science and Mathematics, 86,* 205–222.

Tsuruda, G. (1994). *Putting it together: Middle school math in transition.* Portsmouth, NH: Heinemann.

Vaac, N. N. (1993). Teaching and learning mathematics through classroom discussion. *Arithmetic Teacher, 41,* 225–227.

Whitin, D. J. (1993). Becca's investigation. *Arithmetic Teacher, 41,* 78–81.

Whitin, D. J. (1993). Looking at the world from a mathematical perspective. *Arithmetic Teacher, 40,* 438–441.

Worth, J. (1990). Developing problem-solving abilities and attitudes. In J. N. Payne (Ed.), *Mathematics for the young child* (pp. 39–61). Reston, VA: National Council of Teachers of Mathematics.

Yackel, E. (1995). Children's talk in inquiry mathematics classrooms. In P. Cobb & H. Bauersfeld (Eds.), *The emergence of mathematical meaning: Interaction in classroom cultures* (pp. 131–162). Hillsdale, NJ: Erlbaum.

CHAPTER

5

BUILDING ASSESSMENT INTO INSTRUCTION

To find classrooms where the vision of the *Standards* is most fully actualized, you must find classrooms where the general approach and philosophy of assessment have also changed to reflect that vision. Assessment can and should be an integral component of learning and teaching.

The challenge of the new direction in assessment is significant. Although it is taking time for school districts and teachers to restructure their thinking about assessment, it is clear that the vision of mathematical power in a child-centered, problem-solving environment demands no less. The habit of testing only the lowest-level mathematics skills must be broken.

THE ASSESSMENT STANDARDS

The fourth section of the *Curriculum Standards,* the Evaluation Standards, clearly articulated a need to shift away from a test-oriented view of assessment that effectively penalizes students for what they *do not* know. The shift must be toward a broader view of assessment that attempts to find out and acknowledge what students *do* know. In 1995, NCTM's *Assessment Standards for School Mathematics* enlarged on that theme. The *Assessment Standards* calls for a shift away from "assessing only students' knowledge of specific facts and isolated skills" and toward "assessing students' full mathematical power" (p. 83). The document contains six standards for assessment and details four purposes that assessment practices should serve.

What Is Assessment?

The term *assessment* is defined in the *Assessment Standards* as "the process of gathering evidence about a student's knowledge of, ability to use, and disposition toward mathematics and of making inferences from that evidence for a variety of purposes" (p. 3). It is important to note that assessment is not at all the same as testing, measurement, or evaluation of students. These latter terms include the elements of value or worth. Assessment data are certainly used in evaluation of both students and programs. However, assessment focuses on data collection. There are multiple ways to collect and use this data. Only one of the four uses of data described in the *Assessment Standards* is related to assigning evaluative grades.

Six Assessment Standards

As with the earlier *Standards* documents, these standards are statements against which assessment practices can be judged. They are not prescriptions for how to create assessments. The classroom teacher should periodically reflect on his or her assessment methods using the standards as a benchmark.

1. The Mathematics Standard

Assessment should reflect the mathematics that all students need to know and be able to do (NCTM, 1995, p. 11).

The first standard seems like common sense, yet it has not been fully realized in many classrooms. What students "need to know" is the mathematics articulated in the *Curriculum Standards,* not the outdated arithmetic of computation and procedural skills. Nor can assessment focus only on skills that are easy to assess. Assessment must reflect the four theme standards of mathematics as problem solving, as communication, as reasoning, and as mathematical connections. Mathematics must include the broader vision of the *Standards* content, including a significantly smaller emphasis on computational skills. What we assess communicates what is valued.

2. The Learning Standard

Assessment should enhance mathematics learning (NCTM, 1995, p. 13).

The traditional approach to assessment has been one of summative evaluation, done after instruction to determine if students know what was taught. The Learning Standard suggests that the main purpose of assessment is to improve performance, not merely to audit it. Classroom assessment practices should communicate to students *during* the learning process, guiding students to improve their learning and know what is valued.

In like manner, assessment should guide teachers in their design of instruction by providing a constant stream of information by which decisions can be made during a unit rather than when instruction is finished.

For assessment to support and enhance learning, it must be viewed and designed as an integral part of instruction, not as an addendum or an interruption.

3. The Equity Standard

Assessment should promote equity (NCTM, 1995, p. 15).

Equitable assessment respects the unique qualities, experiences, and expertise of each student. Equity in assessment sets high mathematical standards for all students, including those with special needs. "The challenge posed by the equity principle is to devise tasks with sufficient flexibility to give students a sense of accomplishment, to challenge the upper reaches of every student's mathematical understanding, and to provide a window on each student's mathematical thinking" (MSEB, 1993, p. 12). Equity aims directly at finding out what all students *do* know rather than establishing a narrow hurdle that too often screens students from further mathematics or suggests only that they have not achieved.

4. The Openness Standard

Assessment should be an open process (NCTM, 1995, p. 17).

Students need to know what is expected of them and how they can demonstrate what they have learned. The criteria for quality performance must also be clear to students. In the past, acceptable criteria consisted of a designated percentage of correct responses. Now reasoning, communica-

tion, and problem solving are the main agendas, and performance will be viewed in a holistic and often subjective manner. Students need to be involved in setting the criteria and even using the criteria to assess their own performance. Openness also means that parents and other teachers are aware of the methods and criteria that are valued in the classroom.

5. The Inferences Standard

Assessment should promote valid inferences about mathematics learning (NCTM, 1995, p. 19).

The question that teachers in a developmental approach to instruction must constantly ask is, "What does this performance tell me about this student's understanding or reasoning?" Assessments are based on students' doing mathematics—communicating, reasoning, justifying results, testing hypotheses, looking for patterns. The activity of doing mathematics cannot be expressed as a "number correct." Assessment is rarely "teacherproof." No objectively scored test can determine the workings of children's thought processes or individual understandings.

To live up to this standard requires that teachers reflect seriously and honestly on what students are revealing about what they know. The use of multiple assessment techniques is one way that teachers can improve the validity of their inferences. A classroom with effective discourse will provide ample data for valid assessments. Teachers have a duty to pay attention to this information.

6. The Coherence Standard

Assessment should be a coherent process (NCTM, 1995, p. 21).

In 1989, the *Curriculum Standards* called for "alignment" in assessment. That meant that assessment practices and instructional practices should be coordinated. For example, if calculators or manipulative materials or verbal expressions were part of the instructional process, those same approaches should properly be part of the assessment process. The Coherence Standard builds on the concept of alignment by demanding that assessment also reflect the goals of instruction. Further, the four purposes of assessment should be balanced: to improve learning, inform instruction, inform others including parents (grades), and evaluate the instructional program. Coherence can be translated as balance of purpose and alignment with instruction.

Purposes of Assessment

Even a cursory glance at the six assessment standards suggests a completely integrated view of assessment with instruction. The *Assessment Standards* document outlines four specific purposes of assessment as depicted in Figure 5.1 (p. 64). With each purpose, the rectangle to the outside indicates a corresponding result.

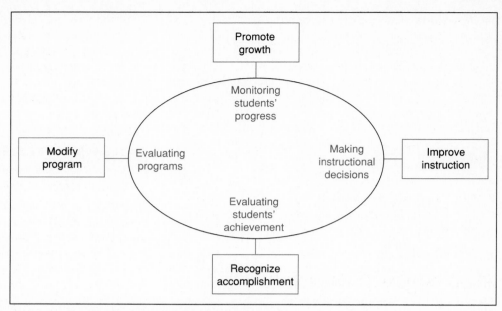

●**FIGURE 5.1** Four purposes of assessment and their results.
Source: NCTM (1995, p. 25). Used with permission.

Monitoring Student Progress

As a teacher, you establish high goals for all of your students. Assessment should provide both teacher and students with ongoing feedback concerning progress toward those goals. Assessment should provide information concerning more than simple mastery of procedural skills. It should inform each individual student and the teacher about growth toward mathematical power and problem-solving ability. Furthermore, the feedback should be received during instruction, not at the end of the unit, when it is perhaps too late. It is this ongoing aspect of assessment that best promotes student learning.

Making Instructional Decisions

In Chapter 4, the teacher-as-decision-maker process was described as a four-stage endeavor that paralleled George Pólya's stages of problem solving (see Figure 5.2). Assessment data are a key element of this process at every stage. Understanding the

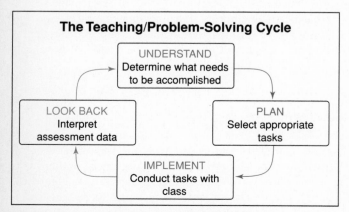

●**FIGURE 5.2** Assessment informs each stage of the teaching/problem-solving cycle.

teaching problem requires information concerning students' current levels of understanding and needs. Data from prior lessons inform the choice of tasks at the second stage. Plans must also be made for gathering new information. At the third stage in the classroom, the constructivist teacher listens to students throughout the lesson and makes judgments on a minute-by-minute basis. As teaching shifts from teacher telling to student doing, assessment data are collected and either used immediately or stored for the next stage. At the fourth stage, the teacher reflects on the day's lesson and interprets the data gathered. This interpretation informs the understanding of the teaching problem, and the cycle continues.

Evaluating Student Achievement

An important distinction should be made between assessment and evaluation. *Assessment* is the collection of data; *evaluation* is "the process of determining the worth of, or assigning a value to, something on the basis of careful examination and judgment" (NCTM, 1995, p. 3). Evaluation involves a teacher's judgment about a student's demonstrated understanding. It may include test data but should take into account a wide variety of sources and types of information gathered during the course of instruction. Most important, evaluation should reflect performance criteria about what students know and understand and should not be used to compare one student with another.

Traditional evaluation was nearly synonymous with the end-of-unit test. There was a clear line between instruction and evaluation. The *Standards* view of appropriate assessment practice is pretty much to eradicate that line by gathering assessment data continuously in informal ways and frequently in more structured ways and by including these data in evaluation. (A more complete discussion of grading can be found near the end of this chapter.)

Evaluating Programs

Assessment data should be used as one significant component in answering the question "How well did this program work to achieve my goals?" In this context, *program* refers to any organized unit of study and need not be restricted to school or district decisions such as which textbook should be adopted. For the classroom teacher, program includes such things as self-designed units of instruction, a chapter from a resource book or text, or even a particular strategy for cooperative groups or learning centers. In evaluation of these as well as larger curricular programs, students' knowledge, understanding, processes, and disposition—based on multiple sources of information—should all be taken into account.

WHAT SHOULD BE ASSESSED?

Effective assessment requires planning to make sure that it happens and that the data reflecting important objectives are actually gathered. Assessment of the long-term, broad goals of mathematical power—of doing mathematics—should be included in assessment of short-term goals that reflect the content of the current unit of instruction.

Mathematical Power

The *Curriculum Standards* defines *mathematical power* as "an individual's abilities to explore, conjecture, and reason logically, . . . to use a variety of mathematical methods effectively to solve non-routine problems" (NCTM, 1995, p. 5). The *Standards* goes on to note that mathematical power also includes personal self-confidence. As different school districts and educators have designed assessment strategies, each has taken a slightly different approach concerning how to focus on this somewhat illusive notion of "power." You will most likely want to make some personal or department-level decisions as you design your own long-term assessment plan. For example, some educators may choose to focus on communication and reasoning throughout the year, with affective factors being assessed at specific times. Others may choose to focus on problem solving. Perhaps the agenda will change in emphasis over the course of the year.

Guidelines for defining the specifics of mathematical power can be found in the first four Curriculum Standards and in the three categories of goals for problem solving as discussed in Chapter 4. After selecting the components you wish to assess, the next step is to write or adapt descriptive statements that can be used to help identify achievement at different levels. For example, Kentucky has chosen to base its portfolio scoring guide around the four theme standards: problem solving, reasoning, communication, and connections (see Figure 5.3). Note, however, that this guide is used for statewide evaluation purposes. As such, it omits many things that the classroom teacher may also want to consider.

KENTUCKY MATHEMATICS PORTFOLIO
HOLISTIC SCORING GUIDE
PROCESS DESCRIPTORS

PROBLEM SOLVING

- Understands the features of a problem (understands the question, restates the problem in own words)
- Explores (draws a diagram, constructs a model and/or chart, records data, looks for patterns)
- Selects an appropriate strategy (trial and error, exhaustive list, simpler but similar problem, works backward, guesses and checks, estimates a solution)
- Solves (implements a strategy with an accurate solution)
- Reviews, revises, and extends (verifies answer, explores and analyzes solutions, formulates a rule.)

REASONING

- Makes mathematical conjectures through observing data and recognizing patterns (inductive reasoning)
- Validates mathematical conjectures through logical verifications or counter-examples: constructs valid arguments (deductive reasoning)

MATHEMATICAL COMMUNICATION

- Uses appropriate mathematical notation and terminology
- Provides quality explanations for the given task
- Communicates concepts, ideas, and reflections clearly
- Provides multiple mathematical representations (models, graphs, tables, diagrams)

INTEGRATION CONNECTIONS

- Evaluates the consequences of solutions, conclusions, or actions from different perspectives
- Makes unique and creative analogies or connections
- Recognizes, makes, or applies the connections among the mathematical core concepts
- Recognizes, makes or applies the connections with mathematics, other disciplines, and the real world

Student work for each of the above processes is rated at one of the following four levels:

NOVICE/APPRENTICE/PROFICIENT/DISTINGUISHED

●**FIGURE 5.3** *The Kentucky Mathematics Portfolio Holistic Scoring Guide.*

Source: Kentucky Department of Education. Used with permission.

For example, metacognitive and affective goals are not represented here. Another difference is that the guide is designed for written work that goes into a portfolio. The teacher also has access to daily work and to data from observations that can tell of students' perseverance and willingness to work.

Concepts and Procedures

You do not need an entirely new assessment scheme and procedure for each unit. You can and should develop a general framework within which you can assess information concerning all content.

Recall that understanding occurs on a continuum determined by the number and quality of connections that an individual has made. A good assessment strategy will provide opportunity for students to demonstrate how they themselves understand the concepts under discussion. The traditional test generally targets only one way to know an idea, that determined by the test designer. Furthermore, traditional tests are generally given at the end of instruction after all further opportunities for growth have passed. If you collect information from students as they complete an activity, while it is being discussed, as results are justified—in short, while students are doing mathematics—you will gain information that provides insight into the nature of the students' understanding of that idea. That information can be used to plan the next lesson, provide feedback and encouragement to students, or design a remedial intervention. After collecting evidence from multiple activities, you should be able to make a qualitative judgment concerning the big ideas for the unit of instruction and build that into your evaluation.

Procedural knowledge, including skill proficiency, should also be examined. Be careful to see that conceptual foundations for skills are there as well. If a student can compute with fractions yet has no idea of why he needs a common denominator for addition but not for multiplication, then the rules that have been "mastered" are poorly connected to meaning. This would indicate only the tenuous presence of a skill. Whereas a routine skill such as mastering addition with regrouping can easily be checked with a traditional test, the desired conceptual connections require assessment of a different nature.

COMBINING INSTRUCTION AND ASSESSMENT

Real change in the classroom cannot be achieved without simultaneously changing and integrating both instruction and assessment. If your instruction becomes more problem-based but your assessment methods focus on recall and closed-response items, the instruction is doomed to failure. Students quickly learn that what is valued is getting answers. Older students tune out or even refuse to participate in the tasks provided. "Just show us how to get the answer." Assessment strategies must reflect our values in exactly the same manner as our instruction.

The reverse situation—to engage in "traditional," teacher-directed instruction with open-ended, problem-solving tasks for assessment—asks children to demonstrate mathematical power without ever having experienced it. Students who are accustomed to being told how to do everything in the mathematics classroom, when facing novel, problem-solving tasks, will understandably complain, "You've never told us how to do this!" Teachers who have tried various "alternative assessments" without significantly altering their instruction find these assessments difficult or impossible for their students, and all involved become frustrated.

What many teachers fail to realize is that quality instruction and appropriate assessment need not be different activities. Assessment and instruction can and should become nearly indistinguishable. We can assess as we provide opportunities for learning. The search for quality assessment tasks is simultaneously a search for quality learning tasks. They are one and the same!

Performance Tasks

As you will recall from Chapter 4, a *performance task* is a problem (sometimes open-ended), a project, or an investigation, always presented in a spirit of inquiry. Furthermore:

- It may be an individual, pair, or group task.
- It may involve hands-on materials or drawings or calculators.
- Justification and explanation for answers and results are the responsibility of students.
- It should include some form of report—oral or written—or a physical product.

Good tasks should permit every student in the class, regardless of mathematical prowess, to demonstrate some knowledge or skill or understanding. Lower-ability students should not be excluded from quality tasks and should be encouraged to use the ideas they do possess to work on the problem even if these are not the same skills or strategies used by others in the room. A forgotten computational procedure should not preclude a student from working on a performance task. At the same time that we consider accessibility, we should strive to select or design tasks that are sufficiently rich to challenge the thinking and reasoning of all students.

The literature abounds with definitions and examples of "performance *assessment* tasks." Differences tend to reflect the authors' desires to stress or not stress real-world or authentic contexts, long-term projects, or the integration of mathematical content. The good news is that this emphasis on assessment tasks has encouraged educators to create some excellent activities. The bad news is that many teachers feel that they must look beyond their good instructional ideas to find assessment tasks. Remember that the first purpose of assessment is to promote learning.

The unfortunate separation of learning and assessment tasks is partly due to our lengthy history of equating assessment with summative, evaluative testing. There may be times when you do decide to use a task as a summative evaluation and therefore choose not to interact with students as they are working. In these instances, you will have already provided students with an opportunity to access and develop the content that is essential to the task. The task should not be identical to a previous learning experience; if it were, the students would simply be following an earlier example, not doing mathematics. Using a task as a summative assessment simply changes the purpose and intent of the task. Taken out of this evaluative context, the task should still look exactly like a learning task.

Examples of Performance Tasks

Anne is a third-grade teacher. During an academic year, she was one of a group of teachers learning to use appropriate assessment techniques in mathematics. Anne used the following task with her class arranged in groups of three or four working together.

> **Find ways to add consecutive numbers in order to reach sums between 1 and 15. For example, 3 + 4 + 5 = 12, and 3, 4, and 5 are consecutive numbers.**

Anne reports:

When I was planning this task, I did a much better job of deciding what I wanted to assess first and then finding a task that would assess it. I wanted to assess if my students were able to both estimate and solve math facts mentally. In addition, I wanted to assess how far my students had come in cooperative learning. I developed a checklist for myself to use when making my observations. Some items on the list included "able to recall basic facts," "able to add mentally," "adding by counting up on fingers," "interacted with peers positively," and "participating with the group." The task was long enough and engaging enough that I was able to spend time with each group listening to the interaction and questioning the members about their thinking.

Like many teachers who have learned to think of assessment and learning as different activities, Anne had earlier in the year searched through books for "assessment" tasks rather than tasks that embodied her objective. By thinking of her objective ahead of time, she was able to listen actively to her students and know what she was looking for. Anne

stated her objectives in very procedural language: "able to recall," "able to add mentally." She might have focused on how children connect facts. For example, do children see that 4 + 5, 5 + 6, and 6 + 7 are odd sums or are each two apart? Do those who are still counting use one fact, say, 4 + 5, to arrive at 3 + 4 + 5? By focusing on behaviors, Anne forgot to plan a discussion that would allow her to see the ideas students may have constructed. She did use this opportunity to assess some group skills.

The important point to note in this example is that a lot of very different information can be gathered from one task. The essential content of this task was addition and number relationships. Yet the focus could be on either procedural or conceptual knowledge and may or may not include attention to problem solving or other skills. Anne also had a written report from each group that she could take home and reflect on for communication skills. Had she entertained a class discussion after the task, she would have opened the door for whatever thoughts students may have had. There would be an opportunity to wonder how many sums were possible for different numbers. "Do all numbers have consecutive sums? How do we know? What else do you notice?"

A Sampling of Performance Tasks

Recall from Chapter 4 that problems or performance tasks cover a wide range of activities. Nine different ways to think about constructing tasks were suggested. Tasks for assessment purposes can be developed in the same manner.

In the examples that follow, consider what might happen when children at the grade level indicated in parentheses are working on the task and what might be discovered in a follow-up discussion.

- What is the essential conceptual content in the task?
- What problem-solving processes might be observed?
- What opportunity might there be to observe communication skills?
- What about reasoning (if-then thinking)?
- Are there opportunities for students to connect the content with other content either in or outside of mathematics?
- Can the task be extended?
- Is it accessible to a range of students in some way?
- How would you begin an after-activity discussion?

> **MENTAL MATH (4–8)**
>
> **Explain two different ways to multiply 4 × 276 in your head. Which way is easier to use? Would you use a different way to multiply 5 × 398? Explain why you would use the same or different methods.**

TYPICAL CLASS (5–8)

Enrollment data for the school provide information about the students and their families as shown here:

	SCHOOL	CLASS
Siblings		
None	36	5
One	89	4
Two	134	17
More than two	93	3
Race		
African-American	49	11
Asian-American	12	0
White	219	15
Travel-to-school method		
Walk	157	10
Bus	182	19
Other	13	0

If someone asked you how typical your class was of the rest of the school, how would you answer? Write an explanation of your answer. Include one or more charts or graphs that you think would support your conclusion.

REMAINDERS (4–6)

Dave says $13 \div 4$ is $3\frac{1}{4}$. Martha says it's 3 R 1. Zach says that they are both wrong. He thinks it's 3.25. Who is correct? Why?

Follow-up: Describe a situation where Dave's answer makes the most sense, one where Martha's answer is reasonable, and one where Zach's idea is probably the best.

BALLPOINTS (2–4)

At the Dollar Store, $1 buys two ballpoint pens. The Pencil Point stationery store offers three of the same pens for $2. Which store has the better buy? Can you explain your answer in two different ways?

TOP AND BOTTOM (4–6)

In the fraction $\frac{3}{4}$, how would you explain the meaning of the top number to a third grader? Do the same for the bottom number. Use two different ways to explain each.

SHARES (K–3)

Leila has 6 gumdrops, Darlene has 2, and Melissa has 4. They want to share them equally. How will they do it? Draw a picture to help explain your answer.

SIX (K–1)

Think about the number 6 broken into 2 different amounts. Draw a picture to show a way that 6 things can be in 2 parts. Think up a story to go with your picture.

DECIMAL FRACTIONS (5–8)

The label on a chunk of cheddar cheese said 0.75 lb. The recipe called for 2 oz. How can you decide where to cut the cheese to get just 2 oz.? Explain your reasoning and, if necessary, draw a picture.

TWO TRIANGLES (4–8)

Tell everything you can about these two triangles.

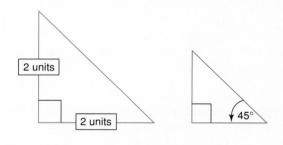

MYSTERY BAG (3–6)

We reached in the bag of colored blocks 10 times and pulled out 1 block each time. Each time we put the block back in the bag. We got 3 reds, 1 yellow, and 6 green blocks. If there are 20 blocks in the bag, what colors and how many of each do you think are in the bag? How sure can you be? Explain (Burns, 1992a).

HAMBURGERS (6–8)

You and a friend have been reading about McDonald's. The article says that 7 percent of Americans eat at McDonald's each day. Your friend thinks this is impossible. You know that there are about 250 million Americans and 9000 McDonald's restaurants. Is the article's statistic reasonable, or is your friend correct?

FRACTION CONFLICT (3–6)

Two students are trying to decide how to figure out what $\frac{1}{6} + \frac{1}{6}$ is. They use a pattern block hexagon and triangles.

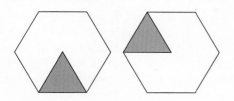

One student says, "Each triangle is $\frac{1}{6}$, so two triangles must be $\frac{2}{6}$."

The other one says, "Yes, but look at this:"

$$\frac{1}{6} + \frac{1}{6} = \frac{1+1}{6+6} = \frac{2}{12}$$

The first one says, "Oh, maybe that's how you do it. Each triangle is $\frac{1}{12}$, so it's $\frac{2}{12}$."

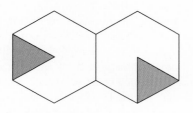

How would you help these two students solve the dilemma of which is correct? Include an explanation they can understand (Ball, 1992).

SUBTRACTION (1–2)

If you did not know the answer to $12 - 7$, what are some ways you could find the answer?

THE WHOLE SET (3–5)

Mary counted 15 cupcakes left from the whole batch that Mother made for the picnic. "We've already eaten two-fifths of these," she noted. How many cupcakes did Mother bake?

HOW MUCH? (1–2)

Gustavo has saved $5 to buy a game that he wants. The game costs $23. How much money does Gustavo still need?

RULER (K–4)

Make a ruler. Use it to measure something shorter than your ruler. Use it to measure something longer than your ruler. Tell about your ruler. Tell about your measurements. (*Directions will vary with the age of the students.*)

ALGEBRA: GRAPHING 1 (7–8)

Create a graph that does not go into the third quadrant on your graphing calculator. What are some ways that you could tell you were correct?

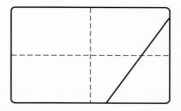

ALGEBRA: GRAPHING 2 (7–8)

Does the graph of $y = x^2$ ever intersect the graph of $y = x^2 + 2$? What are some ways that you could test your idea?

AREA AND PERIMETER (6–8)

Without measuring, how would you expect the areas of these shapes to compare?

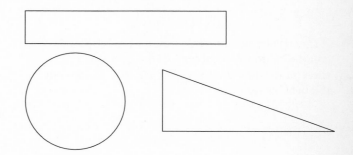

Follow-up: How would you expect the perimeters or circumferences to compare? Explain your reasoning (Stenmark, Beck, & Asturias, 1994).

MEASUREMENT (K–8)

What could we measure about our soccer ball?

FOUR NUMBER BARS (K–3)

Make a bar of connecting cubes for each of these numbers: 3, 9, 6, and 5. Find five things to tell about these numbers. What other numbers can you make with these bars if you do not break them into smaller parts?

CRAYONS (1–3)

If each student in our class has a box of crayons with 8 crayons in it, how many crayons does the class have altogether?

DECIMALS (4–6)

Alan tried to make a decimal number as close to 50 as he could using the digits 1, 4, 5, and 9. He arranged them in this order: 51.49.

Jerry thinks he can arrange the same digits to get a number that is even closer to 50. Do you agree or disagree? Explain.

FRACTIONS (3–6)

Place an X on the number line about where $\frac{11}{8}$ would be. You will need to draw and label points on the line to show your answer. Explain why you put your X where you did (Courtesy of Montgomery County Public Schools, Rockville, MD).

```
|_____|
0                        2
```

BROKEN KEYS (2–4)

If the ⑤ key on your calculator were broken, how could you do this problem: 458 + 548 + 354? Is there more than one way? Which way do you like the best? Why?

ADDITION (1–3)

What are some good ways to add 6 + 5 + 4? Which ways would work for 7 + 4 + 3? What way do you like the best? (Baker & Baker, 1991).

THEME PARK (4–6)

Keisha needs money to go to a theme park. A one-day ticket costs $15.00. She decides to sell lemonade. Her parents agree to donate the paper cups and ice, but Keisha must buy the frozen lemonade.

A can of lemonade costs 79 cents and makes six servings. How much should she charge for a glass of lemonade?

More Thoughts About Performance Tasks

The collection of tasks listed here was purposely mixed in terms of content and grade level to give you a feel for the diversity of possibilities. Every one of these problems could be used as a learning task. In some instances, the real value of the task or what can be learned about students will come only in the discussion that follows. For others, the information will be in the written report (although a discussion remains a good idea).

Some tasks look like straightforward story problems. Still, these offer the opportunity to learn a lot from students if we require some explanation or justification of the answer. Even students in kindergarten can begin to draw pictures to explain their thinking about word problems. In many of Marilyn Burns's books, you will see the phrase "We think the answer is . . . We think this because . . ." If students fail to develop the habit of adding and listening to justifications, they will be unable to supply reasons. But they can learn to do this and even do it without prompting.

Two other variables in the tasks are connections to the "real world" and open-endedness. Several of the problems, such as "Hamburgers" and "Typical Class," involve quite realistic contexts. Some contexts, such as the cupcakes in "The Whole Set" and the money in "How Much?" are more trivial. "Typical Class" and "Theme Park" do not have clearly defined correct answers, which makes them even more realistic. Much of the assessment literature has placed a significant value on situational problems or realistic problems and open-ended problems. There is no doubt that such problems have an important place in the mathematics classroom. But neither open-endedness nor real-world contexts are necessary for students to be meaningfully engaged in constructing mathematics. Nor are these features necessary for quality assessment. An open-ended, very realistic problem can be interesting and engaging and be mathematically trivial. Selecting Christmas gift items out of a catalog, being sure to get something for everyone in the house, and not spending more than a given amount of money is little more than a glorified addition task. Keep your focus on the mathematics. Add or include real connections and open-ended tasks when doing so is possible without sacrificing the mathematics.

Especially at the K–2 level, many activities have no written component and no "answer" or result. For example, students may be playing a game where dice or dominoes are being used or playing a game of war with regular cards. A teacher who sits in on these games will see great differences in how children use numbers. Some will count every dot on the card or domino. Others will use a counting on strategy. Some will recognize certain patterns without counting. Others may be unsure if 13 beats 11. These and other differences constitute assessment data about number concepts.

A geometry activity in which one child tries to describe a shape to a partner who cannot see it is another example where data must come only from the discussion or oral activity. In the past, we never thought about listening to children for the purpose of assessment. Data gathered from listening to a pair of children work on a simple activity or an extended project provide significantly greater insight into students' thinking than almost any written test we could devise. Data from student conversations and observations of student behavior can be recorded and used for the same purposes that written data can, including evaluation and grading. Especially in the case of grading, it is important to keep dated written notes that can be referred to later.

COLLECTING DATA FROM PERFORMANCE TASKS

Remember that assessment is the *gathering* of evidence about students. Many teachers who are just beginning a shift to a more performance-based approach to assessment tend to make generalizations about the class as a whole. "I was very pleased (or disappointed) with how my students did on that task." Exactly what did "they" do? What did "they" know? And more important, what does Jenny know? Where is Desmond's understanding? Assessment to improve learning, inform instruction, and evaluate students requires that you have real data on individuals. Global impressions will leave students who do not fit the class norm somewhat lost in your planning and in your feedback. Without hard evidence gathered from performance tasks, you will find yourself relying on traditional tests to fill out report cards, and the value of data from performance tasks will be significantly diminished.

Students are active in the learning process, and in a community that includes discourse, they talk a lot. Students write solutions and justifications to problems, and they create projects and products that can be examined. These things that you see and hear during class and the products that you can examine after class are the sources of your data. Now you need a framework within which to examine those data. That is the topic of this section.

One warning before you continue: As you read about rubrics and observation schemes, you may find the task overwhelming. Please understand: *Not every performance task needs to be formally assessed with a rubric.*

Performance Indicators and Rubrics

A *rubric* is a framework that can be designed or adapted by the teacher for a particular group of students or a particular mathematical task (Kulm, 1994). A rubric consists of a scale of three to six points that is used as a rating of performance rather than a count of how many items are correct or incorrect. The rating is applied by examining total performance on a task as opposed to counting the number of items correct.

A Simple Three-Point Rubric

The simplest form of a rubric consists of three or four points and is a good type of scale to begin with or even to use on a regular basis; for example:

3 Above and beyond—uses exemplary methods, shows creativity, goes beyond the requirements of the problem

2 On target—completes the task with no more than minor errors, uses expected approaches

1 Not there yet—makes significant errors or omissions, uses inappropriate methods, uses faulty reasoning

Another variation of a simple three-point scale may attend more to development:

3 Understands and applies the concept or process

2 Shows evidence of development of the concept or process

1 Does not yet understand the concept or process

These relatively simple scales are *general* rubrics. They label general categories of performance but do not define the performance that fits the category. For any given task or process, it is usually helpful to create performance indicators for each level. *Performance indicators* are task-specific statements that describe what performance looks like at each level of the rubric and in so doing establish criteria for acceptable performance (Ann Arbor Public Schools, 1993).

Whether your rubric has three points or six, the most important level is the one that describes "on-target" performance, performance that meets your goals. In a three-point rubric, the middle category is always "on target." From there you can establish what exceptional performance looks like at one extreme and performance that indicates a need for assistance or further development at the other. The rubric and its performance indicators should focus you and your students on your goals and away from the self-limiting question "How many can you miss and still get an A?" There is almost always an "above and beyond" at the high end to encourage excellence.

Writing Performance Indicators Before the Lesson

What performance at different levels of your rubric will or should look like may be difficult to predict. Much depends on your experience with children at that grade level, your past experiences with students working on the same task, and your insights about the task itself and the ideas that it embodies or that children may use as they work on it. What constitutes acceptable, on-target performance also varies with your personal goals and expectations.

If possible, it is good to write the indicators before you use the task in class. This is an excellent way to be sure the task is likely to accomplish the purpose you selected it for in the first place. Begin with the on-target descriptors. These will tell you what you want to happen and will provide a good check that students will be able to access your goals through the task. Examine your problem-solving goals as well as your content goals. Think about how children will approach the activity. Consider different materials that might be used, different ways to describe the results, and how the product can be explained or the answer justified. Avoid a singular focus on correct answers and doing the activity in a prescribed manner. Spend the most time brainstorming about variations of acceptable performance.

From acceptable performance, ask yourself how the activity lends itself to extensions, variations, or creative approaches. These descriptors are more difficult to predict. You want to be sure that your activity actually allows for ways to excel. At the same time, you do not want to prescribe in detail what exceptional performance must look like. It is best to allow students to surprise you. Just be sure to provide the opportunity.

Describing less than acceptable performance is generally easier. The description will again reflect your goals and should indicate clearly that they are not being met. Avoid emphasis on less important details such as neatness or spelling, features not related to your goal.

If you write performance indicators ahead of time, do not be afraid to adjust them as you observe your students or examine their performance. Unexpected methods and solutions may force you to modify the on-target performance. Your educational objectives are what are important. Don't box students into demonstrating only the behaviors that you predetermined when there is evidence that they are accomplishing your objectives in different ways.

Writing Performance Indicators After the Fact

There are many times when you simply do not feel that you can adequately describe acceptable performance ahead of time. New teachers with limited experience with children or teachers new to a grade level often have difficulty predicting what children are able or likely to do with a task. The performance indicator can still be profitably written during or after the students have done the activity as a way of focusing your attention on what students did and whether or not they were making progress toward your objectives.

A useful approach is a "three-pile sort." As you read or examine papers or other products such as posters or geometric constructions, separate them into three piles representing three levels of performance. If your rubric framework has more than three points, go back to each pile and sort within the pile. There will almost always be differences across your class. What is most important is to be sure that the student performance actually relates appropriately to your goal. Remember, you should always base assessments on established criteria and not on comparisons of one student with another.

When you have finished your sorting process, write a description of each category you have created. File the descriptors with the activity for future use.

Student Involvement with Rubrics

When mathematics consisted primarily of arithmetic, students knew that correct computation was the goal—the only goal. Today, not only is the curriculum significantly broader than computation, but the focus is on *doing mathematics* and all that that entails. Students need information about what doing good mathematics looks like, and they need to know what your expectations are for acceptable and exceptional performance. This is part of the Openness Standard for assessment.

In the beginning of the year, discuss your general rubric with the class. Post it prominently. Many teachers use the same rubric for all subjects. Others prefer to use a special rubric for mathematics or mathematics and science. In your discussion, let students know that as they do activities and solve problems in class, you will look at their work and provide them with feedback in terms of the rubric, rather than as a letter grade or a percentage. Everyone should strive for the highest ratings, but the goal is to be "on target."

The general rubric provides the same global framework for students as it provides for you. It also has the same limitations until performance indicators are described for a given task. Early in the year, share your performance indicators with students. Sometimes you will want to do this before a task, and other times you may find it useful to do so after the task. Children at the K–2 level need real examples. If possible, make copies of performance from students in a prior year or another class. Remove all names, of course. Alternatively, you can create your own examples of performance at different levels. A third alternative is to use examples of acceptable and exceptional performance from your current class. This requires real sensitivity. All students want their work to be the model.

When students start to understand what the rubric really means, begin to discuss tasks in terms of the general rubric without providing task-specific indicators. You might have students rate their own work according to the general rubric and explain their reasons for the rating. Older students can do this in written form, and you can respond in writing. For all students, you can have class discussions about a task that has been done and what might constitute good and exceptional performance.

Finally, begin to have your class generate performance indicators for tasks before they begin. This has enormous benefits. First, it helps identify the goals of the task and heads students in the correct direction. Second, it helps students begin thinking in terms of going beyond the minimum for good performance and encourages them to strive for excellence. This is the difference between "What do I *have* to do?" and "What are some ways I can really show what I know?" Third, the process of involving students values them. As they help define what is important, they themselves become important in the learning process.

More Examples of Rubrics

The discussion so far has centered on a very simple form of a rubric, one with three levels. For many teachers, this is all that is necessary. While some teachers like the simplicity of a three-point scale, others find that the more detailed scales suit their needs better. Figure 5.4 is an example of a six-point rubric. Regardless of the scale you select, let your needs dictate what to use. Do not waste effort trying to create indicators for a six-point rubric when the complexity of the task does not warrant it. Collapse a few levels. The same rubric need not be used for every task.

The earlier three-point scale and the six-point rubric in Figure 5.4 are examples of *holistic scales,* single scales used to rate a complete task as a whole while possibly covering many subtopics and agendas. One rating on the scale summarizes the full performance. A single grade on a report card is also a holistic rating.

PERFORMANCE LEVELS IN MATHEMATICS

LEVEL 6
Student work demonstrates rigorous mathematical thinking and in-depth understanding of essential mathematical ideas. Responses meet and often exceed expectations; they are consistently correct and complete, and use appropriate representations (for example, works, diagrams, graphs, pictures). Student work extends concepts or produces related conjectures. Generalizations and connections are supported by precise logical arguments using multiple or unique approaches and appropriate mathematical tools and techniques.

LEVEL 5
Student work demonstrates solid mathematical thinking and full understanding of mathematical ideas. Responses fully meet expectations; they are usually correct and complete, and use appropriate representations (for example, works, diagrams, graphs, pictures), although sometimes containing minor flaws. Some of the student work contains generalizations and connections supported by effective arguments using multiple or unique approaches and appropriate mathematical tools and techniques.

LEVEL 4
Student work demonstrates substantial mathematical thinking and understanding of essential mathematical ideas, including appropriate representations (for example, works, diagrams, graphs, pictures). Responses are usually correct although the work may contain flaws. Student work exhibits appropriate use of mathematical tools and techniques.

LEVEL 3
Student work demonstrates partial mathematical thinking and understanding of mathematical ideas. Some responses are correct; however, gaps in conceptual understanding are evident and representations (for example, works, diagrams, graphs, pictures) need elaboration. There is an acceptable use of tools and techniques.

LEVEL 2
Student work demonstrates limited mathematical thinking and understanding of mathematical ideas. Although responses are sometimes correct, student work often falls short of providing workable solutions. Tools and techniques are rarely used or are used inappropriately.

LEVEL 1
Student work demonstrates little or no mathematical thinking and understanding of mathematical ideas. Responses show little or no progress toward accomplishing mathematical tasks. There is little correct or appropriate use of tools, techniques, or representations.

● **Figure 5.4**   A six-point rubric developed by the California Mathematics Council.

Source: California Department of Education © 1993. Used with permission.

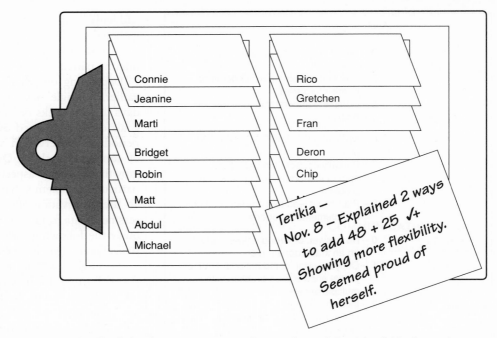

● **FIGURE 5.6**   Cards for observation notes can be taped to a clipboard or folder for quick access.

Making Whole	Given Fraction Part	(3/17)
Super Clear understanding. Communicates concept in multiple representations. Shows evidence of using idea without prompting. *Fraction whole made from* *part in rods and in sets.* *Explains easily.*	Sally ✓ Latania ✓+ Greg	Zal
On Target Understands or is developing well. Uses designated models. *Can make whole in either* *rod or set format (note).* *Hesitant. Needs prompt to* *get unit fraction.*	Lavant Julie George Maria	Tanisha Lee J.B. John H.
Not Yet Some confusion or misunderstands. Only models idea with help. *Needs help to do* *activity. No confidence.*	John S.	Mary

● **FIGURE 5.7**   Record names in a rubric during an activity or for a single topic over several days.

Checklists for Full Classes

Another format involves listing all students in a class on a single page or not more than three pages (see Figure 5.9, p. 77). Across the top of the page are specific things to look for. Pluses and minuses, checks, or codes corresponding to your general rubric can be entered in the grid. A space left for comments is useful. A full-class checklist is more likely to be used for long-term objectives. Topics that might be appropriate for this format include problem-solving processes, communication skills, and such skills as basic facts or estimation. Dating entries or noting specific activities observed is also helpful.

OTHER ASSESSMENT OPTIONS

The use of rubrics and observations of performance tasks are not the only ways to gather valuable assessment data. Data can come from asking open-ended questions and listening carefully. Students themselves can give us a lot of information. Two important methods are journals and self-evaluation instruments. These latter two methods are especially useful for gathering affective information as well as concept and problem-solving process data. Finally, good assessment does not rule out tests as long as the tests are well constructed.

Listening Requires Good Questions

We have a tendency in mathematics classes to ask questions that have very specific right answers. "What is the name of

NAME: Sharon V.	NOT YET	OK	SUPER	NOTES
FRACTIONS				
Understands numerator/denominator		✓		
Area models		✓		
Set models	✓			
Uses fractions in real contexts	✓			
Estimates fraction quantities		✓		getting better
PROBLEM SOLVING				
Understands problem before beginning work		✓		this is good
Is willing to take risks	✓			problem area
Justifies results				

• **FIGURE 5.8** A focused checklist and rubric can be printed for each student with the help of a computer.

this figure?" "What is the decimal equivalent of $\frac{2}{3}$?" These questions can give us very little information concerning a student's understanding. All that can be learned is whether the factual information can be produced.

Another tendency is to explore or follow up only on incorrect responses. Students whose answers are challenged are more likely to change them than to defend them. A questioning technique that looks only for correct answers will fail to help you see how students are constructing ideas. It will intimidate less able students and will be dominated by the top students in your class.

To get more information during classroom interchanges, we need to develop an open-ended questioning technique and use a more inquiring form of response, encouraging students to defend or explain both correct and incorrect answers.

Here are some examples of closed and open questioning for the same situations.

Topic: Mental Computation + of 2 – dis. nos Names	Not Yet Can't do mentally	On Target Has at least one strategy	Wow! Uses different methods with different numbers
Lalie		✓ 3-18 -21	
Pete	✓ 3-20		Needs place value help
Sid		3-12 ✓+	Super
Lakeshia		✓	Good
George		✓	
Pam	✓		Close – getting a tens first idea
Maria		✓ 3-24	Finally!

• **FIGURE 5.9** A full-class observation checklist can be used for longer-term objectives or for several days to cover a short-term objective.

SECOND-GRADE SUBTRACTION ALGORITHM

$$\begin{array}{r} 72 \\ -45 \\ \hline \end{array}$$

Closed: You can't take 5 from 2, so what should we do with the 7?

Open: What would you do first in this problem? (There are a variety of ways to solve this problem.)

FOURTH-GRADE ONE-STEP WORD PROBLEM

Closed: What must you do to solve this problem: add, subtract, multiply, or divide?

Open: **What could we do to help us understand this problem? (Could you draw a picture, perhaps using a number line? Explain how your picture is the same as the problem. What operation goes with your picture?)**

SIXTH-GRADE MEASUREMENT

Closed: **What unit should be used to measure the length of the room?**

Open: **How would you measure the length of this room?** *or* **What are some ways we could measure this room? (Length is now only one option.) What units would you use? Why?**

The first two examples show how a question can be open and yet focused. The last example is much broader. A question such as "What can you tell about this geometric figure (computation, graph, pattern, etc.)?" allows students to tell you what they know rather than what they think you want to hear.

It is a good idea to have students think about their ideas quietly and not blurt out answers. A sequence of think first, talk with a partner, and then share (think-pair-share) is a very useful technique. As discussed in Chapter 4, students who are the most reluctant, least capable, or least creative can be called on first so that their good ideas will not be "taken."

The second part of good questioning is to respond to students in a manner that helps them think and lets you see what they are thinking. You may like some of the following techniques or develop some similar ones of your own.

Waiting (Nonjudgment). An immediate judgment of a response usually stops any further pondering or reflection on the part of the student. If, after a student answers, you simply nod thoughtfully or say "Uh-huh" or "Hmm," the student is encouraged to and often will elaborate on the response. Other students can join in, offer alternative ideas, or continue to think. An accepting yet nonjudgmental response is to record answers on the board without comment. When used consistently, nonevaluative responses indicate to students that the time for thinking is not yet over and you value their additional thoughts. Such responses indicate an interest in more than answers.

Request for Rationale. Most students have learned to expect judgmental responses from teachers and to have teachers tell them if their answer is correct. These students are initially shocked when teachers begin to respond to their answers with phrases such as the following:

"Why do you think that?"

"Are you sure? How do you know that?"

"I see. Would you explain your answer to the rest of us?"

"Show us how you figured that out. Maybe you could use these base 10 blocks to help you."

These responses should be used frequently, with both correct and incorrect answers. Soon the request for justification will become the expected norm, and students even in the lower grades will begin to offer unsolicited explanations along with their answers.

Search for Alternative Ideas. A similar approach is to accept the first response without judgment and then ask if other students may have a different idea. "I see. That's one possible idea. Who else has an idea about this?" Alternative responses by different classmates can then be evaluated in a discussion that looks at the rationale for each. Allow plenty of wait time for the second and third responses because it is during this time that slower or even average students are given an opportunity to think the idea through. Accept repeat answers, since they are quite likely original thoughts and not copies. Students often pay little attention to the responses of others when they are busy working out an idea on their own.

Writing and Journals

Having students write in mathematics is a natural and very important way to help them reflect on what they are learning as well as a good way for you to see what they know or feel about a subject. Writing is a form of communication, a major objective for mathematics instruction. Though many children have difficulty writing in mathematics initially, persistence pays off.

Writing has some real advantages over oral communication. It can include pictures, graphs, and symbols that are powerful communication tools not available orally. Written expression is usually preceded with time spent to organize one's thoughts. It can be revised or edited by scratching out and writing over. Oral responses are immediate and irretrievable. Finally, written expression is private. Students can learn to put trust in your respect for what they write. Trust will come through thoughtful, helpful responses and respect for students' privacy.

Journals

Writing can of course be done on a single sheet of paper and turned in separately, but the use of a journal has real value. A journal may take the form of a composition booklet or, for K–1 children, folded writing paper stapled within a construction-paper cover. Binders and spiral notebooks are other options, but teachers find these bulky, and students are more likely to remove unwanted pages.

Journals are a way to make written communication a regular part of doing mathematics. Journals help you abandon the mistaken, counterproductive myth "If they write it, I must grade it." Journals are a place for students to write about such things as

• Their conceptual understandings and problem solving, including descriptions of ideas, solutions, and justifications of problems, graphs, charts, and observations

- Their questions concerning the current topic, an idea that they may need help with, or an area they don't quite understand
- Their feelings about aspects of mathematics, their confidence in their understanding, or their fears of being wrong

Even if you have students write in their journals nearly every day, be sure that these journals are special places for writing about mathematics. Drill and practice, for example, should not be done in a journal. Lengthy projects done over several days should be separate from journals and given a special presentation. A performance task you plan to use primarily for evaluation purposes should probably not be in a journal. But the work for many of your performance tasks can and should go in the journal as part of the doing of mathematics. In this way, you communicate that the work is important and you do want to see it but you are not going to grade it.

Journals are vehicles for communication, not evaluation. To grade journal writing defeats its purpose as a way to learn about students' ideas and to provide them with valuable feedback and direction. Graded journals would communicate that there is a specific "right" response you are seeking. That would not have the same flavor as communication. It is essential, however, that you read and respond to journal writing. One form of response for a performance task would be to use the classroom's general rubric along with a helpful comment. This is another way to distinguish between rubrics and grades and still provide feedback.

On a regular basis, it is manageable to read and respond to about five journals a night. Following an especially interesting lesson, you might want to read the journal entry of every student in the class. Allow students to flag entries for which they want your special attention or response. If you do not read and respond to journals, students will quickly come to regard them as busywork and conclude that you do not value their efforts. Teachers whose students have learned to communicate honestly through their journals find them a key element in their assessment program, prized above all other sources of information to improve learning and instruction.

Writing Prompts and Ideas

Students should always have a clear, well-defined purpose for writing in their journals. They need to know exactly what to write about and who the audience is (you, an imaginary friend, a student in a lower grade, an adult, a Martian), and they should be given a definite time frame within which to write. Journal writing that is completely open-ended without goal or purpose will be a waste of time. Here are some suggestions for prompts to get you thinking; however, the possibilities are endless.

Affective Ideas
"What I like most (or least) about mathematics is . . ."

Write a mathematics autobiography. Tell about your experiences in mathematics outside of school and how you feel about the subject.

"Mathematics is like a _____ because . . ."

Write to an imaginary friend who is the same age as you and tell how you feel about what we did in mathematics this week.

Concepts and Problem Solving
"I think the answer is _____. I think this because . . ." (The journal can be used to solve and explain any problem. Always be sure to include the problem. Some teachers duplicate the problem and have students tape it into the journal to save time and effort.)

Write an explanation for other students (or for students in a lower grade) of why 4×7 is the same as 7×4 and why this works for 6×49 and 49×6.

Draw four different quadrilaterals that are alike in some way. Tell why they are alike. Draw one that is different. Tell why it is different.

Explain to a student in the _____ grade (or who was absent today) what you learned about decimals today.

What about the work we did today was easy? What was hard? What do you still have questions about?

If you got stuck today in solving a problem, where did you get stuck? Why do you think you had trouble there? If you did not get stuck, what idea helped you solve the problem?

What did you do after you got the answer to today's problem to help you believe your answer was correct? How sure are you that you got the correct answer?

How can addition help you do subtraction facts like $12 - 4$ and $15 - 6$?

Write a story problem that goes with this picture (this graph, this diagram, this equation).

Journals for Early Learners

If you are interested in working with K–1 children, the writing suggestions presented may have sounded discouraging because it is difficult for prewriters and beginning writers to express ideas like those suggested. There are techniques for journals that have been used successfully in kindergarten and first grade.

The Giant Journal. To begin the development of the writing-in-mathematics process, one kindergarten teacher uses a language experience approach. After an activity, she writes the heading "Giant Journal" and a topic or prompt on a large flipchart. Students respond to the prompt, and she writes their ideas, adding the contributor's name and even drawings when appropriate (see Figure 5.10, p. 80).

Drawings and Invented Spellings. All students can draw pictures of some sort to describe what they have done. Dots can represent counters or blocks. Shapes and special figures can be cut out from duplicated sheets and pasted onto the journal page.

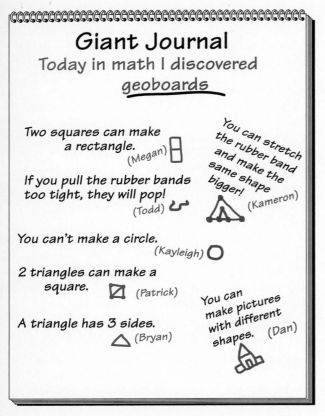

• **FIGURE 5.10** A journal in kindergarten is a class product on a flipchart.

It is important for the "writing" to be a record of something the student has just done and is comfortable with. Figure 5.11 shows problems solved in kindergarten, first grade, and second grade. Do not be concerned about invented spellings to communicate ideas. Have students read their papers to you.

Brainstorming. Young children have difficulty translating what they say and think into written form. One way to help is to use discussion time to help children think about their journal entries. Record ideas on the board as they are contributed by students. For kindergartners and first graders, use very simple abbreviated versions of what they say. For children in grades 2 and 3, you may limit your recording to key phrases and special words. In this manner, the ideas that have been generated are now recorded for students to assemble into their own writing. When a student says "I don't know what to write," have him tell you about his task or idea. Then have him write what he just told you.

Student Self-Assessment

Stenmark (1989) notes that "the capability and willingness to assess their own progress and learning is one of the great-

est gifts students can develop. . . . Mathematical power comes with knowing how much we know and what to do to learn more" (p. 26).

Student self-assessment means just that, students assessing themselves. In a self-assessment, students may tell you

- How well they think they understand a piece of content
- What they believe or how they feel about some aspect of mathematics, perhaps what you are covering right now
- How well they perceive they are working in class or in their group

It is important to see that this is not your measure of their learning, disposition, or behavior but rather it is how *they perceive* these things.

In each of these three possible areas for student self-assessment (content, disposition, behavior), there is potential for interesting and useful inputs into your instructional program. What are the implications when a student feels she knows content better than (or not as well as) she actually does? How do you react to positive attitudes from a poorly performing student or negative attitudes from a generally strong student? How can you use students' assessment of their group behaviors as a tool for improving group behavior? These and similar questions are aimed at getting you to think about why you might want to use periodic self-assessments in your class. It is important to consider how you want the assessment to help you as a teacher before you begin collecting the data. Tell your students why you are having them do this activity. Encourage them to be honest and candid. Though it may seem like fun to collect class information early in the year on a topic such as "Why I like mathematics," do not assign a self-assessment activity just to make yourself feel good about your students.

You can gather self-assessment data in several ways. A common method is to use some form of a questionnaire to which students respond. These can have open-ended questions, response choices (e.g., seldom, sometimes, often; disagree, don't care, agree), mind maps, drawings, and so on. Many such instruments appear in the literature, and many textbook publishers provide examples. Whenever you use a form or questionnaire that someone else has devised, be certain that it serves the purpose you intend. Often these forms are too long or include questions in which you have little interest. Modify them to suit your purposes. The fact that a form was professionally prepared or accompanied your text does not necessarily make it appropriate or useful to you.

An open-ended writing prompt such as was suggested for journals is one method of getting self-assessment data.

How well do you think you understand the work we have been doing the last few days on fractions? If there is something that is causing you difficulty with fractions, please explain what you do not understand.

Write one thing you liked and one thing you did not like about math class today (or this week).

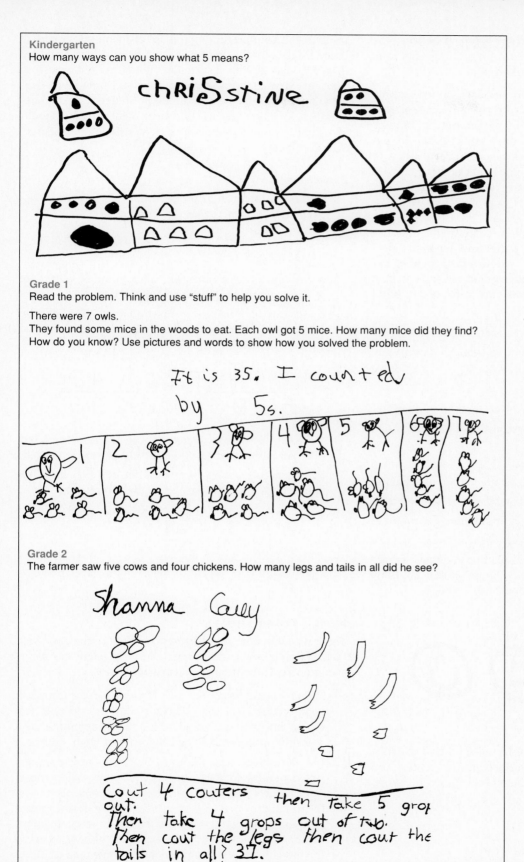

Kindergarten
How many ways can you show what 5 means?

chriSstine

Grade 1
Read the problem. Think and use "stuff" to help you solve it.

There were 7 owls.
They found some mice in the woods to eat. Each owl got 5 mice. How many mice did they find?
How do you know? Use pictures and words to show how you solved the problem.

It is 35. I counted
by 5s.

Grade 2
The farmer saw five cows and four chickens. How many legs and tails in all did he see?

Shanna Caley

Cout 4 couters then take 5 grop
out.
Then take 4 grops out of two.
Then cout the legs then cout the
tails in all? 37.

• **Figure 5.11**   *Journal entries of three early grades children.*

In your group, how well do you think you have followed the rules about helping others? About asking for ideas from others? About keeping the group on task?

These questions indicate how an open-ended writing prompt can be directed at any of the three areas of self-assessment. You may find that a simple prompt can become familiar to students as you use it on a regular basis. For example, midway through a unit is a good time to listen to what students see as things they know and do not know. As students learn that you will react in some way that is helpful to them, they will be more apt to provide you with candid, useful information.

Students may find it difficult to write about attitudes and beliefs. An inventory where they can respond "Yes," "Maybe," or "No" to a series of statements is another approach. Encourage students to add comments under an item if they wish. Here are some items you could use to build such an inventory:

I feel sure of myself when I get an answer to a problem.

I sometimes just put down anything so I can get it over with.

I like to work on really hard math problems.

Math class makes me feel nervous.

If I get stuck, I usually just quit or go to another problem.

I am not as good in math as most of the other students in this class.

Mathematics is my favorite subject.

I do not like to work at problems that are hard to understand.

Memorizing rules is the only way I know to learn mathematics.

I will work a long time at a problem until I think I've solved it.

Another technique is to ask students to write a sentence at the end of any work they do in mathematics class saying how that activity made them feel. Young children can draw a face on each page to tell you about their feelings.

Figure 4.5 on page 58 presents a self-reporting checklist to help students reflect on their metacognitive activities. You may want to use some form of that checklist in your assessment scheme for problem solving.

Tests

A test need not be a collection of low-level skill exercises. Although simple tests of computational skills may have

some role in your classroom, the use of such tests should be limited. Like all other forms of assessment, tests should reflect the goals of your instruction. Tests can be designed to find out what concepts students have and how their ideas are connected. Tests of procedural knowledge should go beyond just knowing how to perform an algorithm and should allow and require the student to demonstrate a conceptual basis for the process.

Examples

1. Write a multiplication problem that has an answer between the answers to these two problems:

$$\begin{array}{cc} 49 & 45 \\ \times 25 & \times 30 \end{array}$$

2. a. In this division exercise, what number tells how many tens were shared among the 6 sets?

   b. Instead of writing the remainder as "R 2," Elaine writes "$\frac{1}{3}$." Explain the difference between these two ways of handling the leftover part.

$$6\overline{)296} \; \text{49 R2} \qquad 6\overline{)296} \; \text{49}\tfrac{1}{3}$$

3. On the grid, draw two figures with the same area but different perimeters. List the area and perimeter of each.

4. For each subtraction fact, write an addition fact that helps you think of the answer to the subtraction.

$$\begin{array}{cccc} 12 & \;^{9}_{+3} & 9 & 14 \\ \underline{-3} & \underline{\;\;} & \underline{-4} & \underline{-7} \\ _{9} & _{12} & & \end{array}$$

5. Draw pictures of arrows to show why $^-3 + {}^-4$ is the same as $^-3 - {}^+4$.

Some Testing Options

There is much more information to be found in a good test than simply correct or incorrect answers. Here are some things to think about when constructing a test.

1. *Permit calculators all the time.* Except for the simplest computation tests, the calculator allows students to focus on what you really want to test. It also communicates a positive attitude about calculator use to your students.

2. *Use manipulatives and drawings.* Students can use appropriate models to work on test questions when those same models have been used to develop concepts. (Note the use of drawings in Example 5.) Simple drawings can be used to represent counters, base 10 pieces, fraction pieces, and the like. Provide examples of how to draw the models before asking students to draw on a test (see Figure 5.12).

3. *Include opportunities for explanations.*

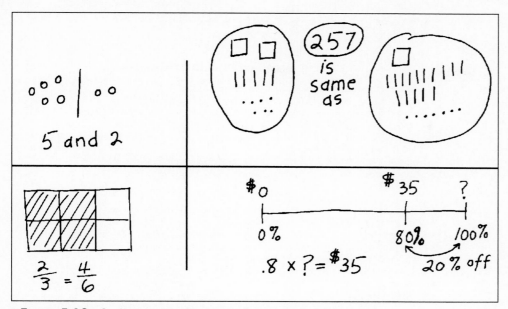

● **FIGURE 5.12** *Students can use drawings to illustrate concepts on tests.*

4. *Assess affective factors on the test.* There are many ways to do this. One idea is to have students rate their personal confidence level on each question as A (high), B (moderate), or C (low). Another idea is to have students draw a face showing how they feel about the question or the test in general. Ask students to complete a sentence that begins "I liked this test because . . ." or "I did not like this test because . . ."

5. *Avoid "preanswered" tests.* These are tests where questions have only one correct answer, whether it is a calculation, a multiple choice, or a fill-in-the-blank. Tests of this type tend to fragment what children have learned and hide most of what they know. Rather, construct tests that allow students the opportunity to show what they know.

PORTFOLIOS IN THE ASSESSMENT PLAN

A *portfolio* is an assemblage of many types of student work selected with both student and teacher input, designed to provide a holistic view of some aspect of mathematics that may not be evident from examination of any single entry. The portfolio should demonstrate and help students reflect on their mathematical power and what that really means. It may be used to focus on progress and growth, understandings, or problem-solving processes. The materials in the portfolio may include assignments, projects, reports, student writing, worksheets from texts or other sources, comments by teachers, observations from interviews, and self-evaluations of group and individual efforts. The portfolio is an excellent form of communication between student and teacher, student and parent, and parent and teacher.

Portfolio Content Suggestions

There are many different ways to design a portfolio assessment program for your classroom, and you should not feel confined by rigid prescriptions. Your own portfolio program should be carried out to serve the particular goals you have in mind and to communicate achievement of these goals to your students and parents. These plans and goals should be discussed with your students from the outset and revisited periodically so that the students are fully involved in the process.

Table 5.2 (p. 84) is taken from a superb NCTM booklet, *Mathematics Assessment: Myths, Models, Good Questions, and Practical Suggestions* (Stenmark, 1991). It provides ideas for the types of entries that could be included to correspond to different goals. Any given portfolio will include only a sampling of these ideas and may contain only eight to ten entries. Be focused in your reason for undertaking portfolio assessment. Do not attempt to cover all goals noted in the table.

A portfolio should be more than a folder of student papers. The portfolio should tell a story that goes beyond the individual entries. Be sure to include problems, tasks, and projects as possible portfolio entries. These are the kinds of things that represent what doing mathematics is all about. Traditional textbook drill exercises or graded computation tests can be included as well, but these are not much fun to look at a second time and do not add to the vision of

TABLE **5.2** GOALS AND SUGGESTED PORTFOLIO CONTENTS

GOAL	EVIDENCE, EXAMPLES, AND COMMENTS
Positive mathematical disposition Motivation Curiosity Perseverance Risk taking Flexibility Self-responsibility Self-confidence	• Journal entries depicting enthusiasm for mathematics • Photographs of large, colorful mathematics graphics by students • Problem solution with an added paragraph beginning with "On the other hand . . ." or "What if . . ." • Log of a week's or month's work showing a single important problem or investigation worked on over a period of time • Homework paper with a description of several approaches to a problem • Student-written planning calendar outlining work to be done • Mathematics autobiography
Growth in mathematical understanding Concept development Problem-solving skills Communication skills Construction of mathematics Reflection on approaches and solutions to problems or tasks	• Similar items collected at regular intervals from the beginning of the year • Written explanation of why an algorithm works • Diagram, table, or similar organized representation that clarifies a problem situation • Solution that defines assumptions, includes counterexamples • Photographs of a mathematics project • Journal entries delineating solution justifications and variations in strategies • Student identification of papers that need more work, with reasons • A paper that starts with "Today in math class I learned . . ." • Inclusion of drafts as well as finished work
Mathematical reasoning in a variety of mathematical topics Estimation, number sense, number operations, and computation Measurement, geometry, and spatial sense Statistics and probability Fractions and decimals Patterns and relationships	• Report on an investigation (e.g., number patterns in sums of sequential numbers) • Student-planned statistical survey, with accompanying graphic designs • Written report of a probability experiment and accompanying theoretical design • Response to an open-ended question regarding measurement of geometric shapes • Student explanation of what $\frac{1}{2}$ minus $\frac{1}{3}$ means • Diagram examples of multiplication using a number line, a rectangular array, and repeated groups of physical objects • Annotated drawing illustrating the Pythagorean theorem • Representation of an area model solution for a statistical problem
Mathematical connections Connecting a mathematical idea to other mathematical topics, to other subject areas, and to real-world situations	• Papers that show authentic use of mathematics in other curricular areas such as science or social studies • Student reflections on how mathematics is meaningful as it is used in the adult world • Examples from nature of occurrences of Pascal's triangle number patterns • A report on the relationship among arithmetic, algebra, and geometry with demonstrative examples on a coordinate grid • Student-constructed table of equivalent fractions, decimal numbers, and percents, with examples of where each type of number is used • Mathematical art project • Report about a person in history or personally known who contributed to mathematics
Group problem-solving Development of skills in working with others Communication	• A task design or plan • Group paper that includes the names of the members of the group and the tasks each did • Group self-assessment sheet • Videotape or audiotape of group working on problems or making oral reports • Group-work report of trying a second or third strategy applied when the first one didn't work
Use of tools Integration of technology—use of calculators and computers and so on Use of manipulatives	• Computer-generated statistical analysis of a problem • Frequent mention of use of calculators on open-ended problems • Diagrams representing use of manipulative material
Teacher and parent involvement Communication between teacher and parent and between parent and student Parental understanding of educational objectives and values	• Consistency of program demonstrated by items from every grading period • Anecdotal report • Informal assessment sheet • Interview of student • Teacher- or parent-written comments • Assessment by teacher of student work • Student presentation of portfolio to parent during parent-teacher conference

Source: National Council of Teachers of Mathematics © 1991. In Stenmark, J. K. (Ed.) in *Mathematics Assessment.* Reprinted by permission.

mathematical power in the same manner as real problem solving and projects.

Teachers who have used portfolios have noted that students begin to take more pride in their work and make extra efforts. Portfolios can add a sense of importance to daily work.

Portfolio Management

At first, the idea of keeping a portfolio for every child is a bit daunting. Included in this section are some ideas found in the Stenmark booklet.

A Working Portfolio

Set up folders for each student, and keep them where students can easily get to them. These folders serve as working portfolios and will hold students' potential portfolio entries. Encourage students to revise or correct work on special projects, but always keep the original versions to indicate progress. The working portfolio is also the place where your observation notes or other items that originate with you can be kept. When groups turn in reports or projects, make copies for each group member's work portfolio.

At the end of the unit or grading period, or whenever it is time to assemble the final portfolio, students select and clip together the items from the working portfolio that they wish to be included in their final portfolio. You will want to have a class discussion about how to select items and what the items should show. Encourage children to pick things that tell about themselves in mathematics: their strengths, weaknesses, points of pride, places they need help, and progress made over the period. Students should include a few sentences explaining each selection and why it was included. You should designate two or three items as "must include," usually the same ones for the whole class.

Students then review their portfolios and write a cover letter that discusses the content as a whole and gives their personal perspective on such things as problem-solving skills, confidence, attitudes, and growth in understanding, depending on the goals you and your class have established. This portfolio is now ready for evaluation and subsequent sharing with parents.

Portfolio Evaluation

You will probably have made comments on most or all of the materials as they were completed. Now you are looking at the portfolio as a whole. It is very important to provide feedback. It is an excellent way to encourage students and to build confidence and communicate perspective about mathematics. Your comments should be made with this in mind. If you plan to include the portfolio in your grading scheme, a rubric will be useful.

DIAGNOSTIC INTERVIEWS

An interview is simply a one-on-one discussion with a child to help you see how children are thinking about a particular subject, what processes they use in solving problems, or what attitudes and beliefs they may have. A structured interview may be as short as five to ten minutes. More open-ended or exploratory interviews may last as long as a half hour.

Reasons to Consider an Interview

There are several reasons why it may occasionally be well worth the time and effort to conduct interviews. The most obvious reason is that you need more information concerning a particular child and how he or she is constructing concepts or using a procedure. Remediation will almost always be more successful if you can pinpoint *why* a student is having difficulty before you try to fix the problem.

A second reason is to get information either to plan your instruction or to assess the effectiveness of your instruction. For example, are you sure that your students have a good understanding of equivalent fractions, or are they just doing the exercises according to rote rules? At the end of Chapter 9, a collection of tasks is suggested to get at students' understanding of place value. Concept tasks such as these might be used in interviews conducted at the beginning of a unit to see what ideas you need to work on. They can be used later in the unit or at the end to assess growth or retention of ideas. Be sure not to include diagnostic tasks as instructional exercises. Practice with the tasks may make them routine and thereby mask understanding.

Another reason is to grow as a teacher, to learn more about the way children learn and think. You might decide to conduct at least one interview a week, changing the topic and the children you interview. In addition to growth in your knowledge of children, you will also grow in your ability to conduct good interviews.

Planning an Interview

There is no magic right way to plan or structure an interview. In fact, flexibility is a key ingredient. You should, however, have some overall game plan before you begin, and be prepared with key questions and materials. Begin an interview with questions that are easy or closest to what the child is likely to be able to do, usually some form of procedural exercise. For numeration or computation topics, begin with a pencil-and-paper task such as doing a computation, writing or comparing numerals, or solving a simple translation problem. When the opening task has been completed, ask the child to explain what was done. "How would you explain this to a second-grader (or your younger sister)?" "What does this (point to something on the paper) stand for?" "Tell me about why you do it that way." At this point, you may try a similar task but with a different feature; for example, after doing 372 − 54 try 403 − 37. The second problem has a zero in the tens place, a possible source of difficulty.

The next phase in the interview involves the use of models or drawings that the child can use to demonstrate understanding of the earlier procedural task. Computations can be done with base 10 materials, blocks or counters can be used, number lines explored, grid paper used for drawing, and so on. Be careful not to interject or teach. The temptation to do so is sometimes overwhelming. Watch and listen. Next, explore connections between what was done with models and what was done with pencil and paper. Many children will do the very same task and get two different answers. Does it matter to the children? How do they explain the discrepancy? Can they connect actions using models to what they wrote or explained earlier?

Alternative beginnings to an interview include making an estimate of the answer to either a computation or a word problem, doing a computation mentally, or trying to predict the solution to a given task. Notice that the interview does not generally proceed the way instruction does. That is, in an interview, the conceptual explanations and discussions in general come after the procedural activity. Your goal is not to use the interview to teach but rather to find out where the child is in terms of concepts and procedures at this time.

Suggestions for Effective Interviews

The following suggestions have been adapted from excellent discussions of interviewing children by Labinowicz (1985, 1987), Liedtke (1988), and Scheer (1980):

1. *Be accepting and neutral as you listen to the child.* Smiles, frowns, or other body language can make the child think that the answer he or she gave is right or wrong. Develop neutral responses such as "Uh-huh," "I see," or even a silent nod of the head.

2. *Avoid cuing or leading the child.* "Are you sure about that?" "Now look again closely at what you just did." "Wait. Is that what you mean?" These responses will indicate to children that they have made some mistake and cause them to change their responses. This can mask what they really think and understand. A similar form of leading is a series of easily answered questions that direct the student to a correct response. That is teaching, not interviewing.

3. *Do wait silently.* Wait after you ask a question. Give the student plenty of time before you give a different question or probe. After the child makes a response, wait again! This second wait time is even more important because it allows and encourages the child to elaborate on the initial thought and provide you with more information. Wait even when the response is correct. Waiting also can be relaxing and give you a bit more time to think about the direction you want the interview to take. Your wait time will almost never be as long as you imagine it is.

4. *Do not interrupt.* Let children's thoughts flow freely. Encourage children to use their own words and ways of writing things down. Interviewing with questions or by correcting language can be distracting to the child's thinking.

5. *Phrase questions in a directive manner to prevent avoidance.* Use "Show me . . .," "Do . . .," or "Try . . .," rather than "Can you . . .," or "Will you . . .." In the latter form, the child can simply say "no," leaving you in a vacuum.

6. *Avoid confirming a request for validation.* Students frequently follow answers or actions with, "Is that right?" This query can easily be answered with a neutral, "That's fine," or "You're doing OK," regardless of whether the answer is right or wrong.

Interviewing is not an easy thing to do well. Many teachers are timid about it and fail to take the time. But not much damage is possible, and the rewards of listening to children, both for you and your students, are so great that you really do not want to pass it up.

GRADING

Myth: A grade is an average of a series of scores on tests and quizzes. The accuracy of the grade is dependent primarily on the accuracy of the computational technique used to calculate the final numeric grade.

Reality: A grade is a statistic that is used to communicate to others the achievement level that a student has attained in a particular area of study. The accuracy or validity of the grade is dependent on the information that is used in preparing the grade, the professional judgment of the teacher, and the alignment of the assessments with the true goals and objectives of the course.

Confronting the Myth

Most experienced teachers will tell you that they know a great deal about their students in terms of what the students know, how they perform in different situations, their attitudes and beliefs, and their various levels of skill attainment. Good teachers have always been engaged in ongoing performance assessment, albeit informal and usually with no recording. In the past, however, even these good teachers believed in the test score as the determinant of grades, essentially forcing themselves to ignore a wealth of information that reflected a truer picture of their children.

The myth of grading by statistical number crunching is so firmly ingrained in schooling at all levels that you may find it hard to abandon. If one thing is clear from the discussions in this chapter, it should be that it is quite possible to gather a wide variety of rich information about students' understanding, problem-solving processes, and attitudes and beliefs. To ignore all of this information in favor of a handful of numbers based on tests, tests that usually focus on low-level skills, is unfair to students, to parents, and to you as the teacher.

This chapter has been about assessment, the gathering of information to find out what our students know. A subjective grading decision carefully made on the basis of daily observations, daily problem solving, student projects, group reports, student self-evaluations, and portfolio evidence of growth will undoubtedly be much more valid than any numeric average even if computed to three decimal places. Remember that there has always been enormous subjectivity in test construction. The determination of the numeric scale for letter grades is completely arbitrary. Let's admit that grading is subjective and arm ourselves with the best information available.

Grading Issues

For effective use of the assessment information gathered from performance tasks and other appropriate methods to assign grades, some hard decisions are inevitable. Some are philosophical, some require school or district agreements about grades, and all require us to examine what we value and the objectives we communicate to students and parents.

Values

In contrast to the many myths of grading, one thing is undeniably true: *What gets graded is what gets valued.* Using rubric scales to provide feedback and to encourage a pursuit of excellence must also relate to grades. However, "converting four out of five to 80 percent or three out of four to a grade of C can destroy the entire purpose of alternative assessment and the use of scoring rubrics" (Kulm, 1994, p. 99). Kulm explains that directly translating rubrics to grades focuses attention on grades and away from the purpose of every good problem-solving activity, to strive for an excellent performance. When papers are returned with less than top ratings, the purpose is to help students know what is necessary

to achieve at a higher level. Early on there should be opportunities to improve based on feedback. When a grade of 75 percent or a C− is returned, all the student knows is that he or she did poorly. If, for example, a student's ability to justify her own answers and solutions has improved, should she be penalized in the averaging of numbers by a weaker performance early in the marking period?

What this means is that grading must be based on the performance tasks and other activities for which you assigned rubric ratings; otherwise, students will soon realize that these are not important scores. At the same time, they need not be added or averaged in any numeric manner. The grade at the end of the marking period should reflect a holistic view of where the student is now relative to your goals and value system. That value system should be clearly reflected in your framework for rating tasks.

Alignment

The grades you assign should reflect all of your objectives. It is difficult to profess a belief in the *Curriculum Standards* and not have grades reflect mathematical power including the goals of problem solving as well as conceptual understanding. Procedural skills remain important but should be weighted in proportion to other goals in keeping with your value system. If you are restricted to assigning a single grade for mathematics, different factors probably have different weights or values in making up the grade. Student X may be fantastic at reasoning and truly love mathematics yet be weak in traditional skills or careless. Student Y may be mediocre in problem solving but possess good communication skills. How much weight should you give to cooperation in groups, to written versus oral reports, to computational skills? There are no simple answers to these questions. However, they should be addressed at the beginning of the grading period and not the night you set out to assign grades.

A multidimensional reporting system is a big help. If you can assign several grades for mathematics and not just one, your report to parents is more meaningful. Even if the school's report card does not permit multiple grades, you can devise a supplement indicating several ratings for different objectives. A place for comments is also helpful. This form can be shared with students periodically during a grading period and can easily accompany a report card.

But even with a single, holistic grade, you can involve students and parents in a discussion of a multidimensional approach to determining a grade based on rubric ratings for different components of your goals. Traditional test averaging has always done this. Not every test covers the same thing, and various scores (quizzes, homework, exams) are often assigned different weights. These are subjective, teacher-made decisions. The same subjective approach can be used with rubric scores without computing numeric averages.

Grading Scales

Many school systems have "standard" grading scales: 94 and above is an A, 87 to 93 is a B, and so on. These scales tend to perpetuate the myth that numbers are needed to produce grades. Such a scale, even if mandated, need not deter you from using appropriate assessment strategies. Simply transfer your subjective grade to a corresponding number. For example, a "high B" might be a 92.

Such games with numbers do not, however, solve the more important issues surrounding grading scales:

• Is progress to be considered, or only final achievement?

• Is ability a factor, or must all students be evaluated on the same scale?

• When different students study different material, are the criteria the same? That is, is excellent performance on material that is perhaps below grade level deserving of the same grade as excellent performance on advanced work?

• Should special-needs children in your collaborative classroom be graded the same as all the rest? To what degree are disabilities to be taken into account?

These and similar issues should be addressed by the faculty in your school and clarified in the reports that you send beyond the classroom. As grading goes beyond the average of test scores, the need for more information than can be delivered by a single number or letter becomes apparent.

REFLECTIONS ON CHAPTER 5: WRITING TO LEARN

1. The six assessment standards are about assessment and *mathematics, learning, equity, openness, inferences,* and *coherence.* For each, describe in your own words what the standard says and what its importance is for you as a teacher.

2. Describe the four purposes of assessment as outlined by the *Assessment Standards.* How do these purposes relate to you as a teacher?

3. What should we look for if we are trying to assess "mathematical power"?

4. In looking at procedural knowledge, what should be assessed in addition to skill proficiency? Why?

5. How can a learning task or problem be an assessment task? Why should these be the same thing?

6. Describe the essential features of a rubric. What are performance indicators? What is the difference? What is the difference between a holistic rubric and an analytic rubric?

7. How can students be involved in understanding and using rubrics to help with their learning?

8. Describe at least two ways that you might gather observation data during a lesson. Why would you want to bother with observation data when you can always look at student papers?

9. How can you use journals in the mathematics classroom? What is the difference between students' writing in journals and their simply solving problems and turning them in?

10. Describe what is meant by student self-assessment. Why would you perhaps want to use this technique in your assessment plans?

11. Describe two ways that tests can be constructed so as to provide more valuable assessments than with traditional end-of-chapter tests.

12. How is a portfolio more than a collection of papers? What goes into a portfolio?

13. Distinguish between assessment and evaluation. Are these completely different procedures? When should evaluation activities take place in a unit?

14. Why is it not necessary to average a collection of test scores to determine a grade? Why, in fact, is this approach to grading probably not even valid?

FOR DISCUSSION AND EXPLORATION

1. How is it possible—even easy—to make invalid inferences about what students understand in mathematics? What are some of the things that would contribute to making incorrect inferences? Do you think that such inferences are made often in the typical classroom? Why or why not? What are the effects of invalid inferences?

2. Examine a few chapter-end tests in various textbooks. How would you describe the alignment of the tests with what is important in the chapter? What about concepts and understanding? What about mathematical power?

3. Select any good performance task for a grade level you are interested in. Try to answer the list of questions on page 67, just above the examples of performance tasks. If possible, get some other people to do the same for the same task. Compare your ideas.

4. Pick a topic and a grade level. Try to write three good test questions for that topic.

5. You will very likely find yourself teaching in a school where other teachers are using a traditional approach to grading. What do you see as the single most important issue or concern surrounding grading? How will you confront this issue and a school environment that is still test-oriented?

SUGGESTED READINGS

Highly Recommended

Kulm, G. (1994). *Mathematics assessment: What works in the classroom.* San Francisco, CA: Jossey-Bass.

Kulm has excellent credentials in the area of both mathematics and science assessment. This book provides perspective, detailed guidance, and models that can be copied for direct use in the classroom. It is one of the best books on assessment in mathematics available.

Lambdin, D. V., Kehle, P. E., & Preston, R. V. (Eds.). (1996). *Emphasis on assessment: Readings from NCTM's school-based journals.* Reston, VA: National Council of Teachers of Mathematics.

This collection of 30 articles on assessment that appeared in various NCTM journals between 1991 and 1995 are organized in four categories: rationale for change, testing and grading, alternative assessment options, and evaluation of teacher effectiveness. At the end of the book are annotated bibliographies for elementary and middle grades teachers, for secondary teachers, and one from the *Journal for Research in Mathematics Education.*

Lambdin, D. V., & Walker, V. L. (1994). Planning for classroom portfolio assessment. *Arithmetic Teacher, 41,* 318–324.

In one of the most practical articles on getting started with portfolios in the classroom, the authors provide tips for planning and for helping students reflect, ideas for management, suggestions for entries, and more, geared primarily to the upper elementary school teacher.

Stenmark, J. K. (Ed.). (1991). *Mathematics assessment: Myths, models, good questions, and practical suggestions.* Reston, VA: National Council of Teachers of Mathematics.

If you want a comprehensive look at new directions in assessment with examples, alternatives, ideas, and formats, this book is a must. Since its publication, it has been one of NCTM's most popular titles. The author is associated with the EQUALS project and has written extensively on assessment. You'll find this an excellent resource.

Zawojewski, J. S. (1996). Polishing a data task: Seeking better assessment. *Teaching Children Mathematics, 2,* 372–378.

Judy Zawojewski does two important things in this article. First, she begins with a performance task that has been published and widely used and shows us its flaws. In the process, you begin to see how a good task can be constructed and the kinds of things to be attentive to. Second, by using a task from the popular assessment literature and pointing to serious flaws found there, she challenges the myth that teachers must spend hours searching for tasks. Use the ideas illustrated in thinking about your own tasks.

Other Suggestions

Ann Arbor Public Schools. (1993). *Alternative assessment: Evaluating student performance in elementary mathematics.* Palo Alto, CA: Dale Seymour.

Badger, E. (1992). More than testing. *Arithmetic Teacher, 39*(9), 7–11.

Burns, M. (1995). *Writing in math class.* White Plains, NY: Cuisenaire (distributor).

Cai, J., Lane, S., & Jakabcsin, M. S. (1996). The role of open-ended tasks and holistic scoring rubrics: Assessing students' mathematical reasoning and communication. In P. C. Elliott (Ed.), *Communication in mathematics, K–12 and beyond* (pp. 137–145). Reston, VA: National Council of Teachers of Mathematics.

Cai, J., Magone, M. E., Wang, N., & Lane, S. (1996). Describing student performance qualitatively. *Mathematics Teaching in the Middle School, 1,* 828–835.

Clarke, D. J., Clarke, D. M., & Lovitt, C. J. (1990). Changes in mathematics teaching call for assessment alternatives. In T. J. Cooney (Ed.), *Teaching and learning mathematics in the 1990s* (pp. 118–129). Reston, VA: National Council of Teachers of Mathematics.

Greenwood, J. J. (1993). On the nature of teaching and assessing "mathematical power" and "mathematical thinking." *Arithmetic Teacher, 41,* 144–152.

Hankes, J. E. (1996). An alternative to basic-skills remediation. *Teaching Children Mathematics, 2,* 452–458.

Harvey, J. G. (1991). Using calculators in mathematics changes testing. *Arithmetic Teacher, 38*(7), 52–54.

Hébert, E. A. (1992). Portfolios invite reflection—from students and staff. *Educational Leadership, 49*(2), 58–61.

Helton, S. M. (1995). I thik the citanre will hoder lase: Journal keeping in mathematics class. *Teaching Children Mathematics, 1,* 336–340.

Hopkins, M. H. (1992). The use of calculators in assessment of mathematics achievement. In J. T. Fey (Ed.), *Calculators in mathematics education* (pp. 158–166). Reston, VA: National Council of Teachers of Mathematics.

Huinker, D., & Laughlin, C. (1996). Talk your way into writing. In P. C. Elliott (Ed.), *Communication in mathematics, K–12 and beyond* (pp. 81–88). Reston, VA: National Council of Teachers of Mathematics.

Joyner, J. J. (1995). NCTM's *Assessment Standards:* A document for all educators. *Teaching Children Mathematics, 2,* 20–22.

Knight, P. (1992). How I use portfolios in mathematics. *Educational Leadership, 49*(2), 71–72.

Lambdin, D. V., & Forseth, C. (1996). Seamless assessment/instruction = good teaching. *Teaching Children Mathematics, 2,* 294–299.

Lindquist, M. M. (1988). Assessing through questioning. *Arithmetic Teacher, 35*(5), 16–19.

Manon, J. R. (1995). The mathematics test: A new role for an old friend. *Mathematics Teacher, 88,* 138–141.

Mathematical Sciences Education Board, National Research Council. (1993). *Measuring up: Prototypes for mathematics assessment.* Washington, DC: National Academy Press.

Mathematical Sciences Education Board, National Research Council. (1993). *Measuring what counts: A conceptual guide for mathematics assessment.* Washington, DC: National Academy Press.

National Council of Teachers of Mathematics. (1992). Alternative assessment [Theme issue]. *Mathematics Teacher, 85*(8).

National Council of Teachers of Mathematics. (1992). Assessment [Focus issue]. *Arithmetic Teacher, 39*(6).

National Council of Teachers of Mathematics: Commission on Teaching Standards for School Mathematics. (1995). *Assessment standards for school mathematics.* Reston, VA: Author.

Newman, V. (1994). *Math journals: Tools for authentic assessment.* San Leandro, CA: Watten/Poe Teaching Resource Center.

Pandey, T. (1991). *A sampler of mathematics assessment.* Sacramento: California Department of Education.

Peressini, D., & Bassett, J. (1996). Mathematical communication in students' responses to a performance-assessment task. In P. C. Elliott (Ed.), *Communication in mathematics, K–12 and beyond* (pp. 146–158). Reston, VA: National Council of Teachers of Mathematics.

Reys, B. J., & Long, V. M. (1995). Teacher as architect of mathematical tasks. *Teaching Children Mathematics, 1,* 296–299.

Richardson, K. (1988). Assessing understanding. *Arithmetic Teacher, 35*(6), 39–41.

Robinson, G. E., & Bartlett, K. T. (1993). Assessment and the evaluation of learning. In R. J. Jensen (Ed.), *Research ideas for the classroom: Early childhood mathematics* (pp. 329–348). Old Tappan, NJ: Macmillan.

South Carolina Educational Television, Kuhs, T. (Dir.). (1992). *Mathematics assessment: Alternative approaches* [video and guide book]. Reston, VA: National Council of Teachers of Mathematics.

Spangler, D. A. (1992). Assessing students' beliefs about mathematics. *Arithmetic Teacher, 40,* 148–152.

Stenmark, J. K., Beck, P., & Asturias, H. (1994). A room with more than one view. *Mathematics Teaching in the Middle School, 1,* 44–49.

Vaac, N. N. (1993). Questioning in the mathematics classroom. *Arithmetic Teacher, 41,* 88–91.

Vermont Department of Education. (1991). *Looking beyond "the answer": The report of Vermont's mathematics portfolio assessment program.* Montpelier, VT: Author.

Vincent, M. L., & Wilson, L. (1996). Informal assessment: A story from the classroom. *Mathematics Teacher, 89,* 248–250.

Webb, N. (Ed.). (1993). *Assessment in the mathematics classroom.* Reston, VA: National Council of Teachers of Mathematics.

Webb, N. L., & Briars, D. (1990). Assessment in mathematics classrooms, K–8. In T. J. Cooney (Ed.), *Teaching and learning mathematics in the 1990s* (pp. 108–117). Reston, VA: National Council of Teachers of Mathematics.

Webb, N. L., & Welsch, C. (1993). Assessment and evaluation for middle grades. In D. T. Owens (Ed.), *Research ideas for the classroom: Middle grades mathematics* (pp. 299–315). Old Tappan, NJ: Macmillan.

Wiggins, G. (1992). Creating tests worth taking. *Educational Leadership, 49*(2), 26–33.

Zawojewski, J. S., & Shannon, A. (1995). Mathematics performance assessment: A new goal for students. *Mathematics Teacher, 88,* 752–757.

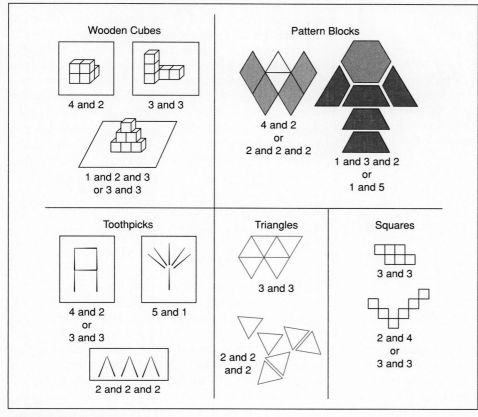

● **FIGURE 6.14**   Designs for 6.

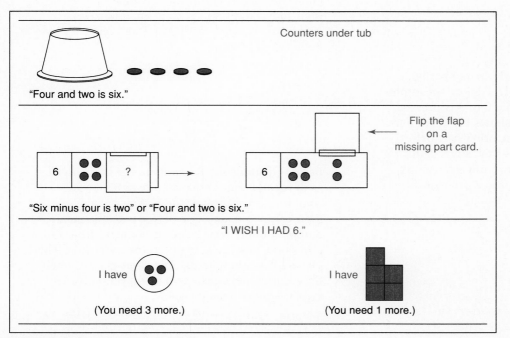

● **FIGURE 6.15**   Missing-part activities.

---ACTIVITY---

6.31 I Wish I Had

Hold out a bar of connecting cubes, a dot strip, a two-column strip, or a dot plate showing 7 or less. Say, "I wish I had seven." The children respond with the part that is needed to make 7. Counting on can be used to check. The game can focus on a single whole, or the "I wish I had" number can change each time.

The following are also missing-part activities but are completely symbolic.

---ACTIVITY---

6.32 Missing-Part Machine

Draw a "machine" on the board similar to the one in Figure 6.10 (p. 102). This time the machine is a "parts of 8" (or any number) machine. A number "goes in," and the students say the other part. If 3 goes in a parts-of-8 machine, a 5 comes out. Do not forget the discussion concerning how the students decided on the outcome.

---ACTIVITY---

6.33 Calculator Missing Part

On the calculator, store the whole number by pressing $\boxed{-}$ 8 $\boxed{=}$, for example. (Ignore the minus sign.) Now if any number from 0 to 8 is pressed followed by $\boxed{=}$, the display shows the other part. Children should try to say the other part before they press $\boxed{=}$. Though this is basically a drill activity, a discussion with any child concerning his or her reasoning returns it to a problem orientation.

Dot Card Activities

Many good number development activities involve more than one of the relationships discussed so far. As children learn about ten-frames, patterned sets, and other relationships, the dot cards found in the Blackline Masters at the back of this book provide a wealth of activities. The cards contain dot patterns, patterns that require counting, combinations of two and three simple patterns, and ten-frames with "standard" as well as unusual placements of dots. When children use these cards for almost any activity that involves number concepts, the cards make them think about numbers in many different ways. The dot cards add another dimension to many of the activities already described and can be used effectively in the following activities (see Figure 6.16).

---ACTIVITY---

6.34 Double War

The game of "Double War" (Kamii, 1985) is played like war, but on each play, both players turn up two cards instead of one. The winner is the one with the larger total number. Children playing the game can use many different number relationships to determine the winner without actually finding the total number of dots.

---ACTIVITY---

6.35 Dot-Card Trains

Make a long row of dot cards from 0 up to 9, then go back again to 1, then up, and so on. Alternatively, begin with 0 or 1 and make a two-more/two-less train.

---ACTIVITY---

6.36 Difference War

Besides dealing out the cards to the two players as in regular war, prepare a pile of about 50 counters. On each play, the players turn over their cards as usual. The player with the greater number of dots wins as many counters from the pile as the difference between the two cards. The players keep their cards. The game is over when the counter pile runs out. The player with the most counters wins the game.

——ACTIVITY——

6.37 Missing-Part Combos

Select a number between 5 and 12 and find combinations of two cards that total that number. When students have found at least ten combinations, one student can then turn one card in each group face down. The next challenge is to name the card that was turned down. ("Before you check, why do you think you are right?")

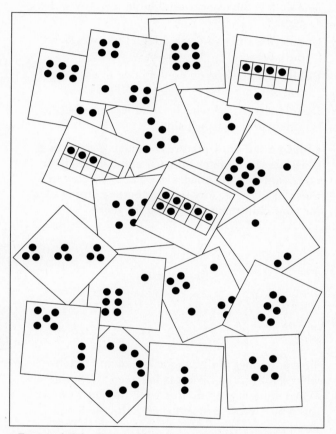

● **FIGURE 6.16** *Dot cards can be made using the Blackline Masters at the back of this book.*

RELATIONSHIPS FOR NUMBERS 10 TO 20

Even though kindergarten, first-, and second-grade children daily experience numbers up to 20 and beyond, it should not be assumed that they will automatically ex-

tend the set of relationships they have developed on smaller numbers to the numbers beyond 10. And yet these numbers play a big part in many simple counting activities, in basic facts, and in much of what we do with mental computation. Relationships on these numbers are just as important as relationships involving the numbers through 10.

A Pre-Place-Value Relationship with 10

A set of ten should play a major role in children's initial understanding of numbers between 10 and 20. When children see a set of six with a set of ten, they should know without counting that the total is 16. However, the numbers between 10 and 20 are not an appropriate place to discuss place-value concepts. That is, prior to a much more complete development of place-value concepts (appropriate for second grade and beyond), children should not be asked to explain the 1 in 16 as representing "one ten." (Stop for a moment and say to yourself: "one ten." Think about it! What would this mean to a 5-year-old? Ten is a lot. How can it be one? This is initially a strange idea.) The inappropriateness of discussing "one ten and six ones" (what's a one?) does not mean that a set of ten should not figure prominently in the discussion of the teen numbers. The following activity illustrates this idea.

——ACTIVITY——

6.38 Ten and Some More

Use a simple two-part mat, and have children count out ten counters onto one side. Next have them put five counters on the other side. Together count all of the counters by ones. Chorus the combination: "Ten and five is fifteen." Turn the mat around: "Five and ten is fifteen." Repeat with other numbers in a random order but without changing the 10 side of the mat.

Activity 6.38 is designed to teach new number names and thus requires a certain amount of directed teaching. Following this activity, explore numbers to 20 in a more open-ended manner. Provide each child with two ten-frames drawn on a construction paper mat, one ten-frame under the other. In random order, have children show numbers to 20 on their mats. There is not a correct way to do this as long as there are the correct number of counters. What is interesting is to discuss how the counters can be placed on the mat so that it is easy to see how many are there. Allow children to share their ideas. Not every child will use a full set of ten, but as this idea becomes more popular, the notion that ten and some more is a teen amount will soon be developed. Do not forget to include numbers less than ten as well. As you listen to your children, you may want to begin challenging them to find ways to show 26 counters or even more.

Extending More and Less Relationships

The relationships of one more than, two more than, one less than, and two less than are important for all numbers. However, these ideas are built on or connected to the same concepts for numbers less than 10. The fact that 17 is one less than 18 is connected to the idea that 7 is one less than 8. Children may need help in making this connection.

──── ACTIVITY ────

6.39 More and Less Extended

On the overhead, show 7 counters, and ask what is two more, or one less, and so on. Now add a filled ten-frame to the display (or 10 in any pattern), and repeat the questions. Pair up questions by covering and uncovering the ten-frame as illustrated in Figure 6.17.

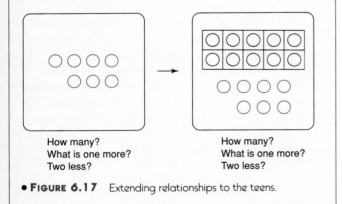

How many?
What is one more?
Two less?

How many?
What is one more?
Two less?

• **FIGURE 6.17**   *Extending relationships to the teens.*

Double and Near-Double Relationships

The use of doubles (double 6 is 12) and near-doubles (13 is double 6 and 1 more) is generally considered a strategy for memorizing basic addition facts. There is no reason why children should not begin to develop these relationships long before they are concerned with memorizing basic facts. Doubles and near-doubles are simply special cases of the general part-part-whole construct.

──── ACTIVITY ────

6.40 Double Images

Relate the doubles to special images. Thornton (1982) helped first graders connect doubles to these visual ideas:

Double 3 is the bug double: three legs on each side.

Double 4 is the spider double: four legs on each side.

Double 5 is the hand double: two hands.

Double 6 is the egg carton double: two rows of six eggs.

Double 7 is the two-week double: two weeks on the calendar.

Double 8 is the crayon double: two rows of eight crayons in a box.

Double 9 is the 18-wheeler double: two sides, nine wheels on each side.

Children can draw pictures or make posters that illustrate the doubles for each number. There is no reason that the images need be restricted to those listed here. Any images that are strong ideas for your children will be good for them.

──── ACTIVITY ────

6.41 What's the Double Number?

Give a number orally, and ask students to tell what double it is. "What is fourteen?" (Double 7!) When students can do this well, use any number up to 20. "What is seventeen?" (Double 8 and 1 more.)

──── ACTIVITY ────

 ### 6.42 The Double Maker

On the calculator, store the "double maker" (2 ⊠ ▣). Now a press of any digit followed by ▣ will produce the double of that number. Children can work in pairs or individually to try to beat the calculator.

NUMBER SENSE AND THE REAL WORLD

So far we have discussed the development of number meanings and some very specific relationships involving numbers. These ideas are very much a part of what is meant by number sense. Here we examine ways to broaden the early knowledge of numbers even further. Relationships of numbers to real-world quantities and measures and the use of numbers in simple estimations can help children develop the flexible, intuitive ideas about numbers that are most desired.

Estimation and Measuring

One of the best ways for children to think of real quantities is to associate numbers with measures of things. In the early grades, measures of length, weight, and time are good places to begin. Just measuring and recording results will not be very effective, however, since there is no reason for children to be interested in or think about the result. To help children think or reflect a bit on what number might tell how long the desk is or how heavy the book is, it would be good if they could first write down or tell you an estimate. To produce an estimate is, however, a very difficult task for young children. They do not understand the concept of "estimate" or "about." For example, suppose that you have cut out of poster board an ample supply of very large footprints, say, about 18 inches long. All are exactly the same size. You would like to ask the class, "About how many footprints will it take to measure across the rug in our reading corner?" The key word here is *about,* and it is one that you will need to spend a lot of time helping children understand. To this end, the request of an estimate can be made in ways that help with the concept of "about" and still permit children to respond. Here are some suggestions that can be applied to this example and to most other early estimation activities.

- *More or less than _____?* Will it be more or less than 10 footprints? Will the apple weigh more or less than 20 wooden blocks? Are there more or less than 15 connecting cubes in this long bar?

- *Closer to _____ or to _____?* Will it be closer to 5 footprints or closer to 20 footprints? Will the apple weigh closer to 10 blocks or closer to 30 blocks? Does this bar have closer to 10 cubes or closer to 50 cubes?

- *Less than _____, between _____ and _____, or more than _____?* Will it take less than 10, between 10 and 20, or more than 20 footprints? Will the apple weigh less than 5 blocks, between 5 and 15 blocks, or more than 15 blocks? Are there less than 20, between 20 and 50, or more than 50 cubes in this bar?

- *About _____.* Use one of these numbers: 5, 10, 15, 20, 25, 30, 35, 40, ... About how many footprints? About how many blocks will the apple weigh? About how many cubes are in this bar?

This list of estimation question formats is arranged from the easiest to the most difficult. However, notice that each clearly indicates to the children that they need not come up with an exact amount or number. Asking for estimates using these formats has several advantages. It helps children learn what you mean by "about." Every child can make an estimate without having to pull a number out of the air.

For almost all measurement estimation activities at the K–2 level, it is good to use an informal measuring unit instead of standard units such as feet, centimeters, pounds, or kilograms. This avoids the problem of children's lack of familiarity with the unit. If, however, you want them to learn about a unit of measure, say, the meter, then by all means include that unit in these exercises.

Another suggestion is to estimate several things in succession using the same unit. This will help children develop an understanding of relative measures. For example, suppose that you are estimating and measuring "around things" using a string. To measure, the string is wrapped around the object and then measured in some unit such as craft sticks. After measuring the distance around Demetria's head, estimate the distance around the wastebasket or around the globe or around George's wrist. Each successive measure helps children with the new estimates.

An alternative approach is to estimate and measure the same item successively with different-sized units. You will be surprised when young children guess that the measure is smaller when the unit gets smaller. The ideas that smaller units produce larger measurements and large units small measurements are difficult relationships for children to construct. (See Chapter 16 for a more complete discussion of measurement.)

More Connections

Here are some additional activities that can help children connect numbers to real situations.

---ACTIVITY---

6.43 Add a Unit to Your Number

Write a number on the board. Now suggest some units to go with it, and ask the children what they can think of that fits. For example, suppose the number is 9. "What do you think of when I say *9 dollars? 9 hours? 9 cars? 9 kids? 9 meters? 9 o'clock? 9 hand spans? 9 gallons?"* **Spend some**

time in discussion of each. Let children suggest units as well. Be prepared to explore some of the ideas either immediately or as projects or tasks to share with parents at home.

---ACTIVITY---

6.44 Is It Reasonable?

Select a number and a unit—for example, 15 feet. Could the teacher be 15 feet tall? Could your living room be 15 feet wide? Can a man jump 15 feet high? Could three children stretch their arms 15 feet? Pick any number, large or small, and a unit with which children are familiar. Then make up a series of these questions.

Once children are familiar with Activity 6.44, have them select the number and the unit or things (10 kids, 20 bananas, . . .) and see what kinds of questions children make up. When a difference of opinion develops, capitalize on the opportunity to explore and find out. Resist the temptation to supply your adult-level knowledge. Rather, say, "Well, how can we find out if it is or is not reasonable? Who has an idea about what we could do?"

---ACTIVITY---

6.45 Things That Are Seven

Pick any number (7 is used here as an example), and have groups of children find ways to tell about that number. Seven might be the days in a week, the number of people in Mandy's family, or the number of kittens in Inky's litter. Other children might want to show 7 in some measurement way, such as a stack of 7 books, 7 glasses of water in a jug, 7 long giant steps, the length of 7 children lying down head to toe, or how many hops they can hop in 7 seconds. Groups can present their ideas orally, make a written report, contribute a page to put on the bulletin board, or present a demonstration.

The last three activities are really problems in the truest sense. Not only are there no clear answers, but children can easily begin to pose their own questions and explore number in the part of the environment most interesting to them.

Children will not have these real-world connections when you begin, and you will be disappointed in their limited ideas about number. Howden (1989) writes about a first-grade teacher of children from very impoverished backgrounds who had explained to her, "They all have fingers, the school grounds are strewn with lots of pebbles and leaves, and pinto beans are cheap. So we count, sort, compare, and talk about such objects. We've measured and weighed almost everything in this room and almost everything the children can drag in" (p. 6). This teacher's children had produced a wonderfully rich and long list of responses to the question "What comes to your mind when I say twenty-four?" In another school in a professional community where test scores are high, the same question brought almost no response from a class of third graders. It can be a very rewarding effort to help children connect their number ideas to the real world.

Graphs

Graphing activities are another good way to connect children's worlds with number. Chapter 19 discusses ways to make graphs with children in grades K–2. Graphs can be quickly made of almost any data that can be gathered from the students: favorite ice cream, color, sports team, pet; number of sisters and brothers, kids who ride different buses, types of shoes, number of pets, and so on. Graphs can be connected to content in other areas. A unit on sea life might lead to a graph of favorite sea animals.

Once a simple bar graph is made, it is very important to take a few minutes to ask as many number questions as is appropriate for the graph. In the early stages of number development (grades K–1), the use of graphs for number relationships and for connecting numbers to real quantities in the children's environment is a more important reason for building graphs than the graphs themselves. The graphs focus attention on counts of realistic things. Equally important, bar graphs clearly exhibit comparisons between and among numbers that are rarely made when only one number or quantity is considered at a time. See Figure 6.18 for an example of a graph and questions that can be asked. At first, children will have trouble with the questions involving differences, but repeated exposure to these ideas in a bar graph format will improve their understanding. These comparison concepts add considerably to children's understanding of number.

LITERATURE CONNECTIONS

Children's literature abounds with wonderful counting books. Involving children with books in a variety of ways can serve to connect number to reality, make it a personal

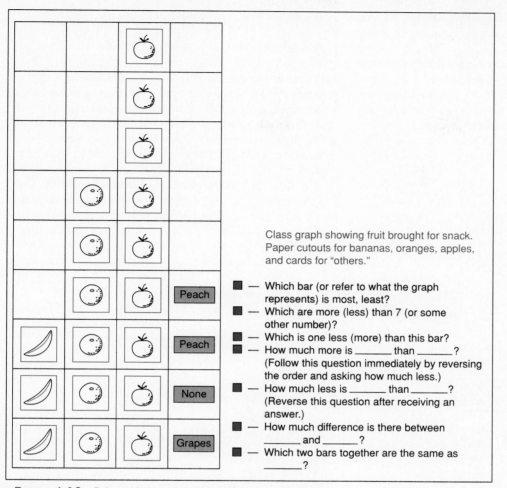

Class graph showing fruit brought for snack. Paper cutouts for bananas, oranges, apples, and cards for "others."

■ — Which bar (or refer to what the graph represents) is most, least?

■ — Which are more (less) than 7 (or some other number)?

■ — Which is one less (more) than this bar?

■ — How much more is _____ than _____? (Follow this question immediately by reversing the order and asking how much less.)

■ — How much less is _____ than _____? (Reverse this question after receiving an answer.)

■ — How much difference is there between _____ and _____?

■ — Which two bars together are the same as _____?

● **FIGURE 6.18** *Relationships and number sense in a bar graph.*

experience, and provide ample opportunities for problem solving. Be sure to go beyond simply reading a counting book or a number-related book and looking at the pictures. Find a way to extend the book into the children's world. Create problems related to the story. Have children write a similar story. Extend the numbers and see what happens. Create a mural, graphs, or posters. The ideas are as plentiful as the books. Here are a few ideas.

Anno's Counting House (Anno, 1982)

In the beautiful style of Anno, this book shows ten children in various parts of a house. As the pages are turned, the house front covers the children, and a few are visible through cutout windows. A second house is on the opposite page. As you move through the book, the children move one at a time to the second house, creating the potential for a 10–0, 9–1, 8–2, . . . , 0–10 pattern of pairs. But as each page shows part of the children through the window, there is an opportunity to discuss how many in the missing part. Have children use counters to model the story as you "read" it the second or third time.

What if the children moved in pairs instead of one at a time? What if there were three houses? What if there were more children? What else could be in the house to count? How many rooms, pictures, windows? What about your house? What about two classrooms or two buses instead of houses?

The Very Hungry Caterpillar (Carle, 1969)

This is a predictable progression counting book about a caterpillar who eats first one thing, then two, and so on. Children can create their own eating stories and illustrate them. What if more than one type of thing were eaten at each stop? What combinations for each number are there? Are seven little things more or less than three very large things? What does all of this stuff weigh? How many things are eaten altogether?

Two Ways to Count to Ten (Dee, 1988)

This Liberian folktale is about King Leopard in search of the best animal to marry his daughter. The task devised involves throwing a spear and counting to 10 before the spear lands.

Many animals try and fail. Counting by ones proves too lengthy. Finally, the antelope succeeds by counting "2, 4, 6, 8, 10."

The story is a perfect lead-in to skip counting. Can you count to 10 by threes? How else can you count to 10? How many ways can you count to 48? What numbers can you reach if you count by fives? The size of the numbers you investigate is limited only by the children. A hundreds board or counters are useful thinker toys to help with these problems. Be sure to have children write about what they discover in their investigations.

Another fun book to use is *The King's Commissioners* (Friedman, 1994), a hilarious tale that also opens up opportunities to count by different groupings or skip counting.

EXTENSIONS TO EARLY MENTAL MATHEMATICS

Teachers in the second and third grades can capitalize on some of the early number relationships and extend them to numbers up to 100. A useful set of materials to help with these relationships is the little base-ten-frames found in the Blackline Masters. Each child should have a set of 10 tens and a set of frames for each number 1 to 9 with an extra 5.

The following three ideas are illustrated with the little ten-frames in Figure 6.19. First are the relationships of one more than and one less than. If you understand that one

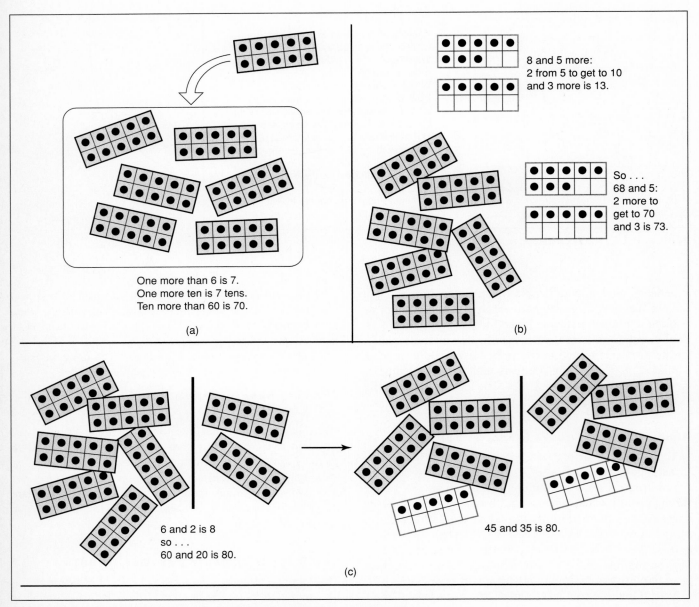

One more than 6 is 7.
One more ten is 7 tens.
Ten more than 60 is 70.

(a)

8 and 5 more:
2 from 5 to get to 10
and 3 more is 13.

So . . .
68 and 5:
2 more to
get to 70
and 3 is 73.

(b)

6 and 2 is 8
so . . .
60 and 20 is 80.

45 and 35 is 80.

(c)

• **FIGURE 6.19**   *Extending early number relationships to mental computation activities.*

more than 6 is 7, then in a similar manner, ten more than 60 is 70 (that is, one more ten). The second idea is really a look ahead to fact strategies. If a child has learned to think about adding on to 8 or 9 by first adding up to 10 and then adding the rest, the extension to similar two-digit numbers is quite simple; see Figure 6.19(b). Finally, the most powerful idea for small numbers is thinking of them in parts. It is a very useful idea (though not one found in textbooks) to take apart larger numbers to begin to develop some flexibility in the same way. Children can begin by thinking of ways to take apart a multiple of 10 such as 80. Once they do it with tens, the challenge can be to think of ways to take apart 80 when one part has a 5 in it, such as 25 or 35.

More will be said about early mental computation in Chapter 10. The point to be made here is that early relationships on number have a greater impact on what children know than may be apparent at first. Even teachers in the upper grades may profitably consider the use of ten-frames and part-part-whole activities.

REFLECTIONS ON CHAPTER 6: WRITING TO LEARN

1. How can you tell if children are attaching any meaning to their counting?

2. Describe an activity that is a "set-to-numeral match" activity, and describe what ideas the child must have to do these activities meaningfully and correctly.

3. What are the four types of relationships that have been described for small numbers? Explain briefly what each of these means, and give at least one activity for each.

4. Describe a missing-part activity, and explain what should happen if the child trying to give the missing part does not know it.

5. Describe how a calculator can be used to develop early counting ideas connected with number. How can a calculator be used to help a child practice number relationships such as part-part-whole or one less than?

6. For numbers between 10 and 20, describe how to develop each of these ideas:

   a. The idea of the teens as a set of 10 and some more

   b. Extension of the one-more/one-less concept to the teens

7. Describe in two or three sentences your own idea of what number sense is.

8. What are three ways that children can be helped to connect numbers to real-world ideas?

9. Describe two examples of how early number relationships can be used to develop some early mental computation skills.

FOR DISCUSSION AND EXPLORATION

1. Examine a textbook series for grades K–2. Compare the treatment of counting and number concept development with that presented in this chapter. What ideas are stressed? What ideas are missed altogether? If you were teaching in one of these grades, how would you plan your number concept development program? What part would the text play?

2. Many teachers in grades above the second find that their children do not possess the number relationships discussed in this chapter but rely heavily on counting. Given the pressures of other content at these grades, how much effort should be made to remediate these number concept deficiencies?

3. Discuss the importance of number sense in the K–4 curriculum. You might want to read "Standard 6: Number Sense and Numeration" in the K–4 section of the NCTM *Standards*. Do you find that teachers and current textbooks are adequately addressing the issue of number sense? Is it really important? Why?

SUGGESTED READINGS

Highly Recommended

Burton, G. (1993). *Number sense and operations: Addenda series, grades K–6*. Reston, VA: National Council of Teachers of Mathematics.

Either this book or the *Number Sense and Operations* addenda series book for your grade level should be a must for developing number concepts. The activities are developed in sufficient detail to give you clear guidance and yet allow considerable flexibility.

Thompson, C. S., & Rathmell, E. C. (Eds.). (1989). Number sense [Focus issue]. *Arithmetic Teacher, 36*(6).

This remains one of the best focus issues of *The Arithmetic Teacher*. It contains the Howden article referenced in this chapter and several others worth reading. It is still timely.

Van de Walle, J. A., & Watkins, K. B. (1993). Early development of number sense. In R. J. Jensen (Ed.), *Research ideas for the classroom: Early childhood mathematics* (pp. 127–150). Old Tappan, NJ: Macmillan.

This chapter includes a discussion of many of the K–2 topics covered in this text as well as a broader discussion of number sense, including mental computation and estimation. It provides a good mix of practical ideas with ample references to the research literature.

Other Suggestions

Burk, D., Snider, A., & Symonds, P. (1988). *Box it or bag it mathematics: Teachers resource guide* [Kindergarten, First–Second]. Salem, OR: Math Learning Center.

Fischer, F. E. (1990). A part-part-whole curriculum for teaching number in the kindergarten. *Journal for Research in Mathematics Education, 21,* 207–215.

Fuson, K. C. (1989). *Children's counting and concepts of number.* New York: Springer-Verlag.

Greenes, C., Schulman, L., & Spungin, R. (1993). Developing sense about numbers. *Arithmetic Teacher, 40,* 279–284.

Kroll, D. L., & Yabe, T. (1987). A Japanese educator's perspective on teaching mathematics in the elementary school. *Arithmetic Teacher, 35*(2), 36–43.

Leutzinger, L. P., & Bertheau, M. (1989). Making sense of numbers. In P. R. Trafton (Ed.), *New directions for elementary school mathematics* (pp. 111–122). Reston, VA: National Council of Teachers of Mathematics.

National Council of Teachers of Mathematics. (1990). *Number sense now! Reaching the NCTM Standards* [Video and teacher's guide]. Reston, VA: Author.

Payne, J. N., & Huinker, D.M. (1993). Early number and numeration. In R. J. Jensen (Ed.), *Research ideas for the classroom: Early childhood mathematics* (pp. 43–71). Old Tappan, NJ: Macmillan.

Schwartz, S. L. (1995). Enchanting, fascinating, useful number. *Teaching Children Mathematics, 1,* 486–491.

Van de Walle, J. A. (1988). The early development of number relations. *Arithmetic Teacher, 35*(6), 15–21, 32.

Van de Walle, J. A. (1990). Concepts of number. In J. N. Payne (Ed.), *Mathematics for the young child* (pp. 63–87). Reston, VA: National Council of Teachers of Mathematics.

Weinberg, S. (1996). Going beyond ten black dots. *Teaching Children Mathematics, 2,* 432–435.

Whitin, D. J. (1989). Number sense and the importance of asking "Why?" *Arithmetic Teacher, 36*(6), 26–29.

Whitin, D. J., Mills, H., & O'Keefe, T. (1994). Exploring subject areas with a counting book. *Teaching Children Mathematics, 1,* 170–174.

Whitin, D. J., & Wilde, S. (1995). *It's the story that counts: More children's books for mathematical learning, K–6.* Portsmouth, NH: Heinemann.

CHAPTER

DEVELOPING MEANINGS

FOR THE OPERATIONS

This chapter is about helping children connect different meanings, interpretations, and relationships to the four operations of addition, subtraction, multiplication, and division so that they can effectively use these operations in other settings.

It should be clear that the activities of this chapter are not designed to produce basic fact mastery (being able to respond quickly to $4 \times 9 = \square$ or $12 - 8 = ?$) or computational skill. Conceptual knowledge of the operations is certainly important in mastering basic facts, but as will be seen in Chapter 8, it takes more than an understanding of the operations to develop mastery. The main thrust of this chapter is helping children develop what might be termed "operation sense," a highly integrated understanding of the four operations and the many different but related meanings these operations take on in real contexts.

 BIG IDEAS

1. **Addition and subtraction are connected. Addition names the whole in terms of the parts, and subtraction names a missing part.**
2. **Models can be used to solve story problems for all operations and to figure out what operation is involved in a problem.**
3. **Multiplication involves counting groups of like size and determining how many are in all (multiplicative thinking).**

4. **Multiplication and division are related. Division names a missing factor in terms of the known factor and the product.**

TWO SOURCES OF OPERATION MEANINGS

For all four operations, word stories or word problems and models (usually sets of counters and number lines) are the two basic tools the teacher has to help students develop operation concepts. As you will see, each of the four operations is a little more involved or complex than you may have thought. For example, as many as 14 different types of word problems have been identified for addition and subtraction.

Operation Meanings from Word Problems

Probably the most important way in which children construct operation meanings is from word problems or word stories. The word problem provides an opportunity for examining a diverse set of meanings for each operation.

We know from research that children as early as kindergarten can and do solve story problems. This is much earlier than is commonly acknowledged in traditional textbooks. Quite simply, children who have not yet learned to grab the numbers in a story problem and perform an operation on these numbers are forced to think very hard about the problem. As long as the numbers are relatively simple, children are usually able to solve these problems by directly modeling the meaning of the problem with counters and counting. In the process, many children also develop new and more efficient counting strategies. What is not so clear is how children should best learn to write symbolic equations to go with the meanings of the problems.

To see the difference between simple models and story problems, consider the action of joining 4 counters with 7 counters to create a set of 11. Although this is a model for $7 + 4 = 11$, word problems for this situation may be quite different. Look at the following two problems:

Molly earned \$4 babysitting. She had already earned \$7. How much does Molly have now?

Jerome was picking apples. He had 7 apples in his bag and then picked some more. When he counted again, he had 11 apples. How many more apples did he pick?

The action with counters is not completely the same for the two problems. In the apple problem, an unknown number of counters must be added to 7 until the total is 11. In the money problem, the 4 is known; it can be counted out and then joined with the 7. How would you solve the apple problem if it were changed like this?

You had 34.8 bushels of apples, received a new shipment, and now have a total of 72.5 bushels. How many bushels were shipped?

To compute the answer or to use a calculator, you will have to perform the operation $72.5 - 34.8$, a subtraction. The action was joining, but subtraction names the amount joined.

Basic Meanings Developed with Models

Counter or set models for the operations include movable objects, pictures of sets in various arrangements, arrays (things arranged in rows and columns), and variations of these basic ideas. Number lines are also a good model at the upper grade levels but can be more confusing than helpful at the primary level.

An activity that involves only models and no word problems is generally much more directive than having children solve word problems. Word problems can and should be handled in a spirit of inquiry, allowing children to use their own methods and justify their solutions. An activity with only models lacks a problem to solve. The teacher must be more directive in explaining what is to be done. Children do something with the model (arrange, separate, join, draw arrows on the number line, count rows and lengths of rows, and so on) and then write number sentences (equations) that mean the same thing as the model. The purpose is to associate or connect a new symbolic language (the equation and operation sign) with the concept of the operation as seen in the model.

In all of the models-only activities, children write complete equations. The activities begin with models, and what is written is a full equation that tells about the model. An equation such as $12 - 8 = 4$ tells something about the model and how it relates the quantities 12, 8, and 4. The child is doing much more than simply filling in the answer to $12 - 8 = \square$, which is more a drill than a concept development activity.

Children soon write equations to go with the story problems they solve. Models serve both as a thinker toy to analyze what the structure of the story problem may be and also as a connection between the meaning in the story problem and the symbolic equation. In the constructivist spirit, the class discussion following a story problem should examine not only the answer but also the equations. Return to the problem of having 7 apples, picking some more, and ending up with 11 apples. One child may write $7 + 4 = 11$ and another $11 - 7 = 4$. The discussion serves to help children see that both make sense and that they are actually equivalent equations. Forcing children to write exactly the equation we have in mind or to solve a problem as we would solve it may be a waste of precious classroom time. The time may better be spent allowing children to solve problems and write equations in ways that make the most sense to them and discussing these solutions to share and develop a rich array of ideas (Gutstein & Romberg, 1995).

Translations: Models, Words, and Symbols

It is useful to think of models, word problems, and symbolic equations as three separate languages. Each language can be used to express the relationships involved in one of the operations. The model and word problem languages more clearly illustrate the relationships involved, whereas the equation is a convention used to stand for ideas. Given these three languages, a powerful approach to helping children develop operation meaning is to have them make translations from one language to another. Once children develop a familiarity with an assortment of models and drawings and

independent work. All children, even the youngest, can produce a written report of their work so that there is evidence to keep and also evidence of written communication skills.

Not only does the mode of the story problem make data gathering easy, but the problems also provide a wonderful opportunity to assess a wide range of information about your students. The obvious data is about the students' conceptual understanding of the operations involved, connections between related operations, connections with operation symbolism (equations), and connections to real-world information.

Another area of conceptual knowledge and understanding is number sense. Though this chapter has not focused on the computation and estimation aspects of solving problems, large quantities of data are available. After students have decided what computation to do in a problem, it is useful to see how they go about doing it. Several programs, most notably CGI (Fennema, Carpenter, Franke, & Carey, 1993; Hankes, 1996), rely almost entirely on solutions to word problems for the development of basic fact mastery and the invention of computational procedures. Regardless of how computational methods are developed in your class, children will exhibit their most spontaneous and personal approaches to computation when solving realistic story problems.

Finally, all aspects of problem solving, including the metacognitive and affective goals, can be "observed as children work on simple story problems. The four theme standards are also visible in these activities.

The message of all that has just been said is that a few story problems each week at all grade levels (including kindergarten and the middle grades) are an excellent way to help children construct meanings of the operations and provide you with a wealth of ongoing feedback that is critical to your overall assessment strategies.

To make all of this happen, it should be clear that the students must focus on more than getting answers. They must be expected to communicate their ideas and defend their solutions. They should, when appropriate, look for alternative paths to a solution or ways to communicate their ideas. Only when these things are part of the story-problem picture will you harvest the many benefits that are possible.

LITERATURE CONNECTIONS

Finding an exciting and fun way to use literature to develop or expand understanding of the operations is extremely easy. There are lots of books with stories or pictures concerning sets of things, buying things, measures, and so on, that can be used to pose problems or, better, to stimulate children to invent their own problems. Perhaps the most widely mentioned book in this context is *The Doorbell Rang*, by Pat Hutchins (1986). You can check that one out yourself. Here are three additional suggestions.

How Many Snails? (Giganti, 1988)

Appropriate for the K–2 set, this book includes a variety of pictures where the objects belonging to one collection have various subcollections (parts and wholes). For example, a sky full of clouds has various types of clouds. The text asks, "How many clouds are there? How many clouds are big and fluffy? How many clouds are big and fluffy and gray?" These pages lead directly to addition and subtraction situations matching the part-part-whole concepts. Of special note is the opportunity to have missing-part thinking for subtraction. Children can think of collections that they would like to draw so that subcollections have a variety of attributes. They can then pose their own questions about the drawing and add appropriate number sentences. In discussion, children could explain why they selected the particular equation and how it fits the picture.

More than One (Hoban, 1981)

The wonderful black-and-white photos of Tana Hoban are designed to introduce group words such as a *crowd* of people, a *herd* of elephants, or a *bundle* of wood. A discussion of group words (animal groups fit nicely with science—*flock, pride, covey,* etc.) beyond those that are in the book can be interesting in and of itself. Do different groups typically contain different numbers of things? Is it likely that there would be two elephants in a herd? Could there be 50? What is typical? These grouping words provide a real opportunity for children to develop *group* as single entity but with separate things inside. Now suppose that there are many groups (herds, flocks, crowds). If we know the size of one, and we know how many herds, do we know how many elephants in all? Imagine a situation where that was always the case—all groups with group names have the same number of things. If there are 87 pieces of wood in 3 bundles, how many in a bundle? Clever one- and two-step multiplication and division stories can be generated.

Each Orange Had 8 Slices (Giganti, 1992)

Each two-page spread shows objects grouped in three ways. For example, one spread has four trees, three bird's nests in each tree, and two eggs in each nest. The author asks three questions: "How many trees? How many nests? How many eggs?" The three questions with each picture extend multiplication to a three-factor product. In the case of the trees, nests, and eggs, the product is $4 \times 3 \times 2$. After children get a handle on the predictable arrangement of the book's pictures, they can not only write multiplication stories that go with the pictures but also make up situations of their own. What similar situations can be found in the classroom? Perhaps desks, books, and pages or bookshelves, shelves, and books. And there is no need to restrict the discussion to three nestings of objects. The same idea is present in measurements: yards, feet, inches or gallons, quarts, pints, cups, ounces. New problems can be posed that require division.

What if there were some boxes with 6 cartons in each? Each carton has 4 widgets. If there are 72 widgets, how many boxes are there?

REFLECTIONS ON CHAPTER 7: WRITING TO LEARN

1. Make up a context for some story problems, and make up six different join and separate problems: three with a join action and three with a separate action. For all six problems, use the same number family: 9, 4, 13.

2. Make up a comparison word problem. Next change the problem to provide an example of all six different possibilities for comparison problems.

3. Make up multiplication word problems to illustrate the difference between equal groups and multiplicative comparison. Can you create problems involving rates or continuous quantities?

4. Make up two different word problems for 36 ÷ 9. For one, the modeling should result in four sets of nine, and for the other, the modeling should result in nine sets of four. Which is which? Which of your problems is a measurement problem, and which is a partition problem?

5. Make up realistic measurement and partition division problems where the remainder is dealt with in each of these three ways: (a) it is discarded (but not left over); (b) it is made into a fraction; (c) it forces the answer to the next whole number.

6. Use three different models to illustrate what 3 × 7 means in terms of repeated addition. What is the meaning of each factor? What is the meaning of 3 × 7 in the combination concept? Make a drawing to illustrate what you mean.

7. Explain how to help students analyze problems when the numbers are not small whole numbers but rather are large or are fractions or decimals that do not lend themselves to using counters.

8. What roles can story problems play in your assessment scheme? What will you have to do in the classroom to make the most of story problems as assessment opportunities?

FOR DISCUSSION AND EXPLORATION

1. In the 1980s, one-step story problems got a bit of a bad reputation as not really being problem-solving tasks. They tended to come at the end of chapters in which an operation was the focus, and most problems matched the operation named in the chapter title. Children knew they were in a multiplication chapter and so could ig-

nore the actual story of the problem and simply pick the numbers and multiply. This chapter suggests a fairly different approach to the use of story problems. Would you consider these problems "problem solving"? Defend your answer.

2. Examine a basal textbook at one or more grade levels. Identify how, and in what chapters, the meanings for the operations are developed. Discuss the relative focus on meanings of the operations with one-step story problems, use of models, and mastery of basic facts.

3. When looking at a basal textbook, see how many different types of story problems you can find. In the primary grades, look for join, remove, part-part-whole, and compare problems. For grades 4 and above, look for the four multiplicative types (look in the multiplication and division chapters and also at special problem-solving lessons). Are the various types of problems well represented?

SUGGESTED READINGS

Highly Recommended

Carpenter, T. P., Carey, D. A., & Kouba, V. L. (1990). A problem-solving approach to the operations. In J. N. Payne (Ed.), *Mathematics for the young child* (pp. 111–131). Reston, VA: National Council of Teachers of Mathematics.

These authors explain in simple, practical terms how to develop a program for the four operations around word problems. Included is a discussion of the various problem types for the four operations, the introduction of symbolism, how children use different number strategies to solve problems, and hints for generating problems. Excellent!

Gutstein, E., & Romberg, T. A. (1995). Teaching children to add and subtract. *Journal of Mathematical Behavior, 14,* 283–324.

A bit more research-oriented than the Carpenter, Carey, and Kouba article and yet very worthwhile reading for a teacher who wants to have a clear understanding of how children develop addition and subtraction concepts. The article explores several research programs that have investigated different strategies for teaching addition and subtraction. It extends beyond operation meaning to the development of computational strategies.

Kouba, V. L., & Franklin, K. (1993). Multiplication and division: Sense making and meaning. In R. J. Jensen (Ed.), *Research ideas for the classroom: Early childhood mathematics* (pp. 103–126). Old Tappan, NJ: Macmillan.

This chapter, which seeks to help teachers understand the intricacies of multiplicative concepts, is complete and readable, providing teachers at the 3–4 level with a good perspective without being too technical.

Other Suggestions

Baroody, A. J., & Standifer, J. D. (1993). Addition and subtraction in the primary grades. In R. J. Jensen (Ed.), *Research ideas for the classroom: Early childhood mathematics* (pp. 72–102). Old Tappan, NJ: Macmillan.

Bell, A., Greer, B., Grimison, L., & Mangan, C. (1989). Children's performance on multiplicative word problems: Elements of a descriptive theory. *Journal for Research in Mathematics Education, 20,* 434–449.

Burk, D., Snider, A., & Symonds, P. (1988). *Box it or bag it mathematics: Teacher's resource guide* [Kindergarten, First–Second]. Salem, OR: Math Learning Center.

Burns, M. (1989). Teaching for understanding: A focus on multiplication. In P. R. Trafton (Ed.), *New directions for elementary school mathematics* (pp. 123–133). Reston, VA: National Council of Teachers of Mathematics.

Burns, M. (1992). *About teaching mathematics: A K–8 resource.* Sausalito, CA: Marilyn Burns Education Associates.

Carey, D. A. (1991). Number sentences: Linking addition and subtraction word problems and symbols. *Journal for Research in Mathematics Education, 22,* 266–280.

Carey, D. A. (1992). Students' use of symbols. *Arithmetic Teacher, 40,* 184–186.

Clark, F. B., & Kamii, C. (1996). Identification of multiplicative thinking in children in grades 1–5. *Journal for Research in Mathematics Education, 27,* 41–51.

Hankes, J. E. (1996). An alternative to basic-skills remediation. *Teaching Children Mathematics, 2,* 452–457.

Huinker, D. M. (1989). Multiplication and division word problems: Improving students' understanding. *Arithmetic Teacher, 37*(2), 8–12.

Kamii, C. (1994). *Young children continue to reinvent arithmetic: 3rd grade.* New York: Teachers College Press.

Katterns, B., & Carr, K. (1986). Talking with young children about multiplication. *Arithmetic Teacher, 33*(8), 18–21.

Mahlios, J. (1988). Word problems: Do I add or subtract? *Arithmetic Teacher, 36*(3), 48–52.

Quintero, A. H. (1985). Conceptual understanding of multiplication: Problems involving combination. *Arithmetic Teacher, 33*(3), 36–39.

Rathmell, E. C., & Huinker, D. M. (1989). Using "part-whole" language to help children represent and solve word problems. In P. R. Trafton (Ed.), *New directions for elementary school mathematics* (pp. 99–110). Reston, VA: National Council of Teachers of Mathematics.

Schwartz, S. L., & Curcio, F. R. (1995). Learning mathematics in meaningful contexts: An action-based approach in the primary grades. In P. A. House (Ed.), *Connecting mathematics across the curriculum* (pp. 116–123). Reston, VA: National Council of Teachers of Mathematics.

Silverman, F. L., Winograd, K., & Strohauer, D. (1992). Student-generated story problems. *Arithmetic Teacher, 39*(8), 6–12.

Sowder, L., Threadgill-Sowder, J., Moyer, M. B., & Moyer, J. C. (1986). Diagnosing a student's understanding of operation. *Arithmetic Teacher, 33*(9), 22–25.

Talton, C. F. (1988). Let's solve the problem before we find the answer. *Arithmetic Teacher, 36*(1), 40–45.

Thompson, C. S., & Hendrickson, A. D. (1986). Verbal addition and subtraction problems: Some difficulties and some solutions. *Arithmetic Teacher, 33*(7), 21–25.

Thompson, C. S., & Van de Walle, J. A. (1984). Modeling subtraction situations. *Arithmetic Teacher, 32*(2), 8–12.

Weiland, L. (1985). Matching instruction to children's thinking about division. *Arithmetic Teacher, 33*(4), 34–35.

CHAPTER

HELPING CHILDREN MASTER
THE BASIC FACTS

Basic facts for addition and multiplication refer to combinations where both addends or both factors are less than 10. Subtraction and division facts correspond to addition and multiplication facts. Thus $15 - 8 = 7$ is a subtraction fact because both parts are less than 10.

Mastery of a basic fact means that a child can give a quick response (in less than 3 seconds) without resorting to non-efficient means, such as counting. Work toward mastery of addition and subtraction facts typically begins in the first grade. Most books include all addition and subtraction facts for mastery in the second grade, although much additional drill is usually required in grade 3 and even after. Multiplication and division facts are generally a target for mastery in the third grade with more practice required in grades 4 and 5. Many children in grade 8 and above do not have a complete command of the basic facts.

The widespread availability of calculators in no way diminishes the importance of basic fact mastery; quite the contrary. With the shift in emphasis from pencil-and-paper computation to mental computation and estimation skills, command of the basic facts is more important than ever. Further, it is true that *all* children are able to master the basic facts—including children with learning disabilities and slow learners. Children simply need to construct efficient mental tools that will help them. This chapter is about helping children develop those tools.

 BIG IDEAS

1. **Number relationships can be used to help remember basic facts.**
2. **For subtraction facts, the concept "think addition" is the most important idea.**
3. **There are patterns and relationships in basic facts. You can figure out new or unknown facts from the ones you already know.**
4. **All the facts can be learned with the help of efficient strategies.**

A THREE-STEP APPROACH TO FACT MASTERY

Every teacher of grades 4 to 10 knows children who are still counting on their fingers, making marks in the margins to count on, or simply guessing at answers. These children have certainly been drilled enough and have been given more than adequate opportunity to practice their facts over their previous years in school. Why haven't they mastered their facts? The simple answer is that they have not developed efficient methods of producing a fact answer. The endless practice they have endured has at best made them very fast counters. Drill of inefficient mental methods does not produce mastery!

Fortunately, we do know quite a bit about helping children develop fact mastery, and it has little to do with quantity of drill or drill techniques. Three components or steps to this end can be identified:

1. Help children develop a strong understanding of the operations and of number relationships.
2. Develop efficient strategies for fact retrieval.
3. Provide practice in the use of and in the selection of the strategies.

The Role of Number and Operation Concepts

Number relationships play a significant role in fact mastery. For example, an efficient mental strategy for 8 + 5 is to think "8 and 2 more is 10. That leaves 3. 10 and 3 is 13." This requires the relationship between 8 and 10 (8 is 2 away from 10), the part-part-whole knowledge of 5 (2 and 3 more makes 5), and the fact that 10 and 3 is 13. For 6 × 7, it is efficient to think "5 times 7 and 7 more." For many children, the efficiency of this approach is lost because they need to count on 7 to get from 35 to 42. With an extension of the number relationships just noted, it is possible to think "35 and 5 more is 40, and 2 more is 42." In addition to the role of 10 and part-part-whole relationships, the relationships of one and two more than, one and two less than, doubles, and visualization of numbers in patterned arrangements to enable thinking of a number as a "single unit" rather than a count all play a significant part in the construction of efficient strategies. Always remember that children construct new ideas integrated with existing ones. When these number relationships are not present, the only existing relationships children have are based in counting.

The meanings of the operations also play a role as children attempt to construct efficient strategies. The ability to relate 6 × 7 to "5 times 7 and 7 more" is clearly based on an understanding of the meanings of the first and second factors. To relate 13 − 7 to "7 and what makes 13" is dependent on a clear understanding of how addition and subtraction are related. The commutative or "turn-around" properties for addition and multiplication are very powerful ideas. The turn-around properties reduce the number of addition and multiplication facts from 100 each to 55 each. Turn-arounds are especially important for the multiplication

facts, where many children do not realize that knowing 3 × 9 means they also know 9 × 3. These are just a few examples of the role that operation sense plays in the mastery of basic facts.

Teachers in the upper grades with students who have not mastered basic facts will do well to first investigate what command of number relationships and operations the students have. Without these relationships and concepts, the strategies discussed throughout this chapter will necessarily be learned in an instrumental manner. The results will not be nearly as effective as they would had these basic ideas been established first.

Development of Efficient Strategies

An efficient strategy is one that can be done mentally and quickly. The emphasis is on *efficient*. Counting is not an efficient strategy. If practice or drill is undertaken when that is the only strategy available to a child, all you are providing is practice in counting.

We have already seen some efficient strategies: the use of building up through 10 in adding 8 + 5 and the use of the related fact 5 × 7 to help with 6 × 7. Consider for a moment how you think about 6 + 6. What about 9 + 5 or 2 + 7? You may think that you just "know" these. What is more likely is that you used some ideas similar to double six (for 6 + 6), 10 and 4 more (for 9 + 5), and your knowledge of the two-more-than relationships (for 2 + 7). Your response may be so automatic by now that you are not reflecting on the use of these relationships or ideas. That is one of the features of efficient mental processes—they become automatic with use.

Many children have learned their facts without being taught efficient strategies. You, for example, were probably not taught strategies for the facts. Research suggests that we develop or learn many of these methods in spite of the drill we may have endured. Relational understanding of numbers and operations permits many individuals to invent their own strategies, probably without conscious thought.

Recognize also that strategies must be meaningful to students. In the pages that follow, you will find a collection of well-researched strategies for mastering the basic facts. What is most important for you to understand is that children must develop their own strategies. You can introduce the ideas presented here; however, there will always be other approaches that children will invent that are equally efficient, or nearly so, for them. The strategies that you and others suggest must be discussed in full-class conversations. "Who has a clever or interesting way to figure out what 6 × 8 is?" The resulting discussion will very likely include the ideas found here, or you may conduct an activity where an efficient idea is likely to be discovered. But if a child tries mindlessly to mimic your strategies, it is very likely that those strategies will not be used effectively.

Drill of Efficient Methods and Strategy Selection

Drill certainly plays a significant role in fact mastery, and the use of old-fashioned methods such as flash cards and fact games can be effective if used wisely.

Avoid Premature Drill

Many activities suggested in this chapter involve drill using simple flash cards. It is critical, however, that you do not introduce or suggest such drill too soon. Suppose that a child does not know the 9 + 5 fact and has no way to deal with it other than to count on his or her fingers or manipulate counters. These are inefficient methods. Practice cannot produce a more efficient strategy because it introduces no new information and encourages no new connections. Practice at that point in the learning process is both a waste of time and a frustration to the child.

The strategies for some facts may not seem completely efficient at first glance. However, if practice is delayed until a strategy has been rather firmly developed, the practice will be *of that strategy* and will not be aimed at rote memory. The repetitious use of the strategy makes its use much quicker. Once again, it is not necessary that the strategies be your strategies, only that they be efficient and meaningful and useful to the child.

The confidence engendered in giving an accurate response allows the strategy itself to fall into the background as the fact response becomes more automatic. Fact responses learned via strategies do become quick and automatic with practice.

Practice Strategy Selection or Strategy Retrieval

Many teachers who have tried teaching fact strategies report that the method works well while the children are focused on whatever strategy they are working on. That is, they acknowledge that children can learn and use strategies. But, they continue, when the facts are all mixed up or the child is not in "fact practice" mode, the strategies tend to go out the window and the old counting habits return. The use of a strategy for basic facts is much like using a problem-solving strategy. We not only need to know how to use the strategy but also how to select the appropriate strategy when it is needed. This selection of a strategy or retrieval of the strategy from our personal repertoire is as important a part of fact strategy instruction as the strategies themselves.

For example, suppose that your children have been practicing the near-doubles facts for addition, those that have addends that are one apart such as 4 + 5 or 8 + 7. The strategy is to derive the unknown 8 + 7 fact from the better-known double, 7 + 7. Children become quite skilled at doubling the smaller addend and adding 1. All of the facts they are practicing are selected to fit this model. On other days, they have learned and practiced strategies for facts like 9 + 4

(make-10 facts) and probably others. Later, on a worksheet or in a mental math exercise, the children are presented with a mixture of facts. In a single exercise, a child might see

```
  7        4        2        8
+ 6      + 9      + 6      + 5
```

There is no mind-set or reminder to use different processes for each. Especially if the children have previously been habituated to counting to get answers, they will very likely revert to counting and ignore the efficient methods they recently practiced. Note that in practicing the strategy, there is no need to decide what strategy may be useful. All of the facts during the near-doubles practice were near doubles, and the strategy worked. Later, however, there is no one to suggest the strategy.

Strategy selection or *strategy retrieval* is the process of deciding what strategy is appropriate for a particular fact. If you don't think to use a strategy, you probably won't. A simple activity that is useful is to prepare a list of facts selected from two or more strategies and then, one fact at a time, ask children to name a strategy that would work for that fact. Once again, the strategies a particular child uses may not be the same as those you emphasized in class. Regardless, children still need to develop the habit of using the relationships they have constructed and not fall back on inefficient methods. Further, they should explain why they picked the strategy and demonstrate its use. This type of activity turns the attention to the features of a fact that lend it to this or that strategy. The children are reflecting first on matching strategies with facts and secondarily on use of the strategy.

Overview of the Approach

The use of strategies is not at all a new idea. Brownell and Chazal (1935) recognized that children use different thought processes with different facts. Since the mid-1970s, there has been a strong interest among mathematics educators in the idea of directly teaching strategies to children (e.g., Baroody, 1985; Bley & Thornton, 1995; Fuson, 1984, 1992; Rathmell, 1978; Steinberg, 1985; Thornton & Noxon, 1977; Thornton & Toohey, 1984;). Many of the ideas that appear in this chapter have been adapted from the work of these researchers.

Regardless of the strategy or the operation, the general approach is roughly the same as outlined here. Most of the remainder of the chapter is devoted to explaining the strategies.

Introduce a Strategy

Initial work with a strategy begins with open discussions. "How would you get the answer to 6 + 9? What other facts would you do the same way? Who knows a fact that you would think about differently?" The idea is to get ideas out in the open and let students develop the general idea that there are ways of thinking about facts.

Models or drawings can be suggested when appropriate. For example, with the 9 + 5 fact, you might ask if anyone can think how the ten-frame might be helpful. Children can use materials at their desks to help construct the new idea and to help talk about how it works. Discussions about the strategies are key in helping every child find strategies that work for him or her. Student explanations require children to reflect on the process and thereby make it their own. Note that the use of materials is to develop the strategy. They are not there as answer-getting devices.

At times, a strategy requires the use of concepts or ideas developed earlier. You need to check to see if your students have these ideas. These prerequisites may be special number relationships, such as the notion that 10 and 3 is 13. Prerequisites may include mastery of a set of facts to which the new set of facts is to be related. One can hardly use the strategy of "double and one more" for 6 + 7 if double 6 is not a known fact. These prerequisites will be pointed out as each strategy is discussed.

Practice the Strategy

When you are comfortable that children are able to use a strategy without recourse to physical models and that they are beginning to use it mentally, it is time to practice it. It is a good idea to have as many as ten different activities for each strategy or group of facts. File folder or boxed activities can be used by children individually, in pairs, or even in small groups. With a large number of activities, children can work on the facts that they need the most.

Flash cards are among the most useful approaches to fact strategy practice. For each strategy, make several sets of flash cards using all of the facts that fit that strategy. On the cards, label the strategy or use drawings or cues to remind the children of the strategy. Examples appear throughout the chapter.

Other activities involve the use of special dice made from wooden cubes, teacher-made spinners, matching activities where a helping fact or a relationship is matched with the new fact being learned, and games of all sorts. Almost any existing game involving fact drill can be modified to drill only one strategy or one collection of facts. A child or group of children may even want to make their own flash cards or drill games to match their own newly invented ideas.

Add New Strategies

As children move into the practice phase with one strategy, the prerequisites and strategy for a new group of facts can be introduced and developed. With each new strategy, more activities and flash cards are prepared, and children work on those strategies for which they need the most help.

Individualize

If you have been successful in creating a mathematical community in which problem-solving discourse takes place regularly, it is not unlikely that children will band together in groups to help each other with fact mastery. Either with or without student input, create small study groups of two to four students where each child has similar needs or is working on similar facts. Let them discuss and practice the strategies for a specific cluster of facts together. Beyond the middle of the second grade, it is extremely unlikely that all students in your class will have the same needs or will approach facts the same way. Plan small periods of time for children to work together. These periods should be interspersed with your ongoing curriculum. Do not make fact mastery a burden that prevents you from moving forward.

Practice Strategy Selection

After children have worked on two or three strategies, strategy selection drills are very important. These can be conducted quickly with the full class or a group, or independent games and activities can be prepared. Examples are described toward the end of the chapter.

STRATEGIES FOR ADDITION FACTS

The strategies for addition facts are directly related to one or more number relationships. In Chapter 6, numerous activities were suggested to develop these relationships. When the class is working on addition facts, the number relationship activities can and should be included with those described here. The teaching task is to help children connect these number relationships to the basic facts.

One-More-Than and Two-More-Than Facts

Each of the 36 facts highlighted in the chart has at least one addend of 1 or 2. These facts are a direct application of the one-more-than and two-more-than relationships.

+	0	1	2	3	4	5	6	7	8	9
0		1	2							
1	1	2	3	4	5	6	7	8	9	10
2	2	3	4	5	6	7	8	9	10	11
3		4	5							
4		5	6							
5		6	7							
6		7	8							
7		8	9							
8		9	10							
9		10	11							

─── ACTIVITY ───

8.1 One More/Two More Is +1/+2

Ask, "What is one more than seven?" As soon as you get a response, ask, "What is one plus seven?" or hold up a 1 + 7 flash card. Be sure to connect the one-more-than-seven relationship to both 1 + 7 and 7 + 1.

─── ACTIVITY ───

8.2 One-/Two-More-Than Dice

Make a die labeled +1, +2, +1, +2, "one more," and "two more." Use with another die labeled 4, 5, 6, 7, 8, and 9. After each roll of the dice, children should say the complete fact: "Four and two is six."

─── ACTIVITY ───

8.3 One-/Two-More-Than Match

In a matching activity, children can begin with a number, match that with the one that is two more, and then connect that with the corresponding basic fact.

─── ACTIVITY ───

8.4 Lotto for +1/+2

A lotto-type board can be made on a file folder. Small fact cards can be matched to the numbers on the board. The back of each fact card can have a small answer number to use as a check.

Figure 8.1 illustrates some of these activities and shows several possibilities for flash cards. Notice as you read through the chapter that activities such as the dice or spinner games and the lotto-type activity can be modified for almost all of the strategies in the chapter. These are not repeated for each strategy. Examples of flash cards are included for every strategy.

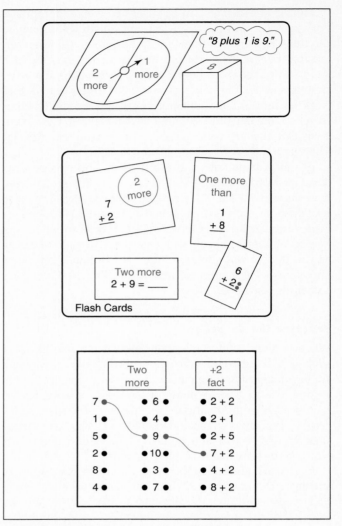

●**FIGURE 8.1** One-more and two-more facts.

Facts with Zero

Nineteen facts have zero as one of the addends. Though such problems are generally easy, some children overgeneralize the idea that answers to addition are bigger. Flash card and dice games should stress the concept of zero (see Figure 8.2).

+	0	1	2	3	4	5	6	7	8	9
0	0	1	2	3	4	5	6	7	8	9
1	1									
2	2									
3	3									
4	4									
5	5									
6	6									
7	7									
8	8									
9	9									

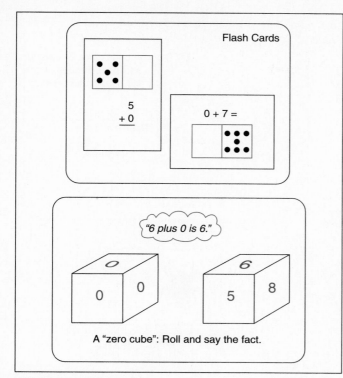

• **FIGURE 8.2**   Facts with zero.

8.6 Double Images

Make picture cards for each of the doubles, and include the basic fact on the card as shown in Figure 8.3 (p. 146).

 ## 8.7 Calculator Doubles

Use the calculator and enter the "double maker" (2 ⊠ ⊜). Let one child say, for example, "Seven plus seven." The child with the calculator should press 7, try to give the double (14), and then press ⊜ to see the correct double on the display. (Note that the calculator is also a good way to practice +1 and +2 facts.)

8.5 What's Alike? Zero Facts

Write about ten zero facts on the board, some with the zero first and some with the zero second. Discuss how all of these facts are alike. Have children use counters and a part-part-whole mat to model the facts at their seats.

Doubles

There are only ten doubles facts from 0 + 0 to 9 + 9, as shown here. These ten facts are relatively easy to learn and become a powerful way to learn the near doubles (addends one apart). Some children use them as anchors for other facts as well.

+	0	1	2	3	4	5	6	7	8	9
0	0									
1		2								
2			4							
3				6						
4					8					
5						10				
6							12			
7								14		
8									16	
9										18

Near Doubles

+	0	1	2	3	4	5	6	7	8	9
0		1								
1	1		3							
2		3		5						
3			5		7					
4				7		9				
5					9		11			
6						11		13		
7							13		15	
8								15		17
9									17	

These facts are also called the "doubles plus one" facts and include all combinations where one addend is one more than the other. The strategy is to double the smaller number and add 1. Be sure students know the doubles before you start this strategy (see Figure 8.4, p. 146).

After discussing the strategy with the class, write 10 or 15 near-doubles facts on the board. Use vertical and horizontal formats, and vary which addend is the smaller. Quickly go through the facts. First have students only identify which number to double. The next time through, have students name the double that will be used. The third time, have students say the double and then the near double.

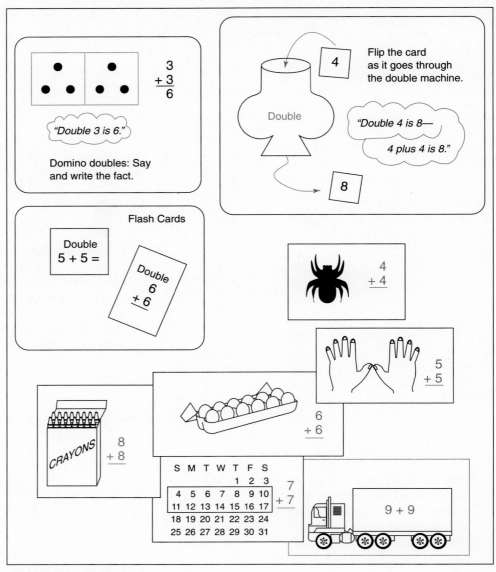

●**FIGURE 8.3** Doubles facts.

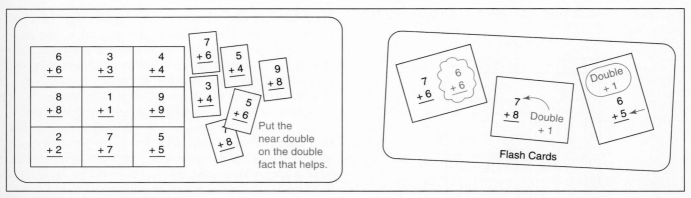

●**FIGURE 8.4** Near-doubles facts.

ACTIVITY

8.8 Match with a Double

Use two sets of doubles cards and a complete set of near-doubles cards. Mix both sets and have students match them up, giving the answer for both facts.

ACTIVITY

8.9 Double Dice + 1

Roll a single die with numerals or dot sets and say the complete double-plus-one fact. That is, for seven, students should say, "Seven plus eight is 15."

Make-10 Facts

+	0	1	2	3	4	5	6	7	8	9
0										
1										10
2									10	11
3									11	12
4									12	13
5									13	14
6									14	15
7									15	16
8			10	11	12	13	14	15	16	17
9		10	11	12	13	14	15	16	17	18

These facts all have at least one addend of 8 or 9. The strategy is to build onto the 8 or 9 up to 10 and then add on the rest. For 6 + 8, start with 8, then 2 more makes 10, and that leaves 4 more for 14.

Before using this strategy, be sure that children have learned to think of the numbers 11 to 18 as 10 and some more. Many second- and third-grade children have not constructed this relationship. (Refer to "Relationships for Numbers 10 to 20" in Chapter 6.)

ACTIVITY

8.10 Make 10 on the Ten-Frame

Give students a mat with two ten-frames (see Figure 8.5). Flash cards are placed next to the ten-frames, or a fact can be given orally. The students should first model each number in the two ten-frames and then decide on the easiest way to show

(without counting) what the total is. The obvious (but not the only) choice is to move counters into the frame showing either 8 or 9. Get students to explain what they did. Focus especially on the idea that 1 (or 2) can be taken from the other number and put with the 9 (or 8) to make 10. Then you have 10 and whatever is left.

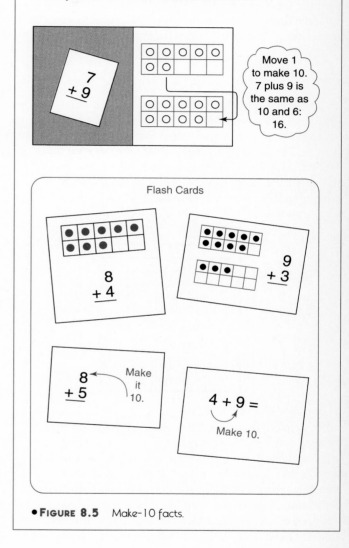

●**FIGURE 8.5** Make-10 facts.

Provide a lot of time with the make-10 activity. Encourage discussion and exploration of "easy ways" to think about adding two numbers when one of them is 8 or 9. Perhaps discuss why this is not a useful idea for a fact such as 6 + 5 where neither number is near 10. Note that children will have many other ways of using 10 to add with 8 or 9. For example, with the fact 9 + 5, some will add 10 + 5 and subtract 1. This is a perfectly good strategy, and it uses 10. You may want to give efficient strategies unique names determined by the children and discuss which ones seem especially useful.

When children seem to have the make-10 idea, try the same activity without counters. Use the little ten-frame cards found in the Blackline Masters. Make a transparency set for the overhead. Show an 8 (or 9) card on the overhead. Place other cards beneath it one at a time. Suggest *mentally* "moving" two dots into the 8 ten-frame. Have students say orally what they are doing. For 8 + 4, they might say, "Take 2 from the 4 and put it with 8 to make 10. Then 10 and 2 left over is 12." The activity can be done independently with the little ten-frame cards.

Make flash cards with either one or two ten-frames, with reminders to "make 10" out of the 8 or the 9.

Other Strategies and the Last Six Facts

To appreciate the power of strategies for fact learning, consider the following. We have discussed only five ideas or strategies (one or two more than, zeros, doubles, near doubles, and make-10), yet these ideas have covered 88 of the 100 addition facts! Further, these ideas are not really new but rather the application of important relationships. The 12 remaining facts are really only six facts, and their respective turn-arounds as shown on the chart.

+	0	1	2	3	4	5	6	7	8	9
0										
1										
2										
3						8	9	10		
4							10	11		
5				8				12		
6				9	10					
7				10	11	12				
8										
9										

To help children with these and perhaps other facts, a variety of additional ideas might be employed. These ideas as well as those already discussed should be considered as a flexible set of possible tools for children's thought processes. Strategies should never be seen as "rules" or required procedures that children must follow. You will undoubtedly find children who use relationships and ideas not discussed here. That is fine! In fact, as your children come up with novel approaches, share these with the class. It is difficult to predict what is best or what will work because different children bring different relationships to the task.

Doubles plus Two or Two-Apart Facts

Of the six remaining facts, three have addends that differ by 2: 3 + 5, 4 + 6, and 5 + 7. There are two possible relationships that might be useful here, each depending on knowledge of doubles. Some children find it easy to extend the idea of the near doubles to double plus 2. For example, 4 + 6 is double 4 and 2 more. A different idea is to take 1 from the larger addend and give it to the smaller. Using this idea, the 5 + 3 fact is transformed into the double 4 fact—*double the number in between.*

Make-10 Extended

Three of the six facts have 7 as one of the addends. The make-10 strategy is frequently extended to these facts as well. For 7 + 4, the idea is *7 and 3 more makes 10 and 1 left is 11.* You may decide to introduce this idea at the same time that you initially introduce the make-10 strategy. It is interesting to note that Japan, mainland China, Korea, and Taiwan all teach an addition strategy of building through 10 and do so in the first grade. The ideas may be easier in these countries because of the languages. The numbers beyond 10 are all named in a regular manner, putting 10 first. Twelve is "ten-two," and 15 is "ten-five." Many U.S. second graders do not know what 10 plus any number is (Fuson, 1992).

Counting On

Counting on is the most widely promoted of the strategies not included here. It is generally taught as a strategy for all facts that have 1, 2, or 3 as one of the addends and thus includes the one- and two-more-than facts. For the fact 3 + 8, the child starts with 8 and counts three counts: *9, 10, 11.* There are several reasons this approach is downplayed in this text. First, it is frequently applied to facts where it is not efficient, such as 8 + 5. It is difficult to explain to young children that they should count for some facts but not others. Second, it is much more procedural than conceptual. Finally, if other strategies are used, it is not necessary.

Ten-Frame Facts

If you have been keeping track, all of the remaining six facts have been covered by the discussion so far, with a few being touched by two different thought patterns. The ten-frame model is so valuable in seeing certain number relationships that these ideas cannot be passed by in thinking about facts. The ten-frame helps children learn the combinations that make 10. Ten-frames immediately model all of the facts from 5 + 1 to 5 + 5 and the respective turn-arounds. Even 5 + 6, 5 + 7, and 5 + 8 are quickly seen as two fives and some more when depicted with these powerful models (see Figure 8.6).

A good idea might be to group the facts shown in the chart here and practice them using one or two ten-frames as a cue to the thought process.

+	0	1	2	3	4	5	6	7	8	9
0						5				
1						6				10
2						7			10	
3						8		10		
4						9	10			
5	5	6	7	8	9	10	11	12	13	14
6					10	11				
7				10		12				
8			10			13				
9		10				14				

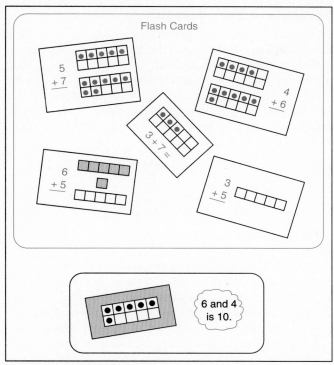

Flash Cards

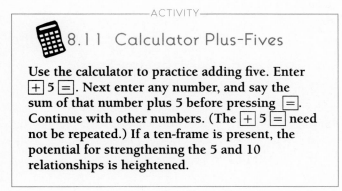

6 and 4
is 10.

● **FIGURE 8.6**   Ten-frame facts.

The next two activities are suggestive of the type of relationships that can be developed.

────── ACTIVITY ──────

8.11 Calculator Plus-Fives

Use the calculator to practice adding five. Enter ⊞ 5 ⊟. Next enter any number, and say the sum of that number plus 5 before pressing ⊟. Continue with other numbers. (The ⊞ 5 ⊟ need not be repeated.) If a ten-frame is present, the potential for strengthening the 5 and 10 relationships is heightened.

────── ACTIVITY ──────

8.12 Say the Ten Fact

Hold up a ten-frame card and have children say the "ten fact." For a card with 7 dots, the response is "seven and three is ten." Later, with a blank ten-frame drawn on the board, say a number less than 10. Children start with that number and complete the "ten fact." If you say, "four," they say, "four plus six is ten." Use the same activities in independent or small group modes.

STRATEGIES FOR SUBTRACTION FACTS

Subtraction facts prove to be more difficult than addition. This is especially true when children have been taught subtraction through a count-count-count approach; for 13 − 5, *count* 13, *count* off 5, *count* what's left. There is little evidence to suggest that anyone who has mastered subtraction facts has used this approach in helping to learn the facts. Unfortunately, many sixth, seventh, and eighth graders are still counting.

Subtraction as Think-Addition

In Figure 8.7, subtraction is shown modeled in such a way that students are encouraged to think, "What goes with this part to make the total?" When done in this *think-addition* manner, the child uses known addition facts to produce the unknown quantity or part. (You might want to revisit missing-part activities in Chapter 6 and part-part-whole subtraction concepts in Chapter 7.) If this important relationship between parts and wholes—between addition and subtraction—can be made, subtraction facts can be much easier. When children see 9 − 4, you want them to think spontaneously, "Four and *what* makes nine?" By contrast, observe a third-grade child who struggles with this fact. The idea of thinking addition never occurs. Instead, the child will begin to count either back from 9 or up from 4. The value of think-addition cannot be overstated.

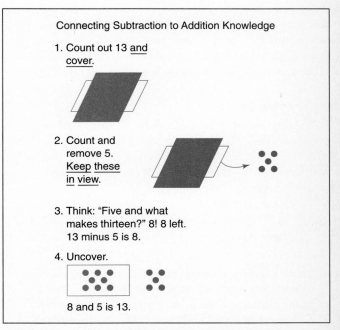

Connecting Subtraction to Addition Knowledge

1. Count out 13 <u>and</u> <u>cover.</u>

2. Count and remove 5. <u>Keep these</u> <u>in view.</u>

3. Think: "Five and what makes thirteen?" 8! 8 left. 13 minus 5 is 8.

4. Uncover.

8 and 5 is 13.

● **FIGURE 8.7**   Using a think-addition model for subtraction.

Subtraction Facts with Sums to 10

Think-addition is most immediately applicable to subtraction facts with sums of 10 or less. These are generally introduced with a goal of mastery in the first grade. Sixty-four of the 100 subtraction facts fall into this category. If think-addition is to be used effectively, it is essential that addition facts be mastered first. Evidence suggests that children learn very few, if any, subtraction facts without first mastering the corresponding addition facts. In other words, mastery of 3 + 5 can be thought of as prerequisite knowledge for learning the facts 8 − 3 and 8 − 5. Rather than lump all of these 64 facts together in one rather formidable bundle, a good idea is to group them in the same way that the corresponding addition facts were grouped.

Facts with Zero

This set of facts includes those involving minus zero and those with a difference of zero (e.g., 7 − 0, 7 − 7). Using the think-addition approach, model these facts on the overhead. You may be surprised to find some children confused by them, especially those involving subtracting zero.

One-Less-Than and Two-Less-Than Facts

This group includes all facts with differences of 1 or 2 as well as those that involve −1 or −2 (e.g., 8 − 7, 8 − 6, 8 − 1, 8 − 2). The relationships of more than and less than must be connected.

Review the one- and two-less-than relationships using any of the ideas in Chapter 6. With these relationships in students' minds, model facts in this group on the overhead projector using the think-addition approach. Frequently follow one fact with its partner. That is, follow 9 − 2 with 9 − 7, and discuss how the two facts are alike. Then write the 7 + 2 = 9 fact. Help children see how the two-more-than and two-less-than relationships are involved in both facts. Use the calculator to practice "minus two" and "minus one" facts. Press ⊟ 2 ⊟ to make a "minus two" machine. Make flash cards for all 36 facts in this group. Use the words *one less* or *two less* on all cards.

Ten-Frame Facts

This group includes all facts with the first number of 10, those involving −5, and those with a difference of 5. Therefore, 10 − 7, 8 − 5, and 8 − 3 are all in this group. Make flash cards for all three types of facts in this group. Use all the cards together.

─────── ACTIVITY ───────

8.13 Plus and Minus 10 Facts

Show a ten-frame card, and have students say a subtraction fact and then an addition fact. For a frame showing 6 dots, students would say, "Ten minus six is four," and then, "Six and four is ten."

Doubles and Near Doubles

This group of facts corresponds to the addition facts of the same name. It is useful to mix doubles and near doubles.

Review the addition doubles and near doubles. Then model the double and near-double subtraction facts on the overhead projector, using the think-addition approach. For each subtraction fact, ask if it was a double or a near double, and have children say both facts. ("Near double! Nine minus four is five. Four plus five is nine.")

─────── ACTIVITY ───────

8.14 Double and Near-Double Search

Write a large number of subtraction facts on a page. Make roughly a third of them doubles, a third near doubles, and the other third other facts. Feel free to repeat facts several times. Have students circle with a crayon all of the doubles facts and then answer them. Next have them circle the facts that are near doubles with a different crayon and answer them. The remaining facts can be left blank. Next to each subtraction fact, have them write the addition double or near double that goes with it.

The 36 "Hard" Subtraction Facts: Sums Greater than 10

Before reading further, look at the three subtraction facts shown here, and try to reflect on what thought process you use to get the answers. Even if you "just know them," think about what a likely process might be.

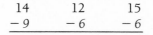

$$\begin{array}{ccc} 14 & 12 & 15 \\ -\,9 & -\,6 & -\,6 \end{array}$$

Many people will use a different strategy for each of these facts. For 14 − 9, it is easy to start with 9 and work up through 10: *9 and 1 more is 10, and 4 more makes 5.* For the 12 − 6 fact, it is quite common to hear "double 6," a think-addition approach. For the last fact, 15 − 6, 10 is used again but probably by working backward from 15—a takeaway process: *Take away 5 to get 10, and 1 more leaves 9.* We could call these three approaches, respectively, build up through 10, think-addition, and back down through 10. Each of the remaining 36 facts with sums of 11 or more can be learned using one or more of these strategies. Figure 8.8 shows how these facts, in three overlapping groups, correspond to these three strategies. Keep in mind that these are not required strategies. Some children may use a think-

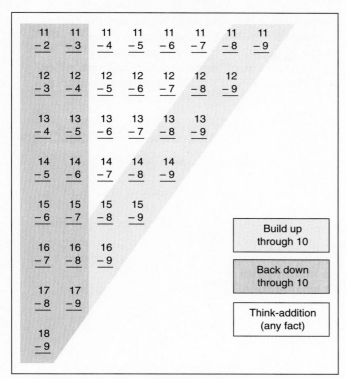

11 −2	11 −3	11 −4	11 −5	11 −6	11 −7	11 −8	11 −9
12 −3	12 −4	12 −5	12 −6	12 −7	12 −8	12 −9	
13 −4	13 −5	13 −6	13 −7	13 −8	13 −9		
14 −5	14 −6	14 −7	14 −8	14 −9			
15 −6	15 −7	15 −8	15 −9				
16 −7	16 −8	16 −9					
17 −8	17 −9						
18 −9							

Build up through 10

Back down through 10

Think-addition (any fact)

● **Figure 8.8** *The 36 "hard" subtraction facts.*

addition method for all. Others may have a completely different strategy for some or all of these. The three approaches suggested here are based on ideas already developed: the relationship between addition and subtraction and the power of 10 as a reference point.

Build Up Through 10

This group includes all facts where the part or subtracted number is either 8 or 9. Examples are 13 − 9 and 15 − 8.

— ACTIVITY —

8.15 Build Up Through the Ten-Frame

On the board or overhead, draw a ten-frame with 9 dots. Discuss how you can build numbers between 11 and 18, starting with 9 in the ten-frame. Stress the idea of *one more to get to 10* and then the rest of the number. Repeat for a ten-frame showing 8. Next, with either the 8 or 9 ten-frame in view, call out numbers from 11 to 18 and have students explain how they can figure out the difference between that number and the one on the ten-frame. Later, use the same approach, but show fact cards to connect this idea with the symbolic subtraction fact (see Figure 8.9).

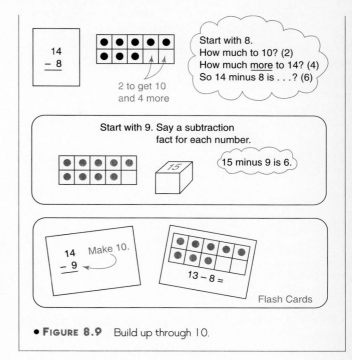

Start with 8.
How much to 10? (2)
How much <u>more</u> to 14? (4)
So 14 minus 8 is . . .? (6)

2 to get 10 and 4 more

Start with 9. Say a subtraction fact for each number.

15 minus 9 is 6.

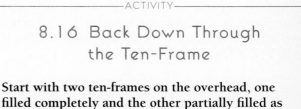

Make 10.

Flash Cards

● **Figure 8.9** Build up through 10.

Back Down Through 10

Here is one strategy that is really take-away and not think-addition. It is useful for all facts that have a difference of 8 or 9, such as 15 − 6 or 13 − 5. For example, with 15 − 6, you start with the total of 15 and take off 5. That gets you down to 10. Then take off 1 more to get 9. For 14 − 6, just take off 4 and then take off 2 more to get 8. Here we are working backward with 10 as a "bridge."

— ACTIVITY —

8.16 Back Down Through the Ten-Frame

Start with two ten-frames on the overhead, one filled completely and the other partially filled as in Figure 8.10 (p. 152). For 13, for example, discuss what is the easiest way to think about taking off 4 counters or 5 counters. Repeat with other numbers between 11 and 18. Have students write or say the corresponding fact.

Extend Think-Addition

Think-addition remains one of the most powerful ways to think about subtraction facts. When the think-addition concept of subtraction is well developed, many children will use that approach for all subtraction facts. (Notice that

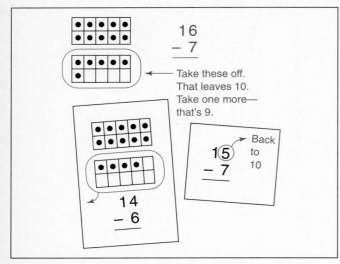

● **FIGURE 8.10**   Back down through 10.

virtually everyone uses a think-multiplication approach for division. Why?)

It does not seem particularly useful to separate the 36 "hard facts" according to the corresponding addition strategies. What may be more important is to listen to children's thinking as they attempt to answer subtraction facts that they have not yet mastered. If they are not using one of the three ideas suggested here, it is a good bet that they are counting—an inefficient method. Work hard at the think-addition concept. Show a fact such as $12 - 5$ and say, "Five and what makes twelve?" Continue using this phrase until it becomes a habit for the child as well. Also return to missing-part activities as found in Chapter 6. Use wholes greater than 10, and have the students write both an addition and subtraction fact for each.

The activities that follow are all of the think-addition variety. There is, of course, no reason why these activities could not be used for all of the subtraction facts. They need not be limited to the "hard facts."

together in the same way. Sometimes the circled number is missing (the sum), and sometimes one of the other numbers is missing (a part). The cards can be made both vertically and horizontally with the sum appearing in different positions. The object is to name the missing number.

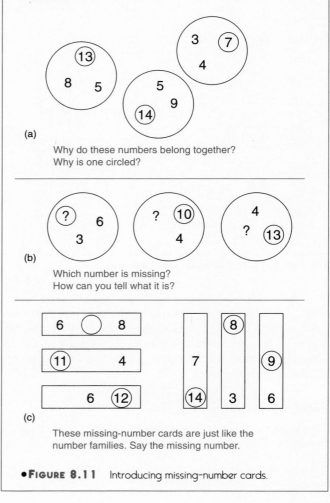

(a)
Why do these numbers belong together?
Why is one circled?

(b)
Which number is missing?
How can you tell what it is?

(c)
These missing-number cards are just like the number families. Say the missing number.

●**FIGURE 8.11**   Introducing missing-number cards.

— ACTIVITY —

8.17 Missing-Number Cards

Show children, without explanation, families of numbers with the sum circled as in Figure 8.11(a). Ask why they think the numbers go together and why one number is circled. When this number family idea is fairly well understood, show some families with one number replaced by a question mark, as in Figure 8.11(b), and ask what number is missing. When students understand this activity, explain that you have made some missing-number cards based on this idea. Each card has two of three numbers that go

— ACTIVITY —

8.18 Missing-Number Worksheets

Make copies of the blank form found in the Blackline Masters to make a wide variety of drill exercises. In a row of 13 "cards," put all of the combinations from two families with different numbers missing, some parts and some wholes. Put blanks in different positions. An example is shown in Figure 8.12. After filling in numbers, run the sheet off, and have students fill in the missing numbers. Another idea is to group facts from one strategy or number relation or perhaps mix facts from two strategies on one page. Actual flash cards can be made this way and put in packets for individual practice. Have students write an addition fact and a subtraction fact to go with each missing-number card. This is an important step because many children are able to give the missing part in a family but do not connect this knowledge with subtraction.

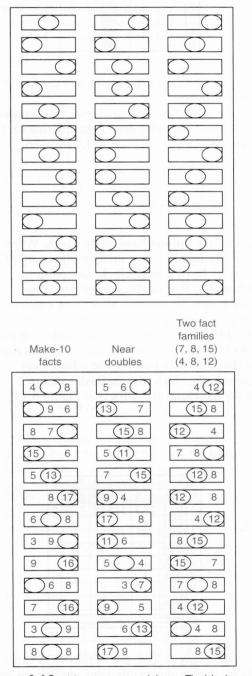

Make-10 facts	Near doubles	Two fact families (7, 8, 15) (4, 8, 12)

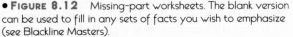

● **FIGURE 8.12** Missing-part worksheets. The blank version can be used to fill in any sets of facts you wish to emphasize (see Blackline Masters).

---ACTIVITY---

8.19 Find a Plus Fact to Help

Select a group of subtraction facts that you wish to practice. Divide a sheet of paper into small cards, about 10 or 12 to a sheet. For each subtraction fact, write the corresponding addition fact on one of the cards. Two subtraction facts can be related to each addition fact. Duplicate the sheet, and have students cut the cards apart. Now write one of the subtraction facts on the board. Rather than call out answers, students find the addition fact that helps with the subtraction fact. On your signal, each student holds up the appropriate fact. For 12 − 4 or 12 − 8, the students would select 4 + 8. The same idea of matching a subtraction fact with a helping addition fact can be made into a matching card game or a matching worksheet and can easily be a small group practice activity.

STRATEGIES FOR MULTIPLICATION FACTS

Multiplication facts can also be mastered by relating new facts to existing knowledge. For example, the facts with a factor of 2 are related to the addition doubles. The fact 4 × 7 can be found from double 7 and then double again. Although models are sometimes used, they are there for constructing relationships, not for getting answers. Counting the elements in six rows of eight will seldom help a child master the 6 × 8 fact.

Since the first and second factors in multiplication stand for different things (7 × 3 is 7 threes and 3 × 7 is 3 sevens), it is imperative that students completely understand the commutative property (go back and review Figure 7.13, p. 134). For example, 2 × 8 is related to the addition fact double 8. But the same relationship also applies to 8 × 2. Most of the fact strategies are more obvious with the factors in one order than in the other, but turn-around facts should always be learned together.

Of the five groups or strategies discussed next, the first four strategies are generally easier and cover 75 of the 100 multiplication facts. You are continually reminded that these strategies are suggestions, not rules, and that the most general approach with children is to have them discuss ways that *they* can use to think of facts easily.

ods that research and experience have proved to be effective. After all the details in this chapter, it may be useful to look again at the fundamentals of a successful approach to helping our students.

Three Steps to Success

We began this chapter with a three-step approach to fact mastery. The first step was to develop a strong understanding of the operations and of number relationships. At this point, you can appreciate even more the value of number concepts and operation meanings in mastering facts. It is never too late to develop some of the really valuable relationships of number and operation sense as described in Chapters 6 and 7, even if you are teaching in the middle grades.

The second step was to develop efficient strategies for fact retrieval. Remember to check to see if the required prerequisite concepts or ideas that a strategy may depend on are actually present. Developing a strategy involves discussion of the strategy and why it works especially for that particular set of facts. Never force a strategy on children, but encourage them, through discussions in class, to find efficient methods themselves. Listen to their ideas and respect them. If a child suggests an approach that seems terribly inefficient to you, respect the idea anyway. As other ideas come from the students and as more efficient strategies are discussed, less effective methods will soon disappear. As you have seen, models and discussions are not a means of getting answers but devices to promote reflective thinking about the strategies.

The third step was to practice the strategy and to practice selection of the strategy. There are two important points to be made here:

1. Do not begin a lot of practice before the strategy seems well developed. That is, practice *efficient strategies,* not inefficient counting.

2. It is absolutely necessary to practice selection or retrieval of appropriate strategies.

The following activities are aimed at strategy selection and can be used with strategies for any operation. These activities should begin soon after you have two or more strategies in place.

---ACTIVITY---

8.24 Circle the Strategy

On a worksheet, have students circle the facts that belong to a strategy they have been working on and then answer only those facts. The same approach can be used for two or even three strategies on one sheet.

---ACTIVITY---

8.25 Sort Them as You Do Them

Mix ordinary flash cards from two or more strategies into a single packet. Prepare simple little pictures or labels for the strategies that are in the packet. For each card, students decide which of the labeled strategies they will use for that fact, place it in the appropriate pile, and then answer the fact.

---ACTIVITY---

8.26 Name It, Then Use It

Orally give facts to the class or group, and have them first select, name, or describe a strategy they will use to answer each fact.

Strategy sorting is a crucial part of your fact strategy program. Children will generally use a strategy consistently when they know that all facts belong to one approach. When taken out of this mind-set, as in a mixed-drill exercise, they forget to use the strategies and revert to inefficient counting.

What About Timed Tests?

Teachers who use timed tests believe that the tests help children learn basic facts. This perspective makes no instructional sense. Children who perform well under time pressure display their skills. Children who have difficulty with skills or who work more slowly run the risk of reinforcing wrong practices under pressure. Also, they can become fearful about, and negative toward, their mathematics learning. (Burns, 1995a, p. 408)

Reflection on this quotation should give us pause whenever we are tempted to give a timed test. Reasoning and pattern searching are never facilitated by restricting time. Some children simply cannot work well under pressure or in situations that evoke stress.

Speed tests have been most popular for tests of basic facts. Although speed may encourage children to memorize facts, it is effective only for students who are goal-oriented and who can perform in pressure situations. Speed in a testing situation is debilitating for many and provides you, the teacher, with no positive benefits. Very short speed drills (say, one row of eight facts), if presented in a lighthearted manner, may be useful. Drills of this nature should not, however, be used as assessments and certainly not for grading purposes. A short, five-fact drill with a soft emphasis on quickness can encourage efficient strategies and provide feedback. But the results should be for the individual child, not your grade book.

In every instance, timed tests reward few and punish many. They can have a lasting negative impact on student attitudes. They should be avoided whenever possible.

Facts No Barrier to Good Mathematics

There is no doubt that a student who has total command of all basic facts will be able to reason more quickly and more flexibly in situations involving any element of computation, especially mental computation and estimation. But such a child does not necessarily reason *better* than a child who, for whatever reason, has not yet mastered the facts. In the outdated curriculum of arithmetic, one in which computation with pencil and paper was the principal goal, basic facts were essential to success. But today, mathematics is not about computation, especially pencil-and-paper computation. Mathematics is about reasoning and patterns and making sense of things. Mathematics is problem solving. There is no reason that a child who has not yet mastered all basic facts should be excluded from real mathematical experiences.

The most obvious alternative is the calculator. It should be on the desk every day for all students. There is absolutely no evidence that the presence of a calculator will impede basic fact mastery. To the contrary, the more students use the calculator, the more proficient they will be with it. This will make many of the calculator fact drills more effective and provide students with a ready access to electronic flash cards. In a classroom climate where most students do know their facts and where students help one another and share thinking strategies as has been suggested, very few students will rely on the calculator for any prolonged period.

Students who are relegated to drill of facts when the rest of the class is engaged in meaningful experiences will soon feel stupid and incapable of doing "real" mathematics. The drill will be disconnected from meaningful experiences so that mathematics will be seen as meaningless also. By contrast, when students who have not mastered facts are engaged in exciting and meaningful experiences, they have real motivation to learn facts and real opportunities to develop relationships that can aid in that endeavor. Do not allow students who are behind in fact mastery to fall behind in mathematics.

FACT REMEDIATION WITH UPPER-GRADE STUDENTS

Children who have not mastered their basic facts by the sixth or seventh grade are in need of something other than more practice. They have certainly seen and practiced those facts countless times over the past several school years. They need a new approach. The following key ideas can guide your efforts to help these older students.

1. *Recognize that more drill will not work.* This is a very difficult concept to get across to upper-grade teachers. Students have not mastered facts because of a failure to develop or to connect important concepts and relationships such as those that have been discussed in this chapter. They are not suffering from a lack of practice. More practice will at best provide temporary results and at worst will cause negative attitudes about learning mathematics.

2. *Inventory the known and unknown facts for each student in need.* Find out from each student what facts are known fairly quickly and comfortably and which are not. Middle grade students can do this diagnosis for you. Provide sheets of all facts for one operation in random order and have them circle the facts they are hesitant about and have them answer all others. Suggest that finger counting or making marks in the margin is not permitted.

3. *Diagnose strengths and weaknesses.* Find out what students do when they encounter one of their unknown facts. Do they count on their fingers? Add up numbers in the margins? Guess? Try to use a related fact? Write down times tables? Are they able to use any of the relationships that might be helpful as suggested in this chapter? Some of this you may be able to accomplish by having students write reflective papers about two or three specific facts. More efficiently, you should conduct a 15-minute diagnostic interview with each student in need. Simply pose unknown facts and ask how the student approaches them. Try an idea from this chapter and see what connections are already there. Don't try to teach, only find out.

4. *Provide hope.* Children who have experienced difficulty with fact mastery can begin to believe that they cannot learn facts or that they are doomed to finger counting forever. Let these children know that you will provide them with some new ideas to help them and that you will help them! Take that burden on yourself and spare them the prospect of more defeat.

5. *Build in success.* As you begin a well-designed fact program for a child who has experienced failure, be sure that successes come quickly and easily. Begin with easy strategies and introduce only a few new facts at a time. Even with pure rote drill, repetitive practice with five facts in three days will provide more success than introducing 15 facts in a week. Success builds success! With strategies as an added assist, success comes even more quickly. Point out to children how one idea, one strategy, is all that is required to learn many facts. Use fact charts to show what set of facts you are working on. It is surprising how the chart quickly fills up with mastered facts. Keep reviewing newly learned facts and those that

were already known. This is success. It feels good, and failures are not as apparent.

6. *Never let lack of fact mastery be a bar to real mathematics.* Design remediation in consultation with the student during study hall or before or after school. If necessary, find an opportunity to talk with the student during a class activity but always aside from the rest of the class. With proper diagnosis and a promise of success, you can feed a student a self-help program in which one new strategy or idea is suggested at a time. Write out a short plan with one strategy and suggested activities. If necessary, provide materials such as flash cards or ten-frames.

Your extra effort beyond class time can be a motivation to a student to make some personal effort on his or her own time. Furthermore, during class, these students are continuing to work with all students on whatever the regular curriculum is. You must personally believe and communicate to these students that the reason they have not mastered basic facts is not a reflection on their ability. Rather, it is due to the fact that good ideas have not been developed. With efficient strategies and individual effort, success will come. Believe!

REFLECTIONS ON CHAPTER 8: WRITING TO LEARN

1. Explain in about one paragraph each part of the three-step approach to fact mastery.

2. For each addition fact strategy:

   a. List at least three facts for which the strategy can be used.

   b. Explain the thinking process and/or concepts that are involved in using the strategy. Use a specific fact as an illustration.

   c. Describe at least one activity that is designed to help children construct the strategy.

3. What is meant by subtraction as "think-addition"? How can you help children develop a think-addition thought pattern for subtraction?

4. For subtraction facts with sums greater than 10, it is reasonable that as many as three different thought patterns or strategies might be used. Describe each of those suggested in the text.

5. Why is the turn-around property (commutative property) so important in multiplication fact mastery?

6. For each multiplication strategy except "use a helping fact," answer the questions in item 2.

7. The "last 25" multiplication facts involve using a fact that has already been learned and working from that fact to the new or harder fact. Four different ways to make this connection with a helping fact were described. Some are applicable only to certain facts. De-

scribe each of these approaches, and list the facts for which the approach is applicable.

8. Why not use speed drills to learn facts?

9. How do you help children who have been drilling their basic facts for years and still have not mastered them?

FOR DISCUSSION AND EXPLORATION

1. Explore a computer software program that drills basic facts. There are perhaps more of these programs than any other area of drill-and-practice software. Many use a variant of an arcade format to encourage speed. Very few, if any, have organized the facts around thinking strategies. Do you think these programs are effective? How would you use such a piece of software in a classroom with only one or two available computers?

2. One view of thinking strategies is that they are little more than a collection of tricks for kids to memorize. This view suggests that direct drill may be more effective and less confusing. Discuss the question, "Is teaching children thinking strategies for basic fact mastery in keeping with a constructivist view of teaching mathematics?" Two successive chapters in *Mathematics for the Young Child* (Payne, 1990) give slightly different views. The chapter on operations is reflective of the CGI school of thought, a highly constructivist program in which almost no direct instruction of strategies is used (Carpenter, Carey, & Kouba, 1990). The following chapter (Thornton, 1990), by a leading researcher in the area of basic-fact strategies, is closer to the spirit of this chapter. Both selections are worthy of your time and consideration.

3. Examine a recently published second-, third-, or fourth-grade textbook to determine how thinking strategies for the basic facts have been developed. Compare what you find with the groupings of facts in this chapter. How would you use the text effectively in your program?

SUGGESTED READINGS

Highly Recommended

Hope, J. A., Leutzinger, L., Reys, B. J., & Reys, R. R. (1987). *Mental math in the primary grades.* Palo Alto, CA: Dale Seymour.

   This first book in a series of three on mental mathematics devotes roughly the first half of its pages to the development of basic facts using strategies similar to those found in this chapter. The lessons include transparency masters as well as activity sheets for children and encourage appropriate use of manipulatives such as ten-frames.

Thornton, C. A. (1990). Strategies for the basic facts. In J. N. Payne (Ed.), *Mathematics for the young child* (pp. 133–151). Reston, VA: National Council of Teachers of Mathematics.

   Carole Thornton was one of the first researchers to test the effectiveness of basic-fact strategies. She has coauthored two series of blackline masters for fact development and has done research in both the United States and Australia. This chapter reflects her recent thinking and is good companion reading to what you have read here.

Other Suggestions

Burns, M. (1995). Timed tests. *Teaching Children Mathematics, 1,* 408–409.

Baroody, A. J. (1984). Children's difficulties in subtraction: Some causes and cures. *Arithmetic Teacher, 32*(3), 14–19.

Baroody, A. J. (1985). Mastery of the basic number combinations: Internalization of relationships or facts? *Journal for Research in Mathematics Education, 16,* 83–98.

Baroody, A. J., & Standifer, D. J. (1993). Addition and subtraction in the primary grades. In R. J. Jensen (Ed.), *Research ideas for the classroom: Early childhood mathematics* (pp. 72–102). Old Tappan, NJ: Macmillan.

Brownell, W. A., & Chazal, C. B. (1935). The effects of premature drill in third-grade arithmetic. *Journal of Educational Research, 29,* 17–28.

Carpenter, T. P., Carey, D. A., & Kouba, V. L. (1990). A problem-solving approach to the operations. In J. N. Payne (Ed.), *Mathematics for the young child* (pp. 111–131). Reston, VA: National Council of Teachers of Mathematics.

Feinberg, M. M. (1990). Using patterns to practice basic facts. *Arithmetic Teacher, 37*(8), 38–41.

Flexer, R. J. (1986). The power of five: The step before the power of ten. *Arithmetic Teacher, 34*(3), 5–9.

Labinowicz, E. (1985). *Learning from children: New beginnings for teaching numerical thinking.* Menlo Park, CA: AWL Supplemental.

Lessen, E. I., & Cumblad, C. L. (1984). Alternatives for teaching multiplication facts. *Arithmetic Teacher, 31*(5), 46–48.

Rathmell, E. C. (1978). Using thinking strategies to teach the basic facts. In M. N. Suydam (Ed.), *Developing computational skills* (pp. 13–38). Reston, VA: National Council of Teachers of Mathematics.

Rightsel, P. S., & Thornton, C. A. (1985). 72 addition facts can be mastered by mid–grade 1. *Arithmetic Teacher, 33*(3), 8–10.

Steinberg, R. M. (1985). Instruction on derived facts strategies in addition and subtraction. *Journal for Research in Mathematics Education, 16,* 337–355.

Thornton, C. A., & Smith, P. (1988). Action research: Strategies for learning subtraction facts. *Arithmetic Teacher, 35*(8), 8–12.

Thornton, C. A., & Toohey, M. A. (1984). *A matter of facts: Addition, subtraction, multiplication, division.* Palo Alto, CA: Creative Publications.

CHAPTER

WHOLE-NUMBER PLACE-VALUE DEVELOPMENT

A full understanding of place value includes a complex array of ideas and relationships that develop over the K–6 grade span. In kindergarten, children begin learning to count to 100. By second grade, they are talking about tens and ones and are using these ideas in many ways. By fourth grade, students are working with numbers involving four or more digits. Numbers are experienced in computations, on calculators, in mental computations and estimations, and in connection with real-world quantities and measures. In fourth and fifth grades, the ideas of whole-number place value are extended to decimals.

In addition to number meanings, students should begin in the early grades to develop some number sense for large numbers. Number sense must continue to be developed throughout the elementary years. Number sense for the whole numbers refers to the following concepts:

- A sense of the relative size of numbers (185 is large compared to 15, small compared to 1219, and about the same as 179)

- A connection to real-world concepts (estimation of quantities, knowing what would be reasonable numbers for the capacity of a football stadium or school cafeteria, the dollars required to purchase a sweatshirt or a TV or a car, or the weight of an adult)

- A flexible use of numbers in estimation (using 250 instead of 243 in a computation because "four 250s" is easy to work with; thinking about 1296 as "about thirteen hundred")

- A knowledge of the effect of operating with large numbers (adding 1000 increases 3472 by less than a third; 1000 times 3472 will be over 3 million; division by 1000 will produce a very small result)

Number sense is a general theme in today's curriculum and deserves much greater attention than it has received in the past. Though pencil-and-paper computation has diminished in importance, the NCTM *Standards* view of computation is much broader. As you will see in Chapter 11, not only are children expected to have some facility with pencil-and-paper computation, but there is real value attached to students' inventing ways of doing computations as well as understanding why the usual methods work. Estimation and mental computation skills round out the computational curriculum. Neither number sense nor computational understanding can possibly be developed without a firm understanding of place value.

 BIG IDEAS

1. **Sets of ten (and tens of tens) must be perceived as single entities. These sets can then be used to describe how many. This is the main principle of base 10 numeration.**
2. **The positions of digits in numbers determine what they represent—which size group they count. This is the main principle of place-value numeration.**
3. **There are patterns to the way numbers are formed.**

4. **The groupings of ones, tens, and hundreds can be taken apart in different ways. For example, 256 can be 1 hundred, 14 tens, and 16 ones.**
5. **"Really big" numbers are best understood in terms of familiar real-world referents.**

EARLY DEVELOPMENT OF PLACE-VALUE IDEAS

It is important for teachers to understand the ideas about numbers that children are likely to have before they develop place-value concepts and to reflect on how these new and complex concepts are built on the early ideas.

Number Ideas Before Place Value

It is tempting to think that children know quite a lot about numbers with two digits (from 10 to 99) even as early as kindergarten. After all, most kindergartners can and should learn to count to 100 and even to count out sets of things that may have 20 or 30 objects in them. They do daily calendar activities, count children in the room, turn to specified page numbers in their books, and so on. Although these students understand these numbers, that understanding is quite different from yours. It is based on a one-more-than or count-by-ones approach to quantity.

A Pre-Place-Value Snapshot of Number

Ask first- or second-grade children to count out 53 tiles, and most will be able to do so or will make only careless errors. It is a tedious but not formidable task. If you watch the children closely, you will note that the tiles are being counted out one at a time and put into the pile with no use of any type of grouping. Have the children write the number that tells how many tiles they just counted. If they remember the number, most children will be able to write it. Some may write "35" instead of "53," a simple reversal.

So far, so good. Now ask the children to write the number that is 10 more than the number they just wrote. Most will begin to count in some manner, either starting from 1 or starting from 53. Those counting on from 53 will also find it necessary to keep track of the counts, probably on their fingers. Many, if not most, children in the first and early second grade will not be successful at this task, and almost none will know immediately that 10 more is 63. Asking for the number that is 10 less is even more problematic. Third-grade children have similar difficulties writing the number that is either 10 more or 100 more than 376 (Labinowicz, 1985).

Finally, show a large collection of cards, each with a ten-frame drawn on it. Discuss how the cards each have ten spaces and that each will hold ten tiles. Demonstrate putting tiles on the cards by filling up one of the ten-frames with tiles. Now ask, "How many cards like this do you think it will take if we want to put all of these tiles [the 53 counted out] on the cards?" A not unusual response is "53." Other children will say they do not know, and a few will try to put the tiles on the cards to figure it out.

Pre-Place-Value Quantity Tied to Counts by Ones

The children just described know that there are 53 tiles "because I counted them." Writing the number and saying the number are usually done correctly, but this procedural knowledge is connected to the count by ones. With minimal instruction, children can tell you that the 5 is in the tens place or that there are "3 ones." It is likely that this is simply a naming of the positions with little understanding. If children have been exposed to base 10 materials, it is reasonable to expect them to name a rod of ten as a "ten" and a small cube as a "one." These same children, however, may not be readily able to tell how many ones are required to make a ten. It is quite easy to attach words to both materials and groups without realizing what the materials or symbols are supposed to represent.

Children do know that 53 is "a lot" and that it's more than 47 (because you count past 47 to get to 53). They think of the "53" that they write as a single number. They do not know that the 5 represents five groups of ten things and the 3 three single things (Ross, 1986, 1989; see Figure 9.1).

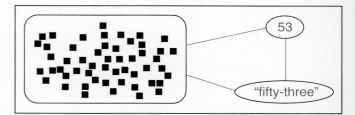

● **FIGURE 9.1** *Before place-value concepts develop, children may be able to count quantities as high as 100 and write numbers accordingly. They do not view either the quantity or the numeral in terms of tens and ones.*

This is where children are before they have constructed place-value ideas. It is on this knowledge that place-value concepts must be built. It is important to realize that children do many things that may suggest they understand these numbers, but that understanding may be rather superficial.

Basic Ideas of Place Value

Place-value understanding requires an integration of new and difficult-to-construct concepts of grouping by tens (base

10 concepts) with procedural knowledge of how groups are recorded in our place-value scheme, how numbers are written, and how they are spoken.

Integration of Groupings by Tens with Counts by Ones

Recognizing that children can count out a set of 53, we want to help them see that making groupings of tens and leftovers is a way of counting or showing that same quantity. Each of the groups in Figure 9.2 has 53 tiles. We want children to construct the idea that all of these are the same and that the sameness is clearly evident by virtue of the groupings of tens.

There is a subtle yet profound difference between two groups of children: those who know that group B is really 53 because they understand the idea that 5 groups of 10 and 3 more is the same amount as 53 counted by ones and those who simply say, "It's 53," because they have been told that when things are grouped this way, it's called 53. The latter children may not be sure how many they will get if they count the tiles in set B by ones or if the groups were "ungrouped" how many there would then be. The children who understand will see no need to count set B by ones. They understand the "fifty-threeness" of sets A and B to be the same.

The ideas in the preceding paragraph are important for you to understand so that the activities discussed later will make sense. Spend some time with these ideas before reading further.

The recognition of the equivalence of groups B and C is another step in the conceptual development that we hope to

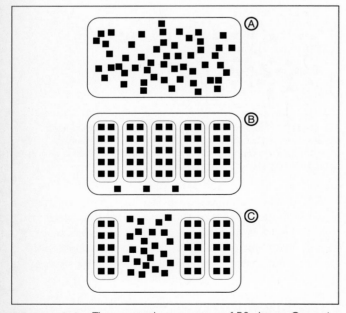

● **Figure 9.2**   Three equivalent groupings of 53 objects. Group A is 53 because "I counted them (by ones)." Group B has 5 tens and 3 more. Group C is the same as B, but now some groups are broken into singles.

obtain. Groupings with fewer than the maximum number of tens can be referred to as *equivalent groupings* or *equivalent representations*. To understand that these representations are equivalent indicates that grouping by tens is not just a rule that is followed but that any grouping by tens, including all or some of the singles, can help tell how many.

The Role of Counting in Constructing Base 10 Ideas

Just as counting is the vehicle with which children construct various relationships with small numbers up to 10, counting plays a key role in constructing base 10 ideas about quantity and connecting these concepts to symbols and oral names for numbers.

Children can count sets such as those in Figure 9.2 in three different ways. Each way helps children think about the quantities in a different way (Thompson, 1990).

1. *Counting by ones.* This is the method children have to begin with. Initially, a count by ones is the only way they are able to name a quantity or "tell how many." All three of the sets in Figure 9.2 can be counted by ones. Before base 10 ideas develop, this is the only way children could be convinced that all three sets are the same.

2. *Counting by groups and singles.* In group B in Figure 9.2, counting by groups and singles would go like this: "One, two, three, four, five bunches of 10, and one, two, three singles." Consider how novel this method would be for a child who had never thought about counting a group of things as a single item. Also notice how this counting does not tell directly how many items there are. This counting must be coordinated with a count by ones before it can be a means of telling "how many."

3. *Counting by tens and ones.* This is the way adults would probably count group B and perhaps group C: "Ten, twenty, thirty, forty, fifty, fifty-one, fifty-two, fifty-three." While this count ends by saying the number that is there, it is not as explicit as the second method in counting the number of groups. Nor will it convey a personal understanding of "how many" unless it is coordinated with the more meaningful count by ones.

Regardless of the specific activity that you may be doing with children, helping them integrate the grouping-by-tens concept with what they know about number from counting by ones should be your foremost objective. That means that children should frequently have the opportunity to count sets of objects in several ways. If first counted by ones, the question might be, "What will happen if we count these by groups and singles (or by tens and ones)?" If a set has been grouped into tens and singles and counted accordingly, "How can we be really certain that there are 53 things here?" or "What do you think we will get if we count by ones?" It is inadequate to tell children that these counts will all be the same. That is a relationship they must construct themselves through reflective thought, not because the teacher says it works that way.

Integration of Groupings with Words

The way we say a number such as "fifty-three" must also be connected with the grouping-by-tens concept. Again, the counting methods provide a connecting mechanism. The explicit count by tens and ones results in saying the number of groups and singles separately: "five tens and three." This is an acceptable, albeit nonstandard, method of naming this quantity. Saying the number of tens and singles separately in this fashion can be called *place-value language* for a number. Children can associate the place-value language with the usual language: "five tens and three—fifty-three."

Notice that there are several variations of the place-value language for 53: 5 tens and 3, 5 tens and 3 ones, 5 groups of 10 and 3 leftovers, 5 tens and 3 singles, and so on. Each may be used interchangeably with the standard name, "fifty-three." For three-digit numbers, the same flexibility is available: 230 can be 23 tens or 2 hundreds and 3 tens. For a number with singles, there are more options.

It can easily be argued that place-value language should be used throughout the second grade, even in preference to standard oral names.

Integration of Groupings with Place-Value Notation

In like manner, the symbolic scheme that we use for writing numbers (ones on the right, tens to the left of ones, and so on) must be coordinated with the grouping scheme. Activities can be designed so that children physically associate a tens and ones grouping with the correct recording of the individual digits, as Figure 9.3 indicates.

Language again plays a key role in making these connections. The explicit count by groups and singles matches the individual digits as the number is written in the usual left-to-right manner. Counting can help with both ways of interpreting the two digits: as a designation of tens and ones and as a single number representing a full amount.

A similar coordination is necessary for hundreds.

A Relational Understanding

Figure 9.4 (p. 166) summarizes the ideas that have been discussed so far.

- The conceptual knowledge of place value consists of the base 10 grouping ideas.

  A collection of objects can be grouped in sets of 10 and some leftover singles.

  There can be equivalent representations with fewer than the maximum groupings.

- The base 10 grouping ideas must be integrated with oral and written names for numbers.

- In addition to counting by ones, children use two other ways of counting: by groups and singles separately and by tens and ones. All three methods of counting are coordinated as the principal method of integrating the concepts, the written names, and the oral names.

What is most important is to remember that these ideas are built on a count-by-ones understanding of number. The notion of sets of 10 as single entities must be constructed as a completely new way of thinking about number. Simply showing children groups of 10 and telling them, even very loudly, that "10 ones is the same as 1 ten" will not construct that idea for them.

The base 10 or grouping ideas are the conceptual knowledge of place value, whereas counting, oral names, and written names fall under the category of procedural knowledge. A relational understanding of place value integrates all of these ideas.

MODELS FOR PLACE VALUE

Appropriate physical models for base 10 concepts can play a key role in helping children develop the idea of "a ten" as both a single entity and as a set of 10 units. What is impor-

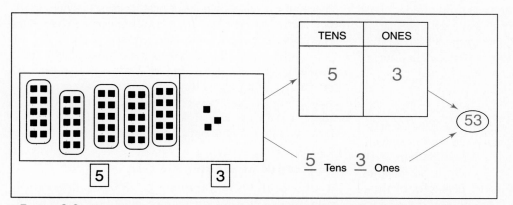

● **FIGURE 9.3**   Groupings by 10 are matched with numerals, placed in labeled places, and eventually written in standard form.

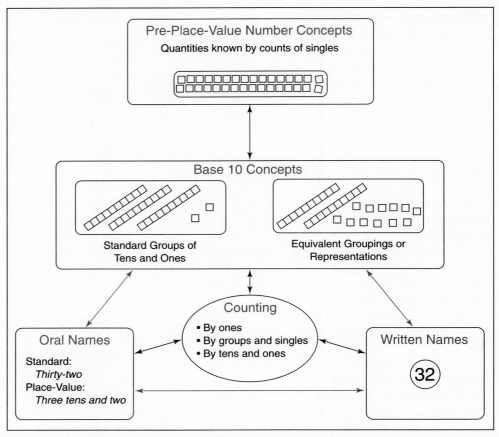

● **FIGURE 9.4** Relational understanding of place value integrates three components shown as the corners of the triangle: base 10 concepts, oral names for numbers, and written names for numbers. Counting is a key activity by which children can construct and integrate these three ideas and connect them to the pre-place-value concepts of number that they have to begin with.

tant to remember is that the models do not "show" the concept to the children. The children must construct the concept and impose it on the model.

Base 10 Models and the Ten-Makes-One Relationship

A good base 10 model for ones, tens, and hundreds is *proportional*. That is, a ten model is physically ten times larger than the model for a one, and a hundred model is ten times larger than the ten model. Base 10 models can be categorized as *groupable* and *pregrouped*.

Groupable Models

Models that most clearly reflect the relationships of ones, tens, and hundreds are those for which the ten can actually be made or grouped from the singles. When you bundle 10 popsicle sticks, the bundle of 10 literally *is the same as* the 10 ones from which it was made. Examples of these "groupable" models are shown in Figure 9.5(a). These could also be called "put-together-take-apart" models.

Of the groupable models, beans or counters in cups are the cheapest and easiest for children to use. (Paper or plastic portion cups can be purchased from restaurant supply houses.) Plastic connecting cubes are attractive and provide a good transition to pregrouped tens sticks. Bundles of Popsicle sticks are perhaps the best-known base 10 model, but small hands have trouble with rubber bands and actually making the bundles. Hundreds are possible with most groupable materials but are generally not practical for most activities in the classroom. Many teachers use plastic connecting chain links and create chains with ten links to represent a ten.

As children become more and more familiar with these models, collections of tens can be made up in advance by the children and kept as ready-made tens. Lids can be purchased for the plastic portion cups, and the connecting cubes or the links can be left prebundled. This is a good transition into the pregrouped models described next.

Pregrouped or Trading Models

At some point, there will be a need to represent hundreds easily. Models that are pregrouped must be introduced. As with all base 10 models, the ten piece is physically equiva-

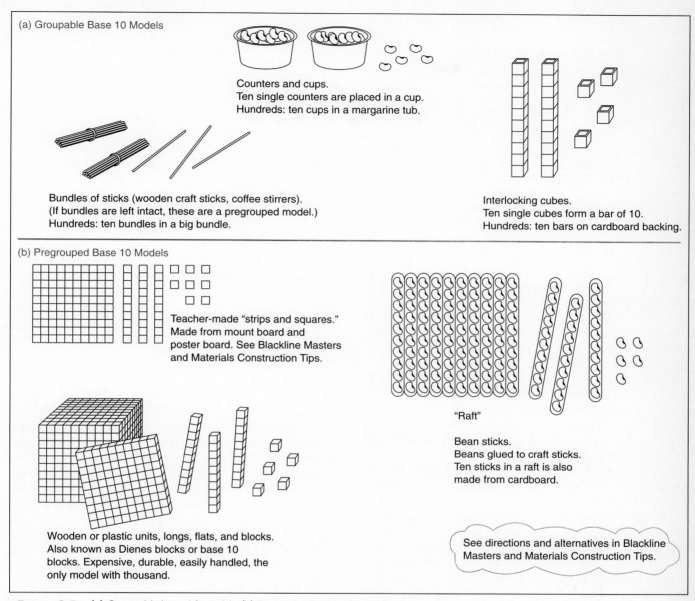

(a) Groupable Base 10 Models

Counters and cups.
Ten single counters are placed in a cup.
Hundreds: ten cups in a margarine tub.

Bundles of sticks (wooden craft sticks, coffee stirrers).
(If bundles are left intact, these are a pregrouped model.)
Hundreds: ten bundles in a big bundle.

Interlocking cubes.
Ten single cubes form a bar of 10.
Hundreds: ten bars on cardboard backing.

(b) Pregrouped Base 10 Models

Teacher-made "strips and squares."
Made from mount board and
poster board. See Blackline Masters
and Materials Construction Tips.

"Raft"

Bean sticks.
Beans glued to craft sticks.
Ten sticks in a raft is also
made from cardboard.

Wooden or plastic units, longs, flats, and blocks.
Also known as Dienes blocks or base 10
blocks. Expensive, durable, easily handled, the
only model with thousand.

See directions and alternatives in Blackline
Masters and Materials Construction Tips.

●**FIGURE 9.5** (a) Groupable base 10 models. (b) Pregrouped base 10 models.

lent to 10 ones, and a hundred piece equivalent to 10 tens, as in Figure 9.5(b). However, children cannot actually take them apart or put them together. When 10 single pieces are accumulated, they must be exchanged or *traded* for a ten, and likewise, tens must be traded for hundreds.

The chief advantage of these models is their ease of use and the efficient way they model numbers as large as 999. Since they do not come apart, there are always readily available tens and hundreds that need not be constructed. The disadvantage is the increased potential for children to use them without reflecting on the ten-to-one relationships. For example, in a ten-for-ones activity, children are told to trade 10 ones for a ten. It is quite possible for children to make

this exchange without attending to the "tenness" of the piece they call a ten. Similarly, children can learn to make the number 42 with 4 tens and 2 ones pieces without really understanding that if the pieces all came apart there would actually be 42 ones pieces that could be counted by ones.

Though no model, including a groupable model, will guarantee that children are reflecting on the ten-to-one relationships in the materials, with pregrouped models we need to make an extra effort to see that children understand that a ten piece really is the same as 10 ones.

(See the Blackline Masters and Materials Construction Tips for making base 10 strips and squares and the little base-ten-frames.)

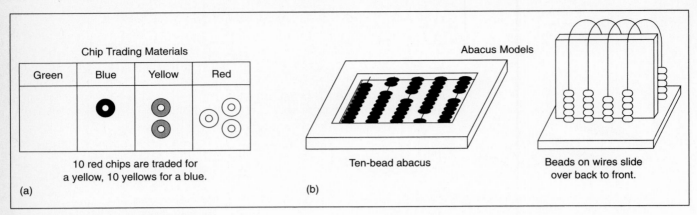

• **Figure 9.6**   *Nonproportional materials.*

Nonproportional Materials

Consider Figure 9.6. In this text, colored counters, abacuses, and money are not considered to model base 10 ideas because the relationships must first exist in the mind of the child, and the materials play no part in helping to develop those relationships. With "chip trading materials" (Davidson, 1975), for example, different-colored chips are used to represent different place values: red for ones, yellow for tens, and so on, as shown in Figure 9.6(a). Trades are made between pieces in a variety of excellent activities, all of which can be done with proportional base 10 models. With the chips, the base can be changed arbitrarily by simply designating different exchange rates.

Somewhat similar to the colored-chip model are the various forms of the abacus, some of which are shown in Figure 9.6(b).

The use of money as a model involves the same issue as colored chips. Pennies, dimes, and dollars are frequently used by teachers and by textbooks as a place-value model. If the relationship that a dime is worth 10 pennies and that a dollar is worth 10 dimes is part of the children's existing understanding, money will model base 10 place value. But if the teacher must explain or impose this relationship, the trade rate between pennies and dimes is simply a "rule of the game" from the children's view. They can learn to obey the rule, but the model is not helping them see why 10 ones is the same as 1 ten. The relationship should be in the model.

The pivotal question may be "Why not just use proportional models?"

DEVELOPING PLACE-VALUE CONCEPTS AND PROCEDURES

Now that you have some idea of what we want to accomplish, we can look at some activities designed to help. This is one area of mathematics where the conceptual and procedural knowledge are both developed in an integrated or coordinated manner. While a particular activity may focus on grouping or on oral or written names, all activities involve models and add to the complete coordination of concepts, oral names, and written symbols as depicted in Figure 9.4 (p. 166).

Grouping Activities

Because children begin their development of base 10 concepts with a count-by-ones idea of number, that is where you must begin. You cannot arbitrarily impose grouping by 10 on children. At the same time, why groups of 10 and not groups of some other number? The decision to use 10 as the base of our numeration system is certainly arbitrary. It most likely stems from the fact that humans have ten fingers. And so we want children to experiment with showing amounts in groups of like size and perhaps to come to an agreement that 10 is a very useful size to use. The following activity could be done in late first grade or second grade and is designed as an example of a first effort at developing grouping concepts.

———ACTIVITY———

9.1 Counting in Groups

Find a collection of things that children might be interested in counting—perhaps the number of eyes in the classroom or the number of shoes, a mystery jar of buttons or cubes, a long chain of plastic links, or the number of crayons in the crayon box. The quantity should be countable and have somewhere between 25 and 100 items. Pose the question, "How could we count our shoes in some way that would be easier than counting by ones?" Whatever suggestions you get, try to implement them. After trying several methods, you can have a discussion of what worked well

and what did not. If no one suggests counting by tens, you might casually suggest that as possibly another idea.

One teacher had her second-grade students find a good way to count all the connecting cubes being held by the children after each had been given a cube for each of their pockets. The first suggestion was to count by sevens. That was tried but did not work very well because none of the second graders could count by sevens. In search of a faster way, the next suggestion was to count by twos. This did not seem to be much better than counting by ones. Finally, they settled on counting by tens and realized that this was a pretty good method, although counting by fives worked pretty well also.

This and similar activities provide you with the opportunity to suggest that materials actually be arranged into groups of tens before the "fast" way of counting is begun. Remember that children may count "ten, twenty, thirty, thirty-one, thirty-two" but not fully realize the "thirty-two-ness" of the quantity. To connect the count-by-tens method with their understood method of counting by ones, the children need to count both ways and discuss why they get the same result.

The idea in the next activity is for children to make groupings of 10 and record or say the amounts. The number word is a feature of the written version so that children will actually count the materials in a way that is meaningful to them. If we use the number word instead of the numeral, children will not be mechanically matching tens and ones with individual digits without confronting the actual quantity in a manner meaningful to them.

If children have difficulty writing the number words, a chart can be displayed for students to copy from (see Figure 9.8, p. 170).

Variations of the "Groups of 10" activity are suggested by the other record sheets in Figure 9.7 (p. 170). In "Get This Many," the children count the dots and then count out the corresponding number of counters. Small cups in which to put the groups of 10 should be provided. Notice that the activity requires students to address quantities in a way they understand, record the amount in words, and then make the groupings.

The activity starts where the students are and develops the idea of groups. Make various countable designs with the dots. "Fill the Tens" and "Loop This Many" each begin with a verbal name (number word), and students must count the indicated amount and then make groups. As you watch children doing these activities, you will be able to learn a lot about their base 10 concept development. For example, how do children count out the objects? Do they make groupings of 10 as they go? Do they count to 10 and then start again at 1? Children who do that are already using the base 10 structure. But what you will more likely see early on is children counting a full set without any stopping at tens and without any effort to group the materials in piles. A second-grade teacher had her students count a jar of small beans. After they had recorded the number, they were to ask for plastic cups in which to make cups of 10. Several children, when asked how many cups they thought they might need, had no idea or made random guesses.

The following activity is another variant but includes an estimation component that not only adds interest but can also contribute to number sense. It is helpful to add estimation to these early counting and grouping activities. Estimates encourage children to think about total quantities. Listening to students' estimates is also a useful assessment opportunity that tells you a lot about children's concepts of numbers in the range of your current activities.

ACTIVITY

9.2 Groups of 10

Prepare bags of counters of different types. Bags may have toothpicks, buttons, beans, plastic chips, connecting cubes, craft sticks, or other items. Each bag should have a label that the children can copy easily. Children have a record sheet similar to the top example in Figure 9.7 (p. 170). The bags can be placed at stations around the room, or each pair of children can be given one. After recording the bag label, the children dump out and count the contents. The amount is recorded as a number word. Then the counters are grouped in as many tens as possible. The groupings are recorded on the form. Bags are traded or children move to another station after returning all counters to the bag.

ACTIVITY

9.3 Estimating Groups of Tens and Ones

Show students a length that they are going to measure—for example, the length of the chalkboard, the length of a student lying down, or the distance around a sheet of newspaper. At one end of the length, line up 10 units (e.g., 10 cubes in a bar, 10 toothpicks, rods, or blocks). On a recording sheet (see Figure 9.9, p. 171), students write down a guess of how many groups of 10 and leftovers they think will fit into the length. Next they find the actual measure, placing units along the full length. These are counted by ones and also grouped in tens. Both results are recorded.

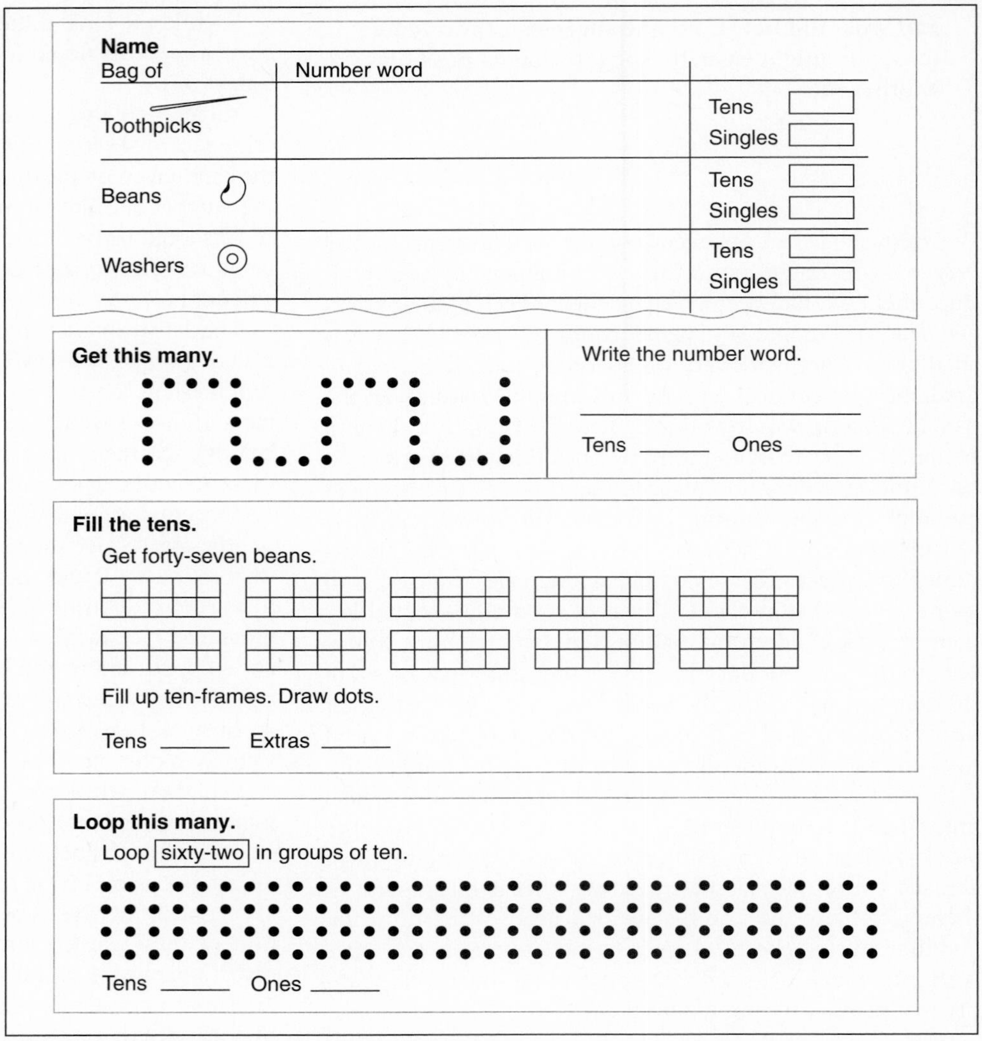

Name _____

Bag of	Number word		
Toothpicks		Tens	☐
		Singles	☐
Beans		Tens	☐
		Singles	☐
Washers		Tens	☐
		Singles	☐

Get this many.

Write the number word.

_____

Tens _____ Ones _____

Fill the tens.

Get forty-seven beans.

Fill up ten-frames. Draw dots.

Tens _____ Extras _____

Loop this many.

Loop ⌷sixty-two⌷ in groups of ten.

Tens _____ Ones _____

● **FIGURE 9.7**   *Number words and making groups of 10.*

Notice that all place-value components are included in Activity 9.3 (p. 169). Children can work in pairs to measure a series of lengths around the room, or this can be a teacher-directed activity focused on a single measure. A similar estimation approach could be added to "Groups of 10" (p. 169), where students first estimate the quantity in the bags. Estimation adds reflective thought concerning quantities expressed in groups.

The Strangeness of Ones, Tens, and Hundreds

As students begin to make groupings of 10, the language of these groupings must also be introduced. At the very start of grouping, language such as "groups of 10 and leftovers" or "bunches of tens and singles" is most meaningful. For tens, use whatever terminology fits: bars of 10, cups of 10, bundles of 10. Eventually you can abbreviate this simply to "ten." Surprisingly, there is no hurry to use the word "ones" for the leftover counters. Language such as "four tens and seven" works very well.

Reflect for a moment on how strange it must sound to say "seven ones." Certainly children have never said they were "seven ones" years old. The use of the word *ten* as a singular group name is even more mysterious. Consider the phrase "Ten ones makes one ten." The first *ten* carries the

Number Words		
eleven	ten	one
twelve	twenty	two
thirteen	thirty	three
fourteen	forty	four
fifteen	fifty	five
sixteen	sixty	six
seventeen	seventy	seven
eighteen	eighty	eight
nineteen	ninety	nine

● **FIGURE 9.8**   *A chart to help children write number words.*

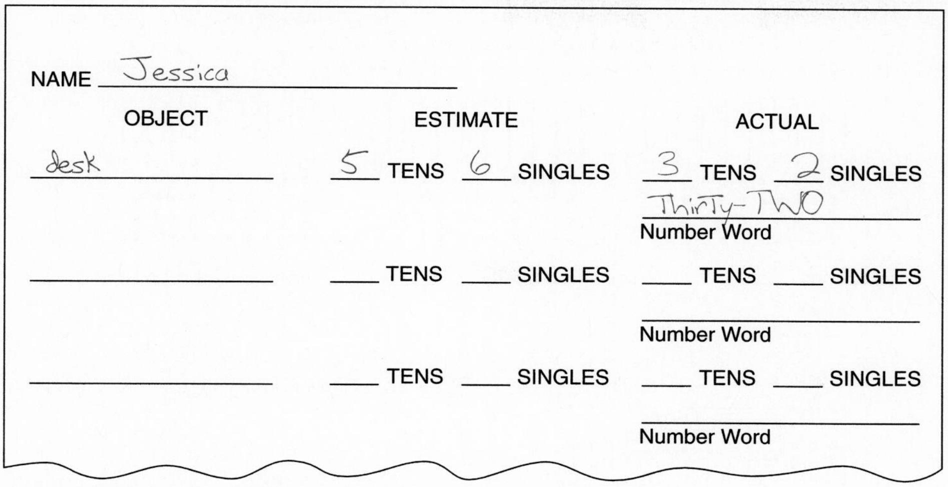

NAME ___Jessica_____

OBJECT	ESTIMATE	ACTUAL

___desk_____   __5__ TENS __6__ SINGLES   __3__ TENS __2__ SINGLES

_____ThirTy-TWO_____
Number Word

_____   ____ TENS ____ SINGLES   ____ TENS ____ SINGLES

_____
Number Word

_____   ____ TENS ____ SINGLES   ____ TENS ____ SINGLES

_____
Number Word

●**FIGURE 9.9**   *Record sheet for "Estimating Groups of Tens and Ones."*

---

usual meaning of 10 things, the amount that is 1 more than 9 things. But the other *ten* is a singular noun, a thing. How can something the child has known for years as the name for a lot of things suddenly become one thing? Bunches, bundles, cups, and groups of 10 make more sense in the beginning than "a ten."

The word *hundred* is equally strange and yet usually gets less attention. It must be understood in three ways: as 100 single objects, as 10 tens, and as a singular thing. These word names are not as simple as they seem!

Equivalent Representations

An important variation of the grouping activities is aimed at the equivalent representations of numbers. (Refer to Figure 9.4, p. 166). For example, if working with the children who have just completed the "Groups of 10" activity for a bag of counters, ask, "What is another way you can show your 42 besides 4 groups and 2 singles? Let's see how many ways you can find." Interestingly, most children will go next to 42 singles. The following activities are also directed to the idea of equivalent representations.

─────────── ACTIVITY ───────────
9.4 Odd Groupings

On the overhead, on a magnet board, or with counters (if working with a small group of children), show a collection of materials that are only partly grouped in sets of 10. For example, you may have 5 chains of 10 links and 17 additional links. Be sure the children understand that the groups each have 10 items. Count the number of groups and also count the singles. Ask,

"How many in all?" Record all responses, and discuss before you count. Let the children use whatever way they wish to count. Next change the groupings (make a ten from the singles, or break apart one of the tens and repeat the questions and discussion. Do not change the total number from one time to the next. Once students begin to understand that the total does not change, ask in what other ways they could be grouped if you use tens and singles.

The next activity is similar but is done using pregrouped materials.

─────────── ACTIVITY ───────────
9.5 Three Other Ways

Students work in groups or in pairs. First they show "four hundred sixty-three" on their desks with strips and squares in the standard representation. Next they find and record at least three other ways of showing this number.

A variation of "Three Other Ways" is to challenge students to find a way to show an amount with a specific number of pieces. "Can you show 463 with 31 pieces?" (There is more than one way to do this.) Students in grades 4 or 5 can get quite involved with finding all the ways to show a three-digit number.

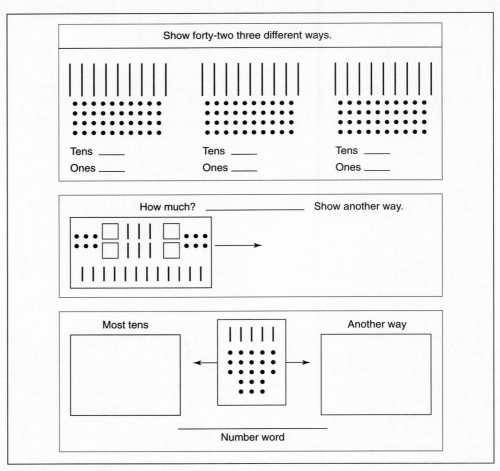

● **Figure 9.10** Equivalent representation exercises using square-stick-dot pictures.

After children have had sufficient experiences with pre-grouped materials, a "dot, stick, and square" notation can be used for recording ones, tens, and hundreds. By third grade, children can use small squares for hundreds, as shown in Figure 9.10. Use the drawings as a means of telling the children what pieces to get out of their own place-value kits and as a way for children to record results.

The next activity begins to incorporate oral language with equivalent representation ideas.

—————ACTIVITY—————

9.6 Base 10 Riddles

Base 10 riddles can be presented orally or in written form. In either case, children should use base 10 materials to help solve them. The examples here illustrate a variety of possibilities with different levels of difficulty.

I have 23 ones and 4 tens. Who am I?

I have 4 hundreds, 12 tens, and 6 ones. Who am I?

I have 30 ones and 3 hundreds. Who am I?

I am 45. I have 25 ones. How many tens do I have?

I am 341. I have 22 tens. How many hundreds do I have?

I have 13 tens, 2 hundreds, and 21 ones. Who am I?

If you put 3 more tens with me, I would be 115. Who am I?

I have 17 ones. I am between 40 and 50. Who am I?

I have 17 ones. I am between 40 and 50. How many tens do I have?

Oral Names for Numbers

The standard name of the collection in Figure 9.11 is "forty-seven." A more explicit terminology is "four tens and seven ones." This latter form, as mentioned earlier, will be referred to as *place-value language*.

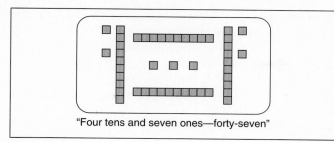

"Four tens and seven ones—forty-seven"

● **Figure 9.11**   *Mixed model of 47.*

The more explicit place-value language is rarely misunderstood by children working with base 10 materials and encourages thinking in terms of groups instead of a large pile of singles.

Two-Digit Number Names

In first and second grade, children need to connect the base 10 concepts with the oral number names they have used many times. They know the words but have not thought of them in terms of tens and ones. The following sequence is suggested:

Start with the names *twenty, thirty, forty,* through *ninety.*

Next do all names *twenty* through *ninety-nine.*

Emphasize the teens as exceptions. Acknowledge that they are formed "backwards" and do not fit the patterns.

Almost always use base 10 models while teaching oral names. Use place-value language paired with standard language.

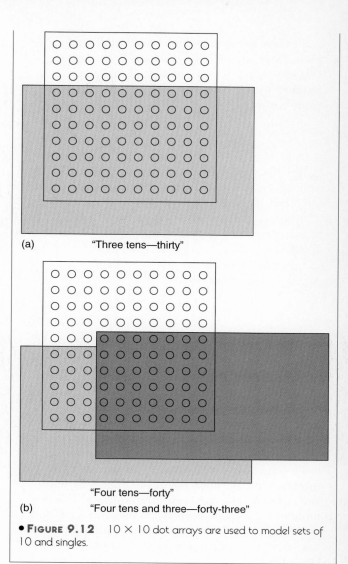

(a)   "Three tens—thirty"

"Four tens—forty"
(b)   "Four tens and three—forty-three"

● **Figure 9.12**   *10 × 10 dot arrays are used to model sets of 10 and singles.*

———ACTIVITY———

9.7 Counting Rows of 10

Use a 10 × 10 array of dots on the overhead projector. Cover up all but two rows, as shown in Figure 9.12(a). "How many tens? (2.) Two tens is called *twenty.*" Have the class repeat. "Sounds a little like *twin.*" Show another row. "Three tens is called *thirty.* Four tens is *forty.* Five tens should have been *fivety* rather than *fifty.*" The names *sixty, seventy, eighty,* and *ninety* all fit the pattern. Slide the cover up and down the array, asking how many tens and the name for that many.

Use the same 10 × 10 array to work on names for tens and ones. Show, for example, four full lines, "forty." Next expose one dot in the fifth row. "Four tens and one. Forty-one." Add more dots one at a time. "Four tens and two. Forty-two." "Four tens and three. Forty-three." This is shown in Figure 9.12(b). When that pattern is established, repeat with other decades from twenty through ninety.

Repeat this basic approach with other base 10 models.

———ACTIVITY———

9.8 Counting with Base 10 Models

Show some tens pieces on the overhead. Ask how many tens. Ask for the usual name. Add a ten or remove a ten and repeat the questions. Next add some ones. Always have children give the place-value name and the standard name. Continue to make changes in the materials displayed by adding or removing 1 or 2 tens and by adding and removing ones. For this activity, show the tens and ones pieces in different arrangements rather than the standard left-to-right order for tens and ones. The idea is to connect the names to the materials, not the order they are in.

> Reverse the activity by having children use place-value pieces at their desks. For example, you say, "Make 63." The children make the number with the models and then give the place-value name.

Note that Activities 9.7 and 9.8 (p. 173) will be much enhanced by entertaining discussions. Whatever responses children give, have them explain their thinking. Without your requiring children to reflect on these responses, base 10 activities can very quickly mask a lack of understanding. Children can learn how to give the response you want, matching number words to models, without actually thinking about the total quantities.

---ACTIVITY---

9.9 Tens, Ones, and Fingers

Ask your class, "How can you show 37 fingers?" (This question is really fun if preceded by a series of questions asking for different ways to show 6 fingers, 8 fingers, and other amounts less than 10.) Soon children will figure out that four children are required. Line up four children and have three hold up 10 fingers and the last child 7 fingers. Have the class count the fingers by tens and ones. Ask for other children to show different numbers of fingers. Emphasize the number of sets of 10 fingers and the single fingers (place-value language) and pair this with the standard language.

In the last three activities, it is important occasionally to count an entire representation by ones. Remember that the count by ones is the young child's principal linkage with the concept of quantity. For example, suppose you have just had children use connecting cubes to make 42. Try asking, "Do you think there really are 42 blocks there?" Many children are not convinced, and the count by ones is very significant.

The language pattern for two-digit numbers is best developed and connected with models using numbers 20 and higher. That is where the emphasis should be. That is not to imply that we should hide the teens from children. Teens can and should appear in the activities but should be noted as exceptions to the verbal rules you are developing.

One approach to the teen numbers is to "back into them." Show, for example, 6 tens and 5 ones. Get the standard and place-value names from the children as before. Re-

move tens one at a time, each time asking for both names. The switch from 2 tens and 5 ("twenty-five") to 1 ten and 5 ("fifteen") is a dramatic demonstration of the "backward" names for the teens. Take that opportunity to point them out as exceptions. Count them by ones. Say them in both languages. Add tens to get to numbers that follow the rules. Return to a teen number. Continue to contrast the teens with the numbers 20 and above.

Three-Digit Number Names

The approach to three-digit number names is essentially the same as for two-digit names. Show mixed arrangements of base 10 materials. Have children give the place-value name and the standard name. Vary the arrangement from one example to the next by changing only one type of piece. That is, add or remove only ones or only tens or only hundreds.

Similarly, have children at their desks model numbers that you give to them orally using the standard names. By the time that children are ready for three-digit numbers, the two-digit number names, including the difficulties with the teens, have usually been mastered. The major difficulty is with numbers involving no tens, such as 702. As noted earlier, the use of place-value language is quite helpful here. The zero-tens difficulty is more pronounced when writing numerals. Children frequently write 7002 for "seven hundred two." The emphasis on the meaning in the oral place-value language form will be a significant help.

Written Symbols

The discussion so far has stressed the ideas of groups of 10 and the connection of these base 10 concepts to oral number names. No one would expect that written numbers are completely absent during this development. At the same time, it is correct to focus on the ideas of base 10 concepts before emphasizing the written numbers. Remember, it is likewise only a convention that we write numbers using the place-value system with which we are all familiar.

Place-Value Mats

Place-value mats are simple mats divided into two or three sections to hold ones and tens or ones, tens, and hundreds pieces as shown in Figure 9.13. You can suggest to your students that the mats are a good way to organize their materials when working with base 10 pieces. Explain that the standard way to use a place-value mat is with the space for the ones on the right and tens and hundreds places to the left.

Though there is no requirement to have anything printed on the mats, it is strongly recommended that two ten-frames be drawn in the ones place as shown. (See Blackline Masters and Materials Construction Tips for directions for making

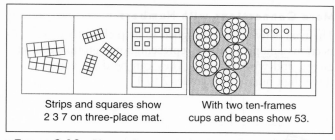

Strips and squares show
2 3 7 on three-place mat.

With two ten-frames
cups and beans show 53.

● **FIGURE 9.13** *Place-value mats with two ten-frames in the ones place to organize the counters and promote the groups-of-10 concept.*

the mats.) As children make a number using materials, the amount of ones on the ten-frames is always clearly evident, eliminating the need for frequent and tedious counting (Thompson & Van de Walle, 1984b). The ten-frame also makes it very clear how many additional counters would be needed to make the next set of 10. If children are modeling two numbers at the same time, one ten-frame can be used for each number. Most illustrations of place-value mats in this book will show two ten-frames, even though that feature is strictly an option and is not commonly seen in standard texts.

As children make or show numbers on their place-value mats, they can be shown how the left-to-right order of the pieces is also the way that numbers are written. The place-value mat becomes a link between the base 10 models and the written form of the numbers the models represent. Once again, you are reminded to be aware of how easy it would be for a child to show a number on a mat using tens and ones

pieces and learn to write the number without any understanding of what the number really represents. Examine first- and second-grade textbooks for situations where a model is shown, and have children record numbers in this manner:

7 tens and 3 ones

73 in all

It is all too easy to copy down the number of sticks and single blocks and rewrite these digits in a single number 73 and not confront what these symbols really stand for.

The 0–99 Chart

A 0–99 chart is a 10 × 10 grid with the numbers written in order from 0 to 99 (see Figure 9.14). It is a good idea to have a large chart like this somewhere prominent in your room. A blank version of the chart is even more important for class discussions and activities. A blank 0–99 chart can be made in several ways. An overhead transparency can be made of the grid in the Blackline Masters, or a transparency master can be purchased. A grid can be drawn on a piece of poster board and laminated. Numbers can be written on either of these blank charts. Some teachers prefer to buy a commercial chart that has pockets into which numeral cards can be inserted. Both the 0–99 chart and blank chart lend themselves to useful activities that involve the written form of numbers. (If you have a chart that goes from 1 to 100, it can be used just as well. There are some minor pros and cons to each version.)

0	1	2	3	4	5	6	7	8	9
10	11	12	13	14	15	16	17	18	19
20	21	22	23	24	25	26	27	28	29
30	31	32	33	34	35	36	37	38	39
40	41	42	43	44	45	46	47	48	49
50	51	52	53	54	55	56	57	58	59
60	61	62	63	64	65	66	67	68	69
70	71	72	73	74	75	76	77	78	79
80	81	82	83	84	85	86	87	88	89
90	91	92	93	94	95	96	97	98	99

● **FIGURE 9.14** A 0–99 chart.

─────ACTIVITY─────

9.16 Who Could They Be?

Label two points on a number line (not necessarily the ends).

Ask students what numbers they think different points labeled with letters might be and why they think that. In the example shown here, B and C are less than 100 but probably more than 60. E could be about 180. You can also ask where 75 might be or where 400 is. About how far apart are A and D? Why do you think D is more than 100?

In the next activity, some of the same ideas are discussed without benefit of a number line.

─────ACTIVITY─────

9.17 Close, Far, and in Between

Put any three numbers on the board.

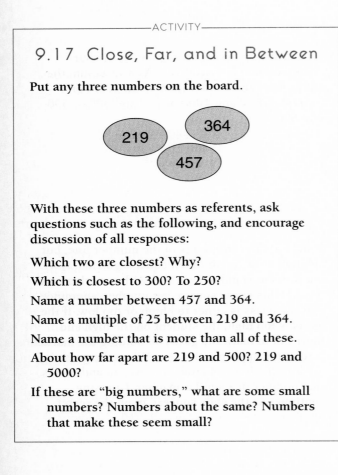

With these three numbers as referents, ask questions such as the following, and encourage discussion of all responses:

Which two are closest? Why?

Which is closest to 300? To 250?

Name a number between 457 and 364.

Name a multiple of 25 between 219 and 364.

Name a number that is more than all of these.

About how far apart are 219 and 500? 219 and 5000?

If these are "big numbers," what are some small numbers? Numbers about the same? Numbers that make these seem small?

Connections to Real-World Ideas

We should not permit our children to study place-value concepts without encouraging them to see number in the world about them. You do not need a prescribed activity to come up with interesting ways to bring real numbers into the classroom.

Children in the second grade should be thinking about numbers under 100 first and soon after, numbers up to 1000. Quantities larger than that are difficult to think about. Where are numbers like this? Around your school there are lots of numbers: the number of children in each class, the numbers on the school buses, the number of minutes devoted to mathematics each day and then each week, the number of cartons of chocolate and white milk served in the cafeteria each day, the numbers on the calendar (days in a week, month, year), the number of days since school has started, and so on. And then there are measurements, numbers at home, numbers on the field trip, . . .

What do you do with these numbers? They can be turned into interesting graphs. Stories can be written, problems made up, contests devised.

As children get a bit older, the interest in numbers can expand to well beyond the school and classroom. Measurement provides a wealth of opportunity to see numbers in action. All sorts of things can and should be measured to create graphs, draw inferences, and make comparisons. For example, what numbers are associated with the "average" fifth grader? Height, weight, arm span, age in months, number of siblings, number of grandparents, distance from home to school, length of standing broad jump, number of pets, hours spent watching TV in a week, . . . How can you find the average for these or other numbers that may be of interest to the students in your room? Is anyone really average?

Finding number in other content areas is a good way to integrate mathematics throughout your school day. For example, in studying another country or culture or time period in social studies, there are always plenty of facts that include numbers. Comparing these facts with the corresponding numbers in your local world is not only a valuable way to make the social studies facts real but also a good way for children to think about numbers. Making graphs and charts and writing about the data in other subjects are always worthwhile activities.

These are just a few ideas to get you going. The particular way you bring number and the real world together in your class is up to you. But do not underestimate the value of connecting the real world to the classroom.

Approximate Numbers and Rounding

In our number system, some numbers are "nice" in that they are easy to think about and work with. The idea of what makes a nice number is sort of fuzzy. However, numbers such as 100, 500, and 750 are easier to use than 94, 517, and 762. Multiples of 100 are very nice, and multiples of 10 are not bad either. Multiples of 25 (50, 75, 425, 675, . . .) are nice because they combine into 100s and 50s rather easily, and we can mentally place those between multiples of 100s. Multiples of 5 are a little easier to work with than those that are not.

Flexible thought with numbers and many estimation skills are related to the ability to substitute a nice number for one that is not so nice. The substitution may be to make a mental computation easier, to compare it to a familiar reference, or simply to store the number in memory more easily.

The choice of a nice number to substitute for a less manageable one is never completely clear-cut. There is not a "correct" or "best" substitute for $327.99 or 57 pounds. The choices depend on the need for clarity and accuracy and how the substitute will be used. For example, nice substitutes for $327.99 might be $300, $320, $325, $328, $330, or even $350. In a given situation there may be more than one good choice of substitutes. (For each of these substitutes, can you think of a situation where using that number might be more useful than the others?)

In the past, rounding numbers was the principal method of selecting a substitute nice number. Students were taught rules for rounding numbers to the nearest 10 or nearest 100. Unfortunately, the emphasis was placed on applying the rule correctly. (If the next digit is 5 or more, round up; otherwise, leave the number alone.) A context to suggest why they may want to round numbers was usually a lesser consideration.

The activities here are designed to help students recognize what nice numbers are and to identify a nice-number substitute. (Note: the term "nice number" is not found in standard textbooks. It is an invention of the author of this book. There is no commonly accepted definition.)

ACTIVITY

9.18 Nice-Number Skip Counts

Count by 5s, 10s, 25s, and 50s with your students. The 5s and 10s are fairly easy, but the skill is certainly worth practicing. Counts by 25s or 50s may be hesitant at first. Students can use a calculator to assist with their counting and connect the counts with numerals (press $+$ 25 $=$ $=$ $=$ . . .). At first, start all counts at zero. Later, start at some multiple of your skip amount. For example, begin at 275 and count by 25s. Counts

by 10s should also begin at numbers ending in 5 as well as multiples of 10. Also count backward by these same amounts (press 650 $-$ 50 $=$ $=$ $=$ . . .).

For children in grades 1 and 2, a 0–99 chart can be used in connection with skip-counting 5s and 10s. Older children should count to at least 1000 and should discuss the patterns that they see in these counts.

Counting Money

Too often, children are expected to count coins without any preparation or background. It is not that money is hard for children but rather that skip-counting by different amounts is difficult. The next activity extends "Nice-Number Skip Counts" in preparation for counting money.

ACTIVITY

9.19 Money Counts

The goal of this activity is to practice shifting from one skip count to another. Explain to the class that they will start counting by one number and at your signal they will shift to a count by a different number. Begin with only two different amounts, say, 25 and 10. Write these numbers on the board. Point to the larger number (25), and have students begin to count. After three or more counts, raise your hand to indicate a pause in the counting. Then lower your hand and point to the smaller number (10). Children continue the count from where they left off but now count by 10s. Use any two of these numbers: 100, 50, 25, 10, 5, 1. Always start with the larger. Later, try three numbers, still in descending order.

Note that the counts in "Money Counts" are the same as are used when counting coins or money. These skills can be applied to bills and coins. Plastic "money" is available for use on the overhead and is an effective substitute.

Rounding

To round a number simply means to substitute a nice number that is close so that some computation can be done more easily. The close number can be any nice number and need not be a multiple of 10 or 100, as has been traditional. It should be whatever makes the computation or estimation easier or simplifies numbers sufficiently in a story or chart or conversation. Note that rounding involves a substitution. You might say, "Last night it took me 57 minutes to do my homework" or "Last night it took me about one hour to do my homework." The first expression is more precise; the second uses a rounded number for better communication. Rounding 57 minutes to 60 minutes did not change the amount of time actually spent on homework.

ACTIVITY

9.20 Near and Nice

The idea is to say or write a number and have students select a close nice-number substitute. Begin by requesting a close multiple of 50. Explain that these are the numbers that you get when you count by 50s. It is a good idea to include a real-world measurement as well. For example, "Instead of 243 feet, let's use _____ feet." Pause at the blank, and students fill in an appropriate number, here 250 feet. The nearest 25 is sometimes difficult. For example, is 463 miles closer to 450 or 475 miles? Actually, either is quite a good substitute. In fact, place your emphasis on selecting a close nice number rather than the closest or best nice number.

A number line with nice numbers highlighted can be useful in helping children select near nice numbers. An unlabeled number line like the one shown in Figure 9.16 can be made using three strips of poster board taped end to end. Labels are written above the line on the chalkboard. The ends can be labeled 0 and 100, 100 and 200, . . . , 900 and 1000. The other markings then show multiples of 25, 10, and 5. Indicate a number above the line that you want to round. Discuss the marks (nice numbers) that are close.

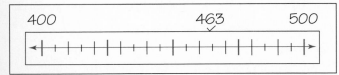

● **FIGURE 9.16**　A blank number line can be labeled in different ways to help students with near and nice numbers.

Looking Toward Computation

An important reason for developing and understanding place value is the impact that place-value concepts have on mental computation, computational estimation, and traditional pencil-and-paper computation. You already saw in Chapter 6 how children can extend part-part-whole ideas to multiples of 10 and even begin to do sums such as 38 + 7 mentally by extending a make-10 process (see Figure 6.19, p. 115). Informal or invented methods of computation and combining and taking numbers apart in different ways contributes to a general flexibility with numbers that will help develop a wide range of efficient computational skills.

Using Tens and Hundreds

Mental computation is an important part of having number sense. As early as the second grade, students can begin to add and subtract tens and hundreds and to combine numbers mentally. In activities such as those suggested here, children are not only beginning mental computation skills but are also simultaneously improving their understanding of place value. The two areas of the curriculum are so closely connected that it is difficult to separate them.

ACTIVITY

9.21 Moving Around the 0–99 Chart

Use a transparent 10 × 10 grid on the overhead projector or a large laminated 10 × 10 grid. Explain that this is a 0–99 chart with the numbers hidden.
　Neighbors. On the blank 0–99 chart, point to a square, and ask students to name the number. Write it in. Next point to squares that surround this number, its neighbors (see Figure 9.17).
　Diagonally Around. Start on a square anywhere on the border of the 0–99 chart, and have students name the number. Then point to successive squares on a diagonal from this starting square as children name the numbers you point to. When you get to the next edge, "bounce" by continuing on a diagonal in the reflected direction. After three such bounces, you will be headed directly toward the number you began with (see Figure 9.17).

Activity 9.21, as well as most activities on a 0–99 chart, can also be done on a hundreds board, a chart numbered from 1 to 100 instead of 0 to 99. The 0–99 chart may be

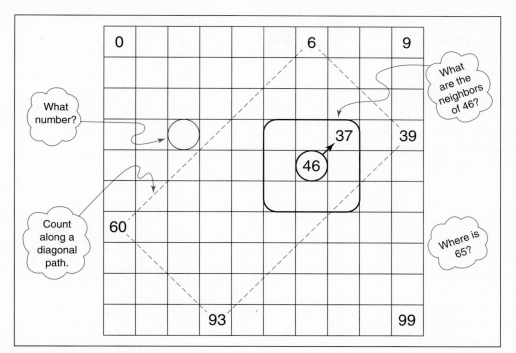

●**FIGURE 9.17** Number names and concepts on a 0–99 chart.

preferable for helping with number patterns; a hundreds board has the advantage of each number corresponding to the number of squares on the board to that point.

---ACTIVITY---

9.22 Arrow Math

With the 0–99 chart in view, write a number on the chart followed by one or more arrows. The arrow can point up, down, left, right, or diagonally. Each arrow represents a move of one square on the board.

63 ↓ ↓ →
Read: "63, 73, 83, 84"

45 ↑ ↑ ↖ ← ←
Read: "45, 35, 25, 14, 13, 12"

After students become adept at "Arrow Math," talk about what each arrow means. The left and right arrows are one-less and one-more arrows. The up and down arrows are the same as 10 less and 10 more. (What do each of the four possible diagonal arrows represent?)*

Adapted from *Mental Math for the Primary Grades* (Hope, Leutzinger, Reys, & Reys, 1988).

The possibility of a 0–999 chart can be discussed with your class, and you may even want to make one. Show a 0–99 chart, and draw a second 10 × 10 grid below it. "What number would go in these squares?" (100 to 199) "And if we had some more charts below this one, what numbers would be in each of them?" Each new grid is the next 100 numbers: 200 to 299, 300 to 399, and so on.

With an extended chart idea, the "Arrow Math" activity can be extended to include "super arrows."

426 ⇓ ⇓ ↓ → →
Read: "426, 526, 626, 636, 637, 638"

In the next example, note how three super up arrows and a regular down arrow are actually a good way to subtract 290.

674 ⇑ ⇑ ⇑ ↓
"674 minus 300 is 374, plus 10 is 384"

---ACTIVITY---

9.23 Calculator Tens and Hundreds

Two students work together with one calculator. They press ⊞ 10 ⊟ to make a "+10 machine." One child enters any number. The other student

says or writes the number that is 10 more. The $\boxed{=}$ is pressed for confirmation. The roles are then reversed. The same activity can be done with plus any multiple of 10 or multiple of 100. On their turn to challenge, students can select what kind of machine to use. For example, they may first press 0 $\boxed{+}$ 300 $\boxed{=}$ and then press 572. The other student would say or write 872 and then press $\boxed{=}$ for confirmation. This game can also be played using $\boxed{-}$ instead of $\boxed{+}$ to practice mentally subtracting tens or hundreds.

Many of the skills and concepts developed so far also appear in the next activity, which combines symbolism with base 10 representation. In all of these activities, good discussion will have children explain how they did the exercises or tell how they thought about them.

─────────ACTIVITY─────────

9.24 Numbers, Squares, Sticks, and Dots

As illustrated in Figure 9.18, prepare a worksheet on which a numeral and some base 10 pieces are shown. Students write the total. Note how "Money Counts" (p. 179) place-value concepts, and symbolism are all included.

Activity 9.24 has children putting numbers together. Another way to develop flexible thinking with numbers is to have children take numbers apart.

─────────ACTIVITY─────────

9.25 Break It in Two Parts

Pick any two- or three-digit number, and have children write down numbers (parts) that together make up the given number. For example, 375 can be 300 and 75 or 215 and 160. Some children may not be thinking in terms of place value and write 3 and 75. Rather than correct such an error, it should be discussed in class. If the word *hundred* is meant to be connected to the 3 (3 hundred and 75), the result makes sense. What word would go with the 75?

The activity can be done with or without the aid of base 10 models. Models may be very useful in the beginning. Also note that it is easier to take 400 apart than it is to take 396 apart.

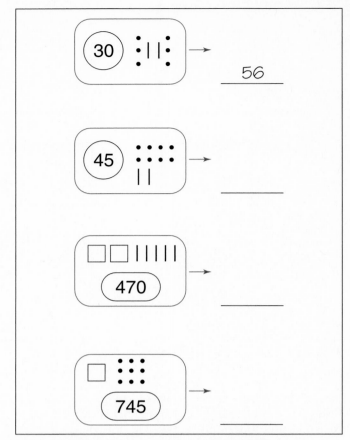

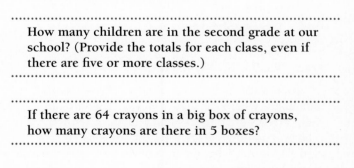

●**FIGURE 9.18**   *Combining models, numerals, and skip counting.*

Computation Without Instruction

Traditionally, children are not asked to solve problems involving computation until they have been taught the usual pencil-and-paper methods of computing. If children are developing good place-value concepts and have access to base 10 models, there is no reason they should not be challenged with problems such as the following:

···

How many children are in the second grade at our school? (Provide the totals for each class, even if there are five or more classes.)

···

···

If there are 64 crayons in a big box of crayons, how many crayons are there in 5 boxes?

···

Problems can involve *all* operations and types of problems discussed in Chapter 7. There is no need to avoid numbers with three digits, especially in the third or fourth grade. Problems involving multiplication of a two- or three-digit number by 3, 4, or 5 can be solved by repeated addition methods. Even division problems such as 586 ÷ 4 can be explored by children in the third grade before any instruction with the usual long-division procedure.

A discussion of methods of solving the problems will produce rich ideas and add to concept development. If a problem turns out to be too difficult, simply set it aside and the next day try a similar one with easier numbers.

Continue with these problems throughout the year. You will be amazed at the wonderful methods children can develop. Self-confidence with problem-solving ability as well as number sense will be enhanced.

NUMBERS BEYOND 1000

For children to have good concepts of numbers beyond 1000, the conceptual ideas that have been carefully developed must be extended. This is sometimes difficult to do because physical models for thousands are not commonly available. At the same time, number sense ideas must also be developed. In many ways, it is these informal ideas about very large numbers that are the most important.

Extending the Place-Value System

Two important ideas developed for three-digit numbers should be carefully extended to larger numbers. First, the grouping idea should be generalized. That is, 10 in any position makes a single thing (group) in the next position, and vice versa. Second, the oral and written patterns for numbers in three digits are duplicated in a clever way for every three digits to the left. These two related ideas are not as easy for children to understand as adults seem to believe. Because models for large numbers are so difficult to have or picture, textbooks must deal with these ideas in a predominantly symbolic manner. That is not sufficient!

----------ACTIVITY----------

9.26 What Comes Next?

Have a "What Comes Next?" discussion with the base 10 strips and squares. The unit or ones piece is a 1-centimeter (cm) square. The tens piece is a 10 × 1 strip. The hundreds piece is a square, 10 cm × 10 cm. What is next? Ten hundreds is called a thousand. What shape? It could be a strip made of 10 hundreds squares. Tape 10 hundreds together. What is next? (Reinforce the idea of "ten makes one" that has progressed to this point.) Ten one-thousand strips would make a square measuring 1 meter (m) on a side. Draw one on butcher paper, and rule off the 10 strips inside to illustrate the ten-makes-one idea. Continue. What is next? Ten ten-thousand squares would go together to make a strip. Draw this 10-cm × 1-m strip on a long sheet of butcher paper and mark off the 10 squares that make it up. You may have to go out in the hall.

How far you want to extend this square, strip, square, strip sequence depends on your class and your needs. The idea that 10 in one place makes 1 in the next can be brought home dramatically. There is no need to stop. It is quite possible with older children to make the next 10-m × 10-m square using masking tape on the cafeteria floor or chalk lines on the playground. The next strip is 100 m × 10 m. This can be made on a large playground using kite string for the lines. By this point, the payoff includes an appreciation of the increase in size of each successive amount as well as the ten-makes-one progression. The 100-m × 10-m strip is the model for 10 million, and the 10-m × 10-m square models 1 million. The difference between 1 million and 10 million is dramatic. Even the concept of 1 million tiny centimeter squares is dramatic.

The three-dimensional wooden or plastic base 10 materials are all available with a model for thousands, which is a 10-cm cube. These models are expensive, but having at least one large cube to show and talk about is a good idea.

Try the "What Comes Next?" discussion in the context of these three-dimensional models. The first three shapes are distinct: a cube, a long, and a flat. What comes next? Stack 10 flats and they make a cube, same shape as the first one only 1000 times larger. What comes next? (See Figure 9.19, p. 184.) Ten cubes make another long. What comes next? Ten big longs make a big flat. The first three shapes have now repeated. Ten big flats will make an even bigger cube, and the triplet of shapes begins again.

A good discussion revolves around the metric dimensions of each successive cube. The million cube is 1 m on an edge. The billion cube is 10 m on an edge, or about the size of a three-story building.

Each cube has a name. The first one is the unit cube, the next is a thousand, the next a million, then a billion, and so on. Each long is 10 cubes: 10 units, 10 thousands, 10 millions. Similarly, each flat shape is 100 cubes.

To read a number, first mark it off in triples from the right. The triples are then read, stopping at the end of each to name the unit (or cube shape) for that triple (see Figure 9.20, p. 184). Leading zeros are ignored. If students can learn to read numbers like 059 (fifty-nine) or 009 (nine), they should be able to read any number. To write a number, use the same scheme. If first mastered orally, the system is quite easy.

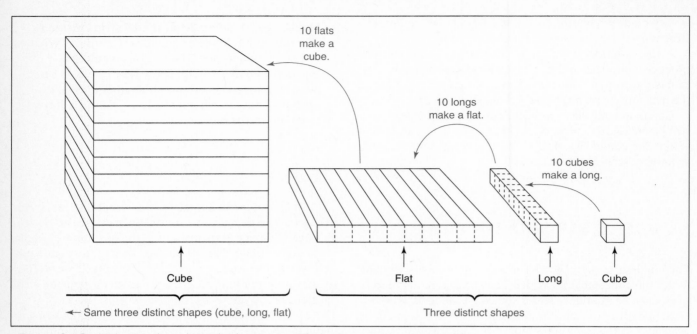

● **FIGURE 9.19** *With every three places, the shapes repeat. Each cube represents a one, each long represents a ten, and each flat represents a hundred.*

It is important for children to realize that the system does have a logical structure, is not totally arbitrary, and can be understood.

Conceptualizing Large Numbers

The ideas just discussed are only partially helpful in thinking about the actual quantities involved in very large numbers. For example, in extending the square, strip, square, strip sequence, some appreciation for the quantities of 1000 or of 100,000 is included. But it is hard for anyone to translate quantities of small squares into quantities of other items, distances, or time.

Creating References for Special Big Numbers

In these activities, numbers like 1000, 10,000, or even 1 million are translated literally or imaginatively into something that is easy or fun to think about. Interesting quantities become lasting reference points or benchmarks for large

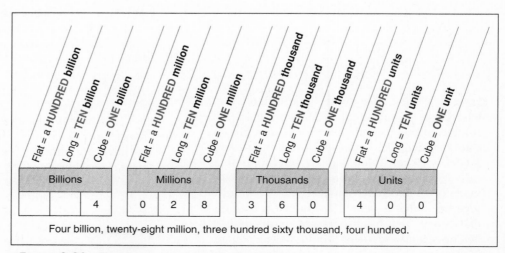

Four billion, twenty-eight million, three hundred sixty thousand, four hundred.

● **FIGURE 9.20** *The triples system for naming large numbers.*

numbers and thereby add meaning to numbers encountered in real life.

— ACTIVITY —

9.27 Collecting 10,000

Collections. As a class or grade-level project, collect some type of object with the objective of reaching some specific quantity—for example, 1000 or 10,000 buttons, walnuts, old pencils, jar lids, or pieces of junk mail. If you begin aiming for 100,000 or 1 million, be sure to think it through. One teacher spent nearly 10 years with her classes before amassing a million bottle caps. It takes a small dump truck to hold that many!

— ACTIVITY —

9.28 Showing 10,000

Illustrations. Sometimes it is easier to create large amounts. For example, start a project where students draw 100 or 200 or even 500 dots on a sheet of paper. Each week, different students contribute a specified number. Another idea is to cut up newspaper into pieces the same size as dollar bills to see what a large quantity would look like. Paper chain links can be constructed over time and hung down the hallways with special numbers marked. Let the school be aware of the ultimate goal.

— ACTIVITY —

9.29 How Long?/How Far?

Real and imagined distances. How long is a million baby steps? Other ideas that address length: toothpicks, dollar bills, or candy bars end to end; children holding hands in a line; blocks or bricks stacked up; children lying down head to toe. Real measures can also be used: feet, centimeters, meters.

— ACTIVITY —

9.30 A Long Time

Time. How long is 1000 seconds? How long is a million seconds? A billion? How long would it take to count to 10,000 or 1 million? (To make the

---

counts all the same, use your calculator to do the counting. Just press the $\boxed{=}$.) How long would it take to do some task like buttoning a button 1000 times?

Estimating Large Quantities

Activities 9.27 through 9.30 focus on a specific number. The reverse idea is to select a large quantity and find some way to measure, count, or estimate how many.

— ACTIVITY —

9.31 Really Large Quantities

Ask how many . . .

Candy bars would cover the floor of your room

Steps an ant would take to walk around the school building

Grains of rice would fill a cup or a gallon jug

Quarters could be stacked in one stack floor to ceiling

Pennies can be laid side by side down an entire block

Pieces of notebook paper would cover the gym floor

Seconds you have lived

Big-number projects need not take up large amounts of class time. They can be explored over several weeks as take-home projects or group projects or, perhaps best of all, be translated into great schoolwide estimation contests. One of the best ways to motivate projects around large numbers is with the many children's books that examine these ideas in inventive ways. A few suggestions follow.

LITERATURE CONNECTIONS

There are lots of different ways to think about using literature to investigate the ideas in this chapter. Books that emphasize groups of things, even simple counting books, are a good beginning to the notion of 10 things in a single group. Lots of books have wonderful explorations of large quantities and how they can be combined and separated. It does not take a great deal of imagination to use these books to begin to explore quantities in the hundreds with first graders up through the elementary years.

Moira's Birthday (Munsch, 1987)

As Moira plans her birthday party, she invites more and more children until she has invited all the children in the kindergarten, first, second, third, fourth, fifth, and sixth grades. Then she needs to order food. She orders 200 cakes and 200 pizzas. Wonderful bedlam ensues as the food and the children all arrive at the party. A second-grade teacher, Diane Oppedal (1995), used this story as a background for the question "How can you show 200 things in different ways?" Children used collections of things, bundles of Popsicle sticks, drawings, and many other ideas to show their way of illustrating too. As children work on this or similar projects, they can be encouraged to use some form of groups to keep track of their collections.

The same book can also be used to motivate a variety of computation situations that could be used prior to structured computation instruction. "How many children are in three classrooms?" "What if everyone at the party got two pieces of pizza?" "If Moira gave 37 of her 94 presents back to the children who helped her clean up, how many presents did she have left?"

How to Count like a Martian (St. John, 1975)

This book explores many different number systems from different ancient cultures (Chinese, Roman, Egyptian, etc.) and so has a culture connection as well as a mathematics connection. The contrast of the different systems, most of which are not place-value systems, can be a good way for children in the fourth and fifth grades to appreciate and discuss the base 10 place-value system. Most other numeration systems do not have a zero, for example. Several numeration systems use the same symbol repeatedly to express multiples of a certain quantity. Children could write numbers in different systems, try to compute in another system, or discuss how they might make up a system of their own. Why is it that most of the world has adopted the system we use?

The King's Commissioners (Friedman, 1994)

The king has so many commissioners he can't keep track of how many there are. In a hilarious tale, the commissioners are marched into the throne room to be counted. One person tries to count them by twos and another by fives. The princess convinces the king that there are many other excellent ways to count. The story is a natural background for place-value concepts, including grouping and different counting methods, large numbers, and informal early computation challenges. Stephanie Sheffield (1995) offers specific suggestions for using this story with children at about the second-grade level.

A Million Fish . . . More or Less (McKissack, 1992)

This story, which takes place in lower Louisiana, is a tall tale of a boy who catches three fish . . . and then a million more. The story is full of exaggerations such as a turkey that weighs 500 pounds and a jump-rope contest (using a snake) where the story's hero wins with 5553 jumps. "Could these things really be? How long would it take to jump 5553 times? Could Hugh put a million fish in his wagon? How do you write half of a million?" Rusty Bresser (1995) suggests a number of excellent ways this tale can be used to investigate large numbers and how they are written. The connections to real things and real ideas is just the ticket to add number sense to an upper-grade unit on place value.

Many other excellent books investigate very large numbers in interesting contexts. How Much Is a Million? (1985) and If You Made a Million (1989), both by David Schwartz, have become very popular. Wanda Gag's Millions of Cats (1928) is a classic that is still worth the time to investigate. Just one more of many possibilities is Six Dogs, Twenty-Three Cats, Forty-Five Mice, and One Hundred Sixteen Spiders (Chalmers, 1986). The imagination that these books inspire can lead children into fascinating investigations of large numbers, and with a bit of guidance, good place-value concepts can be visited along the way.

ASSESSMENT NOTES

Ongoing Assessment

Most of the activities suggested in this chapter serve as opportunities to find out what children know and understand about place value. They are performance tasks. A lot of the assessment information you will need can come from watching and listening as children do these tasks.

- How do children count or estimate quantities? Do they spontaneously use sets of tens?

- When materials are already arranged in groups of 10 (rows on a dot chart, counters in cups, dots in ten-frames) or in groups of 100, do they use these structures to tell how many?

- How flexible are children with their thinking about numbers? Can they take them apart and combine them in ways that reflect an understanding of ones, tens, and hundreds?

- How well are they able to relate numbers appropriate for their age to real quantities, measures, and events?

The following activity is frequently used in interviews with individual students but could easily be a task posed to the whole class or a small group for discussion. As you listen to how children solve these problems, you will realize that there is a lot more information to be found out about their thinking beyond simply getting the answer correct.

— ACTIVITY —

9.32 Mystery Mats

First, show a mat or board with some base 10 pieces covered and some showing. Tell the child how many pieces are hidden under the cover, and ask him or her to figure out how much is on the board altogether, as in Figure 9.21(a).

After that, show a board partially covered as before. Tell the child how many pieces are on the board altogether, and ask how many are hidden, as in Figure 9.21(b).

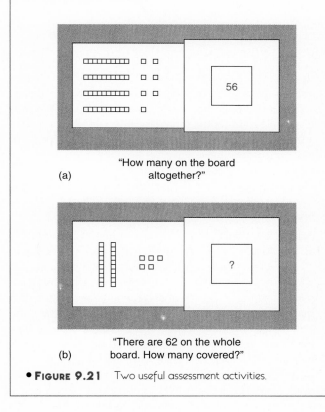

(a)   "How many on the board altogether?"

(b)   "There are 62 on the whole board. How many covered?"

● **FIGURE 9.21**   Two useful assessment activities.

Activity 9.32 could also involve hundreds. The amounts that you tell the child could be given in written form instead of orally.

Diagnosis of Place-Value Concepts

Much information can be had from observation and discussion with your class. However, you may still be curious to know exactly what level of understanding a few particular children in your room may have about place-value concepts. Children are often able to disguise their lack of understanding in this area by following directions, using the tens and ones pieces in prescribed ways, and using the language of place value without really knowing what the words mean.

Another reason for a short diagnostic interview with a few students may be to confirm that the assessments you have made through observation are in fact valid.

The diagnostic tasks presented here are designed to help teachers look more closely at children's understanding of place value. They are not suggested as definitive tests but as means of obtaining information for the thoughtful teacher. These tasks have been used by several researchers and are adapted primarily from Labinowicz (1985) and Ross (1986). The tasks are designed for one-on-one settings. They should not be used as instructional activities.

Counting Skills

A variety of oral counting tasks provide insight into the counting sequence.

- Count forward for me, starting at 77.
- Count backward, starting at 55.
- Count by tens.
- Count by tens, starting at 34.
- Count backward by tens, starting at 130.

In the tasks that follow, the manner in which the child responds is at least as important as the answers to the questions. For example, counting individual squares on tens pieces that are known to the child as "tens" will produce correct answers but indicates that the structure of tens is not being used.

One More and Ten More, One Less and Ten Less

Write the number 342. Have the child read the number. Then have the child write the number that is 1 more than the number. Next ask for the number that is 10 more than the number. Following the responses, you may wish to explore further with models. One less and 10 less can be checked the same way.

Digit Correspondence

Dump out 36 blocks. Ask the child to count the blocks, and then have the child write the number that tells how many there are. Circle the 6 in 36 and ask, "Does this part of your 36 have anything to do with how many blocks there are?" Then circle the 3 and repeat the question exactly. Do not give clues. Based on responses to the task, Ross (1989) has identified five distinct levels of understanding of place value.

1. *Single numeral.* The child writes 36 but views it as a single numeral. The individual digits 3 and 6 have no meaning by themselves.

2. *Position names.* The child identifies correctly the tens and ones positions but still makes no connections between the individual digits and the blocks.

3. *Face value.* The child matches 6 blocks with the 6 and 3 blocks with the 3.

4. *Transition to place value.* The 6 is matched with 6 blocks and the 3 with the remaining 30 blocks but not as 3 groups of 10.

5. *Full understanding.* The 3 is correlated with 3 groups of 10 blocks and the 6 with 6 single blocks.

Using Tens

Dump out 47 counters and have the child count them. Next show the child at least ten cards, each with a ten-frame drawn on it. (Spaces should be large enough to hold the counters used.) Ask, "If we wanted to put these counters in the spaces on these cards, how many cards could we fill up?" (If the ten-frame has been used in class to model sets of 10, use a different frame such as a 10-pin arrangement of circles. Be sure the child knows there are 10 spaces on each card.)

Using Groups of 10

Prepare cards with beans or other counters glued to the cards in an obvious arrangement of 10. Supply at least ten cards and a large supply of the beans. After you are sure that the child has counted several cards of beans and knows there are 10 on each, say, "Show me 34 beans." (Does the child count individual beans or use the cards of 10?) The activity can also be done with hundreds.

REFLECTIONS ON CHAPTER 9: WRITING TO LEARN

1. Explain how a child who has not yet developed base 10 concepts understands quantities as large as, say, 85. Contrast this with a child who understands these same quantities in terms of base 10 groupings.

2. What is meant by *equivalent representations*?

3. Explain the three ways one can count a set of objects and how these methods of counting can be used to co-ordinate concepts and oral and written names for numbers.

4. Describe the two types of physical models for base 10 concepts. What is the significance of the difference between these two types of models? Why is an abacus not considered a model for place value?

5. Describe an activity for developing base 10 grouping concepts, and reflect on how the activity encourages children to construct base 10 concepts.

6. How do children learn to write two- and three-digit numbers in a way that is connected to the base 10 meanings of ones and tens, or ones, tens, and hundreds?

7. How would you describe good place-value number sense? There are a variety of aspects to number sense with large numbers. Describe activities that are designed to help develop these different features of good number sense with larger numbers.

8. What are two different ideas that you would want children to know about very large numbers (beyond 1000)? Describe one or two activities for each.

FOR DISCUSSION AND EXPLORATION

1. Based on the suggestions toward the end of this chapter and on the content of a standard basal textbook, design a diagnostic interview for a child at a particular grade level, and conduct the interview. It is a good idea to take a friend to act as an observer or to use a tape recorder or video recorder to keep track of how the interview went. For a related discussion of children's place-value thinking and suggestions for preparing your interview, read Chapters 10 and 11 of *Learning from Children* (Labinowicz, 1985).

2. A popular collection of activities, sometimes referred to as "trading activities," are done with base 10 models. In all of these activities, children have a place-value mat on which they accumulate materials or from which they remove materials. The activities generally take a game format. Perhaps a die is rolled and the die tells the child how many ones are to be placed on the mat or how many may be removed. Whenever 10 pieces in one section are accumulated, a trade is made for a single piece in the next place: 10 ones for a ten, 10 tens for a hundred. Similarly, in the process of removing pieces, trades are made in the reverse manner: 1 ten for 10 ones.

   Do these trading activities contribute any new connections or ideas to place-value understanding? If so, what are they? Are there any activities in this chapter that get at the same ideas? These activities have been omitted from this chapter (they were included in earlier editions) because they seem so prescriptive that children can do them by following directions rather than by reflecting on and developing the concepts involved. Would you agree?

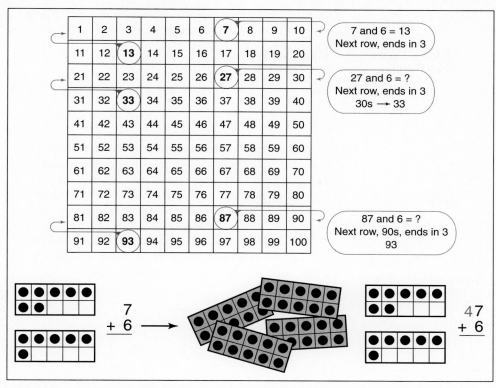

1	2	3	4	5	6	**7**	8	9	10
11	12	**13**	14	15	16	17	18	19	20
21	22	23	24	25	26	**27**	28	29	30
31	32	**33**	34	35	36	37	38	39	40
41	42	43	44	45	46	47	48	49	50
51	52	53	54	55	56	57	58	59	60
61	62	63	64	65	66	67	68	69	70
71	72	73	74	75	76	77	78	79	80
81	82	83	84	85	86	**87**	88	89	90
91	92	**93**	94	95	96	97	98	99	100

7 and 6 = 13
Next row, ends in 3

27 and 6 = ?
Next row, ends in 3
30s → 33

87 and 6 = ?
Next row, 90s, ends in 3
93

$$7 + 6 \rightarrow$$

$$47 + 6$$

● **FIGURE 10.3**   *Two ways of looking at higher-decade addition.*

Front-End Approaches for Addition

Building on the ideas developed so far, there are several ways to add two-digit and three-digit numbers. Rather than force one method, you might pose a problem and have students find at least one or two ways to solve it mentally.

....

Example:

46 + 38

There are at least three equally good methods that might be used.

1. Add tens from one number to the other complete number:

   46 and 30 is 76.
   76 and 8 is 84.

2. Add the tens and the ones separately and then combine:

   40 and 30 is 70.
   6 and 8 is 14.
   70 and 14 is 84.

3. Round one number, add, and then adjust:

   46 and 40 is 86 (round the 38).
   That's 2 too much → 84.

Try these same three approaches with 382 + 75.

Flexible Approaches for Subtraction

As with addition, there are several possibilities for subtraction done mentally. After developing reasonably good addition methods, begin to pose subtraction tasks and discuss various approaches.

....

Example:
Can you find three ways to do this?

83 − 28

1. Add on tens to get close:

   28 and 50 is 78.
   And 5 more is 83 → 55.

2. Add up to the first 10 and then get the rest:

   28 and 2 is 30.
   And 53 more is 83.
   So 2 and 53 → 55.

3. Round the small number, subtract, and then adjust:

   83 − 30 is 53.
   But that was 2 too many off → 55.

The first two methods are based on thinking about the missing part as was discussed in Chapter 8 on basic facts. The only difficulty is in keeping track of the intermediate results, so perhaps these can be written down. The third approach involves an adjustment at the end that can be confusing. Depending on which way you round the small number, you have to adjust accordingly, and there is a tendency to adjust in the wrong direction or at least to be a bit unsure.

Working with Nice Numbers

The ideas presented here are designed to add flexibility with adding and subtracting.

Some numbers are "nice" to work with, like 100 or 700 or 50 or even 450. Try adding nice and not-so-nice numbers. For example, try adding 450 and 27, or add 700 and 248. Subtraction with nice numbers is also easy. For 500 − 73, think "73 and *what* makes 100?" For 650 − 85, first take off 50 from 600 and then 35 more. Notice the two different ways that nice numbers are used in the last two examples. The next two activities help with this type of thinking.

---ACTIVITY---

10.3 The Other Part of 100

Give students a number, say, 28, and have them determine the "other part of 100" (72). Discuss their thought patterns. ("Can you think of two different approaches?") The other part of 50 is just as easy. Later expand the game to get the other part of 600 or 450 or other numbers that end with 00 or 50.

---ACTIVITY---

10.4 50 and Some More

Say a number, and have the students respond with "50 and _____." For 63, the response would be "50 and 13." Use other numbers such as "450 and some more."

Compatible Numbers

Compatible numbers for addition and subtraction are numbers that go together easily to make nice numbers. Numbers that make tens or hundreds are the most common example. Compatibles also include numbers that end in 5, 25, 50, or 75, since these numbers are also easy to work with. The teaching task is to get students accustomed to looking for combinations that work together and then looking for these combinations in computational situations.

---ACTIVITY---

10.5 Searching for Pairs

This activity can be used to help children think about "nice combinations" or compatible numbers. Several searches are presented in Figure 10.4.

Pair searches could be worksheets or could be presented on an overhead projector with students writing down or calling out appropriate pairs. As a variation for an independent activity, the numbers could be written on small cards. Students can see how quickly they can pair up the cards.

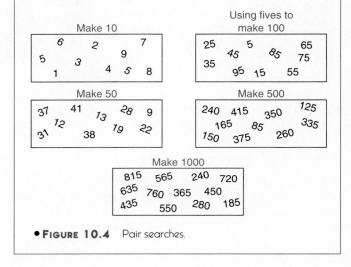

●**FIGURE 10.4**   *Pair searches.*

---ACTIVITY---

10.6 Compatible Calculations for Addition

Present strings of numbers that use compatibles.

30 + 80 + 40 + 50 + 10
25 + 125 + 75 + 250 + 50
95 + 15 + 35 + 5 + 65

Strings such as these can be approached in two ways, and each should be practiced. One way is to search out compatible combinations such as 5 and 95 in the third example. The other way is simply to add one addend at a time, saying the result as you go. For the first example, that would be "30, 110, 150, 200, 210."

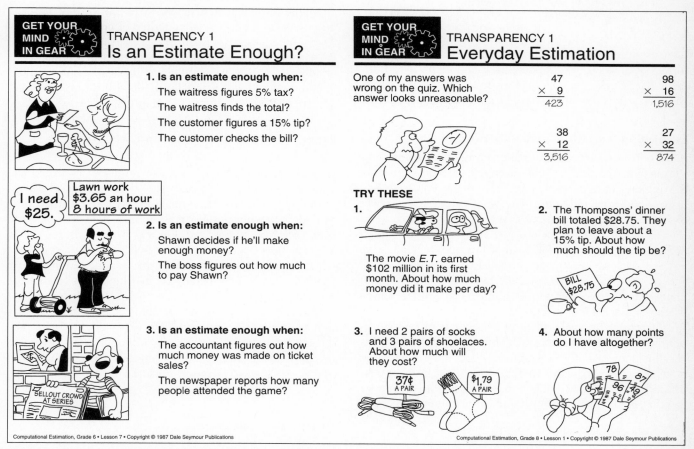

• **FIGURE 10.7**   *Two pages from a teacher resource book relating estimation to real-world situations.*

Source: Reys, Trafton, Reys, & Zawojewski (1987). Reprinted by permission.

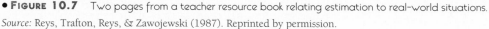

what it means to give an estimate. Two excellent estimators will often produce different estimates for the same computation. Even the same person may give different estimates for the same computation on different days and in different circumstances. The requirements of the situation can change our estimate and our method of producing it. If you want to be sure you have enough money to pay for the five items you've picked up in the drugstore, the accuracy of your estimate depends on how close it appears the total might be to the amount you have in your pocket.

An Early Estimation Alternative

Another way to indicate that estimation is not aimed at one right answer is to avoid the actual estimate altogether. Rather than have students provide an estimate, ask if the result of a particular computation is more or less than a specified value. For example, is 347 + 129 more or less than 500? This is an especially useful technique for the primary grades and when just beginning your estimation program. Obviously, the more-or-less-than approach can be used with any

operation and any size numbers. In fact, we use this method frequently in real life. One example occurs when we look at a few items selected for purchase and wonder if the total is more or less than the amount of cash in our wallet.

A similar way to avoid the one-right-answer syndrome is to provide several computations and a single target number. The task is to determine which computation will be closest to the target. (See Activity 10.11, p. 207.)

COMPUTATIONAL ESTIMATION STRATEGIES

Next, different algorithms or strategies for estimation will be explored. When different methods are used on the same computation, different estimates result. Making adjustments after the mental computation is another factor. Experience and conceptual knowledge will eventually help students make better estimates, but it is crucial that children understand that there is no one answer to an estimation.

Front-End Methods

Front-end methods involve the use of the leading or leftmost digits in numbers and ignoring the rest. After an estimate is made on the basis of only these front-end digits, an adjustment can be made by noticing how much has been ignored. In fact, the adjustment may also be a front-end approach.

Front-End Addition and Subtraction

Front end is a very easy estimation strategy for addition or subtraction. This approach is reasonable when all or most of the numbers have the same number of digits. Figure 10.8 illustrates the strategy. Notice that when a number has fewer digits than the rest, that number is ignored completely.

After adding or subtracting the front digits, an adjustment is made to correct for the digits or numbers that were ignored. Making an adjustment is actually a separate skill. For very young children, practice first just using the front digits. Pay special attention to numbers of uneven length when not in a column format.

When teaching this strategy, present additions or subtractions in column form, and cover all but the leading digits. Discuss the sum or difference estimate using these digits. Is it more or less than the actual amount? Is the estimate off by a little or a lot? Later, show numbers in horizontal form or on price tags that are not lined up. What numbers should be added?

The leading-digit strategy is easy to use and easy to teach because it does not require rounding or changing numbers. The numbers used are there and visible, so children can see what they are working with. It is a good first strategy for children as early as the third grade. It is also useful for older children and adults, especially as they learn to make better adjustments in the front-end sum or difference.

Front-End Multiplication and Division

For multiplication and division, the front-end method uses the first digit in each of the two numbers involved. The computation is then done using zeros in the other positions. For example, a front-end estimation of 48×7 is 40 times 7, or 280. When both numbers have more than one digit, the front ends of both are used. For 452×23, consider 400×20, or 8000.

Division with pencil and paper is almost a front-end strategy already. First determine in which column the first digit of the quotient belongs. For $7\overline{)3482}$, the first digit is a 4 and belongs in the hundreds column, over the 4. Therefore, the front-end estimate is 400. This method always produces a low estimate, as students will quickly figure out. In this particular example, the answer is clearly much closer to 500, so 480 or 490 is a good adjustment.

Rounding Methods

Rounding is the most familiar form of estimation. Estimation based on rounding is a way of changing the problem to one that is easier to work with mentally. Good estimators follow their mental computation with an adjustment to compensate for the rounding. To be useful in estimation, rounding should be flexible and well understood conceptually.

Rounding in Addition and Subtraction

When a lot of numbers are to be added, it is usually a good idea to round them to the same place value. Keep a running sum as you round each number. In Figure 10.9, the same total is estimated two ways using rounding. A combination of the two is also possible.

In subtraction situations, there are only two numbers to deal with. For subtraction and for additions involving only two addends, it is generally necessary to round only one of the two numbers. For subtraction, round only the subtracted number. In $6724 - 1863$, round 1863 to 2000. Then it is easy: $6724 - 2000$ is 4724. Now adjust. You took away a bigger number, so the result must be too small. Adjust to about 4800. For $627 + 385$, you might round 627 to 625 because multiples of 25 are almost as easy to work with as multiples of 10 or 100. After substituting 625 for 627, you may or may not want to round 385 to 375 or 400. The point is that there are no rigid rules. Choices depend on the relationships held by the estimator, on how quickly the estimate is needed, and on how accurate an

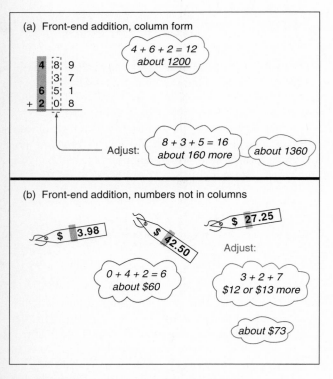

• FIGURE 10.8   Front-end estimation in addition.

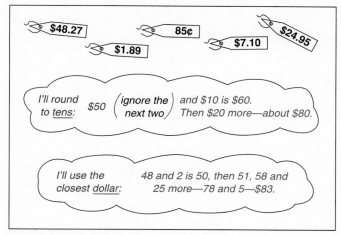

• **FIGURE 10.9** Rounding in addition.

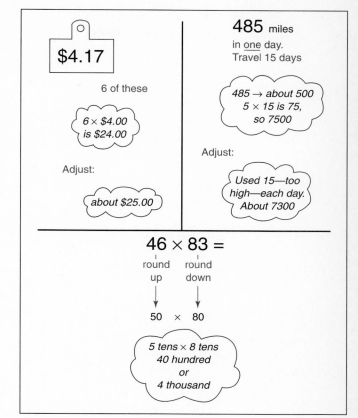

• **FIGURE 10.10** Rounding in multiplication.

estimate is required. The more adjusting and "playing around" with the numbers, the more accurate you are likely to be. After a while, however, you should reach for the calculator.

Rounding in Multiplication and Division

The rounding strategy for multiplication is no different from that for other operations. However, the error involved can be significant, especially when both factors are rounded. In Figure 10.10, several multiplication situations are illustrated, and rounding is used to estimate each.

If one number can be rounded to 10, 100, or 1000, the resulting product is easy to determine without adjusting the other factor.

When one factor is a single digit, examine the other factor. Consider the product 7 × 836. If 836 is rounded to 800, the estimate is relatively easy and is low by 7 × 36. If a more accurate result is required, round 836 to 840, and use a front-end computation. Then the estimate is 5600 plus 280, or 5880 (7 × 800 and 7 × 40). The parts technique relies on the skill of doing the front-end multiplication mentally.

If possible, round only one factor—select the larger one if it is significantly larger. (Why?) For example, in 47 × 7821, 47 × 8000 is 376,000, but 50 × 8000 is 400,000.

Another good rule of thumb with multiplication is to round one factor up and the other down (even if that is not the closest round number). When estimating 86 × 28, 86 is about in the middle, but 28 is very close to 30. Try rounding 86 down to 80 and 28 up to 30. The actual product is 2408, only 8 off from the 80 × 30 estimate. If both numbers were rounded to the nearest 10, the estimate would have been based on 90 × 30, with an error of nearly 300.

With one-digit divisors, it is almost always best to search for a compatible dividend rather than to round off. For example, 7)4325 is best estimated by using the close compatible number, 4200, to yield an estimate of 600. Rounding

would suggest a dividend of 4000 or 4300, neither of which is very helpful. (Recall the contrived examples in the "Mental Division" discussion.)

When the divisor is a two-digit or three-digit number, rounding it to tens or hundreds makes looking for a missing factor much easier. For example, 425)3890, round the divisor to 400. Then think, 400 times *what* is close to 3890?

Using Compatible Numbers

When adding a long list of numbers, it is sometimes useful to look for two or three numbers that can be grouped to make 10 or 100. If numbers in the list can be adjusted slightly to produce these groups, that will make finding an estimate easier. This approach is illustrated in Figure 10.11 (p. 204).

In subtraction, it is often possible to adjust only one number to produce an easily observed difference. The thought process may be closer to addition than subtraction, as illustrated in Figure 10.12 (p. 204).

Frequently in the real world, an estimate is needed for a large list of addends that are relatively close. This might happen with a series of prices of similar items, attendance at a series of events in the same arena, cars passing a point on successive days, or other similar data. In these cases, as il-

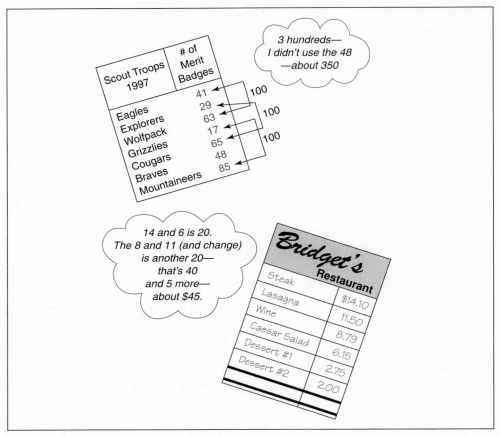

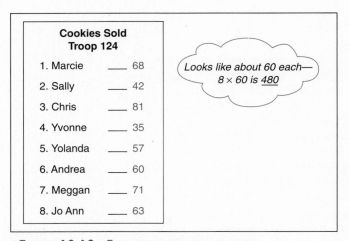

• FIGURE 10.11   Compatibles used in addition.

• FIGURE 10.12   Compatibles can mean an adjustment that produces an easy difference.

lustrated in Figure 10.13, a nice number can be selected as representative of each and multiplication used to determine the total. This is more of an *averaging technique* than a compatible numbers strategy.

One of the best uses of the compatible number strategy is in division. The two exercises shown in Figure 10.14 illustrate adjusting the divisor or dividend (or both) to create a division that comes out even and is therefore easy to do mentally. The strategy is based on whole-number arithmetic

and is not difficult. Many percent, fraction, and rate situations involve division, and the compatible number strategy is quite useful, as shown in Figure 10.15.

Cookies Sold Troop 124	
1. Marcie	____ 68
2. Sally	____ 42
3. Chris	____ 81
4. Yvonne	____ 35
5. Yolanda	____ 57
6. Andrea	____ 60
7. Meggan	____ 71
8. Jo Ann	____ 63

Looks like about 60 each— 8 × 60 is 480

• FIGURE 10.13   Estimating sums using averaging.

●**FIGURE 10.14**   Adjusting to simplify division.

Source: GUESS (Guide to Using Estimation and Strategies) *Box II*, cards 2 and 3. (Reys & Reys, 1983). Reprinted by permission.

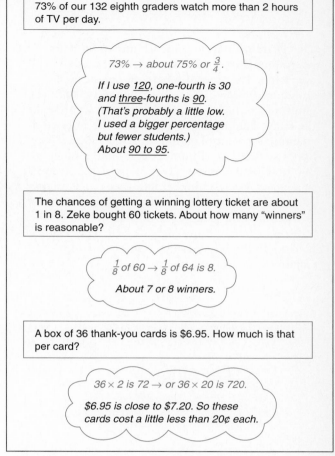

●**FIGURE 10.15**   Using compatible numbers in division.

ESTIMATION EXERCISES

The ideas presented so far illustrate some of the types of estimation and thought patterns you want to foster in your classroom. However, making up examples and putting them into a realistic context is not easy and is very time-consuming. Fortunately, good estimation material is now being included in virtually all textbooks. Text material will provide you with hints and periodic exercises for integrating estimation throughout your program. This exposure, however, will probably not be sufficient to provide an ongoing, intensive program for developing estimation skills with your students. Try adding to the text using one or more of the many good teacher resource materials that are available commercially. Some of these are listed at the end of the chapter.

Teacher's guides, resource books, and professional books and articles on estimation offer good activities or activity models that you can easily adapt to your particular needs without additional resources. The examples presented here are not designed to teach estimation strategies but offer useful formats to provide your students with practice using skills as they are being developed.

Calculator Activities

The calculator is not only a good source of estimation activities but is also one of the reasons estimation is so important. In the real world, we frequently hit a wrong key, leave off a zero or a decimal, or simply enter numbers incorrectly. An estimate of the expected result is one way we can alert ourselves to these errors. The calculator as an estimation-teaching tool lets students work independently or in pairs in a challenging, fun way without fear of embarrassment. With a calculator for the overhead projector, some of the activities described here work very well with a full class.

─ACTIVITY─

10.7 The Range Game

This is an estimation game for any of the four operations. First pick a start number and an operation. The start number and operation are stored in the calculator. Students then take turns entering a number and pressing $=$ to try to make the result land in the target range. The following example for multiplication illustrates the activity: Suppose that a start number of 17 and a range of 800 to 830 are chosen. Press 17 $\times$ $=$ to store 17 as a factor. Press a number and then $=$. Perhaps you try 25. (Press 25 $=$.) The result is 425. That is about half the target. Try 50. The result is 850—maybe 2 or 3 too high. Try 48. The result is 816—in the target range! Figure 10.16 gives examples for all four operations. Prepare a list of

After entering the setup with the start # as shown, players take turns pressing a number, then $=$ to try to get a result in the target range.

Addition:
Press: 0 $+$ (start #) $=$

START		TARGET
153	⟶	790 → 800
216	⟶	400 → 410
53	⟶	215 → 220

Subtraction:
Press: 0 $-$ (start #) $=$

START		TARGET
18	⟶	25 → 30
41	⟶	630 → 635
129	⟶	475 → 485

Multiplication:
Press: (start #) $\times$ 0 $=$

START		TARGET
67	⟶	1100 → 1200
143	⟶	3500 → 3600
39	⟶	1600 → 1700

Division:
Press: 0 $\div$ (start #) $=$

START		TARGET
20	⟶	25 → 30
39	⟶	50 → 60
123	⟶	15 → 20

● **FIGURE 10.16** "The Range Game"—a calculator game.

start numbers and target ranges. Let students play in pairs to see who can hit the most targets on the list (Wheatley & Hersberger, 1986).

"The Range Game" can be played with an overhead calculator with the whole class, by an individual, or by two or three children with calculators who can race one another. The speed element is important. The width of the range and the type of numbers used can all be adjusted to suit the level of the class.

─ACTIVITY─

10.8 Secret Sum

This calculator activity uses the memory feature. A target number is selected—for example, 100. Students take turns entering a number and pressing the $M+$ key. Each of the numbers is accumulated in the memory, but the sum is never displayed on the screen. If one player thinks that the other player has made the sum go beyond the target, he or she announces "over," and the MRC (memory return) key is pressed to check. If a player is able to hit the target exactly, bonus points can be awarded. Interesting strategies quickly develop (Mathematical Sciences Education Board, 1989).

"Secret Sum" can also be played with the $M-$ key. First enter a total amount in the memory. Each player's number is followed by a press of $M-$ and is subtracted from the memory. Here the first to correctly announce that the other player has made the memory go negative is the winner.

─ACTIVITY─

10.9 The Range Game: Sequential Versions

Select a target range as before. Next enter the starting number in the calculator, and hand it to the first player. For addition and subtraction, the first player then presses either $+$ or $-$, followed by a number, and then $=$. The next player begins his or her turn by entering $+$ or $-$ and an appropriate number, operating on the previous result. If the target is 423 to 425, a sequence of turns might go like this:

Start with 119

$\boxed{+}\,350\,\boxed{=}\to 469$ (too high)

$\boxed{-}\,42\,\boxed{=}\to 427$ (a little over)

$\boxed{-}\,3\,\boxed{=}\to 424$ (success)

For multiplication or division, only one operation is used through the whole game. After the first or second turn, decimal factors are usually required. This variation provides excellent understanding of multiplication or division by decimals. A sequence for a target of 262 to 265 might be like this:

Start with 63

$\boxed{\times}\,5\,\boxed{=}\to 315$ (too high)

$\boxed{\times}\,0.7\,\boxed{=}\to 220.5$ (too low)

$\boxed{\times}\,1.3\,\boxed{=}\to 286.65$ (too high)

$\boxed{\times}\,0.9\,\boxed{=}\to 257.985$ (too low)

$\boxed{\times}\,1.03\,\boxed{=}\to 265.72455$ (very close!)

(What would you press next?)

Try a target of 76 to 80, begin with 495, and use only division.

Computer Programs

A number of computer programs that practice estimation skills are available. Computer programs can present problems for estimation, control speed, and compare the result to the actual answer. Most allow the teacher or user to adjust the skill level of the exercises. These programs can be effectively used with a full class using a large monitor or projection system. Students can write down estimates on paper within the allotted time frame. In *Estimation: Quick Solve I* (Minnesota Educational Computing Consortium, 1990), students enter their estimate of a computation in a time frame that can be adjusted by the teacher. Rather than tell students what the exact computation is, the program places the students' response on a number line on which a range of "good enough" values is highlighted. This helps with the idea that there are many good estimates and discourages children from trying to calculate the actual answer, something they have a tendency to do if given the opportunity.

Activities for the Overhead Projector

The overhead projector offers several advantages. You can prepare the computational exercises ahead of time. You can control how long a particular computation is viewed by the

students. There is no need to prepare handouts. Commercial materials such as GUESS cards (Figure 10.14, p. 205) can be copied onto transparencies for instructional purposes.

---ACTIVITY---

10.10 What Was Your Method?

Select any single computational estimation problem and put it on the board or overhead. Allow 10 seconds for each class member to get an estimate. Discuss briefly the various estimation techniques that were used. As a variation, prepare a problem with an estimation illustrated. For example, 139×43 might be estimated as 6000. Ask questions concerning this estimate: "How do you think that estimate was arrived at? Was that a good approach? How should it be adjusted? Why might someone select 150 instead of 140 as a substitute for 139?" Almost every estimate can involve different choices and methods. Alternatives make good discussions, help students see different methods, and learn that there is no single correct estimate.

---ACTIVITY---

10.11 Which One's Closest?

Make a transparency of a page of drill-and-practice computations (see Figure 10.17). Have students focus on a single row or other collection of five to eight problems. Ask them to find the one with an answer that is closest to some round number that you provide. One transparency could provide a week's worth of 5-minute drills.

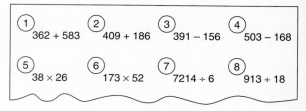

Which of these is closest to 600? To 1000? To 10?

● **Figure 10.17** A textbook drill page can double as an estimation exercise.

—— ACTIVITY ——

10.12 In the Ballpark

Also with a page of problems from a workbook, write in answers to six or seven problems. On one or two problems, make a significant error that can be caught by estimation. For example, write 5408 ÷ 26 = 28 (instead of 208) or 36 × 17 = 342 (instead of 612). Other answers should be correct. Encourage the class to estimate each problem to find those "not even in the ballpark" errors.

—— ACTIVITY ——

10.13 Is This Enough?

Make "Is This Enough?" transparencies. Select an amount such as 10 or 50 (or $10 or $50), and write that at the top of a transparency. Below it, put a variety of computations or realistic situations. The task is to decide quickly if the top amount is *clearly enough* (more) or *clearly not enough* (less) or perhaps *too close to call.* An example is shown in Figure 10.18. Show only one example at a time and only for about 10 seconds. This type of estimation is frequently done in real life and does not always call for a very accurate estimate.

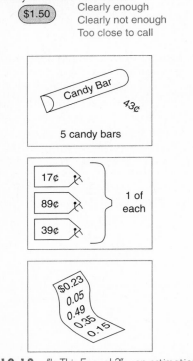

• **FIGURE 10.18**   "Is This Enough?"—an estimation game for the whole class.

ESTIMATING WITH FRACTIONS, DECIMALS, AND PERCENTS

Fractions, decimals, and percents are three different notations for rational numbers. Many real-world situations that call for computational estimation involve the part-to-whole relationships of rational numbers. A few examples are suggested here:

SALE! $51.99. Marked one-fourth off. What was the original price?

About 62 percent of the 834 students bought their lunch last Wednesday. How many bought lunch?

Tickets sold for $1.25. If attendance was 3124, about how much was the total gate?

I drove 337 miles on 12.35 gallons of gas. How many miles per gallon did my car get?

With the exception of a few examples, this chapter has avoided estimations with fractions, decimals, and percents. To estimate with these numbers first involves an ability to estimate with whole numbers. Beyond this, it involves an understanding of fractions and decimals and what these two types of numbers mean. Calculations with percents are always done as fractions or as decimals. The key is to be able to use an appropriate fraction or decimal equivalent.

In the first of the examples just presented, one approach is based on the realization that if $51.99 (or $52) is the result of one-fourth off, that means $52 is three-fourths of the total. So one-fourth is a third of $52, or a little less than $18. Thus about $52 + $18 = $70, or about $69, seems a fair estimate of the original cost. Notice that the conceptualization of the problem involves an understanding of fractions, but the estimation skill involves only whole numbers. This is also the case for almost all problems involving fractions, decimals, or percents.

From a developmental perspective, it is important to see that the skills of estimation are separate from the conceptual knowledge of rational numbers. It would be a mistake to work on the difficult processes of estimation using fractions or percents if concepts of those numbers were poorly developed. In later chapters, where rational number numeration is discussed, it is shown that an ability to estimate can contribute to increased flexibility or number sense with fractions, decimals, and percents.

LITERATURE CONNECTIONS

Children's literature can play a very useful role in the mental computation and computational estimation strands of your mathematics curriculum. It is not always a lot of fun to sit in class and try to do mental computations, and estimations really need a context that provides a need for an estimate. Enter children's books. There are lots of fascinating books that involve large numbers and opportunities to compute. Some are about real data, and others are fictional.

Cookies (Jaspersohn, 1993)

This is the true story of Wally Amos and his Famous Amos Chocolate Chip Cookies. (Are you interested already?) The text includes a large number of color and black-and-white photos that show the production and distribution of Famous Amos cookies. Because it is filled with facts about the cookies—numbers sold, number the average person eats in a year, and so on—it requires little imagination to pose questions that require computation and that children will find interesting. Although actual computations can be done on a calculator, this context clearly suggests that estimates and round numbers make more sense. As you discuss ideas generated by the book, some computations can be done mentally to determine exact answers. Other computations will be estimates. Students can extend the story to a project to research cookie consumption in their home, data from grocery stores about other cookies, or the number of trucks or miles required to get cookies to market. The possibilities are endless. During these projects, suggest that students pay attention to where an estimate makes more sense than an exact computation. Find out if there are places as they are working on their project where they made a quick mental estimate or did a mental computation.

Is a Blue Whale the Biggest Thing There Is? (Wells, 1993)

This is one of the most intriguing books you will find about large things and large distances. Blue whales look small next to Mount Everest, which in turn looks small next to the earth. The data in the book allow children to make other comparisons, such as the number of fourth graders that would have the same weight or volume as a blue whale or would fill the gymnasium. As with the Famous Amos data, these comparisons are the perfect place for estimations and discussions about how much accuracy is necessary to make a meaningful comparison. Bresser (1995) provides excellent insights into the use of this story with fourth-, fifth-, and sixth-grade students.

The 329th Friend (Sharmat, 1979)

This book not only offers the opportunity to examine mental math strategies and practice in the context of the story but is also about friendship and the need to be liked. The story is about Emery Raccoon, who has no friends. Because he is lonely, Emery invites 328 strangers to lunch to make new friends. There are considerations about the number of dishes, knives, forks, and spoons that suggest multiplying 329 by small numbers and different ways of doing this.

The story is easily expanded into other similar number questions. At the end, Emery discovers that although his guests ignored him, there was one friend that was there all along—himself.

ASSESSMENT NOTES

As with any other part of the mathematics curriculum, proper assessment of mental strategies will help you know how well your students are doing, so you will be able to plan your next lessons accordingly. Assessment is also an important method of communicating to students the values that you do (or do not) attribute to mental forms of computation. If mental computation and estimation are to be the most important forms of computation in your curriculum, your overall assessment and grading scheme should reflect this value in a proportionate manner.

Ongoing Assessment

Just as development of mental computation and estimation skills is an ongoing matter, so should the assessment of these areas of the curriculum be ongoing. Giving tests or quizzes of mental methods may likely cause tension and pressure and result in poor performance. Generally, tests of mental computation and estimation are not necessary. In the spirit of integrating assessment and instruction as seen by the *Standards*, make it a point to find out and record how your students are progressing at the same time that they are developing and practicing these skills. A simple checklist with your objectives and a space for comments can work quite well. An example is illustrated in Figure 10.19 (p. 210).

Figure 10.19 is just one example of a checklist. Note that the third column is essentially a minirubric. Students' names can be listed in groups, depending on where they sit in the room or are arranged according to cooperative learning groups.

As you listen to individuals explain their computations or estimation strategies, you will be able to find out all you really need to know. Adjust your checklist periodically to match the ideas and skills you are currently working on. Some teachers may prefer to use cards for each student or some other format such as those suggested in Chapter 5. The format should match your own needs.

If you choose to give a periodic quiz or test of mental skills, compare the results with the information you have gathered through planned observations. Did you get any new information? Were the results consistent? If not, why not? Of course, these questions are always valid, but perhaps more so in this strand of the curriculum than in some others.

Topic: Mental addition and subtraction Names	Adds 2-digit + 1-digit numbers	2-digit + 2-digit Note methods	Flexibility in choosing a method 1 2 3	Comments
Lalie				
Pete				
Sid				
Lakeshia				
George				
Pam				
Maria				
Lucy				

• **FIGURE 10.19** *A checklist can be a good way to record useful observations concerning mental computation.*

Occasional Interviews

It is not always easy to tell what techniques or thought processes are being used by individual students. For example, some students may get overly attached to a particular approach and not be flexible enough to switch to a more efficient method when the numbers call for it. One way to find this out is to conduct a short test on a one-on-one basis. Give perhaps five items for mental computation or estimation. Immediately afterward, return to each answer, and ask the student to explain how the estimate was made. This form of listening to your students will be very valuable in deciding how to pace your program and determining if there are concepts or strategies that require extra emphasis.

REFLECTIONS ON CHAPTER 10: WRITING TO LEARN

1. When a real situation or problem requiring a computation confronts us, what is the first decision that is usually made? Give a personal example of each situation.

2. Four alternatives are generally available if an exact answer to a computation is required. Suggest a situation where each may be reasonable.

3. Explain the statement "Pencil-and-paper algorithms are right-handed and digit-oriented." How are mental methods the opposite of this?

4. Why is it not reasonable to select a single method of computing mentally and have students learn and practice it in the same way that pencil-and-paper algorithms are developed?

5. Explain how each of the following computations can be done in a completely mental way and obtain exact answers. Whenever there is more than one reasonable method, give the others as well.

77 + 6	43 − 7
84 + 57	136 − 64
236 + 479	458 − 89

6. Give an explanation of each of the following mental multiplication methods. For each, select an example that is appropriate for the method.

   a. Front-end digits

   b. Multiples of 10 or 100

   c. Compensation

   d. Halve and double

7. Explain why mental division is actually mental multiplication.

8. What are some of the things that are important to communicate to students about computational estimation in addition to helping them learn various strategies?

9. Name at least one method whereby students can begin to do estimations without having actually to supply an estimate. Why would you want to use this in the classroom?

10. Describe each of these estimation strategies, using an example and an explanation.

   a. Front-end addition or subtraction

   b. Front-end multiplication

   c. Rounding

   d. Compatible numbers

11. How can the calculator be used to practice estimation strategies?

FOR DISCUSSION AND EXPLORATION

1. Examine one of the following teacher resources:

   a. *Computational Estimation (Grades 6, 7, 8)* (Reys, Trafton, Reys, & Zawojewski, 1987)

   b. *Mental Math in the Primary Grades* (Hope, Leutzinger, Reys, & Reys, 1988)

   c. *Mental Math in the Middle Grades* (Hope, Reys, & Reys, 1987)

   d. *Mental Math in the Junior High School* (Hope, Reys, & Reys, 1988)

   e. *GUESS, Boxes I and II* (Reys & Reys, 1983)

   How would the materials you reviewed be used over a school year in your classroom?

2. Select any grade between 2 and 8. At that grade, would you spend more time on pencil-and-paper computation or on mental methods? Why? Would your response be different for different grades? How do you think your choice of emphasis compares with the current emphasis in most classrooms at that level?

SUGGESTED READINGS

Highly Recommended

Hope, J. A., Leutzinger, L. P., Reys, B. J., & Reys, R. E. (1988). *Mental math in the primary grades.* Palo Alto, CA: Dale Seymour.

Hope, J. A., Reys, B. J., & Reys, R. E. (1987). *Mental math in the middle grades.* Palo Alto, CA: Dale Seymour.

Hope, J. A., Reys, B. J., & Reys, R. E. (1988). *Mental math in the junior high school.* Palo Alto, CA: Dale Seymour.

These three books contain blackline masters for making overhead transparencies to guide lessons, worksheets to follow the lessons, and comprehensive reviews. The authors are among the best known in this field, and there are few materials on the market that are as helpful as these books. Even if you only adapt the ideas and do not use the actual pages, the books are a good resource.

Reys, R. E., & Reys, B. J. (1983). *Guide to using estimation skills and strategies (GUESS) Boxes I & II.* Palo Alto, CA: Dale Seymour.

Still among the best materials for teaching computational estimation strategies, these two hefty boxes of cards provide the fourth- through eighth-grade teacher with a complete program. Two of the cards are shown in Figure 10.14. Use them as transparencies, in small groups, or as independent work.

Sowder, J. T., & Kelin, J. (1993). Number sense and related topics. In D. T. Owens (Ed.), *Research ideas for the classroom: Middle grades mathematics* (pp. 41–57). Old Tappan, NJ: Macmillan.

Sowder has long been a leading researcher in the area of number sense. A conference on number sense that she sponsored in 1989 included a lively discussion of how teaching mental algorithms contributes to number sense. This chapter reflects much of the spirit of that conference and provides a comprehensive overview of the topic.

Other Suggestions

Burns, M. (1992). *About teaching mathematics: A K–8 Resource.* Sausalito, CA: Marilyn Burns Education Associates.

Cobb, P., & Merkel, G. (1989). Thinking strategies: Teaching arithmetic through problem solving. In P. R. Trafton (Ed.), *New directions for elementary school mathematics* (pp. 70–81). Reston, VA: National Council of Teachers of Mathematics.

Coburn, T. G. (1987). *How to teach mathematics using a calculator.* Reston, VA: National Council of Teachers of Mathematics.

Coburn, T. G. (1989). The role of computation in the changing mathematics curriculum. In P. R. Trafton (Ed.), *New directions for elementary school mathematics* (pp. 43–56). Reston, VA: National Council of Teachers of Mathematics.

Hazekamp, D. W. (1986). Components of mental multiplying. In H. L. Schoen (Ed.), *Estimation and mental computation* (pp. 116–126). Reston, VA: National Council of Teachers of Mathematics.

Hope, J. A. (1986). Mental computation: Aliquot parts. *Arithmetic Teacher, 34*(3), 16–17.

Hope, J. A., & Sherrill, J. M. (1987). Characteristics of unskilled and skilled mental calculators. *Journal for Research in Mathematics Education, 18*, 98–111.

Lester, F. K. (1989). Mathematical problem solving in and out of school. *Arithmetic Teacher, 37*(3), 33–35.

Leutzinger, L. P., Rathmell, E. C., & Urbatsch, T. D. (1986). Developing estimation skills in the primary grades. In H. L. Schoen (Ed.), *Estimation and mental computation* (pp. 82–92). Reston, VA: National Council of Teachers of Mathematics.

McBride, J. W., & Lamb, C. E. (1986). Number sense in the elementary classroom. *School Science and Mathematics, 86*, 100–107.

Reys, B. J. (1986). Teaching computational estimation: Concepts and strategies. In H. L. Schoen (Ed.), *Estimation and mental computation* (pp. 31–44). Reston, VA: National Council of Teachers of Mathematics.

Reys, B. J. (1992). Estimation. In T. R. Post (Ed.), *Teaching mathematics in grades K–8: Research-based methods,* 2nd ed. (pp. 279–301). Needham Heights, MA: Allyn & Bacon.

Reys, R. E. (1984). Mental computation and estimation: Past, present, and future. *Elementary School Journal, 84*, 547–557.

Reys, R. E. (1986). Evaluating computational estimation. In H. L. Schoen (Ed.), *Estimation and mental computation* (pp. 225–238). Reston, VA: National Council of Teachers of Mathematics.

Reys, R. E., Reys, B. J., Nohda, N., & Emori, H. (1995). Mental computation performance and strategy use of Japanese students in grades 2, 4, 6, and 8. *Journal for Research in Mathematics Education, 26,* 304–326.

Reys, R. E., Trafton, P. R., Reys, B. J., & Zawojewski, J. (1987). *Computational estimation (Grades 6, 7, 8).* Palo Alto, CA: Dale Seymour.

Sowder, J. T. (1989). Developing understanding of computational estimation. *Arithmetic Teacher, 36*(5), 25–27.

Sowder, J. T. (1990). Mental computation and number sense. *Arithmetic Teacher, 37*(7), 18–20.

Sowder, J. T., & Wheeler, M. M. (1989). The development of concepts and strategies used in computational estimation. *Journal for Research in Mathematics Education, 20,* 130–146.

Thornton, C. A., Jones, G. A., & Neal, J. L. (1995). The 100s chart: A stepping stone to mental mathematics. *Teaching Children Mathematics, 1,* 480–483.

Trafton, P. R. (1986). Teaching computational estimation: Establishing an estimation mind-set. In H. L. Schoen (Ed.), *Estimation and mental computation* (pp. 16–30). Reston, VA: National Council of Teachers of Mathematics.

Van de Walle, J. A. (1991). Redefining computation. *Arithmetic Teacher, 38*(5), 46–51.

Van de Walle, J. A., & Watkins, K. B. (1993). Early development of number sense. In R. J. Jensen (Ed.), *Research ideas for the classroom: Early childhood mathematics* (pp. 127–150). Old Tappan, NJ: Macmillan.

CHAPTER

11

PENCIL-AND-PAPER COMPUTATION WITH WHOLE NUMBERS

This chapter concentrates on ways to teach the long-standing, traditional algorithms for whole numbers. As such, it completes the story about computation with whole numbers, a strand that begins with number concepts and continues to add on meanings of the operations, mastery of basic facts, mental algorithms, and number sense.

 BIG IDEAS

1. **Each of the traditional algorithms is simply a clever way to record an operation for a single place value with transitions (trades, "borrows," or "carries") to an adjacent position. They have a digit orientation.**
2. **Ten things in any one place-value position make 1 in the position to the left. Conversely, 1 in any position makes 10 of the things in the position to the right. This idea is the same in all place-value positions, including positions to the right of the decimal point.**

PENCIL-AND-PAPER METHODS IN PERSPECTIVE

As we began the 1990s, pencil-and-paper computation held a dominant position in the curriculum for grades 2 through 6. The revolution in mathematics education that began with the *Curriculum Standards* in 1989 has included a trend toward a somewhat diminished emphasis on these outdated methods. However, as the decade ends, the traditional algorithms continue to have a dominant position in the curriculum.

In the past, computational proficiency was a required skill in our society. We taught computation because it was necessary for everyday living. It was important for both students and adults to be able to compute sums of long columns of four- and five-digit numbers, to find products such as 378×2496, and to do long divisions such as $71.8 \overline{)5072.63}$. Today, computations with numbers as large as these are virtually never required of us, thanks to the readily available calculator.

Algorithms Outside the Classroom

Outside the classroom, in the real world, when a situation calls for an exact answer to a computation, three or four choices are available. Often the quickest and easiest is to do a mental computation. If that is impracticable due to the numbers involved, most people reach for a calculator. Or if there is a long series of repetitive computations, a computer spreadsheet may be appropriate. A pen or pencil is usually the last resort. Even then, if several computations are necessary and they are lengthy or tedious, most reasonable adults will look again for a calculator. In virtually all job situations, a calculator will be available. Considering the limited need for computational proficiency in the contemporary real world, it is quite likely that children spend much more time on pencil-and-paper computation in school than adults do outside of school. Such drills now seem a waste of valuable school time.

Student-Invented Methods

Constructivist theory would suggest that students be provided the opportunity to develop methods of computation through discussion and personal investigations. It is not at all likely that students would ever come naturally to invent the digit-oriented, right-handed methods of the traditional algorithms. These procedures have evolved and been perfected over many years. Students tend to follow their intuition when given free rein in solving a problem. When inventing a computational method, intuition tends to suggest "left-handed" approaches. If the computation involves three-digit numbers, we (and most children) work first with the big pieces—the hundreds. Except for division, the standard algorithms are all right-handed—they begin with the ones or little pieces.

Encouraging Students' Own Methods

If you have read Chapter 10, you have already seen one form of student-invented approaches. Mental methods are very reasonably developed with appropriate tasks suggested. Even there, occasional ideas suggested by the teacher are needed to guide the development. Recall that with mental methods, children should be encouraged to write down intermediate results. The combination of mental computation and written support is actually a form of an algorithm, even if it never gets to be clearly defined and practiced as such.

There are other ways that students can be encouraged to invent algorithms. A method that is strongly suggested in this chapter is to encourage students to complete a given computation with the use of base 10 models—even if they can do the computation mentally. After completing the task, they should work together to decide on a way to record symbolically what they have done. Do not expect that the written records will look anything at all like the traditional methods you plan to teach. What is valuable, however, is that the children begin to see that what is written symbolically is only a way to record something that they can also do

in a very conceptual manner. Children can even be challenged to see if they can solve other computations using their symbolic approaches.

Variations in the way the computational task is posed to the children will influence the kinds of methods they invent. For example, a division problem presented in a word story will very likely be modeled with base 10 pieces according to the structure of the story—fair sharing or measurement. In this chapter, we will see how the standard algorithm for multiplication can be developed based on the area of a rectangle idea for multiplication. If an exploratory problem is posed in an area context, children will pursue that idea. If not, they will more likely pursue a repeated addition approach. You may want to pose tasks that will have a strong likelihood of connecting to the standard algorithm you plan to teach next.

Value of Student-Invented Methods

There are several reasons why the time invested in having students invent their own computational methods is worthwhile.

First, students who are inventing algorithms are clearly *doing mathematics*—looking for relationships and solving problems. Algorithm invention is an excellent form of problem solving. In the real world, engineers and scientists, shopkeepers and housekeepers, all have occasion to invent algorithms. They search for clever and useful methods of performing routine and repetitive tasks when a standard procedure has not already been invented. From searching for the best pattern and tools to mow the lawn to the design of a faster computer chip, real life is full of algorithm invention, and it always will be.

Second, when students see that they can actually figure out computations without being told how and that different students in the same class have done the task in a variety of ways, they also see clearly that mathematics makes sense. It can be invented and mastered by ordinary people.

Third, invented algorithms will always be highly conceptual and reliant on base 10 ideas. They will provide an excellent basis for developing or continuing to work with mental computation methods. Recall that invented algorithms almost always are left-handed. So also are mental procedures.

Finally, as already noted, the invented procedures are a good background for the standard pencil-and-paper procedures that are likely to come next.

In this chapter, discussion of each algorithm will begin with a section titled "Explorations and Invented Algorithms." One or more examples will be provided of tasks that might be used before an algorithm is developed. In a true *Standards*-oriented curriculum, a significant amount of time would be devoted to these explorations or student inventions, and much less time than has been traditional would be spent on the standard algorithms.

Guiding the Traditional Algorithms

The tradition in algorithm instruction is to guide children to learn each algorithmic procedure exactly as we prescribe it. Steps are modeled and practiced in a fairly rigid manner. This guided approach is no less evident when the instruction is completely conceptual. In fact, in this chapter, you will learn how best to conduct such guided development of the algorithms. It is not accidental that this chapter was positioned after those that discuss the much more flexible mental methods. If children can come to see that there are many different ways to do any given computation and that the choice of methods has to do with circumstances, need for accuracy, and the numbers involved, then it may be reasonable to discuss examining the traditional methods as another alternative. The flexibility in thinking that can and should precede this more guided instruction will help enormously in developing the traditional methods.

Note: The development of each of the traditional algorithms as described in this chapter is overly prescriptive and is *not* an example of constructivist teaching. If teachers must, due to their contractual obligations, help children develop these algorithms with the traditional emphasis on skill, a clearly conceptual approach is probably best, even if it guides children more than is perhaps desired.

A Constructivist Alternative

Another alternative to the traditional algorithms views them as problems or puzzles for students to figure out. In classrooms where student-invented approaches to computation have been the norm, teachers sometimes feel pressure to have students learn the algorithms that are in their prescribed curriculum. In a method quite different from the development that follows in this chapter, these teachers show the traditional approach to their students in a manner similar to the following:

> Today we are going to look at the way your parents and I were taught to do subtraction *or* The other day I saw a student doing subtraction this way. (*The traditional approach is illustrated on the board without comment.*) I wonder if we can figure out how this method works. Get in your groups, and see if you can find a way to make sense of this method. What was happening when that 8 was crossed out and a 7 written above it? Why was the 3 in the ones column changed to 13? Maybe you could use your base 10 blocks to help you figure it out. Let's try to figure out why this works.

An approach such as this can be delayed until late in the year as compared to when the algorithm would normally be introduced. In the interim, students are exploring their own methods and discussing the ideas of their fellow students. Figuring out the standard algorithm is then a natural and easy thing to do.

READINESS ACTIVITIES: TRADING

All of the traditional algorithms involve making trades from one position to the next, the process usually referred to as either carrying (a forward trade) or borrowing (a backward trade). Structured activities where students make trades with base 10 pieces on a place-value mat are designed to develop the concept of trading.

In trading activities, students either make or break groups as they add or remove counters from the mat. For example, if you have 4 tens and 8 ones and then add 3 more ones, a trade must be made. The word *trade* is also used when a ten or hundred is broken or unbundled, as when you want to remove 5 ones from 7 tens and 2 ones. Trading activities are described here as either a forward game or a backward game with variations to increase the difficulty.

The Forward Game

The game is described first as a first- or second-grade teacher-directed group activity using counters and cups. Any groupable base 10 material can be substituted. Variations are described later.

Each child has an empty place-value mat, a supply of counters, and small cups. Explain that each time you signal (snap fingers, ring a bell), students are to place one more counter on the ones or singles side of the mat. Whenever a ten-frame is filled (or there are 10 counters on the ones side), they take their counters off the ten-frame, put them in a cup, and place the cup of 10 on the left side or tens place of their mats. Periodically pause and discuss with children how many counters are shown on the mat and how many counters are needed before the next trade. It is important for the children to realize that the number on the mat is the same just before a trade as it is after. Continue adding counters for 10 or 15 minutes or as long as seems appropriate for your class.

The Backward Game

The "backward game" is simply the reverse process from the forward game. Have children place, say, 4 cups of 10 and 6 singles on their mats. Explain that each time you give the signal, they are to remove one counter from their boards instead of putting one on. When there are no more counters on the ones side, a cup of 10 should be dumped out onto the ones side and a ten-frame filled with the counters. Then a counter can be removed. Single counters should never be removed from cups, since cups are to always contain 10 counters. As before, periodically stop and discuss what is happening and what is on their mats.

Variations of the Forward and Backward Games

These four variations provide a bit more interest and can be used for older children who may not have had any experi-

combine numbers such as 348 and 276 in a similar way. All activities should involve trading from the first example.

Madell (1985) has demonstrated that children who have been given ample experiences with base 10 materials will quite readily solve problems with these models, will always begin by working with the largest pieces, and, by third grade, will transfer most of these informal manipulative methods to mental computational skills.

Kamii (1989; Kamii & Joseph, 1988) has also shown that children invariably begin with the tens position instead of the ones position when given addition tasks in a completely symbolic mode—no materials present at all. As discussed in Chapter 10, method details will vary considerably from child to child and also with the particular numbers used.

The value in either approach (with or without models) lies in the student interaction, attention to meaning, and student validation. The students clearly perceive their task as one of "figuring it out" rather than one of following rules that they may or may not understand.

Directed Development of an Addition Algorithm

As you have by now recognized, the usual algorithm for addition (and also subtraction) will be contrary to children's natural inclination to begin with the left-hand numbers. Explain to children that they are going to learn a method of adding on paper that most "big people" use. It is not the only way to add or even the best way; it is just a way that you want them to learn.

Addition with Models Only

Begin with base 10 materials on place-value mats. In the beginning, there is no written work except for the possible recording of an answer. The idea is to make the entire algorithm make sense first. Later, children will learn to write or record what they have already developed conceptually.

Have students make two numbers on their place-value mats. Direct attention first to the ones column, and decide if a trade is necessary (or if a group of 10 can be made). If so, have the children make the trade. Repeat the process in the tens column. If you are working with hundreds, go on to the third column. Explain that from now on, you want them always to begin working right to left, starting with the ones column. An example is shown in Figure 11.5. Children solve the problems with models and record only the answers.

Connections with Symbolism

Reproduce pages with simple place-value charts similar to those shown in Figure 11.6. The charts will help young children record numerals in columns. The general idea is to have children record on these pages each step of the proce-

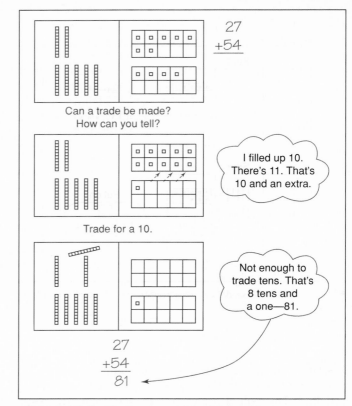

●**FIGURE 11.5**   *Working from right to left in addition.*

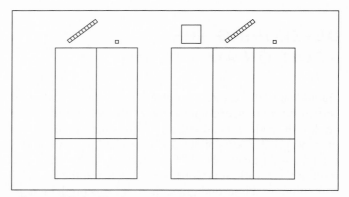

●**FIGURE 11.6**   *Blank recording charts are helpful.*

dure they do with the base 10 models *as it is done*. The first few times you do this, guide each step carefully, as is illustrated in Figure 11.7 and the Blackline Masters. A similar approach would be used for three-digit problems.

A variation of the recording sheet that has been used successfully with children permits them to write down the sum in the ones column and thereby see and think about the total as a two-digit number (see Figure 11.8 and the Blackline Masters). When using models, children trade 10 for 1 but rarely think of the total in the ones column. The bubble on

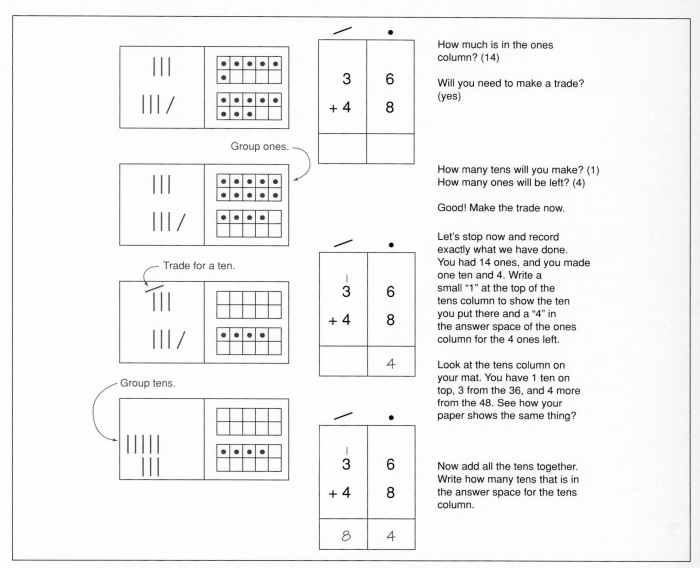

How much is in the ones column? (14)

Will you need to make a trade? (yes)

Group ones.

How many tens will you make? (1)
How many ones will be left? (4)

Good! Make the trade now.

Trade for a ten.

Let's stop now and record exactly what we have done. You had 14 ones, and you made one ten and 4. Write a small "1" at the top of the tens column to show the ten you put there and a "4" in the answer space of the ones column for the 4 ones left.

Group tens.

Look at the tens column on your mat. You have 1 ten on top, 3 from the 36, and 4 more from the 48. See how your paper shows the same thing?

Now add all the tens together. Write how many tens that is in the answer space for the tens column.

• **FIGURE 11.7** Help students record on paper each step that they do on their mats as they do it.

the side provides a linkage that can easily be dropped or faded out later on.

The hardest part of this connecting or record-as-you-go phase is getting children to remember to write each step as they do it. The tendency is to put the pencil down and simply finish the task with the models. One suggestion is to have children work in pairs. One child is responsible for the models and the other for recording the steps as they are done. Children reverse roles with each problem.

To determine if children have adequately made the connection with the models, first see that they can do problems and record the steps. Then ask them to explain the written form. For example, ask what the little 1 at the top of the column stands for and also why they only wrote a 4 in the ones column when the total was 14. When children demonstrate a connection with concepts and also can do the procedure without any assistance, they are ready to do problems without models.

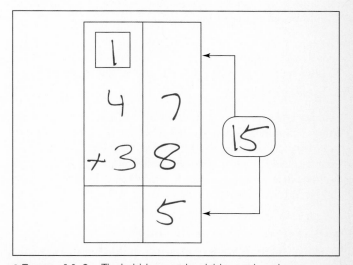

• **FIGURE 11.8** The bubble provides children with a place to write the sum in the ones column.

DEVELOPING THE SUBTRACTION ALGORITHM

The subtraction algorithm is also taught in the second grade, with reteaching and more practice with three digits in the third grade. (Why do you think so much reteaching of these algorithms is necessary?)

Explorations and Invented Algorithms

Although the traditional algorithm that involves "borrowing" is generally more difficult for children than addition, children are just as capable of inventing their own methods of subtraction as they are of inventing addition methods. Both approaches for encouraging student-invented methods that were suggested for addition (with and without models) are also appropriate for subtraction. Instead of presenting these ideas as activities, a few comments are all that are necessary here.

If children are given a take-away type of word problem for subtraction and asked to use their base 10 pieces to solve it, they will be most likely to model only the initial amount. The change or take-away amount is contained in this initial amount. The student task is to figure out how to remove it.

Regardless of whether the children are using models or a strictly mental approach as suggested by Kamii (1989), children will again work first with the tens or the left-hand numbers. In a problem such as $72 - 38$, they will be most likely to begin by removing 3 tens from the 7 tens (or "30 from 70 leaves 40"). This parallels what happens with addition. Their next step may surprise you. They will rarely trade a ten for ones, which in this example would make 12 ones. Rather, they may take 8 from one of the remaining 4 tens ("That makes 30, and 2 and 2 more is 34") or take away the 2 ones that are there and then take 6 more from one of the tens ("Six from 40 is 34"). These ideas are much more in keeping with efficient mental computation procedures and should never be discouraged.

Directed Development of a Subtraction Algorithm

The general approach to developing a subtraction algorithm for pencil and paper is the same as for addition. Children are instructed exactly how to model the exercises first using only models. When the procedure is completely understood with models, a do-and-write approach to connecting it with a written form is used.

Subtraction with Models Only

Start by having children model the top number in a subtraction problem on the top half of their place-value mats. A good method for dealing with the bottom number is to have

children write each digit on a small piece of paper and place these pieces near the bottom of their mats in the respective columns, as in Figure 11.9. The paper numbers serve as reminders of how much is to be removed from each column. Nothing should be removed from any column until the total amount can be taken off. Also explain to children that they are to begin working with the ones column first, as they did with addition. The only justification for this latter rule is that when done symbolically, it is a bit easier to work with the ones first, and that is how most people do subtraction. The entire procedure is exactly the same as the backward-trading games when two dice were used.

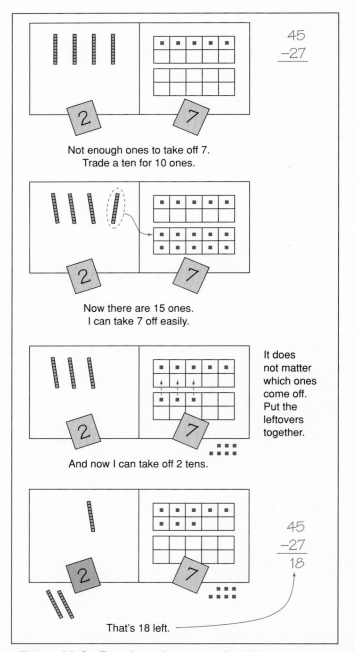

• **FIGURE 11.9** *Two-place subtraction with models.*

Use a set of your own models to follow through the steps in Figure 11.9. Notice how the empty ten-frame is filled with 10 ones when the backward trade is made. Without a frame, many children add onto the 5 ones already there and end up with only 10 ones.

Difficulties with Zeros

Exercises in which zeros are involved anywhere in the problem tend to cause special difficulties, especially in symbolic exercises without models. Enough attention should be given to these cases while still using models to provide an experience base for working with symbols.

A zero in the ones or tens place of the bottom number means there is nothing to take away and leaves some children wondering what they are supposed to do.

With a zero in the ones place of the top number, there are no materials in that column, which presents an unusual situation when done with models. Make a special effort to include problems such as 70 − 36 or 520 − 136 while children are working with models and before they begin learning how to record.

The most difficult zero case is the one with no tens in the top number, as in 403 − 138. With models, children must make a double trade, exchanging a hundreds piece for 10 tens and then one of the tens for 10 ones. With models, it is relatively clear that the hundred should not be exchanged directly for ones. Symbolically, that is a very common error: "Take 1 from the 4 and put it with the 3 to make 13." (Notice the lack of logic.)

If you have not done so already, use base 10 models to do one of these subtraction exercises with zeros.

Connections with Symbolism

Children should continue using materials and recording only answers until they can comfortably do problems without assistance and demonstrate an understanding. At that point, the process of recording each step as it is done can be introduced in the same way as was suggested for addition. The same recording sheets (see Figure 11.6, p. 218) can be used. Figure 11.10 (p. 222) shows a sequence for a three-digit subtraction problem, indicating the recording for each step.

When an exercise has been solved and recorded, children should soon be able to explain the meanings of all of the markings at the top of the problem in terms of base 10 materials. This ability to explain symbolism is a signal for moving children on to a completely symbolic level.

DEVELOPING THE MULTIPLICATION ALGORITHM

The multiplication algorithm is probably the most difficult for children to understand in a conceptual manner, especially when the bottom number or multiplier is a two-digit number. The easier case of a one-digit multiplier is generally developed in the third grade, and multipliers with two digits are introduced in fourth and fifth grades. It is difficult to argue that children need to develop skills with larger multipliers.

Explorations and Invented Algorithms

There are two distinctly different conceptual approaches to the development of the traditional pencil-and-paper algorithm for multiplication. One is based on an area concept of multiplication, where each of the factors is a length of a rectangle and the product is an area—the stuff inside the rectangle. The other approach is based on repeated addition, where one factor indicates the number of sets and the other the size of the sets. The area model will be developed in some detail in this chapter, followed by a much shorter discussion of the repeated addition approach. Regardless of the directed development you may teach later, informal explorations of both ideas are certainly worthwhile.

Area Model

One valuable exploration in preparation for more directed development is to prepare large rectangles for each group of two or three students. The rectangles should be measured carefully, with dimensions between 25 cm and 60 cm, and drawn accurately with square corners. (Use the corner of a piece of poster board for a guide.) The students' task is to determine how many small ones pieces will fit inside. They should be provided with ones, tens, and hundreds pieces. Wooden or plastic base 10 pieces are best, but cardboard strips and squares are adequate.

Groups should be encouraged to figure out clever ways to do the counting. They should draw pictures to explain how they arrived at their result. Most important, have them devise a written record of what they did using numbers.

A Possible Solution. Here is what children might do if given a rectangle to fill in that measures 47 cm by 36 cm. (It would be an excellent idea to draw a rectangle and fill it in yourself so that you can follow this discussion more easily.) Most children will fill the rectangle first with as many hundreds pieces as possible. That would be 12 hundreds, probably in a 3 × 4 array (1200 square ones). While there are many possible ways to fill in the rectangle, one obvious approach is to put the 12 hundreds in one corner. This will leave narrow regions on two sides that can be filled with tens pieces and a final small rectangle that will hold ones. These four regions can each be counted, recorded, and added up using concepts of ones, tens, and hundreds. If you have not actually done this activity yourself, skip forward to Figure 11.18 (p. 228) to see how the pieces would fit into the rectangle. The recording inventions will vary considerably. How would you record what you did, assuming that you did not already know the algorithm? Can you use your

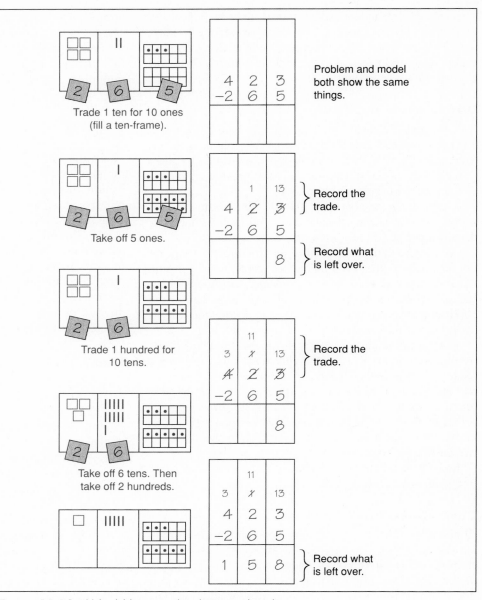

• **FIGURE 11.10**   *Help children record each step as they do it.*

method on a rectangle that measures 68 cm by 37 cm? Can you make a sketch to explain your work?

A Challenge.   A true challenge to students' understanding is next to provide them with only the dimensions of a new rectangle. Can they use the ideas they developed in the first exercise to determine the area of the new rectangle without actually filling it in?

Even children in the middle grades can benefit from this activity. These older students should be given the artificial constraint of devising a way to determine the number of ones without using any multiplication fact beyond 9 × 9.

Repeated Addition

When given a multiplication problem and left to invent their own methods (as was done with addition and subtraction), children are most likely to use a repeated addition approach. For example, consider the following problem:

....

There were four performances of the school play last weekend, and each one was a sellout. The auditorium holds 368 people. How many people attended the play over all four performances?

....

If explored using base 10 materials, students will probably make four collections of 3 hundreds, 6 tens, and 8 ones and combine them in some way. Some children may simply shove all like pieces together and count. Others will look at four groups of 3 hundreds and note (or record) that there are 12 hundreds. Similarly, they will record 24 tens and 32 ones. The exact details of how they combine the 20 tens or the 30 ones will vary from group to group. Encourage children to find ways to record whatever they do. As was suggested with the area model, pose other problems of a similar type, and see if students can use their invented methods without actually using the models.

Directed Development of a Multiplication Algorithm

With more emphasis being placed on understanding computation, the area model for the standard multiplication algorithm has received increased emphasis in many textbooks. Though not necessarily easier to develop than a repeated addition approach, it has some distinct advantages. First, it generalizes much more easily to a two-digit multiplier. (Can you imagine making 57 piles of 86?) Perhaps more important, the area model can be used for products of fractions, products of decimals, and products of algebraic expressions. As the *Curriculum Standards* suggests, it is important to capitalize on connections within mathematics whenever possible.

The development presented here has several distinct steps, each of which must be understood completely before going on to the next. These are listed here and examined in depth in the discussions that follow:

1. Conceptual development of base 10 products. Models are used to fill in actual rectangles, or base 10 grids are used. A correlated oral language is a critical component.

2. Recording base 10 products. The language of ones, tens, and hundreds developed in the first step is used as a guide to determine in which columns to record the numbers.

3. The standard algorithm for multiplying a two-digit by a one-digit number is developed by combining base 10 products with the recording scheme.

One-Digit Multipliers

The steps just listed are explored first to develop the algorithm for one-digit multipliers and then are repeated for two-digit multipliers.

Developing Base 10 Products: Ones × Ones and Ones × Tens

These exercises involve filling in rectangles with base 10 pieces. If the dimensions of the rectangles are in centimeters, centimeter base 10 strips and squares will fit the dimensions. Wooden or plastic models, all in metric dimensions, are much easier to work with for these tasks.

It is probably better if you have students work together in small groups of two or three and give them predrawn rectangles. You will need to use large sheets of paper or tagboard. One way to prepare these rectangles for your class is to cut one of each size you want from poster board and quickly trace around it with a felt-tipped marker.

Give each group of children two rectangles with these dimensions:

Rectangle A: 3 ones by 5 ones (3 ones is 3 cm in length)

Rectangle B: 3 ones by 5 tens

Next have them fill in the rectangles with base 10 pieces, using the largest pieces that will fit, as shown in Figure 11.11. "How many *pieces* are in the small rectangle?" (15.) "What *kind* of pieces are they?" (Ones.) "How many pieces

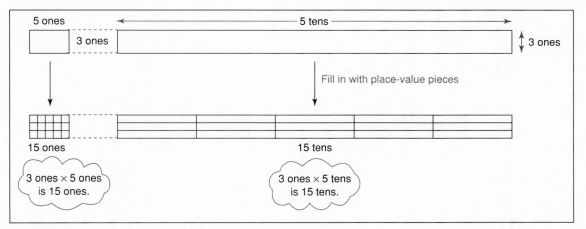

●**FIGURE 11.11**   Fill in rectangles to develop base 10 products.

are in the long rectangle?" (15.) "And what are they?" (Tens.) Have children "read" the dimensions of the rectangles and the area (amount filled inside) using base 10 language, not centimeters: "3 ones by (times) 5 ones is 15 *ones*. 3 ones by 5 tens is 15 *tens*." The goal is to generalize *two base 10 products: ones × ones are ones,* and *ones × tens are tens.*

Draw other rectangles, and label them in terms of tens and ones. Students should measure these with centimeter rulers. Have students read the length, width, and areas using the base 10 language. Factors used are always less than 10. For example, "6 *ones* times 7 *tens* is 42 *tens*." The relationship between rectangle dimensions and the type of base 10 pieces that can fill them is the essential concept behind this approach to the algorithm. Students should know why the product is tens or ones (because the rectangle is filled in with that type of piece). The language used in reading the rectangle will provide an important link with symbolism.

Rectangles could also be drawn on base 10 grid paper (see the Blackline Masters) instead of filling them in with strips and squares. Provide base 10 grid paper, and give the outside dimensions in terms of ones and tens. Students draw the corresponding rectangles on the grid. Each rectangle is filled with *all ones* or *all tens*. Always read the rectangle with the class, as in Figure 11.12. Another good idea is to have children shade in one or two pieces in each rectangle. Talk about how many base 10 pieces would be inside if you had a full-size rectangle filled with physical models.

The language of base 10 products can be drilled orally. The following series relates basic facts with base 10 product language.

Eight times *four* is . . . 32.

Eight *ones* times four *tens* is . . . 32 *tens*.

Eight *ones* times four *ones* is . . . 32 *ones*.

Recording Base 10 Products

When base 10 product language is clearly understood, the next step is to learn to record the products in appropriate place-value columns. Worksheets can be prepared. The base 10 factors are written to the left of the place-value columns, and the products are written in the chart.

The natural place to write the product of 4 ones times 8 tens is in the tens column. Suggest that children write the two-digit products in columns, as in Figure 11.13. "What would you have to do if you had 32 tens all in one column?" (Make a trade.) When the class determines that 32 tens will make 3 hundreds and 2 tens, have them cross out the 32 and show the 3 and 2 in the respective columns as shown. Continue with other factors using ones times ones and also ones times tens. Move quickly to recording a product with only one digit in a column and omitting the step of crossing out to show the trade. Students will discover that the last digit of the product will end in the named column.

Empty columns to the right are not filled with zeros. This makes the language agree with what is written. If 32 tens were written with a zero in the ones column, it would be read as "three hundred twenty" and not as "thirty-two tens."

An understanding of the recording of base 10 products is the principal conceptual basis for the procedural algorithm. If you yourself do not have a good grasp of the links between filling in the rectangles, how that develops a base 10 language, and how these products are recorded in a chart, it would be good to stop here and work through these last two sections again with your own models. Work with a friend, and talk about all of these ideas in your own words. This will also demonstrate to you the value of learning an idea conceptually rather than just learning the rules.

Two-Part Products

Give students a plain rectangle with a long side of 47 cm and a short side of 6 cm. How could this be filled in with base 10 pieces?

As shown in Figure 11.14, this rectangle can be "sliced" or separated into two parts so that one part will be 6 ones by 7 ones, or 42 ones, and the other will be 6 ones by 4 tens, or 24 tens. Have children read each part of the rectangle as before, using base 10 language. Finally, since they already know how to record these products, show how the recording can

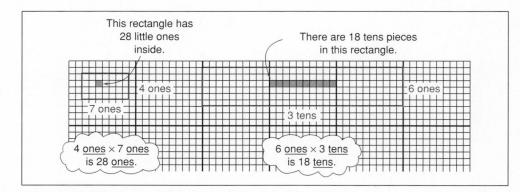

This rectangle has 28 little ones inside.

There are 18 tens pieces in this rectangle.

4 ones

6 ones

7 ones

3 tens

4 ones × 7 ones is 28 ones.

6 ones × 3 tens is 18 tens.

● **FIGURE 11.12** Draw and read rectangles on base 10 grid paper.

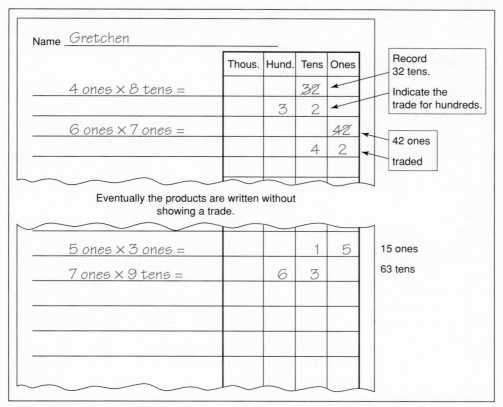

●**FIGURE 11.13**   Children can learn to record base 10 products in the correct columns.

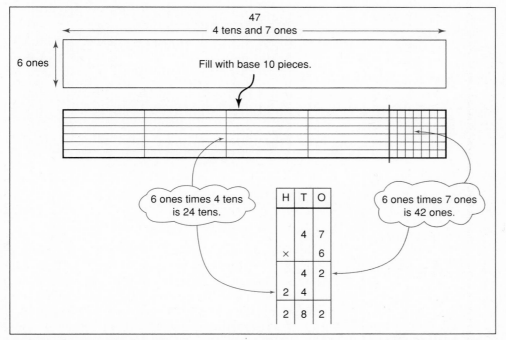

●**FIGURE 11.14**   A model and a record of a two-digit by one-digit product. Notice that the same language is used with the model and the symbolism.

be done in two lines beneath the problem as shown. The area of the entire rectangle is easily found by adding the two parts. Since the whole rectangle represents the product of 47 and 6, each section is referred to as a *partial product.*

Now go to the written record, and repeat the problem orally, pointing to each digit. "Six ones (point to 6) times seven ones (point to 7) is forty-two ones. Six ones (point) times four tens (point) is twenty-four tens." Notice that the base 10 value of the factors is determined by which column the digits are in. Students have also learned how to record each partial product with only one digit per column, so they should already know where each product is to be recorded.

It cannot be stressed too strongly that language is the key connection between the rectangle model and the written form. Care should be taken to develop the language at each step. Notice that when you read the rectangle, you use exactly the same language as when you read the written problem.

Students should soon be able to start with a problem such as 39 × 5, draw the appropriate rectangle on base 10 grid paper, slice it into two parts, write the two partial products, and explain the connection to the drawing. Stop now and try this yourself on a sheet of grid paper.

While still connecting the written form with the rectangle model, students write each partial product separately. It can easily be argued that this is good enough for today's needs. For the few times outside the classroom that we actually use this algorithm, we could certainly get by without worrying about a shorter form of the algorithm (with "carrying"). However, if you feel compelled to teach this to children, make the connections shown in Figure 11.15. Many of the errors that children commonly make with multiplication stem from this regrouping procedure. Is it really necessary?

With this final symbolic change, the two-digit by one-digit algorithm is complete with no special cases to be considered. Problems with three digits in the top number (e.g., 639 × 7) cannot be modeled with this approach, but the extension is relatively easy. *Ones* times *hundreds* are *hundreds.* The product of 7 *ones* times 6 *hundreds* is 42 *hundreds.* The 2 is written in the hundreds column, the 4 in the thousands

column. (Why?) Try the product 639 × 7 yourself. Say each of the three partial products in base 10 language, and record each separately.

Two-Digit Multipliers

If the algorithm for one-digit multipliers is completely understood, the extension to a two-digit multiplier is quite easy. Each discussion here is an exact parallel to the preceding development.

Developing Base 10 Products: Tens × Ones and Tens × Tens

On large sheets of paper, provide students with a rectangle with dimensions 40 cm by 60 cm. Have them fill it in with base 10 pieces. The obvious choice of pieces is hundreds, as in Figure 11.16. Read the rectangle as before: "4 *tens* by 6 *tens* is 24 *hundreds.*" Generalize this new base 10 product: *tens* times *tens* are *hundreds.* The other new base 10 product is the turn-around or commutative partner of the old one: *tens* times *ones* are *tens.* For tens × tens, help students visualize a large rectangle that clearly will hold hundreds. For tens × ones and ones × tens, the rectangles are always long and skinny. These skinny rectangles hold only tens.

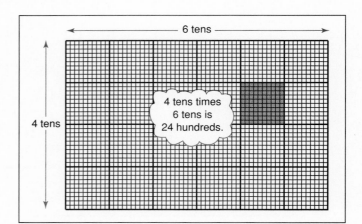

● **FIGURE 11.16**   *Tens × tens = hundreds, a new base 10 product.*

Recording Base 10 Products

Go through exactly the same process as before, teaching children how to record the new base 10 products. Permit or even encourage the recording of two digits in one column, and then make a trade symbolically, as in Figure 11.17. It is important to write the verbal form of the two factors to the left of the place-value columns as indicated. Do not move on until children can correctly record any base 10 product with only one digit in each column. The step where the

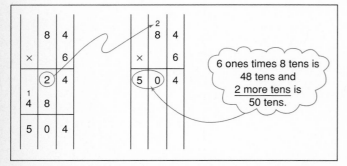

● **FIGURE 11.15**   *Two separate partial products can be added orally and the total written on one line in the standard form.*

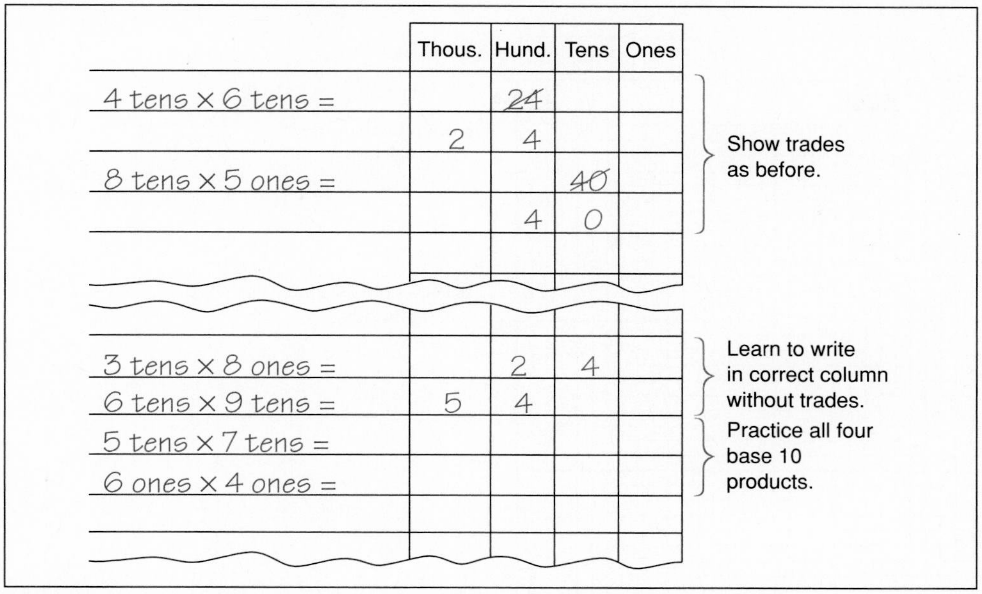

	Thous.	Hund.	Tens	Ones	
4 tens × 6 tens =		24			} Show trades as before.
	2	4			
8 tens × 5 ones =			40		
		4	0		
3 tens × 8 ones =			2	4	} Learn to write in correct column without trades.
6 tens × 9 tens =	5	4			
5 tens × 7 tens =					} Practice all four base 10 products.
6 ones × 4 ones =					

•FIGURE 11.17 *Children learn to record the new base 10 products.*

whole two-digit product is written in one column is only transitional and should be abandoned before continuing.

Four-Part Products

Give students a rectangle (or have them draw one on base 10 paper) with one side measuring 47 and the other side 36. How could this be filled in with base 10 pieces? (Note that we are now at the same place as in the informal exploration—filling in a rectangle and finding out how to record what is inside.)

Nearly everyone begins with hundreds placed in a corner, with a result similar to Figure 11.18 (p. 228). The hundreds pieces could be in any of the four corners, with the other pieces arranged accordingly.

When the rectangle is filled in, notice that there are four separate sections: one with hundreds, two with tens pieces, and one with singles or ones. Have students read each of these sections. As was done for the one-digit multiplier, record each section or partial product in place-value columns under the problem. The order in which the four sections or partial products are recorded is an arbitrary convention of the algorithm. The first two sections are the same as if the tens digit of the multiplier were not there. It is a good idea to record all four partial products separately, as shown in Figure 11.18.

Repeat the language that goes with the problem (reading the rectangles), but this time point to each digit in the problem. As before, the column each digit is in gives it its base 10 name, and the exact same words can be used with the symbolism, as in the rectangle. Students should be able to explain the connection of each partial product and each factor in the problem with the rectangle model.

You might wish to stop at this point, draw a rectangle that is 56 cm by 34 cm, and fill it in with base 10 pieces. Then read the four sections as you point to each. Record all four partial products in order, using the same oral language as you do so. Try another example drawn on a base 10 grid.

A Repeated Addition Development

The area model for developing the multiplication algorithm, as just discussed, is a nontrivial development requiring time and patience. While it has become more prominent in standard textbooks, adequate pictures of rectangles and explanations require a lot of page space. Quality instruction requires considerable effort beyond what a text can offer.

Why not use a repeated addition model? A repeated addition approach would make a lot of sense if the only goal were to develop a one-digit algorithm. For products such as 37×5, it is easy to model five sets of 3 tens and 7 ones. The two products (15 tens and 35 ones) may be computed in either order. The thought process involved transfers nicely to mental computation.

The difficulty with repeated addition begins with the second digit in the multiplier. It is not easy to model or think about 37 sets of 24. Orally (for this example), when you get to the 2×3 part of the computation, it is not correct to say "2 tens times 3 tens" because it is really "20 sets of 3 tens." This is a bit more difficult to handle mentally than "2 tens times 3 tens." Finally, the repeated addition model does not easily carry over to decimal or algebraic computation.

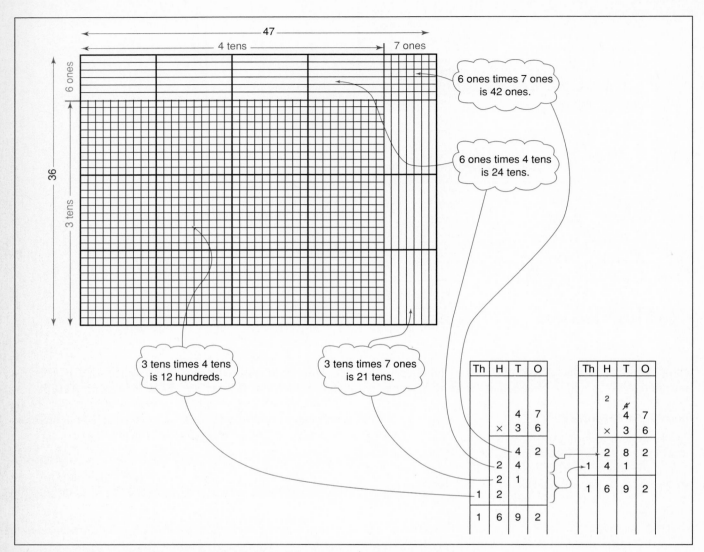

● **FIGURE 11.18** A 47 × 36 rectangle filled with base 10 pieces. Language connects the four sections of the rectangle to the four partial products.

These are simply the arguments on either side of the issue of which approach should be used to develop the algorithm. Figure 11.19 illustrates a typical approach to repeated addition for two-digit multipliers that might be found in a textbook.

For example, the state of Michigan's objectives restrict whole-number divisors to two digits. Even these divisors are to be less than 30 except for multiples of 10 (Michigan State Board of Education, 1988). This restriction allows students to focus on the rationale for the algorithm and avoid much of the stress caused by working with larger divisors. It also allows teachers to make better connections with estimation and mental computation methods.

DEVELOPING A DIVISION ALGORITHM

Division by one digit is traditionally begun in the third grade, with two-digit divisors introduced in the fourth grade. A two-digit divisor substantially increases the difficulty of the task. Fortunately, there is a movement to remove three- and four-digit divisors from the curriculum entirely.

Explorations and Invented Algorithms

Recall that there are two distinct concepts of division, one involving partitioning or fair shares and the other involving measurement or repeated subtraction. If children are presented with division computations without contexts, some children will use a measurement approach, and some will use partition. This provides an excellent opportunity for discussion.

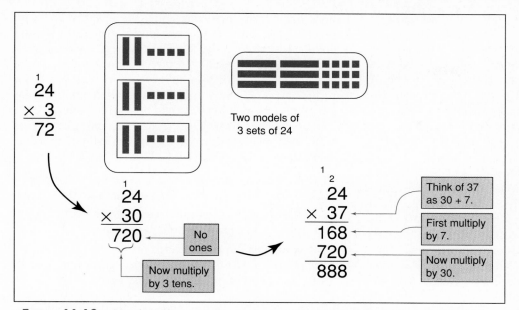

• **FIGURE 11.19**   A traditional sequence to develop the two-digit algorithm with repeated addition.

Have students determine how to solve 4)583 in any way they wish. How you present this task and what suggestions you provide will have a significant impact on what methods students use to solve the problem.

One approach is simply to write the division exercise on the board and have students work in pairs to get a solution. As is always the case with an unstructured activity, it is not possible to predict all of the interesting things that students are likely to do. Some may devise a completely mental method—for example, "One hundred fours is 400, another 25 fours is 500. That leaves 83. Twenty fours is 80. That makes 125 and 20, or 145, and there are 3 left." What is more likely is that children may do a similar form of thinking but write down the intermediate amounts or show appropriate multiplications. The solution just presented is based on measurement: How many fours are in 583?

It is also possible to think about the problem as a partition problem. In that case, the reasoning might be like this: "With 500, that's 125 in each of four sets. The 80 splits up with 20 in each set, so that makes 125 and 20 in each set, or 145 altogether. The 3 is just left over because you can't separate 3 into four sets." Again, the use of some recording is likely, but in neither case will children use the standard algorithm unless they have been taught it.

If you suggest that students use base 10 materials to solve a division problem, it is much more likely that they will use a sharing or partitioning approach. For the problem we have been discussing, children set out 5 hundreds, 8 tens, and 3 ones and try to figure out how to separate these materials into four piles. This is exactly what is suggested for the directed development of the algorithm. It might be a good idea to get out some base 10 pieces right now and see how you would go about using them to solve this problem.

If the exercise is offered in the context of a word problem, students are almost certain to use the conceptual approach suggested by the problem. The use of models remains an option. Consider these two problems, both involving the same division we have been discussing:

....

Mr. Martin, who runs a picture-framing shop, has a piece of framing material that is 583 cm long. If he cuts it into four pieces so that he can make a square frame, what is the largest square he can make?

....

....

Mrs. Martin buys the frame stock for the framing store. The most popular type of frame material costs $4 per yard. Her most recent bill from the supplier indicates that she spent $583 on this material. How many yards of frame stock did she buy?

....

Regardless of how you explore division informally with your class, students will almost certainly approach the task in a left-hand manner, working with the hundreds before the tens before the ones. That is the way both mental and paper-and-pencil algorithms are done. Therefore, informal explorations of division have a big payoff.

If to these explorations you add the additional challenge of finding a way to write down or record the thinking involved, you may decide that your children actually have an adequate algorithm for practical purposes. If we are going to abandon one of the traditional algorithms in the curriculum, it is likely that division will be the first to go.

Directed Development of a Division Algorithm

The division algorithm most often seen in textbooks is based on the partition or fair-share concept of division. As with addition and subtraction algorithms, the division algorithm can be completely developed conceptually with models before any connection to symbolism is undertaken.

Division with Models Only

Provide students with base 10 pieces and six or seven pieces of paper about 6 inches square. (Construction paper cut in fourths is perfect.) Begin with a problem such as 4)583. Discuss the meaning of the task in base 10 language. You have 5 hundreds pieces, 8 tens, and 3 ones to be shared evenly among four sets or piles. Place an emphasis on language that focuses on 5 *things,* 8 *things,* and 3 *things* rather than 583

single items. Have students model the quantity 583 with their base 10 pieces, and set out four of their paper squares to represent the four sets. Explain that it is a good idea always to begin with the largest pieces because if they cannot be completely shared evenly, they can be exchanged for smaller pieces. Figure 11.20 illustrates the complete solution to this task as students would do it with models.

It is very important to get students to talk this process out in their own words. Notice that with each place value, several distinct things happen:

* The number of pieces available is considered, and a decision is made to see if there are enough to be distributed.
* The pieces that each set can get are actually passed out to the sets—that is, placed on the paper mats.
* Any remaining pieces are traded for the next smaller size. The pieces received in trade are added to any that were already there. At this point the process begins over.

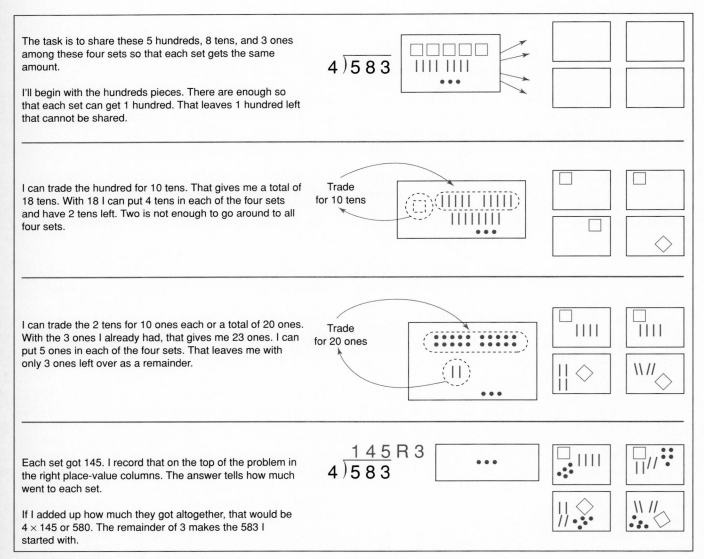

The task is to share these 5 hundreds, 8 tens, and 3 ones among these four sets so that each set gets the same amount.

I'll begin with the hundreds pieces. There are enough so that each set can get 1 hundred. That leaves 1 hundred left that cannot be shared.

I can trade the hundred for 10 tens. That gives me a total of 18 tens. With 18 I can put 4 tens in each of the four sets and have 2 tens left. Two is not enough to go around to all four sets.

I can trade the 2 tens for 10 ones each or a total of 20 ones. With the 3 ones I already had, that gives me 23 ones. I can put 5 ones in each of the four sets. That leaves me with only 3 ones left over as a remainder.

Each set got 145. I record that on the top of the problem in the right place-value columns. The answer tells how much went to each set.

If I added up how much they got altogether, that would be 4 × 145 or 580. The remainder of 3 makes the 583 I started with.

● **FIGURE 11.20**   Long division at the concept level.

The sharing of individual pieces at each place value is the entire conceptual basis for the long-division algorithm. Students should do exercises using only models until they can talk through that process (using their own words) in such a way that the sharing of each type of base 10 piece and trading to the next size is quite clear.

Notice that in this context, the phrase "4 *goes into* 5" has absolutely no meaning. In fact, 5 hundreds are being put into four sets. Teachers especially have difficulty abandoning the "goes into" terminology because it has become such a strong tradition while doing long division.

In making up the exercises that students should do with models, you will have to keep different problem types and nuances in mind. Figure 11.21 illustrates some of these. If excessive trades are avoided, most exercises with dividends through three digits and divisors of one digit can be easily modeled.

Two-digit dividends;
not very challenging or interesting

$$4\overline{)67}$$

Be careful of excessive trades.

$$5\overline{)865}$$

3 hundreds for 30 tens (a lot but OK)
1 ten for 10 ones

$$5\overline{)745}$$

2 hundreds for 20 tens
4 tens for 40 ones (excessively tedious)

No hundreds to distribute

$$4\overline{)372}$$

No trades in one or more places

$$4\overline{)852} \quad 3\overline{)426} \quad 3\overline{)693}$$

No tens to distribute (zero in an answer)

$$4\overline{)832}$$

Zeros in dividend

$$3\overline{)704}$$

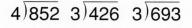
● **FIGURE 11.21** *Consider a variety of special cases to be worked out using models.*

You may wish to stop at this point and try some of these division exercises with your own models. (Use the ones suggested in Figure 11.21.) Pay special attention to the language you are using. Remember, you are simply passing pieces out fairly as you would M&Ms to friends. Avoid the "goes into" terminology. Also stress the language that explains the trading.

Connections with Symbolism

The general approach of having students record on paper each manipulative step as they do it is the way to connect symbolism to division.

Long division is simply a matter of passing out or sharing or distributing pieces in each place-value column and then trading any that may be left over for the next smaller size. When recording, however, two in-between steps must also be written down. All four steps are given here. Notice that steps B and C have no corresponding action with models.

A. *Share* available pieces in the column among the sets. *Record* the number given to each set.
B. *Record* the number of pieces given out in all. Find this by multiplying the number given to each times the number of sets.
C. *Record* the number of pieces remaining. Find this by subtracting the total given out from the amount you began with.
D. *Trade* (if necessary) for equivalent pieces in the next column, and combine those with any that may already have been there. *Record* the total number of pieces now in the next column.

Students must write more than what they do or think about when working manipulatively. In the beginning, students frequently omit steps B and C because there is no apparent reason to do them. The value or necessity of this extra writing may seem obscure to some students while they are still using models.

Two Alternatives for Recording

Along with the traditional method of recording this algorithm, an alternative method is suggested here that helps keep the conceptual meaning more clearly tied to the symbolism. Steps A, B, and C are recorded as usual in both methods, as shown in Figure 11.22(a) (p. 232). In the traditional algorithm, the trade is implied when you "bring down" the next digit. Notice that the total is technically in two columns. In the example, the 2 that stood for the remaining hundreds somehow becomes 20 tens when the 6 is brought down, as shown at the left in Figure 11.22(b). In the alternative explicit-trade version, the trade for tens is made explicit by crossing out the 2, and the total of 26 tens is written completely in the tens column. Next, multiplica-

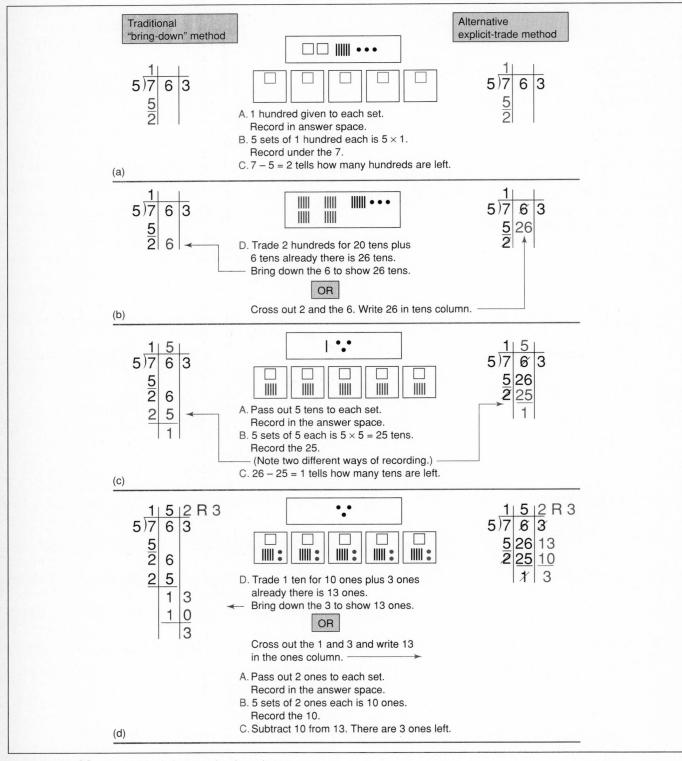

• **FIGURE 11.22**   *Two methods for recording long division.*

tion indicates that 25 tens were passed out in all. In the traditional scheme, the 25 must be recorded part in the hundreds column and part in the tens column. In the alternative method, the 25 tens is recorded in the tens column, clearly representing what was done, as shown in Figure 11.22(c).

The idea of writing a two-digit number in one column is not entirely new. In subtracting 637 − 281, we write a 13 above the 3 to represent 13 tens.

The "bring-down" procedure is difficult to explain to children. The explicit-trade method avoids bring-downs and is a direct match with the modeling of the procedure. It does require that the digits in the dividend be spaced out more and almost necessitates the use of lines to mark the columns, even as a permanent feature of the algorithm. (This method of recording is an invention of the author and does not appear in traditional textbooks.)

The process of doing division problems with models and recording all of the steps is a complex task for young children. Some will get carried away with the materials and forget to record.

In groups of three, one child can be the "doer," one the "recorder," and one the "supervisor." The supervisor's job is to see that all the steps are being written down and to keep the two processes together. All three children should be talking about the problem as it is being solved. Doing three problems in a period gives each student the chance to take on each task.

Avoiding Some Difficulties

Some of the difficulties that young children have with the division algorithm are due to sloppy writing. You can help students by preparing division record sheets. Nine blanks similar to those shown in Figure 11.23 (see also the Blackline Masters) can easily fit on one page. This is especially useful if the alternative recording scheme is used. Similar sheets can be prepared with four columns.

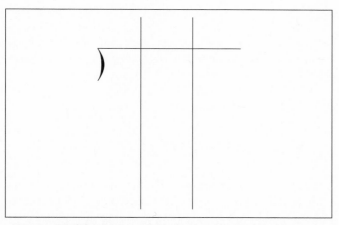

● **Figure 11.23** *Pages with blank charts like this (shown actual size) or with four columns are helpful when children are recording division problems.*

Many children forget to record zeros in the answer. An example is shown in Figure 11.24. To the right of the error, you can see that the practice of drawing place-value columns or using record sheets can be very helpful because the columns mark a space for each place value to be filled in. Perhaps more important, children should be encouraged to check that their answer makes sense. In the example, 642 things would have at least 100 in each of the six sets. The answer 17 is not even in the ballpark.

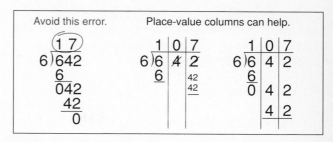

● **Figure 11.24** *Using lines to mark place-value columns can help avoid forgetting to record zero tens.*

Two-Digit Divisors

There is almost no justification for continuing to have children master some symbolic procedure for dividing with two-digit divisors. A large portion of the fourth, fifth, and sometimes sixth grade is frequently spent on this terribly outdated skill. The cost in terms of time and, more important, in terms of students' attitudes toward mathematics is enormous when compared to the few times in any adult's life when an exact result to such a computation is required and a calculator is not available. If you can possibly be of any influence in removing this outdated skill from your school's curriculum, you are encouraged to speak up.

With a two-digit divisor, some form of rounding or a similar trick must be used. Not only is rounding complicated, but it does not always work. This causes frustration and lots of erasures. Consider the problem in Figure 11.25.

The discussions that follow are offered only because you may be obliged to help students with this archaic skill. The suggestions here have been devised by the author and can help students do long division with much more ease than you did when you were in school. If you have to teach this, at least help students avoid the strain.

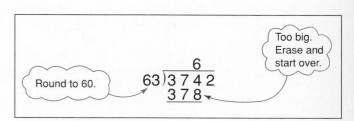

● **Figure 11.25** *Not only is rounding the divisor hard, but it does not always work.*

An Intuitive Idea

Suppose that you were sharing a large pile of candies with 36 friends. Instead of passing them out one at a time, you conservatively estimate that each person could get at least 6 pieces. So you give 6 to each of your friends. What if some are left? If there are enough to go around, you simply pass out more. It would be silly to collect those you have already given out and begin all over. Why not apply this common-sense approach to the sharing of base 10 pieces, the conceptual basis for long division?

The principal lessons of the candy example are, first, never overestimate the first time, and second, distribute more if the first attempt leaves enough to pass around. One way to make an easy but always safe estimate the first time is to pretend there are more sets than there really are. For example, if you have 312 base 10 pieces (candies) for 43 sets ("friends"), pretend you have 50 sets instead. It is easy to determine that you can distribute 6 pieces to each of 50 sets because 6 × 50 is an easy product. Therefore, you must be able to distribute *at least* 6 to each of the actual 43 sets. The point is, to avoid overestimates, always consider a larger divisor; *always round up.*

But what if the result shows you could have distributed more? Simply do what you would do with the candy situation—pass out some more.

Use the Idea Symbolically

These ideas are illustrated in Figure 11.26, using the same problem that presented difficulties in Figure 11.25. Both the traditional and the explicit-trade methods of recording are illustrated. Children should write the 70 in a little "think bubble" above the divisor. It is easy to run through the multiples of 70 and compare them to 374. Follow the illustrated computation as you read what follows.

    3 × 70 is 210 (too small).

    4 × 70 is 280 (too small).

    5 × 70 is 350 (close).

    6 × 70 is 420 (too big; use 5).

"I'll give 5 tens to each set ('friend'). But there are actually only 63 sets to share the tens with. Five times 63 tells how many I actually shared, and subtraction tells how many I have left. The 59 tens is not enough to pass out any more, and so I'll trade these 59 tens for ones. Fifty-nine tens is 590 ones, and 2 ones that were already there makes 592 ones. Pretending 70 piles instead of 63 will suggest 8 ones in each pile (8 × 70 is 560, and 9 × 70 is 630, which is too much). Distributing 8 ones to each of only 63 sets leaves 88. Since that is enough to give one more to each set, that's what I'll do. I can show this by putting a 1 above the 8 ones that I've already shared. I'll multiply the 1 by 63 because I really only distributed 63 additional ones, then subtract steps as always. The result is 5 tens and 9 ones in all, with 25 ones left over."

This approach has proved successful with children in the fourth grade learning division for the first time and with children in the sixth to eighth grades in need of remediation. It reduces the mental strain of making choices and essentially eliminates the need to erase. If an estimate is too low, that's OK. And if you always round up, the estimate will

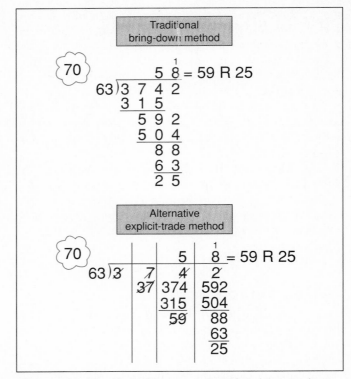

● **FIGURE 11.26**   Think 70 sets instead of 63. In the ones column, pass around 8 to each set and then pass around 1 more.

never be too high. Nor is there any reason ever to change to the more familiar approach. It is just as good for adults as for children. The same is true of the explicit-trade notation. It is certainly an idea to consider.

ASSESSMENT NOTES

It is easy to give a traditional skill test on any of the computational algorithms. Today it seems a lot more important to know if children have any understanding of what they are doing when they do these traditional algorithms. After all, the skill can be replaced by a $4 calculator, but the understanding or lack of it will have enormous implications for what students do in mathematics and how they think about mathematics.

The easiest way to assess understanding of the algorithms is to watch students as they work with base 10 models. If you have discussions about the informal explorations, there is even more information to be gathered. Finally, if you are not certain what ideas a student has, simply spend 10 minutes with the student. First have the child do a computation, and then have him or her use models to explain what he or she did.

REFLECTIONS ON CHAPTER 11: WRITING TO LEARN

1. What is meant by a student-invented algorithm, and why is there value in having students invent algorithms?

2. What is the most obvious difference between the way students intuitively add two numbers and the usual pencil-and-paper algorithm?

3. Describe how to help children connect what they do with models in the addition algorithm with how they do the algorithm in the usual pencil-and-paper way.

4. When doing a subtraction problem such as $394 - 138$ with base 10 pieces, why is only the 394 actually modeled?

5. Use the example of 26×45 to explain the difference between the area model for multiplication and the repeated addition model for multiplication.

6. Four different base 10 products were described. The first was "ones times ones are ones." What are the other three? Select any of these other three, and describe how children can be helped to develop these concepts by filling in rectangles. What discussion would you have about the materials they used to fill in the rectangles? What size rectangles would you have them fill in for each type of product?

7. Describe how children learn to record a product such as 3 tens times 7 hundreds.

8. Draw a picture of an area model for 58×27 that shows each of the four separate partial products. Your drawing should also indicate the arrangement of the base 10 pieces in each of the four sections of the rectangle. Do the computation 58×27 showing each of the four partial products separately, and indicate how each corresponds to your drawing.

9. Do the division problem $6\overline{)748}$ using both the standard algorithm as you learned it in school and the explicit-trade method that was described in this chapter. For the problem as you worked it, answer each of these questions:

   a. How many tens were given to each group?

   b. How many ones were given out in all (to all the groups combined)?

   c. How many groups are being made?

   d. Before any trades were made, but after all hundreds were shared, how many hundreds were left over?

   e. How many ones were received in trade for the leftover tens?

   f. After trading hundreds for tens, how many tens were available to be shared?

10. Explain why, when dividing by a two-digit divisor, the method of rounding the divisor up to the next highest multiple of 10 will always ensure that the first amount shared with each group in a division problem will be either just right or a little low. If the amount shared is too little, what can be done without doing any erasing? Make up an example to illustrate your answers to this question.

FOR DISCUSSION AND EXPLORATION

1. The multiplication algorithm is much more difficult to understand and teach conceptually than any of the other algorithms. With the current deemphasis on pencil-and-paper computation, discuss the proposition that the multiplication algorithm might as well be taught as a rote procedure without any attempt to explain it.

2. Talk with teachers in the upper grades (fifth and above) about how much time they spend teaching algorithms. Do they use base 10 models? Would better development eliminate some of the need for remediation? What about the idea of not teaching the algorithms at all until about fourth grade, when students can handle them?

3. What is the educational cost of teaching students to master pencil-and-paper computational algorithms? Here cost means time and effort required over the entire elementary grade span, in comparison with all other topics that are or could be taught. How much algorithm skill or knowledge do you think is really essential in an age of readily available calculators?

SUGGESTED READINGS

Highly Recommended

Campbell, P. F., & Johnson, M. L. (1995). How primary students think and learn. In I. M. Carl (Ed.), *Prospects for school mathematics* (pp. 21–42). Reston, VA: National Council of Teachers of Mathematics.

Campbell and Johnson describe a project in an urban school system that is completely based in a constructivist paradigm. The purpose of the chapter is to describe how children are able to construct their own ideas. Interestingly, most of the examples provided surround computation and student-invented methods. Absolutely worth reading.

Kamii, C., Lewis, B. A., & Livingston, S. J. (1993). Primary arithmetic: Children inventing their own procedures. *Arithmetic Teacher, 41,* 200–203.

Kamii has been the most vocal critic of teaching the traditional algorithms. In fact, she has written and given talks suggesting that the algorithms are actually harmful to students' development in mathematics. In this short article, Kamii and her colleagues show several invented algorithms of children and discuss how they get children to invent them. It is useful to note that Kamii is not an advocate of using physical models of any sort.

Rathmell, E. C., & Trafton, P. R. (1990). Whole number computation. In J. N. Payne (Ed.), *Mathematics for the young child* (pp. 153–172). Reston, VA: National Council of Teachers of Mathematics.

The authors discuss all forms of whole-number computation and provide excellent activities. The chapter gives a good perspective on how traditional computation can be combined with student methods and mental computation. An excellent chapter.

Other Suggestions

Burns, M. (1991). Introducing division through problem-solving experiences. *Arithmetic Teacher, 38*(8), 14–18.

Kamii, C. (1989). *Double-column addition: A teacher uses Piaget's theory* [videotape]. New York: Teachers College Press.

Kamii, C. (1994). *Young children continue to reinvent arithmetic: 3rd grade.* New York: Teachers College Press.

Kamii, C., & Joseph, L. (1988). Teaching place value and double-column addition. *Arithmetic Teacher, 35*(6), 48–52.

Kamii, C., & Lewis, B. A. (1993). The harmful effects of algorithms in primary arithmetic. *Teaching K–8, 23*(5), 36–38.

Madell, R. (1985). Children's natural processes. *Arithmetic Teacher, 32*(7), 20–22.

Reys, R. E., & Nohda, N. (Eds.). (1993). *Computational alternatives for the twenty-first century: Cross-cultural perspectives from Japan and the United States.* Reston, VA: National Council of Teachers of Mathematics.

Schultz, J. E. (1991). Area models: Spanning the mathematics of grades 3–9. *Arithmetic Teacher, 39*(2), 42–46.

Silver, E. A., Shapiro, L. J., & Deutsch, A. (1993). Sense making and the solution of division problems involving remainders: An examination of middle school students' solution processes and their interpretations of solutions. *Journal for Research in Mathematics Education, 24,* 117–135.

Smith, J. (1996). Assessing children's reasoning: It's an age-old problem. *Teaching Children Mathematics, 2,* 524–528.

Sowder, J. T., & Kelin, J. (1993). Number sense and related topics. In D. T. Owens (Ed.), *Research ideas for the classroom: Middle grades mathematics* (pp. 41–57). Old Tappan, NJ: Macmillan.

Stanic, G. M. A., & McKillip, W. D. (1989). Developmental algorithms have a place in elementary school mathematics instruction. *Arithmetic Teacher, 36*(5), 14–16.

Sutton, J. T., & Urbatsch, T. D. (1991). Transition boards: A good idea made better. *Arithmetic Teacher, 38*(5), 4–9.

Thompson, C. S., & Van de Walle, J. A. (1980). Transition boards: Moving from materials to symbols in addition. *Arithmetic Teacher, 28*(4), 4–8.

Thompson, C. S., & Van de Walle, J. A. (1981). Transition boards: Moving from materials to symbols in subtraction. *Arithmetic Teacher, 28*(5), 4–9.

Thornton, C. A., & Jones, G. A. (1994). *Windows of opportunity: Mathematics for students with special needs* (pp. 205–227). Reston, VA: National Council of Teachers of Mathematics.

Tucker, B. F. (1989). Seeing addition: A diagnosis-remediation case study. *Arithmetic Teacher, 36*(5), 10–11.

Van de Walle, J. A. (1991). Redefining computation. *Arithmetic Teacher, 38*(5), 46–51.

Van de Walle, J. A., & Thompson, C. S. (1985). Partitioning sets for number concepts, place value, and long division. *Arithmetic Teacher, 32*(5), 6–11.

Van Lehn, L. (1986). Arithmetic procedures are induced from examples. In J. Hiebert (Ed.), *Conceptual and procedural knowledge: The case of mathematics* (pp. 133–179). Hillsdale, NJ: Erlbaum.

Wearne, D., & Hiebert, J. (1994). Place value and addition and subtraction. *Arithmetic Teacher, 41,* 272–274.

Weiland, L. (1985). Matching instruction to children's thinking about division. *Arithmetic Teacher, 33*(4), 34–45.

Whitin, D. J. (1993). Becca's investigation. *Arithmetic Teacher, 41,* 78–81.

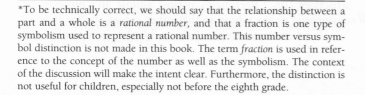

CHAPTER

12

DEVELOPING
FRACTION CONCEPTS

Consider the illustrations of two-thirds in Figure 12.1 (p. 238). Our adult knowledge confirms that each shows two-thirds, yet what do these models have in common? They cannot be matched like seven blocks with seven cards or seven fingers. Some are circles, some are dots, and some are lines. Some have many elements, and some have only one. If shown a rectangle, you cannot say what fraction it is. Some other shape or rectangle must also be identified as the unit or whole. Even the symbolism is a problem. The relationship represented by $\frac{2}{3}$ is represented just as well by $\frac{6}{9}$.

The point of the previous discussion is to heighten your awareness that fractions are not trivial concepts, even for middle school children. A fraction is an expression of a relationship between a part and a whole. Helping children construct that relationship and connect it meaningfully to symbolism is the topic of this chapter.*

---

*To be technically correct, we should say that the relationship between a part and a whole is a *rational number,* and that a fraction is one type of symbolism used to represent a rational number. This number versus symbol distinction is not made in this book. The term *fraction* is used in reference to the concept of the number as well as the symbolism. The context of the discussion will make the intent clear. Furthermore, the distinction is not useful for children, especially not before the eighth grade.

![planet icon] BIG IDEAS

---

1. **Fractional parts are like equal shares of a whole thing or a whole set.**
2. **The size of a fractional part is dependent on the size of the whole.**
3. **The numerator of a fraction tells how many parts are being talked about or considered. The denominator indicates what kind or size of parts the numerator counts.**
4. **Two equivalent fractions are two ways of describing the same amount using different fractional parts.**

FRACTIONS IN THE CURRICULUM

It has been traditional to include some minimal exposure to fractions in grades K–4, with each successive grade spending just a little more time on fraction concepts than the one

―――ACTIVITY―――

12.1 Correct Shares

As in Figure 12.5 (p. 241), show examples and nonexamples of specified fractional parts. Have students identify the wholes that are correctly divided into requested fractional parts and those that are not. For each response, have students explain their reasoning. The activity should be done with a variety of models, including length and set models.

In the "Correct Shares" activity, the most important part is the discussion of the nonexamples. The wholes are already partitioned either correctly or incorrectly, and the children were not involved in the partitioning. It is also useful for children to create designated equal shares given a whole, as they are asked to do in the next activity.

―――ACTIVITY―――

12.2 Finding Fair Shares

Give students models, and have them find fifths or eighths or other fractional parts using the models. (The models should never have fractions written on them.) The activity is especially interesting when different wholes can be designated in the same model. That way, a given fractional part does not get identified with a special shape or color but with the relationship of the part to the designated whole. Some ideas are suggested in Figure 12.6.

Folding paper is another good way to involve children in construction of fractional parts, as in Activity 12.2. Folds into halves, fourths, and eighths are the easiest because they are successive halves. With some help, children can fold strips into three parts and from these thirds fold sixths. Having children draw slices to subdivide a circle or even a rectangle is very difficult and is not recommended. On a rectangle, children will frequently draw four lines for fourths and then realize they have made five parts. Others will make three nice equal parts and then realize that the last one is far too large for fourths. These and other difficulties with eye-hand coordination get in the way of concept development. Children can use models or paper folding and develop fractional part concepts and still not be able to cut a shape into thirds with any accuracy. Try to keep the focus on the number and fairness of the shares and less on the ability to draw them.

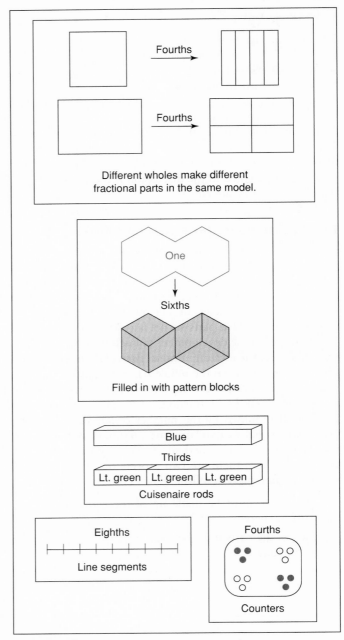

● **Figure 12.6**   *Given a whole, find fractional parts.*

Notice when partitioning sets that children frequently confuse the number of counters in a share with the name of the share. In the example in Figure 12.6, the 12 counters are partitioned into four sets—fourths. Each share or part has 3 counters, but it is the number of shares that makes the partition show fourths.

Counting Fractional Parts

The importance of fractional parts will become increasingly obvious as you read this chapter. As noted already, fractional parts or equal shares are the objects of fractions. Once these objects are developed as ideas, they can then be called fourths or thirds or whatever and counted in the same way one counts apples or other objects. Fractions greater than one whole can similarly be understood this way. Seven-thirds is just seven things called thirds. By counting fractional parts, we can help children develop a completely generalized system for naming fractions before they learn about fraction symbolism. The oral names then can be connected easily to the fraction notation.

Counting fractional parts will play a major role in much of the development of fractional concepts. In the beginning, counting fractional parts can lay the groundwork for several important ideas. The idea that eighths are smaller than thirds, for example, is an elusive idea. Counting different-sized parts and discussing how many parts it takes to make one whole is one opportunity to begin reflection on this idea. "Count three-fourths and then count three-twelfths. Which is more? Why?"

Counts should frequently include sets such as 5 thirds or 11 fourths or other sets greater than one whole. When the count gets to one whole (3 thirds or 4 fourths), stop and discuss other names for that amount. Such counts will dispel the notion that a fraction is something less than 1. With older children, counts can also be stopped at places where equivalent fractions are evident such as 6 twelfths or 9 sixths. These discussions will provide nice forerunners for equivalent fractions and mixed fractions.

ACTIVITY

12.3 Counting with Fractions

Once students have identified fourths, for example, count fourths. Show five or six fourths on the overhead. "How many fourths? Let's count: *one*-fourth, *two*-fourths, *three*-fourths, *four*-fourths, *five*-fourths, *six*-fourths." Count other collections of fourths. Ask if a collection that has been counted is more or less than a whole or more or less than two wholes. As shown in Figure 12.7, make informal comparisons among different counts. "Why did we get almost two wholes with seven-fourths, and yet we don't even have one whole with seven-twelfths? What is another way we could say seven-thirds?" (Two wholes and one-third or one whole and four-thirds.)

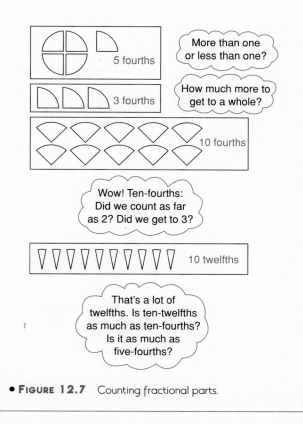

• **FIGURE 12.7** Counting fractional parts.

Connecting Concepts with Symbolism

Fraction symbolism should be delayed as long as possible. The first three activities can all be done orally and with the use of written fraction words such as 7 *fourths* or 3 *eighths*. Eventually, the standard symbolic form must be used.

Always write fractions with a horizontal bar, not a slanted one. Write $\frac{3}{4}$, *not* 3/4.

Meaning of the Top and Bottom Numbers

Consider a grocer who has developed a special way to take orders for his produce. If the order is for "seven apples and three bananas," he simply writes:

$$\frac{7}{A} \qquad \frac{3}{B}$$

The number on the top tells him *how many* items he needs. The letter on the bottom tells him *what* he needs. This analogy can be used for fraction symbolism.

Display several collections of fractional parts, and have children count each set as discussed earlier and write the count using fraction words as in "3 fourths." Explain that you are going to show how these fraction words can be written much more easily than writing out the words. For each collection, write the standard fraction next to the word. Display some other collections, and ask students if they can tell you how to write the fraction. Rather than an explanation, use the already developed oral language both with models and when writing the fraction symbols.

Next have children count by fourths as you write the fractions on the board. Repeat for other parts.

$$\frac{1}{4}, \frac{2}{4}, \frac{3}{4}, \frac{4}{4}, \frac{5}{4}, \frac{6}{4}, \frac{7}{4}, \frac{8}{4}, \frac{9}{4}$$

$$\frac{1}{6}, \frac{2}{6}, \frac{3}{6}, \frac{4}{6}, \frac{5}{6}, \frac{6}{6}, \frac{7}{6}, \frac{8}{6}, \frac{9}{6}$$

$$\frac{1}{8}, \frac{2}{8}, \frac{3}{8}, \frac{4}{8}, \frac{5}{8}, \frac{6}{8}, \frac{7}{8}, \frac{8}{8}, \frac{9}{8}$$

Discuss each row. How are the fractions alike? How are they different? What part of each row is like counting? Why does the bottom number stay the same as you count fourths or sixths or eighths? Finally, ask students:

What does the top number in a fraction tell you?

What does the bottom number in a fraction tell you?

Answer these two questions yourself. Try to think in terms of fractional parts and what has been covered to this point. Write your explanations for the meanings of top and bottom numbers. Try to use children's language. Explore several ways of saying each meaning. Your meaning should not be tied to a particular model.

Here are some reasonable explanations for the top and bottom numbers.

Top number: This is the counting number. It tells how many shares or parts we have. It tells how many have been counted. It tells how many parts we are talking about. It counts the parts or shares.

Bottom number: This tells what is being counted. It tells what fractional part is being counted. If it is a 4, it means we are counting *fourths;* if it is a 6, we are counting *sixths;* and so on.

Notice that if the concept of fractional parts is well developed and children can give an explanation for any fraction word, it is not necessary to include that in the meaning of the bottom number. In fact it is clumsy: "It tells how many of the equal parts being counted that it takes to make a whole." Not only is that clumsy, it detracts from the two simple but important ideas:

The top number *counts.*

The bottom number tells *what is being counted.*

The *what* of fractions are the fractional parts. They can be counted. Fraction symbols are just a shorthand for saying *how many* and *what.*

Numerator and Denominator: A Digression

To count a set is to enumerate it. Enumeration is the process of counting. The common name for the top number in a fraction is the *numerator.*

A $1 bill, a $5 bill, and a $10 bill are said to be bills of different denominations. Similarly, the word *denomination* is used to differentiate among branches of religions (such as Baptists, Presbyterians, Episcopalians, and Catholics). A denomination is the name of a class or type of thing. The common name for the bottom number in a fraction is the *denominator.*

Up to this point, the terms *numerator* and *denominator* have not been used, as will be the case in most of the rest of

the chapter. Why? No child in the third grade would mistake the designations *top number* and *bottom number.* The words *numerator* and *denominator* have no common reference for children. Some teachers may feel that it is important that children use these words. But whether they are used or not, it is clear that the words themselves will not help young children understand the meanings.

Mixed Numbers and Improper Fractions

In the fourth National Assessment of Educational Progress, about 80 percent of seventh graders could change a mixed number to an improper fraction, but fewer than half knew that $5\frac{1}{4}$ was the same as $5 + \frac{1}{4}$ (Kouba et al., 1988a). The result indicates that many children are using a mindless rule that is in fact relatively easy to construct.

--- ACTIVITY ---

12.4 Mixed-Number Names

Use models to display collections such as 13 sixths or 11 thirds. Have children orally count the displays and give at least two names for each. Then discuss how they could write these different names using numbers. They already know how to write $\frac{13}{6}$ or $\frac{11}{3}$. For two wholes and one sixth, a variety of alternatives might be suggested: 2 and $\frac{1}{6}$ or 2 wholes and $\frac{1}{6}$, or $2 + \frac{1}{6}$. All are correct. After doing this with other collections, explain that $2 + \frac{1}{6}$ is usually written as $2\frac{1}{6}$ with the "+" being left out or understood.

Now reverse the process. Write mixed numbers on the board and have students make that amount with models, using only one kind of fractional part. When they have done that, they can write the simple fraction that results. (The term *improper fraction* is an inaccurate yet common term for a simple fraction greater than 1.)

After much back-and-forthing between models and symbols using fractions greater than 1, see if students can figure out a simple fraction for a mixed number and a mixed number for an improper fraction. Do not provide any rules or procedures. Let students work this out for themselves. A good student explanation for $3\frac{1}{4}$ might involve the idea that there are 4 fourths in one whole, so there are 8 fourths in two and 12 fourths in three wholes. Since there is one more fourth, that is 13 fourths in all, or $\frac{13}{4}$.

For fractions greater than 2, it is a good exercise to have students find other expressions besides the usual. For example, $4\frac{1}{5}$ is not only $\frac{21}{5}$ but also $3\frac{6}{5}$, $2\frac{11}{5}$, and $1\frac{16}{5}$. This idea is extremely useful later when subtracting fractions, as in $5\frac{1}{8} - 2\frac{3}{8}$.

ACTIVITY

12.5 Calculator Fraction Counting

Calculators that permit fraction entries and displays are now quite common in schools. The TI-Math Explorer Plus and the Casio FX65 are two examples. If these are available, they can be quite effective in helping children understand fraction symbolism. Counting by fourths, for example, can be done by pressing $\boxed{+}$ **1** $\boxed{/}$ **4** $\boxed{=}$. **The display will show 1/4. Students should have models for fourths to manipulate as they count. When they add successive fourths to the pile, they press** $\boxed{=}$ **for each piece. At four-fourths, the calculator shows 4/4. Continued presses simply add onto the numerator. To see the corresponding mixed number, press the** $\boxed{a\frac{b}{c}}$ **key. The mixed number for** $\frac{6}{4}$ **is shown as 1_2/4. Since the calculator will not reduce the fraction automatically, the count agrees with the physical models.**

Fraction calculators provide an exciting and powerful way to help children develop fractional symbolism. A variation on Activity 12.5 is to show children a mixed number such as $3\frac{1}{8}$ and ask how many counts of $\frac{1}{8}$ on the calculator it will take to count that high. The students should try to stop at the correct number ($\frac{25}{8}$) before pressing the $\boxed{a\frac{b}{c}}$ key.

Exercises with Parts and Wholes

The exercises presented here can help children develop their understanding of fractional parts as well as the meanings of the top and bottom numbers in a fraction. Models are used to represent wholes and parts of wholes. Written or oral fraction names represent the relationship between the parts and wholes. Given any two of these—whole, part, and fraction—the students can use their models to determine the third. As with any exercise, the discussion and explanation of children's answers will provide the greatest value in these activities.

Any type of model can be used as long as different sizes can represent the whole. For region and area models, it is also necessary that single regions or lengths be used to represent nonunit fractions. Traditional pie pieces do not work because the whole is always the circle, and all the pieces are unit fractions.

Sample Exercises

Examples of each type of exercise are provided in Figures 12.8, 12.9, and 12.10 (p. 246). Each figure includes examples with a region model (freely drawn rectangles), a length

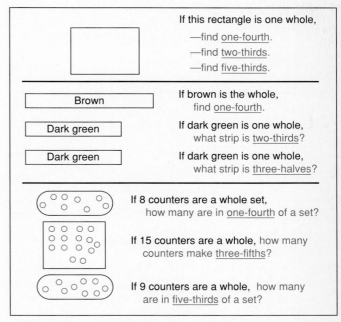

● **FIGURE 12.8** *Given the whole and the fraction, find the part. (Answers are given in Figure 12.11, p 247.)*

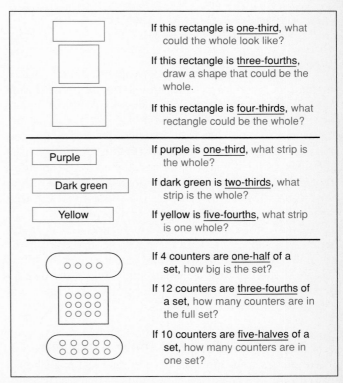

● **FIGURE 12.9** *Given the part and the fraction, find the whole. (Answers are given in Figure 12.12, p. 247.)*

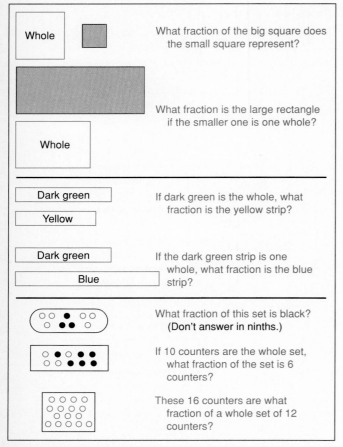

Whole — What fraction of the big square does the small square represent?

What fraction is the large rectangle if the smaller one is one whole?

Whole

Dark green / **Yellow** — If dark green is the whole, what fraction is the yellow strip?

Dark green / **Blue** — If the dark green strip is one whole, what fraction is the blue strip?

What fraction of this set is black? **(Don't answer in ninths.)**

If 10 counters are the whole set, what fraction of the set is 6 counters?

These 16 counters are what fraction of a whole set of 12 counters?

●**FIGURE 12.10**   *Given the whole and the part, find the fraction.* (Answers are given in Figure 12.13, p. 248.)

model (Cuisenaire rods or fraction strips), and set models. It would be a good idea to work through these exercises before reading on. For the rectangle models, simply sketch a similar rectangle on paper. For the rod or strip models, use Cuisenaire rods or make fraction strips. The colors used correspond to the actual rod colors. Lengths are not given in the figures so that you will not be tempted to use an adult-type numeric approach. If you do not have access to rods or strips, just draw lines on paper. The process you use with lines will correspond to what is done with rods.

Answers and explanations are in Figures 12.11, 12.12, and 12.13 (pp. 247–248). The questions that ask for the fraction when given the whole and part require a lot of trial and error and can frustrate young students. Be sure that appropriate fractional parts are available for the region and length versions of these questions.

Part-and-Whole Exercises in the Classroom

The exercises work much better with physical models than with drawings. The models allow students to use a trial-and-error approach to test their reasoning as they go. Also,

younger children have limited ability to partition lines or regions into smaller equal parts.

Care must be taken to ask only questions for which there is an answer within the model. For example, if you were using fraction strips, you could ask students, "If the blue strip (9) is the whole, what strip is two-thirds?" The answer is the strip that is 6 units long, or dark green. You could not, however, ask students to find three-fourths of the blue strip because fourths would each be $2\frac{1}{4}$ units long, and no strip has that length. With rectangular pieces of various sizes, you will likewise need to work out your questions in advance and be sure that they are answerable within the set.

Present each exercise to the full class to observe how different children are approaching the task. It may also be good to have students work in groups. After each task, have the students explain or justify their results.

A *unit fraction* is one that designates a single fractional part. In symbolic form, a unit fraction has a 1 in the numerator. Therefore, $\frac{1}{2}$, $\frac{1}{6}$, and $\frac{1}{12}$ are unit fractions, and $\frac{3}{4}$, $\frac{7}{3}$, and $2\frac{1}{6}$ are nonunit fractions. Questions involving unit fractions are generally the easiest. The hardest questions usually involve fractions greater than 1. For example, "If 15 chips are five-thirds of one whole set, how many chips are in a whole?" The same question can be asked in terms of a mixed number (15 chips are the same as $1\frac{2}{3}$). The mixed-number question is more difficult because it must first be translated to an improper fraction.

Exercise Difficulties

Many students find these part-and-whole activities challenging and even confusing. There is absolutely no benefit in providing students with rules for solving them or even telling them what to do next. Rather, try to focus on the concepts of unit fractions and fractional parts. By way of example, the following hypothetical interchange illustrates the type of problem students may have. Sketch a rectangle on a piece of paper and follow along.

The student has a small rectangle with the accompanying question: "If this is four-thirds of a box, what might one whole box look like?" The student begins by dividing the box into three parts and then is stumped and does not know what to do.

TEACHER: How big is the rectangle?

STUDENT: Four-thirds.

TEACHER: Does that mean it is four things or three things?

STUDENT: Well, thirds means three. So I divided it into three.

TEACHER: So these are thirds?

STUDENT: Yes, thirds.

TEACHER: Let's count. (*together*) One-third, two-thirds, three-thirds. How much is three-thirds?

STUDENT: One whole.

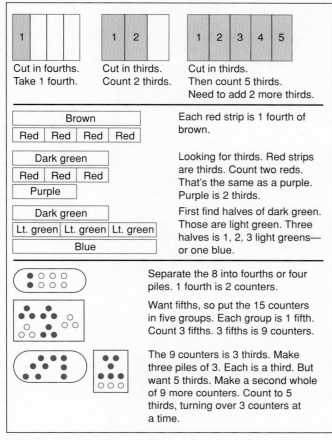

•FIGURE 12.11   *Answers to Figure 12.8 (p. 245).*

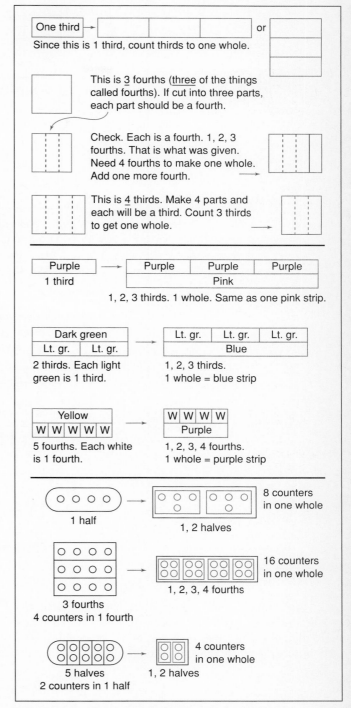

•FIGURE 12.12   *Answers to Figure 12.9 (p. 245).*

TEACHER: But the box is not three-thirds but four-thirds. How many thirds should be in the box you started with?

STUDENT: Four. It's four-thirds. I have to make four parts. (Starts over and draws the box divided into four parts.)

TEACHER: Now count. These are what kinds of pieces?

At this point, the teacher wants the child to stick with the idea that the parts are thirds and there are four of them.

In this and every other example, a unit fractional part comes into play. Once this part is identified in the model, students can count unit parts up to one of the pieces (part or whole) that they had to begin with. This confirms that they are correct. If a student counts four-thirds, that will agree with what was given—namely, that the original box was four-thirds. From that point, counting three-thirds to find the whole is trivial. Again notice the importance of counting parts.

Avoid being the answer book for your students. Make students responsible for determining the validity of their own answers. In these exercises, the results can always be

confirmed in terms of what is given. Students will learn that they can understand these ideas. There are no obscure rules. It makes sense!

When students do a series of exercises of one type, a pattern will begin to set in because each exercise is similar.

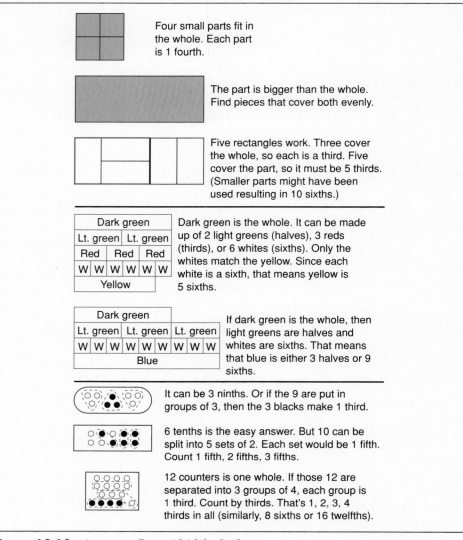

Four small parts fit in the whole. Each part is 1 fourth.

The part is bigger than the whole. Find pieces that cover both evenly.

Five rectangles work. Three cover the whole, so each is a third. Five cover the part, so it must be 5 thirds. (Smaller parts might have been used resulting in 10 sixths.)

Dark green is the whole. It can be made up of 2 light greens (halves), 3 reds (thirds), or 6 whites (sixths). Only the whites match the yellow. Since each white is a sixth, that means yellow is 5 sixths.

If dark green is the whole, then light greens are halves and whites are sixths. That means that blue is either 3 halves or 9 sixths.

It can be 3 ninths. Or if the 9 are put in groups of 3, then the 3 blacks make 1 third.

6 tenths is the easy answer. But 10 can be split into 5 sets of 2. Each set would be 1 fifth. Count 1 fifth, 2 fifths, 3 fifths.

12 counters is one whole. If those 12 are separated into 3 groups of 4, each group is 1 third. Count by thirds. That's 1, 2, 3, 4 thirds in all (similarly, 8 sixths or 16 twelfths).

• **FIGURE 12.13**   *Answers to Figure 12.10 (p. 246).*

When you mix exercises from the first two categories (whole-to-part and part-to-whole), students will experience more difficulty. The goal, however, is not to establish routines but to encourage reflective thought.

FRACTION NUMBER SENSE

The focus on fractional parts is an important beginning because it helps students reflect on the meanings of the part-to-whole relationship and the corresponding meanings of the top and bottom numbers of fractions. But number sense with fractions demands more. In particular, number sense with fractions requires that students have some intuitive feel for fractions. They should know "about" how big a particular fraction is and be able to tell easily which of two fractions is larger. These ideas require building further on the relationships already discussed.

Flexibility with Fractional Parts

Children have a tremendously strong mind-set about numbers that causes them difficulties with the relative size of fractions. In their experience, larger numbers mean "more." The tendency is to transfer this whole-number concept to fractions incorrectly: Seven is more than four, so sevenths should be bigger than fourths. The inverse relationship between number of parts and size of parts cannot be told but must be a creation of each student's own thought process.

---ACTIVITY---

12.6 Ordering Unit Fractions

List a set of unit fractions such as $\frac{1}{3}$, $\frac{1}{8}$, $\frac{1}{5}$, and $\frac{1}{10}$. Ask children to put the fractions in order from least to most. Challenge children to defend the way they ordered the fractions. The first few times you do this activity, have them explain their ideas by using models. Encourage the language of sharing—the more shares in one whole, the smaller each share will be.

This idea is so basic to the understanding of fractions that arbitrary rules ("Larger bottom numbers mean smaller fractions") are not only inappropriate but dangerous. Come back to this basic idea periodically. Children will seem to understand one day and revert to their more comfortable ideas about big numbers a day or two later.

Another way to help children think about fractional parts in a flexible manner is similar to the way we help younger children think about small whole numbers: Take them apart.

---ACTIVITY---

12.7 Taking Fractions Apart

Assign a fraction to work with. For example, consider $1\frac{1}{4}$. The task is to find ways to write the fraction in terms of two parts. $1\frac{1}{4}$ is clearly 1 and $\frac{1}{4}$. But what are some other ways to think about this fraction in two parts? Have children make lists and see what they can find out. You will probably want to let them use a physical model, perhaps one of their own choosing. Or you may suggest that they do the activity without a model as a means of stretching themselves.

How children will approach Activity 12.7 will vary a lot with the age and experience of the children. The activity could be done at any grade from 3 to 8. Consider just a few possibilities for $1\frac{1}{4}$:

All ways to use fourths: $\frac{1}{4}$ and $\frac{4}{4}$, $\frac{2}{4}$ and $\frac{3}{4}$

All ways with some other denominator: $\frac{1}{8}$ and $\frac{9}{8}$, $\frac{2}{8}$ and $\frac{8}{8}$, $\frac{3}{8}$ and $\frac{7}{8}$ . . .

Using two different fractions: $\frac{1}{2}$ and $\frac{3}{4}$, $\frac{1}{3}$ and $\frac{2}{3}$ and $\frac{1}{4}$, or $\frac{1}{3}$ and $\frac{11}{12}$

Thinking in terms of money or decimals: 75 cents and 50 cents, 0.8 and 0.45

These are just a few ideas. There is ample opportunity to develop patterns and relationships among fractions. As a variation, you could supply one part and ask children for one or more ways to determine what the other part is. Children will not think about this as subtraction but will use their own concepts to come up with solutions. This activity is a good assessment of how children are thinking about fractions.

Close to Zero, One-Half, and One

Number sense with whole numbers is partly the ability to understand their relative size. We know that numbers less than 10 are quite a bit smaller than numbers near 100 but that any number less than 100 is relatively small compared to 1000. An analogous familiarity with fractions can be developed by comparing fractions to 0, $\frac{1}{2}$, and 1. For fractions less than 1, this gives quite a bit of information. For example, $\frac{1}{20}$ is small, close to 0, whereas $\frac{3}{4}$ is between $\frac{1}{2}$ and 1. The fraction $\frac{9}{10}$ is quite close to 1. Since any fraction greater than 1 is a whole number plus an amount less than 1, this small range of 0 to 1 is quite helpful when thinking about fractions.

---ACTIVITY---

12.8 Close Fractions

Have your students name a fraction that is close to 1 but not more than 1. Next have them name another fraction that is even closer to 1 than that. For the second response, they have to explain why they believe the fraction is closer to 1 than the previous fraction. Continue for several fractions in the same manner, each one being closer to 1 than the previous fraction. Similarly, try close to 0 or close to $\frac{1}{2}$ (either under or over). The first several times you try this activity, let the students use models to help with their thinking. Later, see how well their explanations work when they cannot use models or drawings. Focus discussions on the relative size of fractional parts.

Establishing fractions close to 0, $\frac{1}{2}$, and 1 is a good beginning for estimation of fractions. If you see an amount that looks to be a bit more than $\frac{1}{2}$, the type of reasoning in Activity 12.8 can help you find a fraction that is a good estimate of the amount you see.

—————————ACTIVITY—————————

12.9 About How Much?

Draw a picture like one of those in Figure 12.14 (or prepare some ahead of time for the overhead). Have each student write down a fraction that he or she thinks is a good estimate of the amount shown (or the indicated mark on the number line). Listen without judgment to the ideas of several students, and engage them in a discussion of why any particular estimate might be a good one. For these situations, there is no single correct answer, but estimates should be "in the ballpark." If children have difficulty coming up with an estimate, ask if they think the amount is closer to 0, $\frac{1}{2}$, or 1.

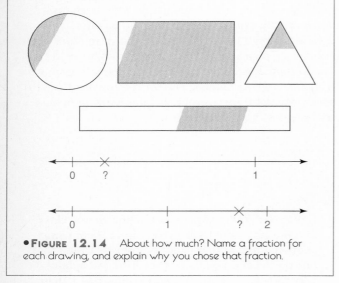

•**FIGURE 12.14**   About how much? Name a fraction for each drawing, and explain why you chose that fraction.

Thinking About Which Is More

The ability to tell which of two fractions is greater is another aspect of number sense with fractions. That ability is built around concepts of fractions, not on an algorithmic skill or symbolic trick.

Concepts, Not Rules

You have probably learned rules or algorithms for comparing two fractions. The usual approaches are finding common denominators and using cross-multiplication. These rules can be effective in getting correct answers but require no thought about the size of the fractions. This is especially true of the cross-multiplication procedure. If children are taught these rules before they have had the opportunity to think about the relative size of various fractions, there is little chance that they will develop any familiarity with or number sense about fraction size. Comparison activities

(which fraction is more?) can play a significant role in helping children develop concepts of relative fraction sizes. But we want to keep in mind that reflective thought is the goal, not an algorithmic method of choosing the correct answer.

Before reading further, try the following exercise. Assume for a moment that you know nothing about equivalent fractions or common denominators or cross-multiplication. Assume that you are a fourth- or fifth-grade student who was never taught these procedures. Now examine the pairs of fractions in Figure 12.15, and select the larger of each pair. Write down or explain one or more reasons for your choice in each case.

Which fraction in each pair is greater?
Give one or more reasons. Try not to use drawings or models.
<u>Do</u> <u>not</u> <u>use</u> common denominators or cross-multiplication.
Rely on concepts.

A. $\frac{4}{5}$ or $\frac{4}{9}$	G. $\frac{7}{12}$ or $\frac{5}{12}$
B. $\frac{4}{7}$ or $\frac{5}{7}$	H. $\frac{3}{5}$ or $\frac{3}{7}$
C. $\frac{3}{8}$ or $\frac{4}{10}$	I. $\frac{5}{8}$ or $\frac{6}{10}$
D. $\frac{5}{3}$ or $\frac{5}{8}$	J. $\frac{9}{8}$ or $\frac{4}{3}$
E. $\frac{3}{4}$ or $\frac{9}{10}$	K. $\frac{4}{6}$ or $\frac{7}{12}$
F. $\frac{3}{8}$ or $\frac{4}{7}$	L. $\frac{8}{9}$ or $\frac{7}{8}$

•**FIGURE 12.15**   Comparing fractions using concepts.

Conceptual Thought Patterns for Comparison

The first two comparison schemes listed here rely on the meanings of the top and bottom numbers in fractions and on the relative sizes of unit fractional parts. The third and fourth ideas use the additional ideas of 0, $\frac{1}{2}$, and 1 as convenient anchors or benchmarks for thinking about the size of fractions.

1. *More of the same-size parts.* To compare $\frac{3}{8}$ and $\frac{5}{8}$, it is easy to think about having 3 of something and also 5 of the same thing. When the fractions are given orally, this is almost trivial. When given in written form, it is possible for children to choose $\frac{5}{8}$ as larger simply because 5 is more than 3 and the other numbers are the same. Right choice, wrong reason. Comparing $\frac{3}{8}$ and $\frac{5}{8}$ should be like comparing 3 apples and 5 apples. Pairs B and G in Figure 12.15 can be compared with this idea.

2. *Same number of parts but parts of different sizes.* This is the case where the numerators are the same, as in $\frac{3}{4}$ and $\frac{3}{7}$. If a whole is divided into 7 parts, the parts will certainly be smaller than if divided into only 4 parts. Many children will select $\frac{3}{7}$ as larger because 7 is more than 4 and the other numbers are the same. That approach

yields correct choices when the parts are the same size, but it causes problems in this case. This is like comparing 3 apples with 3 melons. You have the same number of things, but melons are larger. Pairs A, D, and H in Figure 12.15 can be compared using this idea.

3. *More and less than one-half or one whole.* The fraction pairs $\frac{3}{7}$ versus $\frac{5}{8}$ and $\frac{5}{4}$ versus $\frac{7}{8}$ do not lend themselves to either of the previous thought processes. In the first pair, $\frac{3}{7}$ is less than half of the number of sevenths needed to make a whole, and so $\frac{3}{7}$ is less than a half. Similarly, $\frac{5}{8}$ is more than a half. Therefore, $\frac{5}{8}$ is the larger fraction. The second pair is determined by noting that one fraction is less than 1 and the other is greater than 1. The benchmark numbers of $\frac{1}{2}$ and 1 are useful for making size judgments with fractions. Pairs A, D, F, G, and H in Figure 12.15 can be compared this way.

4. *Closer to one-half or one whole.* Why is $\frac{9}{10}$ greater than $\frac{3}{4}$? Not because the 9 and 10 are big numbers, although you will find that to be a common student response. Each is one fractional part away from one whole, and tenths are smaller than fourths. Similarly, notice that $\frac{5}{8}$ is smaller than $\frac{4}{6}$ because it is only one-eighth more than a half, while $\frac{4}{6}$ is a sixth more than a half. Pairs C, E, I, K, and L in Figure 12.15 can be compared this way. (Can you use this basic idea to compare $\frac{3}{5}$ and $\frac{5}{6}$? *Hint:* Each is half of a fractional part more than $\frac{1}{2}$.)

How did your reasons for choosing fractions in Figure 12.15 compare to these ideas?

Classroom activities should help children develop informal ideas like those just explained for comparing fractions. However, the ideas should come from student experiences and discussions. To teach "the four ways to compare fractions" would be nearly as defeating as teaching cross-multiplication.

---ACTIVITY---

12.10 Compare and Test

Provide students with a familiar fraction model to work with. Present a pair of fractions for comparison. (They should be fractions that can be illustrated with the model.) Have the students think about which is more (compare), write down their choice, and then test their selection with the models. Be sure they make a commitment first, before they use the models.

When students begin to do well with the "Compare and Test" activity, see if they can give reasons without the use of models. Be sure you include fraction pairs that cover all of the possibilities discussed earlier.

---ACTIVITY---

12.11 Why Is It More?

Arrange the class in cooperative groups or pairs of students. Give the class a pair of fractions to compare. The task is to find as many good explanations for their choice as possible within an allotted time. Explanations can be written down and then discussed as a full class. The same exercise is a very good homework assignment and is also a good assessment.

---ACTIVITY---

12.12 Line 'Em Up

Have students put four or five fractions in order from least to most. In this way, a variety of methods for making comparisons can be included within the same exercise. As with all conceptual fraction activities, limit the denominators to reasonable numbers. There are very few reasons to consider fractions with denominators greater than 12.

A word of caution is implicit in the following situation. Mark is offered the choice of a third of a pizza or a half of a pizza. Since he is hungry and likes pizza, he chooses the half. His friend Jane gets a third of a pizza but ends up with more than Mark. How can that be? Figure 12.16 illustrates how Mark got misdirected in his choice. The point of the "pizza fallacy" is that whenever two or more fractions are discussed in the same context, the correct assumption (the one Mark made in choosing a half of the pizza) is that the fractions are all parts of the same whole.

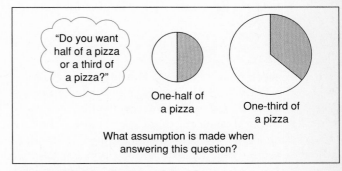

"Do you want half of a pizza or a third of a pizza?"

One-half of a pizza

One-third of a pizza

What assumption is made when answering this question?

● **FIGURE 12.16** *The "pizza fallacy."*

Comparisons with any model can be made only if both fractions are parts of the same whole. For example, $\frac{2}{3}$ of a light green strip cannot be compared to $\frac{2}{3}$ of an orange strip.

Other Methods of Comparison

Not all fractions can be compared by reliance on the conceptual approaches that have been discussed. Most adults would be hard-pressed to compare $\frac{2}{3}$ and $\frac{3}{5}$ without some other methods.

When simple methods fail, a more sophisticated and usually more complex method is required. The most common approach is to convert the fraction to some other form. When the concept and skills related to equivalent fractions are well in place, one or both of the fractions can be rewritten so that both fractions have the same denominator. Another idea is to translate the fraction to a different notation—decimals or percents. Many of these decimal and percent equivalents can and should become second nature and require no computation. In the case of $\frac{2}{3}$ and $\frac{3}{5}$, the equivalents are 66[+] percent and 60 percent, respectively. More will be said in later chapters about helping students make meaningful connections between decimals, percents, and fractions.

Even when common denominator methods are developed, they should be a last resort. Mental methods are frequently much quicker, and the symbolic methods detract from thinking in a conceptual way. There is little or no justification for asking students to compare $\frac{7}{17}$ with $\frac{9}{23}$.

Estimation

A frequently quoted result from the Second National Assessment (Post, 1981) concerns the following item:

Estimate the answer to $\frac{12}{13} + \frac{7}{8}$. You will not have time to solve the problem using paper and pencil.

Here is how 13-year-olds answered:

RESPONSE	PERCENT OF 13-YEAR-OLDS
1	7
2	24
19	28
21	27
Don't know	14

What this result points out all too vividly is that a good concept of fractions is much more significant for estimation purposes than a mastery of the pencil-and-paper procedures. Knowing if a fraction is closer to 0, $\frac{1}{2}$, or 1 proves quite useful. Numbers can be rounded either to the nearest whole or nearest half and then added easily. For example, $2\frac{1}{8} + \frac{4}{9}$ is about the same as $2 + \frac{1}{2}$. A front-end approach is also possible: Deal with the whole numbers, and then look at the fractions using estimates to the nearest half to make an adjustment. The following activities are useful for developing these ideas.

12.13 Pick the Best I

Flash fractions between 0 and 1 on an overhead projector. For each fraction, students should record on their answer sheet 0, $\frac{1}{2}$, or 1, depending on which they think the given fraction is closest to.

12.14 Pick the Best II

Flash sums or differences of proper fractions. Response options can vary with the age and experience of the students. More than 1 or less than 1 is one alternative. Closer to 0, 1, or 2 is also an easy option. A more sophisticated option is to give the result to the nearest half: 0, $\frac{1}{2}$, 1, $1\frac{1}{2}$, or 2.

12.15 Speed Estimates

Provide short speed drills for estimating sums and differences with mixed numbers, as illustrated in Figure 12.17.

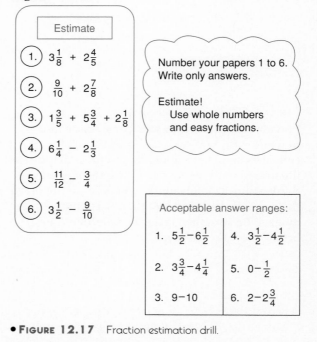

Estimate

1. $3\frac{1}{8} + 2\frac{4}{5}$
2. $\frac{9}{10} + 2\frac{7}{8}$
3. $1\frac{3}{5} + 5\frac{3}{4} + 2\frac{1}{8}$
4. $6\frac{1}{4} - 2\frac{1}{3}$
5. $\frac{11}{12} - \frac{3}{4}$
6. $3\frac{1}{2} - \frac{9}{10}$

Number your papers 1 to 6. Write only answers.

Estimate! Use whole numbers and easy fractions.

Acceptable answer ranges:

1. $5\frac{1}{2} - 6\frac{1}{2}$	4. $3\frac{1}{2} - 4\frac{1}{2}$
2. $3\frac{3}{4} - 4\frac{1}{4}$	5. $0 - \frac{1}{2}$
3. $9 - 10$	6. $2 - 2\frac{3}{4}$

● **FIGURE 12.17** Fraction estimation drill.

When more than two addends are involved, an acceptable range may be a bit wider. Encourage students to give whole-number estimates at first, and later practice refining estimates to the nearest half. Discuss both front-end and rounding techniques.

EQUIVALENT-FRACTION CONCEPTS

Concepts Versus Rules

How do you know that $\frac{4}{6} = \frac{2}{3}$? Here are some possible answers:

1. They are the same because you can reduce $\frac{4}{6}$ and get $\frac{2}{3}$.

2. Because if you have a set of 6 things and you take 4 of them, that would be $\frac{4}{6}$. But you can make the 6 into groups of 2. So then there would be 3 groups, and the 4 would be 2 groups out of the 3 groups. That means it's $\frac{2}{3}$.

3. If you start with $\frac{2}{3}$, you can multiply the top and the bottom numbers by 2, and that will give you $\frac{4}{6}$, so they are equal.

4. If you had a square cut into 3 parts and you shaded 2, that would be $\frac{2}{3}$ shaded. If you cut all 3 of these parts in half, that would be 4 parts shaded and 6 parts in all. That's $\frac{4}{6}$, and it would be the same amount.

These answers, all correct, provide clear examples of the distinction between conceptual knowledge and procedural knowledge. Responses 2 and 4 are very conceptual, although not efficient. The procedural responses, 1 and 3, are quite efficient, yet no conceptual knowledge is indicated. All students should eventually know how to write an equivalent fraction for a given fraction. At the same time, the rules should never be taught or used until the students understand what the result means.

The concept: Two fractions are equivalent if they are representations for the same amount or quantity; if they are the same number.

The rule: To get an equivalent fraction, multiply (or divide) the top and bottom numbers by the same nonzero number.

The rule or algorithm for equivalent fractions has no intuitive connection with the concept. As a result, students can easily learn and use the rule in exercises such as "List the first four equivalent fractions for $\frac{3}{5}$," without any idea of how the fractions in the list are related. It becomes an exercise in multiplication. A developmental approach suggests that students have a firm grasp of the concept and should be led to see that the algorithm is a meaningful and efficient way to find equivalent fractions.

Finding Different Names for Fractions

The general approach to a conceptual understanding of equivalent fractions is to have students use models to generate different names for models of fractions.

Area or Region Models

Examples of equivalent fraction representations using area models are illustrated in Figure 12.18 (p. 254).

---ACTIVITY---

12.16 Different Fillers

Using the same models that students have, draw the outline of several fractions on paper, and duplicate them. For example, if the model is rectangles, you might draw an outline (no subdivisions) of a rectangle for $\frac{2}{3}$, $\frac{1}{2}$, and perhaps $\frac{5}{4}$. Have children try to fill the outlines with unit fraction pieces to determine as many simple fraction names for the regions as possible. In class discussion, it may be appropriate to see if students can go beyond the actual models they have. For example, if the model has no tenths, it would be interesting to ask what other names could be generated if tenths were available. An easier question involves pieces that can be derived from existing pieces. "You found out that $\frac{5}{4}$ and $\frac{10}{8}$ and $\frac{15}{12}$ are all the same. What if we had some sixteenths pieces? Could we cover this same region with those? How many? How can you decide?

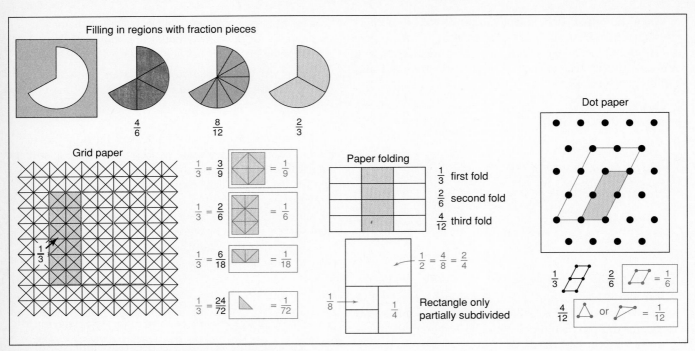

● **FIGURE 12.18**   Area models for equivalent fractions.

ACTIVITY

12.17 Folding and Refolding

Paper folding effectively models the equivalent fraction concept. Have students fold a sheet of paper into halves or thirds. Unfold and color a fraction of the paper. Write the fraction. Now refold and fold one more time. It is fun to discuss, before opening, how many sections will be in the whole sheet and how many will be colored. Open and discuss what fraction names can now be given to the shaded region. Is it still the same? Why? Repeat until the paper cannot be folded any more.

ACTIVITY

12.18 Dot Paper Equivalencies

Use grid paper or dot paper so that regions can easily be subdivided into many smaller parts. Have students draw a model for a whole and shade in some fraction that can be determined using the lines or dots on the paper. Now see how many different names for the shaded part they can find with the aid of the smaller regions

in the drawing (see Figure 12.18). Make a transparency of a grid or dot pattern, and do this exercise with the full class. Teams or individuals can take turns explaining different names for the shaded part.

Although subdivided regions illustrate why there are multiple names for one fractional part, students should learn that the existence of the subdivisions is not required. Half of a rectangle is still $\frac{2}{4}$, even if no subdivisions are present and even if the other half is divided into three parts. Work toward this understanding by drawing models for fractions and then erasing the subdivision lines. "Is this $\frac{2}{3}$ still $\frac{4}{6}$?"

Length Models

Equivalent fractions are modeled with length models in much the same way as area models. One fraction is modeled, and then different lengths are used to determine other fraction names. Some examples are shown in Figure 12.19.

Set Models

The general concept of equivalent fractions is the same with set models as with length and area models, although there

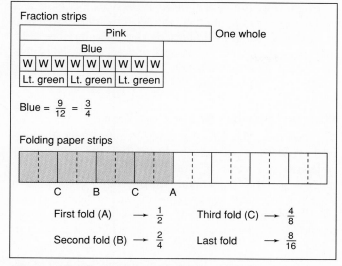

•**FIGURE 12.19**   Length models for equivalent fractions.

12.19 Arrange the Counters, Find the Names

Have students set out a specific number of counters in two colors—for example, 32 counters, 24 of them red and the rest yellow. This set will be the whole. Then have them find as many names as they can for each color by arranging the counters into different subgroups. Drawings can be made using Xs and Os to produce a written record of the activity.

are more limitations to how a particular set can be partitioned. For example, if $\frac{2}{3}$ is modeled with 8 out of 12 counters, then that particular representation shows that it is also $\frac{4}{6}$ and $\frac{8}{12}$. It cannot be seen as $\frac{6}{9}$ or $\frac{10}{15}$. As shown in Figure 12.20, a given number of counters in two colors can be arranged in different arrays or subgroups to illustrate equivalent fractions.

A Transitional Activity

Each of the following four equations is typical of equivalent fraction exercises found in textbooks. Notice the differences among the examples.

$$\frac{5}{3} = \frac{\Box}{6} \qquad \frac{2}{3} = \frac{6}{\Box} \qquad \frac{8}{12} = \frac{\Box}{3} \qquad \frac{12}{8} = \frac{3}{\Box}$$

An excellent exercise is to have students complete equations of this type by using a model to determine the missing number. Some care must be taken to select exercises that can be solved with the model being used. For example, most pie-piece sets do not have ninths. Counters or sets are a model that can always be used. Make students responsible for justi-

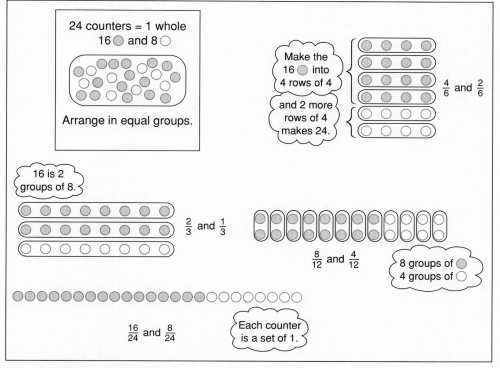

•**FIGURE 12.20**   Set models for equivalent fractions.

fying their results with the use of models or drawings. Explanations should be shared with the class. Later, when symbolic rules are developed, these same exercises will be completed in a more algorithmic but probably less meaningful manner.

Developing an Equivalent-Fraction Algorithm

An Area Model Approach

Though there are many possible ways to model the procedure of multiplying top and bottom numbers by the same number, the most commonly used approach is to slice a square in two directions.

---ACTIVITY---

12.20 Slicing Squares

Give students paper with rows of squares about 3 cm on each side. Have them shade the same fraction in several squares using vertical subdividing lines. Next, slice each rectangle horizontally into different fractional parts, as shown in Figure 12.21. Help students focus on the products involved by having them write the top and bottom numbers in the fraction as a product. Notice that for each model, the top and bottom numbers will always have a common factor. (Paper folding provides a similar result.)

Start with each square showing $\frac{3}{4}$.

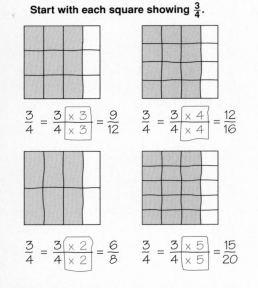

$$\frac{3}{4} = \frac{3 \times 3}{4 \times 3} = \frac{9}{12} \qquad \frac{3}{4} = \frac{3 \times 4}{4 \times 4} = \frac{12}{16}$$

$$\frac{3}{4} = \frac{3 \times 2}{4 \times 2} = \frac{6}{8} \qquad \frac{3}{4} = \frac{3 \times 5}{4 \times 5} = \frac{15}{20}$$

What <u>product</u> tells how many parts are shaded?

What <u>product</u> tells how many parts in the whole?

Notice that the same factor is used for both part and whole.

● **FIGURE 12.21**   A model for the equivalent-fraction algorithm.

Examine examples of equivalent fractions that have been generated with other models, and see if the rule of multiplying top and bottom numbers by the same number holds there also. If the rule is correct, how can $\frac{6}{8}$ and $\frac{9}{12}$ be equivalent? What about fractions like $2\frac{1}{4}$? How could it be demonstrated that $\frac{9}{4}$ is the same as $\frac{27}{12}$?

Writing Fractions in Simplest Terms

The multiplication rule for equivalent fractions produces fractions with larger denominators. To write a fraction in simplest terms means to write it so that numerator and denominator have no common whole number factors. (Some texts use the name *lowest terms* instead of *simplest terms*.) One meaningful approach to this task of finding simplest terms is to reverse the earlier process, as illustrated in Figure 12.22.

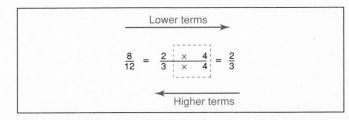
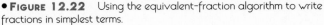

● **FIGURE 12.22**   Using the equivalent-fraction algorithm to write fractions in simplest terms.

Of course, finding and eliminating a common factor is the same as dividing both top and bottom by the same number. The search for a common-factor approach keeps the process of writing an equivalent fraction to one rule: Top and bottom numbers of a fraction can be multiplied by the same nonzero number. There is no need for a different rule for rewriting fractions in lowest terms.

Two additional notes:

1. Notice that the phrase "reducing fractions" was not used. This unfortunate terminology implies making a fraction smaller and is rarely used anymore in textbooks.

2. Many teachers seem to believe that fraction answers are incorrect if not in simplest or lowest terms. This is also unfortunate. When students add $\frac{1}{6} + \frac{1}{2}$ and get $\frac{4}{6}$, they have added correctly and have found the answer. Rewriting $\frac{4}{6}$ as $\frac{2}{3}$ is a separate issue.

The Multiply-by-1 Method

Many junior high textbooks use a strictly symbolic approach to equivalent fractions. It is based on the multiplication identity property of rational numbers that says that any number multiplied by 1 remains unchanged. The number 1 is the identity element for multiplication. Therefore, $\frac{3}{4} = \frac{3}{4} \times 1 = \frac{3}{4} \times \frac{2}{2} = \frac{6}{8}$. Any fraction of the form $\frac{n}{n}$ can be used as the identity element. Furthermore, the numerator and denominator of the identity element can also be fractions. In this way, $\frac{6}{12} = \frac{6}{12} \times (\frac{1}{6} \div \frac{1}{6}) = \frac{1}{2}$.

This explanation relies on an understanding of the multiplicative identity property, which most students in grades 4 to 6 do not fully appreciate. It also relies on the procedure for multiplying two fractions. Finally, the argument uses solely deductive reasoning based on an axiom of the rational number system. It does not lend itself to intuitive modeling. A reasonable conclusion is to delay this important explanation until at least seventh or eighth grade in an appropriate prealgebra context and not as a method or a rationale for producing equivalent fractions.

LITERATURE CONNECTIONS

Fractions in textbooks and even in the activities in this chapter lack context. Context takes children away from rules and the ideas you may have been discussing and encourages them to explore ideas in a more open and informal manner. The way that children approach fraction concepts in these contexts may surprise you.

The Doorbell Rang (Hutchins, 1986)

Often used to investigate whole-number operations of multiplication and division, this book is also an excellent early introduction to fractions. The story is a simple tale of two children preparing to share a plate of 12 cookies. Just as they have figured out how to share the cookies, the doorbell rings and more children arrive. This continues to happen until there are more children than cookies. Grandma saves the day. By changing the number of children to create an uneven division, children have to figure out how to divide the remaining cookies fairly. If given drawings of circles for cookies, investigations of situations such as four cookies for six children provide a variety of ways to solve fraction problems and discuss the need for fractional parts consisting of equal shares.

Gator Pie (Mathews, 1979)

Appropriate even for grades 5 and 6, this delightful book has Alvin, Alice, and other alligators sharing a pie they find in the woods. As more and more gators arrive, the need for cutting the pie into more and more pieces is evident, finally ending in hundredths, making a nice connection between decimals and fractions. An interesting exploration involves cutting a pie (or a rectangle) into halves or thirds and then deciding how to share it among a larger number once already cut. To go from halves to sixths is reasonably easy but may surprise you. What if the pie is cut in thirds and then we want to share it in tenths?

The Man Who Counted: A Collection of Mathematical Adventures (Tahan, 1993)

This book contains a story, "Beasts of Burden," about a wise mathematician, Beremiz, and the narrator, who are traveling together on one camel. They are asked by three brothers to solve an argument. Their father has left them 35 camels to divide among them: half to one brother, one-third to another, and one-ninth to the third. The story provides an excellent context for discussing fractional parts of sets and how fractional parts change as the whole changes. However, if the whole is changed from 35 to, say, 36 or 34, the problem of the indicated shares remains unresolved. The sum of $\frac{1}{2}$, $\frac{1}{3}$, and $\frac{1}{9}$ will never be one whole, no matter how many camels are involved. Bresser (1995) describes three full days of wonderful discussions with his fifth graders, who proposed a wide range of solutions. Bresser's suggestions are worth considering.

REFLECTIONS ON CHAPTER 12: WRITING TO LEARN

1. Give examples of three categories of fraction models. What real models have you used that correspond to each of these?

2. Why are set models more difficult for younger children?

3. Describe fractional parts. What are the two distinct requirements of fractional parts? Explain how children's concepts of partitioning need to be refined to produce a concept of fractional parts.

4. What are children learning in activities in which you count fractional parts? How can this type of activity help children learn to write fractions meaningfully?

5. Give a fourth-grade explanation of the meaning of the top number and the bottom number in a fraction.

6. Use a length model and make up part-and-whole questions for each of the following cases:

   a. Given a part and a nonunit fraction less than 1, find the whole.

   b. Given a part and a nonunit fraction greater than 1, find the whole.

   c. Given a whole and a nonunit fraction less than 1, find the part.

   d. Given a whole and a nonunit fraction greater than 1, find the part.

   Try your questions with a friend. Then change each question so that it is in terms of sets. With sets, be sure that a unit fraction is never a single counter. That is, if the question is about fourths, use whole sets of size 8 or 12 or more.

7. What types of ideas would you want children to develop to foster good number sense? Describe several

types of ideas for number sense with fractions and an activity for each.

8. Make up pairs of fractions that can be compared ("select the largest") without using an algorithm. See if you can make up examples that use the four different ideas that were suggested for comparing fractions.

9. Explain the difference between understanding the concept of equivalent fractions and knowing the algorithm for writing an equivalent fraction.

10. Describe some activities that will help children develop the equivalent-fraction concept.

11. How can you help children develop the algorithm for equivalent fractions?

FOR DISCUSSION AND EXPLORATION

1. A common error that children make is to write $\frac{3}{5}$ for the fraction represented here:

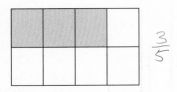

Why do you think that they do this? In this chapter, the notation of fractional parts and counting by unit fractions was introduced before any symbols. How could this help avoid the type of thinking that is involved in this common error?

2. Experiment with rods made of connecting cubes as a model for fractions. For example, if a bar of 12 cubes is a whole, then bars of 3 cubes would be fourths. Since the bars can be taken apart and put together and since the individual cubes can be counted, there are some significant differences between this model and those suggested in the text. Is this a length model or a set model?

3. In an editorial in *Mathematics Teaching in the Middle School*, Patrick Groff (1996) questions the importance of teaching fractions in the upper-elementary and middle grades. His arguments are based in part on the difficulty of learning fraction ideas at this level, the decreased use of fractions in everyday life, and the press for space in the curriculum from other topics that have recently been introduced. His opinion is rebutted in the "Readers Write" section of the September-October 1996 issue by a former physicist and by a current teacher. The discussion has merit and may be of interest. Teachers need to begin to take positions on curriculum.

SUGGESTED READINGS

Highly Recommended

Dorgan, K. (1994). What textbooks offer for instruction in fraction concepts. *Teaching Children Mathematics, 1,* 150–155.

Dorgan asks five important questions about the treatment of fractions in textbooks, concerning amount of instruction, translations among modes, use of models, qualitative reasoning, and use of students' informal knowledge. Although her answers are based on a review of popular text series (grades 1 to 5) in 1992, her observations remain relevant to today's texts. The perspective of an objective reviewer is valuable.

Payne, J. N., Towsley, A. E., & Huinker, D. M. (1990). Fractions and decimals. In J. N. Payne (Ed.), *Mathematics for the young child* (pp. 175–200). Reston, VA: National Council of Teachers of Mathematics.

These authors explore many of the ideas covered in this chapter, provide additional activities or variations on those found here, and show how the early development of fractions can be connected to decimal concepts. Do not be put off by the date; this resource will be timely for many years to come.

Watanabe, T. (1996). Ben's understanding of one-half. *Teaching Children Mathematics, 2,* 460–464.

This provocative article examines three very interesting tasks that were presented to a second-grade child. Even if you are interested in the upper grades, this is a worthwhile article. Not only are the tasks or variations of them quite interesting for all children, but the implications are also worth considering. Listening carefully to children informs us best.

Other Suggestions

Armstrong, B. E., & Larson, C. N. (1995). Students' use of part-whole and direct comparison strategies for comparing partitioned rectangles. *Journal for Research in Mathematics Education, 26,* 2–19.

Behr, M. J., Post, T. R., & Wachsmuth, I. (1986). Estimation and children's concept of rational number size. In H. L. Schoen (Ed.), *Estimation and mental computation* (pp.103–111). Reston, VA: National Council of Teachers of Mathematics.

Behr, M. J., Wachsmuth, I., & Post, T. R. (1985). Construct a sum: A measure of children's understanding of fraction size. *Journal for Research in Mathematics Education, 16,* 120–131.

Bezuk, N. S., & Bieck, M. (1993). Current research on rational numbers and common fractions: Summary and implications for teachers. In D. T. Owens (Ed.), *Research ideas for the classroom: Middle grades mathematics* (pp. 118–136). Old Tappan, NJ: Macmillan.

Bezuk, N. S., & Cramer, K. (1989). Teaching about fractions: What, when, and how? In P. R. Trafton (Ed.), *New directions for elementary school mathematics* (pp. 156–167). Reston, VA: National Council of Teachers of Mathematics.

Groff, P. (1996). It is time to question fraction teaching. *Mathematics Teaching in the Middle School, 1,* 604–607.

Hope, J. A., & Owens, D. T. (1987). An analysis of the difficulty of learning fractions. *Focus on Learning Problems in Mathematics, 9*(4), 25–40.

Kieren, T., Davis, B., & Mason, R. (1996). Fraction flags: Learning from children to help children learn. *Mathematics Teaching in the Middle School, 2,* 14–19.

Kroll, D. L., & Yabe, T. (1987). A Japanese educator's perspective on teaching mathematics in the elementary school. *Arithmetic Teacher, 35*(2), 36–43.

Langford, K., & Sarullo, A. (1993). Introductory common and decimal fraction concepts. In R. J. Jensen (Ed.), *Research ideas for the classroom: Early childhood mathematics* (pp. 223–247). Old Tappan, NJ: Macmillan.

Mack, N. K. (1993). Making connections to understand fractions. *Arithmetic Teacher, 40,* 362–364.

Mack, N. K. (1995). Confounding whole-number and fraction concepts when building on informal knowledge. *Journal for Research in Mathematics Education, 26,* 422–441.

National Council of Teachers of Mathematics. (1984). Rational numbers [Focus issue]. *Arithmetic Teacher, 31*(6).

Post, T. R., Behr, M. J., & Lesh, R. (1982). Interpretations of rational number concepts. In L. Silvey (Ed.), *Mathematics for the middle grades (5–9)* (pp. 59–72). Reston, VA: National Council of Teachers of Mathematics.

Post, T. R., & Cramer, K. (1987). Children's strategies in ordering rational numbers. *Arithmetic Teacher, 35*(2), 33–35.

Pothier, Y., & Sawada, D. (1983). Partitioning: The emergence of rational number ideas in young children. *Journal for Research in Mathematics Education, 14,* 307–317.

Reys, B. J. (1991). *Developing number sense in the middle grades: Addenda series, grades 5–8.* Reston, VA: National Council of Teachers of Mathematics.

Saenz-Ludlow, A. (1994). Michael's fraction schemes. *Journal for Research in Mathematics Education, 25,* 50–85.

Steffe, L. P., & Olive, J. (1991). The problem of fractions in the elementary school. *Arithmetic Teacher, 38*(9), 22–24.

Wearne-Hiebert, D., & Hiebert, J. (1983). Junior high school students' understanding of fractions. *School Science and Mathematics, 83,* 96–106.

Witherspoon, M. L. (1993). Fractions: In search of meaning. *Arithmetic Teacher, 40,* 482–485.

CHAPTER

COMPUTATION WITH FRACTIONS

13

It is possible to argue that of the two chapters in this text dealing with fractions, the one on concepts, Chapter 12, is more important than this one. The *Curriculum Standards* is not explicit about the importance of fraction computation but is consistent in downplaying any emphasis on tedious computations or computations out of context. Whatever your position on the importance of fraction computation, there can be little doubt that it needs to be developed in a much more conceptual manner than has been the practice in the past.

 BIG IDEAS

1. **For fraction computation, use the same ideas developed for whole-number computation. Apply these ideas to fractional parts instead of whole numbers.**
2. **Estimation of computation with fractions helps all fraction computation make sense. Many fraction computations can be done mentally without relying on formal algorithms.**

NUMBER SENSE AND FRACTION ALGORITHMS

Before beginning the discussion of fraction computation, we need to ask ourselves why we want children to have fraction computation skills in the first place. Pencil-and-paper skills with fractions are almost never used outside of school anymore, and certainly children in the sixth and seventh grades do not need much proficiency with pencil-and-paper computation with fractions. There are, however, some real benefits in having children look at fraction computation. Perhaps most important is the value that can be gained in mental computation and estimation skills. These mental approaches are significantly more important than paper methods. Second, if we can help children approach this problem of fraction computation conceptually and with a problem-solving spirit, there is a significant opportunity for children to begin to do some real mathematics—to figure things out and explain the results. Finally, a firm foundation of fraction computation will be helpful when the same patterns and ideas are translated from numbers to algebraic symbols. This last reason is not, however, sufficient in itself. Be careful not to tell children, "You're going to need this to do

260

higher math." That is perhaps the weakest reason for learning any mathematics.

The Danger of Rules

In the short term, the rules for fraction computation can be relatively simple to teach. Students can become quite proficient at finding common denominators during a chapter on adding and subtracting simple fractions. Multiplying fractions is such an easy procedure that some suggest that it should be taught first. The only requirements are third-grade multiplication skills. Division, following the invert-and-multiply rule, is nearly as easy. Fraction rules, too, can easily become the focus of rote instruction and produce artificial feelings of accomplishment on the quiz at the end of the week.

Focusing attention on fraction rules and answer getting has two significant dangers. First, none of the rules help students think in any way about the meanings of the operations or why they work. Students practicing such rules may very well be doing rote symbol pushing in its purest sense. Second, the mastery observed in the short term is quickly lost. When taken as a group of rules, the procedures governing fraction computation become similar and confusing. "Do I need a common denominator, or can you just add the bottoms?" "Do you invert the second number or the first?"

A Number Sense Approach

Without a firm understanding of fraction concepts, the development of computational algorithms for fractions can quickly become superficial, rule-oriented, and confusing. That is why this chapter was written separately from the preceding chapter—to place more emphasis on fraction concepts themselves and not to confuse computation with numeration as an objective.

It may be wise to begin the development of fraction computation with the following ideas in mind:

1. Connect the meaning of fraction computation with whole-number computation. To consider what $2\frac{1}{2} \times \frac{3}{4}$ might mean, we should ask, "What does 2×3 mean?" The concepts of each operation are the same, and benefits can be had by connecting these ideas.

2. Let estimation and informal methods play a big role in all phases of the development, especially during initial explorations. "Should $2\frac{1}{2} \times \frac{3}{4}$ be more or less than 1? More or less than 3?" Estimation keeps the focus on the meanings of the numbers and the operations, encourages reflective thinking, and helps build informal number sense with fractions. For many computations, there is no need for a standard algorithm, and children can, if they are asked to try, find interesting ways to get an-

swers. Here is a simple example: $\frac{7}{8} + \frac{1}{2}$ is 1 whole plus $\frac{1}{8}$ less than $\frac{1}{2}$ so it is $1\frac{3}{8}$.

3. Explore each of the operations using models. Use a variety of models. Have students defend the solutions to computations using the models. You will find that sometimes it is possible to get answers with models that do not seem to help with pencil-and-paper approaches. That's fine! The ideas will help children learn to think about the fractions and the operations, contribute to mental methods, and provide a useful background when you eventually do get to the standard algorithms.

In the discussions that follow, informal exploration is encouraged for each operation. There is also a guided development of each traditional algorithm. You are strongly encouraged to use some models and spend a good bit of time with the exploratory material especially.

ADDITION AND SUBTRACTION

As just suggested, a heavy emphasis should be placed on estimation while developing computation with fractions. Estimation activities can be done at any time—before, during, or after an informal exploration of addition and subtraction. Because addition and subtraction of fractions are operations so basic to fraction number sense, estimation with these operations was discussed in Chapter 12.

The example of the mental computation in item 2 of the list suggests that similar computations should also be explored.

Informal Exploration

Have students add two fractions using a fraction model. The results should come completely from the use of the model even if some of the students have been exposed to symbolic rules and the idea of a common denominator. For example, suggest that students use their model to find the sum of $\frac{3}{4}$ and $\frac{1}{3}$. Exercises such as this should be explored with area, length, and set models. You must be careful that the problems can actually be worked with the materials the students have available. With circular regions, the assumption is that the circle will always represent the whole. However, as seen in Chapter 12, many models allow different representations for the whole. When using these more flexible models (for example, strips or counters), the first task is to determine a whole that permits both fractions to be modeled. (Recall the "pizza fallacy" from Figure 12.16, p. 251.) Figure 13.1 (p. 262) illustrates how beginning addition tasks might be approached using three different models.

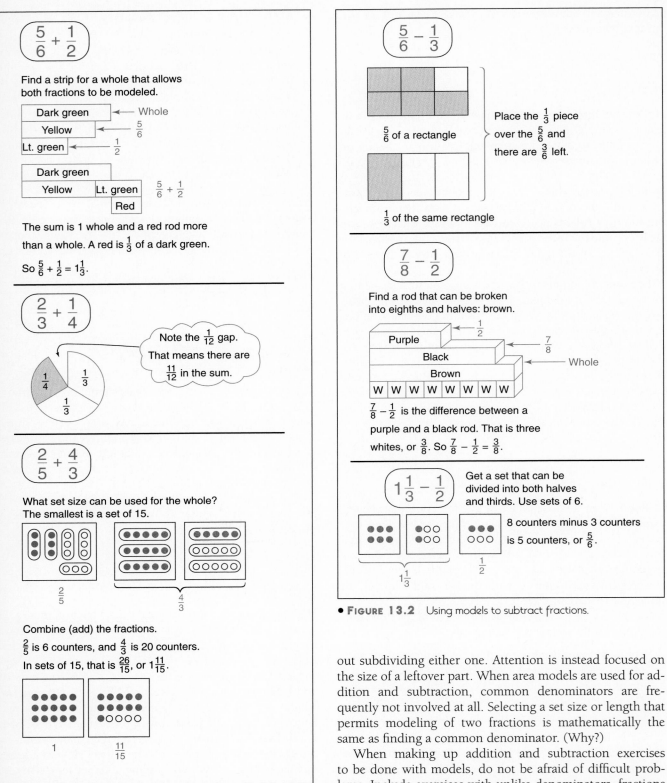

• **FIGURE 13.1** Using models to add fractions.

• **FIGURE 13.2** Using models to subtract fractions.

Subtraction of two fractions with models is a similar process, as shown in Figure 13.2. Notice that it is sometimes possible to find the sum or difference of two fractions with-

out subdividing either one. Attention is instead focused on the size of a leftover part. When area models are used for addition and subtraction, common denominators are frequently not involved at all. Selecting a set size or length that permits modeling of two fractions is mathematically the same as finding a common denominator. (Why?)

When making up addition and subtraction exercises to be done with models, do not be afraid of difficult problems. Include exercises with unlike denominators, fractions greater than 1, and mixed numbers. For subtraction, explore problems such as $3\frac{1}{8} - 1\frac{1}{4}$, where a trade of wholes for eighths might occur. At this stage, avoid directing students with a completely formulated method for arriving at a solution. The problem-solving approach, combined with the use of models, will help students develop relationships. Discuss the solution processes used by different groups. It can be useful to have different groups use different models for their processes.

Developing the Algorithm

Children are not likely to invent the standard algorithms for addition and subtraction without some guidance. At the same time, they can easily build on the informal explorations and see that the common-denominator approach is quite meaningful.

Like Denominators

If students have worked with models to find sums and differences, exercises with like denominators should be trivial. For example, when adding $\frac{3}{4}$ and $\frac{7}{4}$ with circular pie pieces, all that is necessary is to count the fractional parts. In just a few minutes, students should be completely comfortable with adding or subtracting any two fractions of the same type (fractions with like denominators). There is no need to practice these in pencil-and-paper form. In fact, if you stick with models for a while, the next step in the development will make more sense.

Unlike Denominators

When you use an area model to add or subtract two fractions that are not alike, you are very likely to pay attention to a part left over to make a whole (first example in Figure 13.1) or, similarly, to a part that is a bit more than a whole. Although this is excellent thinking, it does not lead to the need for common denominators.

To get students to move to common denominators, consider a task such as $\frac{5}{8} + \frac{2}{4}$. Let students use pie pieces to get the result of $1\frac{1}{8}$ using any approach. Many will note that the models for the two fractions make one whole and there is $\frac{1}{8}$ extra. The key question at this point is, "How can we change this question into one that is just like the easy ones where the parts are the same?" For the current example, it is relatively easy to see that fourths could be changed into eighths. Have students use models to show the original problem and also the converted problem. The main idea is to see that $\frac{5}{8} + \frac{2}{4}$ is exactly the same problem as $\frac{5}{8} + \frac{4}{8}$.

Next try some examples where both fractions need to be changed—for example, $\frac{2}{3} + \frac{1}{4}$. Be sure that the common denominator can actually be modeled with the materials that the students have. Again, focus attention on *rewriting the problem* in a form that is like adding apples and apples, where the parts of both fractions are the same. Students must fully understand that the new form of the problem is actually the same problem. This can and should be demonstrated with models. However, if your students express any doubt about the equivalence of the two problems ("Is $\frac{11}{12}$

really the answer to $\frac{2}{3} + \frac{1}{4}$?"), that should be a clue that the concept of equivalent fractions is not well understood.

As a result of modeling and rewriting fractions to make the problems easy, students should come to understand that the process of getting a common denominator is really one of looking for a way to change the *statement* of the problem without changing the problem itself. After getting a common denominator, it should be immediately obvious that adding the numerators produces the correct answer. These ideas are illustrated in Figure 13.3 (p. 264).

Subtraction of two simple fractions follows exactly the same approach. If the denominators are the same, it is like subtracting apples from apples. When the denominators are different, the problem should be rewritten to make it an easy one.

Common Multiples

Many students have trouble with finding common denominators because they are not able to come up with common multiples of the denominators quickly. That is a skill that can be practiced. It also depends on having a good command of the basic facts for multiplication. Here are two activities aimed at the skill of finding least common multiples or common denominators.

ACTIVITY

13.1 Running Through the Multiples

For this oral drill, give students a number between 2 and 16 (likely denominators) and have them list the multiples in order. At first, writing the multiples may be helpful. Work toward the skill of doing this exercise orally and quickly. Students should be able to list the multiples to about 50 with ease.

ACTIVITY

13.2 LCM Flash Cards

Make flash cards with pairs of numbers that are potential denominators. Most should be less than 16, as before. For each card, students try to give the least common multiple (LCM; see Figure 13.4, p. 264). Be sure to include pairs that are prime, such as 9 and 5; pairs in which one is a multiple of the other, such as 2 and 8; and pairs that have a common divisor, such as 8 and 12.

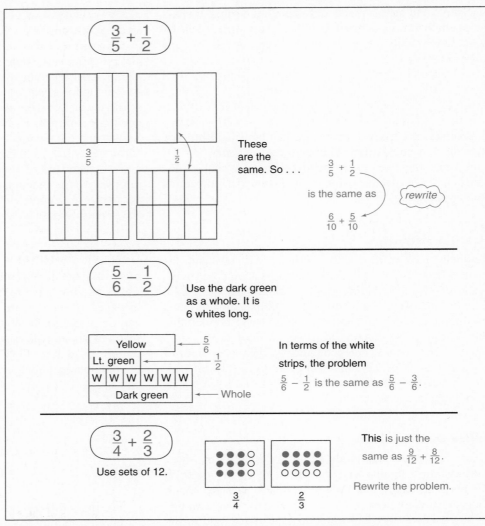

$$\frac{3}{5} + \frac{1}{2}$$

These are the same. So . . .

$$\frac{3}{5} + \frac{1}{2}$$

is the same as

rewrite

$$\frac{6}{10} + \frac{5}{10}$$

$$\frac{5}{6} - \frac{1}{2}$$

Use the dark green as a whole. It is 6 whites long.

Yellow	$\leftarrow \frac{5}{6}$
Lt. green	$\leftarrow \frac{1}{2}$
W W W W W W	
Dark green	$\leftarrow$ Whole

In terms of the white strips, the problem

$\frac{5}{6} - \frac{1}{2}$ is the same as $\frac{5}{6} - \frac{3}{6}$.

$$\frac{3}{4} + \frac{2}{3}$$

Use sets of 12.

This is just the same as $\frac{9}{12} + \frac{8}{12}$.

Rewrite the problem.

$\frac{3}{4}$ $\frac{2}{3}$

• **FIGURE 13.3** *Rewriting addition and subtraction problems involving fractions.*

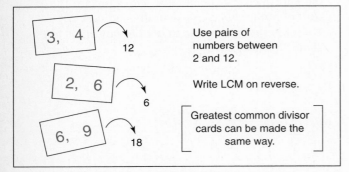

3, 4	→ 12
2, 6	→ 6
6, 9	→ 18

Use pairs of numbers between 2 and 12.

Write LCM on reverse.

[Greatest common divisor cards can be made the same way.]

• **FIGURE 13.4** *Least common multiple (LCM) flash cards.*

"Borrowed" 1 from 5. Changed $\frac{1}{8}$ to $\frac{11}{8}$.

$$\begin{array}{r} \overset{4}{\cancel{5}}\overset{11}{\cancel{\frac{1}{8}}} \\ -3\frac{5}{8} \\ \hline 1\frac{6}{8} \end{array}$$

• **FIGURE 13.5** *A common subtraction error.*

Mixed Numbers

When students do addition and subtraction with mixed numbers, they tend to make errors in converting fractions to whole numbers and whole numbers to fractions. This is especially true in subtraction, as illustrated in Figure 13.5. Students making this error are using a base 10 place-value idea instead of changing a whole for an equivalent set of fractional parts.

When you see students making an error such as this one with mixed numbers, the first thing to do is to find out what ideas are being used. Do they understand what a mixed fraction is? As an assessment, try Activity 12.4, "Mixed-Number Names" (p. 244). Make a fraction model available, and have students explain with the models what they are doing with the symbolic activity. The bottom line for this difficulty is the same as for most others: Listen to children as they talk through their ideas with the help of models. Avoid providing rules that seem to come out of nowhere.

Do not forget to include estimation practice even after you have begun to apply the algorithm. Notice that with mixed numbers, the idea of a left-hand or front-end approach is clearly best for addition and subtraction. That is, deal first with the whole-number part. That alone provides a fairly good estimate. If the situation calls for a better estimate, an adjustment can be made by examining the fractional part.

MULTIPLICATION

With multiplication, there is a greater need to review the meaning of the operation with whole numbers. Many children have developed the mistaken notion that multiplication always results in a bigger number. When one or both of the factors is a fraction, as in $\frac{3}{4} \times 7$ or $\frac{2}{3} \times \frac{1}{2}$, it is very difficult for children to make estimates. Therefore, perhaps the first place to begin is with whole numbers and the meaning of multiplication. However, do not forget to make estimates.

Informal Exploration

Recall with students that for whole numbers, 3×5 means 3 sets with 5 in each set—3 sets of 5 each. "With this in mind, *about* how much do you think $3 \times \frac{4}{5}$ might be?" Encourage students to use models or even a drawing to help them figure out a solution. One possible idea is that it will be less than 3 because there will be 3 sets, each a bit less than 1. Another approach is to use the meanings of the top and bottom numbers: 3 sets of 4 fifths is just 3 sets of 4 things. There will be 12 things in all—12 fifths. Discuss other examples, keeping the first factor a whole number, to elicit a good discussion of techniques.

After a discussion of mental approaches and estimates, have students try to solve some of the same exercises with models. Several examples of how multiplication problems might be modeled are illustrated in Figure 13.6 (p. 266). Help students develop the idea that the first factor tells how many sets and the second factor the size of the sets.

Next, still using models, try examples with a fraction as the first factor and a whole number as the second factor. The meanings remain the same: $\frac{2}{3} \times 4$ means $\frac{2}{3}$ of a set of 4. Try modeling a given product in both orders. For example, try $\frac{1}{6} \times 4$ and $4 \times \frac{1}{6}$. The answers are the same, but the process is quite different.

Finally, see if students can explain the meaning of a fraction times a fraction. For example, what does $\frac{2}{3} \times \frac{3}{4}$ mean? Once again, the meanings remain the same: $\frac{2}{3}$ of a set of $\frac{3}{4}$. That is, with models, one would first make a set of 3 fourths and then determine what is $\frac{2}{3}$ of that set. Notice how easy

that example is compared to $\frac{1}{4} \times \frac{2}{3}$. (Why?) When the first factor is greater than 1, children may have extra difficulty. For example, try solving $\frac{3}{2} \times \frac{1}{4}$ or $\frac{4}{3} \times 1\frac{2}{3}$ using different models and the basic concepts of multiplication.

Frequently, students are perplexed because the answer in multiplication gets smaller instead of larger. When and why a product of two fractions is smaller than either factor are good questions to explore at this preliminary stage.

Developing the Algorithm

More careful development of the usual algorithm will build on the informal techniques just discussed. As with whole-number algorithms, development of a standard algorithm generally involves a more directed approach to instruction. Good discussions can and should continue, however, as you make students responsible for understanding what they are doing.

Both Factors Less than 1

Though not the only way to generate the multiplication algorithm for fractions, an area model where squares or rectangles are used for the whole is one of the most common. The examples that are easiest to understand are those where both factors are fractions less than 1.

Figure 13.7 (p. 267) shows how the square is used first to model the product and then to determine the numerator and denominator of the product in written form. By drawing the lines for each fraction in opposite directions, both the *whole* (the square) and the *product* are arrays made of fractional parts of the same size. The numerator of the product is the *number of parts* in the product, the number of rows times the number of columns. The denominator of the product is the *name of those parts* or the number in one whole. Help students see that these two products are also the products of the numerators and the denominators, respectively. After students model a series of fraction products, the rule of multiplying top and bottom numbers will become obvious.

One Factor a Whole Number

For products where the first factor is a whole number, such as $3 \times \frac{4}{5}$, the intuitive meaning of multiplication is quite easy, as noted earlier. Three sets of 4 fifths is 12 fifths: $3 \times \frac{4}{5} = \frac{12}{5}$. Multiply the whole number by the top number. This rule makes sense even without modeling. Since 3 can be written as $\frac{3}{1}$, the rule of multiplying tops and bottoms does apply. Figure 13.8 (p. 267) illustrates how this product would be modeled using squares as already discussed.

For products where the second factor is a whole number, the result is similar, as illustrated in Figure 13.8. The case where the second factor is a whole number can also be looked at by using the turn-around property: $\frac{3}{4} \times 2$ is the same as $2 \times \frac{3}{4}$. This is especially useful in mental multiplica-

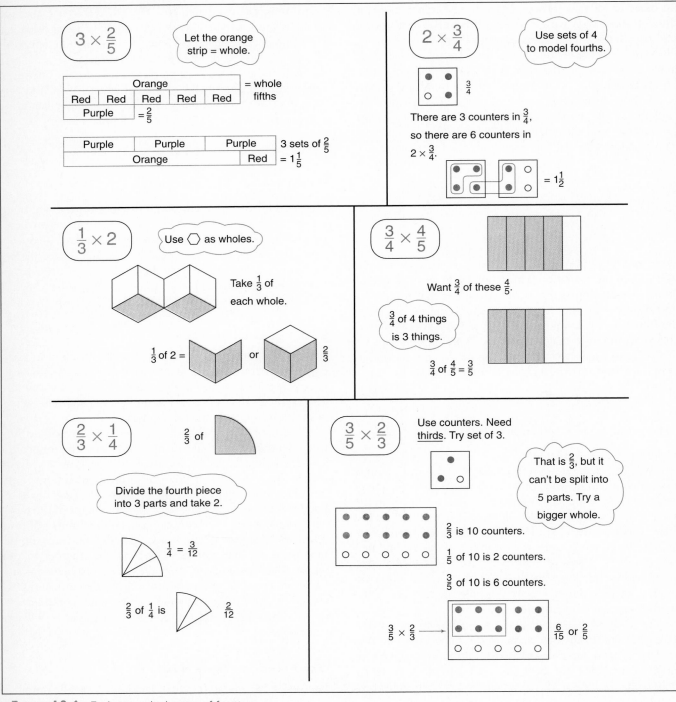

● **FIGURE 13.6** *Exploring multiplication of fractions.*

tion. The modeling is done to make the algorithm complete and to see that the rule does not just apply to a special case. Never let mental computation or estimation slip entirely into the background.

Mixed-Number Factors

Recall that with mixed numbers, mental methods suggest that you work with the whole-number parts first. Consider

the example of $3\frac{2}{3} \times 2\frac{1}{4}$. To get a first estimate of this product, a good place to begin is with 3×2. However, it is not exactly clear what could be done to improve on this estimate. As a problem-solving or performance task, have students work at drawing a picture of the product using the same methods as before. That is, get a picture of $2\frac{1}{4}$ and then show $3\frac{2}{3}$ sets of that $2\frac{1}{4}$. Figure 13.9 (p. 268) shows how this might be done, leading to the use of improper fractions in agreement with the standard algorithm.

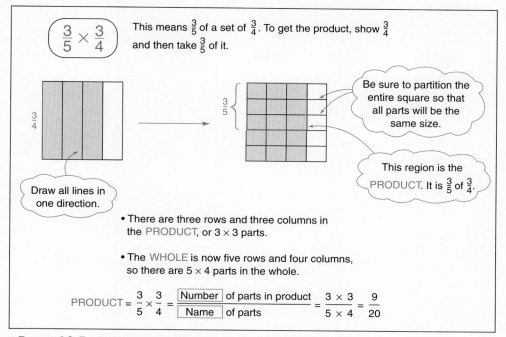

$\dfrac{3}{5} \times \dfrac{3}{4}$

This means $\frac{3}{5}$ of a set of $\frac{3}{4}$. To get the product, show $\frac{3}{4}$ and then take $\frac{3}{5}$ of it.

$\frac{3}{4}$

$\frac{3}{5}$

Draw all lines in one direction.

Be sure to partition the entire square so that all parts will be the same size.

This region is the PRODUCT. It is $\frac{3}{5}$ of $\frac{3}{4}$.

- There are three rows and three columns in the PRODUCT, or 3×3 parts.

- The WHOLE is now five rows and four columns, so there are 5×4 parts in the whole.

$$\text{PRODUCT} = \frac{3}{5} \times \frac{3}{4} = \frac{\boxed{\text{Number}} \text{ of parts in product}}{\boxed{\text{Name}} \text{ of parts}} = \frac{3 \times 3}{5 \times 4} = \frac{9}{20}$$

• **FIGURE 13.7**   *Development of the algorithm for multiplication of fractions.*

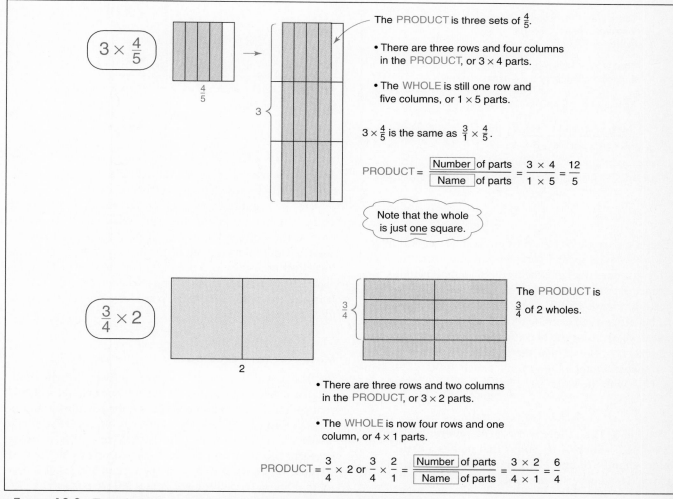

$3 \times \dfrac{4}{5}$

$\frac{4}{5}$

3

The PRODUCT is three sets of $\frac{4}{5}$.

- There are three rows and four columns in the PRODUCT, or 3×4 parts.

- The WHOLE is still one row and five columns, or 1×5 parts.

$3 \times \frac{4}{5}$ is the same as $\frac{3}{1} \times \frac{4}{5}$.

$$\text{PRODUCT} = \frac{\boxed{\text{Number}} \text{ of parts}}{\boxed{\text{Name}} \text{ of parts}} = \frac{3 \times 4}{1 \times 5} = \frac{12}{5}$$

Note that the whole is just *one* square.

$\dfrac{3}{4} \times 2$

2

$\frac{3}{4}$

The PRODUCT is $\frac{3}{4}$ of 2 wholes.

- There are three rows and two columns in the PRODUCT, or 3×2 parts.

- The WHOLE is now four rows and one column, or 4×1 parts.

$$\text{PRODUCT} = \frac{3}{4} \times 2 \text{ or } \frac{3}{4} \times \frac{2}{1} = \frac{\boxed{\text{Number}} \text{ of parts}}{\boxed{\text{Name}} \text{ of parts}} = \frac{3 \times 2}{4 \times 1} = \frac{6}{4}$$

• **FIGURE 13.8**   *The multiplication rule with whole numbers is exactly the same with fractions.*

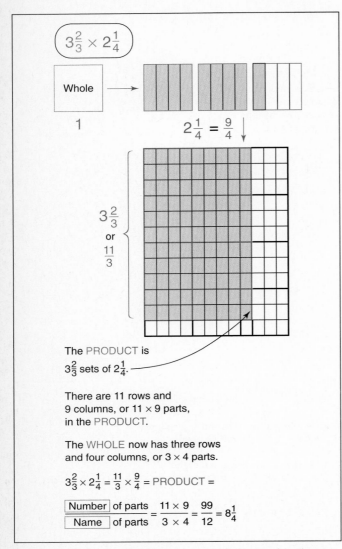

● **FIGURE 13.9** The multiplication rule with two mixed numbers.

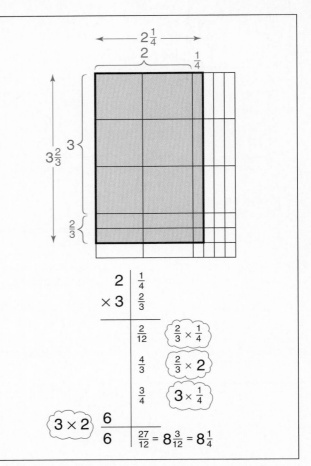

● **FIGURE 13.10** The product of mixed numbers as four partial products.

This last exercise is a good example of an algorithm getting in the way of mental computation and estimation. The process just does not lend itself well to mental methods. Another idea is to make a connection with whole-number multiplication. Figure 13.10 is very much like Figure 13.9 except that it uses the same length × length = area approach as was developed for the two-digit multiplication algorithm in Chapter 11. Notice that there are four partial products, just as there would be for a product such as 36 × 24. Mentally, work with the larger parts first:

- -

3 × 2 is 6. Then there is 3 × $\frac{1}{4}$, or $\frac{3}{4}$ more: 6$\frac{3}{4}$. And 2 × $\frac{2}{3}$ is $\frac{4}{3}$, which is 1$\frac{1}{3}$. So far that makes a little more than 8 (6$\frac{3}{4}$ and 1$\frac{1}{3}$). Then there's 1 fourth of $\frac{2}{3}$ extra. The answer is probably less than 8$\frac{1}{2}$.

- -

Though the mental process is difficult to get exactly, the left-hand approach provides a reasonable estimate.

Another significant benefit of the drawing in Figure 13.10 is the connection made with something the students have learned earlier, the two-digit products of Chapter 11. Later, a similar drawing can be made for a product with decimal fractions such as 3.4 × 2.6. The same area model is also used in algebra for products such as $(2X + 3)(X + 4)$. It is well worth the time to help students see such unifying ideas in mathematics.

More Mental Techniques

In the real world, there are many instances when the product of a whole number times a fraction occurs, and a mental estimate or even an exact answer is quite useful. For example, sale items are frequently listed as "$\frac{1}{4}$ off," or we read of a "$\frac{1}{3}$ increase" in the number of registered voters. Fractions are excellent substitutes for percents, as you will see in the next chapter. To get an estimate of 60 percent of $36.69, it is useful to think of 60 percent as $\frac{3}{5}$ or as a little less than $\frac{2}{3}$.

These products of fractions with large whole numbers can be calculated mentally by thinking of the meanings of the top and bottom numbers. For example, $\frac{3}{5}$ is 3 *one*-fifths. So if you want $\frac{3}{5}$ of 350, for example, first think about *one*-fifth of 350, or 70. If *one*-fifth is 70, then *three*-fifths is 3×70, or 210. Although this example has very accommodating numbers, it illustrates a process for mentally multiplying a large number by a fraction: First determine the unit fractional part, and then multiply by the number of parts you want. Once again, you can see the importance of the fractional-part concept and the meanings of the top and bottom numbers.

When numbers are not so nice, encourage students to use compatible numbers. To estimate $\frac{3}{5}$ of $36.69, a useful compatible is $35. One-fifth of 35 is 7, so three-fifths is 3×7, or 21. Now adjust a bit—perhaps add an additional 50 cents, for an estimate of $21.50.

Students should practice estimating fractions times whole numbers in lots of real contexts: $3\frac{1}{4}$ gallons of paint at $14.95 per gallon or $\frac{7}{8}$ of the 476 students who attended Friday's football game. When working with decimals and percents, these skills will be revisited, and once again mathematics will seem more connected than disconnected.

DIVISION

The division algorithm that you probably learned (invert the divisor and multiply) is one of the most mysterious to children of all the rules in elementary mathematics. Certainly we want to avoid this mystery at all costs. However, first it

makes sense to examine division with fractions from a more familiar perspective.

Concept Exploration

As with the other operations, we want to go back to the meaning of division with whole numbers. Here, recall that there are two meanings of division: partition and measurement. We will review each briefly and look at some real-world situations of the same type that involve fractions. From a number sense perspective or for the purpose of making estimates, we first have to know what the operation means. (Can you make up a word problem right now that would go with the computation $2\frac{1}{2} \div \frac{1}{4}$?)

Partition Concept

In the partition concept for $12 \div 3$, the task is to share 12 things among 3 sets and determine the amount in 1 set. Explore this same idea with fractions, first with the divisor as a whole number. Consider the following word problem:

> **Darlene has $2\frac{1}{4}$ hours to complete three household chores. If she divides her time evenly, how many hours can she give to each?**

In this problem, the task is to separate or partition the quantity $2\frac{1}{4}$ into 3 equal parts. Since $2\frac{1}{4}$ is 9 fourths, 3 fourths can be allotted to each task. That is, Darlene can spend $\frac{3}{4}$ hour per chore. These numbers turned out rather nicely. What if Darlene had only $1\frac{1}{4}$ hours for the three chores? Figure 13.11 shows how this could be modeled in three different ways.

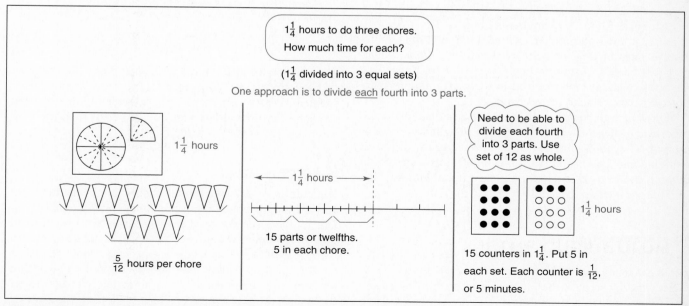

•FIGURE 13.11   Three models of partition division.

Are there partition situations where the divisor is a fraction? Actually, such situations are quite common. Consider the following problem:

> **Elizabeth bought $3\frac{1}{3}$ pounds of tomatoes for $2.50 (that's $2\frac{1}{2}$ dollars). How much did she pay per pound?**

The amount per pound is another way of asking how much 1 pound costs. Put another way, if you share the money among the $3\frac{1}{3}$ pounds evenly, how much money goes to one single pound? (Go ahead, figure this out on your own. The numbers in this problem work out nicely.)

Partition problems can also be made up where the divisor is less than 1. Realistic word problems necessarily must involve contexts where partial sets make sense. Here are a few possibilities:

> **Dad paid $2.00 for a $\frac{3}{4}$-pound box of candy. How much is that per pound?**

(Divide $2.00 into 3 parts—the 3 *fourths*. This tells how much is in 1 fourth. Multiply that by 4 to find out how much in one whole, or 1 full pound.)

> **The runner ran $2\frac{1}{2}$ miles in $\frac{3}{4}$ hour. At that rate, how many miles could he run in 1 hour? That is, what is his speed in miles per hour?**

(Divide the $2\frac{1}{2}$ miles into 3 parts. That tells how many miles in each quarter hour; 4 quarters is a full hour.)

Partition division problems with fraction divisors tend to involve rates of time or price rates. Most of these would probably be done using decimals instead of fractions. The ideas and relationships involved in these explorations may, however, have value in themselves.

If you were to continue this exploration of fair-share approaches to division with fractions, you might try to come up with a symbolic method or algorithm that will do the work for you. This is quite possible. In fact, this approach to division can be used to develop the "invert and multiply" algorithm for fraction division.

Measurement Concept

In the measurement concept for $12 \div 3$, the task is to decide how many sets of 3 things are in a set of 12 things. What would it mean if the problem was $2\frac{1}{4} \div \frac{3}{4}$? The meaning is the same. How many sets of $\frac{3}{4}$ each are in a set of $2\frac{1}{4}$? This might occur in a problem such as the following:

> **Farmer Brown measured his remaining insecticide and found that he had $2\frac{1}{4}$ gallons. It takes $\frac{3}{4}$ gallon to make a tank of mix. How many tankfuls can he make?**

In this problem, both the total amount and the divisor are in the same type of units or parts, fourths. The $2\frac{1}{4}$ is the same as 9 fourths. The question then becomes "How many sets of 3 fourths are in a set of 9 fourths?" The result is 3 sets (not 3 fourths). Farmer Brown can make 3 full tanks of mix. This is relatively easy to model. Try it.

A similar problem is the following:

> **Linda has $4\frac{2}{3}$ yards of material. She is making baby clothes for the bazaar. If each pattern requires $1\frac{1}{6}$ yards of material, how many patterns will she be able to make?**

To make this easier, convert the $4\frac{2}{3}$ to sixths also. The problem then becomes "How many sets of 7 sixths are in a set of 28 sixths?" Once both quantities are in the same units, it really makes no difference what those units are. The problem $5\frac{3}{5} \div 1\frac{2}{5}$ is identical: How many sets of 7 (fifths) are in a set of 28 (fifths)?

The answers in the foregoing examples were whole numbers. Explore for a minute what $13 \div 3$ might mean. There are 4 complete sets of 3 in a set of 13 with 1 left over. That 1 constitutes $\frac{1}{3}$ of a set of 3. What if the 13 and 3 were fractional parts—for example, 13 eighths and 3 eighths? There would still be 4 complete sets of 3 eighths and $\frac{1}{3}$ of a set of 3 eighths. The fact that these are eighths is not relevant. Explore this idea using various fraction models and the following exercises:

$$\frac{7}{5} \div \frac{3}{5} = \square \qquad \frac{7}{12} \div \frac{3}{12} = \square \qquad \frac{3}{4} \div \frac{1}{2} = \square \qquad \frac{5}{3} \div \frac{1}{4} = \square$$

As illustrated in Figure 13.12, once both the dividend and the divisor are converted to the same amounts, the problem is essentially the same as a whole-number division problem. Pay special attention to a problem such as $\frac{1}{2} \div \frac{3}{4}$, where the answer is less than 1.

In the Classroom

Students in your class should explore both measurement and partition problems with fractions. These provide excellent problem-solving situations that can be worked on in groups. Students should be challenged both to come up with an answer and to justify or explain it using a model or a drawing. Even if they have already learned an algorithm for doing the division or are using a fraction calculator to get the results, the explanation of why it makes sense is a terrific performance task. The other important benefit is that these

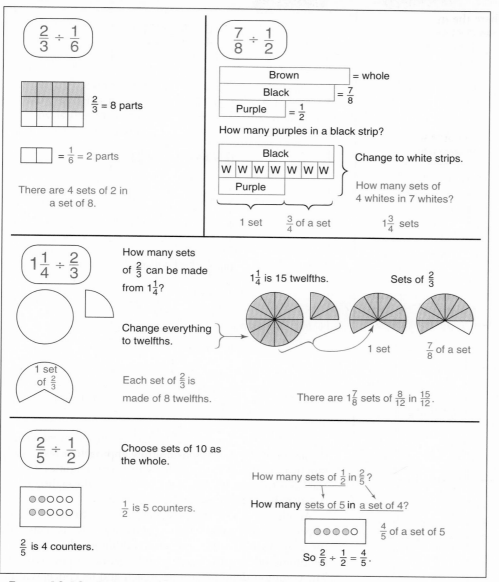

● **FIGURE 13.12** Exploring the measurement concept of fraction division.

problems focus on the meaning of division and will help students with estimation of fraction division much more than the algorithm will.

Developing the Algorithms

There are two different algorithms for division of fractions. Methods of teaching both algorithms are discussed here.

The Common-Denominator Algorithm

The common-denominator algorithm relies on the measurement or repeated subtraction concept of division that was just developed. Consider the problem $\frac{5}{3} \div \frac{1}{2}$. As shown in Figure

13.13 (p. 272), once each number is expressed in terms of the same fractional part, the answer is exactly the same as the whole-number problem $10 \div 3$. The name of the fractional part (the denominator) is no longer important, and the problem is one of dividing the numerators. The resulting rule or algorithm, therefore, is as follows: *To divide fractions, first get common denominators, and then divide numerators.*

Try using pie pieces, fraction strips, and then sets of counters to model $1\frac{2}{3} \div \frac{3}{4}$ and $\frac{5}{8} \div \frac{1}{2}$.

The Invert-and-Multiply Algorithm

The more traditional algorithm for division with a fraction is to invert the divisor and multiply. As noted earlier, it is possible to develop this algorithm by exploring the partition

CHAPTER

DECIMAL AND PERCENT CONCEPTS AND DECIMAL COMPUTATION

There has always been some debate concerning which concepts should be developed first in the curriculum, fractions or decimals. In most U.S. programs, fractions receive earlier attention. What is clear is that the ideas of fractions and decimals must be intimately connected. Most of this chapter is devoted to making that connection.

 ### BIG IDEAS

1. **Decimal numbers are simply another way of writing fractions. Connections between fraction and decimal symbolism can help in understanding both.**
2. **The base 10 place-value system extends infinitely in two directions: to very tiny values as well as to large values.**
3. **The decimal point indicates the units position.**
4. **Percents are simply hundredths and as such are a third way of writing fractions and decimals.**

CONNECTING TWO DIFFERENT REPRESENTATIONAL SYSTEMS

The symbols 3.75 and $3\frac{3}{4}$ both represent the same relationship or quantity, yet on the surface the two appear quite different. For children especially, the world of fractions and the world of decimals are very distinct. Even for adults, there is a tendency to think of fractions as sets or regions (three-fourths *of* something), whereas we think of decimals as being more like numbers. The reality is that fractions and decimals are two different systems of representation that have been developed to represent the same ideas. When we tell children that 0.75 is the same as $\frac{3}{4}$, this can be especially confusing. Even though different ways of writing the numbers have been invented, the numbers themselves are not different.

A significant goal of instruction in decimal and fraction numeration should be to help students see how both systems represent the same concepts. A good connection between fractions and decimals is quite useful. Even though we tend to think of 0.5 as a number, it is handy to know that it is a half. For example, in many contexts, it is easier to think about $\frac{3}{4}$ than 75 hundredths or 0.75. Conversely, the decimal system makes it easy to use numbers that are close to $\frac{3}{4}$, such as 0.73 or 0.78. Other conceptual and practical advantages exist for each system. For example, an obvious use of the decimal system is in digital equipment such as calculators, computers, and electronic meters.

To help students see the connection between fractions and decimals, we can do three things. First, we can use familiar fraction concepts and models to explore those rational numbers that are easily represented by decimals: tenths, hundredths, and thousandths. Second, we can extend the base 10 decimal system to include numbers less than 1 as well as large numbers. Third, we can help children use models to make meaningful translations between fractions and decimals. If two different symbols describe the same model, they must also represent the same idea. These three components are discussed in turn.

Base 10 Fractions

Fractions that have denominators of 10, 100, 1000, and so on will be referred to in this chapter as *base 10 fractions*. This is simply a convenient label and is not one commonly found in the literature. Fractions such as $\frac{7}{10}$ or $\frac{63}{100}$ are examples of base 10 fractions.

Base 10 Fraction Models

Most of the common models for fractions are somewhat limited for the purpose of depicting base 10 fractions. Fraction models for tenths do exist, but generally the familiar fraction models cannot show hundredths or thousandths. It is important to provide models for these fractions using the same conceptual approaches that were used for more familiar fractions such as thirds and fourths.

Two very important area or region models can be used to model base 10 fractions. First, to model tenths and hundredths, circular disks such as the one shown in Figure 14.1 can be printed on tagboard. (A full-sized master is in the

Blackline Masters section.) Each disk is marked with 100 equal intervals around the edge and is cut along one radius. Two disks of different colors, slipped together as shown, can be used to model any fraction less than 1. Fractions modeled on this hundredths disk can be read as base 10 fractions by noting the spaces around the edge but are still reminiscent of the traditional pie model.

The most common model for base 10 fractions is a 10 × 10 square. These squares can be run off on paper for students to shade in various fractions (see Figure 14.2 and Blackline Masters). Another important variation is to use base 10 place-value strips and squares. As a fraction model, the 10-cm square that was used as the hundreds model for whole numbers is taken as the whole or 1. Each strip is then 1 tenth, and each small square is 1 hundredth. The *Decimal Squares* materials (Bennett, 1982) include squares in which each hundredth is again partitioned into ten smaller sections. This permits modeling of thousands by shading in portions of the square. Even one more step is provided by the large square in the Blackline Masters that is subdivided into 10,000 tiny squares. The master can be used to make a transparency. When shown with an overhead projector, individual squares or ten-thousandths can easily be identified and shaded in with a pen on the transparency.

One of the best length models is a meter stick. Each decimeter is one-tenth of the whole stick, each centimeter is one-hundredth, and each millimeter is one-thousandth. Any number-line model broken into 100 subparts is likewise a useful model for hundredths.

Many teachers use money as a model for decimals, and to some extent this is helpful. However, for children, money is almost exclusively a two-place system: Numbers like 3.2 or 12.1389 do not relate to money. Children's initial contact with decimals should be more flexible. Money is certainly an important application of decimal numeration and may be useful in later activities with decimals.

Multiple Names and Formats

Early work with base 10 fractions is primarily designed to acquaint students with the models, to help them begin to

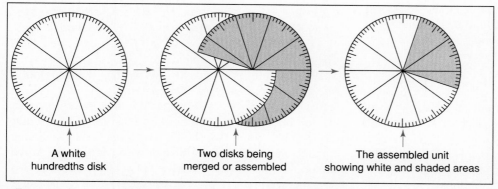

A white hundredths disk

Two disks being merged or assembled

The assembled unit showing white and shaded areas

● **FIGURE 14.1** A hundredths disk for modeling base 10 fractions.

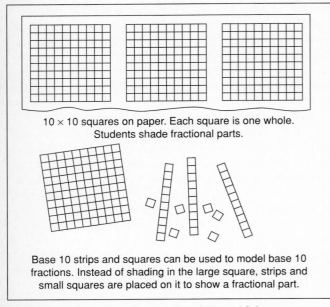

10 × 10 squares on paper. Each square is one whole. Students shade fractional parts.

Base 10 strips and squares can be used to model base 10 fractions. Instead of shading in the large square, strips and small squares are placed on it to show a fractional part.

● **FIGURE 14.2** 10 × 10 squares model base 10 fractions.

think of quantities in terms of tenths and hundredths, and to learn to read and write base 10 fractions in different ways.

Have students show a base 10 fraction using any base 10 fraction model. Once a fraction, say, $\frac{65}{100}$, is modeled, the following things can be explored:

- Is this fraction more or less than $\frac{1}{2}$? Than $\frac{2}{3}$? Than $\frac{3}{4}$? That is, some familiarity with these fractions can be developed by comparison with fractions that are easy to think about.

- What are some different ways to say this fraction using tenths and hundredths? ("6 tenths and 5 hundredths," "65 hundredths.") Include thousandths when appropriate.

- Show two ways to write this fraction ($\frac{65}{100}$ or $\frac{6}{10} + \frac{5}{100}$).

The last two questions are very important. When base 10 fractions are later written as decimals, they are usually read as a single fraction. That is, 0.65 is read "sixty-five hundredths." But to understand them in terms of place value, the same number must be thought of as 6 tenths and 5 hundredths. A mixed number such as $5\frac{13}{100}$ is usually read the same way as a decimal: 5.13 is "five and thirteen-hundredths." For purposes of place value, it should also be understood as $5 + \frac{1}{10} + \frac{3}{100}$. Special attention should also be given to numbers such as the following:

$$\frac{30}{1000} = \frac{0}{10} + \frac{3}{100} + \frac{0}{1000}$$

$$\frac{70}{100} = \frac{7}{10} + \frac{0}{100}$$

The expanded forms will be helpful in translating these fractions to decimals. In oral form, fractions or decimals with trailing zeros are sometimes used to indicate a higher level of precision. Seven-tenths is numerically equal to 70 hundredths, but the latter conveys precision to the nearest hundredth.

Exercises at this introductory level should include all possible connections between models, various oral forms, and various written forms. Given a model or a written or oral fraction, students should be able to give the other two forms of the fraction, including equivalent forms where appropriate.

Extending the Place-Value System

A Two-Way Relationship

Before considering decimal numerals with students, it is advisable to review some ideas of whole-number place value. One of the most basic of these ideas is the 10-to-1 relationship between the value of any two adjacent positions. In terms of a base 10 model such as strips and squares, 10 of any one piece will make one of the next larger, and vice versa. The 10-makes-1 rule continues indefinitely to larger and larger pieces or positional values. This concept is fun to explore in terms of how large the strips and squares will actually be if you move six or eight places out.

If you are using the strip-and-square model, for example, the strip and square shapes alternate in an infinite progression as they get larger and larger. Having established this idea with your students, focus on the idea that each piece to the right in this string gets smaller by one-tenth. The critical question becomes "Is there ever a smallest piece?" In the students' experience, the smallest piece is always the one designated as the ones or unit piece. But what is to say that even that piece could not be divided into 10 small strips? And could not these small strips be divided into 10 very small squares, which in turn could be divided into 10 even smaller strips, and so on? In the mind's eye, there is no smallest strip or smallest square.

The goal of this discussion is to help students see that a 10-to-1 relationship can extend *infinitely in two directions,* not just one. There is no smallest piece and no largest piece. The relationship between adjacent pieces is the same regardless of which two adjacent pieces are being considered. Figure 14.3 illustrates this idea with a strip-and-square model.

The Role of the Decimal Point

An important idea to be realized in this discussion is that there is no built-in reason why any one position should naturally be chosen to be the unit or ones position. In terms of strips and squares, for example, which piece is the ones piece? The small centimeter square? Why? Why not a larger or a smaller square? Why not a strip? *Any piece could effectively be chosen as the ones piece.*

When a number such as 1624 is written, the assumption is that the 4 is in the units or ones position. But if a position to the left of the 4 is selected as the ones position, some method of designating that position must be devised. Enter the decimal point. As shown in Figure 14.4, the same amount can be written in different ways, depending on the choice of the unit. The decimal point is placed between two positions with the convention that the position to the left of the decimal is the units or ones position. Thus the role of

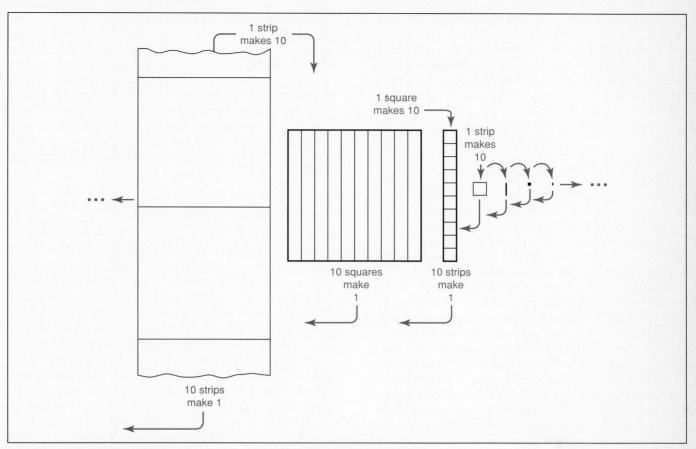

● **FIGURE 14.3** Theoretically, the strips and squares extend infinitely in both directions.

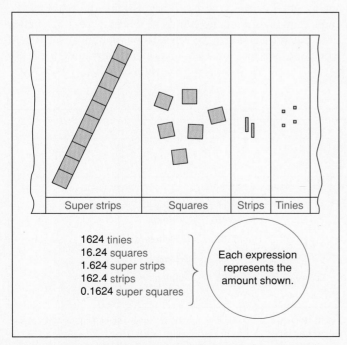

Super strips | Squares | Strips | Tinies

1624 tinies
16.24 squares
1.624 super strips
162.4 strips
0.1624 super squares

Each expression represents the amount shown.

● **FIGURE 14.4** The decimal point indicates which position is the units.

the decimal point is *to designate the units position,* and it does so by sitting just to the right of that position.

A fitting caricature of the decimal is shown in Figure 14.5. The "eyes" of the decimal are always focused up toward the name of the units or ones. A tagboard disk of this

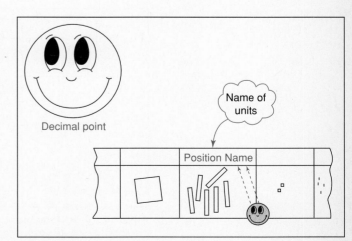

Decimal point

Name of units

Position Name

● **FIGURE 14.5** The decimal point always looks up at the name of the units position.

decimal-point face can be used between adjacent base 10 models or on a place-value chart. If such a decimal point were placed between the squares and strips in Figure 14.4, the squares would then be designated as the units, and the written form 16.24 would be the correct written form for the model.

---ACTIVITY---

14.1 The Decimal Names the Unit

Have students display a certain amount of base 10 pieces on their desks. For example, put out 3 squares, 7 strips, and 4 tinies. (If you want to have students cut up some 1-cm-long pieces of flat toothpicks, they can also model a fourth position.) Refer to the pieces as "squares," "strips," and "tinies," and reach an agreement on names for the theoretical pieces both smaller and larger. To the right of tinies can be "tiny strips" and "tiny squares." To the left of squares can be "super strips" and "super squares." Each student should also have a tagboard smily decimal point (found on the hundredths disk in the Blackline Masters). Now ask students to write and say how many squares they have, how many super strips, and so on, as in Figure 14.4 (p. 277). The students position their decimal point accordingly and both write and say the amounts.

The value of Activity 14.1 is to illustrate vividly how the decimal indicates the named unit and how that unit can change without changing the quantity. A related discussion

could involve multiplication or division of the quantity by powers of 10. If the display shows, for example, 3.74 squares, what would 10 times this amount be? Here the decimal remains looking at the squares position since 10 times 3.74 squares will still be squares. However, while the decimal remains in the same place-value position, each piece in the display would be enlarged 10 times and thus each digit will shift to a position one place to the left. The result would be 37.4 squares, with the 3 squares becoming 3 super strips, the 7 strips becoming 7 squares, and the 4 tinies becoming 4 strips.

The Decimal with Measurement and Monetary Units

The notion that the decimal "looks at the units place" is useful in a variety of contexts. For example, in the metric system, seven place values have names. As shown in Figure 14.6, the decimal can be used to designate any of these places as the unit without changing the actual measure. Our monetary system is also a decimal system. In the amount $172.95, the decimal point designates the dollars position as the unit. There are 1 hundred (of dollars), 7 tens, 2 singles, 9 dimes, and 5 pennies or cents in this amount of money regardless of how it is written. If pennies were the designated unit, the same amount would be written as 17,295 cents or 17,295.0 cents. It could just as correctly be 0.17295 thousands of dollars or 1729.5 dimes. The role of the decimal can be explored in this way using money or metric measures as an example. These systems highlight the idea that the choice of a unit is arbitrary but must be designated. In the case of actual measures such as metric lengths or weights, or the U.S. monetary system, the name of the unit is written after the number. You may be 1.62 meters tall, but it does not make sense to say you are 1.62 tall. In the paper we may read about Congress spending $7.3 bil-

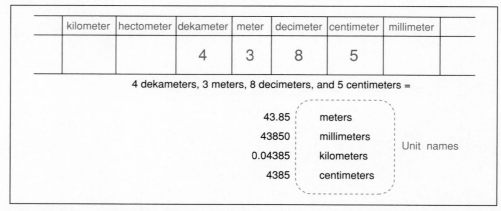

	kilometer	hectometer	dekameter	meter	decimeter	centimeter	millimeter	
			4	3	8	5		

4 dekameters, 3 meters, 8 decimeters, and 5 centimeters =

43.85	meters
43850	millimeters
0.04385	kilometers
4385	centimeters

Unit names

•**FIGURE 14.6** In the metric system, each place-value position has a name. The decimal point can be placed to designate which length is the unit length.

lion. Here the units are billions of dollars, not dollars. A city may have a population of 2.4 million people. That is the same as 2,400,000 individuals.

Reading Decimal Numerals

Consider the example of Figure 14.4 (p. 277). What are appropriate ways to read each of the different designations for these amounts? The correct manner is to read them the same way as one would read a mixed fraction. For example, 16.24 squares is read "sixteen *and* twenty-four hundredths squares." Notice that the word *and* is reserved for the decimal point. It could also be read as "sixteen and two-tenths and four-hundredths squares." The other important feature is that this language is exactly the same as the language that was used for base 10 fractions: 16.24 squares = $16\frac{24}{100}$ squares = $16 + \frac{2}{10} + \frac{4}{100}$ squares.

Help students see that once a place-value position is selected as the unit, the next place to the right is $\frac{1}{10}$ or tenths, the place after that is $\frac{1}{100}$ or hundredths, and so on. As when reading fractions, children should become accustomed to reading decimal numerals in two different forms. The oral language then becomes a useful link between fraction and decimal symbolism.

Other Decimal Models

Technically, any base 10 place-value model can be used as a model for decimals. The strip-and-square model is useful because students can each have a set of these materials at their desks. If the kit includes a tagboard decimal point (see Figure 14.5), no place-value mat is required. Students can arrange their base 10 pieces in order and put the decimal point to the right of whatever piece is the designated unit. Usually, the 10-cm square is selected. This allows students to model decimal fractions to hundredths. Some teachers even cut wooden toothpicks into 1-cm lengths to represent the next smaller strip or thousandths. These show up very nicely on an overhead projector.

The three-dimensional wooden or plastic base 10 blocks have four different pieces. If the 10-cm cube or "block" is designated as 1, then the flats, sticks, and small cubes can be used to model decimals to three places.

Any base 10 fraction model is also a decimal model. This fact is significant because it points out that decimals and fractions are simply two different ways to represent the same amounts. Three-fourths is shown on the hundredths disk as 7 tenths and 5 hundredths. If these pieces could be cut up and put on a place-value chart, they would be shown as 0.75 with the decimal looking up at the circle's place, as in Figure 14.7.

Making the Fraction–Decimal Connection

To connect the two numeration systems, fractions and decimals, students should make concept-oriented translations

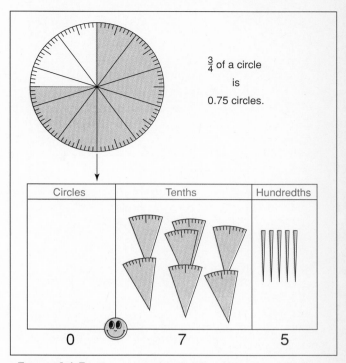

$\frac{3}{4}$ of a circle
is
0.75 circles.

Circles	Tenths	Hundredths
0	7	5

●**FIGURE 14.7** Fraction models could be decimal models.

from one system to the other. The purpose of such activities has less to do with the skill of converting a fraction to a decimal than with construction of the concept that both systems can be used to express the same ideas.

---ACTIVITY---

14.2 Fractions to Decimals

Start with a base 10 fraction, such as $\frac{35}{100}$ or $\frac{28}{10}$. Have students use at least two different base 10 fraction models to show these amounts. Discuss how each model shows the same relationship. Include as one of the models a set of strips and squares with the 10 × 10 square designated as the unit. The strip-and-square model can then be rearranged in standard place-value format indicating how the fraction can be expressed as a decimal (see Figure 14.8, p. 280).

Once a fraction is modeled and written as both a fraction and a decimal, both symbolisms should be read. The oral language for both fraction and decimal will be the same, as has already been discussed.

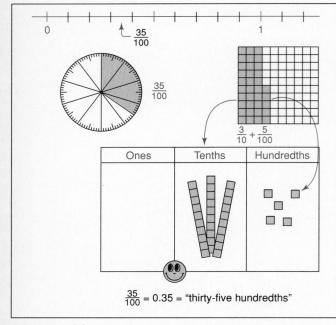

• **FIGURE 14.8** Translation of a base 10 fraction to a decimal.

Activity 14.2 (p. 279) suggests starting with a fraction and ending with a decimal. The reverse activity is equally important. That is, begin with a decimal number, and have students use several models to represent it and then read and write the number as a fraction. As long as the fractions are restricted to base 10 fractions, the conversions are straightforward.

The calculator can also play a significant role in decimal concept development.

---ACTIVITY---

14.3 Calculator Decimal Counting

Recall how to make the calculator "count" by pressing $\boxed{+}$ 1 $\boxed{=}$ $\boxed{=}$ ... Now have students press $\boxed{+}$ 0.1 $\boxed{=}$ $\boxed{=}$ ... When the display shows 0.9, stop and discuss what this means and what the display will look like with the next press. Many students will predict 0.10 (thinking that 10 comes after 9). This prediction is even more interesting if, with each press, the students have been accumulating base 10 strips as models for tenths. One more press would mean one more strip, or 10 strips. Why should the calculator not show 0.10? When the tenth press produces a display of 1 (calculators never display trailing zeros to the right of the decimal), the discussion should revolve around trading 10 strips for a square. Continue to count to

4 or 5 by tenths. How many presses to get from one whole number to the next? Try counting by 0.01 or by 0.001. These counts illustrate dramatically how small one-hundredth and one-thousandth really are. It requires 10 counts by 0.001 to get to 0.01, and 1000 counts will only reach 1.

Activity 14.3 provides an excellent opportunity for class discussion. The calculator should never be cited as the reason for any result or as a source of truth. The fact that the calculator counts 0.8, 0.9, 1., 1.1 instead of 0.8, 0.9, 0.10, 0.11 should give rise to the question "Does this make sense? And if so, why?" After all, experts made the calculator this way. Did they do it right? Why did they make it this way?

---ACTIVITY---

14.4 Double Calculator Counting

A fascinating variation of Activity 14.3 is to use two calculators side by side, the second calculator being one that displays fractions. On the fraction calculator, enter $\boxed{+}$ 1 $\boxed{/}$ 10 $\boxed{=}$, and on the standard calculator, $\boxed{+}$ 0.1 $\boxed{=}$. Repeatedly press $\boxed{=}$ on the two calculators simultaneously. At 10 presses, the standard calculator shows 1., as discussed earlier, but the fraction calculator shows $\frac{10}{10}$ and will continue to increment the numerator to $\frac{11}{10}$ and so on. If the $\boxed{a\frac{b}{c}}$ key is pressed, the mixed number is displayed. The display can be made to toggle back and forth among the mixed number, the improper fraction, and the decimal equivalent. If models are also coordinated with the counting, the activity helps relate two symbol systems and a conceptual model in a powerful illustration.

DEVELOPING DECIMAL NUMBER SENSE

So far, the discussion has revolved around the connection of decimals with base 10 fractions because these are the fractions most directly related to the notation of decimals. Number sense implies more. It means having intuition about or a friendly understanding of numbers. To this end, it is useful to connect decimals to the fractions with which children are familiar, to be able to compare and order decimals readily and comfortably, and to approximate decimals with useful familiar numbers.

Familiar Fractions Connected to Decimals

In Chapter 12, emphasis was placed on helping students develop a conceptual familiarity with simple fractions, especially halves, thirds, fourths, fifths, and eighths. We should try to extend this familiarity to the same concepts expressed as decimals. One way to do this is to have students translate these familiar fractions to decimals by means of a base 10 model.

---ACTIVITY---

14.5 Friendly Decimal Fractions

Have students shade in familiar fractions on a 10 × 10 grid. Because the grid effectively translates any fraction to a base 10 fraction, the fractions can then easily be written as decimals. Under each shaded figure, write the fraction in familiar form, then as a base 10 fraction, and finally as a decimal, as shown in Figure 14.9.

It is good to begin with halves and fifths, since these can be shown with strips of 10 squares. Next explore fourths. Many students will shade $\frac{1}{4}$ by shading in a 5 × 5 square of the grid. See if they can then shade the same amount using strips and fewer than 10 small squares. Repeat for other fourths, such as $\frac{3}{4}$ or $\frac{7}{4}$. Eighths present an inter-

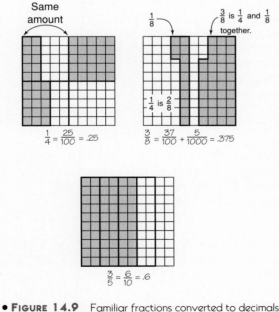

Same amount

$\frac{1}{8}$

$\frac{3}{8}$ is $\frac{1}{4}$ and $\frac{1}{8}$ together.

$\frac{1}{4}$ is $\frac{2}{8}$

$\frac{1}{4} = \frac{25}{100} = .25$

$\frac{3}{8} = \frac{37}{100} + \frac{5}{1000} = .375$

$\frac{3}{5} = \frac{6}{10} = .6$

● **FIGURE 14.9** Familiar fractions converted to decimals using a 10 × 10 square.

esting challenge. One way to find $\frac{1}{8}$ of a 10 × 10 square is to take half of $\frac{1}{4}$. Since $\frac{1}{4}$ is $\frac{2}{10}$ and $\frac{5}{100}$, then $\frac{1}{8}$ is $\frac{1}{10} + \frac{2}{100} + \frac{5}{1000}$. The $\frac{5}{1000}$ part is the same as half of $\frac{1}{100}$. Rather than "explain" all this to students, use the potential difficulty of figuring out $\frac{1}{8}$ as an opportunity for valuable discussion. The result should come from the students.

The exploration of modeling $\frac{1}{3}$ as a decimal is a good introduction to the concept of an infinitely repeating decimal. Try to partition the whole square into 3 parts using strips and squares. Each part receives 3 strips with 1 left over. To divide the leftover strip, each part gets 3 small squares with 1 left over. To divide the small square, each part gets 3 tiny strips with 1 left over. (Recall that with base 10 pieces, each smaller piece must be $\frac{1}{10}$ of the preceding size piece.) Each of the 3 parts will get 3 tiny strips with 1 left over. It becomes obvious that this process is never-ending. As a result, $\frac{1}{3}$ is the same as 0.333333 . . . or $0.\overline{3}$. For practical purposes, $\frac{1}{3}$ is about 0.333. In a similar manner, $\frac{2}{3}$ is a repeating string of sixes, or about 0.667. Later, students will discover that many other fractions cannot be represented by a finite decimal, and this experience is a good background for that idea.

---ACTIVITY---

14.6 Dual Counts with Friendly Fractions

Repeat Activity 14.4, "Double Calculator Counting," but this time begin with a familiar or friendly fraction such as $\frac{1}{5}$ or $\frac{1}{4}$ on the fraction calculator and the corresponding decimal on the other calculator. Again, explore counts beyond 1 or 2 wholes, and also switch between mixed and improper fractions. Notice also that while the $\boxed{\text{F↔D}}$ key changes a fraction to a decimal, when going from a decimal to a fraction it uses a base 10 fraction. Thus 2.6 is changed to $2\frac{6}{10}$. The $\boxed{\text{Simp}}$ key can then be used to find the fraction $2\frac{3}{5}$ that you are working with.

It is common in the seventh and eighth grades for students to memorize the decimal equivalents for halves, thirds, fourths, fifths, and eighths. Kouba et al. (1988a) note that in the fourth NAEP, "60 percent of seventh-grade students could express simple fractions as decimals, but only 40 percent could express an improper fraction as a decimal" (p. 16). An explanation for the discrepancy is that the proper fraction equivalents may have been rotely memorized, whereas to write an improper fraction such as $\frac{7}{5}$ as a decimal would require some conceptual understanding. Even the 60 percent performance indicates a need for better understanding of these translations. If students know conceptually the decimal translation for the unit fractions $\frac{1}{3}, \frac{1}{4}, \frac{1}{5}$, and $\frac{1}{8}$ and apply to these a counting-by-unit-fraction concept, the equivalents for all familiar fractions are nearly immediate. For example, $\frac{3}{5}$ is $\frac{1}{5}$ three times, or $0.2 + 0.2 + 0.2$. Even $\frac{7}{8}$ can be easily thought of as $\frac{1}{8}$ more than $\frac{3}{4}$ or $\frac{1}{8}$ less than 1. An understanding of mixed fractions and improper fractions can easily be applied to find decimal equivalents for familiar fractions greater than 1. For all such exercises, the emphasis should be on conceptual conversions and not on rote memory or other symbolic algorithms.

Approximation with a Nice Fraction

What do you think of when you see a number such as 7.3962? As is, it is an unruly number to think about, perhaps even intimidating. A good approach to decimal numbers that are not "nice" is to think of a close nice number. Is 7.3962 closer to 7 or to 8? Is it more or less than $7\frac{1}{2}$? Is 7 or $7\frac{1}{2}$ good enough for your purposes? If more precision is desired, you might look to see if it is close to a nice fraction. In this case, 7.3962 is very close to 7.4, which is $7\frac{2}{5}$. The fraction $7\frac{2}{5}$ is much easier to think with than a four-digit decimal. In the modern world of digital equipment, decimal numbers frequently reflect much greater accuracy than is necessary. To have good number sense with these decimals implies that you can quickly think of a simple meaningful fraction as a useful approximation for almost any decimal number. This facility is analogous to glancing at your digital watch, seeing 8:48′23″, and announcing that it is about 10 till 9.

To develop this type of familiarity with decimals, children do not need new concepts or skills. They do, however, need the opportunity to apply and discuss the related concepts of fractions, place value, and decimals in exercises and activities such as the following.

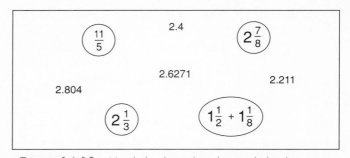

●**Figure 14.10**   Match the decimal numbers with the closest fraction expression.

The activity illustrated in Figure 14.10 has students pair each decimal numeral with the fraction expression that is closest to it. The exercise can be made easier by using fractions that are not as close together.

Ordering Decimal Numbers

Putting a list of decimal numbers in order from least to most is a skill that is closely related to the one just discussed. In the fourth NAEP (Kouba et al., 1988a), only about 50 percent of seventh graders could identify the largest number in the following list: 0.36, 0.058, 0.375, and 0.4. That result is disturbing. It is unfortunately similar to the results of many other studies (e.g., Hiebert & Wearne, 1986). The most common error is to select the number with more digits, which is an incorrect application of whole-number ideas. Some students later pick up the idea that digits far to the right represent very small numbers. They then incorrectly identify numbers with more digits as smaller. Both errors reflect a lack of conceptual understanding of how decimal numbers are constructed. The following activities can help promote useful discussion about the relative size of decimal numbers.

---ACTIVITY---

14.7 Close to a Friendly Fraction

Make a list of decimal numbers that do not have nice fractional equivalents. Have students suggest a decimal number near the given one that does have a nice equivalent. Try this yourself with this list:

24.8025   6.59   0.9003   124.356

Different students may select different fractions for these numbers. The rationale for their choice presents an excellent opportunity for discussion.

---ACTIVITY---

14.8 The Larger Decimal Number

Present two decimal numbers, and have students use models to explain which is larger. A meter stick or a 10 × 10 square is useful for this purpose.

---ACTIVITY---

14.9 Close "Nice" Numbers

Write a four-digit decimal on the board—3.0917, for example. Start with the whole numbers: "Is it closer to 3 or 4?" Then go to the tenths: "Is it closer to 3.0 or 3.1?" Repeat with hundredths and thousandths. At each answer, challenge students to defend their choices with the use of a model or other conceptual explanation. The large number line without numerals described in Figure 14.11 is useful for this activity.

Too often, the process of rounding numbers is taught as an algorithm without any reflection on its purpose or why the algorithm makes sense. Children come to believe that to "round" a number means to do something to it or change it in some way. In reality, to *round* a number means that you *substitute* a "nice" or more easily manipulable number as an approximation for the cumbersome original number. In this sense, we can also round decimal numbers to "nice fractions" and not just to tenths and hundredths. For example, instead of rounding 6.73 to the nearest tenth, a number sense perspective might suggest rounding it to the nearest quarter (6.75 or $6\frac{3}{4}$) or to the nearest third (6.67 or $6\frac{2}{3}$).

---ACTIVITY---

14.10 Line 'Em Up

Prepare a list of four or five decimal numbers that students might have difficulty putting in order. They should all be between the same two consecutive whole numbers. Have students first predict the order of the numbers, from least to most. Next have them place each number on a number line with 100 subdivisions, as in Figure 14.11. As an alternative, have students shade in the fractional part of each number on a separate 10×10 grid using estimates for the thousandths and ten-thousandths. In either case, it quickly becomes obvious which digits contribute the most to the size of a decimal.

Other Fraction-Decimal Equivalents

The only fraction-decimal equivalents that have been discussed so far are those for the nice fractions: halves, thirds, fourths, fifths, and eighths. Also, any base 10 fraction is immediately converted to a decimal, and similarly, simple decimals with two or three decimal places are easily converted to fractions. For the purpose of familiarity or number sense, these fractions and decimal equivalents provide a significant amount of information about decimal numbers. Furthermore, all of this information about decimals can and should be approached conceptually without rules, rote memory, or algorithms. It can be argued that the major focus of decimal instruction should center on these ideas.

At times, however, other fractions must be expressed as a decimal. For example, how do you enter $\frac{5}{6}$ or $\frac{3}{7}$ on a calculator that does not accept fraction notation? The answer, of course, is based on the fact that $\frac{3}{7}$ is also an expression for $3 \div 7$. If this division is carried out on paper, an infinite but repeating decimal will result. The ninths have very interesting decimal equivalents, and looking for a pattern is a worthwhile activity (try $1 \div 9$, $2 \div 9$, . . . , on your calculator). The division process should also be checked out for familiar fraction equivalents. If students have constructed a good understanding of familiar fractions and decimal equivalents, the concept will confirm the division result. If the division $4 \div 5$ is the only explanation students have for why $\frac{4}{5} = 0.8$, a significant lack of a conceptual linkage between fractions and decimals is likely.

Early in the development of decimal numeration, students are often shown how to use division as a means of converting fractions to decimals. Doing a long division or using a calculator for this purpose does not promote firsthand familiarity or number sense with fractions and decimals.

In the seventh or eighth grade, students are frequently taught to convert a repeating decimal to a fraction. These conversions serve the purpose of demonstrating that every repeating decimal can also be represented as a fraction and therefore as a rational number. This important theoretical result is primarily useful in making a distinction between rational and irrational numbers. The contribution such tedious activities have for number sense is rather minimal.

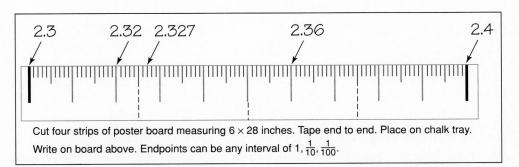

Cut four strips of poster board measuring 6 × 28 inches. Tape end to end. Place on chalk tray.

Write on board above. Endpoints can be any interval of $1, \frac{1}{10}, \frac{1}{100}$.

●**FIGURE 14.11** A decimal number line.

INTRODUCING PERCENTS

Textbooks have traditionally treated percents as a separate topic from fractions and decimals or stuck them in a chapter on ratios. The connection of percents to fraction and decimal concepts is so strong that it makes better sense to discuss percents as students begin to have a good grasp of the fraction-decimal relationships.

A Third Operator System

A major goal that has been stressed so far is to help children understand that decimal numerals and fractions are simply two different symbol systems for the same part-to-whole relationships; that is, they are representations for rational numbers. In this sense, both fractions and decimals are interpreted as real numbers. But when we say "three-fifths of a cake" or "three-fifths of the students," the number meaning comes from the cake or the set of students. Certainly, $\frac{3}{5}$ of 5 students is different from $\frac{3}{5}$ of 20 students. In fact, it is precisely this operator notion that makes it difficult for children to think of fractions as numbers. They initially learn about them as parts of things.

When children have made a strong connection between their concepts of fractions and decimals, the topic of percents can be introduced. Rather than approach percents as a new and strange idea, children should see that percents are simply a different way to write down some of the ideas they have already developed about fractions and decimals. Rather than a third *numeration* system, percents are essentially a third *symbolism for operators.*

Another Name for Hundredths

The term *percent* is simply another name for *hundredths.* If students can express common fractions and simple decimals as hundredths, the term *percent* can be substituted for the term *hundredth.* Consider the fraction $\frac{3}{4}$. As a fraction expressed in hundredths, it is $\frac{75}{100}$. When $\frac{3}{4}$ is written in decimal form, it is 0.75. Both 0.75 and $\frac{75}{100}$ are read in exactly the same way, "seventy-five hundredths." When used as operators, $\frac{3}{4}$ of something is the same as 0.75 or 75 percent of that same thing. Percent is not a new concept, only a new notation and terminology. Connections with fractions and decimal concepts are developmentally appropriate.

Models provide the main link among fractions, decimals, and percents, as shown in Figure 14.12. Base 10 fraction models are suitable for fractions, decimals, and percents, since they all represent the same idea.

Another helpful approach to the terminology of percent is through the role of the decimal point. Recall that the decimal identifies the units. When the unit is ones, a number such as 0.659 means a little more than 6 tenths of 1. The word *ones* is understood (6 tenths of 1 *one*). But 0.659 is also 6.59 tenths and 65.9 hundredths and 659 thousandths.

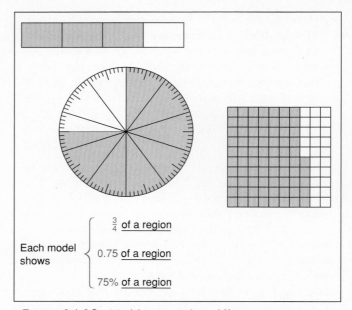

Each model shows	$\frac{3}{4}$ of a region
	0.75 of a region
	75% of a region

● **FIGURE 14.12** *Models connect three different notations.*

In each case, the name of the unit must be explicitly identified, or else the unit ones would be assumed. In 6.59 tenths, the interpretation is similar to an operator. It is 6 and 59 hundredths *of the things called tenths.* Since *percent* is another name for *hundredths,* when the decimal is "identifying" the hundredths position as the units, the word *percent* can be specified as a synonym for *hundredths.* Thus 0.659 (of some whole or 1) is 65.9 hundredths or 65.9 percent or 65.9% of that same whole. As illustrated in Figure 14.13, the notion of placing the decimal point *to identify the percent position* is conceptually more meaningful than the apparently arbitrary rule: "To change a decimal to a percent, move the decimal two places to the right." This rule carries no meaning and is easily confused. "Do I move it right or left?" A better idea is to equate hundredths with percent both orally and in notation.

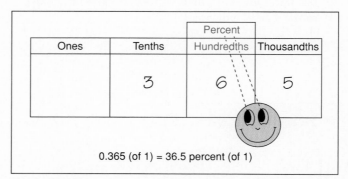

Ones	Tenths	Percent	
		Hundredths	Thousandths
	3	6	5

0.365 (of 1) = 36.5 percent (of 1)

● **FIGURE 14.13** *Hundredths are also known as percents.*

Use Percent with Familiar Fractions

Students should use base 10 models for percents in much the same way as for decimals. The disk with 100 markings around the edge is now a model for percents as well as a fraction model for hundredths. The same is true of a 10 × 10 square. Each tiny square inside is 1 percent of the square. Each row or strip of 10 squares is not only a tenth but 10 percent of the square.

Similarly, the familiar fractions (halves, thirds, fourths, fifths, and eighths) should become familiar in terms of percents as well as decimals. Three-fifths, for example, is 60 percent as well as 0.6. One-third of an amount is frequently expressed as $33\frac{1}{3}$ percent instead of 33.3333 . . . percent. Likewise, $\frac{1}{8}$ of a quantity is $12\frac{1}{2}$ percent or 12.5 percent of the quantity. These ideas should be explored with base 10 models and not as rules about moving decimal points.

Realistic Percent Problems

The Three Percent Problems

Junior high school teachers talk about "the three percent problems." The sentence " _____ is _____ percent of _____ " has three spaces for numbers; for example, "20 is 25 percent of 80." The three classic percent problems come from this sterile expression; two of the numbers are given, and the students are asked to produce the third. Students learn very quickly that you either multiply or divide the two given numbers, and sometimes you have to move a decimal point. This approach to percent is doomed from the start. Students have no way of determining when to do what, which numbers to divide, or which way to shift the decimal. As a result, performance on percentage problems is very poor. Furthermore, the major reason—perhaps the only reason—for learning about percents is that they are commonly used in our society. Such things as sales figures, taxes, census data, political information, and trends in economics and farming and consumption are all expressed in percent terminology. But in almost none of these is the formula version " _____ is _____ percent of _____ " used. So when asked to solve a realistic percent problem, students are frequently at a loss.

In Chapter 12, three types of exercises with fractions were explored. These involved parts, wholes, and fractions. The three types were determined according to which of the three—part, whole, or fraction—was unknown. Students used models and simple fraction relationships in those exercises. Those three types of exercises are precisely the same as the three percent problems. Developmentally, then, it makes good sense to help students make the connection between the exercises done with fractions and those done with percents. How? Use the same types of models and the same terminology of parts, wholes, and fractions. The only thing that is different is that the word *percent* is used instead of *fraction*. In Figure 14.14, three exercises from Chapter 12 have been changed to the corresponding percent terminology. A good idea for early work with percents would be to review (or explore the first time) all three types of exercises

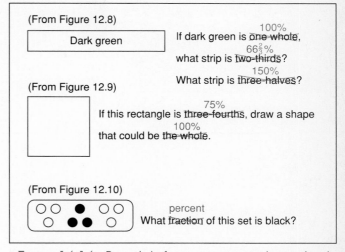

●**FIGURE 14.14**   *Part-whole-fraction exercises can be translated into percent exercises.*

in terms of percents. The same three types of models can be used (refer to Figures 12.8, 12.9, and 12.10, pp. 245–246).

Realistic Percent Problems and Nice Numbers

Though students must have some experience with the noncontextual, straightforward situations in Figure 14.14, it is important to have them explore these relationships in real contexts. Find or make up percent problems and present them in the same way that they appear in newspapers, television, and other real contexts. In addition to realistic problems and formats, follow these maxims for your unit on percents:

- Limit the percents (fractions) to familiar fractions (halves, thirds, fourths, fifths, and eighths) or easy percents ($\frac{1}{10}$, $\frac{1}{100}$), and use numbers compatible with these fractions. That is, make the computation very easy. The focus of these exercises is the relationships involved, not complex computational skills.

- Do not suggest or provide any rules or procedures for different types of problems. Do not categorize or label problem types.

- Utilize the terms *part, whole,* and *percent* (or *fraction*). *Fraction* and *percent* are interchangeable. Help students see these as the same types of exercises they did with simple fractions.

- Require students to use models or drawings to explain their solutions. It is better to assign three problems requiring a drawing and an explanation than to give 15 problems requiring only computation and answers. Remember that the purpose is the exploration of relationships, not computational skill.

- Encourage mental computation.

The following sample problems meet these criteria for easy fractions and numbers. Try working each problem, identifying each number as a part, a whole, or a fraction.

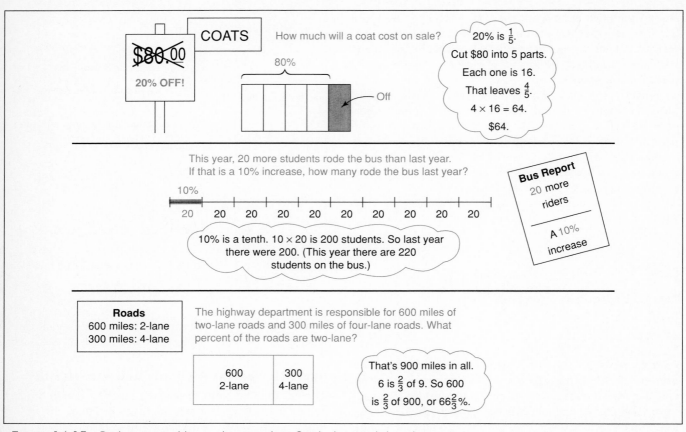

●**FIGURE 14.15** *Real percent problems with nice numbers. Simple drawings help with reasoning.*

Draw length or area models to explain or work through your thought process. Examples of this informal reasoning are illustrated with additional problems in Figure 14.15.

1. The PTA reported that 75 percent of the total number of families were represented at the meeting last night. If children from 320 families go to the school, how many were represented at the meeting?

2. The baseball team won 80 percent of the 25 games it played this year. How many games were lost?

3. In Mrs. Carter's class, 20 students, or $66\frac{2}{3}$ percent, were on the honor roll. How many students are in her class?

4. George bought his new computer at a $12\frac{1}{2}$ percent discount. He paid $700. How many dollars did he save by buying it at a discount?

5. If Joyce has read 60 of the 180 pages in her library book, what percent of the book has she read so far?

6. The hardware store bought widgets at 80 cents each and sold them for $1 each. What percent did the store mark up the price of each widget?

Estimation in Percent Problems

Of course, not all real percent problems have nice numbers. Frequently in real life, an approximation or estimate in percent situations is all that is required or is enough to help one think the situation through. Even if a calculator will be used to get an exact answer, an estimate based on an understanding of the relationship can confirm that a correct operation was performed or that the decimal was positioned correctly.

To help students with estimation in percent situations, two ideas that have already been discussed can be applied. First, when the percent or fraction is not a "nice" one, substitute a close percent or fraction that is easy to work with. Second, in doing the calculation, select numbers that are compatible with the fraction involved to make the calculation easy to do mentally. In essence, convert the not-nice percent problem into one that is nice. Here are some examples. Try your hand at estimates of each.

1. The 83,000-seat stadium was 73 percent full. How many people were at the game?

2. The treasurer reported that 68.3 percent of the dues had been collected, for a total of $385. How much more money could the club expect to collect if all dues are paid?

3. Max McStrike had 217 hits in 842 at-bats. What was his batting average?

Possible estimates:

1. (Use $\frac{3}{4}$ and 80,000)
2. (Use $\frac{2}{3}$ and $380; will collect $\frac{1}{3}$ more.)
3. A bit more than 0.250 ($4 \times 217 > 842$; $\frac{1}{4}$ is 25 percent, or 0.250)

The following exercises are also useful in helping students with estimation in percent situations.

Choose the closest nice fraction. For example, which fraction is closest to 78 percent: $\frac{1}{2}$, $\frac{2}{3}$, or $\frac{4}{5}$? Multiple-choice exercises such as this one can be done with a full class or can be made into worksheet exercises. Later, students can give a nice fraction that is close to the percent without a multiple choice. Have students justify their answers.

Work with "easy percents," especially 1 percent and 10 percent. Begin with exercises where students give 1 percent and 10 percent of numbers. Then show them how to use these easy percents to get other percentages, either exact or approximate. For example, to get 15 percent of $349, think that 10 percent is about $35.00 and 5 percent is half of that, or $17.50. So 15 percent is $35.00 + $17.50, or $52.50. Similar reasoning can be used to adjust an estimate by 1 percent or 2 percent. To find 82 percent of $400, it is easy to think of $\frac{4}{5}$ (80 percent) as $4 \times \frac{1}{5}$ of 400, or $4 \times \$80$, which is $320. Since each 1 percent is $4, add on $8.

Sometimes an exact result, and therefore some calculation, is required. The emphasis on conceptual thinking, nice fractions, and estimation of results will all pave the way for easy work when an exact result is desired. The use of an estimate will determine if the result is in the correct ballpark or if it makes sense. Frequently, the same estimation process will dictate what computation to do so that the problem can be entered on a calculator.

COMPUTATION WITH DECIMALS

Chapter 11 was devoted entirely to the development of computation algorithms for whole numbers. That degree of emphasis is not completely in keeping with the recommendations of the NCTM *Curriculum Standards*. For the next several years, pencil-and-paper computation with whole numbers will probably remain a major thrust of the curriculum for grades 2 to 5. For decimals, however, the corresponding emphasis on pencil-and-paper computation simply cannot be justified in light of readily available calculators and computers, the need for better estimation skills, and the strong recommendations of the *Standards*. "It is no longer necessary or useful to devote large portions of instructional time to performing routine computations by hand. Other mathematical experiences for middle school students deserve far more emphasis" (NCTM, 1989, p. 94). (If you have not yet done so, read and reflect on "Standard 7: Computation and Estimation" in the grades 5–8 section of the *Curriculum Standards*.)

The discussion that follows places a heavy emphasis on estimation of decimal computation. As a transitional step before the day when pencil-and-paper computation with decimals is completely gone from the curriculum, some relatively simple alternatives are suggested.

The Role of Estimation

Students should learn to estimate decimal computations before they learn to compute with pencil and paper. For many decimal computations, rough estimates can be made easily by rounding the numbers to nice whole numbers or simple base 10 fractions. In almost all cases, a minimum goal for your students should be to have the estimate contain the correct number of digits to the left of the decimal—the whole-number part. Select problems for which estimates are not terribly difficult. Before going on, try making easy whole-number estimates of the following computations. Do not spend time with fine adjustments in your estimates.

1. $4.907 + 123.01 + 56.1234$
2. $459.8 - 12.345$
3. 24.67×1.84
4. $514.67 \div 3.59$

Your estimates might be similar to the following:

1. Between 175 and 200
2. More than 400, or about 425 to 450
3. More than 25, closer to 50 (1.84 is more than 1 and close to 2)
4. More than 125, less than 200 ($500 \div 4 = 125$ and $600 \div 3 = 200$)

In these examples, an understanding of decimal numeration and some simple whole-number estimation skills can produce rough estimates. When estimating, thinking focuses on the meaning of the numbers and the operations and not on how many decimal places are involved. However, students who are taught to focus primarily on the pencil-and-paper algorithms for decimals may find even simple estimations difficult.

Therefore, a good *place* to begin decimal computation is with estimation. Not only is it a highly practical skill, but it also helps children look at answers in ballpark terms, can form a check on pencil-and-paper computation, and is one way of placing the decimal in multiplication and division.

A good *time* to begin computation with decimals is well after a firm conceptual background in decimal numeration has been developed. Learning the pencil-and-paper algorithms for decimals will do little or nothing to help students understand decimal numeration.

Addition and Subtraction

From a conceptual standpoint, the addition and subtraction algorithms are nearly identical for decimals and whole numbers. The numbers in like place-value columns are added or subtracted with 10-for-1 trades made when necessary. Although this is a relatively straightforward application of place value, many students do have trouble. Errors tend to occur when problems are presented in horizontal format or are in word problems with different numbers of digits to the right of the decimal. For example, students might compute the sum of 3.45 + 12.2 + 0.807 by lining up the right-hand digits 5, 2, and 7, as they would with whole numbers.

To help students with addition and subtraction, have them first estimate the answer as discussed earlier. For the example just given, the sum should be about 16. Next discuss what the numbers mean in terms of a base 10 model. What does each digit represent? How would the problem be written if the numbers were placed in the appropriate columns of a place-value chart? (See Figure 14.16.) From such a discussion, it should be concluded that like place values should be added or subtracted. When students follow this procedure, they should compare the results with their estimate. The estimate should be a confirmation of the computation (and not the reverse). Under no circumstances should students use the purely rote rule of "lining up the decimal points" without being able to justify it.

Multiplication and Division

Estimation is also a means of locating the decimal point in multiplication or division. For those two operations, one algorithm that is reasonable is the following: *Ignore the decimal points, and do the computation as if all numbers were whole numbers. When finished, place the decimal in the result by estimation.* This approach is illustrated in Figure 14.17. In both examples, notice how a shift of the decimal in either direction just one place would give a result that is not even close to the estimate. Although some explanation for the estimation method is required, it is quite useful except for very

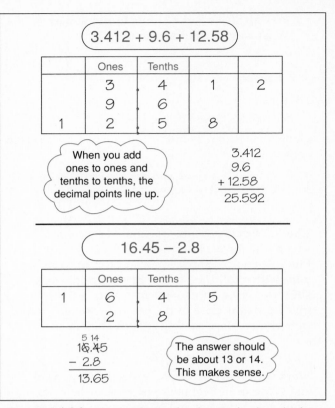

● **FIGURE 14.16** *Using a place-value chart to develop rules for adding and subtracting decimals.*

precise computations such as 0.00987 × 0.000103. Persons who need such precise answers will undoubtedly have a calculator or computer to help them.

Before reading further, estimate each of the following products:

347	34.7	3.47
× 2.6	× 2.6	× 2.6

The first is about 900 (2 × 350 is 700 and 6 tenths of 350 is about 200). Similar reasoning would place the second product at about 90 and the third around 9. The whole-number product 347 × 26 is 9022, or about 9000. Each of these products uses exactly the same digits even though the decimal point makes the numbers quite different. This fact can provoke an excellent discussion and provide a useful introduction to decimal multiplication.

Whole-Number Divisors

For whole-number divisors, the whole-number division algorithm is easily extended to decimal dividends and decimal quotients. In each place-value column, a partition is made, and any leftovers are traded to the next column. Since the trade is always 1 for 10 regardless of which two columns are involved, trading in columns to the right of the decimal point is the same as trading to the left of the decimal. Place-

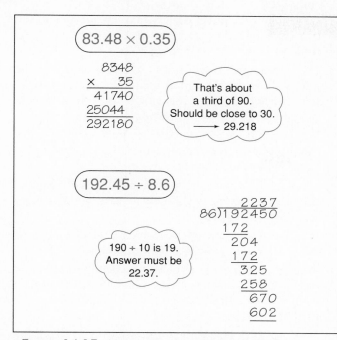

● **FIGURE 14.17** *Using estimation to place decimals.*

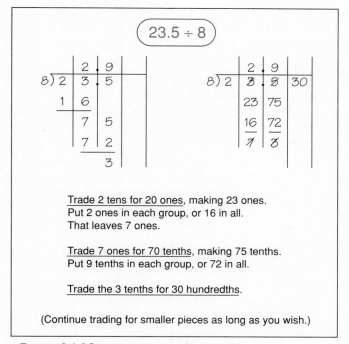

Trade 2 tens for 20 ones, making 23 ones.
Put 2 ones in each group, or 16 in all.
That leaves 7 ones.

Trade 7 ones for 70 tenths, making 75 tenths.
Put 9 tenths in each group, or 72 in all.

Trade the 3 tenths for 30 hundredths.

(Continue trading for smaller pieces as long as you wish.)

● **FIGURE 14.18** *Extension of the division algorithm.*

value columns in the quotient correspond to those in the dividend. These ideas are illustrated in Figure 14.18.

Decimal Divisors

Division with a decimal divisor, especially one with two or more digits, is probably a good place to draw the line

with paper-and-pencil computation. There are almost no instances outside of classrooms where ordinary people perform divisions with decimal divisors using pencil and paper. This is not to say that such computation cannot be taught meaningfully. It simply means that such computation is not a productive use of school time.

LITERATURE CONNECTIONS

There are not many interesting stories that inspire an exploration of decimals and percents for children in the fifth grade and higher. One notable exception is *The Phantom Tollbooth,* a story that should not be missed regardless of its mathematical significance.

If you expand the notion of literature to the daily paper and weekly magazines, you will find decimal and percent situations that can help you make endless connections with the real world. One issue with percents in news stories is the frequent omission of the base amount or the whole on which the percent is determined. "March sales of widgets were reported to be up 3.6 percent." Does that mean an increase over February or March of the previous year? Lots of increase and decrease uses of percents are interesting to project over several years. If the consumer price index rises 3 percent a year, how much will a $50 basket of groceries cost by the time your students are 21 years old?

The Phantom Tollbooth (Juster, 1961)

There are numerous references to mathematical ideas throughout this book. Milo enters a world of crazy places and very imaginative creatures after driving his toy car through a model of a turnpike tollbooth. Several chapters involve adventures in Digitopolis, where everything is number-oriented. In Digitopolis, Milo meets a boy who is only half of a boy, appearing in the drawing to be the left half of a boy cut top to bottom. As it turns out, the boy is actually 0.58 since he is a member of the average family: a mother, father, and 2.58 children. The boy is the 0.58. One advantage, he explains, is that he is the only one who can drive the $\frac{3}{10}$ of a car, the average family owning 1.3 cars. This section of the tale involves a great discussion of averages that come out in decimal numbers.

An obvious extension of the story is to explore averages of things that are interesting to the students (average number of siblings, average arm span, etc.) and see where these odd decimal parts come from. In the case of measures of length, for example, an average length can be a real length even if no one has it. But an average number of something like cars or sisters can be very humorous as discussed in the story. Where else are fractions and decimals used in this way?

ASSESSMENT NOTES

The real danger in teaching the topics discussed in this chapter is to focus on skills instead of the concepts and big ideas. Traditional programs will test children's ability to round numbers, order decimals, compute with pencil-and-paper, and solve sterile percent problems. The focus of these assessments is far too skill-oriented.

Many of the activities described in this chapter involve discussions and explanations. For example, Activity 14.7, "Close to a Friendly Fraction" (p. 282), will very likely produce an array of answers from your students as they select a "nice" decimal and fractional equivalent. How did they make that choice? Which seems "best"? Is there always a best answer? When students use a 10×10 square to find a decimal equivalent for $\frac{3}{8}$ or $\frac{2}{3}$ (see Activity 14.5, p. 281), there will be lots of discussion if you are not overly directive. From these discussions, you will be able to gather a lot of data about your students' understanding of concepts.

You may like an assessment that gets at several concepts and permits some independent work rather than relying on listening to discussions. You can and should have students write out explanations and draw pictues to support their answers to many of the activities that are suggested. Here are two questions that could serve as assessments or as instructional tasks:

1. **Consider these two computations: $3\frac{1}{2} \times 2\frac{1}{4}$ and 2.276×3.18. Without doing the calculations, which do you think is larger? Provide a reason for your answer that can be understood by someone else in this class.**

2. **How much larger is 0.76×5 than 0.75×5? How can you tell without doing the computation? (Kulm, 1994)**

Realistic percent problems are still the best way to assess a student's understanding of percent. Don't assign a list of these problems as exercises; rather give one or two and have students explain why they think their answer makes sense. You might consider taking a realistic percent problem and substituting fractions for percents (e.g., use $\frac{1}{8}$ instead of 12.5 percent) to see how students handle fractions in these problems compared to decimal numbers.

If your focus is on reasons and justifications rather than number of problems correct, you will be able to collect all the information you need.

REFLECTIONS ON CHAPTER 14: WRITING TO LEARN

1. Describe three different base 10 models for fractions and decimals, and use each to illustrate how base 10 fractions can easily be represented.

2. Explain how the place-value system extends infinitely in two directions. How can this idea be developed with students in the fifth or sixth grade?

3. Use an example involving base 10 pieces to explain the role of the decimal point in identifying the units position. Relate this idea to changing units of measurement as in money or metric measures.

4. What are the suggested "familiar fractions," and how can these fractions be connected to their decimal equivalents in a conceptual manner?

5. What kinds of things should be emphasized regarding decimals if you want children to have good number sense with decimals?

6. Describe one or two ways in which a calculator can be used to develop number ideas with decimals.

7. What does rounding mean? What type of rounding can we do that is different from rounding to the nearest tenth or hundredth? Explain how a number line can be used in rounding.

8. Make up three realistic percent problems in which the percents are actually nice fractions and the numbers involved are compatible with the fractions. One problem should ask for the part, given the whole and the percent. One should ask for the percent, given the whole and the part. The third should ask for the whole, given the part and the percent. Model each, and show how each can be solved using fraction ideas.

9. Why should we not spend a lot of time with pencil-and-paper computation with decimals?

10. For addition and subtraction, the line-up-the-decimals rule can be reasonably taught without much trouble. Explain.

11. Give an example explaining how, in most problems, multiplication and division with decimals can be replaced with estimation and whole-number methods.

FOR DISCUSSION AND EXPLORATION

1. For each of the four operations, discuss what computational skill with decimals is necessary for children to have. For example, if you believe that division with decimal numbers is important, what is the most tedious problem you would consider having students master? What alternatives to traditional pencil-and-paper computation do you think should be included in the curriculum?

2. One way to order a series of decimal numbers is to annex zeros to each number so that all numbers have the same number of decimal places. For example, rewrite

0.34	as	0.3400
0.3004	as	0.3004
0.059	as	0.0590

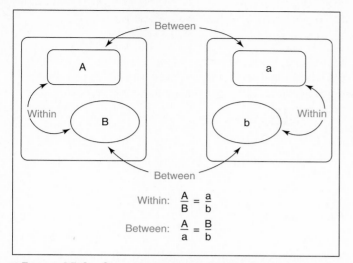

Within: $\dfrac{A}{B} = \dfrac{a}{b}$

Between: $\dfrac{A}{a} = \dfrac{B}{b}$

● **FIGURE 15.8** Given a proportional situation, the two between ratios and the two within ratios will be the same.

When there is an even multiple within, the ratio can easily be converted to a unit ratio. For example, 3 to 12 is the same as 1 to 4. Pairs that involve between but not within multiples lend themselves to the factor-of-change approach: 6 to 14 is an even multiple of the 3-to-7 ratio.

Scaling Activities

Scaling activities involve filling in charts where paired entries are related in some way. The format of a chart is not important, and different formats can be used. Scaling up is a matter of providing entries with larger numbers, and scaling down is entering smaller numbers. The following are some examples of scaling up:

1 foot → 12 inches   1 can → $0.55

2 feet → 24 inches   2 cans → $1.10

3 feet → ? inches   3 cans → $?

As in these examples, the items in the charts can be related measures such as time (minutes to hours), money (nickels to quarters), weight (pounds to ounces or kilograms), or common pairings such as crayons to boxes, hands to fingers, or wheels to tricycles. They can also be arbitrary ratios, such as a man who eats three bagels for every two bananas.

In a scaling-down activity, one or two later entries in the list or table are given, and students are asked to provide entries earlier or at the beginning of the list:

28 days → 4 weeks   12 cups → 24 sugars

21 days → 3 weeks   11 cups → 22 sugars

 ? days → 2 weeks   10 cups → ? sugars

Be careful not to make these exercises too long or tedious. Allow students to use repeated addition or subtrac-

tion as well as multiplication and division. Also, be sure to permit the use of calculators to make computation easy.

Notice that in the examples so far, the unit ratio is easy to determine without the use of fractions. As long as unit ratios are easily found, scaling activities can be done at an early grade. Later, fractions and decimals can be used in a scaling-type exercise. Students can scale down with one division to get a unit ratio and multiply to get a particular requested entry. This is illustrated in the following example:

> 3 boxes for $2.25 → 5 boxes for ?
>   1 box is $0.75 (unit ratio), so 5 boxes is 5 × $0.75 = $3.75.

Suppose that the price of nine boxes or some other multiple of 3 was requested in this example. Then scaling can be done using multiples of the given ratio. Scaling can be done up or down without using a unit ratio.

Minutes:	5	?	15	20	25	30	35
Widgets made:	?	14	21	?	?	?	?

The next two activities are related to scaling but are less structured.

---ACTIVITY---

15.4 What's in the Bag?

This activity involves informal probability concepts as well as ratio. Put colored cubes or other counters of two colors in a bag. For example, use 4 red and 8 blue. Explain that there are cubes of different colors in the bag, but do not tell students the number of cubes or number of colors. Shake the bag, and have students draw out a cube, record the color, and return the cube to the bag. After 10 or 15 trials, ask students how many of each color they think might be in the bag, and record the guesses. After some more trials, you could ask what is the fewest possible number of cubes that they think could be in the bag. Then you can give them one of the following clues: the total counters that are in the bag or the number of cubes of one color. See if with this information they can predict how many of each color are in the bag. "What if there were more cubes? What are other numbers of each color that might be in the bag?" The discussion is useful even if the students do not guess the correct ratio of colors. You can continue pulling out blocks to see that the ratio stays approximately, but not exactly, the same. Besides changing the ratio of colors on different days, you can add a third color. After seeing the actual contents of the bag, discuss what other numbers of each color would produce the same result. Groups might explore drawing cubes from bags with equal ratios of colors but different numbers and compare the results.

Construction and Measurement Activities

In these activities, measurements are made to construct physical models of equivalent ratios in order to provide a tangible example of a proportion as well as look at numeric relationships.

---ACTIVITY---

15.5 Graphs Showing Ratios

Have students make a graph of the data from a collection of equal ratios that they have scaled or discussed. Similar to Figure 15.3 (p. 296), which is a graph of price-to-item ratios, the graph in Figure 15.9 is of the ratios of two sides of similar rectangles. If only a few ratios have actually been computed, the graph can be drawn carefully and then used to determine other equivalent ratios. This is especially interesting when there is a physical model to coincide with the ratio. In the rectangle example, students can draw rectangles with sides determined by the graphs and compare them to the original rectangles. A unit ratio can be found by locating the point on the line that is directly above or to the right of the number 1 on the graph. (There are actually two unit ratios for every ratio. Why?) Students can then use the unit ratio to scale up to other values and check to see that they are on the graph as well. Note that the slope of any line through the origin is a ratio.

---ACTIVITY---

15.6 Different Units, Equal Ratios

Cut strips of adding machine tape all the same length, and give one strip to each group in your class. Each group is to measure the strip using a different unit. Possible units include different Cuisenaire rods or fraction strips, a piece of chalk, a pencil, the edge of a book or index card, or standard units such as inches or centimeters. When everyone has measured the strip, ask for the measure of one of the groups, and display the unit of measure. Next, hold up the unit of measure used by another group, and have the class compare it with the first unit. See if the class can estimate the measurement that the second group found. The ratio of the measuring units should be the inverse of the measurements made with those units. For example, if two units are in a ratio of 2 to 3, the respective units will be in a ratio of 3 to 2. Examine measurements made with other units. Finally, present a unit that no group has used, and see if the class can predict the measurement when made with that unit.

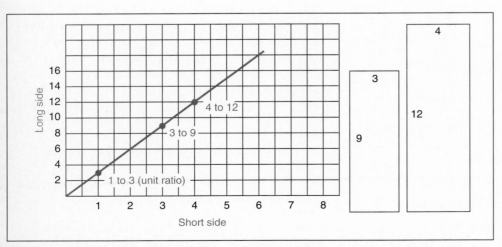

● FIGURE 15.9 Graphs show ratios of sides in similar rectangles.

---ACTIVITY---

15.7 Measurement, Graphs, and Percentages

An expansion of Activity 15.6 is to provide each group with an identical set of four strips of quite different lengths. Good lengths might be 20, 50, 80, and 120 cm. As before, each group measures the strips using a different unit. Next, have each group make a bar graph showing the group's measurements. Have all groups use the same scale for their graphs so that those with short units will have long bars in their graphs and those with long units will have short bars. Before displaying the graphs, have each group also make a circle graph representing the total length of all four strips. This is easily done by adding the measured lengths of the strips and then using a calculator to divide the length of each strip by the total. The results, rounded to two decimal places, will give the percentage of the total contributed by each strip. By tracing a circle around a hundredths disk (see the Blackline Masters) and using the hundredths marks, you can graph the percentage of each strip as a part of the circle. Have all groups make their bar and circle graphs with the strips in the same order and color them with the

same colors. All of the bar graphs will be different heights due to the use of units, but the pie graphs will all be nearly identical. Now you can discuss a variety of ratios and proportions as suggested in Figure 15.10. The fact that certain ratios are the same and that the pie graphs are all the same provides vivid examples of proportionality.

---ACTIVITY---

15.8 Density Ratios

An activity involving weight and density can be conducted in a manner similar to Activity 15.7. Instead of four different-length strips, provide each group with four small containers of different sizes. The four containers must be the same for each group. Have each group fill its containers with a different filler. Select fillers that vary greatly in density—for example, dry oatmeal, rice, sand, and small metal washers. Each group weighs the contents of its containers (not including the containers) to the nearest gram and makes a bar graph of the results. A pie graph is made of the total weight of all containers. The results will be similar to the length experiment. Here, instead of different units of measure, the different densities

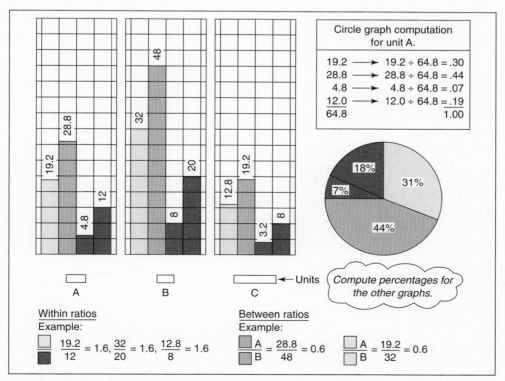

• **FIGURE 15.10** Three groups measure four strips of 80, 120, 20, and 50 cm. Each group uses a different measuring unit. What like ratios can be observed? Can you find inverse ratios?

of the fillers will produce different weights. Since the volumes are the same, the ratios of weights for each group will be the same, and each group should get about the same pie graph.

15.9 Scale Drawings

On dot paper (see the Blackline Masters), have students draw a simple shape using straight lines with vertices on the dots. After one shape is complete, have them draw a larger or smaller shape that is the same as or similar to the first. This can be done either on the same size or on a different-sized grid, as in Figure 15.11. After completing two or three pictures of different sizes, the ratios of the lengths of different sides can be compared. Corresponding sides from one figure to the next should all be in the same ratio. The ratio of two sides within one figure should be the same as the ratio of the corresponding two sides in another figure. This activity connects the geometric idea of similarity with the numeric concept of ratio.

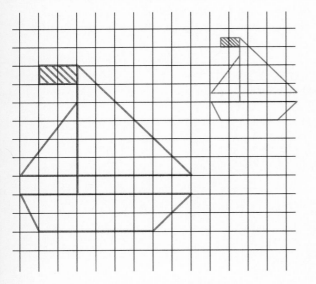

Use a metric ruler
• Choose two lengths on one boat and form a ratio (use a calculator). Compare to the ratio of the same parts of the other boats.
• Choose two boats. Measure the same part of each boat, and form a ratio. Compare with the ratios of another part.
• Compare the areas of the big sails with the lengths of the bottom sides.

● **FIGURE 15.11**   Comparing similar figures drawn on grids.

15.10 Length, Surface, and Volume Ratios

A three-dimensional version of Activity 15.9 can be done with blocks, as shown in Figure 15.12. Using 1-inch or 2-cm wooden cubes, make a simple "building." Then make a similar but larger building, and compare measures. A different size can also be made using different-sized blocks. To measure buildings made with different blocks, use a common unit such as centimeters. (Notice that volumes and surface areas do not vary proportionally with the edges of solids. However, these are relationships that are interesting to observe.)

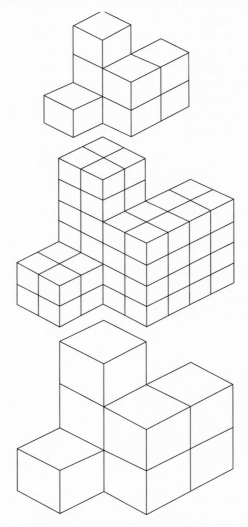

Similar "buildings" can be made by changing the number of blocks in each dimension (factor of change) or by using different-sized blocks.

● **FIGURE 15.12**   Similar constructions.

Activities 15.9 and 15.10 (p. 302) involve area and volume as well as the lengths of various dimensions. Comparisons of corresponding lengths, areas, and volumes in proportional figures lead to some interesting ratios. If two figures are similar or proportional, any linear dimension you measure will be in the ratio on each, say 1 to k. Corresponding areas, however, will be in the ratio of 1 to k^2 and corresponding volumes in the ratio of 1 to k^3. Try this with some constructions of your own.

As a means of contrasting proportional situations with additive ones, try starting with a figure on a grid or a building made with blocks and adding two units to every dimension in the figure. The result will be larger but will not look the same at all. Try this with a simple rectangle that is 1 cm by 15 cm. The new rectangle is twice as "thick" (2 cm) but only a bit longer. It will not appear to be the same shape as the original.

In all these activities, measurements have been made to observe equal ratios or proportions. In Activity 15.11, visual perception is used without measurement to create a proportionate length or shape. Measurement follows the perceptual judgment to see how good the estimate is.

—ACTIVITY—

15.11 Stop When They're the Same

On the board, draw two lines, labeled A and B, as shown in Figure 15.13. Draw a third line, C, that is significantly different from A. Begin drawing a fourth line, D, under C. Have students tell you when to stop drawing so that the ratio of C to D is the same as the ratio of A to B. Measure all four lines, and compare the ratios with a calculator. (Notice that here a single decimal number represents a ratio. How do you explain that?)

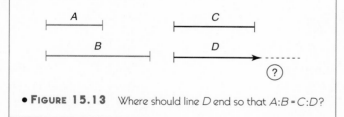

● **FIGURE 15.13**   Where should line D end so that A:B = C:D?

Other activities that have been explored can also be transformed into estimation activities. For example, prepare a figure on plain paper using graph paper placed underneath as a guide. The figure can be as simple as a right triangle or more complicated, such as a drawing of a truck or a house. Make a transparency of the drawing. Students will see a very large figure with no measurements or grid. On paper with a very small grid, perhaps 0.5 cm, students attempt

---

to draw a figure similar to the one on the overhead. Producing a perfectly similar figure may be difficult, but many may be close or even exact.

SOLVING PROPORTIONS

Notice that everything that has been discussed so far has been aimed at helping students develop an intuitive concept of ratio and proportion, to help in the development of proportional reasoning.

One practical value of proportional reasoning is to use observed proportions to find unknown values. Given that two ratios are equivalent, knowledge of one ratio can often be used to find a value in the other. Comparison pricing, using scales on maps, and solving percentage problems are just a few everyday instances where solving proportions is common. Students need to learn to set up proportions symbolically and to solve them.

An Informal Approach

The traditional textbook will show students how to set up an equation of two ratios involving an unknown, "cross-multiply," and solve for the unknown. As you saw earlier, this can be a very mechanical or instrumental approach and will almost certainly lead to confusion and error. Although you may wish eventually to cover the cross-product algorithm, it is well worth the time to encourage students to find ways to solve proportions using their own ideas first. If you have been exploring proportions in activities such as those described so far, students will have a good foundation on which to build or invent their own approaches.

Try solving each of the following problems. If you don't have an immediate idea of what to do, sketch a little drawing of two ratios similar to Figure 15.8 (p. 299). Think about within or between ratios matching up. Do not use cross-multiplication.

> **A rabbit and a turtle have a race. The turtle gets to start 20 feet from the finish line. The rabbit starts 100 feet from the finish line. If the turtle can get to the finish line in 8 minutes, how fast does the rabbit need to run so that the race is a tie? Answer in feet per minute.**

> **The price of a box of two dozen candy bars is $4.80. Bridget wants to buy five candy bars. What will she have to pay?**

> **Brian can run 5 km in 18.4 minutes. If he keeps on running at the same speed, how far can he run in 23 minutes?**

For the turtle-and-rabbit problem, you are looking at two situations involving distance and time. The within ratio for the turtle is 20 to 8 and for the rabbit 100 to t (it takes t minutes for the rabbit to run 100 feet). The rabbit's 100 feet may be recognized as 5 times the turtle's 20 feet (between comparison), so the times must be in the same ratio. Multiply 8 by 5. The rabbit must run at 100 feet per 40 minutes or 2.5 feet per minute.

The candy problem has a nice within ratio that may be used in a similar manner.

Before thinking about the third problem, change the numbers in the turtle-and-rabbit problem to these: Turtle runs 17 feet in 3.8 minutes. The rabbit still must go 100 feet to catch the turtle. How would you solve the problem now? Use your diagram to help you.

Change the numbers in the candy problem to some odd amounts that do not "come out nicely" and decide how you would solve the new problem. If you are having difficulty, discuss the problems with a friend.

Finally, sketch a diagram for Brian and the 5-km race, and see if you can find a way to solve that one. (Do this now before reading on.)

The first situation for your sketch is Brian's 5-km run (5 km and 18.4 minutes). The second situation is the unknown distance and 23 minutes. There are at least two possible things you might have considered, and one is no more likely or easier than the other. First, you may have looked at the between ratios and wondered what you would need to multiply 18.4 by to get 23 ($23 \div 18.4$). The calculator yields 1.25, the factor of change. Now $5 \times 1.25 = 6.25$.

The second possibility is to get a unit rate for the 5 km and multiply by 23. That would mean divide both the 5 and the 18.4 by 18.4 (like reducing a fraction to a denominator of 1). The calculator yields 0.2717391, or about 0.27 km per minute. Multiply this unit rate by 23 minutes and you get 6.2499993 km. In both cases, the longer distance is 6.25 km.

What is important here is to see how to use multiplication to solve the proportional situation. Further, notice that the calculations are based on ideas already developed. If not everyone in the class figures this out on the first few problems, the discussion and justification should help all students begin to understand. The sketch of the two ratios helps keep things straight and avoids any ambiguous cross-multiplying.

The Cross-Product Algorithm

The methods just described come very close to being well-defined algorithms. The fact that they are a bit more flexible than cross-product methods and that they can be understood as you are doing them makes them quite desirable.

The reality is that the computations involved are exactly the same as in cross-multiplication. Some teachers may still want to teach cross-multiplication.

Draw a Simple Model

Given a ratio word problem, the greatest difficulty students have is setting up a correct proportion or equation of two ratios, one of which includes the missing value. Since many apparently different equations can be written for the same situation, some students become even more confused. "Which fractions do I make? Where does the x go?"

Rather than drill and drill in the hope that they will somehow eventually get it, show students how to sketch a simple model or picture that will help them determine what parts are related. In Figure 15.14, a simple model is drawn for a typical rate or price problem. The two equations in the figure come from setting up within and between ratios.

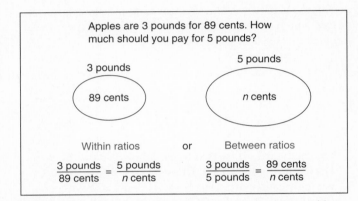

● **FIGURE 15.14**   *A simple drawing helps in a price-ratio problem.*

Solve the Proportion

Examine the left (within) ratios in the same way as for Brian's 5-km race. We could find out what to multiply the left fraction by to get the right. To do this, we would divide 5 by 3 and then multiply that result by 89:

$$\frac{5}{3} \times 89$$

Looking at the same left equation in Figure 15.14, we could also determine the unit price or the price for 1 pound by dividing the 89 cents by 3 and then multiplying this result by 5 to determine the price of 5 pounds:

$$\frac{89}{3} \times 5$$

Now look what happens if we cross-multiply in the original equation:

$$3n = 5 \times 89$$
$$n = \frac{5 \times 89}{3}$$

This equation can be solved by dividing the 5 by 3 and multiplying by 89 or dividing 89 by 3 and multiplying by 5. These are exactly the two devices we employed in our more intuitive approach. If you cross-multiply the between ratios,

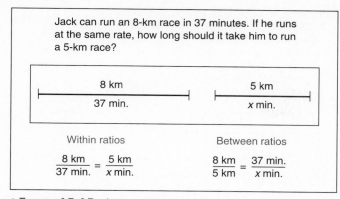

Jack can run an 8-km race in 37 minutes. If he runs at the same rate, how long should it take him to run a 5-km race?

Within ratios

$$\frac{8 \text{ km}}{37 \text{ min.}} = \frac{5 \text{ km}}{x \text{ min.}}$$

Between ratios

$$\frac{8 \text{ km}}{5 \text{ km}} = \frac{37 \text{ min.}}{x \text{ min.}}$$

• **FIGURE 15.15** *Line segments can be used to model both time and distance.*

you get exactly the same result. Furthermore, you get the same result if you had written the two ratios inverted, that is, with the reciprocals of each fraction. Try it!

So if you want to develop a cross-product algorithm, it is not unreasonable to do problems like these with students using their own methods. If you write out the computations involved, a very small amount of direct teaching can develop the cross-product approach. But why hurry?

In Figure 15.15, a problem involving rates of speed is modeled with simple lines representing the two distances. The distance and the time for each run is modeled with the same line. You cannot see time, but it fits into the distance covered. All equal-rates-of-speed problems can be modeled this way. There really is no significant difference from the drawing used for the apples. Again, it is just as acceptable to write between ratios as within ratios, and students need not worry about which one goes on top as long as the ratios are written in the same order. The model helps with this difficulty.

In Figure 15.16, a scale drawing is being made. As before, with the use of the simple sketch, students can easily find two like ratios. The drawing provides security without being a meaningless trick. It also helps illustrate that there is more than one correct way to set up the equation.

Percent Problems as Proportions

In most sixth- through eighth-grade textbooks, you will find a chapter on ratio, proportion, and percent. Percent has traditionally been included as a topic with ratio and proportion because percent is one form of ratio, a part-to-whole ratio. In many older programs, the unit on ratio and proportion focused on solving percent problems as a proportion and devoted relatively little attention to developing proportional thought. In Chapter 14, it was shown that the solution to percent problems can be connected to concepts of fractions. Here the same part-to-whole fraction concept of percent will be extended to ratio and proportion concepts. Ideally, all of these ideas (fractions, decimals, ratio, proportion, and percent) should be conceptually integrated. This integration of related ideas is an excellent example of the network of ideas that increases understanding. The better that students connect these ideas, the more flexible and useful their reasoning and problem-solving skills will be.

Equivalent Fractions as Proportions

Before considering percents specifically, consider first how equivalent fractions can be interpreted as a proportion using the same simple models already suggested. In Figure 15.17, a line segment or bar is partitioned in two different ways: in fourths on one side and in twelfths on the other. In the previous examples, proportions were established based on two amounts of apples, two different distances or runs, and two different sizes of drawings. Here only one thing is measured—the part of a whole—but it is measured or partitioned two ways: in fourths and in twelfths.

The within ratios are ratios of part-to-whole within each measurement. Within ratios result in the usual equivalent fraction equation, $\frac{3}{4} = \frac{9}{12}$ (3 fourths are to 4 fourths as 9 twelfths are to 12 twelfths). The between proportion equates a part-to-part ratio with a whole-to-whole ratio, or $\frac{3}{9} = \frac{4}{12}$ (3 fourths are to 9 twelfths as 4 fourths are to 12 twelfths). The between ratios here might be confusing to children. They illustrate, however, that this drawing is in fact like those of Figures 15.14 through 15.16.

A simple line segment drawing similar to the one in Figure 15.17 could be drawn to set up a proportion to solve any equivalent-fraction problem, even ones that do not re-

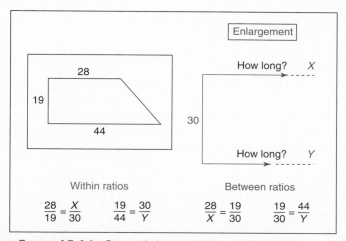

Within ratios

$$\frac{28}{19} = \frac{X}{30} \qquad \frac{19}{44} = \frac{30}{Y}$$

Between ratios

$$\frac{28}{X} = \frac{19}{30} \qquad \frac{19}{30} = \frac{44}{Y}$$

• **FIGURE 15.16** *Pictures help in establishing equal ratios.*

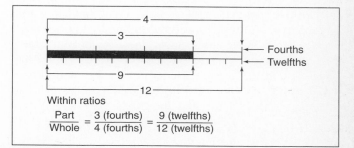

Within ratios

$$\frac{\text{Part}}{\text{Whole}} = \frac{3 \text{ (fourths)}}{4 \text{ (fourths)}} = \frac{9 \text{ (twelfths)}}{12 \text{ (twelfths)}}$$

• **FIGURE 15.17** *Equivalent fractions as proportions.*

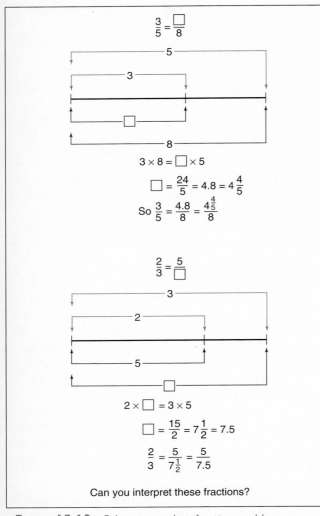

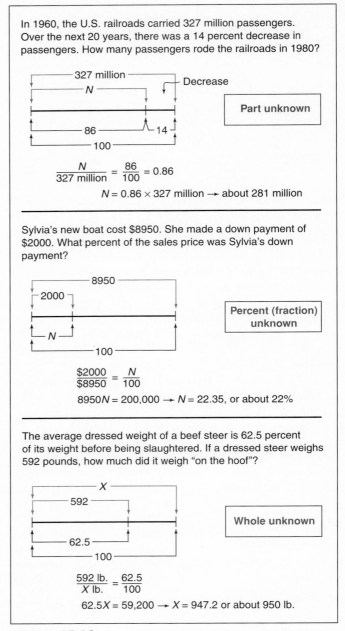

• **FIGURE 15.18** Solving equivalent-fractions problems as equivalent ratios using cross-products.

• **FIGURE 15.19** The three percentage problems solved by setting up a proportion using a simple line segment model.

sult in whole-number numerators or denominators. Two examples are shown in Figure 15.18.

Percent Problems

The equivalent-fraction examples illustrate how any fraction can be sketched easily on a simple line segment showing the part and the whole measured or partitioned two different ways. All percent problems are exactly the same as this. They involve a part and a whole measured in some unit and the same part and whole measured in hundredths—that is, in percents. A simple line segment drawing can be used for each of the three types of percent problems. Using this model as a guide, a proportion can then be written and solved by the cross-product algorithm. Examples of each type of problem are illustrated in Figure 15.19.

It is tempting to teach all percent problems in this one way. That is, whenever there is a percent problem, make a little drawing, set up a proportion, and solve by cross-products. Developmentally, such an approach is not recommended. First, and most important, even though the approach is conceptual, it does not translate easily to intuitive ideas, mental arithmetic, or estimation as discussed in Chapter 14. Second, research does not seem to support the notion of focusing on a single algorithmic approach to solving percent problems (Callahan & Glennon, 1975). The modeling and proportion approach of Figure 15.19 is suggested only as a way to help students connect percent concepts with fraction and proportion ideas and analyze problems that may verbally present some difficulty. The approach of Chapter 14, which relates percent to part-whole fraction concepts, should probably receive the major emphasis in teaching percent.

LITERATURE CONNECTIONS

Literature brings an exciting dimension to the exploration of proportional reasoning. Many books and stories discuss comparative sizes; concepts of scale as in maps; giants and miniature people who are proportional to regular people; comparative rates, especially rates of speed; and so on. A book may not appear to explore proportions, and the author may not have had that in mind at all, but comparisons are the stuff of many excellent stories and are at the heart of proportional ideas. The suggestions here are only to give you an idea of what you might look for.

How Big? How Fast? How Hungry? (Waverly, 1990)

This book provides all sorts of comparisons of various cats to the common house cat. The tiger is bigger (600 pounds to 8 pounds). The cheetah can reach a speed of 70 miles per hour, whereas the house cat can run 30 miles per hour. (That's not exactly slow.) One way to explore these ideas is to look at one ratio (perhaps 75 pounds of meat for the lion to $\frac{1}{3}$ pound for the cat at one meal) and apply the same ratio to some other measure of the house cat. Does that mean that the length of the lion's and the cat's tails are in the same ratio? How much would the lion and the cat eat in a year? Another idea is to apply these ratios to some other species, even humans, and see what the counterpart would be like. Take speed, for example. The cat is to the cheetah as 30 mph is to 75 mph. Michael Johnson runs the 100 meters in about 9.8 seconds. How fast would a man be who was compared to Johnson in the same way as the cheetah is to the cat?

Counting on Frank (Clement, 1991)

We will refer to this wonderful book again when we discuss measurement in Chapter 16. It is hard to imagine that more mathematics could spring from 24 pages mostly covered with pictures. But the ideas appeal to all ages, and the potential for good investigations is clearly there for older children. The narrator and his pet dog, Frank, estimate, figure, and ponder interesting facts, usually about large numbers in odd settings (enough green peas to be level with the kitchen tabletop). But three spreads of the book are wonderful fantasies of proportions that could easily inspire an entire unit of proportional reasoning projects.

"If I had grown at the same speed as the tree—6 feet per year—I'd now be almost 50 feet tall!" How fast do we grow? What if we kept growing at the same rate? At what rates do things grow? How old is the narrator? How old would he be when he is 75 feet tall?

If the mosquito that bothers him were 4 million times bigger . . . What would any common object be like if it were a million times bigger?

If the toaster that shoots toast 3 feet in the air were as big as the house . . .

The Borrowers (Norton, 1953)

This is the classic tale of little folk living in the walls of a house. The furnishings and implements are created from odds and ends from the full-size human world. The potential to make scale comparisons is endless.

A similar tale unfolds in Shel Silverstein's poem "One Inch Tall" (1974), in which you are invited to imagine being 1 inch tall.

At the other extreme are stories about giants and dinosaurs, but the concepts of scale are similar. Why are there no real giants, and how large could a dinosaur possibly be? Suppose that a giant were 18 feet tall, or three times the height of a tall man. All linear dimensions (arm span, foot length, etc.) would also be three times that of the man. But the surface area would be 3^2 or 9 times as large and the giant's volume and hence his weight would be 3^3 or 27 times as much as the man's. That would make the giant weigh about 5400 pounds. Would the bones (cross-sectional area only 9 times more) be able to hold the weight?

ASSESSMENT NOTES

Proportional reasoning is more than acquiring a collection of concepts and skills. It is a way of thinking that includes the ability to understand and compare ratios. It is one of the hallmarks of Piaget's formal operational stage of development. One thing we know about this form of reasoning is that it may not develop in persons who have not had ample opportunities to experience and reflect on proportional situations.

As you work with your students in solving proportional reasoning tasks, it will be useful for you to think about the type of reasoning that students are using.

CHAPTER 16

DEVELOPING MEASUREMENT CONCEPTS

There is a tendency to teach children *how* to measure rather than teaching *what it means* to measure. True, it is very difficult to separate the procedural activity of measurement from the concept. The concept of measurement is best embodied by the process. A typical group of first graders measures the length of their classroom by laying strips 1 meter long end to end. But the strips sometimes overlap, and the line weaves in a snakelike fashion around the desks. Which do these children not understand: how to measure or the meaning of measurement?

 BIG IDEAS

1. Measurement involves a comparison with a unit that has the same attribute as the item which is being measured (length, volume, weight, etc.). There are many ways to make these comparisons. To measure anything meaningfully, the attribute to be measured must be understood.
2. Meaningful measurement and estimation of measurements depend on a personal familiarity with the unit of measure being used.
3. Measurement instruments are devices that replace the need for actual measurement units in making comparisons.
4. Area and volume formulas are ways of using length measures to count more easily the area or volume units in an object without actually using area or volume units.

THE MEANING AND PROCESS OF MEASURING

Suppose that you were asked to measure an empty bucket. The first thing you would need to know is *what* about the bucket is to be measured. Various lengths could be measured: height or depth, diameter (distance across), circumference (distance around). The surface area of the side could be determined. A bucket also has volume and weight. Each of these *aspects that can be measured* is an *attribute* of the bucket.

Once the attribute to be measured is determined, a unit of measure can be chosen. The unit must have the attribute that is being measured. Length is measured with units that have length, volume with units that have volume, and so on.

Technically, a *measurement* is a number that indicates a comparison between the attribute of the object being measured and the same attribute of a given unit of measure. A gross comparison might indicate that the measured attribute was more or less, longer or shorter, heavier or lighter, and so on, than the unit of measure. It is much more common to use small units of measure and to determine in some way a numeric relationship (the measurement) between what is measured and the unit. These comparisons are done in many different ways, depending on what is being measured. For example, to measure a length, the comparison can be done by lining up copies of the unit directly against the length being measured. Notice that this is what you do when you use a ruler or tape measure. To measure weight, which is a pull of gravity or a force, the weight of the object might first be applied to a spring. Then the comparison is made by finding out how many units of weight produce the same effect on the spring. In either case, the number of units is the measure of the object.

For most of the attributes that are measured in schools, we can say that *to measure* means that the attribute being measured is "filled" or "covered" or "matched" with a unit of measure that has the same attribute (as illustrated in Figure 16.1). This concept of measurement will adequately serve the purposes of this chapter and is a good way to discuss with children what a measurement is. It is appropriate with this understanding, then, to say that the measure of an attribute is a count of how many units are needed to fill, cover, or match the attribute of the object being measured.

In summary, to measure something, one must perform three steps:

1. Decide on the attribute to be measured.
2. Select a unit that has that attribute.
3. Compare the units, by filling, covering, matching, or some other method, with the attribute of the object being measured.

Measuring instruments such as rulers, scales, protractors, and clocks are devices that make the filling, covering, or matching process easier. A ruler lines up the units of length and numbers them. A protractor lines up the unit angles and numbers them. A clock can be thought of as lining up units of time and marking them off.

DEVELOPING MEASUREMENT CONCEPTS AND SKILLS

Return to the children measuring the length of the classroom. Did they understand the concept of length as an attribute of the classroom? Did they understand that each strip of 1 meter has this attribute of length? Did they understand that their task was to fill smaller units of length into the longer one? What they most likely understood was that they were supposed to be making a line of strips stretching from wall to wall (and from their vantage point, they were

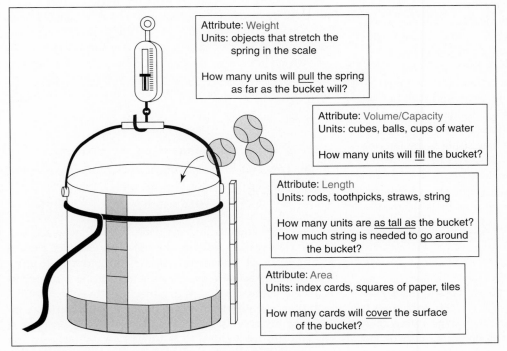

•FIGURE 16.1   *Measuring different attributes of a bucket.*

doing quite well). They were performing a procedure instrumentally, without a conceptual basis.

A General Plan of Instruction

A basic understanding of measurement suggests how to help children develop a conceptual knowledge of measuring.

CONCEPTUAL KNOWLEDGE TO DEVELOP	TYPE OF ACTIVITY TO USE
1. Understand the attribute being measured.	1. Make comparisons based on the attribute.
2. Understand how filling, covering, matching, or otherwise making comparisons of an attribute with units produces what is called a measure.	2. Use physical models of measuring units to fill, cover, match, or make the desired comparison of the attribute with the unit.
3. Understand the way measuring instruments work.	3. Make measuring instruments and use them along with actual unit models to compare how each works.

Each of the types of instructional activities will be discussed briefly.

Making Comparisons

When students compare objects on the basis of some measurable attribute, that attribute becomes the focus of the activity. For example, is the capacity of one box more than, less than, or about the same as the capacity of another? No measurement is required, but some manner of comparing one volume to the other must be devised. The attribute of "capacity" (how much a container can hold) is inescapable.

Many attributes can be compared directly, such as placing one length directly in line with another. In the case of volume or capacity, some indirect method is probably required, such as filling one box with beans and then pouring the beans into the other box. Using a string to compare the height of a wastebasket to the distance around is another example of an indirect comparison. The string is the intermediary. It is impossible to compare these two lengths directly.

Constructing or making something that is the same in terms of a measurable attribute is another type of comparison activity—for example, "Cut the straw to be just as long as this piece of chalk" or "Draw a rectangle that is about the same size (has the same area) as this triangle."

Using Models of Units

For most attributes that are measured in elementary schools, it is possible to have physical models of the units of measure. Time and temperature are exceptions. (Many other attributes not commonly measured in school also do not have physical units of measure. Light intensity, speed, loudness, viscosity, and radioactivity are just a few examples.) Unit models can be found for both informal units and standard units. For length, for example, drinking straws (informal) or tagboard strips 1 foot long (standard) might be used as units.

Unit models can be used in two ways. The most basic and easily understood method is actually to use as many copies of the unit as are needed to fill or match the attribute measured. To measure the area of the desktop with an index card unit, you can literally cover the entire desk with index cards. Somewhat more difficult, especially for younger children, is to use a single copy of the unit with an iteration process. The same desktop area can be measured with a single index card by moving it from position to position and keeping track of which areas the card has covered.

Another type of activity that helps children focus on measurement in a conceptual way is to make or construct objects with the same measure as a given object. Making (drawing, building, finding) an object with the same measure as a given one is quite different from simply measuring a series of objects and writing the results. For example, to cut a piece of paper that has just as much area as the surface of a can is an effective way to focus on the attribute of area as well as on the meaning of area units of measure. It is also possible, when using units, to talk about a numeric difference in the attributes of two objects instead of just making more, less, and same comparisons. "The capacity of the bucket is $2\frac{1}{2}$ liters larger than the capacity of this box."

It is useful to measure the same object with different-sized units. Results should be predicted in advance and discussed afterward. This will help students understand that the unit used is as important as the attribute being measured. It makes no sense to say, "The book weighs 23," unless you say 23 of what unit. The fact that smaller units produce larger numeric measures, and vice versa, is very hard for young children to understand. This inverse relationship can only be constructed by reflecting on measurements with varying-sized units. Predictions and discussions of results add to the reflective nature of the activities.

Making and Using Measuring Instruments

In the fifth National Assessment of Educational Progress (Mullis, Dossey, Owen, & Phillips, 1991), the correct measure of an object not aligned with the end of a ruler, as in Figure 16.2, was given correctly by only 24 percent of fourth-grade students and 61 percent of eighth-grade students. These results point to the difference between using a measuring device and understanding how and why it works.

If students actually make simple measuring instruments using the same unit models that they have already measured with, it is more likely that they will understand how an instrument actually measures. A ruler is a good example. If students line up physical units along a strip of tagboard and

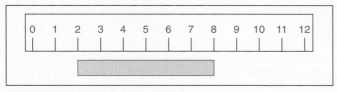

•**FIGURE 16.2**   *"How long is this segment?"*

mark them off, they can see that it is the *spaces* on rulers and not the marks or numbers that are important. It is essential that the measurement with actual unit models be compared with the measurement using an instrument. Without this comparison, students may not understand that these two methods are really two means to the same end. Always have students explain what the ruler, scale, or other device means and how it compares to using actual units.

A discussion of student-made measuring instruments for each attribute is provided in the text that follows. Of course, children should also use standard, ready-made instruments such as rulers and scales. The use of these devices should still be compared directly with the use of the corresponding unit models.

Informal Units and Standard Units: Reasons for Using Each

It is common in primary grades to use nonstandard or informal units to measure length and sometimes area. Unfortunately, measurement activities in the upper grades, where other attributes are measured, frequently do not begin with informal units. There are a number of values in using informal units for beginning measurement activities at all grade levels.

- Informal units make it easier to focus directly on the attribute being measured. For example, instead of using square inches to measure area, an assortment of different units, some of which are not square, can be used to help understand the essential features of area and units of area.

- By selecting units carefully, the size of the numbers in early measurements can be kept reasonable. The measures of length for first-grade students can be kept less than 20 even when measuring long distances. An angle unit much larger than a degree can be significantly easier for a sixth grader to use because a degree is very small and it is hard to make individual copies.

- The use of informal units can avoid conflicting objectives in the same beginning lesson. Is your lesson about what it means to measure area or understanding square centimeters? Learning to measure is different from learning about the standard units used to measure.

- Informal units provide a good rationale for standard units. A discussion of the need for a standard unit can be quite

meaningful after each of the groups in your class has measured the same objects with their own units.

- Informal units can be fun.

The use of standard units is also important in your measurement program at any grade level.

- Students must eventually develop a familiarity with the most common standard units. That is, knowledge of standard units is a valid objective of a measurement program and must be addressed. Students must not only develop a familiarity with standard units, but they must also learn appropriate relationships between them.

- Once a measuring concept is fairly well developed, it is frequently just as easy or even easier to use standard units. If there is no good instructional reason for using informal units, why not use standard units and provide the exposure?

There is no simple rule for when or where to use standard or informal units. Children's initial measurement of any particular attribute should probably begin with informal units and progress over time to the use of standard units and standard measuring tools. The amount of time that should be spent using informal unit models varies with the age of the children and the attributes being measured. For example, first-grade children need a lot of experience with a variety of informal units of length, weight, and capacity. Informal units might be used at this level all year. Conversely, the benefits of nonstandard measuring units may be diminished in two or three days for measurements of mass or capacity at the middle school level.

The Role of Estimation in Learning Measurement

It is very important to have students estimate a measurement before they make it. This is true with both informal and standard units. There are three reasons for including estimation in measurement activities:

- Estimation helps students focus on the attribute being measured and the measuring process. Think how you would estimate the area of the front of this book with standard playing cards as the unit. To do so, you have to think about what area is and how the units might be fitted into the book cover.

- Estimation provides intrinsic motivation. It adds fun and interest to measurement activities. It is fun to see how close you can come to estimating a measurement or if your team can make a better estimate than the other teams in the room.

- When standard units are used, estimation helps develop familiarity with the unit. If you estimate the height of the door in meters before measuring, you have to devise some way to think about the size of a meter.

Helping Children with Measurement Estimates

Having said that estimating measures is very important and should be included in almost all measurement activities, there remains the problem of how to go about doing so. Later we will discuss teaching children specific estimating strategies that can be used throughout life. However, until these strategies are developed along with familiarity with standard units, children will have a great deal of difficulty making estimates. Here are three ways to ask for estimates that avoid asking children to come up with an actual number or measure estimate before they are capable.

1. Ask for a comparison estimate rather than a measure. For example, is the teacher taller, shorter, or about the same as 2 meters? Does the book weigh more, less, or about the same as 1 pound? The same can be done with informal units. Is the area of the desktop more, less, or about the same as 20 index cards?

2. Ask which of two or more suggested measures the actual measure is closer to. For example, is the angle measure closer to 15, 60, or 90 degrees? Is the capacity of the box closer to 1 liter or 3 liters?

3. Provide an actual unit or set of units as a comparison. The children can make an initial estimate privately on paper. Then show the unit or set of 10 or 100 units, and let them adjust their first estimate accordingly. The use of the provided set of units allows them mentally to mark off or compare in some way without having to make a blind guess. Making the first estimate adds a bit of interest. For example, if estimating the length of the chalkboard in connecting-cube units, the number may be rather large and quite difficult for children. After seeing 10 cubes placed at one end of the chalkboard, the children can count by tens as they visually mark off these bars along the board. The use of 10 or 100 is suggested for place-value reasons. For large units such as a meter or a kilogram, one copy of the unit can be placed directly alongside the object being estimated. Of course, with an attribute such as weight, the children should be able to handle the unit as well as the object.

Notice that there is a progression to these three ideas in terms of how specific an estimate is requested. Use this progression as you develop estimation skills with children. These techniques can be applied to almost any measurement activities.

The Approximate Nature of Measurement

In all measuring activities, emphasize the use of approximate language. The desk is *about* 15 orange rods long. The chair is *a little less than* 4 straws high. The use of approximate language is very useful with younger children using large units because many measurements do not come out even. Older children will begin to search for smaller units or will use fractional units to try to measure exactly. Here is an opportunity to develop the idea that all measurements include some error. Each smaller unit or subdivision does produce a greater degree of precision. For example, a length measure can never be more than one-half unit in error. And yet, since there is mathematically no "smallest unit," there is always some error involved.

The notion of precision related to the size of the unit is an important idea in all measuring tasks. There are times when precision is not required, and a larger unit is much easier to deal with. At other times, the need for precision is significant, and smaller units become important. For example, measuring a pane of glass for a window requires a different precision than measuring a wall to decide how many 4-by-8-foot panels are needed to cover it. An awareness of precision due to unit size and the need for precision in different situations is an important aspect of measurement, especially at the upper grades.

Suggested Measurement Sequence

For each attribute that we want children to measure, we can identify the three types of activities that have been discussed. Comparison activities should generally precede the use of units, and measuring instruments should be dealt with last. Within each of these categories, there is also a rough guideline of progression that can be considered as shown in the following chart:

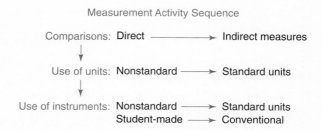

Measurement Activity Sequence

Comparisons: Direct ⟶ Indirect measures

Use of units: Nonstandard ⟶ Standard units

Use of instruments: Nonstandard ⟶ Standard units
Student-made ⟶ Conventional

Almost all activities should include an estimation component. Familiarity with standard units is a separate objective related to understanding the measurement process.

Notice especially that estimation and standard-unit familiarity are important considerations. In the discussions that follow, the focus is on activities for comparison, use of units, and use of instruments for each attribute. Separate discussions of standard units and estimation are also provided, pointing to the importance of these objectives as well.

MEASURING LENGTH

Comparison Activities

At the kindergarten level, children should begin with direct comparisons of two or more lengths.

---ACTIVITY---

16.1 Longer, Shorter, Same

Make a sorting-by-length station at which students sort objects as longer, shorter, or about the same as a specified object. It is easy to have several such stations in your room. The reference object can be changed occasionally to produce different sorts. A similar task is to put objects in order from shortest to longest.

---ACTIVITY---

16.2 Length Hunt

Go on a length hunt. Give pairs of students a strip of tagboard, a stick, a length of rope, or some other object with an obvious length dimension. The task on one day might be to find five things in the room that are shorter than or longer than or about the same as their object. They can draw pictures or write the name of the things they find. (Label things in the room to help.)

It is important to compare lengths that are not in straight lines. One way to do this is with string or rope. Students can wrap string around objects in a search for things that are, for example, just as long around as the distance from the floor to their belly button. Body measures are always fun. A child enjoys looking for things that are just as long as the distance around his or her head or waist.

Indirect comparisons are a next step in length comparisons.

---ACTIVITY---

16.3 Crooked Paths

Make some crooked or curvy paths on the floor with masking tape. The task is to determine which path is longest, next longest, and so on. The students should find a way to make straight paths that are just as long as following the crooked paths so that they can be compared easily. (You may or may not wish to offer this suggestion.) Provide pairs of students with a long piece of rope. The task is easier if the rope is longer than the crooked paths, but that is a choice you should make. The students can draw their straight paths on the board or mark them with tape on the floor or using some other method that you devise. Have students explain to the class how they solved the problem and demonstrate why they think their straight path is just as long as the crooked one. (This is a good outdoor activity also.)

The "Crooked Paths" activity can also be done with the small distances at students' desks. A simple worksheet like the one in Figure 16.3 might be prepared. Instead of crooked paths, students can make straight paths that are as long as the distance around simple shapes (their perimeters).

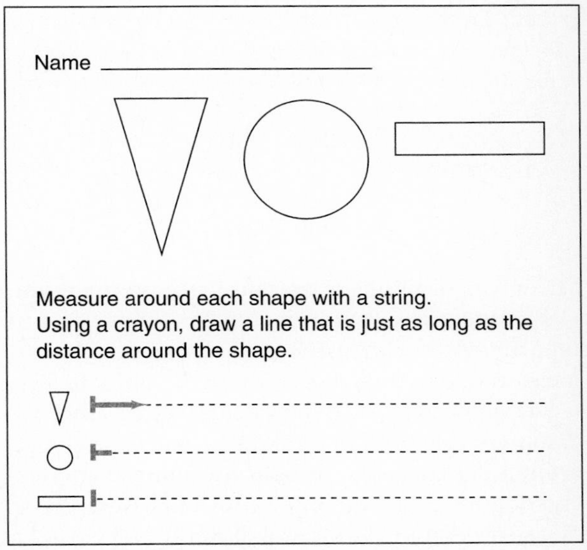

●**Figure 16.3** Making a straight path just as long as a crooked path.

Using Units of Length

Students can use a wide variety of informal units to begin measuring length. Some examples of units of different lengths are suggested here:

Giant footprints: Make about 20 copies of a large footprint about $1\frac{1}{2}$ to 2 feet long cut out of poster board.

Measuring strips: Cut strips of poster board about 5 cm wide. Several sets can be made to provide different units. Some can be the long dimension of the poster board, some the short, and a third set about 1 foot long. Make each set of a different color.

Measuring ropes: Cut cotton clothesline into lengths of 1 meter. These are useful for measuring curved lines and the circumference of large objects such as the teacher's desk.

Plastic straws: Drinking straws are inexpensive and provide large quantities of a useful unit. Straws are easily cut into smaller units. A good idea is to string straws together with a long string. The string of straws is an excellent bridge to a ruler or measuring tape.

Short units: Toothpicks, connecting cubes, strips of tagboard, wooden cubes, and paper clips are all useful as units for measuring shorter lengths. Cuisenaire rods are one of the nicest sets of units because they come in ten different lengths, are easily placed end to end, and can be related to each other. Paper clips can readily be made into chains of about 20 clips for easier use.

For young children, initial measurements should be along lines or edges. If different teams of students measure the same distances and get different results, discuss why they may have gotten these differences. The discussion can help focus on the reason why units need to be lined up end to end and in a straight line and why units such as ropes must be stretched to their full length.

explanations will be the most educational part of the activity. The first few times you do this activity, the larger unit should be a simple multiple of the smaller unit. If the two units are not related by a whole-number multiple, the task becomes difficult numerically and can be frustrating.

Two Units and Fractional Parts of Units

As children begin to develop a need for more precision, two units can be used at the same time. The second unit should be a smaller subunit of the first. For example, with connecting cubes, the first unit can be bars of 10 cubes, and the second can be individual cubes. With measuring strips, make subunits that are one-fourth or one-tenth as long as the longer strip. Cut plastic straws so that an even number of paper clips is equal to one straw. Cuisenaire rods allow for a variety of possibilities. For example, 4 reds make a brown,

---ACTIVITY---

16.4 Guess and Measure

Make lists of things to measure around the room. For younger children, run a piece of masking tape along the dimension of each object to be measured. On the list, designate the units to be used. Do not forget to include curves or other distances that are not straight lines. Distances around desks, doors, or balls are some examples (see Figure 16.4). Include estimates before the measures. Young children will not be very good at estimating distances at first.

---ACTIVITY---

16.5 Changing Units

Have students measure a distance with one unit, then provide them with a different unit and see if they can predict the measure with the new unit. Students should write down their predictions and explanations of how they were made. Then have them make the actual measurement. In the class discussions that follow, the predictions and

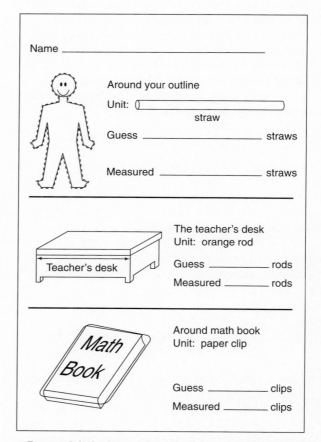

• **FIGURE 16.4**   *Record sheet for measuring with informal length units.*

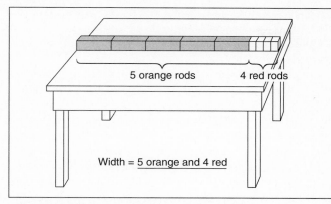

● **Figure 16.5** *Using two units to measure length.*

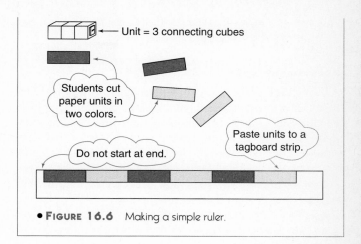

● **Figure 16.6** *Making a simple ruler.*

or 10 whites make an orange. Have children measure with the larger unit until no more of that unit will fit and then add on sufficient smaller units to fill up the distance (see Figure 16.5). Report measures in two parts: "8 straws and 3 clips long." For older students, smaller units can simply be fractional parts of longer units.

After a measurement with two related units has been made and recorded, have students figure out how to report the same measurement in terms of either unit—for example, $5\frac{2}{3}$ blue rods or 17 light green rods (3 light green = 1 blue). This provides a readiness exercise for standard units. For example, a measurement of 4 feet 3 inches is sometimes reported as 51 inches or as $4\frac{1}{4}$ feet. The use of two units is also good readiness for subdivision marks on a ruler.

Making and Using Rulers

Rulers or tape measures can be made for almost any unit of measure that students have used. It is important that students have used the actual unit models before making the rulers.

─────ACTIVITY─────

16.6 Ruler Construction

After doing some measuring with orange Cuisenaire rods (or any unit not shorter than about 5 cm), give students narrow strips of construction paper in two contrasting colors. Have students use a unit model as a guide and cut the strips into lengths as long as the unit. Discuss how the paper strips could be used for measuring instead of the actual units. Have students paste the paper unit strips end to end along the edge of a long tagboard strip about 5 cm wide, as shown in Figure 16.6.

Pasting down copies of the units on a ruler maximizes the connection between the spaces on a ruler and the actual units. Older children can make rulers by using a real unit to make marks along a tagboard strip and then coloring in the spaces. Rulers made with very small units are more difficult for students to make simply because they require better fine-motor skills. If the first unit on a ruler does not coincide with the end of the ruler, the student is forced to attend to aligning the units on the ruler with the object measured. Children should not be encouraged to use the end of a ruler as a starting point because many real rulers are not made that way.

Students should eventually put numbers on their homemade rulers, as shown in Figure 16.7. For young children, numbers might be written in the center of each unit to make it clear that the numbers are a way of precounting the units. When numbers are written in the standard way, at the ends of the units, the ruler becomes a number line. This format is more sophisticated and should be carefully discussed with

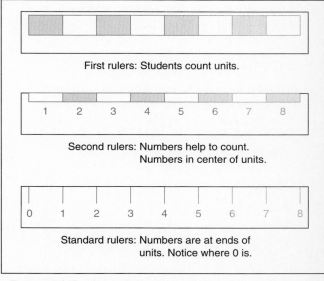

● **Figure 16.7** *Give meaning to numbers on rulers.*

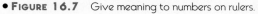
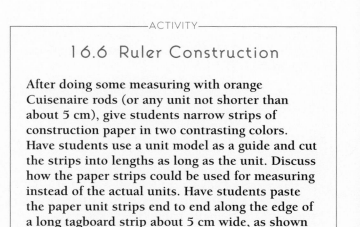

children. (Number lines are generally a poor number model for children below the third grade.)

Assessment Note

Although the progression shown in Figure 16.7 (p. 317) illustrates a developmental progression, children should be encouraged to make and number their rulers in ways that make sense to them. By having students make their own rulers in their own way and by having them use and explain the measures obtained by using their rulers, you receive an enormous amount of assessment data concerning how well students understand the measurement process. By contrast, if you carefully direct how children should construct and use their rulers, they may very well use the rulers instrumentally, blindly following directions with no understanding of what they are doing.

Putting measurement tasks into problem-solving exercises increases this information flow. For example, how could you explain in a letter to a class in another state just how large your classroom is or the size of the model of a blue whale you have been building? Let different groups decide how to do this and make the measurements. Now compare results and see if each solution actually conveys the meaning.

Using Rulers and Tape Measures

After students have made rulers, it is important to use them. In addition to the estimate-and-measure activities mentioned earlier, some special activities should be done with rulers.

Have teams measure items once with a ruler and a second time with actual unit models. Although the results should theoretically be the same, inaccuracies or incorrect use of the ruler may produce differences that are important to discuss.

Use the ruler to measure lengths that are longer than the ruler.

----ACTIVITY----

16.7 More than One Way

Challenge students to find different ways to measure the same length with one ruler. (Start from either end; start at a point not at the end; measure different parts of the object and add the results.)

Tape measures, especially for measuring around objects, can be made in a variety of ways using the same approach as rulers. With long units such as meters, a clothesline can be marked with a piece of masking tape or a marking pen at the end of each meter. Grosgrain ribbon is easily marked with a ballpoint pen. Even adding-machine tape can be used to make temporary tape measures.

After working with simple rulers and tapes, have students make rulers with subunits or fractional units. This should follow the use of two units for measuring as described earlier.

Much of the value of using student-made rulers can be lost if careful attention is not given to transfer of this knowledge to standard rulers. Give children a standard ruler, and discuss how it is alike and how it is different from the ones they have made. What are the units? Could you make a ruler with paper units the same as this? Could you make some cardboard units and measure the same way as with the ruler? What do the numbers mean? What are the other marks for? Where do the units begin?

MEASURING AREA

Comparison Activities

When comparing two areas, there is the added consideration of shape that causes difficulties not present in length measures. One of the purposes of early comparison activities with areas is to help students distinguish between size (or area) and shape, length, and other dimensions. A long, skinny rectangle may have less area than a triangle with shorter sides. This is an especially difficult concept for young children to understand. (Piagetian experiments with conservation of area indicate that many children 8 or 9 years old do not understand that rearranging areas into different shapes does not affect the amount of area.)

Direct comparison of two areas is nearly always impossible except when the shapes involved have some common dimension or property. For example, two rectangles with the same width can be compared directly, as can any two circles. Comparison of these shapes, however, fails to deal with the attribute of area. Instead of comparison activities for area, activities in which one area is rearranged are suggested. By cutting a shape into two parts and reassembling it in a different shape, the intent is that students will understand that the before and after shapes have the same area, even though they are different shapes. This idea is not at all obvious to children in the K–2 grade range.

----ACTIVITY----

16.8 Two-Piece Shapes

Give children a rectangle of construction paper, and have them fold and cut it on the diagonal, making two identical triangles. Next have them rearrange the triangles into different shapes, including the original rectangle. The rule is that only sides of the same length can be matched up and must be matched exactly. Have each group find

all the shapes that can be made this way, pasting the triangles on paper as a record of each shape (see Figure 16.8). Discuss the size and shape of the different results. Is one shape bigger than the rest? How is it bigger? Did one take more paper to make, or do they all have the same amount of paper? Help children conclude that although each figure is a different shape, all the figures have the same *area*. (*Size* in this context is a useful substitute for *area* with very young children, although it does not mean exactly the same thing.)

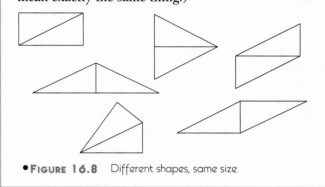

●**FIGURE 16.8**   *Different shapes, same size.*

Activity 16.8 can be extended to three or four triangles to produce even more shapes. If two each of two colors are used, it is also exciting to find all the different color patterns for each shape (Burns & Tank, 1988). Tangrams, a very old and popular set of puzzle shapes, can be used in a similar way. The standard set of seven tangram pieces is cut from a square, as shown in Figure 16.9. The two small triangles can be used to make the parallelogram, the square, and the medium triangle. Four small triangles will make the large triangle. This permits a similar discussion about the pieces having the same size (area) but different shapes (Seymour, 1971). (A Blackline Master for tangram pieces is provided at the back of this book.)

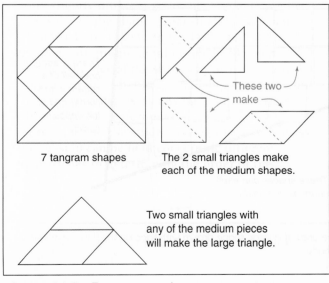

7 tangram shapes

The 2 small triangles make each of the medium shapes.

Two small triangles with any of the medium pieces will make the large triangle.

●**FIGURE 16.9**   *Tangrams provide a nice opportunity to investigate size and shape concepts.*

In the following activities, two different methods are used for comparing areas without measuring.

---ACTIVITY---

16.9 Tangram Areas

Draw the outline of several shapes made with tangram pieces, as in Figure 16.10. Let students use tangrams to decide which shapes are the same size, which are larger, and which are smaller. Shapes can be duplicated on paper, and children can work in groups. Let students explain how they came to their conclusions. There are several different approaches to this task, and it is best if students determine their own solutions rather than blindly follow your directions. You might stop here, get a set of tangrams, and make the area comparisons suggested in Figure 16.10.

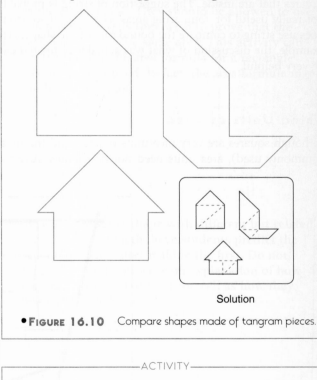

Solution

●**FIGURE 16.10**   *Compare shapes made of tangram pieces.*

---ACTIVITY---

16.10 Fill and Compare

Draw two or three shapes on a piece of paper and duplicate them. The shapes can be irregular "blobs" or more familiar shapes such as triangles, circles, or rectangles. In pairs or small groups, have students decide which of the shapes is largest and which smallest simply by observation. Then have them find a way to determine if their original estimates are correct. You can suggest methods of comparison, or you can leave the methods completely to the students' invention.

stuffed duffel bags, I estimate it would take 3000 bags. Altogether these bags would weigh over 15,000 pounds. If the duffel bags were each as big as my dad's car, they would take a space as big as the football stadium." Ideas such as this are fun to imagine but can also be tested against reality through measurement and calculations. One idea is to have class members contribute to their very own Frank book and provide an appendix that explains their estimates.

8,000 Stones (Wolkstein, 1972)

This is an interesting folktale concerning the Supreme Governor of China, who wishes to find a method of weighing an elephant that has been received as a gift. The emperor's son solves the problem by putting the elephant in a boat and noticing the water level on the side. The amount of weight to produce the same effect is that of the elephant. This is a wonderful introduction to indirect methods of measurement for middle grade students. Not only can the same weighing method be explored, but students can research other measurements and find out how they are made. For example, how do we measure temperature with a mercury thermometer, and how is it done with a bimetal thermometer, the kind that causes a dial to rotate?

REFLECTIONS ON CHAPTER 16: WRITING TO LEARN

1. Explain what it means to measure something. Does your explanation work equally well for length, area, weight, volume, and time?

2. A general instructional plan for measurement has three parts. Explain how the type of activity to use with each part accomplishes the instructional goal.

3. Five reasons were offered for using informal units instead of standard units in instructional activities. Which of these seem most important to you, and why?

4. For each of the following attributes, describe a comparison activity, one or two possible informal units, and a group activity that includes an estimation component:

  a. Length

  b. Area

  c. Volume

  d. Weight

  e. Capacity

5. With a straightedge, draw a triangle, a quadrilateral, and a five-sided figure. Make each about as large as a sheet of notebook paper. Make a waxed-paper protractor, and measure each interior angle. Did the sum of the angles for each figure come close to what is predicted?

6. What is a degree? How would you help children learn what a degree is?

7. What do students need to know about standard units? Of these, which is the most and least important?

8. Develop in a connected way the area formulas for rectangles, parallelograms, triangles, and trapezoids. Draw pictures and provide explanations.

9. Explain how the volume formula for a right rectangular prism can be developed in a completely analogous manner to the area formula for a rectangle.

10. Explain how the area of a circle can be determined using the basic formula for the area of a parallelogram. (If you have a set of fraction "pie pieces," these can be used as sectors of a circle.)

11. Describe the differences between the typical approach or sequence for teaching clock reading and the one-handed approach discussed in this chapter.

FOR DISCUSSION AND EXPLORATION

1. Make your own measuring instrument for an informal unit of measure. Select one attribute, or make one for each attribute. Use your instrument to measure with, and then make the same measurement directly with a unit model. What are some of the values and limitations of each method? Can you see the importance of having children do this both ways?

2. Frequently, the textbook chapter on measurement will cover length, area, volume, and capacity with both metric and customary units. This means a very light treatment of each. An alternative for the publisher is to focus on one area of measurement in each grade and risk not matching the curriculum guides for many states and districts. Get a teacher's edition of a basal textbook for any grade level, and look at the chapters on measurement. How well does the book cover measurement ideas, and how would you modify or expand on the lessons found there?

3. Read Chapter 10, "Foot Activities," in *A Collection of Math Lessons from Grades 3 Through 6* (Burns, 1987). Identify two good ideas in the sequence of lessons. Modify the activities to suit your own needs, and try them out with a class of children.

SUGGESTED READINGS

Highly Recommended

Nitabach, E., & Lehrer, R. (1996). Developing spatial sense through area measurement. *Teaching Children Mathematics, 2,* 473–476.

This is a superb article. The authors describe six principles of measurement, giving special attention to area measurement. They then proceed to describe some nice activities with first and second graders and the children's responses. Too often we take simple measurement ideas for granted. This article provides a research-based view of reality.

Rubenstein, R. N., Lappan, G., Phillips, E., & Fitzgerald, W. (1993). Angle sense: A valuable connector. *Arithmetic Teacher, 40,* 352–358.

This is an important article for the middle grades teacher. The authors describe a series of investigations of angles in various polygons using pattern blocks and an angle-measuring device called a *goniometer.* Among other interesting ideas is a discussion of the question "Why are there 360° in a circle?" and a graphical exposition of the interior angles of polygons that goes beyond the usual.

Wilson, P. S., & Rowland, R. E. (1993). Teaching measurement. In R. J. Jensen (Ed.), *Research ideas for the classroom: Early childhood mathematics* (pp. 171–194). Old Tappan, NJ: Macmillan.

There is an interesting, research-based idea for every teacher in this well-written review of measurement in the classroom. All areas of measurement are discussed, with clear descriptions of some of the difficulties children experience. The chapter contains great activities as well.

Other Suggestions

Clopton, E. L. (1991). Area and perimeter are independent. *Mathematics Teacher, 84,* 33–35.

Coburn, T. G., & Shulte, A. P. (1986). Estimation in measurement. In H. L. Schoen (Ed.), *Estimation and mental computation* (pp. 195–203). Reston, VA: National Council of Teachers of Mathematics.

Corwin, R. B., & Russell, S. J. (1990). *Used numbers: Real data in the classroom.* Palo Alto, CA: Dale Seymour.

Gerver, R. (1990). Discovering pi: Two approaches. *Arithmetic Teacher, 37*(8), 18–22.

Hart, K. (1984). Which comes first—length, area, or volume? *Arithmetic Teacher, 31*(9), 16–18, 26–27.

Hiebert, J. (1984). Why do some children have trouble learning measurement concepts? *Arithmetic Teacher, 31*(7), 19–24.

Kliman, M. (1993). Integrating mathematics and literature in the elementary classroom. *Arithmetic Teacher, 40,* 318–321.

Liedtke, W. W. (1990). Measurement. In J. N. Payne (Ed.), *Mathematics for the young child* (pp. 229–249). Reston, VA: National Council of Teachers of Mathematics.

Rhone, L. (1995). Measurement in a primary-grade integrated curriculum. In P. A. House (Ed.), *Connecting mathematics across the curriculum* (pp. 124–133). Reston, VA: National Council of Teachers of Mathematics.

Shaw, J. M. (1983). Student-made measuring tools. *Arithmetic Teacher, 31*(3), 12–15.

Shaw, J. M., & Cliatt, M. J. P. (1989). Developing measurement sense. In P. R. Trafton (Ed.), *New directions for elementary school mathematics* (pp. 149–155). Reston, VA: National Council of Teachers of Mathematics.

Szetela, W., & Owens, D. T. (1986). Finding the area of a circle: Use a cake pan and leave out the pi. *Arithmetic Teacher, 33*(9), 12–18.

Thompson, C. S., & Van de Walle, J. A. (1981). A single-handed approach to telling time. *Arithmetic Teacher, 28*(8), 4–9.

Thompson, C. S., & Van de Walle, J. A. (1985). Learning about rulers and measuring. *Arithmetic Teacher, 32*(8), 8–12.

Van de Walle, J. A., & Thompson, C. S. (1985). Estimate how much. *Arithmetic Teacher, 32*(9), 4–8.

Whitin, D. J. (1994). Exploring estimation through children's literature. *Arithmetic Teacher, 41,* 436–441.

Wilson, P. S. (1990). Understanding angles: Wedges to degrees. *Mathematics Teacher, 83,* 294–300.

Wilson, P. S., & Adams, V. M. (1992). A dynamic way to teach angle and angle measure. *Arithmetic Teacher, 39,* 6–13.

Wilson, P. S., & Osborne, A. (1992). Foundational ideas in teaching about measure. In T. R. Post (Ed.), *Teaching mathematics in grades K–8: Research-based methods* (2nd ed.) (pp. 89–121). Needham Heights, MA: Allyn & Bacon.

Zweng, M. J. (1986). Introducing angle measurement through estimation. In H. L. Schoen (Ed.), *Estimation and mental computation* (pp. 212–219). Reston, VA: National Council of Teachers of Mathematics.

CHAPTER 17

GEOMETRIC THINKING AND GEOMETRIC CONCEPTS

The geometry curriculum in grades K–8 should provide an opportunity to reflect on and experience shapes in as many different forms as possible. These should include shapes built with blocks, sticks, or tiles; shapes drawn on paper or with a computer; and shapes observed in art, nature, and architecture. Hands-on, reflective, and interactive experiences are at the heart of good geometry activities at the elementary and middle school levels. The geometry curriculum should aim at the development of geometric reasoning and spatial sense. The three Big Ideas parallel three levels of thinking that characterize appropriate development over the K–8 school years.

 BIG IDEAS

1. **Shapes, both two-dimensional and three-dimensional, exist in a very wide variety. There are many different ways to see and describe likenesses and differences among shapes. The more ways that one can classify and discriminate shapes, the better one understands them.**

2. **Shapes have properties that can be described, and these can be used to describe and analyze shapes. Awareness of these properties helps us appreciate shapes in our world. Properties can be explored and analyzed in a wide variety of ways.**

3. **An analysis of geometric properties leads to deductive reasoning in a geometric environment.**

THREE EXPLORATORY ACTIVITIES

It is likely that most of you have quite different ideas about geometry in the elementary school. To provide some common view of the nature of elementary and middle school geometry and how young children approach geometric concepts, three simple activities are offered here for you to do and experience. The activities will provide some idea of the spirit of informal elementary school geometry as well as background for a discussion of children's geometric thinking. All you will need is a pencil, several pieces of paper, scissors, and 15 to 20 minutes.

Different Triangles

Draw a series of at least five triangles. After the first triangle, each new one should be different in some way from those already drawn. Write down why you think each is different.

Shapes with Triangles

Make a few copies of the 2-cm isometric grid found in the Blackline Masters. As an alternative, you can simply place a sheet of paper over the grid. Draw three or four different figures by following the grid lines. Make each figure so that it has an area of 10 triangles. Count to find the distance around each figure (the perimeter), and record this next to each drawing. Examine your results for any ideas you may observe. You may want to explore any ideas you have by drawing additional figures.

A Tiling Pattern

First make at least eight copies of any shape in Figure 17.1. An easy way to do this is to fold a piece of paper so there are eight thicknesses. Trace the shape on an outside section, and cut through all eight thicknesses at once. You may want more copies of these shapes.

Think of the shapes you cut out as tiles. The task is to use the tiles to make a regular tiling pattern. A tiling pattern made with one shape has two basic properties. First, there are no holes or gaps. The tiles must fit together without overlapping and without leaving any spaces. Second, the tiles must be arranged in a repeating pattern that could be extended indefinitely. That is, if you were to tile an endless floor with your pattern, the design in one section of the floor would be the same as that found in any other section. Experiment with the paper tiles to decide on a pattern that you like. Several different tiling patterns are possible for each of the three tiles.

Notice that each of the tile shapes is made up of triangles and can be drawn on a triangle grid such as the 2-cm iso-metric grid in the Blackline Masters (used in the "Shapes with Triangles" activity) or on the isometric dot grid also found in the Blackline Masters. When you have decided on a tiling pattern, place a piece of paper over one of these two grids, and draw your tiling pattern using the grid as a guide. Cover most of the grid with your pattern.

Finally, suppose that your tiles came in two colors, and you want to add a color pattern to your tile pattern. With a pen or pencil, shade in some of the tiles to make a regular pattern in two colors.

Reflections on the Activities

Rather than discuss these three activities in detail, the following are some observations on which you might reflect. These comments are about geometry in the elementary school in general as well as reflections or observations about the activities themselves.

Different People Think About Geometric Ideas in Different Ways

Compare your response to the three exploration activities with those of your peers. Are there qualitative differences as well as objective differences? How would primary-age children's approaches to these activities compare to an eighth grader's? Figure 17.2 (p. 344) shows how two students, one in the fifth grade and one in the eighth grade, responded to the triangle task. Research indicates that age is not the major criterion for how students think geometrically. The kinds of experiences a child has may be a more significant factor. What were your grade school experiences with geometry?

Explorations Can Help Develop Relationships

The more you play around with and think about the ideas in these activities, the more there is to think about. A good teacher might be able to extend each of these activities to develop the ideas beyond the obvious. For example:

For "Different Triangles": **How many different ways can two triangles be different? Could you draw five or more** *quadrilaterals* **that were each different?**

For "Shapes with Triangles": **What did you notice about the shapes that had smaller perimeters as opposed to those with the larger perimeters? If you tried the same activity with rectangles on a square grid, what would the shapes with the largest and smallest perimeters look like? What about three-dimensional boxes? If you build different boxes with the same number of cubes, what could you say about the surface areas?**

For "A Tiling Pattern": **How many different tiling patterns are there for this shape? Can any shape be used to tile with? Can you see any larger shapes within your pattern?**

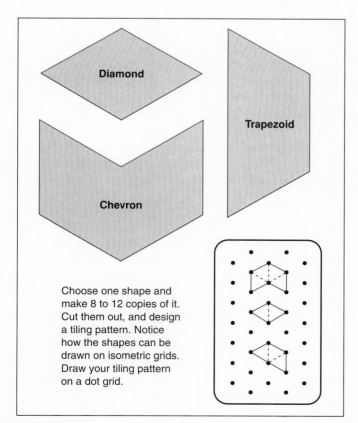

Choose one shape and make 8 to 12 copies of it. Cut them out, and design a tiling pattern. Notice how the shapes can be drawn on isometric grids. Draw your tiling pattern on a dot grid.

• **FIGURE 17.1**   *Three tile patterns.*

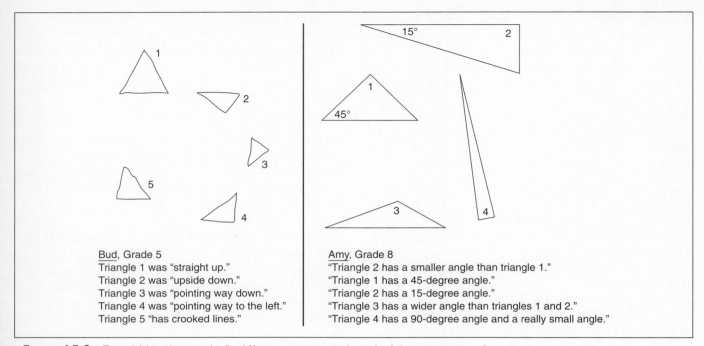

Bud, Grade 5
Triangle 1 was "straight up."
Triangle 2 was "upside down."
Triangle 3 was "pointing way down."
Triangle 4 was "pointing way to the left."
Triangle 5 "has crooked lines."

Amy, Grade 8
"Triangle 2 has a smaller angle than triangle 1."
"Triangle 1 has a 45-degree angle."
"Triangle 2 has a 15-degree angle."
"Triangle 3 has a wider angle than triangles 1 and 2."
"Triangle 4 has a 90-degree angle and a really small angle."

●**FIGURE 17.2**   Two children show markedly different responses to the task of drawing a series of different triangles.
Source: Burger & Shaughnessy (1986, pp. 38–39).

Notice that it takes more than just doing an activity to learn or create a new idea. The greatest learning occurs when you stop and reflect on what you did and begin to ask questions or make observations.

Geometry Activities Are Problem-Solving Activities

Good geometry activities almost always have a spirit of inquiry or problem solving. Many of the goals of problem solving are also the goals of geometry. Reconsider each of the three activities as examples of problem solving. Can you identify at least one problem in each that needs to be solved? In the context of those problems, consider the goals of problem solving (see Chapter 4). In particular, consider the strategy goals of problem analysis and extending or generalizing a solution and the affective goals of perseverance, willingness to try, and enjoyment of mathematics. Like all mathematics, geometry is best developed in a spirit of problem solving and in that spirit contributes to general mathematical power.

Geometry Activities and Hands-On Materials

Even the simple paper tiles used in "A Tiling Pattern" gave you the opportunity to explore spatial relationships and search for patterns much more easily than without them.

Activities on paper such as the dot grid in "Shapes with Triangles" are a second-best alternative to real physical objects. The same area and perimeter activity is much more effective with a collection of cardboard triangles that can be rearranged to form different shapes. The first activity is the least enticing of the three, but at least you could freely draw pictures. Virtually every activity that is appropriate for K–8 geometry should involve some form of hands-on materials, models, or at least paper, such as graph paper or dot paper, that lends itself to easy spatial explorations.

INFORMAL GEOMETRY

The three exploration activities are simple examples of informal geometry activities. What are some of the characteristics of these and similar activities that make them important enough for us to do with children?

What Is Informal Geometry?

Most, if not all, the geometry that is taught in grades K–8 can be referred to as *informal geometry*. This term suggests more about the general nature of geometry activities than it does about the goals or the content of the geometry curriculum. Good informal geometry activities are exploratory and hands-on.

Informal geometry activities provide children with the opportunity to explore, to feel and see, to build and take apart, to make observations about shape in the world around them as well as in the world they create with drawings and models. Activities involve constructing, measuring, visualizing, comparing, transforming, and classifying geometric figures. As we will see, the experiences and explorations can take place at different levels: from shapes and their appearances, to properties of shapes, to relationships between and among these properties. Good activities will avoid teacher telling and student memorizing.

Virtually every good activity at any level of informal geometry involves something to do with your hands. The materials may be tiles, sticks, blocks, paper with line or dot grids, computer programs, rulers, mirrors, clay—the list of materials, some very specialized and some with many different uses, is nearly endless. Activities that focus on notation or emphasize words and definitions in preference to student activity and student descriptions should be discouraged.

In addition to being exploratory and hands-on, frequently, informal geometry will involve a problem-solving or an artistic flavor. Students may figure out how to solve a puzzle, discover why shapes are alike and different, find ways to construct shapes with certain characteristics, or discover that certain combinations of properties are impossible. Many excellent geometry activities involve the construction of artwork. Color and pattern are combined with shape and form at various levels of sophistication to let students at any level see from a personal perspective a distinct connection between art and mathematics.

Regardless of the specifics, informal geometry can be just plain fun. Tedious exercises of memorizing definitions or trying to remember the correct symbol for congruence can be boring, even disheartening. In contrast, informal geometry activities should always be enjoyable for teacher and students alike.

Why Study Geometry?

Informal geometry is aimed at the development of spatial sense, "an intuitive feel for one's surroundings and objects in them" (NCTM, 1989, p. 49). This spatial sense grows and develops over the entire time children are in school. Students should have several in-depth geometric experiences every year. As you will learn in the discussion to follow, rich geometric experiences are the most important factor in the development of children's spatial thinking and reasoning.

Unfortunately, geometry frequently takes a backseat to other topics in school mathematics, and so "Why study geometry?" is a fair question. In fact, if you were to decide that you really enjoyed doing informal geometry activities with your students (some of the most fun that you can have), you may feel the need to justify your actions. The following list of reasons for studying geometry is not intended to be complete or definitive, but it is a good place to begin.

1. Geometry can provide people with a more complete appreciation of the world in which they live. Geometry can be found in the structure of the solar system, in geological formations, in rocks and crystals, in plants and flowers, even in animals. It is also a major part of our synthetic universe: Art, architecture, cars, machines, and virtually everything that humans create have an element of geometric form.

2. Geometric explorations can develop problem-solving skills. Spatial reasoning is an important form of problem solving, and problem solving is one of the major reasons for studying mathematics.

3. Geometry plays a major role in the study of other areas of mathematics. For example, fraction concepts are related to geometric part-to-whole constructs. Ratio and proportion are directly related to the geometric concept of similarity. Measurement and geometry are clearly related topics, each adding to the understanding of the other.

4. Geometry is used by many people daily in their professional and everyday lives. Scientists of all sorts, architects and artists, engineers, and land developers are just a few of the professions that use geometry regularly. In the home, geometry helps build a fence, design a dog house, plan a garden, or even decorate a living room.

5. Geometry is fun and enjoyable. While fun may not be a reason in and of itself, if geometry entices students into loving mathematics more in general, then that makes much of the effort worthwhile.

THE DEVELOPMENT OF GEOMETRIC THINKING

Until recently, the geometry curriculum in the United States has been very poorly defined. Children in the early grades learned to identify a few basic shapes. Beyond that primitive bit of knowledge, teachers have had little guidance on what is important. However, the work of two Dutch educators, Pierre van Hiele and Dina van Hiele-Geldof, is beginning to have an impact on the design of geometry instruction and curriculum.

The van Hiele Levels of Geometric Thought

The van Hieles' work began in 1959 and immediately attracted a lot of attention in what was then the Soviet Union, but for nearly two decades, it got little notice in this country (Hoffer, 1983; Hoffer & Hoffer, 1992b). Though research continues, the van Hiele theory (or some variant of it) has become the most influential formative factor in our geometry curriculum.

The most prominent feature of the model is a five-level hierarchy of ways of understanding spatial ideas. Each of the five levels is descriptive of the thinking processes that one uses in geometric contexts. The levels describe how one thinks and what types of geometric ideas one thinks about rather than how much knowledge a person has. As people progress from one level to the next, a significant characteristic difference is the object of their geometric thinking. What follows is a very brief description of the five van Hiele levels of geometric thinking.

LEVEL 0: VISUALIZATION

The objects of thought at level 0 are shapes and what they "look like."

Students recognize and name figures based on the global, visual characteristics of the figure—a gestaltlike approach to shape. Students operating at this level are able to make measurements and even talk about properties of shapes, but these properties are not explicit in their thinking. It is the appearance of the shape that defines it for the student. A square is a square "because it looks like a square." Because appearance is dominant in the student's thinking at this basic level, appearances can actually overpower properties of a shape. For example, a square that has been rotated so that all sides are at a 45° angle to the vertical may not appear to be a square for a level 0 thinker. Students at this level will sort and classify shapes based on their appearances—"I put these together because they all look sort of alike."

The products of thought at level 0 are classes or groupings of shapes that seem to be "alike."

LEVEL 1: ANALYSIS

The objects of thought at level 1 are classes of shapes rather than individual shapes.

Students at the analysis level of thinking are able to pay more attention to all shapes within a class rather than to a single shape. By focusing on a class of shapes—for example, rectangles—they are able to think about what makes a rectangle a rectangle (four sides, opposite sides parallel, opposite sides same length, four right angles, congruent diagonals, etc.). The irrelevant features (e.g., size or orientation) fade into the background. At this level, students begin to appreciate that the reason a collection of shapes goes together has something to do with properties. Ideas about an individual shape can now be generalized to all shapes that fit that class. Rather than talk about *this* rectangle, it is possible to talk about *all* rectangles. It now makes sense to describe shapes using these properties rather than the appearances of individual shapes. If a shape belongs to a particular class such as cubes, it has the corresponding properties of that class. "All cubes have six congruent faces, and each of those faces is a square." These

properties were only implicit or subsurface at level 0. Students operating at level 1 may be able to list all the properties of squares, rectangles, and parallelograms but not see that these are subclasses of one another, that all squares are rectangles and all rectangles are parallelograms. In defining a shape, level 1 thinkers are likely to list as many properties of a shape as they know.

The products of thought at level 1 are the properties of shapes.

LEVEL 2: INFORMAL DEDUCTION

The objects of thought at level 2 are the properties of shapes.

As students begin to be able to think about properties of shapes or geometric objects without the constraints of a particular object, they are able to develop relationships between and among these properties. "If all four angles are right angles, the shape must be a rectangle. If it is a square, all angles are right angles. If it is a square, it must be a rectangle." With greater ability to engage in "if-then" reasoning, shapes can be classified using only minimum characteristics. For example, four congruent sides and at least one right angle can be sufficient to define a square. Rectangles are parallelograms with a right angle. Observations go beyond properties themselves and begin to focus on logical arguments *about* the properties. Students at level 2 will be able to follow and appreciate an informal deductive argument about shapes and their properties. "Proofs" may be more intuitive than rigorously deductive. However, there is an appreciation that a logical argument is compelling. An appreciation of the axiomatic structure of a formal deductive system, however, remains under the surface.

The products of thought at level 2 are relationships among properties of geometric objects.

LEVEL 3: DEDUCTION

The objects of thought at level 3 are relationships among properties of geometric objects.

At level 3, students are able to examine more than just the properties of shapes. Their earlier thinking has produced conjectures concerning relationships among properties. Are these conjectures correct? Are they "true"? As this analysis of the informal arguments takes place, the structure of a system complete with axioms, definitions, theorems, corollaries, and postulates begins to develop and can be appreciated as the necessary means of establishing geometric truth. At this level, students begin to appreciate the need for a system of logic that rests on a minimum set of assumptions and from which other truths can be derived. The student at this level is able to work with abstract statements about geometric properties and make conclusions based more on logic than intuition. This is the level of the traditional tenth-grade geometry course. A student operating at level 3 can clearly observe that the diagonals of a rectangle bisect each other, just as a student at a lower level of thought can. However, at level 3, there is an appreciation of the need to prove this from a series of deductive arguments. The level 2 thinker, by contrast, follows the argument but fails to appreciate the need.

The products of thought at level 3 are deductive axiomatic systems for geometry.

LEVEL 4: RIGOR

The objects of thought at level 4 are deductive axiomatic systems for geometry.

At this fifth and highest level of the van Hiele hierarchy, the object of attention is now axiomatic systems themselves, not just the deductions within a system. There is an appreciation of the distinctions and relationships between different axiomatic systems. This is generally the level of a college mathematics major who is studying geometry as a branch of mathematical science.

The products of thought at level 4 are comparisons and contrasts among different axiomatic systems of geometry.

Characteristics of the Levels of Thought

You no doubt have noticed that the products at each level of thinking are the same as the objects of thought at the next level. This object-product relationship between levels of the van Hiele theory is illustrated in Figure 17.3. The objects (ideas) must be created at the previous level so that relationships among these objects can become the focus of the next level. In addition to this key concept of the van Hiele theory, four related characteristics of the levels of thought merit special attention.

1. The levels are sequential. That is, to arrive at any level above level 0, the basic level, students must move through all prior levels. To move through a level means that one has experienced geometric thinking appropriate for that level and has created in his or her own mind the types of objects or relationships that are the focus of thought at the next level. To skip a level would break the chain. This rarely occurs.

2. The levels are not age-dependent in the sense of the developmental stages of Piaget. A third grader or a high school student could be at level 0. Indeed, some students and adults remain forever at level 0, and a significant number of adults never reach level 2. But age is certainly related to the amount and types of geometric experiences that we have. Therefore, it is reasonable for all children in the K–2 range to be at level 0, as well as the majority of children in grades 3 and 4.

3. Geometric experience is the greatest single factor influencing advancement through the levels. Activities that permit children to explore, talk about, and interact with content at the next level, while increasing their experiences at their current level, have the best chance of advancing the level of thought for those children.

4. When instruction or language is at a level higher than that of the student, real learning may not occur. Students required to wrestle with ideas above their level (objects of thought that have not been constructed at the earlier level) may be forced into rote learning and achieve only temporary and superficial success. A student can, for example, memorize that all squares are rectangles without having constructed that relationship. At another level, a student may memorize a geometric proof but fail to create the steps or understand the rationale involved (Crowley, 1987; Fuys, Geddes, & Tischler, 1988).

Implications for Instruction

The van Hiele theory provides the thoughtful teacher with a framework within which to conduct geometric activities. The theory does not specify content or curriculum but can

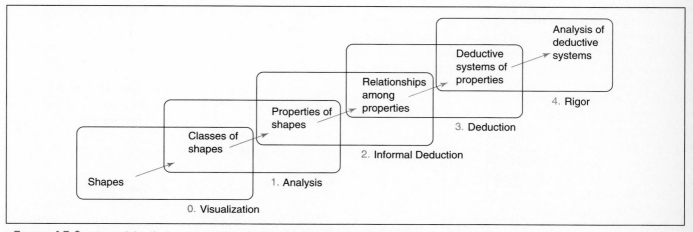

● **FIGURE 17.3** At each level of geometric thought, the ideas created become the focus or object of thought at the next level.

be applied to most activities. Most activities can be designed to begin with the assumption of a particular level and then be raised or lowered by means of the types of questioning and guidance provided by the teacher.

Instructional Goals: Content and Levels of Thought

If you examine just the bold-print portion of the K–4 and 5–8 geometry standards in the NCTM *Standards* (see Appendix A), you will find the following 16 verbs used:

describe	model	develop (an appreciation)
classify	investigate	draw
relate	apply	predict
identify	compare	visualize
represent	explore	understand
	recognize (geometry in the world)	

Only one of these, *identify*, suggests the age-old "knowing the names of the basic shapes." The *Curriculum Standards* describes an active, process-oriented view of what children should be doing and learning in geometry. The goal is much broader than a more traditional collection of facts and bits of knowledge about various geometric ideas. It is best summed up as *spatial sense*.

The van Hiele theory fits very nicely with a *Standards* view of geometry. It focuses our attention on how students think in geometric contexts and the object of their thinking: shapes → properties → informal logic → deductive principles. If the van Hiele theory is correct—and there is much evidence today to support it—then a major goal of the K–8 curriculum must be to advance students' level of geometric thought. If students are to be adequately prepared for the deductive geometry curriculum of high school, their thinking should have advanced to at least level 2. (As mentioned, level 3 is assumed in the traditional tenth-grade course.)

This is not to say that content knowledge is no longer appropriate. Spatial sense is clearly enhanced by an understanding of shapes, what they look like, and even what they are named. The concepts of symmetry, congruence, and similarity play a major role in understanding our geometric world. And the interaction with measurement that allows us to analyze angle measure and relationships between geometric entities is equally important. But these must all be seen and developed not in the context of "things to master" but rather as ways of knowing and understanding the geometric world in which we live.

Therefore, as we design geometry lessons for children, it is good to build them around identifiable content but with a view toward the thought levels of our children. Each lesson should be seen as an opportunity to challenge students to begin to think at the next level: Those at level 0 can be encouraged to consider properties of shapes; those at level 1 can be challenged to formulate and engage in informal arguments or deductions; and so on.

Teaching at the Student's Level of Thought

A developmental approach to instruction demands that we listen to children and begin where we find them. The van Hiele theory highlights the necessity of teaching at the child's level. Almost any activity can be modified to span two levels of thinking, even within the same classroom. This can be done by respecting the types of responses and observations made by children that suggest a lower level of thought while encouraging and challenging children to operate at the next level of thought. Remember that it is the type of thinking that children are required to do that makes a difference in learning, not the specific content.

The following are some suggestive features of instruction appropriate for each of the first three van Hiele levels.

LEVEL 0 ACTIVITIES SHOULD

Involve lots of sorting, identifying, and describing of various shapes.

Use lots of physical models that can be manipulated by the students.

Include many different and varied examples of shapes so that irrelevant features do not become important (many students, for example, believe that only equilateral triangles are really triangles or that squares turned 45° are no longer squares).

Provide opportunities to build, make, draw, put together, and take apart shapes.

LEVEL 1 ACTIVITIES SHOULD

Begin to focus more on properties of figures rather than on simple identification. Define, measure, observe, and change properties with the use of models.

Use problem-solving contexts in which properties of shapes are important components.

Continue to use models, as with level 0, but include models that permit the exploration of various properties of figures.

Classify figures based on properties of shapes as well as by names of shapes. For example, find different properties of triangles that make some alike and others different.

LEVEL 2 ACTIVITIES SHOULD

Continue to use models, with a focus on defining properties. Make property lists, and discuss which properties are necessary and which are sufficient conditions for a specific shape or concept.

Include language of an informal deductive nature: *all, some, none, if-then, what if,* and the like.

Investigate the converse of certain relationships for validity. For example, the converse of "If it is a square, it must have four right angles" is "If it has four right angles, it must be a square."

Use models and drawings as tools to think with, and begin to look for generalizations and counterexamples.

Encourage the making and testing of hypotheses.

Most of the content of the elementary school curriculum can be adapted to any of the three levels. An exception may be an inappropriate attention to abstract concepts such as point, line, ray, and plane as basic elements of geometric forms. These abstract ideas are not even appropriate at level 2.

Listen to your children during a geometry activity. Compare the types of comments and observations that they make with the descriptions of the first two van Hiele levels. Be sure that the activities you plan do not require that students reason above their level of thought.

The activities suggested in the remainder of this chapter have been grouped according to the first three van Hiele levels. These are just suggestions for getting started. Most activities have the potential of being addressed at slightly lower or higher levels.

The activity descriptions are generally rather brief. There are so many excellent geometry activities in the literature that this entire book could easily be filled with them. The intent here is to get you started and to illustrate the wide variety of things that can be done. Find ideas that you like, and develop them fully. Search out additional resource books to help you.

INFORMAL GEOMETRY ACTIVITIES: LEVEL 0

The emphasis at level 0 is on shape and form experiences. Though properties of figures are included, they are explored only informally. Remember that a level 0 activity does not necessarily mean a primary-grade activity. Not all students in the upper grades have had sufficient opportunity to experience ideas and develop their thinking beyond a beginning level.

Any categorization of informal geometry activities according to van Hiele levels is likely to be a bit fuzzy. You may think some activities represent level 1 better, and many can be extended easily to include that level.

Exploring Shapes and Properties

The activities here all begin with shapes already made or drawn, and students work with them in various ways. The shapes may be two- or three-dimensional. Some activities can be done either with a set of flat two-dimensional shapes or equally well with a set of solid shapes.

Sorting and Classifying Shapes

Sorting or classifying shapes using models is a good way to introduce geometric ideas. Names of shapes and properties can be provided as students begin to recognize and discuss them in their own words.

ACTIVITY

17.1 Shape Sort 1

Make collections of poster board shapes similar to those in Figure 17.4. You will want many more shapes than those shown. Have groups of children find sets of shapes that are alike in some way. If you prepare the pieces so that the ideas you want the children to learn are represented by at least four or five different examples, it is likely that students will notice that concept. When students

• **FIGURE 17.4** An assortment of shapes for sorting.

have sorted out some shapes, indicating that they recognize some idea that is common, you have an opportunity to label the concept or provide the proper name of a shape without trying to define it formally. Figure 17.5 (p. 350) suggests some concepts that can be explored in this way. Notice the use of varied examples of each idea.

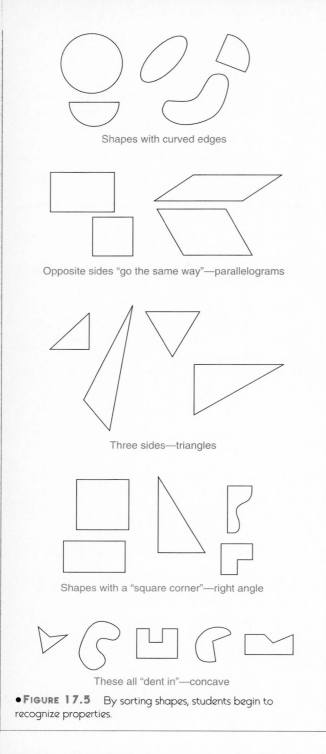

Shapes with curved edges

Opposite sides "go the same way"—parallelograms

Three sides—triangles

Shapes with a "square corner"—right angle

These all "dent in"—concave

● **FIGURE 17.5**   By sorting shapes, students begin to recognize properties.

If students omit shapes from a category they have identified or fail to create a category you had hoped they would discover, it is a clue to their perceptual thinking. Interact informally by selecting an appropriate shape, and have children discuss why they think it may be different or the same as other shapes. Avoid definitions and right or wrong answers at this level.

Shape sorts can be done with three-dimensional shapes. Wooden or plastic collections are available as one option. Another is to make some solids from tagboard or modeling clay. Real objects such as cans, boxes, balls, or Styrofoam shapes are another source of three-dimensional models. Figure 17.6 illustrates some classifications of solids.

Matching Shapes

---ACTIVITY---

17.2 Feel-It Match

Prepare two identical collections of shapes. One set is placed in view. Out of children's sight, place a shape from the other set in a box or bag. Children reach in the box, feel a shape without looking, and attempt to find the matching shape from those that are displayed. The activity can be done with either two-dimensional tagboard shapes or with solids. The shapes in the collection determine what ideas will be focused on and how difficult the activity is. For example, all shapes may have different numbers of sides or faces, or all shapes may be different but belong to one category, such as quadrilaterals, triangles, pyramids, prisms, curved surfaces, curved edges.

A variation is to have the hidden shapes be small versions of the shapes the students see. Matching a small shape with a larger one provides an informal introduction to the notion of similarity: same shape, different size.

The following matching activity is similar but can be done with the entire class and provides more opportunity for informal discussion of how shapes are alike and what their properties are.

---ACTIVITY---

17.3 What's Like This?

Display a collection of shapes (either two- or three-dimensional) for all to see. Show the class a shape that has something in common with one or more of the shapes in the collection. Students are to select the shape that is like your shape in some way and explain their choice. The target shape may be another example of a particular shape, or it may be entirely different, with only some property in common with another shape. There may be excellent choices and reasons that you did not even think about. Figure 17.7 illustrates only a few of the many possibilities for this activity.

Matching activities can also match solid shapes with copies of the faces. "Face cards" can be made by tracing around the different faces of a solid shape, as in Figure 17.8.

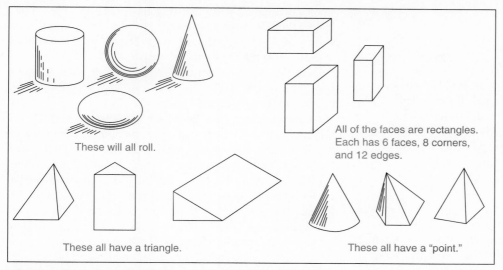

These will all roll.

All of the faces are rectangles. Each has 6 faces, 8 corners, and 12 edges.

These all have a triangle.

These all have a "point."

•**FIGURE 17.6**   Early classifications of three-dimensional shapes.

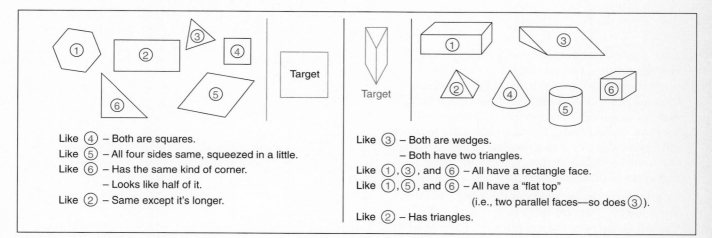

Like ④ – Both are squares.
Like ⑤ – All four sides same, squeezed in a little.
Like ⑥ – Has the same kind of corner.
     – Looks like half of it.
Like ② – Same except it's longer.

Like ③ – Both are wedges.
     – Both have two triangles.
Like ①,③, and ⑥ – All have a rectangle face.
Like ①,⑤, and ⑥ – All have a "flat top"
          (i.e., two parallel faces—so does ③).
Like ② – Has triangles.

•**FIGURE 17.7**   Playing "What's like This" involves finding a shape that's like the target. There are usually many good solutions.

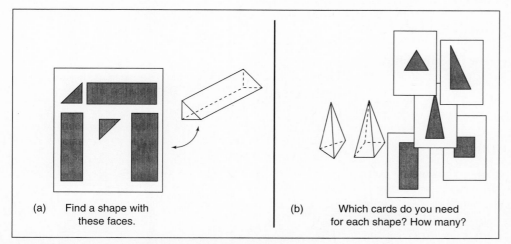

(a) Find a shape with
     these faces.

(b) Which cards do you need
     for each shape? How many?

•**FIGURE 17.8**   Matching face cards with solid shapes.

---ACTIVITY---

17.4 Face Match

Two different matching activities can be done with face cards: Given a face card, find the solid, or given a solid, find the face card. If cards are made with only one face per card, students can select from a larger collection those faces that belong with a particular shape. Another variation is to show only one face at a time as clues.

Going on a "shape hunt" is a well-worn but still worthwhile activity. Notice that an activity can be modified to accommodate different levels of thought within the same classroom by altering what is being searched for. Discussions of objects in the environment contribute to the geometric experiences of all students.

---ACTIVITY---

17.5 Shape Hunt

Have students search not just for triangles, circles, squares, and rectangles but also for properties of shapes. (What you have students look for is a way to make this either a level 0 activity or a level 1 activity.) A shape hunt will be much more successful if you let students look for either one thing or a specific list. Different groups can hunt for different things. Here are some examples of things to search for:

Parallel lines (lines "going in the same direction")
Right angles ("square corners")
Curved surfaces or curved lines
Two or more shapes that make another shape
Circles inside each other (concentric)
Shapes with "dents" (concave) or without dents (convex)
Shapes used over and over in a pattern (brick wall, chain link fence)
Solids that are somehow *like* a box, a cylinder (tube), a pyramid, a cone
Five shapes that are alike somehow (specify solid or flat)
Shapes that are symmetrical

Constructing Shapes

These activities all have children building, drawing, or constructing shapes in some other way. With a new set of materials to work with, it is good to begin by letting students freely make whatever shapes or designs they wish. This permits children to experience the new materials and to create the construction they want to. Prepared activities can then go beyond this free-play level and challenge children to build

shapes that have a particular property or feature. These challenges promote reflective thinking about the properties involved and are a good way to encourage level 1 thinking without pushing children too hard.

Several commercial materials are now available that permit fairly creative building of geometric solids (for example, 3D Geoshapes, Polydron, and D-Stix). Pattern blocks, Color Tiles, and tangrams are among the most popular sets of "tiles." In addition to commercial products, all sorts of other materials can be used to build shapes. Modeling clay is an obvious choice for solids. Plastic straws can be fastened together in different ways to make skeletal models. Special tiles such as a collection of right triangles made by cutting on the diagonal of a rectangle can be constructed from poster board. Geoboards and various grid papers (see the Blackline Masters) provide excellent methods for children to make drawings of shapes.

Using Tiles to Make Shapes

A good way to explore shapes at level 0 is to use smaller shapes or tiles to create larger shapes. Different criteria or directions can provide the intended focus for the activity. Among the best materials for this purpose are pattern

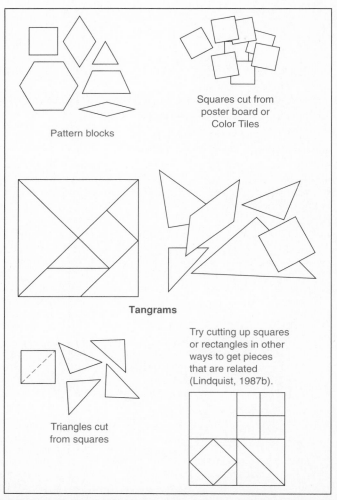

Pattern blocks

Squares cut from poster board or Color Tiles

Tangrams

Triangles cut from squares

Try cutting up squares or rectangles in other ways to get pieces that are related (Lindquist, 1987b).

● **FIGURE 17.9** Activities with tiles can involve an assortment of shapes or can be designed with just one shape.

blocks, but many teacher-made materials can be used. A variety of shapes are suggested in Figure 17.9. Class sets can be cut from poster board and placed in plastic bags for individual or group use. Some of the activities that follow can be repeated using a different set of tiles to provide not only variety but also a different perspective.

Geoboard Explorations

The geoboard is one of the best devices for drawing two-dimensional shapes. Literally hundreds of activities, task cards, and worksheets have been developed for geoboards. Here are just a few activities for a beginning level.

---ACTIVITY---

17.6 Geoboard Copy

Copy shapes, designs, and patterns from prepared cards as in Figure 17.10. Begin with designs shown with dots as on a geoboard, and later have students copy designs drawn without dots.

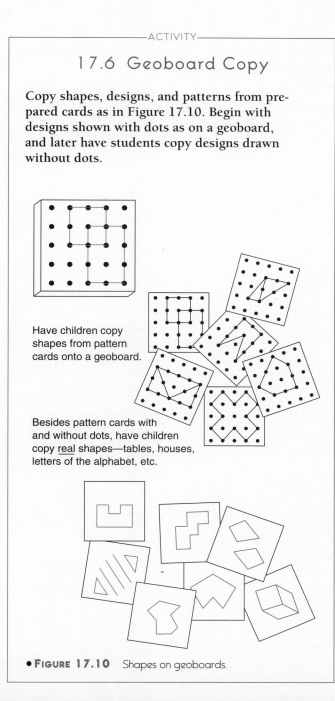

Have children copy shapes from pattern cards onto a geoboard.

Besides pattern cards with and without dots, have children copy <u>real</u> shapes—tables, houses, letters of the alphabet, etc.

● **FIGURE 17.10** Shapes on geoboards.

---ACTIVITY---

17.7 Geoboard Tiles

Challenge the students to make shapes on the geoboard using combinations of only one smaller shape as if the smaller shape were a tile (Figure 17.11). Cards with the smaller shapes can be prepared to direct the activity.

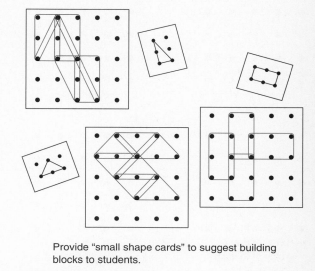

Provide "small shape cards" to suggest building blocks to students.

● **FIGURE 17.11** Bigger shapes from smaller shapes.

---ACTIVITY---

17.8 Congruent Parts

Copy a shape from a card, and have students subdivide or cut it into smaller shapes. Specify the number of smaller shapes. Also specify whether they are all to be congruent or simply of the same type as shown in Figure 17.12 (p. 354). Depending on the shapes involved, this activity can be made quite easy or relatively challenging.

---ACTIVITY---

17.9 Geoboard Challenges

Challenge students to see how many different shapes they can make of a specific type or with a particular property. (Very young children will feel more comfortable searching for three shapes or four shapes rather than "many" shapes.) Here are some appropriate ideas for level 0:

Make shapes with five sides (or some other number of sides).

Make shapes with all square corners. Can you make one with three sides? Four sides? Six, seven, eight sides?

> **Make some trapezoids that are all different (or suggest any other shape that students can identify).**
>
> **Make a shape that has a line of symmetry. Check it with a mirror.**

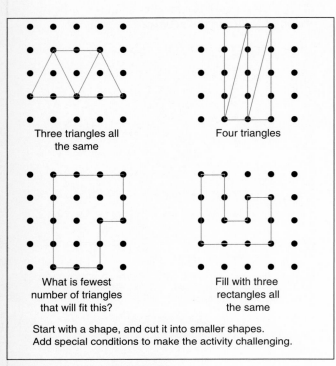

Three triangles all the same

Four triangles

What is fewest number of triangles that will fit this?

Fill with three rectangles all the same

Start with a shape, and cut it into smaller shapes. Add special conditions to make the activity challenging.

● **FIGURE 17.12** Subdividing shapes.

Two practical comments should be made about the use of geoboards. First, have lots of them available in the classroom. It is better for two or three children to have 10 or 12 boards at a station than for each to have only one. That way, a variety of shapes can be made and compared before they are changed.

This leads to the second point. Teach students from the very beginning to copy their geoboard designs onto paper. Paper copies permit students to create complete sets of drawings that fulfill a particular task. If a student wants to make a series of different six-sided shapes but has only one geoboard, the paper lets the child copy the entire series. Drawings can be placed on the bulletin board for classification and discussion, made into booklets illustrating a new idea that is being discussed, and sent home to show parents what is happening in geometry.

Younger students can use paper with a single geoboard on each sheet. At the kindergarten or first-grade level, the paper geoboard can be the same size as the real board. Later, a paper board about 10 cm square is adequate. Older children can use centimeter dot paper or a page of small boards, each about 5 cm square. (See the Blackline Masters.)

In the very early grades, children will have some difficulty copying geoboard designs onto paper, especially designs with slanted lines. To help, suggest that they first mark the dots for the corners of their shape ("Second row, end peg"). With the corners identified, it is much easier for them to draw lines to make the shape.

Dot and Grid Paper Explorations

Geoboards are excellent due to the ease with which drawings can be made and changed, but they have limitations in terms of size, arrangement, and number of pegs. Assorted dot and grid papers provide an alternative way to make drawings and explore shapes. Virtually all of the activities suggested for tiles and geoboards can also be done on dot or grid paper. Changing the type of paper changes the activity and provides new opportunity for insight and discovery. Figure 17.13 shows several possibilities for dot and grid papers, included in the Blackline Masters.

Besides the geoboard and tile activities mentioned so far, here are some additional ideas that lend themselves particularly well to dot and grid paper.

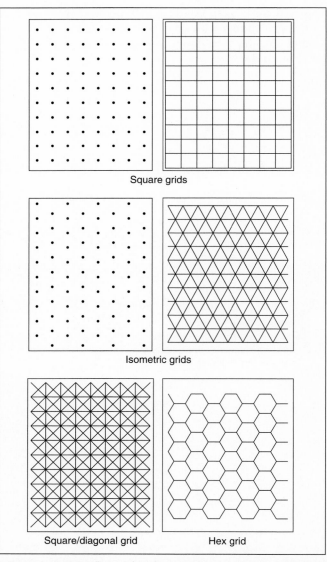

Square grids

Isometric grids

Square/diagonal grid

Hex grid

● **FIGURE 17.13** Dot and grid paper of various types and sizes can be used for many geometric explorations.

—ACTIVITY—

17.10 Three-Dimensional Drawings

Isometric dot paper is an effective way to draw solid shapes that are built with cubes. Square dot paper can be used to draw side and top views, as shown in Figure 17.14. Building a simple shape with cubes and then drawing plan and perspective views is an excellent activity for middle grade students to help with perspective. (See Winter, Lappan, Phillips, & Fitzgerald, 1986, for a series of activities.)

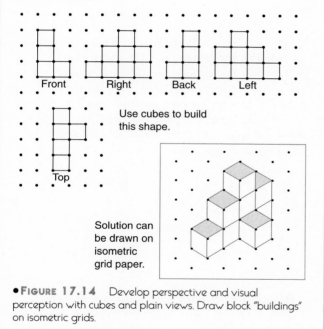

Front   Right   Back   Left

Use cubes to build this shape.

Top

Solution can be drawn on isometric grid paper.

●**FIGURE 17.14** Develop perspective and visual perception with cubes and plain views. Draw block "buildings" on isometric grids.

A slightly different idea is essentially to reverse Activity 17.10. Provide students with a perspective drawing that you have made, and have them build the structure with blocks. Drawings can be prepared on worksheets, or you can begin to develop a collection of cards to be used at workstations. Although an answer key is possible in the form of a top view with the number of cubes indicated in each square, it is best to let students work together to decide if they have made an accurate construction.

—ACTIVITY—

17.11 Slides, Flips, and Turns

Slides, flips, and turns can be investigated on any grid. Start with a simple shape. Draw the same shape flipped over, turned, or placed in a different orientation. Trace the original shape, and cut it out. This copy can be flipped or reoriented to test the drawings that are made (see Figure 17.15).

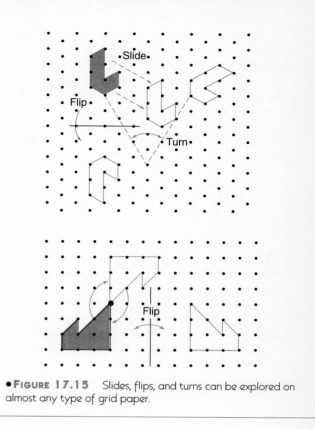

●**FIGURE 17.15** Slides, flips, and turns can be explored on almost any type of grid paper.

Building Solids

Building solid or three-dimensional shapes presents a little more difficulty than two-dimensional shapes but is perhaps even more important. Building a model of a three-dimensional shape is an informal way to get to know and understand the shape intuitively in terms of its component parts.

As noted earlier, there are several commercial plastic building sets that can be used to build a wide variety of solids. The pieces are all equilateral polygons (triangles, squares, pentagons, and hexagons) with all edges the same length. The resulting shapes are quite rigid.

Skeleton models are three-dimensional "solids" that are built using sticks of some sort. This can be done in many ways. In addition to commercial materials such as D-Stix, the following two ideas are highly recommended.

- *Plastic drinking straws with flexible joints.* Cut the straws lengthwise with scissors from the top down to the flexible joint. These slit ends can then be inserted into the uncut bottom ends of other straws, making a strong but flexible joint. Three or more straws are joined in this fashion to form two-dimensional polygons. To make skeletal solids, use tape or wire twist ties to join two polygons side to side. When more and more polygons are connected, a three-dimensional solid can be formed (Prentice, 1989).

- *Rolled newspaper rods.* Fantastic superlarge skeletons can be built using newspaper and masking tape. Roll three large sheets of newspaper on the diagonal to form a rod approximately 1 meter long. The more tightly the paper is rolled, the less likely the rod is to bend. Secure the roll at the center with a bit of tape. The ends of the rods are thin and flexible for about 6 inches where there is less paper. Connect rods by bunching this thin part together and fastening with tape. Use the tape freely, wrapping it several times around each joint. Additional rods can be joined after two or three are already taped. Structures will very soon become quite large (see Figure 17.16).

Regardless of the method used, students should first experience the rigidity of a triangle and compare it with the lack of rigidity of polygons with more than three sides. Point out that the rigidity of the triangle is used in many bridges, in the long booms of construction cranes, in gates and screen doors, and in the structural parts of many buildings. As children begin to build large skeleton structures, they will find that they need to add diagonal members to form triangles. The more triangles, the less likely their structure will collapse.

The newspaper rod method is quite exciting because the structures quickly become large. Even primary-grade students can benefit from creating free-form structures. Let students work in groups of four or five. What makes a structure rigid and ideas of balance and form are all included in such an activity. Older students can be challenged to make more well-defined shapes.

—ACTIVITY—

17.12 Unfolded Solids

Have students design and test nets for various solids. (A *net* for a solid is a flat shape that will fold up to make a solid.) If a square centimeter grid is used, parallel lines and angles can be drawn without tedious measuring (see Figure 17.17). Paper nets can be traced or pasted onto tagboard for a sturdier solid. Circular cones are easily made by cutting a sector from a circle. Experiment with different circle sizes and different sectors. Much of the value in folding up a solid from tagboard is planning what shape the faces will be and where the faces can be connected. Encourage groups to solve these problems themselves; provide only as much help as is necessary.

Plastic building sets like Polydron provide a great way to explore nets since every possible solid made with these sets can be unfolded into a flat net. A potential net is made by linking the desired faces together in a flat array on the desk. If the construction is actually a net, the shape will fold to the desired shape. There is real spatial visualization value in predicting if a given potential net will in fact create the specified shape. In a reverse manner, a shape can be unfolded to

its net. The potential challenges here are to predict in advance the shape of the net or to try to find how many different nets for a shape there are. For example, how many distinct nets are there for a simple cube? Is every arrangement of six squares a net of a cube?

Solids can also be built from blocks such as wooden cubes (1 inch or 2 cm). Plastic connecting cubes are ideal because they can be linked on any side and then turned in other orientations. The following tasks can make such activities challenging and valuable.

—ACTIVITY—

17.13 Block Boxes

In groups, have students see how many different rectangular solids can be made using just 12 cubes each. (A rectangular solid has six faces, and each face is a rectangle.) Try other numbers of cubes. When are two rectangular solids congruent (exactly the same)? How would you have to turn one solid to get it in the same orientation as another that is the same shape?

—ACTIVITY—

17.14 Building Plans

From a simple building that you have built, make a task card with five views of the building, as in Figure 17.18 (p. 358). Students use trial and error to try to build the same building from the five views. Slightly harder is to omit the top view but give the total number of cubes. This is a good exercise in spatial perception.

Geometric Problem-Solving Activities

Many excellent geometry activities are essentially spatial process problems. Content of a traditional nature may be minimal while the problem-solving value is significant. These geometric problem-solving activities are just as important as verbal problem solving and also provide opportunity for growth in geometric thinking and spatial sense.

At level 0, geometric problems involve the manipulation, drawing, and creation of shapes of all types. The tasks revolve around global features of shapes rather than any analysis of properties or relationships between classes or figures. Many activities already suggested have a problem-solving orientation. The following are additional suggestions.

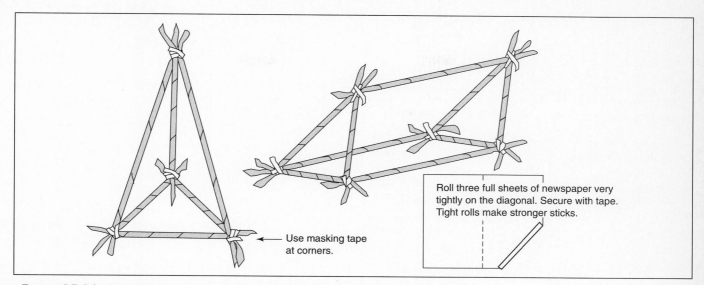

Roll three full sheets of newspaper very tightly on the diagonal. Secure with tape. Tight rolls make stronger sticks.

← Use masking tape at corners.

●**FIGURE 17.16** Large skeletal structures and special shapes can be built with tightly rolled newspaper. Young children can build free-form sculptures. Older children can be challenged to build shapes with specific properties. Overlap the ends about 6 inches to ensure strength.

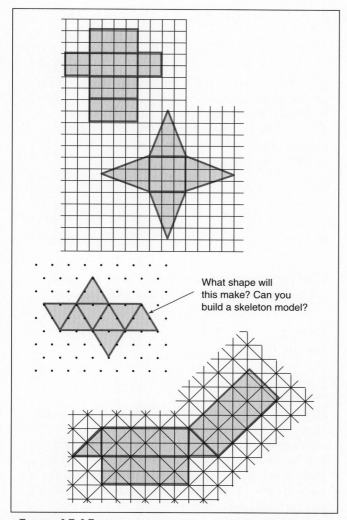

What shape will this make? Can you build a skeleton model?

●**FIGURE 17.17** Nets are easily drawn on grid paper. After making one net for a solid, try to find others that will fold up to make the same solid.

Geometric Puzzles

17.15 Tangram Puzzles

Tangrams have been popular geometric puzzles for years. Figure 17.19 (p. 359) shows tangram puzzles of different difficulties. Easy ones are appropriate even for preschool children. Several good books, including Fair (1987) and Seymour (1971), have a wide assortment of tangram puzzles.

17.16 Pentominoes

Pentominoes are the set of all shapes that can be made from five squares connected as if cut from a square grid. Each square must have at least one side in common with another square. It is an excellent geometric puzzle: Students find the complete set of 12 different pentominoes shown in Figure 17.20 (p. 359). (Do not tell students how many different shapes there are. Good discussions can come from deciding if some shapes are really different and if all shapes have in fact been found.)

Once students have decided that there are just 12 pentominoes, the 12 pieces can then be used in a variety of

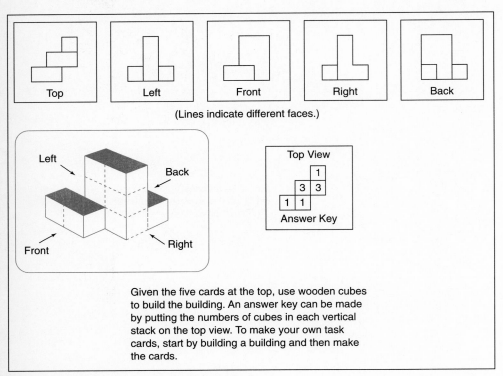

(Lines indicate different faces.)

Given the five cards at the top, use wooden cubes to build the building. An answer key can be made by putting the numbers of cubes in each vertical stack on the top view. To make your own task cards, start by building a building and then make the cards.

● **FIGURE 17.18**   Views of a simple building.

activities. Paste the grids with the children's pentominoes onto tagboard, and let them cut out the 12 shapes. These can be used in the next two activities.

---ACTIVITY---

17.17 Pentomino Puzzles

A variety of puzzles can be made from the pentominoes. Students can make puzzles to challenge their classmates by selecting four or more pieces and putting them together into a single shape. The outline of this shape is then drawn on grid paper. The challenge is to find a way to create the shape without knowing which pieces were used. The more pieces there are, the more difficult the puzzle will be. Many puzzles will have more than one solution. Much harder is to use all 12 pieces to construct a rectangle. It is possible to make a 6 × 10, 5 × 12, and 4 × 15 rectangle using the 12 pieces.

---ACTIVITY---

17.18 Pentomino Squeeze

Play "Pentomino Squeeze" on an 8 × 8 grid of squares. Pieces are dealt out randomly to two players. The player with the cross places it on the board. In turn, players place pieces on the board without overlapping any piece that is already placed. The last player to be able to play is the winner. Smaller boards can be used to make the game more difficult.

---ACTIVITY---

17.19 Hexominoes

Find out how many hexominoes there are (made with six squares). This is quite a challenge.

---ACTIVITY---

17.20 Triangle Patterns

Use six equilateral triangles to make shapes in the same way as pentominoes. An even more challenging activity is to see how many shapes can be made from five 45-degree right triangles (halves of squares). Sides that touch must be the same length. (There are 14 shapes when only four right triangles are used.)

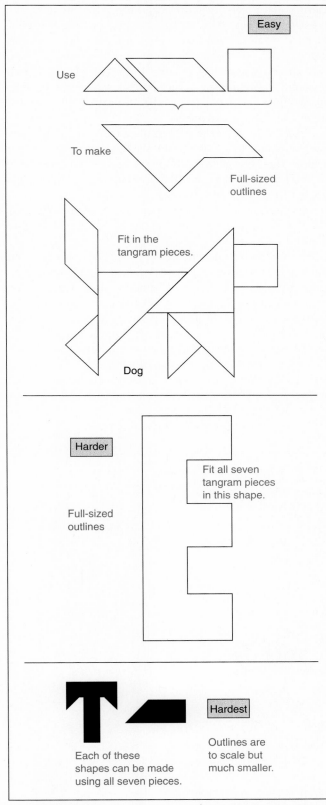

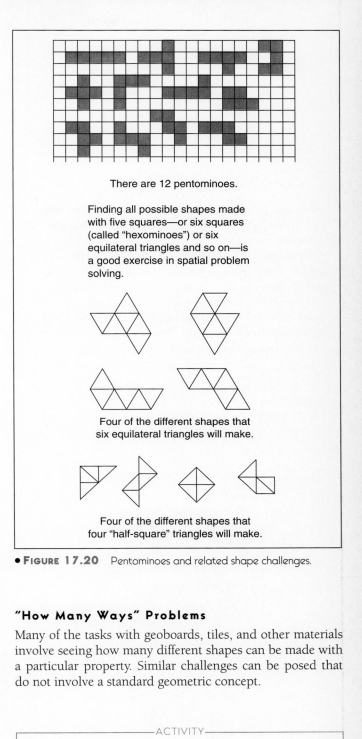

There are 12 pentominoes.

Finding all possible shapes made with five squares—or six squares (called "hexominoes") or six equilateral triangles and so on—is a good exercise in spatial problem solving.

Four of the different shapes that six equilateral triangles will make.

Four of the different shapes that four "half-square" triangles will make.

• **FIGURE 17.20** Pentominoes and related shape challenges.

● **FIGURE 17.19** Four types of tangram puzzles illustrate a range of difficulty levels.

"How Many Ways" Problems

Many of the tasks with geoboards, tiles, and other materials involve seeing how many different shapes can be made with a particular property. Similar challenges can be posed that do not involve a standard geometric concept.

---ACTIVITY---

17.21 How Many Ways on Geoboards?

On a geoboard, how many shapes can you make

a. That have no pegs inside (or exactly one peg, or two pegs)?

b. That will fit around this shape (any cardboard shape)?

c. That will touch exactly five pegs (or some other number)?

d. That can be cut into two identical parts with one line on the geoboard?

―ACTIVITY―

17.22 How Many Buildings?

How many different buildings can you make with exactly five cubes? Touching cubes must have a complete face in common. This is a three-dimensional version of pentominoes. (With plastic interlocking cubes, the number of possibilities increases. Why?) How many ways can you build a building using eight cubes if they must all touch on a whole face and no more than three cubes can be in any one row? (The numbers can be changed to change the problem.)

Tessellations

A *tessellation* is a tiling of the plane using one or more shapes in a repeated pattern with no holes or gaps. The "Tiling Pattern" activity at the beginning of the chapter was a tessellation activity. Making tessellations, or tiling patterns, is a good way for level 0 students from first grade to eighth grade to engage in geometric problem solving. Such nonanalytic interaction with geometric form also provides challenge and artistic interest. One-shape or two-shape tessellation activities can vary considerably in relative difficulty and still remain level 0 activities.

Some shapes are easier to tessellate than others, as illustrated in Figure 17.21. When the shapes can be put together in more than one pattern, both the problem-solving level and the creativity increase. Literally hundreds of shapes can be used as tiles for tessellations. Every one of the 12 pentominoes will tessellate. It is fun to create shapes on various grid papers and then test them to see if they can be used to tessellate.

Most children will benefit from using actual tiles with which to create patterns. Tiles can be cut from construction paper. Simple tiles can be cut quickly on a paper cutter. Other tiles can be traced onto construction paper and several thicknesses cut at once with scissors. Older children may be able to use various dot or line grids and plan their tessellations with pencil and paper. Spend one period with tiles or grids, letting children experiment with various tiling patterns. To plan a tessellation, use only one color so that the focus is on the spatial relationships. To complete an artistic-looking tessellation, add a color design. Use only two colors with younger children and never more than four.

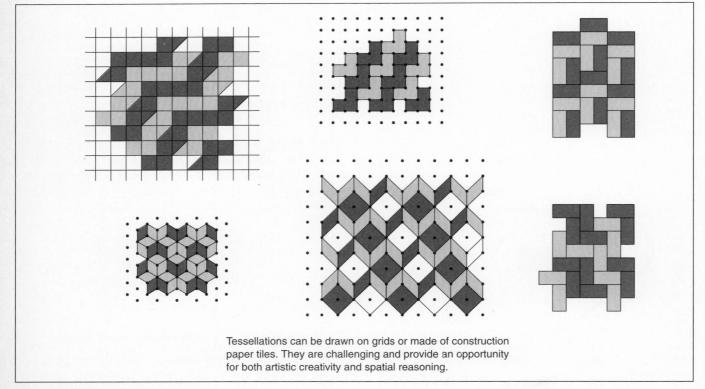

Tessellations can be drawn on grids or made of construction paper tiles. They are challenging and provide an opportunity for both artistic creativity and spatial reasoning.

● **FIGURE 17.21**   Tessellations.

Color designs should also be repeated regularly all over the tessellation.

Tessellations can be made by gluing construction paper tiles to large sheets of paper, by drawing them on dot or line grids, or by tracing around a poster board tile. Do not worry about the edges of tessellations. Work from the center out, leaving ragged edges to indicate that the pattern should go on and on.

INFORMAL GEOMETRY ACTIVITIES: LEVEL 1

The activities at level 1 begin to focus more on the properties of shapes and include some analysis of those properties. For example, at level 0, triangles might have been sorted by "big" and "little," "pointy" and "not as pointy," or even "with square corners" and "without square corners." At level 1, the same set of triangles can be sorted by the relative sizes of the angles or the relative lengths of the sides. Combinations of these categories give rise to even more relationships.

Transitions to Level 1

Most of the materials in the suggested activities are the same as those used at level 0, and many level 0 activities are easily extended to level 1. For example, consider Activity 17.6, "Geoboard Copy" (p. 353)." If students who seem to be ready for more challenging work have successfully copied a parallelogram, talk briefly about what makes that shape special. Can other shapes be made that also have sides that are parallel? Make at least five different parallelograms, and copy them onto dot paper. What is alike about all five? Now this activity has begun to focus the attention on the *class* of *all* parallelograms and the properties of that class.

It is quite reasonable to have several similar but related investigations proceeding in the same classroom, with different groups pursuing tasks at different van Hiele levels.

Classifying Shapes by Properties

Sorting activities are grouped here in a manner similar to that used for level 0 activities. To promote the kind of thinking that is appropriate for level 1, shapes are presented so that specific properties and categorizations are clearly evident. For example, the shapes used might be quadrilaterals or even a collection of two or three types of quadrilaterals. In other words, the children are looking at a class of shapes and producing the ideas that make the class special—properties of the class and all potential members.

You may have to be more direct in pointing out particular properties or categories that students do not notice. When a classification of shapes has been made and discussed and is well understood, the appropriate name for the classification can be supplied.

Special Categories of Two-Dimensional Shapes

Listed in the following table are some important categorizations (or definitions) of two-dimensional shapes. Examples of these shapes can be found in Figure 17.22 (p. 362).

SHAPE	DESCRIPTION
Simple Closed Curves	
Concave, Convex	An intuitive definition of concave might be "having a dent in it." If a simple closed curve is not concave, it is convex. A more precise definition of concave may be interesting to explore with older students.
Symmetrical, nonsymmetrical	Shapes may have one or more lines of symmetry and may or may not have rotational symmetry. These concepts will require more detailed investigation, as discussed later.
Polygons concave, convex symmetrical, nonsymmetrical	Simple closed curves with all straight sides
Regular polygon	All sides and all angles congruent
Triangles	
Triangles *–classified by sides*	Polygons with exactly three sides
Equilateral	All Sides congruent
Isosceles	Only two sides congruent
Scalene	No two sides congruent
–classified by angles	
Right	Has a right angle
Acute	All angles smaller than a right angle
Obtuse	One angle larger than a right angle
Convex Quadrilaterals	
Convex Quadrilaterals	Convex polygons with exactly four sides
Kite	Two opposing pairs of congruent adjacent sides
Trapezoid Isosceles Trapezoid	At least one pair of parallel sides A pair of opposite sides congruent
Parallelogram Rectangle Rhombus Square	Two pairs of parallel sides Parallelogram with a right angle Parallelogram with all sides congruent Parallelogram with a right angle and all sides congruent

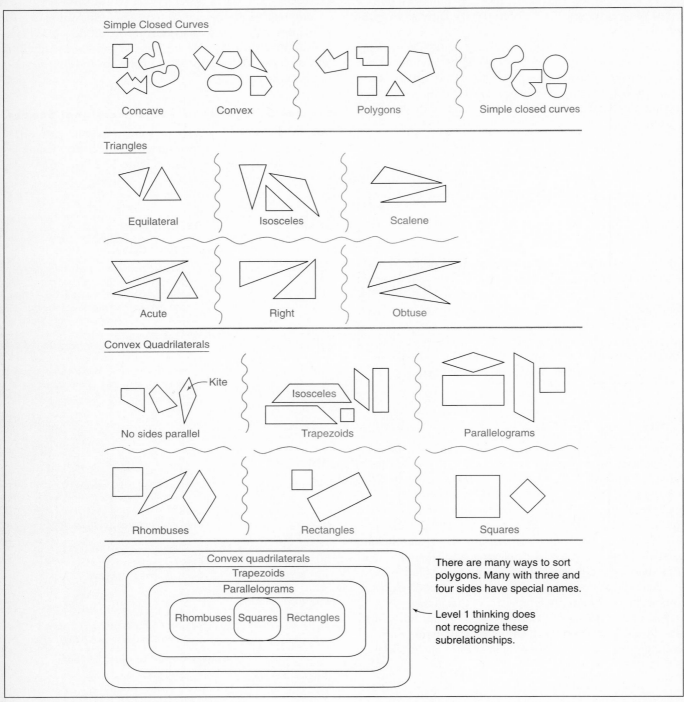

● **FIGURE 17.22** Classification of polygons.

In the classification of quadrilaterals and parallelograms, the subsets are not all disjoint. For example, a square is a rectangle that is a rhombus. All parallelograms are trapezoids, but not all trapezoids are parallelograms.* Children at level 1 have difficulty seeing this type of subrelationship. They may quite correctly list all the properties of a square, a rhombus, and a rectangle and still identify a square as a "nonrhombus" or a "nonrectangle." Is it wrong for students to refer to subgroups as disjoint sets? By fourth or fifth grade, it is only wrong to promote or encourage such thinking. Burger (1985) points out that upper elementary stu-

---

*Some definitions of trapezoid specify *only one* pair of parallel sides, in which case parallelograms would not be trapezoids.

dents correctly use such classification schemes in other contexts. For example, individual students in a class can belong to more than one club. A square is an example of a quadrilateral that belongs to two other clubs.

Several specific approaches to sorting activities can help students grow in their understanding of how shapes are related to one another.

ACTIVITY

17.23 Shape Sort II

Sort shapes by naming properties and not by names of the shapes. When two or more properties are combined, sort by one property at a time. "Find all of the shapes that have opposite sides parallel." (Find these.) "Now find those that also have a right angle." (This group should include squares as well as nonsquare rectangles.) After sorting, discuss what the name of the shapes is. Also try sorting by the same combinations of properties but in a different order.

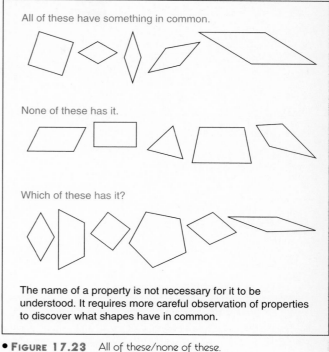

All of these have something in common.

None of these has it.

Which of these has it?

The name of a property is not necessary for it to be understood. It requires more careful observation of properties to discover what shapes have in common.

● **FIGURE 17.23** *All of these/none of these.*

Use loops of string to keep track of shapes as you sort them. Lay two loops out on a flat surface. Have students put all of the shapes with four congruent sides in one loop and those with a right angle in the other. Where do squares go? Let them wrestle with this dilemma until they realize that the two loops must be overlapped, with the squares placed in the overlapping region.

ACTIVITY

17.24 Mystery Definition

Use an "all of these, none of these" type of activity as in Figure 17.23.

Special Categories of Three-Dimensional Shapes

There are a wide variety of important and interesting shapes and relationships in three dimensions. Some classifications of solids are given here. At least an example or two of each of these can be made with clay or with tagboard. Other suggestions for making solids are given later.

All Solids. Three-dimensional figures can be sorted in a variety of ways without resorting to those classes with special names.

Sorted by edges and vertices (corners). No edges and no vertices, edges but no vertices, edges and vertices. Students can find real-world examples and use clay to make unusual examples.

Sorted by faces and surfaces. (A face is a flat surface of a solid.) Solids can be sorted by various combinations of faces and curved surfaces. Some have all faces, all curved surfaces, some of each, with and without edges, with and without vertices.

Sorted by parallel faces. Find, sort, or make solids with one or more pairs of parallel faces. Since faces are two-dimensional, students can refer to the shapes of the faces—for example, solids with two square faces that are parallel and two pairs of rectangle faces that are parallel.

Cylinders. Examples of cylinders are shown in Figure 17.24. Two properties separate cylinders from other solids. First, cylinders have two congruent faces called *bases*. The bases are in parallel planes. Second, all lines joining corresponding points on the bases are parallel. These parallel lines are called *elements*. In verbal form, this description is quite difficult. Models are very useful for discussion.

Right cylinders and oblique cylinders. In a right cylinder, the elements are perpendicular to the bases.

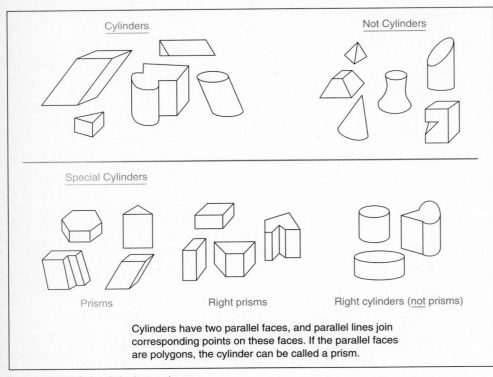

Cylinders have two parallel faces, and parallel lines join corresponding points on these faces. If the parallel faces are polygons, the cylinder can be called a prism.

● **FIGURE 17.24** Cylinders and prisms.

Prisms. If the two bases of a cylinder are polygons, the cylinder is a prism. If the bases are rectangles, the prism is called a *rectangular prism* or *rectangular solid.*

Cubes. A cube is a square prism with square sides. A cube is the only possible solid with all square faces.

Cones. A *cone* is a solid with at least one face, called the *base,* and a vertex that is not on the face. It is possible to draw a straight line (*element*) from any point on the edge of the base to the vertex.

Sorted by the shape of the base. If the base is a circle, the cone is a circular cone, which is the type most people associate with the word *cone.* But the base can be any shape and the figure is still a cone, as shown in Figure 17.25.

Pyramids. A *pyramid* is a special cone in which the base is a polygon. All of the faces of a pyramid are triangles except, possibly, the base.

It is interesting to note that both cylinders and cones contain straight lines called *elements.* A special type of both cylinders and cones occurs when the base is a polygon: A *prism* is a cylinder with polygon bases; a *pyramid* is a cone with a polygon base.

Constructing and Measuring Shapes

Constructing shapes in both two and three dimensions is still one of the most profitable activities that can be done in geometry. As children begin to demonstrate level 1 thinking, the tasks for construction activities can be posed in terms of the properties of shapes rather than their appearance.

In addition to geometric properties, measurements of shapes can help students recognize even more relationships. Area, perimeter, surface area, volume, angle, radius, and circumference are examples of things that can be measured on various shapes. For example, students can measure interior angles of various polygons and discover that when the number of sides of two polygons is the same, so is the sum of the measures of the interior angles. Direct comparisons, informal units, and simple student-made measuring devices are sufficient for exploring almost all interesting relationships involving measures. Do not let sophisticated measurements interfere with the activities.

Two-Dimensional Constructions

Tiles, geoboards, and dot and grid paper continue to be the best construction materials for two-dimensional shapes.

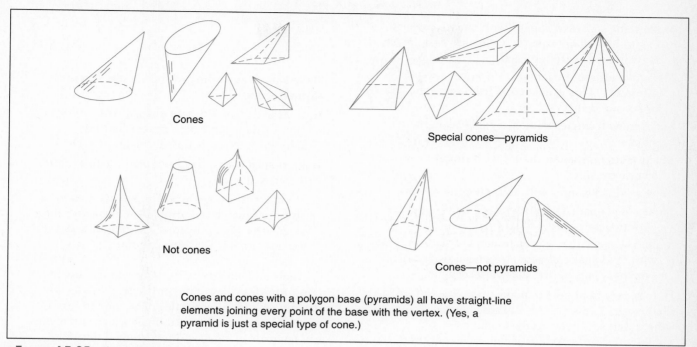

Cones

Special cones—pyramids

Not cones

Cones—not pyramids

Cones and cones with a polygon base (pyramids) all have straight-line elements joining every point of the base with the vertex. (Yes, a pyramid is just a special type of cone.)

● **FIGURE 17.25** Cones and pyramids.

However, in the first activity here (adapted from the 5–8 section of the NCTM *Standards*), ordinary flat toothpicks are used to draw lines.

————ACTIVITY————

17.25 Toothpick Triangles

Provide children with a supply of toothpicks. They are to arrange the toothpicks in straight lines to make triangles. Begin with three picks, then move to four, then five, and so on. For each number of picks, the children first decide if any triangle is possible. If so, they sketch it (showing each pick) and then see if there are other possible triangles that can be made with the same number of picks. For example, only one triangle is possible with three picks, none are possible with four picks, and two different triangles can be made with seven picks.

"Toothpick Triangles" is a good example of an opportunity to extend the reasoning to level 2. If students are asked

to explain why certain triangles are impossible ("Why is only one triangle possible with eight picks?"), students may get beyond just looking at properties of triangles and begin to do some informal reasoning. The sum of any two sides of a triangle must be greater than the third side. (Why?)

————ACTIVITY————

17.26 Property Challenge

This activity can be done with almost any materials that allow students to draw or construct shapes easily. Give students properties or relationships, and have them construct as many shapes as possible that have those properties or exhibit those relationships. Compare shapes made by different groups. Here are some examples:

Make a four-sided shape with two opposite sides the same length but not parallel.

Make some six-sided shapes. Make some with one, two, and then three pairs of parallel sides and some with no parallel sides.

Make shapes with all square corners. Can you make one with three sides? Four sides? Five sides? Six, seven, or eight sides?

Make some six-sided shapes with square corners. Count how many squares are inside each. What is the distance around each?

Make five different triangles. How are they different? (This is also good for four-, five-, or six-sided shapes.)

Make some triangles with two equal (congruent) sides.

Make some four-sided shapes with three congruent sides.

Try five-sided shapes with four congruent sides.

Make some quadrilaterals with all sides equal (or with two pairs of equal sides).

Make a shape with one or more lines of symmetry or with rotational symmetry. (A longer discussion of symmetry is provided later in the chapter.)

It is easy (and fun) to make up property challenges. Explore some of these, and make up others that suit your needs. One idea is to use combinations of previously explored concepts.

Can you make a triangle with two right angles?

Can you make a rhombus that has a right angle? A parallelogram with only two equal sides?

Make a chart like the one shown here:

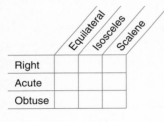

Challenge children to draw or construct triangles that fit into each of the nine cells. Of the nine, two are impossible. (Can you tell which ones?)

Combination challenges can also include the notions of perpendicular, angle measurement, area, perimeter, similarity, concave and convex, regularity, and symmetry, to name just a few. Using the materials that your students will use, prepare a series of combination challenges. Also encourage your students to come up with some of their own. Notice that some of the challenges in Activity 17.26 are not possible. Discovering that some combination of relationships is not possible and why is just as valuable as learning the relationships themselves.

17.27 Measure Investigation

Make shapes according to special measurement requirements.

Make at least five different shapes with an area of _____ (approximate number for your materials). What is the perimeter of each?

Make shapes with a fixed perimeter, and examine the area of each.

Try to make the shape with the largest area for a given perimeter or the smallest perimeter for a given area. (For polygons, the largest area for a fixed perimeter is always regular. Try it.)

Angle and side specifications provide lots of opportunities to examine properties. Angles can usually be kept to multiples of 30 and 45, or informal units can be used. Length measurements can be made using grid dimensions if diagonal segments are avoided.

Make several different triangles that all have one angle the same. Next make some different triangles with two angles the same (for example, 30 and 45 degrees). What do you notice?

Can you make a parallelogram with a 60-degree angle? Make several. Are they all alike? How? How are they different?

Make some parallelograms with a side of 5 and a side of 10. Are they all the same?

Draw some polygons with 4, 5, 6, 7, and 8 sides. Divide them all up into triangles, but do not let any lines cross or triangles overlap. What do you discover? Measure the angles inside each polygon.

Draw an assortment of rectangles, and draw the diagonals in each. Measure the angles that the diagonals make with each other. Measure each part of each diagonal. What do you observe? Try this exercise with squares, rhombuses, other parallelograms, and kites (quadrilaterals with two pairs of adjacent sides congruent).

Three-Dimensional Constructions

Shapes are so difficult to visualize in drawings that the only way to experience some of the truly interesting relationships in three dimensions is to build models. The following activities suggest different ways to construct solids and potential explorations to go with the constructions.

─────────ACTIVITY─────────

17.28 String Cylinders and Cones

An easily made model for exploring cylinders and cones (and prisms and pyramids) is a string model with poster board bases. Students can help you make your initial collection of models, and soon you will have a wide assortment. Directions are in Figure 17.26. When both bases are held together, the vertex can be adjusted up, down, or sideways to produce a family of cones or pyramids with the same base (see Figure 17.27, p. 368). By moving one base up to the knot and adjusting the other base, you can model a family of cylinders or prisms. The bases can also be tilted (not kept parallel) and/or twisted so that noncylindrical shapes are formed. Be sure that students notice that for cylinders and prisms, the elements (strings) remain parallel regardless of the position of the bases. The angle that each makes with the base is the same for all elements. For cones and pyramids, examine how the angles change relative to each other as the vertex is moved. String models like these are well worth the small cost and effort simply for the opportunity to explore how these related solids change as the bases or vertices are moved.

─────────ACTIVITY─────────

17.29 Clay Shapes and Slices

Modeling clay is useful for making almost any shape. Use an oil-based craft clay that will not dry out. Perhaps the best reason to go to this trouble is that clay models can be sliced to investigate the resulting faces on the slices. An inexpensive tool called a *piano wire,* a wire with two handles, is used to cut the clay. This works much better than a knife and can be purchased at an art supply store. Have students make cubes, cones, prisms, cylinders, a torus (doughnut shape), and other

shapes. Precision is not important as long as the essential features are there. There are two types of challenges. First, suggest where to make a slice, and see if students can predict what the face of the slice will be. Second, given a solid, ask students to find a way to slice the shape to produce a slice face with a particular shape. For example, how could you slice a cube so that the slice face is a trapezoid? Will it be isosceles? Always? Figure 17.28 (p. 368) suggests a few ways that different solids can be cut. (Carroll, 1988)

Materials: Soft cotton string or embroidery yarn, metal washers about $\frac{3}{4}$ inch in diameter (about 15 per model), poster board, hole punch

Directions

1. Cut two identical models of the base from poster board. There are no restrictions on the shape. The size should be roughly 4 to 6 inches across.

2. Place the two bases together, and punch an <u>even number</u> of holes around the edges, punching both pieces at the same time so that the holes line up. The holes should be about 1 cm apart.

3. Cut pieces of string about 5 inches long. You will need half as many pieces as holes.

4. Run each piece of string through a washer, and thread the two ends up through two adjacent holes of both bases. Pull all the ends together directly above the base, and tie in a knot.

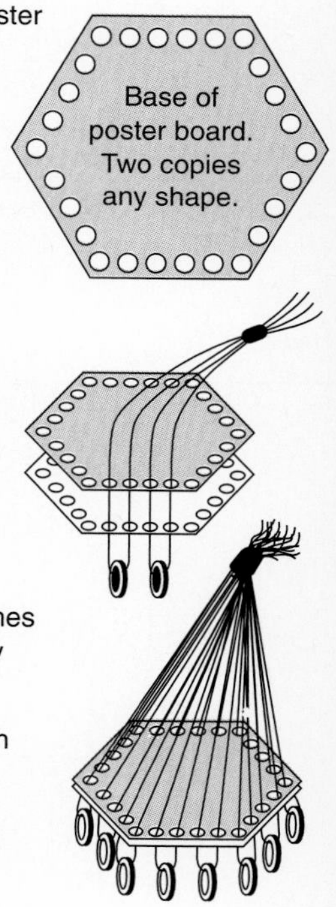

Base of poster board. Two copies any shape.

●**FIGURE 17.26** *A model for cylinders and cones.*

Using cubes to build shapes was a suggestion for level 0. At level 1, it is interesting to examine rectangular prisms (box shapes) using cubes because surface area and volume

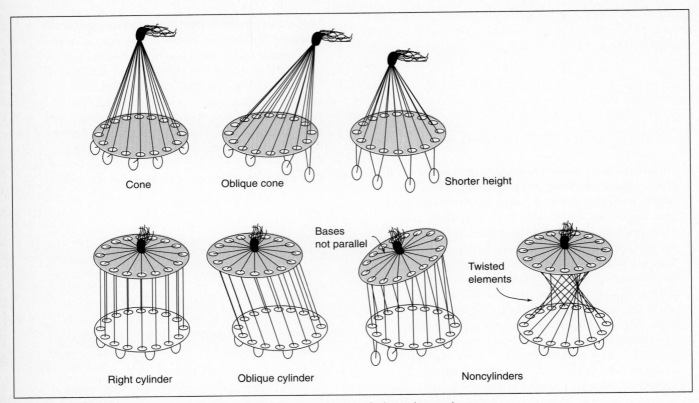

Cone

Oblique cone

Shorter height

Right cylinder

Oblique cylinder

Bases not parallel

Twisted elements

Noncylinders

• **FIGURE 17.27** The string cone or cylinder model illustrates a variety of relationships and can even show solids that are noncylinders.

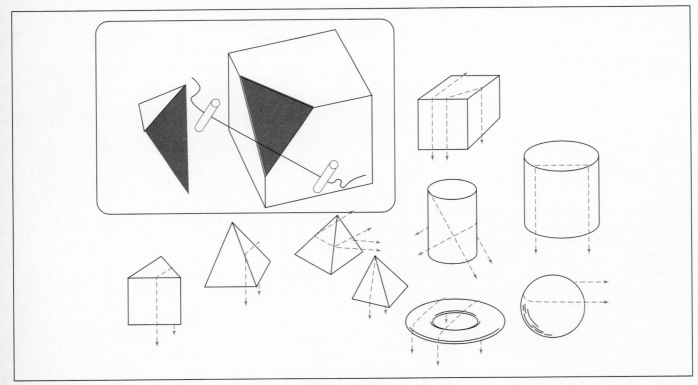

• **FIGURE 17.28** Predict the slice face before you cut a clay model with a piano wire.

are so easily determined. Tasks involving surface area and volume are analogous to tasks in two dimensions that involve perimeter and area.

---ACTIVITY---

17.30 Generating Solids

Students can "generate" imaginary solids by sliding or revolving a plane surface, as shown in Figure 17.29. The resulting shapes can be made with clay. Notice that all cylinders can be generated by sliding a base. Of all cones, only a right circular cone can be spun from a right triangle, but many other shapes can be made by spinning a shape about an edge. Why can't an oblique cone or a noncircular cone be made by spinning? Is there any way to generate these cones? How would you generate a torus or other shapes with holes in them? What shapes around the room could be generated by rotating or sliding a surface? Which ones cannot? How are the shapes that can be generated in this manner

different from those that cannot? From one triangle or rectangle, how many different shapes can be generated by sliding? How many by rotation? Are the answers the same for all triangles? All rectangles?

---ACTIVITY---

17.31 Surface and Volume Inquiry

Working with 36 cubes, have students figure out how many boxes (rectangular prisms) they can make that use all 36 cubes. For each, they should list the dimensions and the total surface area. What can you say about boxes with larger surface areas? Smaller surface areas? Try 60 cubes and then 64 cubes. (Good numbers to use will have several factorizations into three factors.) Later, reverse the problem. Have students construct boxes that have a given surface area. Can boxes with the same surface area have different volumes? Try surface areas of 24, 54, or 96 squares.

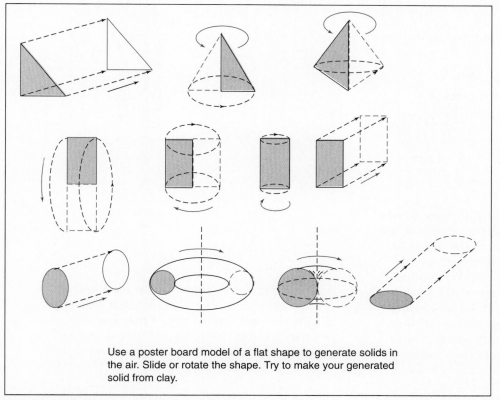

Use a poster board model of a flat shape to generate solids in the air. Slide or rotate the shape. Try to make your generated solid from clay.

● **FIGURE 17.29** *Generating imaginary solids.*

One general conclusion from the "Surface and Volume Inquiry" activity is that boxes that are the closest to cubical will have the smallest surface areas. (Recall that rectangles with the smallest perimeters were squares.) If the experiment could be carried out for boxes with more and more sides, you would see that shapes with the most volume and least surface area tend to get closer and closer to the shape of a sphere. (A cube is sort of a six-sided "sphere.") This, then, explains why soap bubbles are spherical. The volume of air is fixed (trapped inside), and the soap film tends to contract. When the surface is minimal for the amount of air, the bubble is a sphere.

Exploring Special Properties and Relationships

Some geometric properties of shape are worthy of special attention. Here you will recognize some of the more traditional content of geometry. The activities are generally adaptable to several levels of thought in the van Hiele scheme. Since the activities are designed to investigate properties, they are suitable for level 1 thinking. Students still at level 0 will be able to work at the activities but may not arrive at general principles or be able to recognize the same ideas when they appear in different contexts. Those at or ready for level 2 thinking can be challenged to see how properties are related or what conditions give rise to particular properties.

Line Symmetry

Line symmetry (bilateral or mirror symmetry) is fun and challenging to explore using a variety of materials.

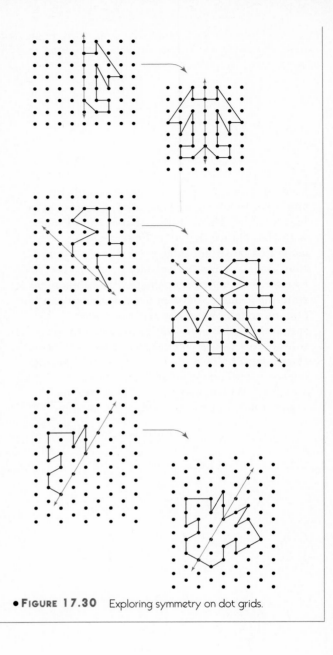

● **FIGURE 17.30** Exploring symmetry on dot grids.

---ACTIVITY---

17.32 Symmetry on a Grid

On a geoboard or on any dot or grid paper, draw a line to be a mirror line. Next draw a shape on one side that touches the line, as in Figure 17.30. Try to draw the mirror or symmetric image of the shape on the other side of the line. Try starting with two intersecting lines of symmetry. Draw the beginning shape between two of the rays formed by these lines. Reflect the shape across each line, a step at a time, until further reflections produce no new lines on your drawing. Mirrors can be used to test the results.

---ACTIVITY---

17.33 Line Symmetry Analysis

On a piece of dot paper, use the technique of Activity 17.32 to create a symmetric drawing. Fold the paper on the mirror line, and notice how corresponding points on each side of the line match up. Open the paper, and connect several corresponding points with a straight line. Notice

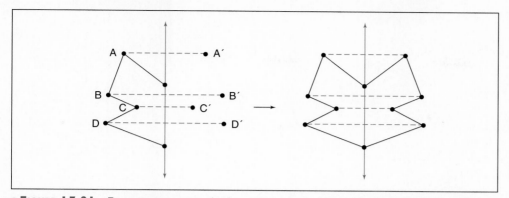

● **Figure 17.31**   From points on one side, draw perpendicular lines to the mirror line and extend them an equal distance beyond.

that the mirror line is a perpendicular bisector of the lines joining the points. Use this property to create a symmetric drawing on plane paper. Draw the line and half of the figure as before. From several critical points, draw perpendicular lines to the mirror line and extend them an equal distance beyond (see Figure 17.31).

A *flip* or *reflection* of a shape through a line is very similar to the concept of symmetry. If you plan to investigate transformations (slides, flips, and turns), the last two activities are good beginnings.

A very useful device for studying symmetry and transformations is the Mira, a piece of red Plexiglas (see Figure 17.32), that stands perpendicular to the table surface. The Mira is essentially a see-through mirror. You can reach behind the Mira and draw the image that you see in the mirror. Since you can see the image behind the Mira as well as the reflected image, it is possible to match images with reflections and draw the mirror line at the base of the Mira. This feature of the Mira allows one to draw perpendicular bisectors and angle bisectors, reflect images, and make a variety of constructions more easily than with a compass and straightedge and in a very conceptual manner.

The following activity offers a slightly different view of symmetry and provides a good preparation for rotational symmetry.

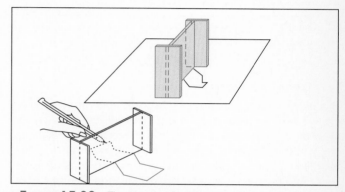

● **Figure 17.32**   The Mira is a "see-through mirror" that allows you to draw the image that you see in the glass.

─────ACTIVITY─────

17.34 Flip into the Box

Cut out a small rectangle from paper or cardboard. Color one side and label the corners A, B, C, and D so that they have the same label on both sides. Place the rectangle on a sheet of paper, and trace around it. Refer to the traced rectangle as a "box" for the cutout rectangle. The question is, "How many different ways can you flip the rectangle over so that it fits in the box?" Before each flip, place the rectangle in the box in the initial orientation. As shown in Figure 17.33, each flip into the box is a flip through a line, and these lines are also lines of symmetry. Students can discover that for a plane shape, there are as many lines of symmetry as there are ways to flip a figure over and still have it fit into its box. Try with other figures: square, nonsquare rhombus, kite, parallelogram with unequal sides and angles, triangles, regular pentagons, and others.

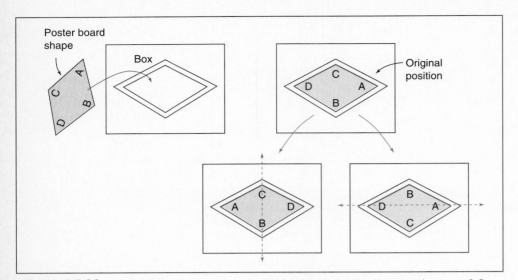

● **FIGURE 17.33**   There are at least two ways to flip this diamond into its box. Are there more? Cut one out and try it!

Rotational Symmetry

One of the easiest introductions to rotational symmetry is to create a box for a shape by tracing around it, as in Activity 17.34 (p. 371). If a shape will fit into its box in more than one way without flipping it over, it has *rotational symmetry*. The *order of rotational symmetry* is the number of different ways it can fit into the box. Thus a square has rotational symmetry of order 4, as well as four flip lines or lines of symmetry. A parallelogram with unequal sides and angles has rotational symmetry of order 2 but no lines of symmetry (see Figure 17.34).

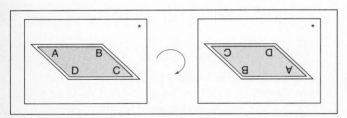

● **FIGURE 17.34**   This parallelogram fits in its box two ways without flipping it over. Therefore, it has rotational symmetry of order 2.

── ACTIVITY ──

17.35 Building "Rotatable" Shapes

Use tiles, geoboards, or dot or grid paper to draw a shape that has rotational symmetry of a given order. Except for regular polygons, this can be quite challenging. To test a result, trace around it, and cut out a copy of the shape. Try to rotate it on the drawing.

Symmetries in Three-Dimensional Figures

A plane of symmetry in three dimensions is analogous to a line of symmetry in two dimensions. Each point in a symmetric solid corresponds to a point on the other side. The plane of symmetry is the perpendicular bisector of the line segments joining each pair of points. Figure 17.35 illustrates a shape built with cubes that has a plane of symmetry.

── ACTIVITY ──

17.36 Plane Symmetry Buildings

With cubes, build a building that has a plane of symmetry. If the plane of symmetry goes between cubes, the shape can be sliced by separating the building into two symmetrical parts. Try making buildings with two or more planes of symmetry. Examine various prisms that you can build. Do not forget that a plane can slice diagonally through the blocks. Try using clay to build solids with planes of symmetry, and slice through these planes with a piano wire.

Rotational symmetry in the plane also has an analogous counterpart in three dimensions. Whereas a figure in a plane is rotated about a point, a three-dimensional figure is rotated about a line. Such a line is called an *axis of symmetry*. As a solid with rotational symmetry revolves around an axis of symmetry, it will occupy the same position in space (its box), but in different orientations. Whereas plane figures have only one center of rotation, a solid can have more than one axis of

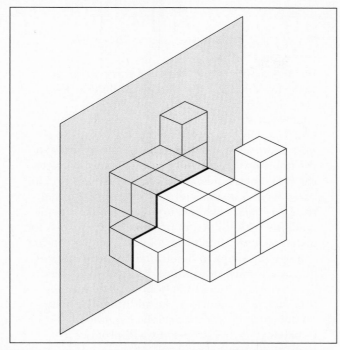

•**FIGURE 17.35**   A block building with one plane of symmetry.

axes of symmetry: three (through opposite faces) of order 4, four (through diagonally opposite vertices) of order 3, and six (through midpoints of diagonally opposite edges) of order 2.

—ACTIVITY—

17.37 Spinning on an Axis

To investigate an axis of symmetry, use a small tagboard model of the solid, and insert a long pin or wire through an axis of symmetry. Color or label each face of the solid to help keep track of the different positions. Hold the axis (pin) vertically, and rotate the solid slowly, observing how many times it fills the same space as it did in the original position, as shown in Figure 17.36. (Bruni, 1977)

---

rotation. For each axis of symmetry, there is a corresponding order of rotational symmetry. A regular square pyramid has only one axis of symmetry that runs through the vertex and the center of the square. A cube, by contrast, has a total of 13

Diagonals of Quadrilaterals

The usual approach to quadrilaterals is in terms of the sides (parallel or not, congruent or not) and angles. Another way to analyze quadrilaterals is in terms of the diagonals. The diagonals of quadrilaterals provide a wealth of interesting relationships to observe. Consider the following relationships for diagonals of quadrilaterals:

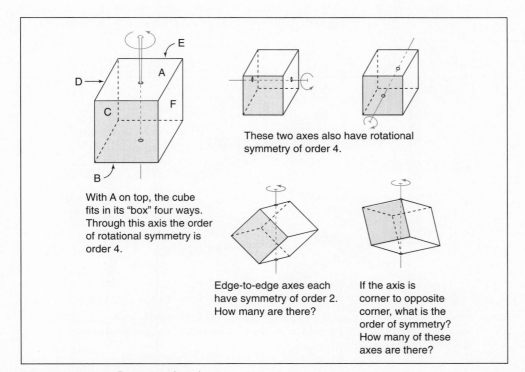

These two axes also have rotational symmetry of order 4.

With A on top, the cube fits in its "box" four ways. Through this axis the order of rotational symmetry is order 4.

Edge-to-edge axes each have symmetry of order 2. How many are there?

If the axis is corner to opposite corner, what is the order of symmetry? How many of these axes are there?

•**FIGURE 17.36**   Rotations of a cube.

Length: either equal in length or not (two possibilities)

Angle of intersection: either right angle or not (two possibilities)

Ratio of parts (from the corners to the intersection): one diagonal bisected, both bisected, neither bisected but parts proportional, or none of these (four possibilities)

17.38 Diagonal Investigation

Have students select a particular type of quadrilateral (say, parallelogram) and draw several different examples of it. Use dot or grid paper to make drawing parallel lines and congruent angles easy. For each example, students should draw the diagonals and make whatever measurements and calculations they desire. The goal is to discover what properties the diagonals of that particular type of quadrilateral might have. Different groups of students can investigate different quadrilaterals, and information can be shared and discussed as a class.

In Activity 17.38, the students begin with a quadrilateral and examine properties of the diagonals. A similar activity begins with the diagonals.

17.39 Diagonal Strips

For this activity, students need three strips of tagboard about 2 cm wide. Two should be the same length (about 30 cm) and the third somewhat shorter (about 20 cm). Punch nine holes equally spaced along the strip. (Punch a hole near each end. Divide the distance between the holes by 8. This will be the distance between the remaining holes.) Use a brass fastener to join two strips. A quadrilateral is formed by joining the four holes as shown in Figure 17.37. Provide students with the list of possible relationships for angles, lengths, and ratios of parts, and see if they can use the strips to determine the properties of diagonals that will produce different diagonals. The strips are there to help in the exploration. Students may want to make additional drawings on dot grids to test the various hypotheses. (Challenge: What properties will produce a nonisosceles trapezoid?)

Every type of quadrilateral can be uniquely described in terms of its diagonals using only the conditions listed earlier.

Angles, Lines, and Planes

The relationships between angles within a figure can be explored quite well by tracing angles for comparisons, by

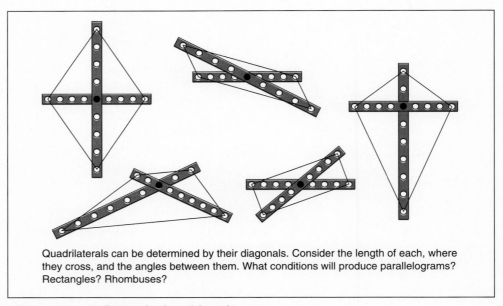

Quadrilaterals can be determined by their diagonals. Consider the length of each, where they cross, and the angles between them. What conditions will produce parallelograms? Rectangles? Rhombuses?

● **FIGURE 17.37** *Diagonals of quadrilaterals.*

comparing angles to a square corner, and by using informal units. With only such simple techniques, students can begin to look at relationships such as the following:

- The angles made by intersecting lines or by lines crossing two parallel lines: Which angles are equal? Which add up to a straight angle?
- The sum of the interior angles of polygons of different types: Is there a relationship in the number of sides and the sum of the angles? What if the shape is concave?
- The exterior angles of polygons: Extend each side in the same direction (for example, clockwise) and observe the sum of these angles. How is the exterior angle related to the interior angle?

In three dimensions, students can begin to observe the angles formed by intersecting planes and between lines and planes. How can two lines not intersect but not be parallel? Can a line and a plane be parallel? How could you describe a line that is perpendicular to a plane? Where would you find examples of these relationships in the real world?

Similar Figures

In both two and three dimensions, two figures can be the same shape but be different sizes. At level 0, students can sort out shapes that look alike. At that level, the concept of similar is strictly visual and not likely to be precise. At level 1, students can begin to measure angles, lengths of sides, areas, and volumes (for solids) of shapes that are similar. By investigation, relationships between similar shapes can be observed. For example, students will find that all corresponding angles must be congruent, but other measures vary proportionately. If one side of a larger yet similar figure is triple that of the smaller figure, so will all linear dimensions be triple those of the smaller figure. If the ratio of corresponding lengths is 1 to n, the ratio of areas will be 1 to n^2, and the ratio of volumes will be 1 to n^3.

In Chapter 15, similar rectangles were used to help students observe equal ratios. Recognition of similar figures and proportional reasoning are very much connected and are a good place to make connections in the mathematics curriculum.

---ACTIVITY---

17.40 Building Similar Figures

Have students build or draw a series of similar shapes. Start with one shape, and pick one side (or for solids, one edge) to be the control side. Make the corresponding side of the similar figures in easy multiples of the control side. For example, make shapes with a corresponding side 2, 3, and 4

times as long as the control (see Figure 17.38). **Make measures of lengths, areas, and volumes (for solids), and compare ratios of corresponding parts. If the control sides are in the ratio 1 to 3, then all linear dimensions will be in the same ratio, areas in the ratio 1 to 9, and volume in the ratio 1 to 27.**

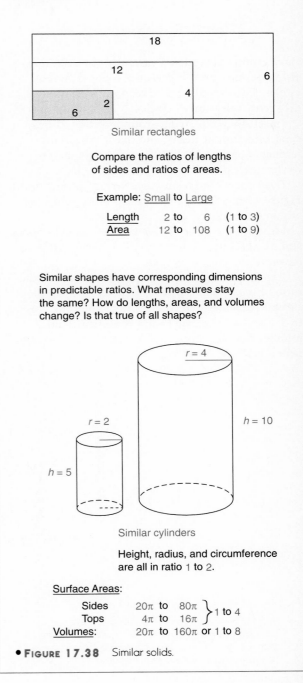

Similar rectangles

Compare the ratios of lengths of sides and ratios of areas.

Example: <u>Small</u> to <u>Large</u>

<u>Length</u>	2 to	6	(1 to 3)
<u>Area</u>	12 to	108	(1 to 9)

Similar shapes have corresponding dimensions in predictable ratios. What measures stay the same? How do lengths, areas, and volumes change? Is that true of all shapes?

Similar cylinders

Height, radius, and circumference are all in ratio 1 to 2.

Surface Areas:

Sides	20π to	80π	}	1 to 4
Tops	4π to	16π		
<u>Volumes:</u>	20π to	160π or 1 to 8		

● **FIGURE 17.38** Similar solids.

Circles

The circle, an apparently simple shape, is also very important. Consider the world around you. What are some of the ways the circle is used? Why do you think it is so frequently used instead of other shapes? Many interesting relationships can be observed between measures of different parts of the circle (see Bruni, 1977). Among the most astounding and important is the ratio between measures of the circumference and the diameter.

---ACTIVITY---

17.41 Discovering π

Have groups of students carefully measure the circumference and diameter of many different circles. Each group can be responsible for a different collection of circles.

Carefully wrap string around jar lids, tubes, cans, and similar items, and mark the circumference. Measure the string and the diameter to the nearest millimeter.

Draw larger circles using a string, as shown in Figure 17.39. String can be used to measure the circumference.

Measure the large circles marked on gym floors and playgrounds. Use a trundle wheel or rope to measure the circumference.

Using a calculator, students should record the ratio of the two measures for each circle. With careful measurement, the results should be close to 3.1 or 3.2. The exact ratio is an irrational number that is represented by the Greek letter π, which is about 3.14159.

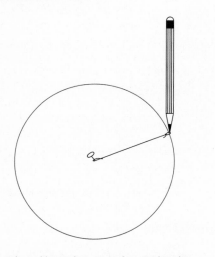

A string with two loops can be used to draw very large circles that are larger than those drawn with a compass. Two students working together will have better success than just one.

●FIGURE 17.39   *Drawing a circle.*

What is most important in Activity 17.41 is that students develop a clear understanding of π as the ratio of circumference to diameter in any circle. The quantity π is not some strange number that appears in math formulas.

There are many other explorations that can be done with circles. For example, a short article by Gerver (1990) describes some interesting area activities that also get at the value of π in an intuitive manner. Drawing circles with compasses and then drawing arcs with the same radius through the center has delighted students for ages. By making three folds of a circular disk into the center, we form a very nice equilateral triangle, complete with flaps on each edge. These can then be glued together to make three of the five Platonic solids (to be discussed in connection with level 2). It is interesting to notice that all triangles drawn with two vertices on opposite ends of a diameter and the third at some other point on the circle have something in common. These and many other explorations suggest that the circle is a good place to look for geometric experiences.

Geometric Problem-Solving Activities

Problem solving continues to be an important feature of geometry activities at level 1. Many activities already suggested are explorations posed as problems. A few additional explorations of a problem-solving nature are suggested here.

---ACTIVITY---

17.42 Triangle Communication

Draw any triangle. Choose three measurements of either angles or lengths of sides, and use only these to tell a partner how to draw a triangle that is congruent to yours. What combinations of angles and sides will work?

---ACTIVITY---

17.43 Area Problems

Determine the areas of odd shapes and surfaces such as those in Figure 17.40 for which there are no formulas or for which dimensions are not provided.

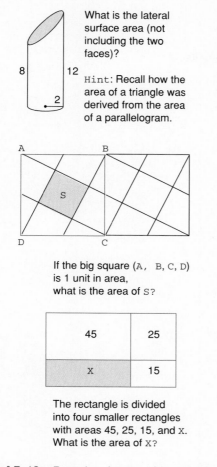

What is the lateral surface area (not including the two faces)?

8   12

2

Hint: Recall how the area of a triangle was derived from the area of a parallelogram.

If the big square (A, B, C, D) is 1 unit in area, what is the area of S?

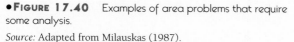

45	25
X	15

The rectangle is divided into four smaller rectangles with areas 45, 25, 15, and X. What is the area of X?

•FIGURE 17.40 *Examples of area problems that require some analysis.*

Source: Adapted from Milauskas (1987).

---ACTIVITY---

17.44 A Geometric Probability Problem

If a dart has an equal chance of landing at any point on a circular target, is it more likely to land closer to the center or closer to the edge?

Tessellations Revisited

Earlier you saw that a tessellation was a regular tiling pattern that covers the plane. Students at level 1 can begin to create more interesting or complex tessellations with attention being given to certain geometric properties.

The Dutch artist M. C. Escher is well known for his tessellations, where the tiles are very intricate and usually take the shape of things like birds, horses, angels, or lizards. What Escher did was take a simple shape such as a triangle, parallelogram, or hexagon and perform transformations on the sides. For example, a curve drawn along one side might be translated (slid) to the opposite side. Another idea was to draw a curve from the midpoint of a side to the adjoining vertex. This curve was then rotated about the midpoint to form a totally new side of the tile. These two ideas are illustrated in part (a) of Figure 17.41(p. 378). Dot paper is used to help draw the lines. Escher-type tessellations, as these have come to be called, are quite popular projects for students in the sixth to eighth grades. Once the tile has been designed, it can be cut from two different colors of construction paper instead of drawing the tessellation on a dot grid.

A regular tessellation is made of a single tile that is a regular polygon (all sides and angles congruent). Each vertex of a regular tessellation has the same number of tiles meeting at that point. A checkerboard is a simple example of a regular tessellation. A semiregular tessellation is made of two or more tiles, each of which is a regular polygon. At each vertex of a semiregular tessellation, the same collection of regular polygons come together in the same order. A vertex (and therefore the complete semiregular tessellation) can be described by the series of shapes meeting at a vertex. Under each example of these tessellations in part (b) of Figure 17.41, the vertex numbers are given. Students can figure out what polygons are possible at a vertex and design their own semiregular tessellations.

TesselMania! (Minnesota Educational Computing Consortium, 1994), a computer software program, has become quite popular as a way to produce intricate tessellations that are similar in spirit to those of Escher. The program begins with a tessellation using a standard shape such as a parallelogram. With the mouse, sides of a single tile can be distorted or rotated or translated, and the entire plane of shapes is distorted accordingly. Color can be added, and the printed results are striking. Intriguing and motivating, a program such as this must be judged in terms of the mathematics that students learn. It is strongly suggested that students work on analysis and development of the ideas found in tessellations before playing with *TesselMania!*

Books by Ranucci and Teeters (1977) and Bezuszka, Kenney, and Silvey (1977) are among a number of excellent resources that can be used to explore this fascinating topic further with junior high students.

An alternate method of tiling the plane is to consider *reptiles*. A rep-tile is a geometric figure for which congruent copies can be made and assembled to produce a larger yet similar figure. All squares, rectangles, parallelograms, and triangles are clearly rep-tiles. Take any one of these shapes,

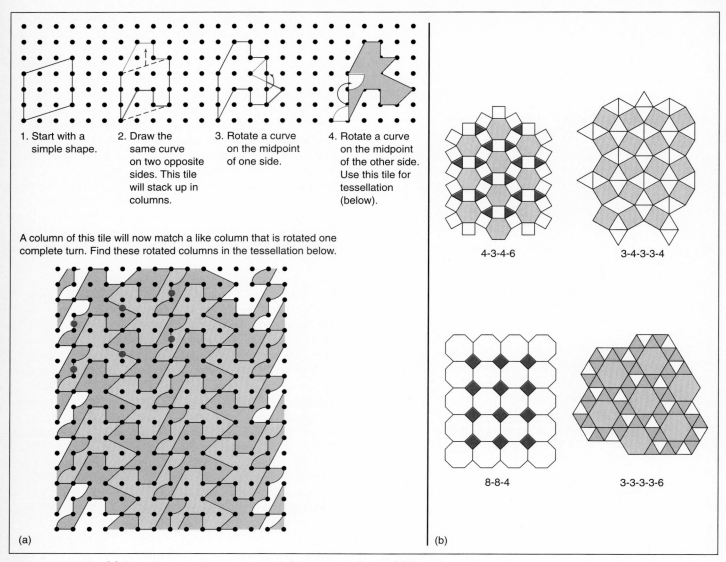

1. Start with a simple shape.

2. Draw the same curve on two opposite sides. This tile will stack up in columns.

3. Rotate a curve on the midpoint of one side.

4. Rotate a curve on the midpoint of the other side. Use this tile for tessellation (below).

A column of this tile will now match a like column that is rotated one complete turn. Find these rotated columns in the tessellation below.

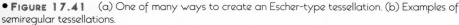

4-3-4-6

3-4-3-3-4

8-8-4

3-3-3-3-6

(a)

(b)

● **FIGURE 17.41** (a) One of many ways to create an Escher-type tessellation. (b) Examples of semiregular tessellations.

cut out four copies of it, and you can rearrange them so that the larger figure is like (similar to) the smaller one.

Now consider beginning with a small triangle. Put four together to make a larger one. Make three copies of the new larger triangle and with the first four small triangles make an even larger triangle—the third generation. Make three copies of this and assemple with the third-generation triangle to make the fourth-generation triangle, and so on. This process will theoretically tile the entire plane but is not a tessellation. After the first four triangles, there are never more than three tiles of any one size. See Fosnaugh and Harrell (1996) for further discussion of this unique idea.

INFORMAL GEOMETRY ACTIVITIES: LEVEL 2

At the van Hiele level 2 of geometric thinking, students begin to use informal deductive reasoning. That is, they can follow and use logical arguments, although they will have a difficult time constructing a proof of their own as in tenth-grade geometry. Physical models and drawings are still important, but for different reasons. At level 1, students' explorations lead to inductive conclusions about shapes. For example, the diagonals of parallelograms bisect each other. Students at level 1 are satisfied that such results are so because it seems to happen that way when they try it. At level 2, students can use a drawing to help them follow a deductive argument supplied by the teacher. They may also use models to test conjectures or to find counterexamples. Models become more a tool for thinking and verification than one for exploration.

Many topics in the seventh- and eighth-grade curriculum lend themselves to projects that promote level 2 thinking. It is important that students be challenged to reason through these topics and not just memorize formulas and procedures. Eighth-grade geometry may be one of the last opportunities for good activities that prepare students for the level 3 thinking required in a high school geometry course.

Definitions and Properties

Classification activities at level 2 can begin to focus on the definitions of shapes and how different classes of shapes are related one to another.

---ACTIVITY---

17.45 Property Lists

Consider a particular type of shape—for example, a rectangle—and list all of the properties of that shape that students can think of. One possible list is suggested here. What is the smallest number of items that can be chosen from this list that will still determine a rectangle? Are there different sublists that will work? Which property or properties are necessary if the rectangle is to be nonsquare?

Four sides

Four right angles

Opposite sides parallel

Diagonals bisect each other

Adjacent sides perpendicular

Opposite sides equal in length

Diagonals congruent

Only two lines of symmetry

Diagonals not perpendicular

---ACTIVITY---

17.46 If-Then, True or False

Explore statements in these forms:

If it is a _____, then it is also a __.

All _____ are _____.

Fill the blanks with names of shapes or statements of properties and relationships. Let students use drawings or models to decide if the statements are true or to find counterexamples. A few examples are suggested here.

If it is a cylinder, then it is a prism.

If it is a prism, then it is a cylinder.

If it is a square, then it is a rhombus.

All parallelograms have congruent diagonals.

All quadrilaterals with congruent diagonals are parallelograms.

If two rectangles have the same area, then they are congruent.

All prisms have a plane of symmetry.

All right prisms have a plane of symmetry.

If a prism has a plane of symmetry, then it is a right prism.

Obviously, not all of these statements are true. For those that you think may be false, find a counterexample. You and your students can make up similar puzzles to stump the class.

Informal Proofs

Perhaps the notion of geometric proof in the seventh or eighth grade seems a bit difficult. That may be because your personal experience with proof and geometry stems from activities in the typical tenth-grade course where proofs are formal. The typical high school geometry proof is based on axioms, definitions, and theorems that have already been established. Each tiny statement must be defended.

What is quite possible at the middle grade level is to require students to build informal arguments that involve everyday logic and that are compelling. These arguments can easily be made by middle grade students if they are given the opportunity to explore an idea and get a good feel for what is involved. Here are some simple examples.

---ACTIVITY---

17.47 Two Congruent Parts

"I have a rectangle that has been divided into two congruent parts. What could the parts be?" There is no single answer to this question, and some answers depend on the specific rectangle in question. How students respond will depend somewhat on what materials you provide. If you suggest that students use a rectangular dot grid, you will likely get different answers than if you simply have them make sketches on plain paper.

The interesting part of "Two Congruent Parts" is the discussion that can surround any given answer. Many answers can be generalized to apply to any original rectangle or to a specific rectangle. A generalized answer is now a conjecture that can potentially be proved. You may want to explore this activity on your own for a while before reading further. Here are a few possible conjectures that are probable results of such an investigation:

1. The two shapes could be right triangles.

2. The two shapes could be squares.

3. The two shapes could be rectangles with one side the same as the given rectangle and the other half the length of the given rectangle.

4. The line dividing the rectangle will always go through the center of the rectangle (the intersection of the diagonals).

Each of these statements is open to some scrutiny, even though most seem to be true on the surface. Consider statement 1. Here is a possible argument: If you draw a line from one corner to the opposite corner, there will be two triangles. Because the shape is a rectangle, the remaining two corners are right angles and are angles in the two triangles. Therefore, they are right triangles. The two shapes are congruent because all of the sides are congruent: One side is the same—the diagonal; the two legs of one triangle are adjacent sides of the rectangle. These sides match the opposite sides of the rectangle and are the legs of the second triangle.

Statement 2 is true only for a special class of triangles but can be proved just as easily. Statement 4 is the toughest to prove but is certainly worthy of a class struggle.

Another opportunity for proof is found in the next activity.

---ACTIVITY---

17.48 Two Polygons from One

Begin with a convex polygon with a given number of sides. Connect two points with a segment. How many sides do the two resulting polygons have altogether (see Figure 17.42)? (Sconyers, 1995)

The answer to the question of course depends on how many sides the original polygon has. It also depends on how the segment is drawn. However, with some exploration, it is reasonable to discover that for any polygon with more than three sides, there are three cases to consider for the segment and for each case a clear answer to how many sides will result. (The proof is left to you.) As students work together, perhaps with some hints or suggestions from you, they will be able to construct a good argument for a generalized answer to the question posed.

What is significant about these last two activities is that the generalizations come from the students after doing some

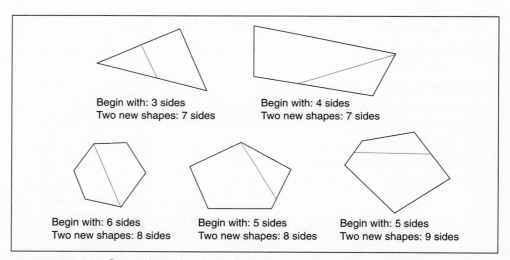

•FIGURE 17.42   Start with a polygon, and draw a segment to divide it into two polygons. How many sides will the two new polygons have?

exploration. If you write a theorem on the board and ask students to prove it, you have already told them the statement is true. The proof becomes an uninteresting exercise. If, by contrast, a student makes a statement about a geometric situation the class is exploring, it can be written on the board with a question mark—it is a *conjecture,* a statement whose truth has not yet been determined. "Is it true? Always? What do you think? Can we prove it? Can you find a counterexample?" Out of discussions such as this, good deductive arguments can be developed by the class. Write the arguments on the board or overhead as students construct them.

As students begin to construct and analyze arguments such as these fairly simple ones, they will begin to develop an appreciation for what a logical or deductive argument is about. Notice that what is happening is in keeping with level 2 of the van Hiele theory. Students are looking at properties of shapes (objects of thought) and constructing logical arguments (products of thought).

The Pythagorean Theorem

An area interpretation of the Pythagorean theorem states that if a square is made on each side of a right triangle, the areas of the two smaller squares will together be equal to the area of the square on the longest side or hypotenuse. Figure 17.43 illustrates two proofs that students can follow and begin to appreciate.

As a variation to the Pythagorean theorem, have students explore what happens if the squares formed on each side of a right triangle are replaced by triangles or semicircles. Will the same relationship between the three areas hold? What about other shapes (pentagons, hexagons, etc.)?

Area and Volume Formulas

Chapter 16 contains suggestions for helping students develop formulas for areas and volumes of common shapes. Formula development is a major connection between measurement and geometry and is also a good bridge between level 1 and level 2 of geometric thinking.

The Platonic Solids

The *Platonic solids* are *completely regular polyhedra.* "Completely regular" means that each face is a regular polygon and every vertex has exactly the same number of faces joining at that point. It is reasonable for level 2 students to work through an informal argument that demonstrates there can

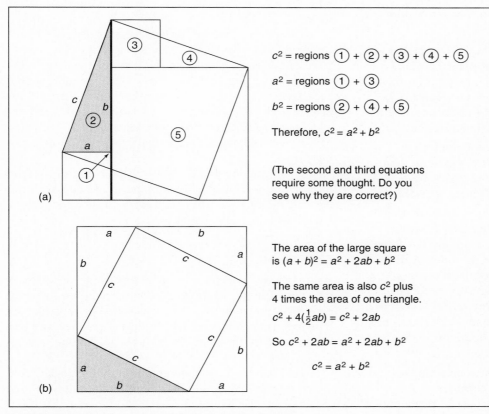

c^2 = regions ① + ② + ③ + ④ + ⑤

a^2 = regions ① + ③

b^2 = regions ② + ④ + ⑤

Therefore, $c^2 = a^2 + b^2$

(The second and third equations require some thought. Do you see why they are correct?)

The area of the large square is $(a + b)^2 = a^2 + 2ab + b^2$

The same area is also c^2 plus 4 times the area of one triangle.

$c^2 + 4(\frac{1}{2}ab) = c^2 + 2ab$

So $c^2 + 2ab = a^2 + 2ab + b^2$

$$c^2 = a^2 + b^2$$

● **FIGURE 17.43** *Two proofs of the Pythagorean theorem.*

be only five such completely regular polyhedra and also allows the excitement of constructing them. To examine these solids, students need a supply of congruent equilateral triangles cut from tagboard, some tagboard squares, tagboard regular pentagons, and a few regular hexagons. One possible approach to the Platonic solids might go as follows:

....

Since the polyhedra must have regular faces, begin with the simplest possible face, an equilateral triangle, and see what polyhedra can be constructed.

1. Put three triangles together at a point. Tape all edges together to form a pyramid. This will leave a space for one more triangle to be inserted as a base forming a *tetrahedron* (tetra = four). Observe that this is a completely regular polyhedron. (Why is a six-sided polyhedron made of two tetrahedra placed face to face not completely regular?)

2. Start over, this time with four triangles coming together at a point. Taping these together will form a square pyramid. Tape another triangle to each edge of the square and bring these four to a point. This will result in a completely regular eight-sided polyhedron or *octahedron* (octa = eight).

3. Begin again with triangles. Tape five together at a point forming a pentagonal pyramid. Continue to add triangles on open edges until there are five at each vertex. It is very exciting to see and feel this form into a ball-like structure of 20 triangles, an *icosahedron* (icosa = twenty).

4. When you try six triangles at a point, they make a flat surface, not a solid. No more than six will work either. Therefore, there are no more completely regular polyhedra possible with triangular faces.

5. The next regular polygon after a three-sided one is a four-sided polygon, a square. Put three together at a point, and tape the sides. Add an additional square at the three open vertices, and you have formed a cube. Now, however, you know to call it a *hexahedron* (hex = six). In a similar argument as was made with the triangles, it should be clear that no other polyhedra can be made with squares.

6. The next polygon to work with is a regular pentagon. Three can be put together at one vertex, and you can continue to add pentagons on open edges with three coming together at every point until 12 pentagons form a complete polyhedron, a *dodecahedron* (dodeca = twelve).

7. Finally, conclude by experimentation that there are no other polyhedra possible with pentagons or with hexagons. After seeing that three hexagons lay flat, it is fairly clear that three septagons would not fit around a point. Thus there are no other possible regular polyhedra, and you have found all five of the Platonic solids.

....

Finding the five Platonic solids has real potential in the development of level 2 thinking. Although you could certainly guide your students through the development, you would be doing all of the thinking for them. If you have access to a plastic building set, all necessary materials for this investigation are not only available but quite easy to assemble. Rather than direct students in these constructions, discuss the meaning of regular polygons and completely regular polyhedra. Along with this discussion, have students work in small groups to find as many completely regular solids as possible using the building kits. As a class, decide if each construction is completely regular and why. Let students decide when they think they have found them all.

An absolutely fantastic skeletal icosahedron can be built out of the newspaper rods described earlier in this chapter. Start with five at a point, and join the other ends with five rods to form a pentagonal pyramid. Add two more rods at each vertex of the base, and continue from there. If you keep in mind that you want five rods at each vertex and that all faces make triangles, the result is guaranteed. The icosahedron will be about 4 feet in diameter and will be amazingly rigid.

Another way to make all of the Platonic solids in skeletal form is to use the bendable drinking straws described earlier. There is enough rigidity that even the cube and dodecahedron will turn out all right.

Constructions

Too frequently, students are taught to perform constructions with a straightedge and compass but have no idea why the constructions work. In most instances, the constructions represent simple theorems that students can follow and provide reasons for the steps. An example of bisecting an angle is illustrated in Figure 17.44.

The Mira offers a different approach to doing many constructions that have traditionally been done with compass and straightedge. With either set of tools, having students determine on their own how to do these constructions is also a valuable form of deductive reasoning.

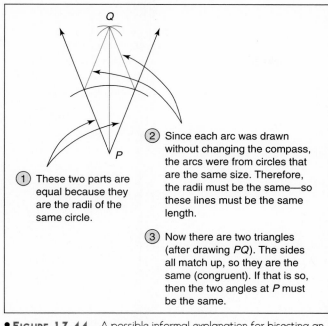

① These two parts are equal because they are the radii of the same circle.

② Since each arc was drawn without changing the compass, the arcs were from circles that are the same size. Therefore, the radii must be the same—so these lines must be the same length.

③ Now there are two triangles (after drawing *PQ*). The sides all match up, so they are the same (congruent). If that is so, then the two angles at *P* must be the same.

●**FIGURE 17.44** A possible informal explanation for bisecting an angle with compass and straightedge.

INFORMAL GEOMETRY ON THE COMPUTER

More and more, the computer offers interesting and powerful methods of exploring geometric ideas. While there are many programs available, three categories of geometric software deserve some attention in this chapter, although this is not intended to be an exhaustive presentation. The intention is to give some indication of how the computer has a particular impact on geometry in schools.

The first category includes software that approximates similar materials available in the physical environment. The second category contains geometric tools that permit drawings to be created with user-specified relationships. This type of software expands considerably the investigative aspect of learning geometry and is especially suited for students at level 2 of the van Hiele theory. Finally, there are Logo environments. Logo itself is a computer programming language with many uses. However, its easily accessible graphics mode has made it a natural medium for investigating shapes in ways that are generally not found in any other mode.

Computer Versions of Geometric Models

Graphics environments on computers provide the ability to use a mouse and manipulate shapes on the screens. Chil-

dren usually find these screen manipulations more fascinating, faster-paced, and more interesting than physical materials. There are several advantages of the computer versions over the physical models.

- Student dexterity is enhanced as shapes "snap" into place.
- Incomplete work can be saved in a student's own file so that a project can be continued from one day to the next.
- Work can be printed out to create a record of the activity or drawing.
- Some programs permit students to type stories or comments about the work onto the picture so that communication in that form is enhanced.
- Many programs come with built-in challenges or activities and provide a free-form use of the electronic manipulative.
- Measurements or counts of objects or other symbolic connections are frequently connected with the drawings.

Computer Geometric Blocks

Several programs are available that offer an electronic variation of pattern blocks. Two examples are "Patterns and Shapes," a separate package within *Exploring Math with Manipulatives—Level II* (EduQuest, 1993) and *Hands-On Math, Volumes 1, 2, and 3* (Ventura Educational Systems, 1991, 1992, 1993). In these and similar programs, a palette of shapes is provided from which selections can be placed onto the screen. These can be flipped, rotated, and copied. Two or more shapes can be put together to create new shapes that can then be manipulated as a single shape. Programs provide outlines to be filled in as a geometric puzzle, patterns to complete or extend, mirror images to complete, and free-form use of the blocks. It is not immediately clear that geometric concepts are made more accessible in this environment, but the advantages listed earlier are clearly present. If computers are available, these programs can be advantageous additions to the geometry program.

Electronic Geoboards

A popular software package that has been around awhile is called *Elastic Lines* (Harvey, McHugh, & McGlathery, 1989). Even though this is an early program, it has clear advantages not available to students using a conventional geoboard with rubber bands. The program provides the options of rectangular and isometric grids in various sizes. This is like having the dot or grid papers from the Blackline Masters on the computer screen and not needing a ruler to draw nice lines. For any shape drawn, the area and perimeter can be displayed automatically. This may not be desirable in some activities, but it opens up explorations not otherwise available to young children: "What shapes can you make that have an area of 36? What can you find out about the perimeter of these shapes?" The flexibility of the computer version of geoboards makes this program a valuable extension of the physical versions.

Tools to Explore Relationships

The first programs in this category were a collection called *The Geometric Supposers* (Schwartz & Yerushalmy, 1985) that ran on Apple II computers. With the *Supposers* (there is one for triangles, one for quadrilaterals, and one for circles), a student can begin to explore possible relationships in geometric shapes without tedious drawing. The *Supposers* and the significantly more powerful software that has followed have added a truly new dimension to geometric exploration by students. These programs fit precisely into a constructivist view of learning by making musings such as "What can I find out about . . . ?" and "I wonder if it always works this way" open to active exploration with powerful visual feedback. These programs provide opportunities for middle and high school students that were not available before.

Geometric Explorations

The Geometer's Sketchpad (Key Curriculum Press, 1995) is designed to provide the same conjecturing and exploration needs originally envisioned for the *Supposers* but is much more powerful. The *Sketchpad* offers a palette of drawing tools (points, circles, segments/rays/lines) that are used with a mouse to draw almost any geometric shape. Objects can be drawn freehand or in a specified relationship to existing objects. Once drawn, any object (point, line, circle, etc.) can be moved or dragged with the mouse, making the drawing dynamic. Freely drawn objects can be moved anywhere on the screen. This allows for polygons to be stretched and positioned in almost any imaginable manner. When objects are created in relationship to other objects, those relationships remain even when the objects are moved. Parallel lines remain parallel, perpendicular lines stay perpendicular, midpoints stay at the midpoint. If a new segment is constructed to be congruent to a model segment, its length will not change unless the model segment is changed. Figures can be translated, rotated, reflected, and dilated. When a figure changes, so does any transformation of that figure. Consider two very simplified examples.

Follow these steps in Figure 17.45:

1. Points A, B, and C were placed freely, and a segment was drawn between A and B.

2. A line was drawn through C parallel to AB.

3. A point D was placed on the line through C, and segments AD and DB were drawn.

(At this time, the line through C can be moved, but it will remain parallel to AB. If A or B is moved, C remains fixed, but the line through C will rotate so that it remains parallel

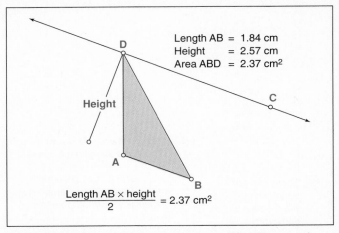

Length AB = 1.84 cm
Height = 2.57 cm
Area ABD = 2.37 cm²

$$\frac{\text{Length AB} \times \text{height}}{2} = 2.37 \text{ cm}^2$$

●**FIGURE 17.45** A *Sketchpad* construction. When D is moved along the line DC, all measures are updated.

to AB. Through all of this, the point D will remain on the line, and triangle ABD will adjust accordingly.)

4. A segment is constructed (some steps are omitted here) so that it runs from D to a hidden line through AB and is always perpendicular to AB. This line is clearly the height of triangle ABD. The *Sketchpad* permits labeling any way you wish.

5. Measures are made of AB, the height, and the area of ABD. The formula AB × height/2 is also calculated.

Now D can be dragged along line DC, and the height of ABD will remain constant, as will the length of AB. It can clearly be seen that the area of the triangle remains fixed as long as the base and height remain fixed.

In Figure 17.46, the midpoints of a freely drawn quadrilateral ABCD have been joined. The diagonals of the resulting quadrilateral (EFGH) are also drawn and measured. No matter how the points A, B, C, and D are dragged around the screen, even inverting the quadrilateral, the other lines will maintain the same relationships (joining midpoints and diagonals), and the measurements will be instantly updated on the screen.

These two examples provide a small hint of the dynamic features of the *Sketchpad* without your actually experiencing it. In addition, the *Sketchpad* permits drawings to be saved and programs that produce drawings to be created and saved. Objects can also be animated, and designated objects can leave a path on the screen as they move.

At least two other programs can be considered to be in the same family of geometric software: *Geometry Inventor* (LOGAL, 1994) and *Cabri Geometry II* (Texas Instruments, 1994) are both similar to the *Sketchpad*. *Geometry Inventor* is easier to use, especially for middle grade students, and offers a wider palette of drawing options. Shapes and measures can be linked quite clearly with graphs and charts to examine relationships

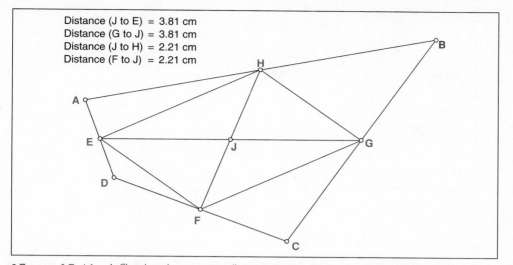

Distance (J to E) = 3.81 cm
Distance (G to J) = 3.81 cm
Distance (J to H) = 2.21 cm
Distance (F to J) = 2.21 cm

●**FIGURE 17.46** A *Sketchpad* construction illustrating several properties of quadrilaterals.

in symbolic and graphic form. *Cabri* is perhaps not as easy for the younger child to use. It is nicely connected to a coordinate view of geometry. Most significant, a version of *Cabri* is incorporated into the TI-92 calculator so that geometric drawings and explorations can be done on a handheld device.

In the Classroom

Tools such as the *Sketchpad* and *Geometry Inventor* can be used in a laboratory setting where all students or students working in pairs have access to their own computers. In this mode, the class should have discussed a potential exploration or defined a problem to solve. For example, the students can create (or have prepared for them) on the computer a rectangle, a parallelogram, and a kite. These shapes can be constructed so that they can be stretched, rotated, and changed in every way imaginable yet still remain rectangles, parallelograms, and kites through every change. In a sense, this is a look at "all" shapes in these three categories. Students can be asked to explore the diagonals of these shapes and see what conjectures about the diagonals they can make. Later, the conjectures from different class members can be discussed and possibly proved.

Worksheets on which students are guided as to what types of constructions to make and what measurements to look for are very helpful. An excellent book of guided explorations (Bennett, 1992) is available for the *Sketchpad,* and each of the other programs comes with activities intended for student use.

These geometry tools are also very effective under teacher direction with just a single computer and an overhead liquid crystal display panel. In this mode, the programs become high-tech electronic blackboards. Students can make conjectures in groups or as a class. Their ideas can be tested or explored on the computer. The verbal interaction between

students and with the teacher is so powerful in this mode that it is difficult to argue that the lab setting is better.

Logo and Informal Geometry

Logo is a highly accessible yet powerful computer language that has many uses other than geometry. However, the ease with which Logo can be used to draw pictures on the monitor makes it a natural vehicle for geometric explorations. Since Logo is both very easy to use and very powerful, it can be used by children as young as kindergarten and also be a challenging medium for college students. Very briefly, in Logo graphics, a tiny triangle or picture of a turtle is controlled with simple keyboard commands. It can be made to go forward or backward any distance. A FORWARD 50 command makes the turtle move forward about 5 cm and draw a line in its path. The turtle can also be turned in its place. The command RIGHT 90 turns the turtle 90 degrees to its right. With these and other commands coupled with the ability to put lists of commands into procedures (little programs), children have both power and flexibility with which they can draw on the computer screen.

The purpose here is to illustrate some of the ways that Logo can be used in an informal geometry program. No attempt is made to explain the details of the Logo programming involved. (For a more detailed explanation of the Logo language, see Chapter 24.)

Shapes in Logo

Children can learn to use regular Logo commands and Logo programming as early as the first grade. Second and third graders can learn to define procedures to create shapes of their own. In the simplest turtle graphics programming, children develop intuitive understandings of angles and distances.

Logo adds much more to a child's experiences with geometric shape than simply drawing shapes on the computer screen. Unlike packages that are designed to make drawing easy and intuitive, Logo requires that a drawing be conceptualized in terms of its component parts—dimensions of sides, angle sizes, turn directions, and orientation in the plane. Shapes are drawn by directing the turtle and not by moving the mouse.

Consider a child who is trying to write a procedure to draw a rectangle. The child has a visual image of "rectangle" and may even have one drawn on paper. But the turtle must be "taught" to draw each part separately, and the relationship between the parts must be clearly understood. The resulting procedure is a form of definition of a rectangle developed by the child. Further, it is a definition based on component parts and relationships rather than a gestalt visual image.

A more profound difference between visualizing shapes and defining procedures to draw shapes can be observed when watching children who want the turtle to draw a circle. The turtle moves only in straight lines, not curves. A common technique for helping children translate shapes into turtle actions is to have them "play turtle" or walk the shape as if they were the turtle on the screen. How can you walk in a circle if you can only move forward? Children quickly conclude that they should go forward just a little bit, and then turn a little bit, and repeat this over and over. Logo includes a REPEAT function, which makes it easy to do a series of actions over and over. A common "first circle" is produced by the line

REPEAT 360 [FD 1 RT 1]

Compare the following Logo procedures:

TO SQUARE
    REPEAT 4 [FD 50 RT 90]
    END
TO EIGHTSIDES
    REPEAT 8 [FD 10 RT 45]
    END
TO 36 SIDES
    REPEAT 36 [FD 2 RT 10]
    END

Each procedure draws a regular polygon. The 36-sided polygon looks exactly like a circle, and yet it was conceived as a polygon. "Circles" of different sizes can be made by changing the amount of the turn or the forward step (or both). This example illustrates a completely different form of thinking and analysis of shape than is provided in other media. How do you know how much to turn? What if you wanted to make a triangle or a hexagon? How is a circle like an octagon or even a square? How do you make different triangles? Can you make a curve that is not a circle?

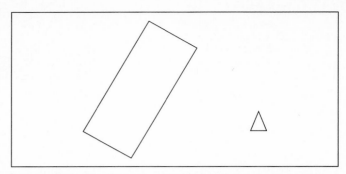

● **FIGURE 17.47**   Drawing a tilted rectangle in Logo demands a different understanding of rectangles and angles.

As another simple example, consider the task of duplicating the rectangle already drawn on the screen as shown in Figure 17.47. Although the orientation of a rectangle does not alter its definition, is this completely clear to a level 0 thinker? Most children know that before they begin to draw this figure, they should turn the turtle to the right a bit, perhaps RT 30. They proceed to enter FD 80 (for FORWARD 80). Now, even though they have previously drawn rectangles in a vertical or horizontal orientation using 90-degree turns, many children begin to guess at how much to turn the turtle to make the first corner of the rectangle.

As Clements and Battista (1989) have found, the concept of angle is much more complex than might be thought. Their studies show that, in comparison with students who have not had Logo experiences, children who have been in Logo environments tend to have more accurate concepts of angle and are more likely to discriminate or classify shapes based on geometric properties.

Easy Versions of Logo

Logo requires that children do a minimal amount of typing to create commands. This is sometimes a limiting feature, especially for the very young.

One solution for the K–2 set is to begin with a modified version of Logo that uses a teacher-written program. Programs in Logo can be written that permit very young children to press only a single key, possibly followed by RETURN, to control the turtle. Most of these so-called instant Logo routines have a key for each of the following actions: FORWARD 10, BACK 10, RIGHT 30, and LEFT 30.

The drawing in Figure 17.48 was made using an instant program that includes single keystrokes for those four commands as well as for square, triangle, and rectangle. Two other keys are programmed for PENUP and PENDOWN.

All major versions of Logo include a simple instant program in the manuals. Excellent versions are presented in the article "Microcomputers in the Primary Mathematics Classroom" (Campbell, 1988) and the book *Learning with Logo* (Watt, 1983).

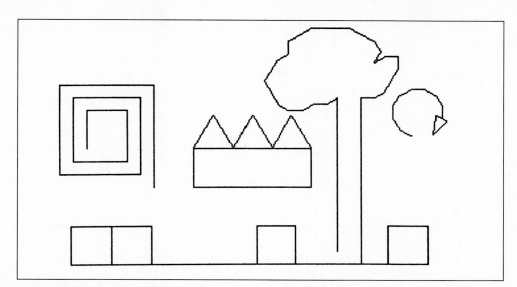

•FIGURE 17.48 *An instant Logo program allows young children to experiment with lines, shapes, and angles on the computer.*

Instant Logo activities are appropriate for level 0 thinking and provide a nice bridge to level 1 activities and to regular versions of Logo.

For children in the 8- to 12-year-old range, there are versions of Logo that have taken some of the tedium out of the language and added environments that enhance learning and exploration. Though not a complete Logo environment, *Crystal Rain Forest* (Terrapin, 1994) combines adventure games, problem solving, and simple Logo language in an environment that attracts children. The program introduces children to the basic commands of Logo, including the REPEAT command, and has a reduced version of the full Terrapin Logo language. This may be an option for those who want to explore Logo in geometry but do not wish to invest heavily in instructional time.

Clements and Meredith (1994) have developed a version of Logo called *Turtle Math*. In addition to regular Logo commands, this program provides a complete array of explorations in the Logo environment that are designed to get students to wrestle with a variety of ideas. In addition, a command menu at the top of the screen and the integration of a command window, a drawing window, and a program window make using this version of Logo much easier than the standard versions.

More Ideas with Logo

The following ideas are intended to give an indication of what can be done with Logo in geometry.

Variables can be used in procedures to create many shapes with the same characteristics. For example, the following procedure will draw rectangles of any dimensions. Executing RECTANGLE 20 20 will produce a square. How are RECTANGLE 20 60 and RECTANGLE 60 20 alike? How are they different?

TO RECTANGLE :L :W
   REPEAT 2 [FD :L RT 90 FD :W]
   END

Not only can forward distances be variable, but angles can be, too. How would you write a procedure to draw any parallelogram?

Symmetry can be explored in Logo to provide a different perspective. A mirror image of a shape (reflection) is achieved by changing all right turns to left and vice versa. It is also easy to create shapes, images, and rotational symmetry.

Try writing a procedure with no variables to create a small shape or drawing. Next, write a new procedure from the original in which all distances are multiplied by the same variable. By changing the value of the variable, proportional drawings (similar figures) are produced.

ASSESSMENT NOTES

What to Assess

An understandable conflict arises when we examine the breadth of engaging activities that are available in the area of geometry. On the one hand, our intuition suggests that these are good experiences for children as they explore the geometric world around them. On the other hand, the question "Exactly what did they learn?" gnaws at the back of our minds. Many good geometric experiences, especially those suitable for level 0 and level 1 students, are explorations in which children have the opportunity to develop their spatial sense.

If students are filling in outlines with tangram pieces or finding all of the 12 pentominoes (see Figures 17.19 and 17.20, p. 359), we are certainly not concerned that they "master" these skills. It is not a curricular objective to find the 12 shapes that can be made with five squares on a grid. Perhaps it is precisely because these activities do not show up on lists of objectives that schools and textbooks in the United States have traditionally not allocated much time to geometry in the elementary and middle grades.

Many teachers find themselves trying to apply a grade to geometry activities that have no right or wrong answers and for which there is no clear objective. Even when the activity is aimed at a particular geometric concept, such as line symmetry or similarity, there is a lot of fuzziness when asking, "Do they know it?" In level 2, many activities invite class or group discussions of informal proofs and conjecture making. Again, the objective is often unclear.

Clarifying Your Geometry Objectives

The greatest mistake that can be made is to take the fuzziness of geometry goals to mean that geometry is not important. Rather, it is important to articulate clearly just what the goals of your geometry program are and to find ways to assess these goals. By so doing, you will know when you are being successful, know how to defend or explain what you are doing in your geometry program, and also be able to make well-documented evaluations of your students.

The most important geometric agenda of the K–8 teacher is to provide experiences that move students from level 0 thinking to level 2 thinking by the end of the eighth grade. Not every teacher will be able to move his or her children to the next level. However, all teachers should be cognizant of the fact that the experiences they provide are the single most important factor in moving children up this developmental ladder. Every teacher should be able to see some growth in geometric thinking over the course of the year.

Spatial Sense

"Spatial sense is an intuitive feel for one's surroundings and the objects in them" (NCTM, 1989, p. 49). If you read the general suggestions for geometry and spatial sense at the K–4 level of the *Curriculum Standards,* you will see that a curriculum aimed at improving spatial sense will also be one aimed at improving growth in geometric thought according to the van Hiele theory.

Spatial sense or growth in geometric thought can be articulated in objectives such as the following:

- Attends to a variety of characteristics of shapes in sorting and building activities

- Uses language that is descriptive of geometric shapes (appropriate to the level of thought)
- Shows evidence of geometric reasoning in solving puzzles, exploring shapes, creating designs, and analyzing shapes
- Recognizes shape in the environment
- Solves spatial problems

This list is not meant to be exhaustive or prescriptive. At any grade level, statements such as these need to be considered general goals for the grade and coordinated with objectives for other grades. Nearly any activity in this chapter can be partly assessed in terms of spatial sense using similar statements. Anecdotal statements can be made on observation sheets or note cards for individual students so that evidence across the class will begin to show an emerging pattern of growth, for both the individual student and the class as a whole.

It is not reasonable for students at the K–1 level to begin to evidence level 1 thinking (using and describing geometric properties of classes of sets). However, by grade 3 or 4, teachers should aim their activities to encourage more thinking at level 1. The objectives for these grade levels should include evidence of level 1 thinking: use of properties to describe shapes, categorization of shapes based on geometric properties and not on appearance or irrelevant attributes, and evidence of understanding geometric properties beyond identification of the property in a given particular shape. Again, there will be a differentiation in sophistication from one grade to the next as long as each grade is providing quality geometric experiences.

Middle Grades Geometry Objectives

By about the sixth grade, students who have clearly developed level 1 thinking should begin to move toward level 2 thought. This means that reasoning and logic should play a greater role in their activities, and hence that type of reasoning should be among the things you look for in your assessment. The following are suggestive of the objectives you should be aware of at this level:

- Shows improvement in spatial visualization skills
- Has an inclination to make and test conjectures in geometric situations
- Makes use of logical explanations in geometric problem solving
- Justifies conclusions in geometric contexts
- Assesses the validity of logical arguments in geometric situations
- Is aware of applications of geometric principles and concepts in real-world situations

Geometric Concept Objectives

The attention to growth in geometric thinking includes the development of specific concepts and ideas. Like concepts in other strands of mathematics, geometric concepts can be assessed. As with other concepts, understanding of most ideas will vary considerably from one student to the next, and you will want to be aware of different levels of understanding.

Children should begin at level 0 and continue in level 1 to attach appropriate names to special classifications of shapes that they readily recognize. It will be useful to see if the ideas are present even if the actual names are not. Shape recognition, however, should not be a major focus of your program and certainly should not dominate your assessment agenda.

Many textbooks in the intermediate grades focus on ideas such as *point, line, ray, segment,* and *angle.* These geometric elements are so primitive that they are difficult to define. Rather than focus on mastery of definitions, be more aware of the appropriate use of these terms in student activities. A student who can give you a memorized definition of a ray and an angle but shows little understanding when using these terms in an activity has not learned much of value. Similar statements can be made about a host of other geometric terms and relationships (*parallel, perpendicular, diameter, radius, tangent, skew, congruence, supplemental angles,* etc.).

There are some larger concepts for which understanding grows over the years as new connections and sophistication with the concepts develop. These include *line symmetry, rotational symmetry, similarity,* and *transformations (slides, flips, turns).* Each of these has been addressed in this chapter. The concept of line symmetry, for example, may be introduced as early as the second grade and continue to be developed in sophistication through the eighth grade. It is not reasonable to say that Johnny "knows symmetry." It may be appropriate to note that Johnny can recognize line symmetry in simple geometric designs and can produce a symmetric image if given a simple design and a line of symmetry. Johnny may not, for example, use or even recognize the relationship of corresponding elements in a symmetrical pattern to the line of symmetry or know how symmetry and the reflection transformation are related. For the purpose of assessment, descriptive statements about the concepts need to be made that indicate what a student does know about them. Your objectives should also be articulated in similar descriptive form.

Mathematical Power in Geometry

Mathematical power as defined by the *Curriculum Standards* includes the ability to explore, conjecture, and reason logically. Of course, it includes problem solving. These agendas should be evident in your assessment of geometry as well as other areas of the curriculum.

Perhaps the best way to get a handle on mathematical power is to consider the four theme standards: problem solving, communication, reasoning, and connections. Each

of these can and should be a part of every good geometry activity. Geometry as problem solving is seen in nearly every activity in this chapter as students are given a situation to wrestle with or make sense of. The goals of problem solving (see Chapter 4) can also be considered. Do not overlook the affective goals of confidence, willingness to try, and perseverance. Your assessment of individual children with respect to these goals may turn up differences in geometry when compared with other areas of the curriculum.

How do children represent and talk about geometric ideas? The level of that talk and the sophistication of the terminology and notation should be in keeping with students' developmental levels. "Sharp," "wide," and "square" are appropriate categories for angles in the second grade. "Pointy" and "not so pointy" might be appropriate in kindergarten or first grade. "Acute," "obtuse," and "right" and the use of standard symbolism for angles is appropriate in the intermediate and middle grades. These are aspects of the communication standard.

The reasoning and connections standards have already been addressed implicitly. Children's geometric reasoning is obviously related to their level of development as described by the van Hiele theory. Geometry is very much a part of the world we live in, and children should recognize and apply these connections.

Putting It All Together

Not every idea that has been discussed in these rather lengthy assessment notes needs to be included in your assessment program. However, in deciding what to assess and how, it is best to take a long-term view of geometry rather than a more traditional mastery-oriented approach. Three large perspectives have been suggested:

1. Growth in spatial sense and/or geometric thought
2. Understanding of geometric concepts and the corresponding terminology and notation
3. Development of mathematical power: geometric problem solving, communication, reasoning, and connections

As a teacher, you should establish and articulate goals for your geometry program in these areas. Share them with others at your grade level. Do not try to assess everything but create checklists, observation schemes, and rubrics that reflect long-range objectives. In this way, you can gather data that will inform and support your geometry program. By thinking in terms of long-range objectives, you will be able to articulate the value of a pentomino activity or other geometric challenge. Furthermore, you will learn what kinds of things to look for and listen for during a geometry exploration. What a child "knows" in geometry is not just a list of mastered terms but a way of thinking in geometric contexts.

REFLECTIONS ON CHAPTER 17: WRITING TO LEARN

Note: There are so many activities in this chapter that you may feel overwhelmed. The best way to get excited about and comfortable with informal geometry is to start doing activities, the same ones that are designed for students. Do not worry about being "right." What is right is to *do something,* to think about what you are doing, and to have fun. If you get interested, you will begin to search for ideas and relationships, and you may even decide you want to do further reading. Good geometry resource books for teachers are plentiful, and articles in the journals *Teaching Children Mathematics* and *Mathematics Teaching in the Middle School* are often excellent. You could not go wrong by simply exploring activities from this chapter. A possible limitation may be materials. An effort has been made to include many activities that use only teacher-made materials.

1. Describe what is meant by informal geometry. How is it different from the geometry usually taught in high school? How is it different from what you remember from school?

2. What do you think are the two best reasons for studying geometry? Explain.

3. Describe in your own words the first three van Hiele levels of geometric thought (levels 0, 1, and 2). Note in your description the object of thought and the product of thought. How do these ideas create a progression from one level to the next?

4. Describe the four characteristics of the van Hiele levels of thought. For each, reflect on why each characteristic might be important for teachers.

5. How would activities aimed at levels 0, 1, and 2 be different?

6. Select an activity from each of the levels, and do it (perhaps with a friend). Describe your experiences. If you were a child operating at the corresponding level, how would you describe your approach to the activity?

7. What do you do when the students in your classroom are at different van Hiele levels of thought?

8. Assessment in geometry involves much more than checking to see what students have mastered. What are the long-range goals of geometry, and how can these goals be incorporated into your assessment program?

FOR DISCUSSION AND EXPLORATION

1. How important should geometry be in the primary grades, the intermediate grades, and the middle school grades? Consider, at each of these levels, the competing demands of other areas of the mathematics curriculum and suggest how many of the roughly 36 weeks of the year should be spent on geometry. What justification can you give for your position?

2. Examine the teacher's edition of a basal textbook at any grade level. Select any lesson on geometry. Remember that the authors of the pupil's book are restricted to the printed page by the very nature of books. Teachers are not so restricted. How would you teach this lesson so that it was a *good* informal geometry lesson? Your lesson should include a hands-on activity and have a problem-solving spirit.

3. Get access to a computer software program for geometry such as *The Geometer's Sketchpad, Geometry Inventor, Elastic Lines,* or *Turtle Math* and play around with it. Try suggested explorations in the manuals or perhaps an article or other book that discusses the software you are exploring. What value should be given to a program like this in the grades for which the software was designed?

SUGGESTED READINGS

Highly Recommended

Bertheau, M. (1994). The most important thing is . . . *Teaching Children Mathematics, 1,* 112–115.

This short article reminds us that children's literature is a wonderful springboard for mathematics even if the book is not about mathematics. In addition to a nice idea for a good geometry lesson, the suggested discussion about shapes and what is important about them makes a good activity to begin moving children from level 0 to level 1 thinking. It is also a good assessment activity in the spirit of finding out what children know.

Crowley, M. L. (1987). The van Hiele model of the development of geometric thought. In M. M. Lindquist (Ed.), *Learning and teaching geometry, K–12* (pp. 1–16). Reston, VA: National Council of Teachers of Mathematics.

Crowley's chapter helped provide the rationale for the categorization of activities as presented in this text. It is a readable and informative view of the van Hiele theory, accompanied by excellent activities.

Del Grande, J. (1993). *Geometry and spatial sense: Addenda series, grades K–6.* Reston, VA: National Council of Teachers of Mathematics.

Geddes, D. (1992). *Geometry in the middle grades: Addenda series, grades 5–8.* Reston, VA: National Council of Teachers of Mathematics.

These two *Addenda* books are outstanding. Each provides useful perspective on geometry for the grade span and exciting activities. As with all the *Addenda Series* books, the activities are accompanied by discussions of how to "get into" the activity and develop the ideas with children. Blackline masters are provided when appropriate. The K–6 activities are also found in each of the elementary grade-level *Addenda* books from NCTM.

Geddes, D., & Fortunato, I. (1993). Geometry: Research and classroom activities. In D. T. Owens (Ed.), *Research ideas for the classroom: Middle grades mathematics* (pp. 199–222). Old Tappan, NJ: Macmillan.

Geddes and Fortunato bring a well-informed research perspective to the issue of geometry in the upper elementary and middle grades. This chapter clearly illustrates the van Hiele perspective for the classroom teacher and provides useful activities as examples along the way. The bibliography is extraordinary.

Other Suggestions

Beaumont, V., Curtis, R., & Smart, J. (1986). *How to teach perimeter, area, and volume*. Reston, VA: National Council of Teachers of Mathematics.

Bennett, D. (1992). *Exploring geometry with* The Geometer's Sketchpad. Berkeley, CA: Key Curriculum Press.

Bezuszka, S. J., Kenney, M., & Silvey, L. (1977). *Tessellations: The geometry of patterns*. Palo Alto, CA: Creative Publications.

Bidwell, J. K. (1987). Using reflections to find symmetric and asymmetric patterns. *Arithmetic Teacher, 34*(7), 10–15.

Bruni, J. V., & Seidenstein, R. B. (1990). Geometric concepts and spatial sense. In J. N. Payne (Ed.), *Mathematics for the young child* (pp. 203–207). Reston, VA: National Council of Teachers of Mathematics.

Burger, W. F. (1982). Graph paper geometry. In L. Silvey (Ed.), *Mathematics for the middle grades (5–9)* (pp. 102–117). Reston, VA: National Council of Teachers of Mathematics.

Carroll, W. M. (1988). Cross sections for clay solids. *Arithmetic Teacher, 35*(7), 6–11.

Chazan, D. (1989). *How to use conjecturing and microcomputers to teach geometry*. Reston, VA: National Council of Teachers of Mathematics.

Confer, C. (1994). *Math by all means: Geometry, grade 2*. White Plains, NY: Cuisenaire (distributor).

Dana, M. E. (1987). Geometry: A square deal for elementary teachers. In M. M. Lindquist (Ed.), *Learning and teaching geometry, K–12* (pp. 113–125). Reston, VA: National Council of Teachers of Mathematics.

Dana, M. E., & Lindquist, M. M. (1978). Let's try triangles. *Arithmetic Teacher, 26*(1), 2–9.

Ernie, K. T. (1995). Mathematics and quilting. In P. A. House (Ed.), *Connecting mathematics across the curriculum* (pp. 170–176). Reston, VA: National Council of Teachers of Mathematics.

Flores, A. (1993). Pythagoras meets van Hiele. *School Science and Mathematics, 93,* 152–157.

Fosnaugh, L. S., & Harrell, M. E. (1996). Covering the plane with rep-tiles. *Mathematics Teaching in the Middle School, 1,* 666–670.

Fuys, D. J., & Liebov, A. K. (1993). Geometry and spatial sense. In R. J. Jensen (Ed.), *Research ideas for the classroom: Early childhood mathematics* (pp. 195–222). Old Tappan, NJ: Macmillan.

Giganti, P., Jr., & Cittadino, M. J. (1990). The art of tessellation. *Arithmetic Teacher, 37*(7), 6–16.

Hill, J. M. (Ed.). (1987). *Geometry for grades K–6: Readings from* The Arithmetic Teacher. Reston, VA: National Council of Teachers of Mathematics.

Hoffer, A. R., & Hoffer, S. A. K. (1992). Geometry and visual thinking. In T. R. Post (Ed.), *Teaching mathematics in grades K–8: Research-based methods* (2nd ed.) (pp. 249–277). Needham Heights, MA: Allyn & Bacon.

Kaiser, B. (1988). Explorations with tessellating polygons. *Arithmetic Teacher, 36*(4), 19–24.

Kleiman, G. M. (1995). Seeing and thinking mathematically in the middle school. In P. A. House (Ed.), *Connecting mathematics across the curriculum* (pp. 153–158). Reston, VA: National Council of Teachers of Mathematics.

Lappan, G., & Even, R. (1987). Scale drawings. *Arithmetic Teacher, 35*(9), 32–35.

Lufkin, D. (1996). The incredible three-by-five card. *Mathematics Teacher, 89,* 96–98.

National Council of Teachers of Mathematics. (1990). Spatial sense [Focus issue]. *Arithmetic Teacher, 37*(6).

Pollack, P. (1996). My application of the Pythagorean theorem. *Mathematics Teaching in the Middle School, 1,* 814–816.

Ranucci, E. R., & Teeters, J. L. (1977). *Creating Escher-type drawings*. Palo Alto, CA: Creative Publications.

Rectanus, C. (1994). *Math by all means: Geometry, grade 3*. White Plains, NY: Cuisenaire (distributor).

Rubenstein, R. N., & Thompson, D. R. (1995). Making connections with transformations in grades K–8. In P. A. House (Ed.), *Connecting mathematics across the curriculum* (pp. 65–78). Reston, VA: National Council of Teachers of Mathematics.

Sconyers, J. M. (1995). Proof and the middle school mathematics student. *Mathematics Teaching in the Middle School, 1,* 516–518.

Senk, S. L., & Hirschhorn, D. B. (1990). Multiple approaches to geometry: Teaching similarity. *Mathematics Teacher, 83,* 274–280.

Serra, M. (1993). *Discovering geometry: An inductive approach*. Berkeley, CA: Key Curriculum Press.

Shaw, J. M. (1983). Exploring perimeter and area using centimeter-squared paper. *Arithmetic Teacher, 31*(4), 4–11.

Shroyer, J., & Fitzgerald, W. (1986). *Mouse and elephant: Measuring growth*. Menlo Park, CA: AWL Supplemental.

Skinner, J. (1987). Extracts from a teacher's diary. *Mathematics Teaching, 121,* 23–26.

Teppo, A. (1991). Van Hiele levels of geometric thought revisited. *Mathematics Teacher, 84,* 210–221.

Van de Walle, J. A., & Thompson, C. S. (1980). Concepts, art, and fun from simple tiling patterns. *Arithmetic Teacher, 28*(3), 4–8.

Van de Walle, J. A., & Thompson, C. S. (1981). A triangle treasury. *Arithmetic Teacher, 28*(6), 6–11.

Van de Walle, J. A., & Thompson, C. S. (1984). Cut and paste for geometric thinking. *Arithmetic Teacher, 32*(1), 8–13.

Walter, M. J. (1970). *Boxes, squares, and other things*. Reston, VA: National Council of Teachers of Mathematics.

Willcutt, B. (1987). Triangular tiles for your patio. *Arithmetic Teacher, 34*(9), 43–45.

Winter, J. J., Lappan, G., Phillips, E., & Fitzgerald, W. (1986). *Middle grades mathematics project: Spatial visualization*. Menlo Park, CA: AWL Supplemental.

CHAPTER

LOGICAL REASONING: ATTRIBUTE AND PATTERN ACTIVITIES

In Chapter 2, mathematics was described as the science of pattern and order. The search for and analysis of pattern and order are an integral part of doing mathematics, whether it is developing a computational algorithm, exploring properties of shapes, or figuring the solution to a probability problem. Children can learn the processes of doing mathematics as they learn mathematics content. However, the ability to reason is so important in this science of pattern and order that attention should be given explicitly to helping children develop their reasoning skills.

Note that the activities in this chapter are *not* just for early childhood classrooms. The tradition has been that work with patterns and attribute materials is done only in K–1 classrooms. Put that notion aside. There are activities in this chapter for all students in grades K–8. The objectives of these activities are integral to *all* mathematics learning.

BIG IDEAS

1. **The same set of objects can be considered in different ways, leading to the creation of different classifications. A single object can belong to more than one class.**
2. **Logical patterns exist and are a regular occurrence in mathematics. They can be recognized and extended.**
3. **The same logical pattern can exist or be found in many different forms.**

OBJECTIVES OF ATTRIBUTE AND PATTERN ACTIVITIES

We saw in Chapter 4 that in addition to the knowledge base of mathematics, a good mathematics program has three sets of problem-solving goals: (1) strategy and process goals, (2) metacognitive goals, and (3) affective goals. The objectives of attribute and patterning activities are nearly identical to those found in these three categories.

Strategy Goals

The activities in this chapter are aimed at higher-order thinking skills. Logical reasoning of some form is important in nearly every activity. Students are encouraged to formulate and check hypotheses. Because many of these logic problems are posed with manipulative materials or calculators, the strategy of "try and adjust" or "guess and check" is encouraged. Attribute activities get specifically at the skills of classification (observing likenesses and differences). Patterning activities develop a sense of pattern and regularity and practice the skills of searching for pattern, extending patterns, and making pattern generalizations.

Another feature of all of these activities is that correctness can always be determined by the students. Certainly students will ask, "Is this right?" but you can always respond, "How can you tell? Does what you did fit the pattern?" The ability to self-assess is absolutely crucial in all of mathematics. The habit and the process of self-assessment are developed in these activities along with the expectation that it can be done.

Metacognitive Goals

In all of these tasks, there is a clear sense of working toward a goal—figuring out the classification scheme, discerning the pattern, extending the pattern. Thus it is quite natural to ask students the three questions suggested in Chapter 4: *What* are you doing? *Why* are you doing it? *How* does it help you? If you keep the habits of self-monitoring in mind, you can get as much mileage out of these activities as any problems in the curriculum. Students learn from these experiences to reflect on their own activity, to be aware of their progress or lack of progress, and to change their strategies or approaches as need dictates.

Affective Goals

Affective goals, you will recall, fall under two headings: attitudes and beliefs. Under attitudes we find *willingness* to try, *enjoyment* in solving problems, and *perseverance* in the face of difficulty. The difficulty level of most attribute or pattern problems can be adjusted so that there is just sufficient difficulty to be challenging and interesting but not disheartening. When the tasks are set at the right level, children love to work on them. They are fun things to do in groups. There is a lot of natural give-and-take between children as they work. As a result, children learn that they really can solve tough problems and enjoy doing it. They learn that occasionally it takes time, but the work pays off.

Under the heading of beliefs we find *self-confidence,* faith in *personal abilities,* and the belief that *methods can be discovered.* Again, the good-spirited, fun approach, coupled with the use of manipulatives, makes attribute and pattern activities ideally suited to addressing these goals.

ATTRIBUTE MATERIALS AND ACTIVITIES

Attribute activities help students reason about likenesses and differences. Classifications or groupings are discovered. Schemes for presenting these groupings are developed. The problems and materials help children understand that things can be looked at in a number of ways. (An object has several attributes. It may be like another object when thought about one way but different when considered in another way.) Classification skills are also science skills. Many good science programs, especially those that are process-oriented, include a heavy emphasis on classification.

In the 1960s and early 1970s, classification activities became very popular as readiness activities for number. They were viewed as "prenumber" activities. The view adopted in this book is that there is no demonstrated relationship between classification activities and number concept development. The activities presented here should not be considered prenumber experiences.

Attribute Materials

Attribute materials are sets of objects that lend themselves to being sorted and classified in different ways. Natural or *unstructured* attribute materials include such things as seashells, leaves, the children themselves, or the set of the children's shoes. The *attributes* are the ways that the materials can be sorted. For example, hair color, height, and gender are attributes of children. Each attribute has a number of different *values:* for example, blond, brown, or red (for the attribute of hair color); tall or short (for height); male or female (for gender).

A *structured* set of attribute pieces has exactly one piece for every possible combination of values for each attribute. For example, several commercial sets of plastic attribute materials have four attributes: color (red, yellow, blue), shape (circle, triangle, rectangle, square, hexagon), size (big, little), and thickness (thick, thin). In the set just described, there is exactly one large, thin, red triangle, just as there is one each of all other combinations. The specific values, number of values, or number of attributes that a set may have is not important.

Three teacher-made sets of attribute pieces are illustrated in Figure 18.1 (p. 394). The attribute shapes are easily made in nice large sizes out of poster board and laminated for durability. A Woozle Cards master is in the Blackline Masters. These can be duplicated on tagboard and quickly colored in two colors before laminating. The ice-cream cones can be made from construction paper and laminated or could be duplicated on paper and cut out by the students.

The value of using structured attribute materials (instead of unstructured materials) is that the attributes and values are very clearly identified and easily articulated to students. There is no confusion or argument concerning what values a particular piece possesses. In this way, we can focus our attention in the activities on the reasoning skills that the materials and activities are meant to serve. Even though a nice set of attribute pieces may contain geometric shapes of different colors and sizes, they are not very good materials for teaching shape, color, or size. A set of attribute shapes does not provide enough variability in any of the shape attributes to help students develop anything but very limited geometric ideas. In fact, simple shapes, primary colors, and two sizes are chosen because they are most easily discriminated and identified by even the youngest students.

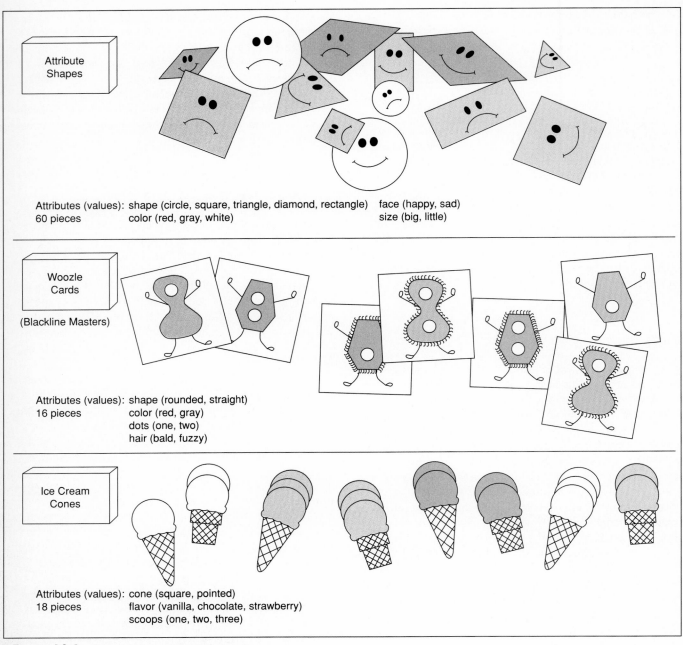

Attribute Shapes

Attributes (values): shape (circle, square, triangle, diamond, rectangle)   face (happy, sad)
60 pieces   color (red, gray, white)   size (big, little)

Woozle Cards

(Blackline Masters)

Attributes (values): shape (rounded, straight)
16 pieces   color (red, gray)
                   dots (one, two)
                   hair (bald, fuzzy)

Ice Cream Cones

Attributes (values): cone (square, pointed)
18 pieces   flavor (vanilla, chocolate, strawberry)
                   scoops (one, two, three)

● **FIGURE 18.1**   Three teacher-made attribute sets.

Activities with Attribute Materials

Most attribute activities are best done in a teacher-directed format. Young children can sit on the floor in a large circle where all can see and have access to the materials. Older children can work in groups of four to six students, each group with its own set of materials. In that format, problems can be addressed to the full class, and groups can explore them independently. All activities should be con-

ducted in an easygoing manner that encourages risks, good thinking, attentiveness, and discussion of ideas. The atmosphere should be nonthreatening, nonpunitive, and nonevaluative.

Most of the activities here will be described using the geometric shapes in Figure 18.1. However, each could be done with any structured set, and some could be done with nonstructured materials.

Learning Classification Schemes

Several attribute activities involve using overlapping loops, each containing a designated class of materials. Loops are made of yarn or are drawn on paper to hold a designated class of pieces such as "red" or "not square." When two loops overlap, the area that is inside both loops is for the pieces that have both properties. Children as young as kindergarten can have fun with simple loop activities. With the use of words such as *and, or,* and *not,* the loop activities become challenging for children in the upper grades as well.

Before children can use these loops in a problem-solving activity, the scheme itself must first be understood. A good way to accomplish this is simply to do a few activities that involve the loops. Children find these interesting and fun. After several days of working with these initial activities, you will be able to move on to the logic problems that involve the same formats. Children will be able to attend to the problems because they are familiar with the way the loops are used.

Once the idea of how a loop can be used to hold a particular type of piece, "strings" or loops can be drawn on poster board or on large sheets of paper. If you happen to have a magnetic blackboard, try using small magnets on the backs of the pieces and conduct full-class activities with the pieces on the board. Students can come to the board to place or arrange pieces inside loops drawn on the board with colored chalk.

ACTIVITY

18.2 Labeled Loops

Label the overlapping loops with cards indicating values of different attributes. Let children take turns randomly selecting a piece from the pile and deciding in which region it belongs. Pieces belonging in neither loop are placed outside. Let other students decide if the placement is correct, and occasionally have someone else explain. Do this even when the choice of regions is correct.

ACTIVITY

18.1 The First Loops

At the beginning level, give children two large loops of yarn or string. Direct them to put all the red pieces inside one string and all triangles inside the other. Let the children try to resolve the difficulty of what to do with the red triangles. When the notion of overlapping the strings to create an area common to both loops is clear, more challenging activities can be explored.

A significant variation of Activity 18.2 is to introduce negative attributes such as "not red" or "not small." Also important is the use of the *and* and *or* connectives, as in "red and square" or "big or happy." The use of *and, or,* and *not* significantly widens children's classification schemes. It also makes these activities quite difficult for very young children. In Figure 18.2, three loops are used in a string game illustrating some of these ideas.

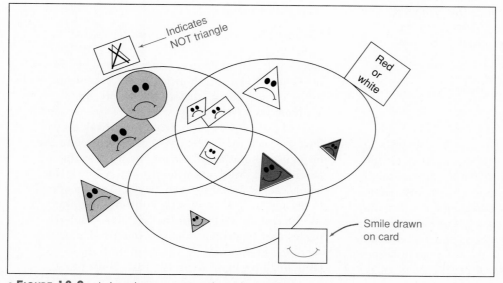

● **FIGURE 18.2**   A three-loop activity with attribute pieces.

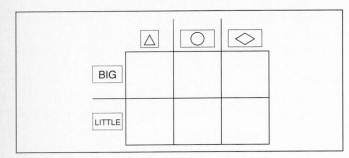

● **FIGURE 18.3**   A two-way classification grid.

In addition to using loops to arrange or display overlapping classes of objects, a matrix or grid can be used, as shown in Figure 18.3. The values for one attribute are listed across the top and for another attribute down the side. Each region in the grid holds all objects that share the two corresponding values.

---ACTIVITY---

18.3 Attribute Grids

Draw a large grid on a poster board or on a large sheet of butcher paper. If you draw a 3 × 3 or a 3 × 4 grid, the same drawing can be used regardless of the attributes and values selected. Use cards as was done with the loops to designate the attribute values. Place the value cards face up so that the students can see them. Have the children take turns selecting a piece at random from the full set and placing it in the grid. Students, not the teacher, should decide if the piece is correctly placed. If not all values of an attribute are included among the labels placed on the grid, some pieces may not fit in the grid at all. Instead of simply placing pieces correctly in the grids, students can be asked to find a piece that fits in a particular cell of the grid.

Solving Logic Problems

The activities described so far have students attempting to classify materials according to *our* schemes. That is, the teacher creates a classification, and the children fit pieces into it. While this is important for the purpose of understanding classifications by more than one attribute (the overlapping loops), the activities make relatively few cognitive demands. All that is required in these activities is an understanding of the loop method of classification and the ability to discriminate the attributes. When the words *and, or,* and *not* are used,

children gain experience with those logical connectives. However, very limited logical reasoning or problem solving is actually going on. A much more significant mental activity is to infer how things have been classified when the scheme is not clearly articulated. The following activities are examples of those that require students to make and test conjectures about how things are being classified. These activities move classification squarely into the domain of problem solving.

---ACTIVITY---

18.4 Guess My Rule

For this activity, try using students instead of shapes as attribute "pieces." Decide on an attribute of your students such as "wearing blue jeans" or "has stripes on clothing," but do not tell your rule to the class. Silently look at one child at a time and move the child to the left or right according to this attribute rule. After a number of students have been sorted, have the next child come up and ask students to predict which group he or she belongs in. Before the rule is articulated, continue the activity for a while so that others in the class will have an opportunity to determine the rule. This same activity can be done with virtually any materials that can be sorted. When unstructured materials such as students, students' shoes, shells, or buttons are used, the classifications may be quite obscure, providing an interesting challenge.

---ACTIVITY---

18.5 Hidden Labels

The same inference approach can be applied to "Labeled Loops" (Activity 18.2, p. 395). Select label cards for the loops of string, and place the cards face down. Begin to sort pieces according to the turned-down labels. As you sort, have students try to determine what the labels are for each of the loops. Let students who think they have guessed the labels try to place a piece in the proper loop, but avoid having them guess the labels aloud. Students who think they know the labels can be asked to "play teacher" and respond to the guesses of the others. Point out that one way to test an idea about the labels is to select pieces that you think might go in a particular section. Do not turn the cards up until most students have figured out the rule. Notice that some rules or labels are equivalent: "not large" is the same as "small." With the use of three loops and logical connectives, this activity can become quite challenging even for middle school students. With simple, one-value labels and only two loops, it can easily be played in kindergarten.

---ACTIVITY---

18.6 Secret Grids

"Attribute Grids" (Activity 18.3) can be converted to require inference too. Select labels for each row and column, but turn the cards face down. Place pieces on the grid where they belong. The object is to determine what the attribute values (on the cards) are for each row and column. Encourage students to use trial and error to test what they think the cards say.

---ACTIVITY---

18.7 Which One Doesn't Belong?

The *Sesame Street* game "One of These Things Is Not like the Others" is easily conducted with any attribute set. Select four pieces so that three of the pieces have some feature in common that is not a feature of the fourth. The students try to decide which piece is different. In Figure 18.4, there are two pieces that are each different from the other three. Frequently, there can be three or even four possible choices, each for a different reason. The students should explain their reasons, and classmates should decide if the reason is good. Be sure that you emphasize good reasoning and not right answers.

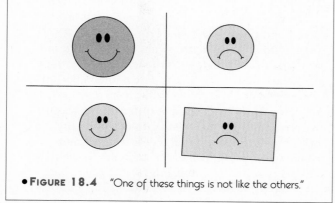

●**FIGURE 18.4**   *"One of these things is not like the others."*

---ACTIVITY---

18.8 Sets of Four

Choose one value of any two attributes, such as "happy triangles" or "large red pieces." Select any four pieces that share both values, and arrange them in a 2 × 2 array. The challenge is to make more arrays similar to or like the original one. To make new arrays, you must first decide how the pieces in the original array are alike, and use those same attributes but with different values to make the other arrays. Look at the example in Figure 18.5. The original array was all happy triangles: attributes of face and shape. The values of color and size are mixed. Within each new array, face and shape values are the same. Corresponding pieces each match the original

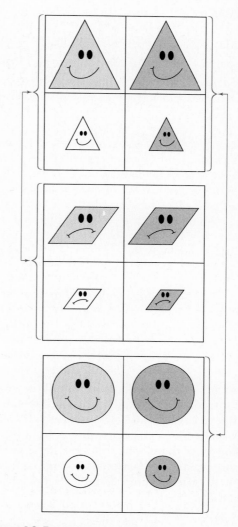

●**FIGURE 18.5**   *Making sets of four.*

array in color and size. If this activity is done with sets such as the Woozle Cards or People Pieces (Elementary Science Study, 1966), where each of the attributes has exactly two values, four arrays will use up all of the pieces.

Be prepared to adjust the difficulty of these and similar activities according to the skills and interests of your children. Remember that children like to be challenged, but an activity that is either too easy or too difficult is likely to result in restless children and discipline problems.

Difference Games

As an introduction to these activities, let each child select an attribute piece. Then you hold up one piece for all to see and ask questions such as these:

Who has one that is like mine? How is it like mine?

Who has one that is different? Explain how it is different.

Look at your neighbor's piece. Tell how yours is like that one. Let your partner explain how your neighbor's is different from your piece.

Students will soon find that sometimes a piece differs in three or four ways and other pieces will differ in perhaps one or two ways. To focus attention on this, ask, "Who has a piece that is different in *just exactly one way* from mine? Who has a piece that is different in *exactly two ways?*" Notice that for a set with four attributes, a piece differing in three ways is alike in one way. It is usual to limit attention to either one difference or two differences.

on it. Place the first piece in one of the sections. Subsequent pieces can be placed to the right or the left around the track but must differ in one way from the adjacent piece. Placing the last piece may be difficult or even impossible; it must differ in exactly one way from the piece on either side. A sample is shown in Figure 18.6.

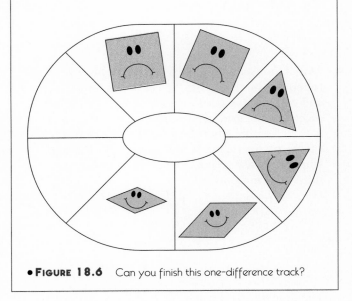

● **Figure 18.6**   *Can you finish this one-difference track?*

Difference train and track games can be two-difference games as well as one-difference games. These are not significantly more difficult but add variety.

ACTIVITY

18.9 Difference Trains and Tracks

Place an attribute piece in the center of the group. The first student finds a piece that is different from this piece in exactly one way. Let students take turns finding a piece that differs from the *preceding* piece in just one way, creating a "one-difference train." The train can be made as long as the students wish or until no more pieces will fit the one-difference rule.

As a variation, draw a circular track on a piece of paper or poster board with six to ten sections

---

ACTIVITY

18.10 Difference Grids

Draw a 4 × 5 grid on poster board so that each space will hold an attribute piece. Select one piece, and place it anywhere on the board. In turn, students try to put pieces on the board in any space above, below, to the left, or to the right of a space that is filled. The rule is that adjacent pieces up and down must differ in two ways; to the left and right, they must differ in one way. It will frequently be impossible to complete the grid, but establishing that fact is a significant challenge. It is important for students to see that not every problem is solvable.

REPEATING PATTERNS

Identifying and extending patterns is an important process in mathematical thinking. Simple repetitive patterns can be explored as early as kindergarten. Young children seem to love to work with patterns such as those made with colored blocks, connecting cubes, and buttons, extending the patterns across an entire room. The internal positive feedback they receive from knowing they are right and successful is significant.

Using Materials in Patterning

Almost all patterning activities should involve some form of physical materials to make up the pattern. This is especially true of repeating patterns in grades K–4, but it is also true of virtually all patterning activities, even at the junior high level. When patterns are built with materials, children are able to test the extension of a pattern and make changes as they discover errors without fear of being wrong. The materials permit experimentation or trial-and-error approaches that are almost impossible without them.

Many kindergarten and first-grade textbooks have pages where students are given a pattern such as a string of colored beads. The task may be to color the last bead or two in the string. There are two differences between this and the same activity done with actual materials. First, by coloring or marking a space on the page, the activity takes on an aura of right versus wrong. There is clearly a correct way to finish the pattern. If a mistake is made, correction on the page is difficult and can cause feelings of inadequacy. With materials, a trial-and-error approach can be used. Second, pattern activities on worksheets prevent children from extending patterns beyond the few spaces provided by the page. Most children enjoy using materials such as colored blocks, buttons, and connecting cubes to extend their patterns well beyond the printed page. Children are frequently observed continuing a pattern with materials halfway across the classroom floor. In doing so, children receive a great deal of satisfaction and positive feedback from the activity itself. "Hey, I understand this! I can do it really well. I feel good about how I solved my pattern problem."

The same benefit of using materials can be built into patterning activities at the upper grades. There the satisfaction comes not so much from extending a repeating pattern as it does from seeing how an observed relationship actually exists in a particular design or arrangement of materials. Thus patterning is not only a form of problem solving and logical reasoning but also a satisfying and self-rewarding pursuit. It is very important that students connect such positive feelings with mathematical thinking.

Repeating-Pattern Activities

The concept of a repeating pattern and how a pattern is extended or continued can be introduced to the full class in several ways. One possibility is to draw simple shape patterns on the board and extend them in a class discussion. Oral patterns can be joined in by all children. For example, "do, mi, mi, do, mi, mi, . . ." is a simple singing pattern. Up, down, and sideways arm positions provide three elements with which to make patterns: up, side, side, down, up, side, side, down, . . . Boy-girl patterns or stand-sit-squat patterns are also fun. From these ideas, the youngest children learn quickly the concept of patterns. Students can begin to work more profitably in small groups or even independently once a general notion of patterns is developed.

---ACTIVITY---

18.11 Pattern Strips

Students can work independently or in groups of two or three to extend patterns made from simple materials: buttons, colored blocks, connecting cubes, toothpicks, geometric shapes, and a wide variety of other materials, most of which you can gather easily. For each set of materials, draw two or three complete repetitions of a pattern on strips of tagboard about 5 cm by 30 cm. The students, using actual materials, copy the pattern shown and extend it as far as they wish. Discussions with students will help them describe their patterns, and uncover errors. Soon you can encourage students to make up patterns on their own. Figure 18.7 (p. 400) illustrates some possible patterns for a variety of materials. It is not necessary to have class-sized sets of materials. Make 10 to 15 different pattern strips for each set of materials. With six to eight sets, your entire class can work at the same time, with small groups working with different patterns and different materials.

The *core* of a repeating pattern is the shortest string of elements that repeats. Notice in Figure 18.7 that the core is always fully repeated, and never only partially shown. If the core of a pattern is –oo, a card might have –oo–oo (two repetitions of the core), but it would be ambiguous if the card showed –oo–oo– or –oo–.

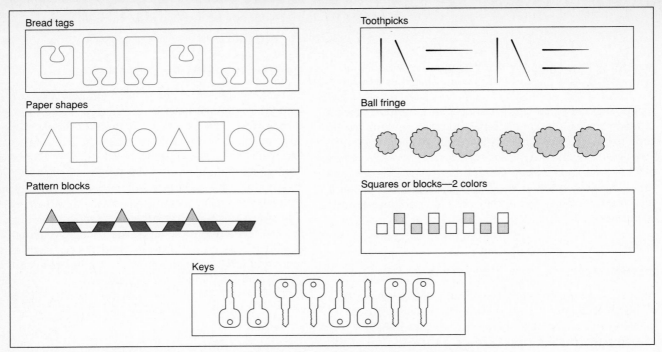

Bread tags

Paper shapes

Pattern blocks

Toothpicks

Ball fringe

Squares or blocks—2 colors

Keys

● **FIGURE 18.7** Examples of pattern cards drawn on tagboard. Each pattern repeats completely and does not split in the middle of a core.

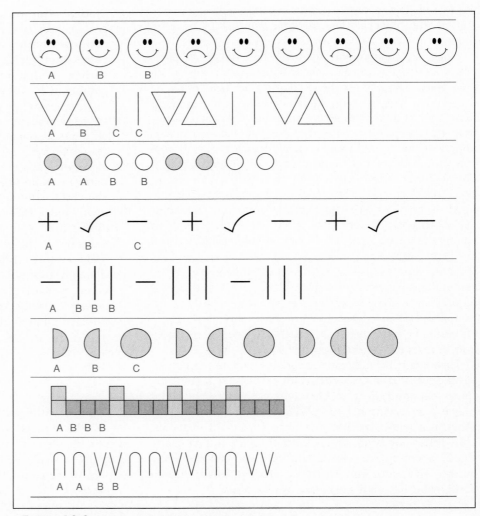

A B B

A B C C

A A B B

A B C

A B B B

A B C

A B B B

A A B B

● **FIGURE 18.8** More examples of repeating patterns.

A significant step forward mathematically is to see how two patterns constructed with different materials can actually be the same pattern. For example, the first pattern on the left in Figure 18.7 and the first pattern in Figure 18.8 can both be "read" A-B-B-A-B-B-, and the pattern below those in both figures is A-B-C-C-A-B-C-C-. Challenging students to translate a pattern from one medium to another or to find two patterns that are alike, even though made with different materials, is an important activity that helps students focus on the relationships that are the essence of repeated patterns.

---ACTIVITY---

18.12 Pattern Match

Using a chalkboard or an overhead projector, show six or seven patterns with different materials or pictures. Teach students to use an A, B, C method of reading a pattern. Half of the class can close their eyes while the other half uses the A, B, C scheme to read a pattern that you point to. After hearing the pattern, the students who had their eyes closed examine the patterns and try to decide which pattern was read. If two of the patterns in the list have the same structure, the discussion can be very interesting.

The following independent activity involves translation of a pattern from one medium to another, which is another way of helping students separate the relationship in a pattern from the materials used to build it.

---ACTIVITY---

18.13 Same Pattern, Different Stuff

Have students make a pattern with one set of materials given a pattern strip showing a different set. This activity can easily be set up by simply switching the pattern strips from one set of materials to another. A similar idea is to mix up the pattern strips for four or five different sets of materials and have students find strips that have the same pattern. To test if two patterns are the same, children can translate each of the strips into a third set of materials or can write down the A, B, C pattern for each.

Two-Dimensional Patterns

Figure 18.9 illustrates how patterns can be developed on a grid instead of a straight line. Children at the primary level find completion of these patterns quite challenging. Pattern cards can be made by coloring or drawing on a piece of grid paper. If blank grids the same width as the pattern cards are laminated, students can use colored blocks or colored squares of construction paper on the blank grids. This provides the same trial-and-error potential that was noted with repeating patterns.

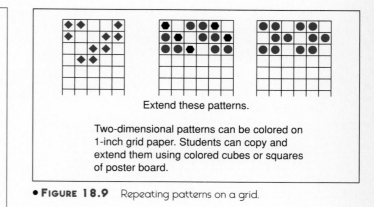

Extend these patterns.

Two-dimensional patterns can be colored on 1-inch grid paper. Students can copy and extend them using colored cubes or squares of poster board.

● **FIGURE 18.9** *Repeating patterns on a grid.*

GROWING PATTERNS

Beginning at about the fourth or fifth grade and extending through the junior high years, students can explore patterns that involve a progression from step to step. In technical terms, these are called *sequences;* we will simply call them *growing patterns.* With these patterns, students not only extend patterns but also look for a generalization or an algebraic relationship that will tell them what the pattern will be at any point along the way. Therefore, not only do these activities develop the mathematical processes noted at the outset of the chapter, but they are also an excellent example of the concept of function and can be used as one way to provide meaningful experiences with this very important mathematical idea.

Figure 18.10 (p. 402) illustrates some growing patterns that are built with various materials or drawings. The patterns consist of a series of separate elements or *frames,* each new frame related to the previous one according to the pattern.

As just noted, the most significant reason for exploring these patterns is that they are an excellent introduction to the concepts of function (the rule or pattern involved is a function) and also variable. In Chapter 21, these same growing patterns are discussed in terms of their potential for

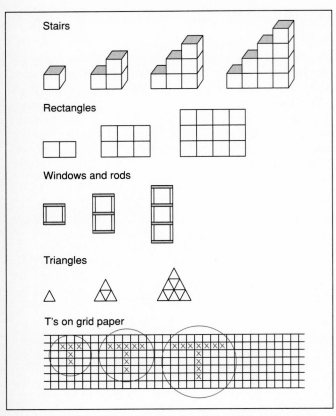

Stairs

Rectangles

Windows and rods

Triangles

T's on grid paper

● **FIGURE 18.10**   *Growing patterns with materials or drawings.*

helping children develop function and variable concepts. Even though those algebraic ideas are generally part of the seventh- or eighth-grade curriculum, children can profitably explore growing patterns as early as the fourth grade.

OTHER PATTERNS TO EXPLORE

Patterns pervade all of mathematics and much of nature. It would be an error to leave the impression that repeated patterns and growing patterns as discussed so far are all that children need to know about patterns. Here you will be exposed to some other patterns or approaches to looking at patterns. But there really is no end to the variation. Mathematicians continue to search for and discover new patterns and relationships. Applications of mathematical patterns have led to solutions of real-world problems that were once thought to be unsolvable. Patterns are powerful ideas.

The Fibonacci Sequence

For a growing pattern that is just a little bit different, see Figure 18.11. It begins with a little square. Each successive

frame is formed by building a new and larger square onto the previous design. (Can you see how to continue drawing this pattern?) If the side of the first two little squares is 1 each, then the sides of each new square are the numbers of most interest in this pattern. For those squares shown in the figure, the sides are 1, 1, 2, 3, 5, 8, and 13. What would the side of the next square be? This series of numbers, known as the *Fibonacci sequence,* is named for the Italian mathematician Leonardo Fibonacci (c. 1180–1250). The sequence occurs in a variety of living things. For example, if you count the sets of spirals that go in opposite directions on a pineapple or the seeds of a sunflower, the two numbers will be adjacent numbers in the Fibonacci sequence, usually 8 and 13 for a pineapple and 55 and 89 for sunflowers.

Another interesting fact about the Fibonacci sequence is that the ratio of adjacent numbers in the sequence gets closer and closer to a single fixed number known as the *golden ratio,* a number very close to 1.618. Each larger rectangle in Figure 18.11 has sides in ratio a little closer to the golden ratio. A rectangle in that ratio is called a *golden rectangle,* examples of which can be found in most of the prominent examples of ancient Greek architecture as well as in much art and architecture through the ages. The spiral that is drawn in the last rectangle shown (made from quarter circles drawn in each square) is the same spiral found in the shell of the chambered nautilus.

The usual Fibonacci sequence begins with 1, 1. After these first two terms, the next term is found by adding the two preceding terms: $1 + 1 = 2$, $1 + 2 = 3$, $2 + 3 = 5$, $3 + 5 = 8$, and so on. What happens if you use the same rule for generating each new number but you begin with numbers

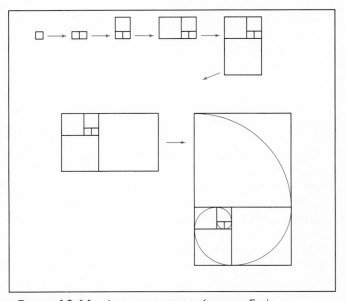

● **FIGURE 18.11**   *A growing pattern of squares: Each new rectangle is a little closer to a "golden rectangle."*

other than 1 and 1? This is an interesting exploration. Among other things you may discover is that the ratio of successive pairs of terms also gets closer and closer to the same golden ratio, 1.618 . . . , as the regular Fibonacci sequence. On a graphing calculator, the following simple program will produce successive numbers in the sequence and the current ratio of the last two terms with every press of the Enter key.

```
ClrHome
ClrList L₂,L₁
1→N
Disp "ENTER 1ST"
Disp "SEED"
Input H
1→L₁(N)
Disp "ENTER 2ND"
Disp "SEED"
Input Y
H/Y→L₂(1)
ClrHome
Disp "FIRST 2 NOS.",H,Y
Disp "RATIO",H/Y
Pause
ClrHome
Lbl 1
N+1→N
H+Y→A
Y→Z
H→Y
A→H
Disp "LAST 3 NOS.",Z,Y,H
Disp "RATIO OF LAST 2",H/Y
N→L₁(N)
H/Y→L₂(N)
Pause
ClrHome
Goto 1
```

The Fibonacci sequence and the golden ratio are fascinating phenomena of mathematics. For those who would like to learn more about the connections of this sequence with nature, art, and mathematics, books by Runion (1990) and by Garland (1987) are highly recommended.

Numeric Patterns

Drawings and manipulative objects should be a principal feature of patterning programs because they permit experimentation and trial-and-error approaches without threat. Students can validate their observations and conjectures without recourse to the teacher or answer book. However, many worthwhile patterns can be observed with numbers alone. These can be simple repeating patterns such as 1, 2, 1, 2, . . . Even very young children can use numbers in patterns like these. Generally, however, numeric patterns involve some form of progression. The pattern 1, 2, 1, 3, 1, 4, 1, 5, . . . is a simple example that even young students can discover. Here are some more numeric patterns:

2, 4, 6, 8, 10, . . .	(even numbers; add 2 each time)
1, 4, 7, 10, 13, . . .	(start with 1; add 3 each time)
1, 4, 9, 16, . . .	(squares: 1^2, 2^2, 3^2, etc.)
0, 1, 5, 14, 30, . . .	(add the next square number)
2, 5, 11, 23, . . .	(double the number and add 1)
2, 6, 12, 20, 30, . . .	(multiply successive pairs)
3, 3, 6, 9, 15, 24, . . .	(add the two preceding numbers—a Fibonacci sequence)

The challenge in these patterns or sequences of numbers is not only to find and extend the pattern but also to try to determine a general rule to produce the *n*th number in the sequence. Informal or exploratory approaches are similar to those described for growing patterns.

Patterns with the Calculator

The calculator provides a powerful approach to patterns. A few examples are presented here, but there are many more.

---ACTIVITY---

18.14 Skip Count
Patterns

Choose a start number between 0 and 9, and add a constant (skip number) repeatedly to that number. Remember to use the automatic constant feature. For example, to start with 7 and add 4 repeatedly, you press 7 ⊞ 4 ⊟ ⊟ ⊟ . . . What digits appear in the ones place? (1, 5, 9, 3, 7, 1, 5, 9, 3, 7, . . .) How long is the pattern before it repeats? Are all patterns the same length? Are there shorter ones? Can you find one that is length 6? Why not? How does this change when the start number changes? How does it change when the skip number changes?

To supplement Activity 18.14, supply children with 0–99 charts. Small versions of these charts can be found in the Blackline Masters. For each pattern (start number and skip number), have students color in all of the results. Visual patterns will appear on the charts as well as in the numbers. Also, do not forget to look for other patterns in these series of numbers. There are more patterns than those you may find in the ones digits.

—ACTIVITY—

18.15 Creating Matching Patterns

In Activity 18.12, "Pattern Match" (p. 401) children learned that patterns in different forms can be coded using letters. They learned to talk about an AAB pattern or an ABBC pattern. Young children can use the calculator to create number patterns that match these letter patterns that you suggest—for example, "Make an AAB pattern on your calculator." Some may key in 448448448. Another might be 992992992. (Note that 299299 would be an ABB pattern, not AAB.) The pattern cannot be extended on the eight-digit display. However, you can share these different results for the same pattern form by writing them on the board, and asking how they should be extended and how the patterns are alike. As an added twist, you might look for all the patterns that match the form and have the same "core sum," the sum of the digits making up the core. The core sums for the two examples here are 16 and 20, respectively.

—ACTIVITY—

18.16 Secret Function I

This game can be modified for any grade level, K–8. It can be introduced using an overhead calculator with the full class, and then pairs of children can play independently. Without the class looking, store a one-step operation (secret function) in the calculator. Here is an example for each operation.

Addition:	Secret = + 8	Press 0 ⊞ 8 = ± =
Subtraction:	Secret = −24	Press 0 ⊟ 4 = ± =
Multiplication:	Secret = ×36	Press 6 ⊠ 0 =
Division:	Secret = ÷3	Press 0 ⊡ 3 =

The display will show 0 after the function has been stored. After a secret function has been entered, students try to guess the secret rule or function. They can get up to three clues. To get the first clue, they enter any number and press = to see what the secret function does to the entered number. They can get a second clue to the secret by pressing = again and the third clue by

pressing = a third time. After each clue, they should try to guess the secret function and predict the display after the next = press.

"Secret Function I" can be played at any grade level with addition and subtraction. Be prepared to talk about numbers less than zero. When division is used, decimals will appear. At the upper grade levels, the multiplication and division functions may be decimals or fractions. Consider the discussion when the rule is ×0.5 and a student guesses ÷2. As a variation, instead of pressing = successively, a different number can be entered each time before pressing =. If any of the operation keys are pressed, the function will no longer be stored.

Your calculator must have a sign-change key ± to enter addition or subtraction functions. Some calculators store the second rather than the first factor for multiplication. In that case, reverse the order in the hidden function.

—ACTIVITY—

18.17 Secret Function II

A graphing calculator allows for a different version of "Secret Function I." Compound functions such as $(2x + 1)/2$ or $x^2 - 4x$ can be stored. Students attempt to guess the rule by entering different numbers and seeing the output. The goal is to try to guess the function using as few input trials as possible. On the TI–81, TI–82, or TI–83, the following simple program will take an entry, display the output, and continue to accept inputs until you press Quit.

```
Prgm 1: GUESS
:Lbl 1
:Disp "ENTER X"
:Input X
:2x+5⇒A   (This line stores the secret function.)
:Disp A
:Goto 1
```

Students using the program will see only

```
Prgm 1: GUESS
"ENTER X"
?3
            11
ENTER X
?5
            15
```

The function line of the program is easily changed.

---ACTIVITY---

18.18 Amazing Digits

Enter 9 ⊠ *n*, where *n* is any number from 1 to 9. Press ⊡. Now press other numbers followed by ⊡. Even if students know their nines facts, this step will serve to clarify the process and illustrate that each new press of ⊡ multiplies the display by 9. Now enter 99 ⊠ *n* ⊡. Try other values of *n* followed by ⊡. What is the pattern? Try 999 ⊠ *n* and even 9999 or 99999 ⊠ *n*. Students should play with and explore this idea as long as they wish. Next try using repeating digits for *n* (3333 or 66). Instead of using nines for the multiplier, try using 0.009 or 99.9. Also experiment with other repeat-digit multipliers. If students are interested, the patterns with nines might be analyzed by looking at 999 as 1000 − 1 or as 9 × 111.

---ACTIVITY---

18.19 More Amazing Digits

Especially if students have shown interest in "Amazing Digits," try division by 9. Begin by just dividing single-digit numbers by 9. (The calculator remembers the last divisor, so after the first division, just enter the new number and press ⊡.) After this, there are all sorts of variations to try:

   a. Divide by 99, 999, . . .
   b. Divide by 0.9, 0.09, 0.009, . . .
   c. Divide by 9, but use two-digit dividends. Can you predict the results?
   d. Try three-digit dividends and a divisor of 9.
   e. Combine (a) or (b) with (c) or (d).

The patterns in "More Amazing Digits" are spectacular and interesting by themselves, but you may want to also try using a digit other than 9 in that exercise.

---ACTIVITY---

18.20 Consecutive Odd Numbers

Before doing this activity, you will need to explain what consecutive odd numbers are and how to add them on the calculator. Consecutive odd numbers are odd numbers that come together in the counting order. Thus, 1, 3, 5, 7, . . . are consecutive odd numbers, as are 27, 29, 31, . . . To add a string of these numbers, some students may benefit by writing the numbers down before they begin to add them on the calculator. Young students are confused when adding more than two numbers in a row. When they press ⊞ after the second addend, the display shows the sum as if ⊡ had been pressed.

Part 1

Have students use their calculators to make a chart that lists the sums of the first *n* consecutive odd numbers.

1	1
1 + 3	4
1 + 3 + 5	9
1 + 3 + 5 + 7	16
and so on	

The sums should look familiar. If students (around grades 5 to 8) do not recognize these as squares, suggest that they press the ⎷ key after they get the sum. It would be a good idea for them to express the sums as squares (1^2, 2^2, 3^2, 4^2, . . .). Can they predict the sum of the first 20 or first 50 consecutive odd numbers?

Part 2

If the consecutive odd numbers are written in a triangular list as shown here, and the sum of each horizontal row is recorded, there is an interesting result:

1

3   5

7   9   11

13   15   17   19

and so on.

As follow-up to the odd sum activity, students may want to examine consecutive even numbers or simply consecutive numbers. For example, what can you tell about the sum of any four consecutive numbers? Any five? Pick a number less than 100. Can you find a string of consecutive numbers that add up to your number? Can you find two different consecutive strings of numbers that have the same sum? (3 + 4 + 5 + 6 = 5 + 6 + 7). What numbers have only one sum?

As you can see, the calculator can be used not only to create patterns but also to hide patterns for discovery, and it can help with the tedium of uncovering patterns that students might otherwise be unwilling to explore. The extent to which the patterns are explored depends on the interest and age level of the students. Encourage students to explore as much as they are able. Within these patterns are some very nice mathematical ideas.

LITERATURE CONNECTIONS

Children generally find pattern and attribute activities to be so much fun that there is little need for literature to provide motivation. What literature can do is connect these logic activities to the real world and perhaps provide a different activity or perspective.

Frog and Toad Are Friends (Lobal, 1970)

As Frog and Toad go walking, Frog loses a button. As they search to find the button, they find many buttons. Whenever one of Frog's friends asks, "Is this your button?" Frog responds (with a touch of anger), "No, that is not my button! That button is _____, but my button was _____." The phrase is repeated with each newly found button. It turns out that Frog did not lose the button on the walk but in his own home before they left. This provides another value to the story as Frog must find a way to make up for being so angry with his friends.

The approach to finding the button is very much like the game "One of These Things Is Not like the Others." It is also a perfect lead-in to secret sorting activities as described in this chapter. Young students can model the story directly with sets of buttons, shells, attribute blocks, Woozle Cards, or other objects with a variety of attributes. With a highly varied set of geometric shapes, the children could play the game and explore their geometric language and perceptions of geometric attributes.

Pattern (Pluckrose, 1988)

This book brings pattern from the real world to the classroom in the form of brilliantly colored photographs. Pattern is seen in the soles of tennis shoes, dishes, butterflies, leaves, and flowers. The book provides a jumping-off point for an exploration of pattern in the world around us. A photo collage could be made of patterns found by the children. Drawings of patterns with explanations of the source and descriptions of the patterns can be assembled into a book. A display of patterns from your class activities and those found in nature, in the home, and in the neighborhood would make an excellent show for parents.

Anno's Mysterious Multiplying Jar (Anno & Anno, 1983)

Like all of the books illustrated by Mitsumasa Anno, this one is beautiful. It's an imaginative story of a mysterious jar that contains a sea. On the sea is one island. The island has two mountains. Each mountain has three countries. Within each country are four walled kingdoms. . . . Finally, each of nine boxes contains ten jars. The illustrations help develop the quickly expanding numbers of factorials. After the story, the authors help conceptualize the size of each factorial with arrays of tiny stars and suggest other ways to explore this fascinating number pattern.

Children of almost any age are likely to be interested in exploring the factorial concept due to the large numbers. A simple idea is to create a multiplying story and illustrate it or collect objects to show how many items are involved. Another idea is to examine nested situations in the real world even if they are not factorials. For example, talk to a grocery store about how small items such as chewing gum are shipped to the store. There will likely be cartons in which there are smaller boxes. In each box there may possibly be packages. Each package might contain several packs of gum and then finally single sticks. How many in all is determined by the same multiplication process.

REFLECTIONS ON CHAPTER 18: WRITING TO LEARN

1. Explain how attribute activities and patterning activities meet the goals of problem solving in each of these categories: (a) strategies and processes, (b) metacognition, and (c) affective considerations.

2. What is the difference between a structured and an unstructured set of attribute materials? Give an example of each to support your distinctions.

3. Loop activities, in which children sort items into categories inside loops of string, can be done in two different ways. First they can be done with the category label cards showing, and later they can be done with the label cards face down, in which case the teacher decides on the correct placement of each piece. Explain why the latter activity is a logic activity but the first really is not.

4. How is a two-difference game played on an oval track? Draw a picture showing a two-difference solution for a track with seven spaces.

5. Make up three pattern strips showing repeating patterns for some common objects that might be found in the classroom. Label each using an ABC scheme. No two schemes should be alike, but all should use the same materials. What is the core of each?

6. Make your calculator store each of these secret functions: +3 and ×5. Explain how to do this and how to play "Secret Function I."

7. Explore one other of the suggested ideas for calculators, and explain your results briefly.

FOR DISCUSSION AND EXPLORATION

1. In the *Curriculum Standards,* the third standard in both the K–4 and 5–8 sections is "Mathematics as Reasoning." Read these two standards. Discuss briefly how the activities of this chapter fit those goals. What else is meant by "mathematics as reasoning"?

2. Explorations of patterns such as the number and calculator patterns or the Fibonacci sequence are not presented in typical textbooks except as enrichment or extras, especially in the upper grades. (Repeat patterns are quite popular in grades K and 1.) Is it reasonable to spend time in the fourth through eighth grades on explorations of this sort? Take a position and defend it.

3. The Disney film *Donald in Mathmagic Land* is a classic from the 1940s that is now available in video and occasionally aired on the Disney Channel. This film explores pattern and several related beauties of mathematics in a timeless manner. Your mathematics education is not quite complete if you haven't seen it. It will intrigue children from third grade to high school, and a creative teacher can find many ways to follow up with explorations. View it if you can, and share an idea for using the film with children.

SUGGESTED READINGS

Highly Recommended

Coburn, T. G. (1993). *Patterns: Addenda series, grades K–6.* Reston, VA: National Council of Teachers of Mathematics.

This is one of the best resource books on patterns for the K–6 grades. Examples of virtually every type of pattern activity are included. As with other elementary *Addenda* books, the same activities are found in each of the grade-level books. What you get in this book are not only good activities but also a view of how pattern can easily progress from kindergarten to grade 6.

Pagni, D. (Ed.). (1991). *Calculators and Mathematics Project, Los Angeles (CAMP-LA).* (4 vols.: K–2, 3–4, 5–6, 7–8). Fullerton, CA: Cal State Fullerton Press. (Distributed by Didax Educational Resources.)

Many of the ideas found in our discussion of calculator patterns were adapted from the *CAMP-LA* books. Each book has a chapter on patterns and functions and is complete with lesson plans and worksheets. These volumes are among the best calculator resources available.

Other Suggestions

Baratta-Lorton, M. (1976). *Mathematics their way.* Menlo Park, CA: AWL Supplemental.

Bezuszka, S. J., & Kenney, M. (1982). *Number treasury: A sourcebook of problems for calculators and computers.* Menlo Park, CA: Dale Seymour.

Burk, D., Snider, A., & Symonds, P. (1988). *Box it or bag it mathematics: Teachers resource guide (K–2).* Salem, OR: Math Learning Center.

Burns, M. (1992). *About teaching mathematics: A K–8 resource.* Sausalito, CA: Marilyn Burns Education Associates.

Creative Publications. (1986). *Hands-on attribute blocks.* Palo Alto, CA: Author.

Johnson, J. J. (1987). Do you think you might be wrong? Confirmation bias in problem solving. *Arithmetic Teacher, 34*(9), 13–16.

Masalski, W. J. (1975). *Color cube activities.* Fort Collins, CO: Scott Scientific.

Perl, T. (1974). *Relationshapes activity cards.* White Plains, NY: Cuisenaire.

Phillips, E. (1991). *Patterns and functions: Addenda series, grades 5–8.* Reston, VA: National Council of Teachers of Mathematics.

Speer, W. R., & Brahier, D. J. (1995). What comes nex _____? *Teaching Children Mathematics, 1,* 100–108.

Thompson, A. G. (1985). On patterns, conjectures, and proof: Developing students' mathematical thinking. *Arithmetic Teacher, 33*(1), 20–23.

Thompson, C. S., & Van de Walle, J. A. (1985). Patterns and geometry with Logo. *Arithmetic Teacher, 32*(7), 6–13.

Trotter, T., Jr., & Myers, M. D. (1980). Number bracelets: A study in patterns. *Arithmetic Teacher, 27*(9), 14–17.

Van de Walle, J. A. (1988). Hands-on thinking activities for young children. *Arithmetic Teacher, 35*(6), 62–63.

Van de Walle, J. A., & Holbrook, H. (1987). Patterns, thinking, and problem solving. *Arithmetic Teacher, 34*(8), 6–12.

Van de Walle, J. A., & Thompson, C. S. (1985). Promoting mathematical thinking. *Arithmetic Teacher, 32*(6), 7–13.

Williams, S. E., & Copley, J. V. (1994). Promoting classroom dialogue: Using calculators to discover patterns in dividing decimals. *Mathematics Teaching in the Middle School, 1,* 72–75.

CHAPTER

EXPLORING CONCEPTS OF PROBABILITY AND STATISTICS

The related topics of probability and statistics represent two of the most prominent uses of mathematics in our everyday lives. We hear about the possibility of contracting a particular disease, having twins, winning the lottery, or living to be 100. Simulations of complex situations are frequently based on simple probabilities used in the design of highways, storm sewers, medical treatments, sales promotions, and spacecraft. Graphs and statistics bombard the public in advertising, opinion polls, reliability estimates, population trends, health risks, and the progress of students in schools and schools in school systems, to name only a few areas.

To deal with this information, students should have ample opportunity throughout their school years to have informal yet meaningful experiences with the basic concepts involved. The emphasis from the primary level into high school should be placed on activities leading to intuitive understanding and conceptual knowledge rather than computations and formulas.

 BIG IDEAS

1. **The possible occurrence of a future event, compared to the chance of its nonoccurrence, can be characterized as impossible, less likely, equally likely, more likely, or certain. To determine the likelihood of an event along this continuum is to determine the probability of its happening.**
2. **Data sets can be analyzed in various ways to provide different kinds of information, including how spread**

out the data are (e.g., range, variance) and how they cluster (mean, median, mode).
3. **Data are organized so as to help with the making of decisions or inferences or the development of new ideas about situations or the populations from which the data are drawn.**
4. **Data gathered and analyzed from observations, experiments, random sampling, and surveys have an enormous impact on our everyday lives. It is important to know and understand how data are collected and analyzed so that informed decisions can be made.**

PROBABILITY AND STATISTICS IN SCHOOLS

Organizations such as the Joint Committee on the Curriculum in Statistics and Probability of the American Statistical Association and the NCTM have promoted attention to the topics of probability and statistics in schools. A number of factors can be identified that indicate an increase in the quantity and quality of probability and statistics instruction in elementary and middle schools in recent years:

Increased awareness of the importance of probability and statistics concepts and methods

An emphasis on experimental or simulation approaches to probability (instead of rules and formulas)

The use of simplified yet powerful plotting techniques to describe data visually without complicated procedures

The use of readily available calculators and computers, especially graphing calculators, to conduct thousands of random trials of experiments, from flipping coins to simulating baseball batting performances; to do the tedious work of constructing graphs; and to perform computations on large sets of numbers almost instantly

The terms *probability* and *statistics* may sound overly mathematical or perhaps even frightening to people who are unfamiliar with the simple basic ideas involved. NCTM's *Addenda* series booklets use the titles *Making Sense of Data* (the K–6 book) and *Dealing with Data and Chance* (the middle grades book). This terminology is less intimidating, and the books themselves bring these important ideas to the classroom level in nonthreatening ways. With new approaches and attitudes toward the development of the conceptual knowledge of probability and statistics, it is almost certain that even more emphasis will be placed on these topics in the near future.

INTRODUCTION TO PROBABILITY

Here you will experiment with some basic ideas of probability before considering how to help children develop these ideas.

Two Experiments

Consider answering the following two questions by actually performing the experiments enough times to make a reasonable guess at the results.

TOSSING A CUP

Toss a paper or Styrofoam cup once or twice, letting it land on the floor. Notice that there are three possible ways for the cup to land: upside down, right side up, or on its side. If the cup were tossed this way 100 times, about how many times do you think it would land in each position?

FLIPPING TWO COINS

If you were to flip one coin 100 times, you would expect that it would come up heads about as many times as tails. If two coins were tossed 100 times, about how many times do you think that they would both come up heads?

A quick way to conduct these experiments is to work in groups. If ten people each do ten trials and pool their data, the time needed for 100 trials is not long. Even if you do not actually do the experiments, jot down your predictions now before reading on.

Theoretical Versus Experimental Probability

In the cup toss, there is no practical way to determine the results before you start. However, once you had results for 100 flips, you would undoubtedly feel more confident in predicting the results of the next 100 flips. If you gathered data on that same cup for 1000 trials, you would feel even more confident. Say that your cup lands on its side 78 times out of 100. You might choose a round figure of 75 or 80 for the 100 tosses. If, after 200 flips, there were 163 sideways landings, you would feel even more confident of the 4-out-of-5 ratio and predict about 800 sideways landings for 1000 tosses. The more flips that are made, the more confident you become. You have determined an *experimental probability* of $\frac{4}{5}$ or 80 percent for the cup to land on its side. It is experimental because it is based on the results of an experiment rather than a theoretical analysis of the cup.

In a one-coin toss, the best prediction for 100 flips would be 50 heads, although you would not be too surprised if actual results were between 45 and 55 heads. The prediction of 50 percent heads could confidently be made before you flipped the coin, based on your understanding of a fair coin. Your prediction for two heads in the two-coin version may be more difficult. It is quite common for people to observe that there are three types of outcomes: both heads, both tails, and one of each. Based on this analysis they predict that two heads will come up about one-third of the time. (What did you predict?) The prediction is based on their analysis of the experiment, not on experimental results. When they conduct the experiment, however, they are surprised to find that two heads come up only about one-fourth of the time. With this experiential base, they might return to their original analysis and look for an error in their thinking.

There is only one way for two heads to occur and one way for two tails to occur, but there are *two* ways that a head and a tail could result: Either the first coin is heads and the second tails, or vice versa. As shown in Figure 19.1 (p. 410), that makes a total of four possible outcomes, not three. The assumption that each outcome is equally likely was correct. Therefore, the correct probability of two heads is 1 out of 4, or $\frac{1}{4}$, not $\frac{1}{3}$. This *theoretical probability* is based on a logical analysis of the experiment, not on experimental results.

When we talk about probabilities, we are assigning some measure of chance to an experiment. An *experiment* is any

First Coin	Second Coin
Head	Head
Head	Tail
Tail	Head
Tail	Tail

● **FIGURE 19.1**   Four possible outcomes of flipping two coins.

activity that has two or more clearly discernible results or *outcomes*. Both tossing the cup and tossing the two coins were experiments. Observing tomorrow's weather and shooting ten free throws on the basketball court are also experiments. The collection of all outcomes is generally referred to as the *sample space*. As you have already seen, the toss of two coins has four outcomes in the sample space. Tomorrow's weather can be described in many ways: precipitation or no precipitation, or dry, rain, sleet, or snow. An *event* is any subset of the outcomes or any subset of the sample space. For the two-coin experiment, the event we were concerned with was getting two heads. For the free-throw shoot, we might be interested in the event of getting five or more baskets out of the ten tosses.

When all possible outcomes of a simple experiment are equally likely, the *theoretical probability* of an event is

Number of outcomes in the event

Number of possible outcomes

In real-world situations, outcomes frequently cannot be determined to be equally likely, as they are for coin flips or dice rolls. The cup-tossing experiment, though not a practical situation, is "muddy" and real. The outcomes are difficult to predict, and they are not equally likely. In situations like these, we can determine the observed relative frequency of the event by performing the experiment a lot of times. The relative frequency of an event is

Number of observed occurrences of the event

Total number of trials

It should be clear that the relative frequency is not a good predictor of the chance of the event's happening unless the number of trials is very large. The *experimental probability* of an event is the ratio that the relative frequency approaches as the number of trials gets infinitely large. Because it is impossible to perform an infinite number of trials, we must be satisfied with some large number of trials. The more trials, the more confident we might be that the experimental probability is close to the actual probability.

Implications for Instruction

There are many reasons why an experimental approach to probability, actually conducting experiments and examining outcomes, is important in the classroom. An experimental approach has these advantages:

- It is significantly more intuitive and conceptual. Results begin to make sense and do not result from some abstract rule.

- It eliminates guessing at probabilities and wondering, "Did I get it right?" Counting or trying to determine the number of elements in a sample space can be very difficult without some intuitive background information.

- It provides an experiential background for examining the theoretical model. When you begin to sense that the probability of two heads is $\frac{1}{4}$ instead of $\frac{1}{3}$, the analysis in Figure 19.1 seems more reasonable.

- It helps students see how the ratio of a particular outcome to the total number of trials begins to converge to (get closer and closer to) a fixed number. For an infinite number of trials, the relative frequency and theoretical probability would be the same.

- It develops an appreciation for a simulation approach to solving problems. Many real-world problems are actually solved by conducting experiments or simulations.

- It is a lot more fun and interesting! It even makes searching for a correct explanation in the theoretical model more interesting.

Whenever possible, then, we should try to use an experimental approach in the classroom. If a theoretical analysis (such as with the two-coin experiment) is possible, it should also be examined, and the results should be compared. Rather than correcting a student error in an initial analysis, we can let experimental results guide and correct student thinking.

Sometimes it is possible to develop theoretical explanations from results of experiments. For example, the results of the cup toss might be compared with the ratio of the height of the cup to the diameter of the opening. The cup can then be cut to different heights and the experiment repeated. A reasonable connection can be made between the ratio of height to top opening and the probability of a side landing. (For a better-controlled experiment, try a variety of open-ended cylinders such as paper tubes and tin cans.)

DEVELOPING PROBABILITY CONCEPTS

It is no longer reasonable to wait until high school to begin helping children develop informal ideas about probability.

Informal ideas developed early provide necessary background for concepts to be constructed at the middle and secondary levels.

Early Concepts of Chance

Children in kindergarten and the primary grades need to develop an intuitive concept of chance: the idea that some events, when compared with others, have a better or worse chance or an approximately equal chance of happening.

Many young children believe that an event will happen because "it's my favorite color" or "because it's lucky" or "because it did it that way last time." Many games such as CandyLand or Chutes and Ladders are very exciting for young children who do not comprehend that the outcomes are entirely random. When they finally learn that they have no control over the outcome, children begin to look for other games where there is some element of player determination.

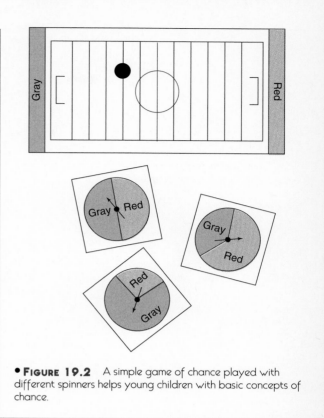

● **FIGURE 19.2** A simple game of chance played with different spinners helps young children with basic concepts of chance.

---ACTIVITY---

19.1 Is It Likely?

Ask students to judge various events as *certain,* *impossible,* or *maybe.* Consider these examples:

It will rain tomorrow.

Drop a rock in water, and it will sink.

Trees will talk to us in the afternoon.

The sun will rise tomorrow morning.

Three students will be absent tomorrow.

George will go to bed before 8:30 tonight.

You will have two birthdays this year.

---ACTIVITY---

19.2 Who Will Win?

Play simple games where the chance of one side's winning can be controlled. Before playing the games, have students predict who will win and why. Afterward, discuss why they think things turned out as they did. For example, the hockey game in Figure 19.2 starts with a counter in the center. Two players take turns spinning a spinner. The counter moves one space toward the goal that comes up on the spinner. Play the game with different spinners. As a variation, let students choose a spinner on each turn. Ask them to explain their choices.

---ACTIVITY---

19.3 Predictions

Have students make predictions about the outcomes of simple experiments using the terms *more, less, all,* and *none.* For example, show children how many each of red and yellow cubes you have in a bag. You will let children draw cubes one at a time and put them back each time. "If we do this ten times, will there be more reds, less reds, all reds, or no reds?" Change the number of each color cube and repeat. The same activity can be done by spinning spinners, rolling dice, drawing cards, or using any random device that you can adjust. Include situations that are certain, such as placing all yellow cubes in the bag.

Determining Probabilities for Simple Events

From a basic understanding that one event can be more or less likely than another, students can begin to predict specific ratios of outcomes of simple events. Before students

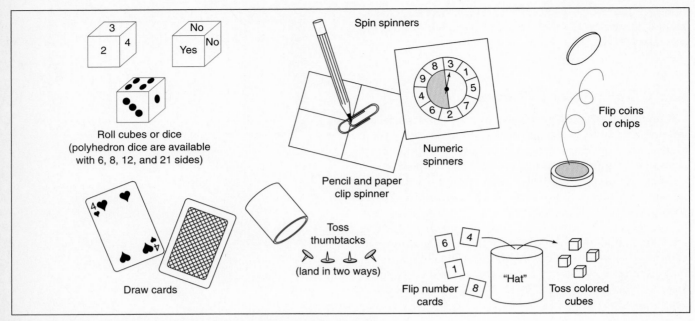

● **FIGURE 19.3**   *There are many simple ways to produce random outcomes.*

have worked with part-to-whole ratios, use language such as "65 out of 100" instead of using fractional probabilities. A discussion of reasons for students' predictions is always important. The experiment should then be conducted and the results compared with expected outcomes.

Figure 19.3 illustrates a number of simple random devices that can be used for experiments. To get large numbers, let groups of students conduct the same experiment and tally their results. Group results can quickly be combined to get larger numbers. Ask students to notice that the results for smaller numbers of trials are all different and that they are frequently quite different from what might be expected.

Random Numbers and Electronic Devices

If a coin is tossed repeatedly, the long run will produce a ratio very close to one-half heads and one-half tails, but what happens in the short run? Do heads and tails alternate? If heads come up six times in a row, what is the probability that tails will come up next? The answers to questions such as these reflect an understanding of randomness and are worth discussing.

Occasionally have students list the outcomes of their experiments in a row, to show the order of the outcomes. Interestingly, truly random events do not alternate. They frequently appear in clusters or runs. If eight odd numbers in a row come up on a die roll, the chance remains exactly $\frac{1}{2}$ (1 out of 2) that the next roll will be odd. The die has no memory. The previous roll of a die cannot affect the next roll. It is very unlikely that even numbers will come up seven times in a row (1 chance in 128). However, if that does happen, the chance for an even number on the next roll is still $\frac{1}{2}$.

Hands-on random devices such as those in Figure 19.3 provide an intuitive feel for randomness. It is important to conduct experiments using these because students can believe in the unbiased outcomes. The downside is that the use of these devices requires a lot of time to produce a large number of trials and keep track of the results. This is where certain relatively simple calculators, graphing calculators, or the computer can help out enormously. These electronic devices are designed to produce random numbers. Usually, these numbers are in the form of decimal numbers between 0 and 1. Students who are going to use these random number generators should understand what these numbers look like and how to use them. One idea is simply to make the computer or calculator produce a series of these one at a time. The outcome might look like this:

0.0232028877

0.8904433368

0.1693227117

0.1841957303

0.5523325715

How could a list of decimals like this replace flipping a coin or spinning a spinner? If you multiplied each of these numbers by 2, they would then be numbers between 0 and 2 (not including 2). If you then ignored the decimal part of the number, you would get a series of zeros and ones. These might stand for heads and tails or boys and girls or true and false or any other pair of outcomes that are equally likely. If we wanted to get outcomes that were the same as a $\frac{1}{4}$ versus $\frac{3}{4}$ spinner, we could multiply the random numbers by 4, throw out the decimal parts (producing zeros, ones, twos, and threes). We could assign one of the digits to the $\frac{1}{4}$ color on the spinner and the other three to the other color. How could you use random digits like these to simulate dice throwing?

Students who are going to use an electronic random number device (calculator or computer) should understand how the numbers can be used to simulate a physical device. It may even be a good idea to compare the outcomes of the two devices for a small run before using the electronic version for a large run.

The program in Figure 19.4 is for a TI-82 or TI-83 calculator. It will electronically "roll" as many dice as you request as many times as you request. For each roll, a count is recorded for that sum. At the end of the program, a histogram is displayed that gives the totals for each sum. If you then use the TRACE command, the value represented by each bar of the histogram is displayed. The figure shows the result of rolling two dice 1000 times. It took about $2\frac{1}{2}$ minutes to run the program and produce the graph.

Experiments with Two or More Independent Events

Flipping two coins and observing the result of each is an example of an experiment with two independent events. The flip of one coin has no effect on the other. The events are *independent*. Another example is that of drawing a card and spinning a spinner. Many interesting experiments involve two or more separate, independent events.

Determining the experimental probability of compound events is no different than for simple events. The experiment is performed numerous times, and the number of favorable results is compared to the total trials as before. The challenge comes in trying to reconcile experimental results with theoretical ones.

To illustrate, suppose that a class is conducting an experiment to determine the probability of rolling a 7 with two dice. They might tally their results in a chart showing each sum from 2 to 12 as a single event, as in part (a) of Figure 19.5 (p. 414).

The results of their experiment will show clearly that these events are not equally likely and that in fact the sum of 7 has the best chance of occurring. To explain this, they might look for the combinations that make 7: 1 and 6, 2 and 5, and 3 and 4. But there are also three combinations for 8. It seems as though 8 should be just as likely as 7, and yet it is not.

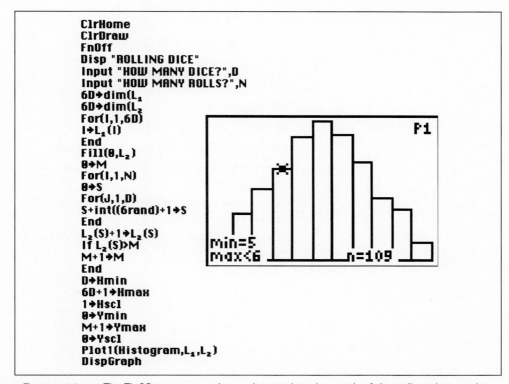

● **FIGURE 19.4** This TI–82 program can be used to simulate thousands of dice rolls and accumulate the results.

Sum of Two Dice

2	卌 \
3	卌 卌
4	卌 卌 卌 ||||
5	卌 卌 卌 ||||
6	卌 卌 卌 卌 卌 ||||
7	卌 卌 卌 卌 卌 卌 卌 ||||
8	卌 卌 卌 卌 卌 卌 ||||
9	卌 卌 卌 卌 卌
10	卌 卌 卌 |
11	卌 ||
12	卌 卌

(a)

Red Die

	1	2	3	4	5	6
1	卌	卌 |	卌 |||	卌 ||	卌 ||||	卌 ||
2	卌 ||||	卌 |||	卌 |	卌 |||	卌 |||	卌 ||
3	卌 卌	卌 |||	卌 ||	卌 ||	卌 卌 ||	卌 ||||
4	卌 ||	卌 卌 ||	卌 ||||	卌 卌 ||	卌 卌 ||	卌 |||
5	卌 ||||	卌 卌 ||	卌 卌 |||	卌 |||	卌 |||	卌 ||||
6	卌 |||	卌 ||||	卌 |||	卌 ||	卌 |||	卌 |||

Green Die

There are six ways to get 7.

(b)

• **FIGURE 19.5** *Tallies can account only for the total (a) or keep track of the individual dice (b).*

Now suppose that the experiment is repeated. This time, for the sake of clarity, suggest that students roll two different-colored dice and that they keep the tallies in a chart like the one in part (b) of Figure 19.5. A TI-83 program very similar to the one in Figure 19.4 can roll two dice and record the outcomes of each die in a matrix rather than adding the outcomes.

The results of a large number of dice rolls indicate what one would expect, namely, that all 36 cells of this chart are equally likely. But there are more cells with a sum of 7 than any other number. Therefore, students were really looking for the event that consists of any of the six ways, not three ways, that two dice can add to 7. There are six outcomes in the desired event out of a total of 36, for a probability of $\frac{6}{36}$, or $\frac{1}{6}$.

When investigating the theoretical probability of a compound event, it is useful to use a chart or diagram that keeps the two independent events separate and illustrates the combinations. The matrix in Figure 19.5(b) is one good

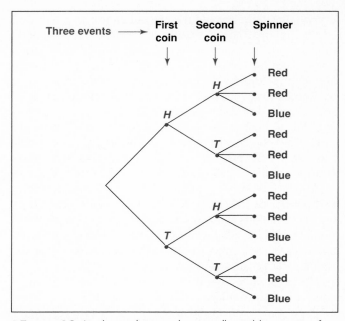

• **FIGURE 19.6** *A tree diagram showing all possible outcomes for two coins and a spinner that is $\frac{2}{3}$ red.*

suggestion when there are only two events. A tree diagram (Figure 19.6) is another method that can be used with any number of events.

---ACTIVITY---

19.4 Compound Experiments

The following are examples of compound experiments with independent events. Determine the probability of each event:

   a. **Rolling an even sum with two dice**

   b. **Spinning blue and flipping a cup on end**

   c. **Getting two blues out of three spins (depends on spinner)**

   d. **Having a tack or a cup land up if each is tossed once**

   e. **Getting *at least* two heads from a toss of four coins**

Words and phrases such as *and, or, at least,* and *no more than* can also cause children some trouble. Of special note is the word *or,* since its everyday usage is generally not the same as its strict logical use in mathematics. In mathematics, *or* includes the case of *both.* So in the tack-and-cup example, the event includes tack up, cup up, and *both* tack *and* cup up.

Theoretical Probabilities with an Area Model

The method just suggested for determining the theoretical probability of a compound event is to list all possible outcomes and count those that are favorable, that is, those that make up the event. This is very useful and intuitive as a first approach. However, it has some limitations. First, what if the events are not all equally likely and are not made up of smaller events? An example is the cup toss. Second, it is difficult to move from that approach to even slightly more sophisticated methods. An area model approach has been used successfully with fifth-grade students. It is quite useful for some reasonably difficult problems (Armstrong, 1981). The following example will illustrate how an area model works.

Suppose that after many experiences, you have decided that your cup lands on its side 82 percent of the time. The experiment is to toss the cup and then draw a card from a deck. What is the probability that the cup will land on the side *and* you will draw a spade? Draw a square to represent one whole. First partition the square to represent the cup toss, 82 percent and 18 percent, as in Figure 19.7(a). Now partition the square in the other direction to represent the four equal card suits and shade $\frac{1}{4}$ for spades, as in Figure 19.7(b). The overlapping region is the proportion of time

that both events, sideways and spades, happen. The area of this region is $\frac{1}{4}$ of 82 percent, or 20.5 percent.

You can use the same drawing to determine the probability of other events in the same experiment. For example, what is the probability of the cup landing on either end *or* drawing a red card? As shown in Figure 19.7(c), half of the area of the square corresponds to drawing a red card. This section includes the case of drawing a red card *and* an end landing. The other half of the 18 percent end landings happen when a red card is not drawn. Half of 18 percent is 9 percent of the area. The total area for a red card *or* an end landing is 59 percent.

The area approach is easy for students to use and understand for experiments involving two independent events where the probability of each is known. For more than two independent events, further subdivision of each region is required but is still quite reasonable. The use of *and* and *or* connectives is easily dealt with. It is quite clear, without memorization of formulas, how probabilities should be combined.

Exploring Dependent Events

The next level of difficulty occurs when the probability of one event depends on the result of the first. For example, suppose that there are two identical boxes. In one box is a dollar bill and two counterfeit bills. In the other box is one of each. You may choose one box and from that box select one bill without looking. What are your chances of getting a genuine dollar? Here there are two events: selecting a box and selecting a bill. The probability of getting a dollar in the second event depends on which box is chosen in the first event. These events are *dependent*, not independent.

As another example, suppose that you are a prisoner in a faraway land. The king has pity on you and gives you a chance to leave. He shows you the maze in Figure 19.8 (p. 416). At the start and at each fork in the path, you must spin the spinner and follow the path that it points to. You may request that the key to freedom be placed in one of the two rooms. In which room should you place the key to have the best chance of freedom? Notice that the probability of ending the maze in any one room is dependent on the result of the first spin.

Either of these two problems could be solved with an experimental approach, a simulation. A second approach to both problems is to use the area model to determine the theoretical probabilities. An area model solution to the prisoner problem is shown in Figure 19.9 (p. 416). How would the area model for the prisoner problem be different if the spinner at Fork II were a $\frac{1}{3}$ versus $\frac{2}{3}$ spinner?

It would be good to stop at this point and try the area approach for the problem of the counterfeit bills. (The chance of getting a dollar is $\frac{5}{12}$.)

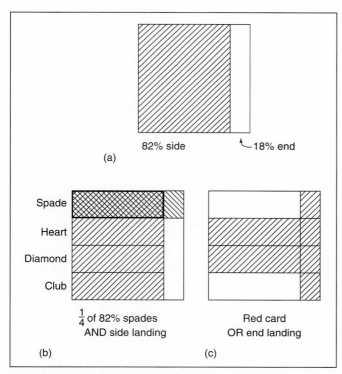

● **Figure 19.7** An area model for determining probabilities.

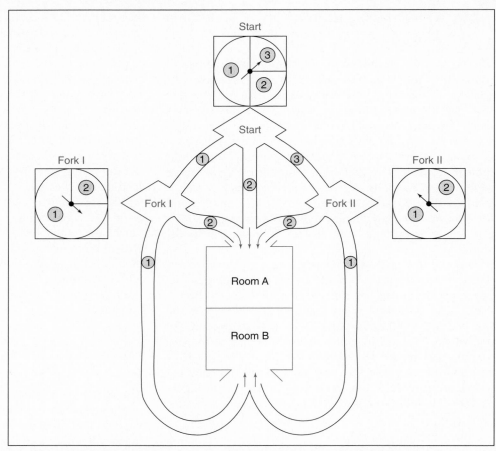

• **FIGURE 19.8**   Should you place your key to freedom in Room A or Room B? At each fork, the spinner determines your path.

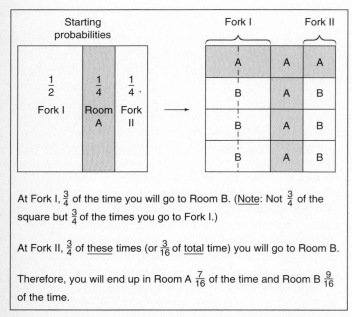

At Fork I, $\frac{3}{4}$ of the time you will go to Room B. (Note: Not $\frac{3}{4}$ of the square but $\frac{3}{4}$ of the times you go to Fork I.)

At Fork II, $\frac{3}{4}$ of these times (or $\frac{3}{16}$ of total time) you will go to Room B.

Therefore, you will end up in Room A $\frac{7}{16}$ of the time and Room B $\frac{9}{16}$ of the time.

• **FIGURE 19.9**   Using the area model to solve the maze problem.

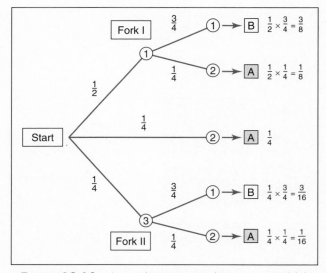

• **FIGURE 19.10**   A tree diagram is another way to model the outcomes of two or more dependent events.

The area model will not solve all probability problems. However, it fits very well into a developmental approach to the subject because it is conceptual, it is based on existing knowledge of fractions, and more symbolic approaches can be derived from it. Figure 19.10 shows a tree diagram for the same problem, with the probability of each path of the tree written in. After some experience with probability situations, the tree diagram model is probably easier to use and adapts to a wider range of situations. You should be able to match up each branch of the tree diagram in Figure 19.10 with a section of the square in Figure 19.9. Use the area model to explain why the probability for each complete branch of the tree is determined by multiplying the probabilities along the branch.

SIMULATIONS

Simulation is a technique used for answering questions or making decisions in complex situations where an element of chance is involved. A simulation is very much like solving a probability problem by an experimental approach. The only difference is that one must design a model that has the same probabilities as the real situation. For example, in designing a rocket, a large number of related systems all have some chance of failure. Various combinations of failures might cause serious problems with the rocket. Knowing the probability of serious failures will help determine if redesign or backup systems are required. It is not reasonable to make repeated tests of the actual rocket. Instead, a model that simulates all of the chance situations is designed and run repeatedly, most likely with the help of a computer. The computer model can simulate hundreds or even thousands of flights, and an estimate of the chance of failure can be made.

Many real-world situations lend themselves to simulation analysis. In a business venture, the probability of selling a product might depend on a variety of chance factors, some of which can be controlled or changed and others not. Will advertising help? How much chance is there that a competitor will enter the market? Should high-cost materials be used? What location provides the best chance of sales? If a reasonable model can be set up that simulates these factors, an experiment can be run before actually entering into the venture to determine the best choices.

The following problem and model are adapted from the excellent materials developed by the Quantitative Literacy Project (Gnanadesikan, Schaeffer, & Swift, 1987). In Figure 19.11, a diagram shows water pipes for a pumping system connecting A to B. The five pumps are aging, and it is estimated that at any given time, the probability of pump failure is $\frac{1}{2}$. If a pump fails, water cannot pass that station. For

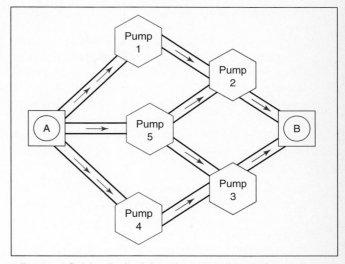

●**FIGURE 19.11** Each of these five pumps has a 50 percent chance of failure. What is the probability that some path from A to B is working?

example, if pumps 1, 2, and 5 fail, water can flow through 4 and 3. Consider the following questions that might well be asked about such a system:

What is the probability that water will flow at any time?

On the average, about how many stations need repair at any time?

What is the probability that the 1–2 path is working at any time?

For any simulation, a series of steps or a model can serve as a useful guide.

1. *Identify key components and assumptions of the problem.* The key component in the water problem is the condition of a pump. Each pump is either working or not. The assumption is that the probability that a pump is working is $\frac{1}{2}$.

2. *Select a random device for the key components.* Any random device can be selected that has outcomes with the same probability as the key component—in this case, the pumps. Here a simple choice might be tossing a coin, with heads representing a working pump.

3. *Define a trial.* A *trial* consists of simulating a series of key components until the situation has been completely modeled one time. In this problem, a trial could consist of tossing a coin five times, each toss representing a different pump.

4. *Conduct a large number of trials, and record the information.* For this problem, it would be good to keep the record of heads and tails in groups of five because each set of five is one trial and represents all of the pumps.

5. *Use the data to draw conclusions.* There are four possible paths for the water, each flowing through two of the five pumps. As they are numbered in the drawing, if any one of the pairs 1–2, 5–2, 5–3, and 4–3 is open, it makes no difference whether the other pumps are working. By counting the trials in which at least one of these four pairs of coins both came up heads, we can estimate the probability of water flowing. To answer the second question, the number of tails per trial can be averaged. How would you answer the third question concerning the 1–2 path's being open?

Steps 4 and 5 are the same as solving a probability problem by experimental means. The interesting problem-solving aspects of simulation activities are in the first three steps, where the real-world situation is translated into a model. Translation of real-world information into models is the essence of applied mathematics.

Here are a few more examples of problems that can be solved by simulation and are easy enough to be tackled by middle school students.

In a true-or-false test, what is the probability of getting 7 out of 10 questions correct by guessing alone? (*Key component:* answering a question. *Assumption:* Chance of getting it correct is $\frac{1}{2}$.) What if the test were multiple choice with 4 choices?

In a group of five people, what is the chance that two were born in the same month? (*Key component:* month of birth. *Assumption:* All 12 months are equally likely.)

Casey's batting average is .350. What is the chance he will go hitless in a complete nine-inning game? (*Key component:* getting a hit. *Assumptions:* Probability of a hit for each at-bat is .35. Casey will get to bat four times in the average game.)

Krunch-a-Munch cereal packs one of five games in each box. About how many boxes should you expect to buy before you get a complete set? (*Key component:* getting one game. *Assumption:* Each game has a $\frac{1}{5}$ chance. *Trial:* Use a $\frac{1}{5}$ random device repeatedly until all five outcomes appear; the average length of a trial answers the question.) What is the chance of getting a set in eight or fewer boxes?

GATHERING AND MAKING SENSE OF DATA

The NCTM *Curriculum Standards* includes a standard for statistics at both the K–4 and 5–8 levels. This does not mean that elementary school children should be engaged in using complex formulas. It does mean that students should be involved in the following activities:

- Collecting and describing data
- Constructing and interpreting charts and graphs
- Making inferences and arguments based on their analysis of data
- Examining arguments based on data that others have analyzed

For children in school, not only are these processes relevant, interesting, and important for daily living, but they also constitute a real form of problem solving. A variety of techniques for graphing and making sense of data are simple and accessible to elementary school children. These same techniques can be applied directly to the real world.

One of the most important rules to follow in conducting graphing and statistics activities is to let students gather their own data. Tables of numbers in textbooks tend to be sterile and uninteresting. Real data, gathered by children, are almost always more interesting. For example, one class of students gathered data concerning which cafeteria foods were most often thrown in the garbage. As a result of these efforts, certain items were removed from the regular menu. The activity illustrated to students the power of organized data, and it helped them get food they liked better.

There are all sorts of ways for students to gather data that may be of interest to them. Some examples are suggested here, but these represent only the tip of the iceberg. Use your imagination, the interests of your students, and special events and activities in your class, school, and community.

Classroom Surveys

One of the easiest ways to collect data in the primary grades is to get one piece of information from each student in your class. The resulting information will have manageable numbers, and everyone will be interested. When there are lots of possibilities, restrict the number of choices. Here are some ideas:

Favorites. TV shows, fruit, season of the year, color, football team, pet, ice cream.

Numbers. Bus number, number of pets or sisters, hours of sleep, birthday (month or day in month), bedtime

Measures. Height, weight, other body measures, long-jump distances, letters in name, time to button sweater, number of beans in a "handful" or seeds in a slice of watermelon, weight of a potato, measures of objects that students bring from home

Schoolwide or Grade-Level Surveys

The news media frequently use the phrase "A survey shows that the typical _____ . . ." when describing families, businesses, teenagers, drug addicts, or other groups. Two things in these stories can be used to attract the attention of your students. First, how did they survey everyone? Of course, they sampled only a small percentage and used those data to describe the whole group. Second, what does "typical" mean? Are all people in the group typical? Is anyone in the group typical? Do the students in your class believe they are typical of children at that grade level? An excellent activity is to get children involved in describing the typical student at their grade level. What questions should they ask to help them decide? How many questions? Should they use multiple-choice answers, or if not, how will they group the responses? Will they survey everyone in the class or in the grade level? Is your class typical of other classes? These and many related decisions are an integral part of using statistics in real situations.

Gathering school data can involve sampling techniques such as randomly selecting ten students per grade level instead of surveying everyone. Consider school issues such as cafeteria likes and dislikes, preferred lunch order, or use of the playground or gym. Political or social issues that all students may know about are also useful and allow you to integrate other subject areas.

Besides surveys, the school has a wealth of interesting data. Attendance by day of week, by grade level, and by month is one example. What materials are used and how much, how many tests are given in what grades and in what subjects, and how many parents attend PTA meetings are a few additional ideas. Some "people data" can be compared to similar statistics for the population at large. Examples include left-handedness, eye color, average family size, or years living at the present address.

Consumer Data

The ingredients, prices, weights, and volumes of popular grocery items such as cereal, candy bars, paper towels, or laundry soap provide all sorts of interesting data. Catalogs and menus are good sources of consumer data for the classroom.

Other Sources

Count various things in the newspaper (number of letters in headlines, number of vowels in 100 words, number of common words such as *and* used on a page). Almanacs, sports records, and assorted government publications can provide a wide variety of interesting statistics.

GRAPHICAL REPRESENTATIONS

Once data have been gathered, what are you going to do with them? Students should be involved in the decisions that go into answering this question. To whom do you want to communicate the information? What ideas in the data are most important, and what are some good ways to show these off?

Children with little experience with the various ways of picturing data will not even be aware of the many options that are available to them. Sometimes you can suggest a new way of displaying data and have children learn to construct that type of graph or chart. Once they have made the display, they can discuss its value. Did this graph (or chart or picture) tell about our data in a clear way? Compared to other ways of displaying data, how is this better?

The emphasis or goal of our instruction should be to help children see how graphs and charts tell about information, that different types of representations tell different things about the same data. The value of having students actually construct their own graphs is not so much that they learn the techniques but that they are personally invested in the data and that they learn how a graph conveys information. Once a graph is constructed, the most important activity is discussing what it tells the people who see it, especially those who were not involved in making the graph. Discussions about graphs of real data that the children have themselves been involved in gathering will help them interpret other graphs and charts that they see in newspapers and on TV.

What we should *not* do is get overly anxious about the tedious details of graph construction. The issue of communication is your agenda and is much more important than the technique! In the real world, technology will take care of details.

There are two equally good possibilities you may consider when planning to have your students construct graphs or charts. First, you can simply encourage students to do their best and make charts and graphs that make sense to them and that they feel communicate the information they wish to convey. This is not to say that children do not need guidance. They should have seen and been involved in group constructions of various types of graphs and charts. This provides them with some ideas from which to choose for their own graphs. This informal approach may be best with younger students because they will be more personally invested in their work and not distracted by the techniques of the technology. Care should be taken not to worry about fancy labeling or nice, neat pictures. The intent is to get the students involved in communicating a message about their data.

The second option is to use technology. The computer and graphing calculators have provided us with many tools for constructing simple yet powerful representations. With the help of technology, it is possible to construct several different pictures of the same data with very little effort. With virtually no effort involved in displaying the same data in several formats, the discussion can focus on the message or information that each format provides. Here students can be very much involved in making their own selections of various graphs and can justify their choice based on their own intended purposes. As just one example, Figure 19.12 shows four graphs produced by the program The Graph Club (Tom Snyder, 1993). When two or more graphs are being created from the same data, it is possible to see all graphs change accordingly. How does a pie graph show information differently than a picture graph?

Bar Graphs

Bar graphs and tally charts are one of the first ways to group and present data and are especially useful in grades K–3. At this early level, bar graphs should be made so that each bar consists of countable parts such as squares, objects, tallies, or pictures of objects. No numeric scale is necessary. Graphs should be simple and quickly constructed. Figure 19.13 illustrates a few techniques that can be used to make a graph quickly with the whole class.

A "real graph" uses the actual objects being graphed. Examples include types of shoes, seashells, and books. Each item can be placed in a square so that comparisons and counts are easily made.

Picture graphs use a drawing of some sort that represents what is being graphed. Students can make their own drawings, or you can duplicate drawings to be colored or cut out to suit particular needs.

Symbolic graphs use something like squares, blocks, tallies, or Xs to represent the things being counted in the graph. An easy idea is to use sticky notes as elements of a graph. These can be stuck directly to the chalkboard or other chart and rearranged if needed.

To make a quick graph of class data, follow these steps:

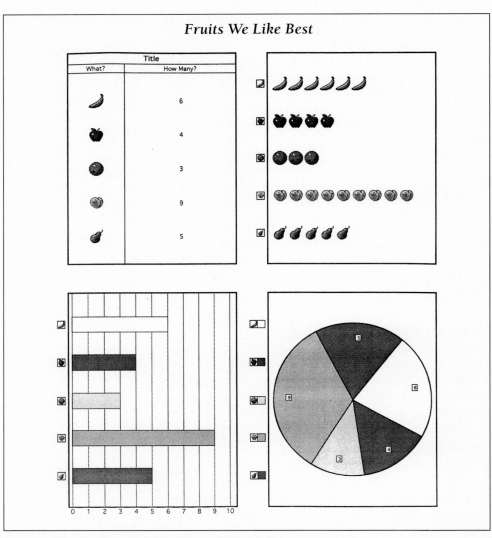

• **FIGURE 19.12** Four graphs produced with Graph Club software.

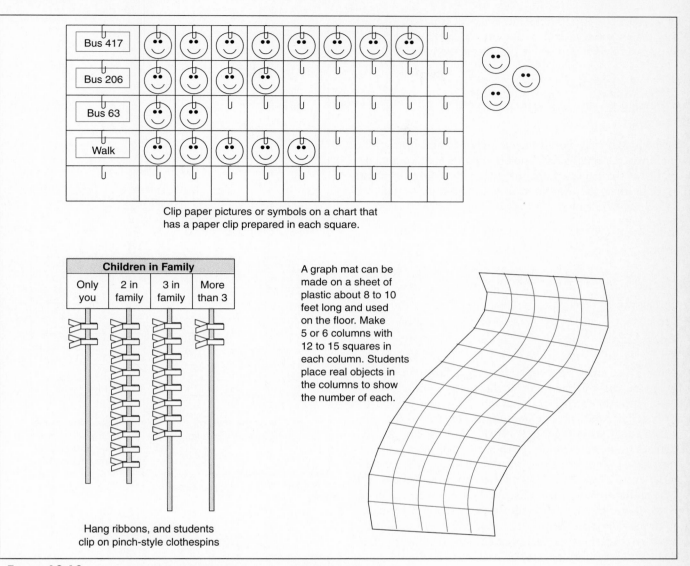

Clip paper pictures or symbols on a chart that
has a paper clip prepared in each square.

Children in Family

Only you	2 in family	3 in family	More than 3

A graph mat can be made on a sheet of plastic about 8 to 10 feet long and used on the floor. Make 5 or 6 columns with 12 to 15 squares in each column. Students place real objects in the columns to show the number of each.

Hang ribbons, and students
clip on pinch-style clothespins

●**FIGURE 19.13** Some ideas for quick graphs that can be used again and again.

1. Decide on what groups of data will make up the different bars. It is good to have two to six different bars in a graph.

2. Have everyone decide on or prepare his or her contribution to the graph before you begin. For real or picture graphs, the object or picture should be ready to be placed on the graph. For symbolic graphs, students should write down or mark their choice.

3. Have students, in small groups, quickly place or mark their entry on the graph. A graph mat can be placed on the floor, or a chart can be prepared on the wall or chalkboard. If tape or pins are to be used, have these items ready.

Following these steps, a class of 25 to 30 students can make a graph in less than 10 minutes, leaving ample time to use it for questions and observations.

Once a graph has been constructed, engage the class in a discussion of what information the graph tells or conveys. "What can you tell about our class by looking at this shoe graph?" Graphs convey factual information (more people wear sneakers than any other kind of shoe) and also provide opportunities to make inferences that are not directly observable in the graph (kids in this class do not like to wear leather shoes). The difference between actual facts and inferences is an important idea in graph construction and is also an important idea in science. Older students can examine graphs found in newspapers or magazines and discuss the *facts* in the graphs and the *message* that may have been intended by the person who made the graph.

As children begin to see different types of graphs, they can begin to make their own graphs of information gathered independently or by a group. A simple way to move graphing from the entire class to a small group is to assign different data collection tasks to different groups of children. The task is to gather the data and decide on and make a graph that displays as clearly as possible the information found.

STEM-AND-LEAF PLOTS

Stem-and-leaf plots are an increasingly popular form of bar graph where numeric data is plotted by using the actual numerals in the data to form the graph. By way of example, suppose that the American League baseball teams had posted the following record of wins over the past season:

Baltimore	45	Milwaukee	91
Boston	94	Minnesota	98
California	85	New York	100
Chicago	72	Oakland	101
Cleveland	91	Seattle	48
Detroit	102	Toronto	64
Kansas City	96	Texas	65

If the data are to be grouped by tens, list the tens digits in order and draw a line to the right, as in Figure 19.14(a). These form the "stem" of the graph. Next, go through the list of scores and write the ones digits next to the appropriate tens digit, as in Figure 19.14(b). These are the "leaves." There is no need to count or group the data ahead of time. The process of making the graph does it all for you. Furthermore, every piece of data can be retrieved from the graph. (Notice that stem-and-leaf plots are best made on graph paper so that each digit takes up the same amount of space.)

To provide more information, the graph can be quickly rewritten, ordering each leaf from least to most, as in Figure 19.14(c). In this form, it may be useful to identify the number that belongs to a particular team, indicating its relative place within the grouped listing.

Stem-and-leaf graphs are not limited to two-digit data. For example, if the data ranged from 600 to 1300, the stem could be the numerals from 6 to 13 and the leaves made of two-digit numbers separated by commas. If the ones digit is not important, round the data to the nearest 10, and use only the tens digit in the leaves. Figure 19.15 shows the same data in two different stem-and-leaf plots.

Figure 19.16 illustrates two additional variations. When two sets of data are to be compared, the leaves can extend in opposite directions from the same stem. In the same example, notice that the data are grouped by fives instead of tens. When plotting 62, the 2 is written next to the 6; for 67, the 7 is written next to the dot below the 6.

Stem-and-leaf plots are significantly easier for students to make than bar graphs, all of the data are maintained, they provide an efficient method of ordering data, and individual elements of data can be identified. For these reasons, stem-and-leaf plots are preferred over bar graphs by many authorities (Landwehr, Swift, & Watkins, 1987).

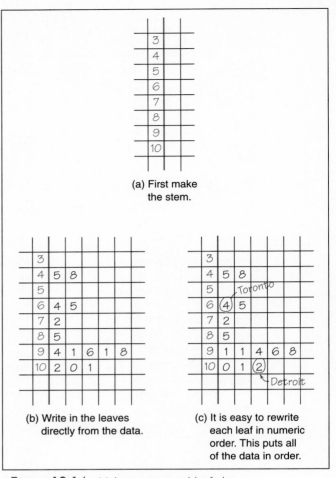

(a) First make the stem.

(b) Write in the leaves directly from the data.

(c) It is easy to rewrite each leaf in numeric order. This puts all of the data in order.

● **FIGURE 19.14** *Making a stem-and-leaf plot.*

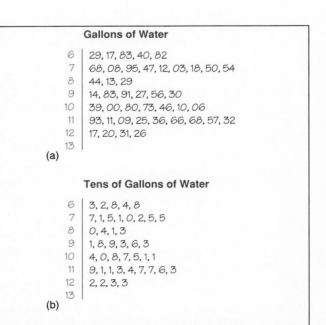

Gallons of Water

6	29, 17, 83, 40, 82
7	68, 08, 95, 47, 12, 03, 18, 50, 54
8	44, 13, 29
9	14, 83, 91, 27, 56, 30
10	39, 00, 80, 73, 46, 10, 06
11	93, 11, 09, 25, 36, 66, 68, 57, 32
12	17, 20, 31, 26
13	

(a)

Tens of Gallons of Water

6	3, 2, 8, 4, 8
7	7, 1, 5, 1, 0, 2, 5, 5
8	0, 4, 1, 3
9	1, 8, 9, 3, 6, 3
10	4, 0, 8, 7, 5, 1, 1
11	9, 1, 1, 3, 4, 7, 7, 6, 3
12	2, 2, 3, 3
13	

(b)

● **FIGURE 19.15** *In the plot shown in (b), the data from (a) are rounded to the nearest 10.*

mark and label entries of particular interest. For example, Joe B. and Whitney might be the class officers.

Making box-and-whisker plots is quite simple. First, put the data in order. An easy and valuable method is to make a stem-and-leaf plot and order the leaves, providing another visual image as well. Next, find the median. If the data are listed in a single row or column, young students can put their fingers on the ends and move each toward the middle one step at a time. Older children will simply count the number of values and determine the middle one. This can be done directly on the stem-and-leaf plots as was done in Figure 19.20. To find the two quartiles, ignore the median itself, and find the medians of the upper and lower halves of the data. Again, this can be done on the stem-and-leaf plots. Mark the two extremes, the two quartiles, and the median above an appropriate number line. Draw the box and the lines. Box plots can also be drawn vertically.

Note that the means for the data in our example are each just slightly higher than the medians (class = 132.4; boys = 133.9; girls = 130.8). For this example, the means themselves do not provide nearly as much information as the box plots. In Figure 19.21 the means are shown with small segments extending above and below each box.

Graphing calculators as well as several computer programs draw box-and-whisker plots making this relatively simple process even more accessible. The TI-82 and TI-83 calculators can draw box plots for up to three sets of data on the same axis. This provides for excellent discussions. In Figure 19.22, the data for the top box plot is based on 23 items. The second plot has 122 items. The third plot has 48 items of data. When you compare both large and small sets of data in this manner, the spread or lack of spread of the data becomes much more obvious.

Box-and-whisker plots are graphical representations, and yet they are pictures of statistics perhaps more than pictures of data. They show the range and the median and pictorially indicate a sense of the spread. The more traditional measures of spread, the *variance* and the *standard deviation,* are not necessary to consider at the elementary level. However, once a concept of spread or dispersion of data is developed informally with box-and-whisker plots, the standard deviation may have more meaning. This statistic is rather tedious to compute but is available on most scientific calculators at the press of a button.

Understanding the Mean

Due to ease of computation and stability, the median when compared to the mean has some advantages as a practical average. However, the mean will continue to be used in popular media and in books, frequently along with the median. For smaller sets of data such as your test scores, the mean is perhaps a more meaningful statistic. Finally, the mean is used in the computation of other statistics such as the standard deviation. Therefore, it remains important that students have a good concept of what the mean tells them about a set of numbers. How do you describe the mean other than how to compute it? The two activities in this section will help students construct intuitive ideas about the mean.

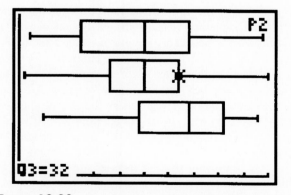

• **FIGURE 19.22**   Three box plots of data falling between the values of 0 and 50. Twenty-three items are represented by the top plot, 122 by the middle plot, and 48 by the bottom plot. The cursor on the middle plot shows that the third quartile is 32. What other information can be determined from this plot?

—ACTIVITY—

19.5 Leveling the Bars

Make a bar graph using wooden cubes for the bars. Choose a graph with five or six bars with lengths of no more than 10 to 12. (The graph in Figure 19.23 (p. 428) represents the prices of six toys chosen so that the total of the prices is a multiple of 6.) Sketch a picture of the graph on the board as a record. Have students compute the mean using the usual numeric methods. Discuss with them what they think this number called the mean tells them about the data. After listening to their ideas, compare the process of adding up the numbers to the process of piling all the cubes into one stack. Dividing the sum by the number of values is the same as separating the one big stack of block into equal stacks. Rearrange the cubes into bars of equal length. The mean, then, is the number you get if all of the values are leveled off. Make different graphs with cubes, and let students find the mean by leveling out the stacks rather than using any computation.

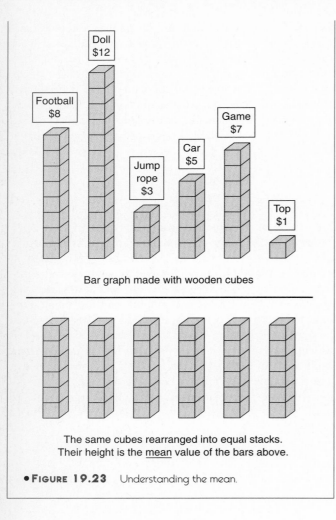

Bar graph made with wooden cubes

The same cubes rearranged into equal stacks.
Their height is the <u>mean</u> value of the bars above.

• FIGURE 19.23   Understanding the mean.

estimated mean line and record this number. Similarly, for bars that are below their estimated mean line, add up the spaces between the tops of the bars and the mean line (see Figure 19.24). Compare the two sums. Should they be the same or different, or is it impossible to know? Now have students compute the actual mean with a calculator, draw a new line, and check the totals of the bars above and below as before. The two sums should be exactly the same when the mean line is drawn accurately. Notice that the pieces that stick up above the mean could be cut off and fitted into the spaces below the line to make the bars all equal (as with the blocks). Visually estimating the mean of a bar graph is a fun challenge.

Technology provides teachers with an effective method for examining the mean with their classes. Even very simple spreadsheets are easy to use for things such as adding lists of numbers, ordering them, and computing the mean. It is easy to add one "far-out" number to the data, delete numbers, or change the data in any way at all to observe the effect on the mean. The program Data Insights has a spreadsheet function built right into it that requires no programming and allows for this same sort of exploration. (It also draws box-and-whisker plots.) Also, do not forget the graphing calculator. Data sets can be entered in much the same way as on a spreadsheet.

This bar graph mean activity can also be done by making the original bar graph on paper. Numbers of any size can be used. After computing the mean, cut out all the bars, and tape them together end to end. The length of the total strip is the sum of the numbers. Fold the long strip into as many equal parts as there are bars in the graph. The length of each part is the mean.

The next activity is a good follow-up to Activity 19.5.

SCATTER PLOTS AND RELATIONSHIPS

The graphs and descriptive statistics discussed so far in this chapter are designed to describe single sets of data or to make comparisons between two sets of data. Data are also analyzed to search for or demonstrate relationships between two sets of data or phenomena. For example, what are the relationships, if any, between time spent watching television and overall grade point average? Does the size of a college have anything to do with the cost of attending?

All sorts of real situations exist where we are interested in relationships between two variables or two numeric phenomena. The following three categories are simply to get you thinking about what kinds of things might be examined for potential relationships.

• *Social phenomena.* These include people's habits, likes and dislikes, and age; money spent, saved, or earned; and physical abilities (e.g., sports). The data for these things

─────ACTIVITY─────

19.6 Over and Under the Mean

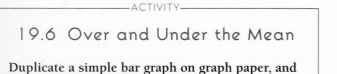

Duplicate a simple bar graph on graph paper, and pass it out to the class. Without doing any computation, ask students to draw a line across the graph where they estimate the mean to be. Next, using the scale on the graph, have them add up the pieces of the bars that are above their

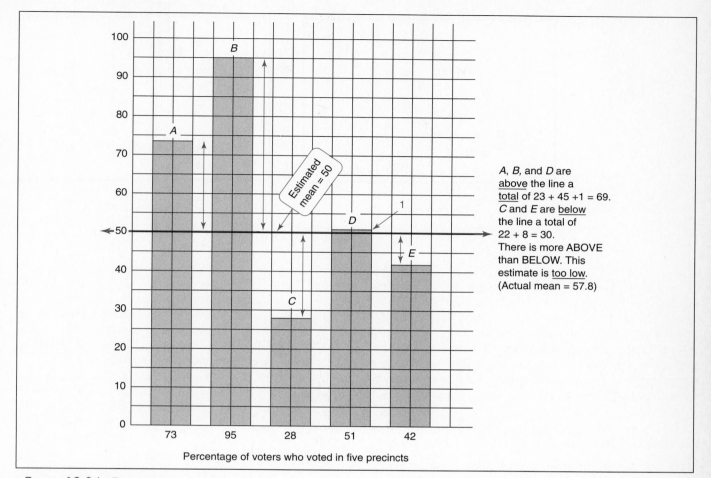

● **FIGURE 19.24**   *Estimating the mean on a bar graph.*

come from surveys (rate your approval of candidate *X* on a scale of 1 to 10) and from various records or observations. The numbers generally do not follow any hard rules but frequently follow trends.

- *Experiments.* The world of science abounds with experimental data. How far does a toy car roll down an inclined plane as compared to the angle of the plane? How fast does the corn grow over a 21-day period from the day it sprouts? Such data are generally gathered from some sort of experiment that is set up and observed, with measurements taken. The experiment defines the various variables to look at.

- *Data from a mathematical formula or physical law.* Here the data can be generated on paper. A common example is to determine the relationship between the area of a rectangle and the width of one side if the total distance around the rectangle (perimeter) is held fixed.

Data from all of these situations are available in pairs. For example, if you were going to examine the possible relation-

ship between hours of TV watched and grades, each person in the survey or sample would produce a pair of numbers, one for TV time and one for grade point average.

Scatter Plots

Regardless of the source of the data, a good first attempt at examining them for possible relationships is to create a *scatter plot* of the two variables involved, a graph of points on a coordinate grid with each axis representing one of the two variables. Each pair of numbers from the two sets of data, when plotted, produces a visual image of the data as well as a hint concerning any possible relationships. Suppose that the following information was gathered from 25 eighth-grade boys: height in inches, weight in pounds, and number of letters in their last name. The two graphs in Figure 19.25 (p. 430) show two possibilities. The first is a scatter plot of height to weight, and the second is a plot of name length to weight.

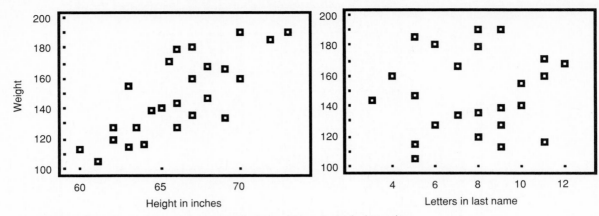

●**FIGURE 19.25**   Scatter plots show potential relationships or lack of relationships.

As you would expect, the boys' weights seem to increase as their heights increase. However, the relationship is far from perfect. We all know there are short chubby people and tall lanky people and many variations in between. However, the dots in the graph illustrate a general trend. Similarly, there is no reason to expect any relationship between name length and weight, and indeed the dots appear to be almost randomly distributed.

Best-Fit Lines

If your scatter plot indicates a relationship, it can be simply described in words. "As boys get taller, they tend to get heavier." This is correct but not particularly useful. What exactly is the relationship? If I knew the height of a boy, could I predict what his weight might be based on this information? Like much of statistical analysis, the value of a statistic is to predict what has not yet been observed. We poll a small sample of voters before an election to predict how the full population will vote. Here, can a sample of 30 students predict the weights of other students?

The relationship in these cases is not a number like a mean or a standard deviation but rather a line or curve. Is there a line that can be drawn through the scatter plot that represents the "best" approximation of all of the dots and reflects the observed trend? If the scatter plot seems to indicate a steadily increasing or steadily decreasing relationship (as in the height-weight graph), you would probably try to find a straight line that approximates the dots. Sometimes the plot will indicate a curved relationship, in which case you might try to draw a smooth curve like a parabola to approximate the dots.

What Determines Best Fit?

From a strictly visual standpoint, the line you select defines the observed relationship and could be used to predict other values not in the data set. The more closely the dots in the scatter plot "hug" the line you select, the greater the confidence you would have in the prediction value of the line. Certainly you could draw a straight line somewhere in the name length–weight graph, but you would not have much faith in its predictive capability because the dots would be quite dispersed from any line you might draw.

In Figure 19.26, the height-weight plot is redrawn in a larger scale. Imagine that you had duplicated this plot for all students in the room. Provide each student with a piece of spaghetti to use as a line. The task is to tape the line on the graph so that it is the "best" line to represent the dots. Further, the students are to come up with a rationale for why they positioned their line where they did. (Groups or pairs are suggested.) You might try to decide on a best-fit line yourself before reading further. Once you have decided on a line, what reasons can you give for your choice? This is an excellent source of discussion with your students. Many will say things like "It just looks the best." Others will try to see how many dots they can make their line pass through. Still other students will try to get the same number of points on each side of the line.

Consider all of these ideas for best fit, and note that none of them actually takes all points into consideration and also leads to a single best line. Two different people using the same criteria could come up with different lines.

Encourage students to use a more "mathematical" reason for why a line might be best. Since a good line is one around which most dots cluster, a good-fitting line is one where the distances from all of the dots to the line is minimal. This general notion of least distance to the line for all points can lead to an algorithm that will always produce a unique line for a given set of points. Two such algorithms are well known and used in statistics. The more complicated approach is called the *least squares regression* line. It is an algebraic procedure not accessible to middle grade students and is also rather tedious to compute. The second algorithm produces what is called the *median-median* line and is quite easy to determine.

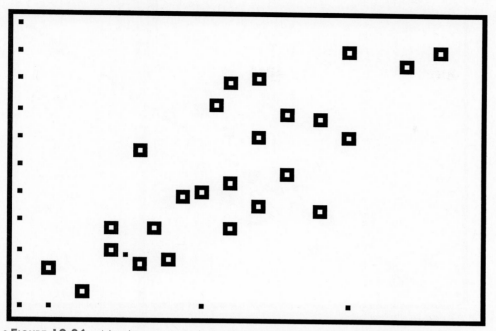

● **FIGURE 19.26**   A height–versus–weight scatter plot. Determine the median–median line on this graph.

Median-Median Line

The median-median line can be determined directly from the graph or from the data. It is based on the simple median statistic. The method for determining the median-median line essentially consists of these steps:

1. Separate the data into three "equal" sets of points along the horizontal axis. (In the example of Figure 19.26, since there are 25 points, put the extra point into the middle third.)

2. Find the *median point* in each third of the points. (This is described in the text that follows.)

3. Connect the median points in the first and third sets of data. This line takes into consideration all points in these two sections but ignores the points in the middle third.

4. Draw a parallel line one-third of the distance between this first line and the center median point. This gives the center collection of points a proportional influence on the position of the line.

A *median point* in a scattered collection of points is the point with its first coordinate equal to the median of all the first coordinates and its second coordinate equal to the median of all the second coordinates. Another way of saying this is that the median point is one that is midway vertically and midway horizontally. Using this second formulation,

the median point can be found by counting points from the bottom up until you have half the points below and half above. With an odd number of points, draw a horizontal line through the middle point. With an even number of points, draw the line halfway between the two middle points. The median point will fall on this horizontal line. Repeat the process moving from left to right. The vertical line you find this way will intersect the horizontal line at the median point. Note that it is not necessary for the median point to be a data point.

In Figure 19.26, the median point in the left-hand third of the data (the first eight points counting left to right) is shown as a single pixel. Find the other two median points on your own.

To complete the median-median line for this example, draw the line joining the left and right median points. It should be just a small amount above the center median point. Draw a new line parallel to the first and about one-third of the distance down toward the center median point.

Median-Median Lines with a Calculator

The TI-82 and TI-83 calculators will compute the median-median line for you. The data are entered in two lists, one for the first coordinates of each point and one for the corresponding second coordinates. Figure 19.27 (p. 432) shows the calculator plot of the median-median line for the same height-versus-weight data as in Figure 19.26..

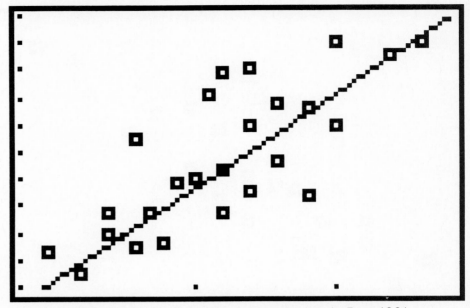

● **FIGURE 19.27**   *The median-median line for the points plotted in Figure 19.26.*

Thinking About Functional Relationships

A median-median line for a collection of points that students can actually plot can be found without knowing anything about the equation of a line. However, it is worth noting that the line found is a graphical representation of a function relating the variable on the horizontal axis to the variable on the vertical axis. Using the height-weight example, it is appropriate to say that *the weight of a boy is a function of his height.* The best-fit line is a mathematical method of determining what the function might be. Different methods of finding the best-fit line will likely develop slightly different lines.

Note that if the function (line) that we found accurately predicted the weight of a boy based on his height, all of the data points in Figure 19.26 would fall along a perfectly straight line. That they do not is a vivid picture of the difference between data found in the world (the points on the graph) and a mathematical model of the real world (the line).

Scatter plots and best-fit lines will be discussed again in Chapter 21 on functions and variables. The connection between the real world, statistics, and algebraic ideas is a valuable one to make.

Ideas for Investigations

The best investigations of potential relationships are probably found in the interests of your students and the subjects they are studying. Data can frequently be found in your own classroom or taken from surveys. Science units generate data from experiments. Beyond data actually collected, books of lists, almanacs, books of sports records, and encyclopedias have data that may be related to your students' current interests. Here are some ideas to get you started thinking, but do not be limited by these suggestions:

SCHOOL DATA

Participation in sports, band, drama, out-of-school activities, scouts (compared to grades, time spent doing other things)

Grades (overall, in a specific subject, in one subject related to another)

Money spent in the cafeteria (on lunch, on snacks)

PERSONAL DATA

Body data (weight, arm span, shoe size, hair length, reach, age in months)

Abilities (speed in 40-yard dash, free throws out of 50, maximum jump height)

TV watching time, time go to bed, hours of sleep

SOCIAL DATA

Prices (CDs, fast foods, sneakers, cars; over time, who buys, etc.)

Ratings of household or consumer products such as found in trade magazines or *Consumer Reports*

Food data (fat, protein, calories, salt)

College data (SAT or ACT scores, number of students, tuition)

Notice that all things that are related are not necessarily related in the same way. The height-weight example exhibited a *positive linear* relationship since it was approximated by a straight (linear) line with an upward (positive) slope. Weight tends to rise directly as height increases. Some other linear relationships are negative. For example, sales tend to decrease as price increases. Furthermore, not all relationships are linear. Some scatter plots represent a very definite curve. Whereas a straight line can always be determined by following the median-median method, that does not always mean that the line is a good representation of the data. In a more sophisticated analysis, a statistic is often computed that tells how well the line of best fit represents the data. At the middle grade level, an "eyeball test" is sufficient.

ASSESSMENT NOTES

Care should be taken in assessment of probability and statistical ideas to distinguish between the use of related algorithms and techniques and the quite different kind of knowledge that involves judgment and interpretation.

Probability

The skills that are easy to assess involve the computation of probabilities. Even young children should be able to tell if an event is possible or impossible or is very likely or not very likely. Older children should be able to determine probabilities in well-designed experiments such as those discussed in this chapter.

You also want to be aware of students' understanding of chance and probability. What does it mean that an event has a probability of 89 percent or $\frac{2}{3}$? How many times should a simulation or an experiment be conducted before you can have confidence in the results? What does "confidence in the results" mean? Can knowing the probability of an event ever predict what will happen on the next trial? How are probability ideas used in the real world?

These more subtle ideas can be determined by having class discussions and listening for the reasoning of students and making efforts to check students' understanding of the key ideas you are looking for. You might use a three-point rubric to rate students quickly on their understanding.

Middle school students can write short reports about a situation that includes your main ideas, and you can have them specifically address the issues you want to assess.

Statistics

In the area of statistics and data analysis, the same distinction is important. Of course, you want your students to know how to make a stem-and-leaf plot and a box plot or find the mean and the median. But many students can learn to do these things without interpreting them. Choice and interpretation of graphs and statistics are more important than the ability to construct and compute.

Choice

Computers and calculators will make the graphs we want even when they are inappropriate to our needs. We must be able to select appropriate graphs and statistics to suit the purposes. It is important to pose situations that include a real context and have students decide what statistics and what graphs would best serve the purposes. Is a bar graph or a line graph more appropriate? Why? Which statistic is better in this situation, the mean or the median?

Interpretation

In a similar manner, making the graph or computing the best-fit line does not help me understand what it tells me about the data. There are a number of ways to get at interpretation. For example, several graphs and statistics for the same situation and data can be presented. "Suppose you were a newspaper editor. Which of these statistics and graphs should you use in your story? Explain your selection. Are any of these statistics of no value to the message?" In this type of interpretation, several options are provided, and the choice is based on the intended audience and purpose. There is no need actually to compute the statistics or create the graphs.

Another idea is to provide graphs and statistics for two related situations: your class and the rest of the school, your state and the rest of the country, hamburgers at McDonald's and hamburgers at Burger King. What can be determined for sure from these data? What inferences can be made? What would help you make a decision about _____ that you cannot determine from the information gathered? How could you use this information to argue in favor of _____? How could you use the same information to argue on the reverse side of the issue?

Selection and interpretation of graphs and statistics rarely involves one right answer. There are very few absolutes. What is important is to be able to make reasoned judgments and arguments based on the choices we make and the interpretations of the data we have before us.

REFLECTIONS ON CHAPTER 19: WRITING TO LEARN

1. Describe the difference between theoretical probability, relative frequency, and experimental probability.

2. Why do you think it is a good idea to have students conduct experiments before trying to figure out probabilities?

3. What are the first ideas that young students should develop about the concept of chance? How can this be done?

4. Describe how you could use a random-number generator on a computer or calculator to produce a simulation of a three-part spinner with all parts equal.

5. What is the purpose of a simulation? Set up a simulation for at least one of the examples on page 418. Conduct a few trials.

6. Use an area model and a tree diagram to determine the theoretical probability for the following experiment:

> Dad puts a $5 bill and three $1 bills in the first box. In a second box, he puts another $5 bill but just one $1 bill. Junior, for washing the car, gets to take one bill from the first box without looking and put it in the second box. After these have been well mixed, he then gets to take one from the second box without looking. What is the probability that he will get $5?

Design a simulation for the problem, and try it out. Does it agree with your theoretical probability?

7. Draw a picture of a line plot, a histogram, and a line graph. How are all of these alike?

8. Put at least 30 numbers in a stem-and-leaf plot, and use it to determine the median, the upper and lower quartiles, and the range and to draw a box-and-whisker plot.

9. What are three ways to make a circle graph? What does a circle graph tell you that a bar graph does not? What does it not tell?

10. What are three different forms of averages? Which is the most stable? Explain. What is meant by the mean?

11. Describe what is meant by a best-fit line. When would you want to find such a line?

12. On a grid, make a scatter plot of about 30 points that appear to have a negative linear relationship or correlation. Use these points to draw the median-median line. Suppose that your points represented number of yearly visits to the mall as related to miles between home and mall. How could your best-fit line be used to predict the number of visits to the mall for a person who was not included in your data set? How much potential error would you assign to your prediction based solely on the scatter plot that you drew?

FOR DISCUSSION AND EXPLORATION

1. Examine one of six books from the Used Numbers Project (see Suggested Readings). These books have some of the best statistics activities for elementary students. You might share an activity or idea in the book that excited you, react to a lesson described in the book, or share an idea in the book with a teacher and get his or her reaction.

2. How important is it, in your opinion, to teach probability concepts in the early grades (K–4)? What about in the middle grades? Does your answer change if you substitute statistics for probability? Explain your position. Some experts have argued that the ability to understand probability and statistical ideas is so much more important than the related skills that being able to compute probabilities and statistics or to make graphs are skills that we could skip in favor of increased reasoning in this area. What position would you take on this issue?

SUGGESTED READINGS

Highly Recommended

Shulte, A. P. (Ed.). (1981). *Teaching statistics and probability*. Reston, VA: National Council of Teachers of Mathematics.

It may seem unusual to recommend a book published in 1981, but this NCTM yearbook remains timely. With the exception of the use of graphing calculators and currently available software, all of the ideas discussed in this chapter are included and then some. Several specific chapters are noted in Other Suggestions, but as an overall reference, this is a good one.

Used numbers: Real data in the classroom. Palo Alto, CA: Dale Seymour.

This set of six books, each covering two or three grades between kindergarten and sixth, is a result of an NSF-supported project at Technical Education Research Centers (TERC) and Lesley College. The books are an excellent resource for elementary statistics activities. Each book is a unit of study, most with subtopics that can be used independently. The authors (authorship varies with each book) include ample detail to help you get a feel for what might happen in the classroom. The spirit of these activities is excellent! The suggestions are realistic and can all be implemented as suggested. Blackline masters are included when needed. (All six titles are included in Other Suggestions.)

Zawojewski, J. S. (1991). *Dealing with data and chance: Addenda series, grades 5–8*. Reston, VA: National Council of Teachers of Mathematics.

Middle school teachers interested in teaching probability and statistics must have this book. It is not timid in its suggestions for demanding activity, yet all activities are appropriate for middle grade students. The book is organized around the four theme standards of the *Curriculum Standards*.

Other Suggestions

Armstrong, R. D. (1981). An area model for solving probability problems. In A. P. Shulte (Ed.), *Teaching statistics and probability* (pp. 135–142). Reston, VA: National Council of Teachers of Mathematics.

Bright, G. W., Harvey, J. G., & Wheeler, M. M. (1981). Fair games, unfair games. In A. P. Shulte (Ed.), *Teaching statistics and probability* (pp. 49–59). Reston, VA: National Council of Teachers of Mathematics.

Bright, G. W., & Hoeffner, K. (1993). Measurement probability, statistics, and graphing. In D. T. Owens (Ed.), *Research ideas for the classroom: Middle grades mathematics* (pp. 78–98). Old Tappan, NJ: Macmillan.

Bruni, J. V., & Silverman, H. J. (1986). Developing concepts in probability and statistics—and much more. *Arithmetic Teacher, 33*(6), 34–37.

Bryan, E. H. (1988). Exploring data with box plots. *Mathematics Teacher, 81,* 658–663.

Burns, M. (1995). *Math by all means: Probability, grades 3–4.* White Plains, NY: Cuisenaire (distributor).

Corwin, R. B., & Friel, S. N. (1990). *Statistics: Prediction and sampling.* (A unit of study for grades 5–6 from *Used numbers: Real data in the classroom.*) Palo Alto, CA: Dale Seymour.

Corwin, R. B., & Russell, S. J. (1990). *Measuring: From paces to feet.* (A unit of study for grades 3–5 from *Used numbers: Real data in the classroom.*) Palo Alto, CA: Dale Seymour.

Dessart, D. J. (1995). Randomness: A connection to reality. In P. A. House (Ed.), *Connecting mathematics across the curriculum* (pp. 177–181). Reston, VA: National Council of Teachers of Mathematics.

Fair, J., & Melvin, M. (1986). *Kids are consumers, too! Real-world mathematics for today's classroom.* Menlo Park, CA: AWL Supplemental.

Friel, S. N., Mokros, J. R., & Russell, S. J. (1992). *Middles, means, and in-between.* (A unit of study for grades 5–6 from *Used numbers: Real data in the classroom.*) Palo Alto, CA: Dale Seymour.

Gnanadesikan, M., Schaeffer, R. L., & Swift, J. (1987). *The art and techniques of simulation: Quantitative literacy series.* Palo Alto, CA: Dale Seymour.

Goldman, P. H. (1990). Teaching arithmetic averaging: An activity approach. *Arithmetic Teacher, 37*(7), 38–43.

Karp, K. S. (1994). Telling tales: Creating graphs using multicultural literature. *Teaching Children Mathematics, 1,* 87–91.

Kelly, I. W., & Bany, B. (1984). Probability: Developing student intuition with a 20 × 20 array. *School Science and Mathematics, 84,* 598–604.

Landwehr, J. M., Swift, J., & Watkins, A. E. (1987). *Exploring surveys and information from samples: Quantitative literacy series.* Palo Alto, CA: Dale Seymour.

Landwehr, J. M., & Watkins, A. E. (1987). *Exploring data: Quantitative literacy series.* Palo Alto, CA: Dale Seymour.

Leutzinger, L. P. (1990). Graphical representation and probability. In J. N. Payne (Ed.), *Mathematics for the young child* (pp. 251–263). Reston, VA: National Council of Teachers of Mathematics.

Lindquist, M. M. (1992). *Making sense of data: Addenda series, grades K–6.* Reston, VA: National Council of Teachers of Mathematics.

Martin, H. M., & Zawojewski, J. S. (1993). Dealing with data and chance: An illustration from the middle school addendum to the standards. *Arithmetic Teacher, 41,* 220–223.

National Council of Teachers of Mathematics. (1990). Data analysis [Minifocus issue]. *Mathematics Teacher, 83*(2).

Newman, C. M., Obremski, T. E., & Schaeffer, R. L. (1987). *Exploring probability: Quantitative literacy series.* Palo Alto, CA: Dale Seymour.

Phillips, E., Lappan, G., Winter, M. J., & Fitzgerald, W. (1986). *Middle grades mathematics project: Probability.* Menlo Park, CA: Addison-Wesley Publishing Co.

Russell, S. J., & Corwin, R. B. (1989). *Statistics: The shape of the data.* (A unit of study for grades 4–6 from *Used numbers: Real data in the classroom.*) Palo Alto, CA: Dale Seymour.

Russell, S. J., & Corwin, R. B. (1990). *Sorting: Groups and graphs.* (A unit of study for grades 2–3 from *Used numbers: Real data in the classroom.*) Palo Alto, CA: Dale Seymour.

Russell, S. J., & Friel, S. N. (1989). Collecting and analyzing real data in the elementary classroom. In P. R. Trafton (Ed.), *New directions for elementary school mathematics* (pp. 134–148). Reston, VA: National Council of Teachers of Mathematics.

Russell, S. J., & Stone, A. (1990). *Counting: Ourselves and our families.* (A unit of study for grades K–1 from *Used numbers: Real data in the classroom.*) Palo Alto, CA: Dale Seymour.

Schultz, H. S., & Leonard, B. (1989). Probability and intuition. *Mathematics Teacher, 82,* 52–53.

Shaughnessy, J. M., & Dick, T. (1991). Monty's dilemma: Should you stick or switch? *Mathematics Teacher, 84,* 252–256.

Stevens, J. (1993). Generating and analyzing data. *Mathematics Teacher, 86,* 475–478, 487–489.

Uccellini, J. C. (1996). Teaching the mean meaningfully. *Mathematics Teaching in the Middle Grades, 2,* 112–115.

Wallace, E. C. (1993). Exploring regression with a graphing calculator. *Mathematics Teacher, 86,* 741–743.

Watkins, A. E. (1981). Monte Carlo simulation: Probability the easy way. In A. P. Shulte (Ed.), *Teaching statistics and probability* (pp. 203–209). Reston, VA: National Council of Teachers of Mathematics.

CHAPTER

20

PREPARING FOR ALGEBRA

Much of the middle grades curriculum has been discussed in previous chapters, including decimals, ratio and proportion, percent, measurement, geometry, probability, and statistics. Each of those topics has its initial development in earlier grades but continues in the middle school. The most significant ideas of algebra, functions and variables, are explored in the next chapter. But some important ideas about numbers that extend or build on each of the topics discussed and provide useful background information for the study of functions remain. Specifically, students in the middle grades need to develop a more complete understanding of the number system, extend whole numbers to integers, start to think of fractions as rational numbers (both positive and negative), and begin to appreciate the completeness of the real number system. In addition, some ideas about numbers are simply interesting in themselves and add to the continued development of mathematics as a science of pattern and order.

 BIG IDEAS

1. **Whole numbers exhibit some interesting patterns and relationships that can be observed, explored, and understood.**

2. **Exponential notation is a powerful way to express repeated products of the same number. Specifically, exponents of 10 help us express very large and very small numbers in an economical and useful manner.**

3. **The integers add to number the idea of opposite, so that every number has both size and a positive or**

negative relationship to other numbers. A negative number is the opposite of the positive number of the same size.

4. **Every fraction, both positive and negative, is a rational number. Furthermore, every rational number can be expressed as a fraction.**

5. **There are many numbers that are not rational and can only be expressed symbolically with special symbolism or approximately as a close rational number.**

EXPLORING TOPICS IN NUMBER THEORY

Number theory is the study of relationships found among the natural numbers. At the elementary level, number theory includes the concepts of prime number, odd and even numbers, and the related notions of factor, multiple, and divisibility. Prime factorization is frequently connected with finding common denominators and reducing fractions. More important, the concepts of prime, factor, and multiple are also used in algebraic expressions. Students should develop an intuitive understanding of these topics with numbers so that the algebraic generalizations can be built on them. Number theory topics also provide an opportunity for problem solving and for student discovery of many fascinating relationships.

Primes and Factorization

Prime numbers can be viewed as fundamental building blocks of the other natural numbers. Simply defining a prime number and searching for primes can be a rather dull experience. The activities described here are examples of interesting things we can explore with children and still have fun while developing basic concepts of prime, factor, and multiple.

---ACTIVITY---

20.1 Looking for Rectangles

Have students work in groups using square tiles or cubes or just square grid paper. Begin with the number 12 or 16. Have students find as many different rectangles as possible made up of that many squares. Share results. Students should agree that 1 × 12 and 1 × 16 rectangles should be included and that a square (4 × 4) is also a special kind of rectangle. When the process is understood completely, have students try to build as many rectangles as possible for each number up to 100. Give different groups different numbers to work on. Draw pictures on graph paper for each number, and make a display. Students will discover that some numbers (primes) have only one rectangle. The dimensions of each rectangle are two factors of that number. Use this idea to develop a definition of factor and of prime number. (A number other than 1 is a *prime* number if its only factors are itself and 1.) Help students use the idea of rectangular dimensions to develop definitions of prime numbers and factors. Rectangles are a way to think of numbers as a product of two factors. Rectangular solids are a model for a number expressed as a product of three factors.

Once students have an idea of what a prime number and a factor are, they can explore a variety of other relationships involving primes. Calculators should be available for all explorations.

- Given a number, is it a prime or not a prime? (Nonprime numbers other than 1 are called *composite* numbers.) What are some ways to test if a number is a prime?

- Explore Goldbach's conjecture: Any even number greater than 2 can be written as the sum of two prime numbers. For example: $38 = 31 + 7$. Goldbach's conjecture has never been proved or disproved. (Goldbach lived between 1690 and 1764.)

- Have students make up and explore different conjectures of their own. They might consider the difference of primes or the sum of three primes. Can they find a formula that will always produce primes? For example, $2n - 1$ works for quite a few values of n. The formula $n^2 - n + 41$ yields prime numbers for any value of n between 1 and 40. Let students try to find other "prime generators."

- Have students write down all of the prime factors of a number, including repeats. Write the number as a product of these prime factors, placing them in order from least to most. For example, $360 = 2 \times 2 \times 2 \times 3 \times 3 \times 5$. Before comparing results from different groups, discuss the various strategies or approaches that were used. If a different approach is used, will it still result in the same factorization? (The answer, of course, is yes. This result is known as the *fundamental theorem of arithmetic*.) Three ways to find the prime factorization of a number are shown in Figure 20.1.

- The terms *divisor* and *factor* are synonyms. For a non-prime number, find all of the *proper divisors* (divisors other than the number itself), and add them up. (See which groups can come up with the cleverest ways of finding all the factors of a number.) If the sum is less than

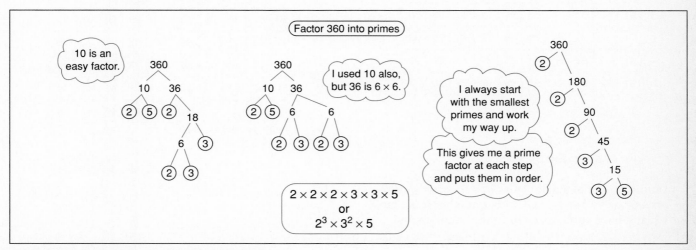

• **FIGURE 20.1**   *Different routes to the same factors.*

the number, it is called *deficient;* if it is more than the number, it is called *abundant;* and if it is equal to the sum of its proper divisors, it is called *perfect.* For example, 6 is perfect, 8 is deficient, and 12 is abundant. Those are the easy ones. What are the next three of each type?

- Students can also explore looking for twin primes, those that are two apart, such as 11 and 13.

Patterns on a Hundreds Chart

One of the truly fascinating aspects of mathematics is the way that numbers tend to appear in patterns. In Chapter 18, the calculator was suggested as a good way to explore some interesting numeric patterns. The Fibonacci sequence was also discussed as an intriguing source of patterns and relationships. In the following activities, students can use a hundreds chart to discover other interesting phenomena of numbers. As you explore these ideas, consider how prime numbers and factors play a role in the results. How are these patterns like the calculator patterns in Chapter 18? Encourage students to explore some of these ideas and make their own observations. A self-discovered pattern is much more exciting than one that is pointed out to students.

all multiples of it. For every number, some pattern will emerge (see Figure 20.2). Which numbers make diagonal patterns, and which produce only columns or parts of columns? Notice that the pattern for sixes is made up of numbers that are also in the threes pattern. How can you tell if one pattern will be a part of another? Do they ever overlap, or is one always completely inside another? What happens if you start a jump-by-threes pattern at 2 instead of at 0?

---ACTIVITY---

20.3 Changing the Charts

Change the dimensions of the chart in Activity 20.2 by changing the lengths of the rows (see Figure 20.3). If the rows have six squares, which numbers will make patterns in rows and which in columns? If there are seven squares in the row, only one number will make a column pattern, the multiples of 7. Why? Try other row lengths, including rows with more than ten squares. All patterns seem to be either columns or diagonals. What does row length have to do with the patterns involved? Consider looking at primes and factors.

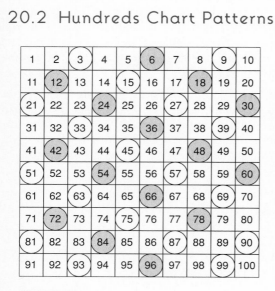

Circle the threes.
Color the sixes.
What columns are these in?

- **FIGURE 20.2** *Patterns of multiples.*

Duplicate lots of small copies of a hundreds chart (or a 0-to-99 chart). Start with a number less than 10, and have students color in that number and

Fours on a 5-wide chart

Threes and fives
on a 4-wide chart

- **FIGURE 20.3** *Looking for patterns on different hundreds charts.*

---ACTIVITY---

20.2 Hundreds Chart Patterns

Tests for Divisibility

It is easy to tell whether or not a number is divisible by 10. For example, 198,456 is not, but 650,270 is. The test for divisibility by 10 is to look at the last digit, the digit in the ones position. You probably know this already. Experience indicates that products with a factor of 10 end in 0. Divisibility by 5 is similar: If the last digit is either 5 or 0, the number is divisible by 5.

There are similar tests for divisibility by other numbers.

A Number Is Divisible by

3 if the sum of the digits is divisible by 3

9 if the sum of the digits is divisible by 9

2 if the last digit is even (divisible by 2)

4 if the last *two* digits are divisible by 4

8 if the last *three* digits are divisible by 8

6 if it is divisible by both 3 and 2

Many students find these intriguing. The limited practical value of such tests indicates that they should be investigated as a problem-solving task rather than as a topic of mastery. The more intriguing and more valuable question is "Why do these tests work?" Since the answer lies in the base 10 place-value representation of the numbers, divisibility rules also provide an opportunity to review place-value concepts (see Figure 20.4). One approach is to give students the divisibility rule and suggest that they use base 10 materials or drawings to figure out why it works. Having discovered one rule, the students can then be asked to find a rule that is similar. For example, the argument for divisibility by 3 is identical to that for 9, and the arguments for 4 and 8 are similar to that for 2.

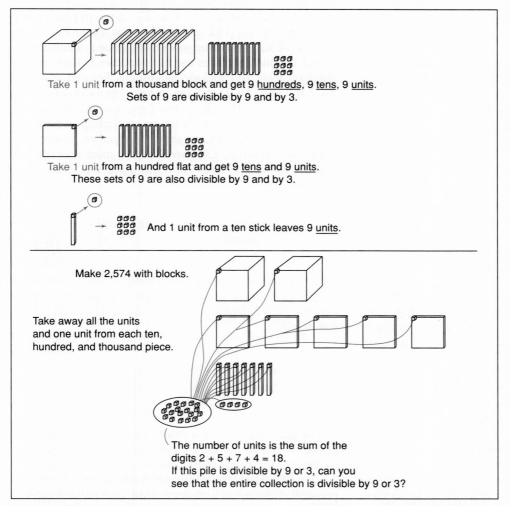

Take 1 unit from a thousand block and get 9 <u>hundreds</u>, 9 <u>tens</u>, 9 <u>units</u>.
Sets of 9 are divisible by 9 and by 3.

Take 1 unit from a hundred flat and get 9 <u>tens</u> and 9 <u>units</u>.
These sets of 9 are also divisible by 9 and by 3.

And 1 unit from a ten stick leaves 9 <u>units</u>.

Make 2,574 with blocks.

Take away all the units and one unit from each ten, hundred, and thousand piece.

The number of units is the sum of the digits 2 + 5 + 7 + 4 = 18.
If this pile is divisible by 9 or 3, can you see that the entire collection is divisible by 9 or 3?

● **Figure 20.4**   Divisibility by 9 and 3 shown with base 10 blocks. Can you show that every block larger than a 10 can be divided by 4? Use this fact to establish a divisibility-by-4 rule.

The other commonly used model is the number line. It is a bit more traditional and mathematical, yet many students find it somewhat confusing. The football field model provides an intuitive background. Positive and negative numbers are measured distances to the right and left of 0. It is important to remember that signed values are *directed distances* and not points on a line. The points on the number line are not models of integers; the directed distances are. To emphasize this for students, represent all integers with arrows, and avoid referring to the coordinates on the number line as "numbers." Poster board arrows of different whole-number lengths can be made in two colors, blue pointing to the right for positive quantities and red to the left for negative quantities (see Figure 20.8). The physical arrows help students think of integer quantities as directed distances. A positive arrow never points left, and a negative arrow never points right. Furthermore, each arrow is a quantity with both length (magnitude or absolute value) and direction (sign). These properties remain for each arrow regardless of its position on the number line. Small versions of the arrows can easily be cut from poster board and distributed as kits for students to work with.

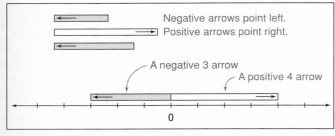

● **FIGURE 20.8**   *Number-line model for integers.*

Why Bother?

Before discussing how these models are used to explain the operations, it is worth pointing out that the rules (procedural knowledge) for operations on the integers are generally easier simply to give to students than explanations with a model are. The conceptual explanations do not make the rules easier to use, and it is never intended that students continue to think in terms of these models as they practice integer arithmetic. Rather, it is important that students not view the procedural rules for manipulating integers as arbitrary and mysterious. Here, then, is a case where we must remember to make students responsible for the conceptual knowledge. If we emphasize only the procedural rules, there is little reason for students to attend to the conceptual justifications. In your discussions with students, do not be content to get right answers; always demand explanations. You might even try giving students the answers and having them explain with a model why they must be so.

Which Model?

Many teachers who have tried both of these models with their students frequently report that they much prefer one model over the other or that their students find one model easy and the other hard. (The counter model seems to be the clear favorite.) As a result, they decide to use only the model that students like or understand better. This is a mistake! Remember that the concept is not in the model but must be a construction of the students in their own minds. For example, it may be that students find the operations to be easier "to do" when they use the counter model. This is not the same thing as understanding integer operations. The concept of "opposite" is expressed in one model as different color and in the other as different direction. Students should experience both models and, perhaps most important, discuss how the two are alike. A parallel development using both models at the same time may be the most conceptual approach.

A PROBLEM-SOLVING APPROACH

The discussion that follows is more a quick explanation of how counters and arrows can be used to model operations with integers than a suggested pedagogical approach. Once your students understand how integers are represented by each of the models, the operations for the integers can be presented to your students in the form of problems. In other words, rather than *explain* how addition of integers works and showing students how to solve exercises with the models, you can pose an integer computation and let students use their models to find a solution. It may be useful to assign half of the class the arrow model and the other half the counters. When solutions have been reached, the groups can compare and justify their results. Many incorrect ideas will surface, but the learning that will come from the discussion and clarification will be far superior to an expository approach by you.

Addition and Subtraction

Adding or subtracting integers with the models is straightforward and analogous to the corresponding debit-credit model or the football model. Since middle school or junior high students will not have used counters or number lines for some time, it would be good to begin work with either of these models using positive whole numbers. After a few examples to help them become familiar with the model for addition or subtraction with whole numbers, have them work through an example with integers using exactly the same reasoning. Remember, the emphasis should be on the rationale and not how quickly students can get correct answers.

Several examples of addition are modeled in Figure 20.9, each in two ways: with positive and negative counters and with the number-line-and-arrow model. First examine the counter model. After the two quantities are joined, any pairs of positive and negative counters cancel each other out, and students can remove these, making it easier to see the result.

To add using the arrow model, note that each added arrow begins at the point end of the previous arrow. If you help students with the analogy between these arrows and the football situation, when the arrows change direction, that is like the ball changing teams. Addition is the advance of a team from the previous position. In the $^+3 + {}^-5$ exam-

ple, the positive arrow (+ team) starts at 0 and ends at positive 3. From that point, the negative arrow begins (the − team takes over and *advances* in the negative direction). The result, then, is an arrow beginning at 0 and ending where the second arrow ended. The same change of direction (change of ball possession) takes place in the $^-6 + {}^+2$ example. If a negative were added to a negative, the arrows would each go toward the left or negative (no change of possession), just as there was no change of direction for the $3 + 5$ example.

Subtraction is interpreted as "remove" in terms of the counter model and "back up" in terms of the arrow model.

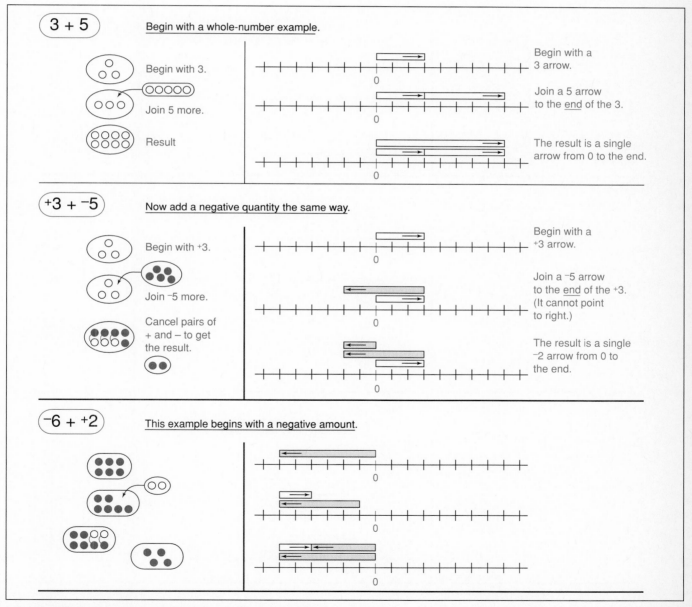

• **FIGURE 20.9**   *Relate integer addition to whole-number addition.*

In Figure 20.10, for ⁻5 − ⁺2, both models begin with a representation of −5. To remove two positive counters from a set that has none, a different representation of ⁻5 must first be made. Since any number of neutral pairs (one positive, one negative) can be added without changing the value of the set, two pairs are added so that two positive counters can be removed. The net effect is to have more negative counters. This is like removing credits from your ledger if you are already in debt. The result is to leave you further in debt. A similar change in the representation of the begin-

ning amount is always necessary when you need to subtract a quantity of a different sign.

With the number-line-and-arrow model, subtraction means to back up or to move in the opposite direction. Using the football field analogy, either team moves backward when it is penalized or loses yardage. Each team moves in the opposite direction from its goal. In the example of ⁻5 − ⁺2, the first arrow ends at ⁻5. If the ⁺2 were to be added, it would be in the dotted position, ending at ⁻3. But it backs up instead. The result of the operation is an arrow from 0 to

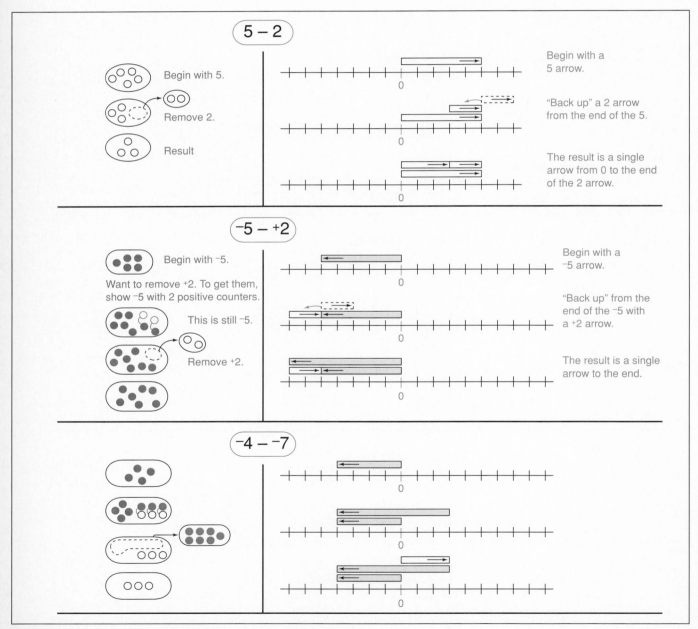

the back end of the $^+2$ arrow. In the football analogy, the ball is first at the $^-5$-yard line, changes hands to the positive team, which proceeds to lose 2 yards, leaving the ball at the $^-7$-yard line. In the second example, $^-4 - ^-7$, the ball does not change hands, but the negative team loses yardage.

You want your students to draw pictures to accompany computations that they do with integers. Set pictures are easy enough. They may consist of Xs and Os, for example. For the arrow model, there is no need for anything elaborate either. Figure 20.11 illustrates how a student might draw arrows for simple addition and subtraction exercises without even sketching the number line. Directions are shown by the arrows, and magnitudes are written on the arrows. For your initial modeling, however, the poster board arrows in two colors will help students see that negative arrows always point left and that addition is a forward movement and subtraction is a backward movement for either type of arrow.

An effort is usually made to see that $^+3 + ^-5$ is the same as $^+3 - ^+5$ and that $^+2 - ^-6$ is the same as $^+2 + ^+6$. With the method of modeling addition and subtraction described here, these expressions are quite discernible and yet have the same result as they should have.

On graphing calculators, these expressions are entered using a separate key for "negative" and the usual key for "subtraction." The difference is also evident in the display. The redundant superscript plus signs are not shown. Students can see that $3 + ^-5$ and $3 - 5$ each results in -2, and $3 - ^-5$ and $3 + 5$ are also alike.

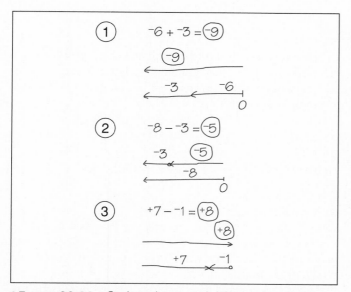

●**FIGURE 20.11** *Students do not need elaborate drawings to think through the number-line model.*

Multiplication and Division

Multiplication of integers should be a direct extension of multiplication for whole numbers, just as addition and subtraction were connected to whole-number concepts. We frequently refer to whole-number multiplication as repeated addition. The first factor tells how many sets there are or how many are added in all, beginning with 0. This translates to integer multiplication quite readily when the first factor is positive, regardless of the sign of the second factor. The first example in Figure 20.12 (p. 450) illustrates a positive first factor and a negative second factor.

What could the meaning be when the first factor is negative, as in $^-2 \times ^-3$? If positive first factor means repeated addition (how many times added to 0), a negative first factor should mean repeated subtraction (how many times subtracted from 0). The second example in Figure 20.12 illustrates how multiplication with the first factor negative can be modeled. The success of your students in understanding integer multiplication depends on how well they understood integer addition and subtraction. Notice that there really are no new ideas, only an application of addition and subtraction to multiplication.

The deceptively simple rules of "like signs yield positive products" and "unlike signs yield negative products" are quickly established. However, one more time, it is not as important that your students be able to produce answers correctly and skillfully as that they be able to supply a rationale.

With division of integers, it is again a good idea to explore the whole-number case first. Recall that $8 \div 4$ with whole numbers has two possible meanings corresponding to two missing-factor expressions: $4 \times ? = 8$ asks, "Four sets of *what* make eight?" whereas $? \times 4 = 8$ asks, "How many fours make eight?" Generally, the measurement approach ($? \times 4$) is the one used with integers, although both concepts can be exhibited with either model. (Students should be permitted to explore the meaning in whatever manner makes most sense to them, as long as they can justify it.) It is helpful to think of building the dividend with the divisor from 0 in the same way that we fill units into an amount when we measure it. The first example in Figure 20.13 (p. 451) illustrates how the two models work for whole numbers. Following that is an example where the divisor is positive but the dividend is negative. How many sets of $^+2$ will make $^-8$, or $? \times ^+2 = ^-8$. With the set model, if we try to add positive counters, the result will be positive, not negative. The only way to use sets of $^+2$ to make $^-8$ is to remove them from 0. This means that we must first change the representation of 0 as illustrated. For the arrow model, consider how $^+2$ arrows can be placed end to end to result in a distance 8 to the left of 0. Starting at 0, the arrows must be backed up. In both models, the arrows are being repeatedly subtracted, or added a negative number of times. Try now to model $^+9 \div ^-3$ using both models. The approach is very similar to this example. Then try a negative divided by

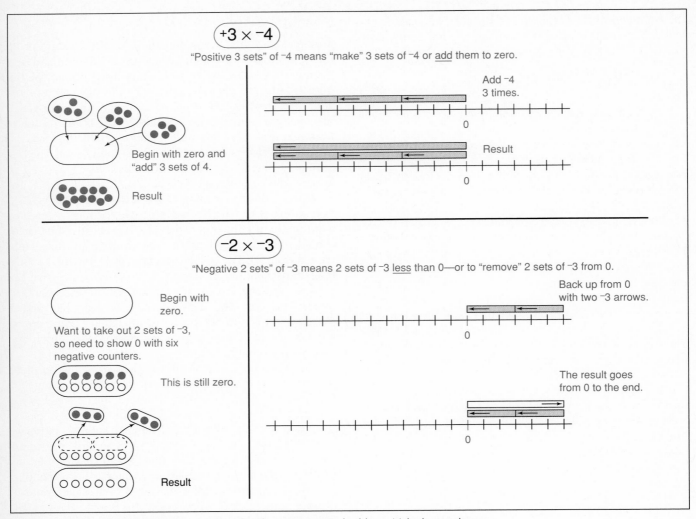

● **FIGURE 20.12**   *Multiplication by a positive first factor is repeated addition. Multiplication by a negative first factor is repeated subtraction.*

a negative. That case is much easier to understand. However, the entire understanding of integer division rests on a good concept of a negative first factor for multiplication and a knowledge of the relationship between multiplication and division.

There is no need to rush your students on to some mastery of use of the models. It is much better that they first think about how to model the whole-number situation and then figure out, with some guidance from you, how to deal with integers.

RATIONAL NUMBERS

Several number ideas that students have been exposed to in earlier grades, coupled with the ideas of the integers, need

to come together in the middle grades. A complete understanding of the rational numbers as positive and negative decimals and equivalently as positive and negative fractions is an important development.

Fractions as Indicated Division

If four people were to share 12 candies, the number that each would get can be expressed by $12 \div 4$. If four people were to share three pizzas, the amount that each would get can be expressed similarly by $3 \div 4$; that is, three things divided four ways. In the pizza example, each person would receive three-fourths of a pizza. So $\frac{3}{4}$ and $3 \div 4$ are both expressions for the same idea: 3 things divided by 4. Similarly, in the candy example, $\frac{12}{4}$ expresses the number each will receive just as well as $12 \div 4$.

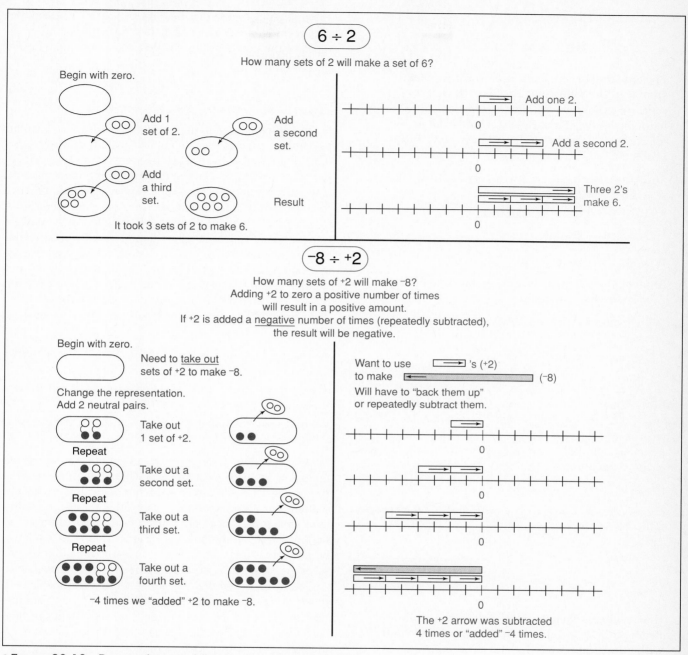

● **FIGURE 20.13** *Division of integers following a measurement approach.*

Put simply, a fraction $\frac{a}{b}$ is another way of writing $a \div b$. Students understandably find this meaning of fractions unusual. First, the indicated division is different from the meaning that has been carefully developed. Second, fractions are commonly thought of as amounts of parts of wholes, not as operations. Similarly, expressions such as $7 \div 3$ are thought of as operations (things to be done), not numbers. In fact, however, 4, 2 + 2, 12 ÷ 3, and $\frac{8}{2}$ are all symbolic expressions for the same number. 12 ÷ 3 is not the question and 4 the answer; both are expressions for 4. Likewise, 2 ÷ 3 and $\frac{2}{3}$ are both expressions for the quantity two-thirds. Do you find this a little hard to swallow? So do children. For the first time in seven or eight years of schooling you are telling students that a symbol can represent two different ideas. This is a relatively sophisticated idea.

How can we help students develop the idea that a fraction is another way of expressing division? Here are some possibilities.

─────── ACTIVITY ───────

20.8 How Do You Write It?

Present students with a simple word problem similar to the following: *Zach has 18 meters of rope. He cuts off one-fifth of the rope to make a leash for his dog, Sam. How much rope did he use for the leash?* Three "students" have solved this problem.

Student A: Zach cut off 3.6 meters because $18 \div 5 = 3.6$.

Student B: I did $\frac{1}{5} \times 18$ like this:

$$\frac{1}{5} \times \frac{18}{1} = \frac{18}{5} = 3\frac{3}{5}$$

so the answer is 3 and $\frac{3}{5}$ meters.

Student C: I did the same thing, but I just said the answer was $\frac{18}{5}$ meters.

Which student is correct? Which has the "best" answer?

─────────────────

In the discussion of a problem situation like the one in Activity 20.8, you can lead students to see that $18 \div 5$ and $\frac{18}{5}$ mean exactly the same thing.

A similar approach is to discuss the difference between these three expressions:

$\frac{1}{4}$ of 24 $\frac{24}{4}$ $24 \div 4$

In the spirit of looking for patterns, here is a further idea.

─────── ACTIVITY ───────

20.9 Division Patterns

Have students do a series of divisions as follows: Begin with 18 and divide by 4. Record the result with a fraction remainder and as an improper fraction. Repeat with 17, then 16, and so on. What can you find out about this?

─────────────────

In Activity 20.9, students are thinking about division but are recording fractions. In the improper form, each fraction is written as equal to the corresponding division. This becomes more obvious when the dividend (resulting numerator) is less than 4 ($3 \div 4 = \frac{3}{4}$, $2 \div 4 = \frac{2}{4}$, $1 \div 4 = \frac{1}{4}$). Some children will explore $0 \div 4 = \frac{0}{4} = 0$ and continue to negative numbers: $^-1 \div 4 = \frac{-1}{4}$. This gives rise to even further possibilities. What happens if you divide numbers by negative integers instead of positive numbers? Is $\frac{-1}{4}$ the same as $\frac{1}{-4}$? And what about the fraction $\frac{-2}{-3}$?

Any or all of these discussions can lead to a general development of the idea that a fraction can be thought of as division of the numerator by the denominator or that $\frac{a}{b}$ is the same as $a \div b$.

Fractions as Rational Numbers

In the early grades, children develop the idea that fractions are "things" such as parts of circular regions or shaded sections of rectangles. Even when fractions are seen as parts of sets, they remain, in the minds of children, more physical object than number. This is one reason that children have such a difficult time placing fractions on a number line. A significant leap toward thinking about fractions as numbers is made when students begin to understand that a decimal is a representation of a fraction. In Chapter 14, we explored the idea of the "friendly" fractions (halves, thirds, fourths, fifths, eighths) in terms of their decimal equivalents. The connection was largely based on the use of region models for fractions.

In the middle grades, it is time to combine all of these ideas:

- $4\frac{3}{5}$ is 4.6 because $\frac{3}{5}$ is six-tenths of a whole, so 4 wholes and six-tenths is 4.6.
- $4\frac{3}{5}$ is $\frac{23}{5}$, and that is the same as $23 \div 5$, or 4.6 if I use decimals.
- 4.6 is read "four and six-tenths," so I can write that as $4\frac{6}{10} = 4\frac{3}{5}$.

What becomes clear in a discussion that is open and builds on students' existing ideas is that any number, positive or negative, that can be written as a fraction can also be written as a decimal number. It is perhaps worth the effort of reversing this idea and converting decimal numbers to fractions. Keep in mind that the purpose is to see that it can be done, that there are different symbolic notations for the same quantities; it is not to become skilled at conversions.

The end result of this full discussion is a reasonable definition of rational numbers: A *rational number* is any number that can be expressed as a fraction. And equivalently, a *rational number* is any number that can be written as either a terminating or repeating decimal number.

─────── ACTIVITY ───────

20.10 How Close Is Close?

Have students select any two fractions or any two decimals that they think are "really close." It makes no difference what numbers students pick or even how close together they really are. Now challenge them to find at least ten more numbers (fractions or decimals) that are between these two numbers. Do not be tempted to show students any clever methods for finding the numbers.

Activity 20.10 is an opportunity to find out a lot about how your students understand fractions and decimals. (The activity should be done in both forms eventually.) There are quite obvious ways of getting as many fractions as you wish between two given fractions. But if you haven't been told a method, you must rely on your own ideas to come up with a solution. The activity offers a great opportunity for discussion, assessment of individual students' fraction and decimal concepts, and an opportunity to introduce perhaps the most interesting feature of the rational number system: density. The rational numbers are said to be *dense* because between any two rational numbers there exists an *infinite* number of other rational numbers. In other words, if you tried to plot all of the rationals between 0 and 1, you would have no gaps at all.

A true understanding of the density of the rationals makes the irrationals even more amazing.

REAL NUMBERS

As just noted, there are *irrational* numbers, numbers that are not rational. The irrationals together with the rational numbers make up the *real* numbers. The real numbers fill in all the holes on the number line even though the holes are infinitesimally small.

Introducing the Concept of Roots

How could you use a calculator to estimate the sides of the second square or the edges of the second cube shown in Figure 20.14 without using the square-root key? These are excellent challenges for students and provide a good introduction to the process of finding the root of a number. The solutions will satisfy these equations:

$$\square \times \square = 45, \text{ or } \square^2 = 45$$

and

$$\square \times \square \times \square = 30, \text{ or } \square^3 = 30$$

The calculator permits students to guess at a solution and quickly test to see if it is too big or too small. For example, to solve the cube problem, you might start with 3.5 and find that 3.5^3 is 42.875, much too large. You will quickly find that the solution is between 3.1 and 3.2. But where? Again, try halfway: 3.15^3 is a bit more than 31.255. The next try should be lower. By continued trial and error, a simple calculator can get the result correct to six decimal places.

From a simple introduction such as this, students can be challenged to find solutions to equations such as $\square^6 = 8$. These students are now prepared to understand the general definition of the *nth root* of a number N as the number that when raised to the *n*th power equals N. The square and cube roots are simply other names for the second and third roots. With this approach, the concept of the *n*th root is de-

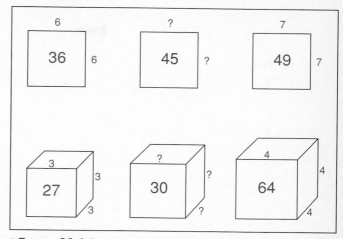

● **FIGURE 20.14** *A geometric interpretation of square roots and cube roots.*

veloped in general. The notation involving the radical sign can come last in this development. It should then be clear that $\sqrt{6}$ is a number and not an exercise to be done. The cube root of eight is the same as $\sqrt[3]{8}$, which is just another way of writing 2.

Real Numbers

Though it may be open to argument, eighth-grade students probably do not need a very sophisticated knowledge of the real number system. A few powerful ideas, however, deserve to be explored or discussed informally.

Irrational Numbers

One characterization of a rational number is that of a number that can be written as a decimal where the decimal part is either finite or repeats infinitely. Thus both 3.45 and 87.19363636 . . . are rational numbers and can each be converted to fractional form. But what about a decimal number that just goes on and on and on, with no repetition? Or what about the number 3.101001000100001000001 . . . ? These never repeat and are not finite and therefore are not rational. A number that is not rational is called *irrational*.

The numbers π and $\sqrt{2}$ are both irrational numbers. The number π is a ratio of two measures in one of the most common shapes we know, the circle. Although it is not possible to prove the irrationality of π at this level, the fact that it is irrational implies that it is impossible to have a circle with the lengths of both the circumference and the diameter rational. (Why?) A proof that $\sqrt{2}$ is irrational is generally explored at the junior high level. The usual argument assumes that $\sqrt{2}$ is rational, which then leads to a contradiction.

Density

If the density of the rationals is impressive, even more astounding is that the irrationals are also dense. And the irrationals and the rationals are all mixed up together. The density of the irrationals is not as easy to demonstrate and is not within the scope of the middle school.

Rational Roots

One reason it is difficult to comprehend irrational numbers is that we have very little firsthand experience with them. The irrational numbers we are most familiar with are roots of numbers. For example, it has already been noted that students are frequently shown a proof for the irrationality of $\sqrt{2}$. An intuitive notion of that fact is difficult to come by. Most calculators will show only eight digits, requiring at least some leap of faith to accept that the decimal representation is infinite and nonrepeating.

What can unfortunately happen is that whenever students see the radical sign, they think the number is irrational. A possible approach is to consider the concept of roots from the opposite direction. Rather than ask what is the square root of 64 or the cube root of 27, we might suggest that *every* number is the square root, the cube root, the fourth root, and so on, of some number (for example, 3 is the second root of 9, the third root of 27, etc.). From this vantage point, students can see that "square root" is just a way of indicating a relationship between two numbers. That the cube root of 27 is 3 indicates a special relationship between 3 and 27.

LITERATURE CONNECTIONS

The topics in this chapter present a wonderful opportunity for exploration and "playing around" with ideas and numbers. Although most teachers in the middle grades do not think of using literature as a springboard for mathematics, here are a few ideas that are worthy of a change of pace in the upper grades.

The Phantom Tollbooth (Juster, 1961)

Milo's remarkable journey through the lands beyond the magic tollbooth are so full of wonderful words and ideas that the story is a must to read and discuss with adolescents regardless of the potential mathematical content. But the first page of Chapter 14, with its road sign indicating three directions to Digitopolis, is worthy of time in your mathematics class. The sign reads:

DIGITOPOLIS

5	Miles
1,600	Rods
8,800	Yards
26,400	Feet
316,800	Inches
633,600	Half inches

AND THEN SOME

The discussion about which road is shorter or quicker is just great. Three pages later, Milo is told, "Why, did you know that if a beaver two feet long with a tail a foot and a half long can build a dam twelve feet high and six feet wide in two days, all you would need to build Boulder Dam is a beaver sixty-eight feet long with a fifty-one foot tail?" (p. 175). In the next chapter is an equally humorous discussion of infinity. That is followed by the chapter in which Milo meets the 0.58 boy.

Not only are these fanciful ideas in a story filled with excellent language, but there are also opportunities to wonder what if or to create similar fantasies based on numbers. For example, students could write a new chapter for the book in which Milo journeys to a world in outer space where the distances are enormous and everyone uses scientific notation.

In One Day (Parker, 1984)

This is not literature but an amazing book of 365 facts concerning things that occur in one day in the United States. For example, in one day, Americans "fill in, or at least try to, 50 acres of crossword puzzles" and "buy at least 5 million things that are shaped like Mickey Mouse, or have a picture of Mickey Mouse on them." (That has probably increased since 1984.)

It is difficult not to wonder at the amazing numbers in the book. Students may want to test the facts in some way or perhaps do a bit of research to add new facts that they find interesting. For example, how many footballs are thrown on an average fall day? If there is any interest in finding real numbers in the real world through some simple research, sharing this book with the class is probably worth the time.

Math Curse (Scieszka & Smith, 1995)

This book was an instant hit probably because there are so many people out there who have math phobias. The first page sets the tone: "On Monday in math class Mrs. Fibonacci says, 'You know, you can think of almost everything as a math problem.' On Tuesday I start to have problems." Some may argue that this book is so antimathematics that it has no place in the middle grades. But it does provide an opportunity to show your human side as you discuss a wide range of mathematical ideas.

ASSESSMENT NOTES

Middle school teachers frequently get bogged down in the minutia of the prealgebra curriculum. Many books emphasize rules and exercises when there are so many opportunities for explorations and for doing mathematics. The content of this chapter is a great place to focus on your students' mathematical power rather than their acquisition of skills.

For example, in the area of number theory, searching for primes by building rectangles, searching for a prime-number-generating formula, and generalizing observed patterns on different-sized hundreds charts provide good opportunities to see how students reason, communicate ideas, go beyond the answer to generate their own ideas, and generally *do mathematics.*

The same is true of the discussion of exponents. Once students have learned the relatively simple definition of what an exponent is, the search for easy tricks for multiplying and dividing should be left to students' discovery and their own reasoning. The discussions that will no doubt ensue will be better than drilling rules about adding exponents when you multiply numbers with like bases. These are good opportunities to assess mathematical power.

With respect to integers, you have already been warned about focusing on the rules for operations with them. Certainly, the rules are important and will be needed in algebra. However, if the rules for operating on the integers are developed by the students themselves, not only will they have a deeper understanding of them, but you will have an opportunity to observe and assess their mathematical power.

Similar comments can be made about fractions and decimal relationships and rational numbers as discussed in this chapter. The development of reasoning ability and students' belief that they can do mathematics is far more important than drilling on tedious rules.

REFLECTIONS ON CHAPTER 20: WRITING TO LEARN

1. How does building rectangles with square tiles help distinguish between prime and nonprime (composite) numbers?

2. Why might it be valuable for students to examine the patterns of multiples on a hundreds chart or to explore the rules for divisibility?

3. Explain the value of the graphing calculator's ability to display a complete arithmetic expression (with or without a variable) on a single line and to evaluate it on another line.

4. Explain how powers of 10 are used to write very small and very large numbers. What is the particular form of the power-of-10 symbolism used in scientific notation and on calculators? What is the value of this notation?

5. Why is it probably better to use two different models for the integers even if one of the two seems to cause students some confusion?

6. Use both the arrow model and the counter model to demonstrate the following:

$$^-10 + {}^+13 = {}^+3 \qquad ^-4 - {}^-9 = {}^+5 \qquad ^+6 - {}^-7 = {}^+13$$

$$^-4 \times {}^-3 = {}^+12 \qquad ^+15 \div {}^-5 = {}^-3 \qquad ^-12 \div {}^-3 = {}^+4$$

7. How can you help students understand that a fraction such as $\frac{7}{8}$ means the same thing as $7 \div 8$?

8. How would you explain the difference between a rational and an irrational number to a middle school student?

9. What does $\sqrt{6}$ mean? How is $\sqrt{6}$ different from $\sqrt{4}$? How are they the same?

10. What does it mean to say that the rational numbers are dense?

FOR DISCUSSION AND EXPLORATION

1. Read the article "Why Elementary Algebra Can, Should, and Must Be an Eighth-Grade Course for Average Students" (Usiskin, 1987). In this article, Usiskin argues for moving the curriculum forward to algebra in the eighth grade for all students. His position is somewhat different from that of the NCTM *Standards.* What is your view?

2. Use a calculator for the following exercises:

   a. Estimate the cube root of 10 to five decimal places.

   b. What do you think will happen if you enter 1000 in your calculator and then press ÷ 2 = = ...? Try it.

   c. What do you think will happen if you enter 1000 in your calculator and then repeatedly press the √ key? Before you try it, try to explain why you think it will happen.

   d. See if you can find a prime number that is between 500 and 1000, and prove that it is prime.

3. Examine the table of contents in sixth-, seventh-, and eighth-grade books from two or three different publishers or books specifically intended for middle school mathematics. Using these books as a guide, how would you define "prealgebra"? How much of the curriculum of these three grade levels seems repetitious? Is this the same for all publishers?

SUGGESTED READINGS

Highly Recommended

Fitzgerald, W., Winter, M. J., Lappan, G., & Phillips, E. (1986). *Middle grades mathematics project: Factors and multiples.* Menlo Park, CA: AWL Supplemental.

This book is one in a series of five that has stood the test of time. The related topics of prime, factor, composite, prime factorization, divisor, multiple, common multiple, common factor, and relatively prime number are all developed in a series of interesting games and activities for the middle grades. The focus is on pattern development and logical connections. This is a good way to involve students in good mathematics without overwhelming them with tedious algebraic ideas.

Graeber, A. O., & Baker, K. M. (1992). Little into big is the way it always is. *Arithmetic Teacher, 39*(8), 18–21.

This is one of the few articles that discuss the issue of a fraction as an indicated division. The authors look at practices in the elementary school that suggest why the difficulty exists and make practical suggestions for working with middle school students.

Phillips, E., Gardella, T., Kelly, C., & Stewart, J. (1991). *Patterns and functions: Addenda series, grades 5–8*. Reston, VA: National Council of Teachers of Mathematics.

Again, the *Addenda Series* is the place to go for excellent activities. In this volume, you will find sections on exponents and growth patterns, number theory and counting patterns, and rational number patterns. Other topics in the book are related more to the concepts of function and variable.

Other Suggestions

Battista, M. T. (1983). A complete model for operations on integers. *Arithmetic Teacher, 30*(9), 26–31.

Bennett, A., Jr. (1988). Visual thinking and number relationships. *Mathematics Teacher, 81,* 267–272.

Bennett, A., Jr., Maier, E., & Nelson, L. T. (1989). *Modeling integers: Unit 6, Math in the mind's eye*. Salem, OR: Math Learning Center.

Edwards, F. M. (1987). Geometric figures make the LCM obvious. *Arithmetic Teacher, 34*(7), 17–18.

Hirschhorn, D. B., & Senk, S. (1992). Calculators in the UCSMP curriculum for grades 7 and 8. In J. T. Fey (Ed.), *Calculators in mathematics education* (pp. 79–90). Reston, VA: National Council of Teachers of Mathematics.

Kieran, C., & Chalouh, L. (1993). Prealgebra: The transition from arithmetic to algebra. In D. T. Owens (Ed.), *Research ideas for the classroom: Middle grades mathematics* (pp. 179–198). Old Tappan, NJ: Macmillan.

Martinez, J. G. R. (1988). Helping students understand factors and terms. *Mathematics Teacher, 81,* 747–751.

Paulos, J. A. (1988). *Innumeracy: Mathematical illiteracy and its consequences*. New York: Hill & Wang.

Rubenstein, R. N. (1996). The function game. *Mathematics Teaching in the Middle Grades, 2,* 74–78.

Shilgalis, T. W. (1994). Are most fractions reduced? *Mathematics Teacher, 87,* 236–238.

Sobel, M. A., & Maletsky, E. M. (1988). *Teaching mathematics: A sourcebook of aids, activities, and strategies* (2nd ed.). Upper Saddle River, NJ: Prentice Hall.

CHAPTER

21

FUNCTIONS AND VARIABLES

The concept of function is one of the big ideas or common threads that runs through much of mathematics. Students in the middle grades and in first-year algebra courses should begin their exploration of function concepts by learning to express functional relationships found in situations they are investigating and that make sense to them.

In the past, a symbolic, abstract approach to function, including vertical-line tests, identification of range and domain, and $y = f(x)$ notation, was part of the traditional effort to learn about functions. The result was a lot of student difficulties and a wide array of misunderstandings (Markovits, Eylon, & Bruckheimer, 1988). More important, that symbolic study of functions did not give students the power to use functions to understand and describe the patterns found in the world around them.

In this chapter, you will see how an investigation of a meaningful context can result in the development and articulation of function concepts in ways that make sense to students.

 BIG IDEAS

1. Functions are relationships or rules that uniquely associate members of one set with members of another set.
2. Functional relationships can be expressed in real contexts, graphs, algebraic equations, tables, and words. All representations for a given function are simply different ways of expressing the same idea, yet each representation provides a different view of the function.
3. Variables are symbols that take the place of numbers or ranges of numbers. Variables have different meanings depending on whether they are being used as representations of quantities that vary or change, representations of specific but unknown values, or placeholders in a generalized expression or formula.

FUNCTION CONCEPT AND REPRESENTATIONS

The underlying concept of a function is that of a relationship or rule of correspondence. To get an idea of what a function is and how it can be represented in different ways, let's consider a simple, real-world relationship.

Brian is trying to make money to help pay for college by selling hot dogs from a hot-dog cart at the coliseum during major performances and ball games. He pays the cart owner $35 per night for the use of the cart. He sells hot dogs for $1.25 each. His costs for the hot dogs, condiments, napkins, and other paper products are about 60 cents per hot dog on average. The profit from a single hot dog is therefore 65 cents.

Five Representations of a Function

There are at least five different ways to "see" or represent a function. Each representation is a different way of communicating the same rule of correspondence or relationship. It is important to see that although the representations are quite different, each expresses the same idea. And yet each provides a different way of looking at or thinking about the relationship. We will use the hot-dog vendor situation as an example to illustrate all five representations.

Contextual Representations of Functions

This function begins with a context: selling hot dogs and the resulting profit. We are interested in Brian's profit in terms of the number of hot dogs sold. It is fairly easy to see that the more hot dogs Brian sells, the more profit he will make. Brian does not begin to make a profit immediately because he must pay the $35 rent on the vending cart. Nonetheless, Brian's profit is dependent on—is a function of—the number of hot dogs he sells.

Not every function has a real-world context, but at the middle school level, it is a good idea to place functions in contexts that make sense to students. Here are some other contexts in which functional relationships are to be found:

* Suppose that the value of a new car depreciates at the rate of 20 percent each year. There is a definite relationship between the age of the car and the current value of the car. The original cost of the car is the maximum value, and each year the value decreases.

* If you measure the height and arm span of a lot of different people, from very short to very tall, you will likely find that there is a predictable relationship between these two measures. Arm span is related to height.

* A ride on a roller coaster has several possible relationships. As time passes from the beginning of the ride to the end of the ride, the height of the cars above the ground changes. It increases slowly at first, then most likely has a fast decrease followed by a series of lesser increases and decreases. The speed of the cars on the roller coaster is also a function of time. The speed of the cars has an effect on how loud the passengers scream, and so it is reasonable to say that speed and screams are related although perhaps not as precisely as the height is related to the time.

* If you build rectangles so that all have the same fixed perimeter, the length of the rectangles will decrease as the widths increase. If you begin with a very small width and a longer length, the area of the rectangles first increases as the width increases from zero and then decreases.

These are all contexts in which there is a functional relationship. Some, such as the hot-dog vendor's profit and the height of the roller coaster car, exist in the real world. The rectangle example is a context for a relationship, but there is no real-world aspect to it. That context comes up in a geometric investigation of areas and perimeters of rectangles. In the height versus arm span and the loudness of the roller coaster passengers, the relationship is there but is not easy to determine in as precise a manner. The crowd will not always scream at exactly the same decibel level, nor will everyone's height–to–arm span ratio be the same. However, all of these situations illustrate functions in meaningful contexts that make sense. Each has at least two values that change, with one being dependent on or related to the other.

Table Representations of Functions

Brian the hot-dog vendor might well sit down and calculate some possible income figures based on hypothetical sales. This will give him some idea of how many franks he must sell to break even and what his profit might be for an evening. For example, if he sells no hot dogs, he will be $35 in the hole, or his profit will be negative $35. If he sells 70 hot dogs, that would yield a profit of 70 × 0.65 − 35 = 45.50 − 35, or $10.50. A table of similar values might look like this:

HOT DOGS	PROFIT
0	−35.00
70	10.50
100	30.00
150	62.50

The numbers used in the table for the number of hot dogs are purely a matter of choice. It is possible to calculate the profit for 10,000 hot dogs (10,000 × 0.65 − 35) and enter that value in the table even though it is not reasonable to expect Brian to sell that many. One of the values of contexts in thinking about functions is to see how mathematical representations, in this case a table of related values, can ignore reality. The person who interprets the table must take the context into consideration.

To make a table for the car depreciation example, all we need to know is the sale price of the car. If the car was purchased for $15,000, how would you determine the value of the car after 1 year, 2 years, 5 years? The area of the rectangle can similarly be determined in terms of either the length or the width if we know what the fixed perimeter is. In the case of the roller coaster, some information about the physics of roller coasters would be necessary, or else we would actually have to measure what happens as the roller coaster travels its course.

In the height–arm span situation, a table could be created from actual measurements of a lot of people. For any given person, there will be a specific height and a specific arm span. However, this table only approximates the "general" relationship. One person who is 5 feet 10 inches tall may have an arm span of 69 inches, while another of the exact same height might have an arm span of 72 inches. Later we will see how a function can be determined that is a good predictor of the height–arm span relationship. The table for that function can be used to predict or make a guess at any person's arm span if we know that person's height.

Language Expressions for Functions

Functional relationships are dependent relationships or rules of correspondence. In the hot-dog vendor situation, Brian's profit depends on the number of hot dogs that are sold. In functional language, we can say, "Profit *is a function of* the number of hot dogs sold." The phrase "is a function of" expresses the dependent relationship. The profit *depends on* or *is a function of* the hot-dog sales.

Looking at the other contextual examples, we would say that the current value of a car is a function of its age or the value of the car depends on its age. The speed of the roller coaster is a function of the time since the ride started. If someone were to ask what speed the roller coaster is going, you might respond, "It depends on the time since the ride began," or, in functional terms, "That depends. The speed is a function of the time since the ride began." See if you can express the relationships in the other examples in functional terms.

What variables in your own world are dependent on other variables? Express one of these relationships in functional terms. The language of functions helps us think about the relationships. As you move from one representation to the other, the language that expresses the relationship can remain the same and help tie the representations together.

Language can also help us think about the reverse relationships in a situation. Brian's hot-dog profit is a function of sales. Are his sales a function of profits? Yes, in this sense. If you know how much profit he made in one evening, you can determine precisely how many hot dogs he sold. However, reverse relationships are not always functions. Consider the speed of the roller coaster. Though speed is a function of time, it is not true that time is a function of speed. Why? Suppose you had a table of the roller coaster speed for every 5 seconds from the beginning of the 2-minute ride to the end. If you were asked, "At what time did the roller coaster go 35 mph?" it may be that that speed was reached at eight or ten different times during the ride, as the car accelerated down a hill or slowed going up a hill. Here time cannot be determined by the speed, but the speed can be uniquely determined by the time. Try reversing the functional relationships for all of the examples. Which reverse relationships are functions?

Graphical Representations of Functions

The old saying goes that a picture is worth a thousand words. This is certainly true of functions. An important representation of a function is with a graph. In Figure 21.1, six different values of hot-dog sales are plotted on a graph. The

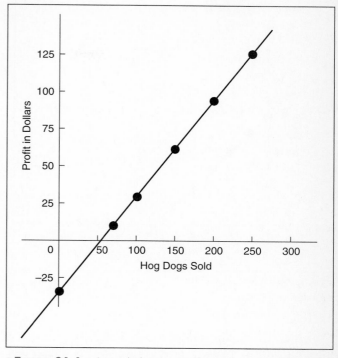

● **FIGURE 21.1** A graph showing profit as a function of hot-dog sales.

horizontal axis represents the number of hot dogs sold, and the vertical axis, the profit. As we have already established, the profit goes up as the sales go up. There is, in this situation, a very clear pattern to the six values. A straight line can be drawn through them as in the figure.

The graph shows that the relationship between sales and profits is *linear*—a straight line—and is increasing. It also allows us easily to answer questions about Brian's profits. How many hot dogs must be sold to break even? The graph shows zero profit (the break-even point) where the line crosses the horizontal axis. (Why?) It looks to be near 53 or 54. What is Brian's profit for 130 hot dogs? How many hot dogs must be sold to make a profit of $100? The context gives meaning to the graph, and the graph adds understanding to the context.

The graph is another mathematical model that, in terms of the context, does not make sense for all portions of the picture. If the line is extended indefinitely, there would be values where Brian's sales were negative (to the left of the vertical axis). This clearly does not make sense. Nor is it reasonable to talk about sales of millions of hot dogs even though the graph can extend as far as is wished.

Not all graphs of functions are straight lines. Consider the rectangle situation. If you start with a rectangle that has a fixed perimeter of 24 inches and increase the length beginning at 1 inch, the graph that shows the corresponding width and the graph showing the area will be different. You will see that the width graph is linear. It decreases at a constant rate. By contrast, the area graph rises in a curve, reaches a maximum value, and then goes back down. (See Figure 21.2, p. 460.).

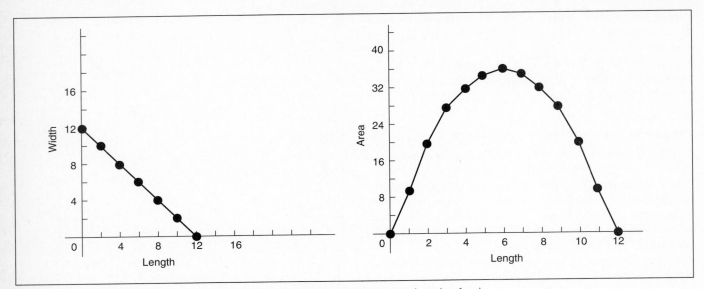

● **FIGURE 21.2**   The width and area graphs as functions of the length of a rectangle with a fixed perimeter of 24 units.

Figure 21.3 shows a simple roller coaster. Suppose that it takes just 100 seconds to ride. Try to sketch a graph that shows the *height* of the roller coaster throughout the ride. Why will your graph not be exactly the same as the path of the roller coaster? Now make another graph that shows the *speed* of the car over the 100 seconds of the ride. Share your sketches with a friend. How are these two graphs related to each other?

If the average man is a "square," meaning that his arm span is the same as his height, what would a graph of this relationship look like? What portions of the graph would make sense, and what portions are not very reasonable?

Equations to Represent Functions

Suppose that we pick a letter, say, *H,* to represent the number of hot dogs Brian sells. For each hot dog sold, his income is $0.65 \times H$ dollars. But to determine his profit, we have to subtract from his income the rental cost of the cart.

Therefore, Brian's profit is represented by $0.65 \times H - 35$. To make an equation, we can assign another letter to stand for profit: $P = 0.65 \times H - 35$. This equation defines a mathematical relationship between two values or two variables, P for profit and H for hot dogs. Taken out of context, it is simply a relationship between P and H. It is exactly the same as the relationship between x and y in the equation $y = 0.65x - 35$.

By expressing a function as an equation, it can be examined in its most abstract form. Equations can be categorized and described in terms of the properties that the entire class of equations possesses. When the properties of a class of equations are understood, the specific equation representing a realistic context can also be understood in a similar manner. In our hot-dog example, the equation has the general form of a linear equation, $Y = mX + b$. In this form, the value of m tells us how quickly or steeply the line goes up or down moving from left to right. The value of b tells where the graph will cross the vertical axis.

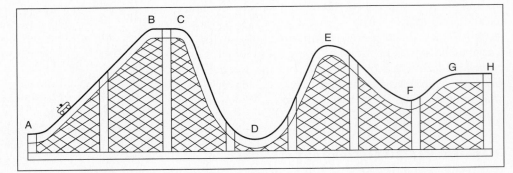

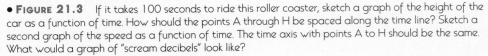

● **FIGURE 21.3**   If it takes 100 seconds to ride this roller coaster, sketch a graph of the height of the car as a function of time. How should the points A through H be spaced along the time line? Sketch a second graph of the speed as a function of time. The time axis with points A to H should be the same. What would a graph of "scream decibels" look like?

In the rectangle context, the following two equations represent the width and area, respectively, as functions of the length (assuming that the perimeter is fixed at 24 units):

$$W(L) = \frac{(24 - 2L)}{2} = 12 - L \qquad A(L) = L(12 - L)$$

By expressing the relationship or function in an equation, the symbols can be manipulated according to appropriate rules to make it easier to see what is happening. In this example, the function notations $W(L)$ and $A(L)$ were used instead of a single letter for each. $W(L)$ stands for the width. Within this efficient notation is an indication that the width is a function of the length L. "The width when the length is 3" can now be represented symbolically as $W(3)$. The symbolic name for the function itself—the relationship between the length and width—is represented by the letter W. Similarly for the area function A: $A(L)$ is the area for any given value of L; $A(4)$ is the area when the length is 4. The area is a function of the length.

Equations also make it easier to calculate values of the function. The rule or equation can be entered into a graphing calculator, and the calculator can do the calculations to produce a table or draw a graph. Without the equation representation of the function, the graphing calculator is much less useful. Figure 21.4 shows the screen of a TI–83 calculator with both the perimeter and the area graphs drawn. The table to the right computes the area for every length in steps of one-half. It requires very little expertise to do this on the calculator and allows the middle school child the chance to see and explore interesting graphs without the tedium of having to plot points.

In the roller coaster example, the equations are not so easily determined, but someone with a knowledge of the laws of physics could create equations for each section of the roller coaster. Sometimes equations come from selecting a curve (and its corresponding equation) that seems to "fit" the data available. That is how an equation for the height–arm span relationship would be determined. A "best-fit curve" would be determined to fit the data. You may recall finding a median-median line for height and weight data in Chapter 19.

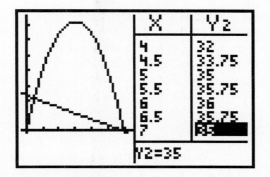

● **Figure 21.4**   This graphing calculator shows graphs of both the width and the area of a rectangle of fixed perimeter as functions of the length. The table can show all possible length and area values.

Developing Function Concepts in the Classroom

If the discussion you have read so far in this chapter had focused only on one example, say, Brian and the hot-dog vendor, the development would be similar to the approach in a middle school classroom. Begin with a context, explore the relationships, and develop different representations to show what has been found. The following text suggests some general principles for exploring function concepts with students.

Begin with Meaningful Contexts

Algebra has traditionally been thought of as generalized arithmetic, with the emphasis on learning how to manipulate symbols and equations. Only a minority of students would survive the symbol pushing to arrive much later (often in college) to see what value there was in knowing algebra. Although this view of algebra has been resistant to change, change is beginning to happen. Today algebra should be dominated by the study of functions and should begin with meaningful situations in which the functions are found. There are numerous contexts that contain functional relationships that are completely accessible to students, even as early as sixth grade. By exploring a context and making sense of it, the function relationship is already developed.

In the context of Brian's sales, a discussion can involve finding the number of hot dogs to sell to make a given amount of money and how much profit is made by selling a particular number of hot dogs. By working on and explaining these questions, students are using the functional relationship between hot dogs sold and profit made. They are actually using a function before they have been asked to worry about symbols and definitions.

As you will see, there are a variety of contexts to begin with. The search for functional relationships is part of the science of pattern and order—the doing of mathematics. Some contexts can be tied to other strands of the curriculum, providing important connections within mathematics.

- Statistics explorations lead to collecting data and making scatter plots. A function (curve) is found to approximate the data.

- Patterns that grow (also known as *sequences*) combine the direct search for pattern with the idea of functional relationships.

- Proportional situations can be graphed and tables made (see Chapter 15). This produces a special class of linear functions with all graphs passing through the origin.

- Geometry and measurement come together in an assortment of formulas. These formulas take on new meaning when expressed as functions. You have already seen how area and length can be related in a rectangle with a fixed perimeter.

Just as important as these mathematical connections are the connections to the real world. Our lives abound with situations that involve functional relationships. Select ones that students are interested in. Making money and the ideas related to profit and loss are not only realistic but also interesting. Social studies has many interesting relationships. For example, populations of various regions of the world may be related to health, income, production levels, education levels, death rates, and so on. Science offers another area of investigations. Pendulums can be swung to investigate period (time for one full swing) as a function of length. The distance a toy car will roll down a ramp can be compared to the angle of the ramp. Plant growth can be related to time in the light, to quantities of fertilizer, or to the number of days since germination. These are just a few ideas of real contexts that provide connections to other disciplines and can make the study of functions meaningful.

Connect Different Representations

Figure 21.5 illustrates the five representations of functions that we explored earlier. The most important idea is to see that for a given function, each of these representations illustrates the same relationship. The *context* provides an embodiment of the relationship outside the world of mathematics. Though not every function has a real-world context, it certainly adds to the meaning and value of doing mathematics when contexts are involved. *Language* helps express the relationship in a meaningful and useful manner. *Tables* very explicitly match up selected elements that are paired by the function or rule of correspondence. The rule of correspondence or function is implicit in the pairings of numbers. The *graph* translates the number pairs into a picture. Any point on the graph of a function has two coordinates. The function is the rule that relates the first coordinate to the second. These two coordinates are possible entries in the function table. The *equation* expresses the functional relationship with the economy and power of mathematical symbolism, yet it is the same relationship.

Use Technology

In the past, when students had to plot points and do by hand all the computations that were involved, functions were limited to extremely simple examples. Eighth-grade students would probably never see a function with an equation much more complicated than $y = 3x + 2$. Algebra I would focus on learning tricks and techniques for graphing equations that were a bit more complex, but even then, the tedium of computing and plotting function values meant that examples had to use numbers that were small and relatively easy to work with, making the link to real contexts almost impossible. Realistic contexts frequently involve not-so-nice numbers or not-so-simple functions. Thanks to technology, we need no longer be restricted to overly simple functions. Students can and should investigate all sorts of functions as long as the relationship can be understood.

Consider only the examples in the first part of this chapter. The profit example is the easiest to work with and could probably be examined without technology. Even there, however, the numbers are somewhat large. The car depreciation is an exponential function. The area for a fixed perimeter is a parabolic function. If students can come up with an equation to go with a function rule, technology can be used to make a graph and do the necessary number crunching to make a table. The technology is not thinking for the students; on the contrary, student effort is focused on the thinking and not on the tedium of computation and plotting points.

Students who have talked about exponents and about percents—both middle grades topics—are equipped to develop a formula or equation for the car depreciation situation. That exploration might go like this: If the car loses 20 percent of its value in 1 year, then it must be worth 80 percent of its value after a year. So after 1 year, the $15,000 car is worth $15,000 × 0.8. In the second year, it loses 20 percent of that value, so it will be worth only 80 percent of its value at the end of year one: ($15,000 × 0.8) × 0.8 = $15,000 × 0.8^2. At the end of the third year, the value will be $15,000 × 0.8^3 and so on. So in general, at the end of n years, the value of the car can be expressed in this equation:

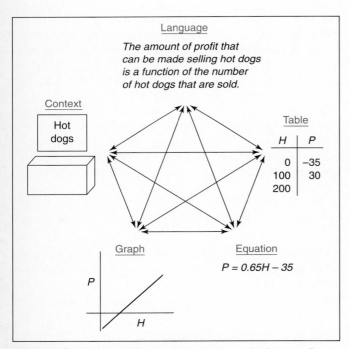

Language

The amount of profit that can be made selling hot dogs is a function of the number of hot dogs that are sold.

Context

Hot dogs

Table

H	P
0	–35
100	30
200	

Graph

Equation

$P = 0.65H - 35$

● **FIGURE 21.5**   *Five different representations of a function. For any given function, students should see that all these representations are connected and illustrate the same relationship. Each representation provides a different perspective on the function.*

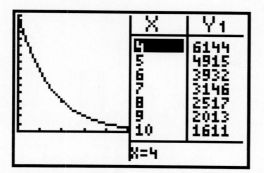

● **FIGURE 21.6**   The graph and table for $V = 15,000 \times .8.^n$. The graph shows n for values 0 to 15. The vertical axis runs from 0 to 15,000.

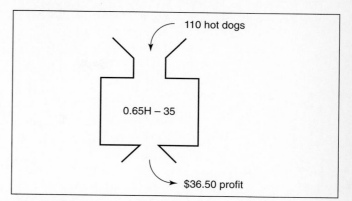

● **FIGURE 21.7**   A function machine illustrates the idea that a single input value from the domain of the function produces a unique value in the range of the function. Each in-out pair corresponds to an entry in the function table and a point on the graph of the function.

$V = \$15,000 \times 0.8^n$. Figure 21.6 shows the graph and the table of values on a graphing calculator.

This equation is no more difficult to enter into a graphing calculator or a computer graphing utility than $y = 3x + 2$. An early study of functions is not a detailed functional analysis endeavor. The idea is to see that there are functional relationships and that these can be expressed in different ways.

Real data from measurements, experiments, and surveys can be entered into a graphing calculator or any number of computer programs, and a scatter plot can be easily produced. The same technology can then be used to find a curve that approximates the data. At the middle school level, it is not necessary to know how the calculator determines the quadratic or exponential curve that seems to fit best. But at the same time, there is no reason to hide from students the idea that a curve can be created, along with an equation, to approximate data that makes sense to them.

Use Function Machines

Another illustration of a function has come into common use: the *function machine*. A function machine can be thought of as a "black box" with input and output slots as shown in Figure 21.7. Inside the box is the function rule—the rule of correspondence between the input numbers and the output numbers. The function machine representation helps illustrate what makes a function a function. Specifically, it highlights that a function is a rule of correspondence (the rule inside the box), that for any input there is a unique output value, that the elements that the machine will accept are the elements for which the function is defined (also known as the *domain* of the function), and that the set of all possible outputs is the set known as the *range* of the function.

These ideas tend to focus on generic aspects of function and do little to illustrate the specific function that is "in the box." The function machine is most like the table representation of a function. In fact, a table is often generated by recording the inputs and outputs of a function machine.

Whatever information is necessary to generate a table is precisely what is necessary to make a function machine "work." It is not clear that it is a distinctly different representation of a particular function.

FUNCTIONS FROM PATTERNS

You might begin an exploration of functions with students in the middle grades in any number of places. In fact, it may be useful to engage in several "beginnings" to functions to help students come to see the same basic ideas from different perspectives. Here we will see how function concepts can be developed from an exploration of growing patterns.

Materials, Frames, and Tables

You may recall reading about growing patterns in Chapter 18. In a physical or picture form, each part of a growing pattern is a separate design representing a progression of some sort from the previous part of the pattern. Each section of a growing pattern will be referred to in this chapter as a *frame*. Growing patterns are best developed with materials or, at the very least, drawings. Examples of this type of pattern are shown in Figure 21.8 (p. 464)..

The first thing to do with patterns in the upper and middle grades is to get students comfortable with building patterns and talking about how they can be extended in a logical manner. Building the patterns with physical materials such as tiles, counters, or flat toothpicks is extremely useful because students can make changes if necessary and build on to one frame to make a new frame. It is also more fun!

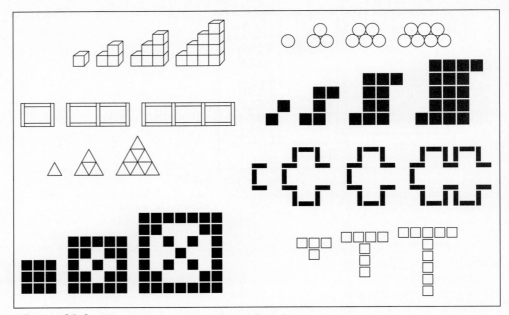

● **FIGURE 21.8** "Growing patterns" with materials or drawings.

21.1 Extend and Explain

As an introduction to growing patterns, show students the first three or four elements or frames of a pattern. Provide them with appropriate materials or grid paper, and have them extend the patterns and explain why their extension indeed follows a pattern. For some patterns, there may be more than one way to extend the first two or three frames. If, for example, you were to suggest only the first two elements of the block pattern at the top of Figure 21.8, students might well develop four or five patterns that are different from the stairsteps shown in the figure. The purpose would simply be to explore the idea of a progression from one frame or part of a growing pattern to the next.

When discussing a pattern, students should try to determine how each frame in the pattern differs from the preceding frame. If each new frame can be built by adding on to the previous frame, the discussion should include how this can be done. For example, each stairstep in Figure 21.8 can be made by adding a column of blocks to the preceding stairsteps. The square with the diagonals cannot be made by adding on to the previous frame. That pattern involves a form of expansion rather than adding on.

Growing patterns also have a numeric component, the number of objects or elements in each frame. As shown in Figure 21.9, a table can be made for any growing pattern. One row of the table or chart is always the frame number, and the other is for recording how many elements are in that frame. Frequently, a pattern grows so quickly and requires so many blocks or spaces to draw it that it is only reasonable to build or draw the first five or six frames. A good question then becomes "How many items will be in the next frame? How many in the 10th frame? The 20th?"

Searching for Relationships

There are two places in the chart and the physical patterns where you and your students can look for numeric relationships: first, in the progression from one frame to the next; and second, in the relationship between the frame number and the number of objects in that frame.

Patterns from Frame to Frame

For most students, it is easier to see the patterns from one frame to the next. When you have a table constructed, the differences from one frame to the next can be written next to or below the table, as in Figure 21.9. In that example, the number in each frame can be determined from the previous frame by adding successive even numbers.

Whenever there is a pattern in the table, see if students can find that same pattern in the physical version. In Figure 21.9, notice that in each frame, the previous frame has been outlined. That lets you examine the amount added and see how it creates the pattern of adding on even numbers. The picture or physical pattern and the table should be as closely connected as possible in the students' minds.

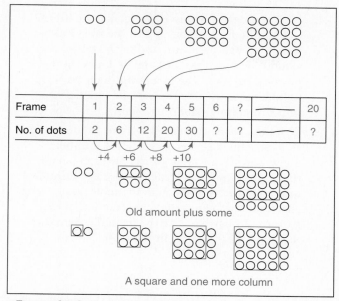

• **FIGURE 21.9** *Two different relationships in a visual pattern.*

There is no systematic or prescribed method for finding this relationship between frame number and frame. Some students may get insight by simply "playing around" with the numbers in the table and asking, "How can I operate on the frame number to get the corresponding number in the table?" Most will benefit from examining the physical pattern for regularities. At the bottom of Figure 21.9, a square array is outlined for each frame. Each successive square is one larger on a side. Once a regular physical idea can be observed, see what relationship might exist between this piece or subset of the pattern and the frame numbers. In the case of Figure 21.9, the side of each square is the same as the frame number. The row to the right of each square is also the frame number. With that information, how would you describe the 20th frame? Can you determine how many elements will be in it without drawing the picture? At this point, a significant activity is to write a numeric expression for each frame number using the same pattern. For example, the first four frames in Figure 21.9 are $1^2 + 1$, $2^2 + 2$, $3^2 + 3$, and $4^2 + 4$.

It may take much searching and experimenting for students to come up with an expression that is similar for each frame. The search can be an exciting class or group activity. Do not be nervous or upset if students have difficulty. Encourage the search for relationships to continue, even if it takes more than one day. The search for and discovery of relationships is the most significant portion of these activities.

Patterns from Frame Number to Frame

The frame-to-frame pattern is a powerful pattern and almost certainly will be the first that your students observe. However, if you want to find the table entry for the 100th frame, the only way a frame-to-frame pattern can help is to find all of the prior 99 entries in the table. If a rule can be discovered that relates the number of objects in a frame to the frame number, any frame can be determined without building or calculating all of the intermediate frames in the pattern.

Moving from Patterns to Function and Variable

When students have discovered numeric expressions for each frame using frame numbers, write them with brackets around the frame numbers as shown in Figure 21.10. If

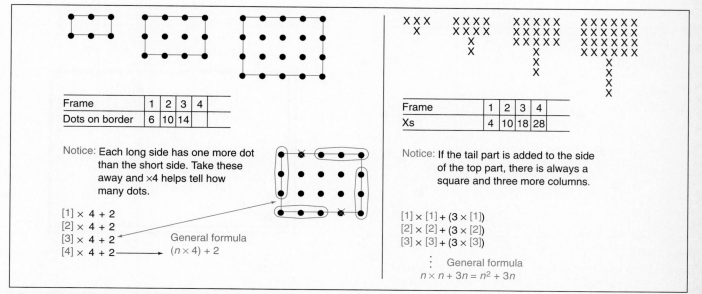

• **FIGURE 21.10** *Finding functional relationships in patterns.*

this results in a pattern, the bracketed numbers will change from one frame to the next while the other numbers in the expressions remain the same. Now the bracketed numbers can be replaced by a letter or variable resulting in a general formula. The formula then defines a functional relationship between frame numbers and frame values.

It would be a good idea for you to explore each of the patterns in Figure 21.8 to see if you can find formulas (functional relationships) for each. You should be able to "plug in" the frame numbers in your formulas and get the value for that frame.

The discussion to this point is summarized in the following activity.

——ACTIVITY——

21.2 Find the Function in the Pattern

Give students the beginning of a pattern, usually at least three frames. Their tasks with the pattern are as follows:

1. **Extend the pattern several more frames until they are sure they understand the pattern. They should always look backward to the beginning of the pattern to see that their idea works for all frames. Record this in a drawing.**

2. **Make a table that shows frame numbers and elements in each frame for every frame they have constructed.**

3. **Find and describe in writing as many patterns as possible in the table and in the physical pattern. For each pattern found in the table, they should see how that idea can be found in the physical pattern. The most important pattern to look for is the one from frame number to frame, the functional relationship.**

4. **Write the frame number–to–frame relationship as a formula in terms of the frame number. Show how the formula works for each part of the table already constructed. Use the formula to predict the next entry in the table, and check this with an actual construction of the pattern, if possible. Use the formula to predict the 10th or 20th entry in the table.**

It is a good idea to have students work in groups so that ideas can be generated more freely. A student working alone may not have the insight at that moment to see the function in the pattern and as a result become frustrated.

Graphing the Pattern

So far, four of the five representations of function have been used in this pattern exploration. Why not add the graph? The individual points in a pattern can be plotted even if the physical pattern has not been discovered. Figure 21.11 shows the graph for each of the two patterns in Figure 21.10. Notice that the first is a straight-line (linear) relationship and the other is a curved line that would make half of a parabola if the points were joined. Do not forget how easy it

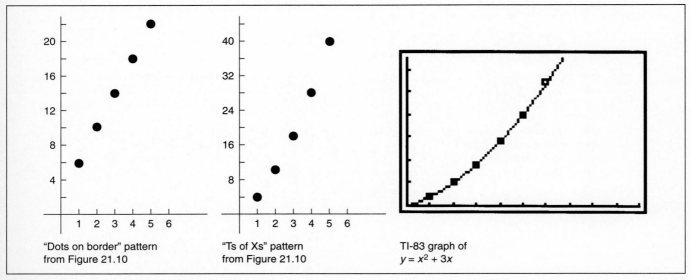

"Dots on border" pattern from Figure 21.10

"Ts of Xs" pattern from Figure 21.10

TI-83 graph of $y = x^2 + 3x$

• **FIGURE 21.11** Graphs of functions from patterns.

is both to plot points and to draw curves on the graphing calculator. The second graph in Figure 21.11 is also shown on a graphing calculator with the function $y = x^2 + 3x$ (same as $n^2 + 3n$) drawn through it.

FUNCTIONS FROM THE REAL WORLD

Patterns are but one way to get students into an investigation of functions and variables. Here you will encounter some other ideas that develop the same concepts.

Relationships Found in the Real World

The earlier example of Brian selling hot dogs was an example of a function that was developed out of a "real" situation. A situation such as this is explored with children by having them make tables of data based on the information given. By computing several entries in the table, the students will begin to see a pattern or a formula develop. Consider the following activity.

---ACTIVITY---

21.3 How Many Gallons Left?

Present this situation to students: A car gets 23 miles per gallon of gas. It has a gas tank that holds 20 gallons. Suppose that you were on a trip and had filled the tank at the outset. Make a table showing the number of gallons remaining in the tank for at least three different points in a trip of 350 miles. Plot the data on a graph. Show how you calculated each entry in your table, and be prepared to discuss what you did with the class.

Notice that very little direction is given in this activity. However, the situation presented to the students is fairly clear. Some teachers may prefer to use numbers that would be easier to compute, but that takes much of the realism out of the situation. If a student decides to make a table entry for 50 miles, he or she will first have to figure out what to do. On a calculator, $50 \div 23 = 2.173913$. This amount should be subtracted from 20 to find out how many gallons remain in the tank. Should you subtract 2 or 2.17 or 2.173913? This is a good example to discuss numbers in real contexts and let students make reasonable decisions. Avoid being prescriptive because different students will do things differently, providing you with the opportunity for good class dis-

cussions. If you are overly prescriptive, the students will focus on following your directions rather than doing their own thinking. Depending on the situation presented, students are bound to make errors in reasoning as well as in computation. The class discussion will sort things out.

As part of the discussion with students, help them develop functional language to represent the situation. Here the number of gallons in the tank is dependent on how far the car has been driven. The number of gallons remaining *is a function of* the miles driven. In addition to the language, work toward student development of an equation that represents the relationship in the situation being discussed. In this case, one possible equation is $g = 20 - \frac{m}{23}$. Or, using functional notation, you might say $G(m) = 20 - \frac{m}{23}$.

Students can draw a line through their plotted points, or with a graphing calculator, they can enter the equation and have the calculator do the graphing. In either case, the graph should be used to answer questions about the situation. "How can you tell from the graph how much gas will be left after driving 300 miles?" "How many miles can you drive before the gas tank has only 3 gallons left?" "What will happen to the graph if the driver stops to fill the tank after driving 350 miles?"

Here are a few suggestions for situations that you might explore in a similar manner.

....

Mr. Calloway wants to build a fenced pen against one side of his shed. The shed is 15 feet long, and he wants to use the full side of the shed. The pen is to be in the shape of a rectangle with two sides 15 feet long. How much fence will he have to buy if he knows how long the other two sides of the pen will be (side versus fence length)? Add in a gate that is 3 feet long and costs $32. If fencing is $4.25 per foot, rethink the problem in terms of side versus cost. You can also discuss area and side length.

....

Yolanda's mother agrees to loan her the price of a new lawn mower so that Yolanda can earn money over the summer cutting grass. The lawn mower costs $285. Yolanda has determined that she can average $24 per lawn after paying for gasoline. She thinks she will be able to cut about five lawns per week. Examine Yolanda's profit in terms of number of lawns mowed and then in terms of weeks that she works. Suppose that the family takes a vacation during the third and fourth weeks of summer. What will the graph of Yolanda's profit in terms of weeks worked look like during this time? Use the graph to figure out when Yolanda will break even and how much profit she will make during the summer.

....

Mark is an avid cyclist. He can average 17 miles per hour for about 4 hours. He leaves home and travels for $2\frac{1}{2}$ hours at this rate, stops for lunch for $\frac{1}{2}$ hour, and then starts home. What is his distance from home at any given time? Suppose he goes faster for 1 hour and slower for 2 more hours and then returns home. Suppose he has a flat tire and has to stop for 15 minutes to repair it. How fast will he have to go in order to return home at the same time as scheduled, including the same lunch break? Does it make any difference where the breakdown occurs?

Pleasant's Hardware buys widgets for $4.17 each, marks them up 35 percent over wholesale, and sells them at that price. Relate widgets sold to total income. Consider profit instead of income. Incorporate a sale using a reduced price.

Proportional Situations

In the same spirit as the preceding discussion, there are many relationships involving rates or proportions that offer a valuable opportunity for examining functions. The following is a typical proportion problem. Students are usually expected to set up a proportion and solve for the unknown.

Two out of every three students who eat in the cafeteria drink a pint of white milk. If 450 students eat in the cafeteria, how many gallons of milk are consumed?

As the problem is stated, there is a fixed number of students (450) and a single answer to the problem. If only the first sentence of the problem is provided, students can be asked to create a table showing the number of pints (or gallons) of milk consumed for four or five different numbers of students, plot the data on a graph, and create an equation that shows the relationship between students in the cafeteria and milk consumed. Functional language can be discussed: The number of pints of milk consumed in the cafeteria *is a function of* the number of students who eat there. The graph can be used to answer the question about milk for 450 students. Students can be challenged to find an equation that gives the amount of milk in terms of the number of students.

Each of the following problems has been converted to a function investigation by asking for an answer in terms of an unknown instead of a specific number.

Mr. Schultz pays $4.00 for a box of 12 candy bars, which he then sells in his store for 45 cents each. How much profit will he make on *n* boxes of candy bars?

If each recipe of lemonade will serve 20 people, how many recipes are needed to serve *n* people? If it takes three cans of concentrate to make one recipe, how many cans should be purchased to serve *n* people?

The second example has two questions. One equation can be written to relate the number of recipes as a function of the number of people—$R = f(p)$—and a second equation to give the number of cans of concentrate as a function of the number of recipes—$C = g(R)$. Can you see how the recipe equation can be used in the can equation to produce an equation that gives cans of concentrate as a function of the number of people? This is a simple example of compound functions. For example, the slope of the line relating students to pints of milk is $\frac{2}{3}$. (What would the slope be for the line relating students to gallons of milk?)

It is useful to notice that the graphs of all proportional situations are straight lines that pass through the origin. Later, students will find that the slope of these lines is also the rate between the two variables.

Functions from Formulas

Geometric formulas relate various dimensions, areas, and volumes of shapes. Each of these formulas involves at least one functional relationship.

Consider any formula for measuring a geometric shape with which students are familiar. For example, $V = \frac{1}{3}\pi r^2 h$ is the formula for the volume of a circular cone. Here the volume is related to both the height of the cone and the radius. If, for example, the radius is held constant, the volume is a function of the height. Similarly, for a fixed height, the volume is a function of the radius. Figure 21.12 shows how both of these ideas might be illustrated and the graph that would be associated with each.

The following activity is frequently proposed as an early example of using functions in a practical way.

---ACTIVITY---

21.4 Designing the Largest Box

Begin with a rectangular sheet of cardboard, and from each corner, cut a square. The four resulting flaps are then folded up and taped together to form an open box. The volume of the box will vary depending on the size of the squares. Assume that your sheet of cardboard is 9 by 12 inches, as shown in Figure 21.13. Write a formula

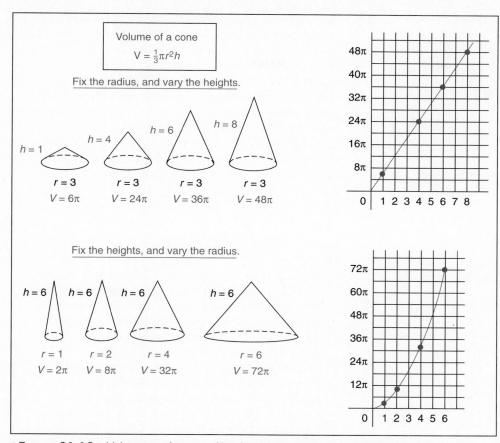

Volume of a cone

$V = \frac{1}{3}\pi r^2 h$

Fix the radius, and vary the heights.

$h = 1$ $h = 4$ $h = 6$ $h = 8$

$r = 3$ $r = 3$ $r = 3$ $r = 3$
$V = 6\pi$ $V = 24\pi$ $V = 36\pi$ $V = 48\pi$

Fix the heights, and vary the radius.

$h = 6$ $h = 6$ $h = 6$ $h = 6$

$r = 1$ $r = 2$ $r = 4$ $r = 6$
$V = 2\pi$ $V = 8\pi$ $V = 32\pi$ $V = 72\pi$

• **FIGURE 21.12** *Volume as a function of height or radius. If the radius is fixed, changes in height produce a straight-line graph, but if the height is fixed, changes in the radius produce a curved line.*

that gives the volume of the box as a function of the size of the cutout squares. Use the function to determine what size the squares should be to create the box with the largest volume.

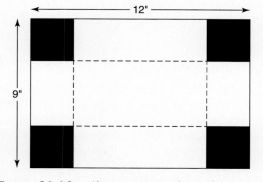

• **FIGURE 21.13** *If squares are cut from a 9-by-12-inch piece of cardboard so that the four flaps can be folded up, what size squares should be cut so that the volume of the box is the largest possible?*

In "Designing the Largest Box," the resulting equation is a cubic or third-power polynomial. However, any seventh-grade student who knows that the volume of a box is the product of the three dimensions could develop this formula. A table of values and a graph are easily produced on a graphing calculator. Another interesting feature of this problem is that the function is defined for values of the variable that do not make sense in the context. For example, the largest square that could be cut out is 4.5 inches on a side, in which case the squares from adjacent corners would touch and there would be no flap to turn up. But the function will produce "negative volumes" for values between 4.5 and 6 and positive volumes for values of the variable greater than 6. The equation representation of the function makes sense in this context *only* for values of the unknown between 0 and 4.5. This is a useful discussion for students to help them realize that a mathematical model cannot be completely divorced from the context. Figure 21.14 (p. 470) shows the graph on a calculator. The tracer point is near the point at which a maximum volume will occur.

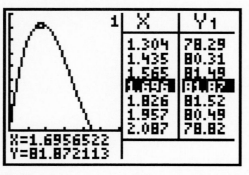

● **FIGURE 21.14** A graphing calculator plot of the volume function for the problem in Figure 21.13.

Functions from Scatter Plot Data

In the contexts discussed so far, patterns and real-world situations, the context gave rise to a specific formula or equation that represented the functional relationship. Often in the real world, phenomena are observed that seem to suggest a dependent relationship or functional relationship but not necessarily as clean or as well defined as the situations we have observed so far. In these cases, what is generally done is to plot the data on a graph to produce a scatter plot of points. A visual inspection of the data when graphed may suggest what kind of relationship, if any, exists. When a functional relationship seems to be suggested by the data, an equation can be sought that defines a function approximating the data.

A situation like this was explored in Chapter 19. Data representing the heights and weights of people in a sample were plotted on a graph as a set of points, one for each person in the sample. The plot suggested a straight-line relationship between the heights and weights. A median-median line was found. In that case, the median-median line was the function (in graphical form) that approximated the data and was used to define the observed relationship between height and weight. In functional language, we could say that weight appeared to be a function of height.

Students in the middle grades might easily gather data found in an interesting context and use the data to perform this same type of analysis—that is, plot the data, look for a possible relationship, and find a best-fit line. When a line is drawn on the scatter plot that approximates the data, all representations of the function are present except the equation. The context produced the data. The graph of the best-fit line is a graphical representation of the function, and functional language can easily be used. A table can be made from points on the best-fit line. (Why would the table be made from the line and not from the actual data?) All that remains is to devise an equation to complete the representations of the function.

The position in this chapter is that functional relationships can be explored as early as the sixth grade. However, in cases where a simple equation is not readily accessible, as

it has been in earlier examples, either that symbolic representation can be overlooked or technology can be used to produce the equation. With the existence of graphing calculators or curve-fitting software, there seems little reason to stop students from seeing that methods do exist for finding best-fit curves. Each method results in a different type of graph. Some are straight lines, some are parabolas, and some are other curves. The calculator permits students to see what these curves and equations may look like even though exploring the techniques of actually finding the equations without technology will have to wait.

ACTIVITY

21.5 Pendulum Swings

Give pairs of students string and a small weight that can be tied to the string (a large washer or a tennis ball, for example). Assign each pair a different length for their pendulum from about 30 cm to 3 m (if the room is tall enough). The pendulum should be measured from the suspension point to the bottom of the weight. Have students carefully time the swing of the pendulum through ten full (back-and-forth) swings. If time permits, they can perform the experiment several times and take an average of their times to report to the class.

In the pendulum experiment, the data will form a surprisingly accurate curve without much variation. Students can use their hand-drawn curve to predict the times for other pendulum lengths. (Theoretically, the curve is the top half of a parabola that opens to the right. It can be found on the graphing calculator by experimenting with the equation $y = a\sqrt{x}$ for different values of a until a curve is found that fits nicely.) What is most important at this level is not finding the equation but seeing how a physical law can be expressed as a function and represented in table and graphical form.

Electronic Data Gathering

Technology now offers students a new way to gather physical data that has exciting implications for connecting function concepts to the real world. The Texas Instruments Calculator-Based Laboratory or (CBL) is a device that interfaces between the graphing calculator and data sensors to gather and record real data directly into the calculator. Experiments that measure things such as temperature of a liquid, motion of a rolling car or a bouncing ball, light intensity, pH, and force can be conducted, and no pencil-and-paper record keeping is necessary. What is exciting is that theories of science that before could only be described can now be observed with real data gathered and analyzed.

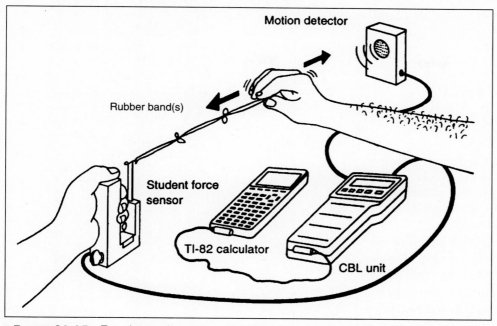

Motion detector

Rubber band(s)

Student force sensor

TI-82 calculator

CBL unit

● **FIGURE 21.15**   *Two data probes are used to deliver force and motion data directly to a graphing calculator. (Courtesy of Texas Instruments)*

Figure 21.15 shows a simple experiment using two different sensors connected through the CBL to the TI-82. The motion detector senses the motion back and forth as the hand stretches the rubber bands. The force sensor is connected to the rubber bands and measures the force applied and transmitted through them. A program available with Texas Instruments' manual (Brueningsen, Bower, Antinone, & Brueningsen, 1994) is loaded into the TI-82. The program directs the CBL to collect data at regular intervals and store them in the calculator. Like any other data, these can then be plotted and a best-fit line determined. Figure 21.16 shows a scatter plot of data from running this experiment. It is fairly clear that there is a linear relationship and that a best-fit line would likely go through the origin. It is appropriate to say that the force applied to the rubber band is directly proportional to the distance the rubber band is stretched. In functional language, the force *is a function of* the amount the rubber band is stretched.

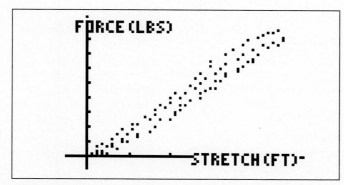

FORCE (LBS)

STRETCH (FT)

● **FIGURE 21.16**   *A graphing calculator scatter plot of data gathered in a rubber-band-stretching experiment as depicted in Figure 21.15.*

Other Scatter Plot Ideas

Do not forget to consider gathering information that may be of personal interest to students. For example, do grades earned in social studies predict grades earned in mathematics? What about science and mathematics? What would the functional relationships be here? Even if a scatter plot of some information that was gathered showed no particular trend, functional language could still be employed—for example, "The grades on last week's mathematics test do *not* appear to be a function of the number of hours' sleep students got the night before the test."

Data can also be obtained from sports records, census reports, the business section of the newspaper, and many other sources. The U.S. Department of Commerce publishes reports listing a wide variety of data for each state and often over a series of years. For example, is there a functional relationship over the years between the gross domestic product and the population of the United States?

Graphs Without Equations

It is important that a study of functions in the middle school not get bogged down in techniques of graphing and analysis of equations. That is one reason that the graphing calculator is such an effective tool for early explorations: Points are quickly plotted, and tables can be generated instantly from simple formulas.

The graph is one of the most powerful representations of a function. It is both fun and profitable to interpret and construct graphs related to real situations but without using any specific data, equations, or numbers. The advantage of activities such as these is the focus on the relationships involved and how the graph can express them.

─────── ACTIVITY ───────

21.6 Sketch a Graph

Sketch a graph for each of these situations. No numbers or formulas are to be used.

a. The temperature of a frozen dinner from 30 minutes before it is removed from the freezer until it is removed from the microwave and placed on the table (Consider time 0 to be the moment the dinner is removed from the freezer.)

b. The value of a 1970 Volkswagen Beetle from the time it was purchased to the present (It was kept by a loving owner and is in top condition.)

c. The level of water in the bathtub from the time you begin to fill it to the time it is completely empty after your bath

d. Profit in terms of number of items sold

e. The height of a baseball in terms of time from when it is thrown straight up to the time it hits the ground

f. The speed of the baseball in the situation in (e)

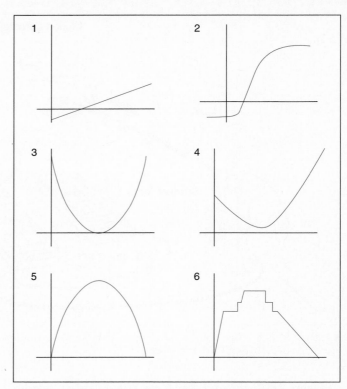

●FIGURE 21.17 Match each graph with the situations described in Activity 21.6. Talk about what is happening in each case.

It would be a good idea for you to stop here and try to sketch graphs for each of the situations in the activity. In a classroom, it is fun to have students sketch their graphs on transparencies without identifying which situation is being graphed (no labels on the graphs). Let students examine the graphs to see if they can determine which situation goes with each graph that is presented. Examine the graphs for one situation drawn by several students to decide which graph represents a situation best and why. In Figure 21.17 are six graphs that match the six situations described in the "Sketch a Graph" activity. Can you match these graphs with the six situations? How do these graphs compare to the graphs that you sketched?

The next activities are similar but begin to develop the idea of rate of change—how rapidly or slowly something changes.

─────── ACTIVITY ───────

21.7 Bottles and Volume Graphs

Figure 21.18 shows six bottles and six graphs. Assume that the bottles are filled at a constant rate. Because of their shapes, the height of the liquid in the bottles will increase either more slowly or more quickly as the bottle gets wider or narrower. Match the graphs with the bottles.

Find some bottles or glassware that have different shapes. One place to look is in the science lab. Using a small container such as a medicine cup, pour water into each bottle. Measure the height after each small containerful is poured. Make a graph of the heights as a function of the volume. If students do an actual experiment, the discussion of which graph fits which bottle and why will be much more meaningful.

A similar example of rates is found in situations involving time and distance. Consider the following:

⋯⋯⋯⋯⋯⋯⋯⋯⋯⋯⋯⋯⋯⋯⋯⋯⋯⋯⋯⋯⋯⋯⋯⋯⋯⋯⋯⋯⋯⋯⋯

A car is traveling along a road at about 45 mph and comes to a stop sign. It stops for the sign and then accelerates to the same 45-mph speed.

⋯⋯⋯⋯⋯⋯⋯⋯⋯⋯⋯⋯⋯⋯⋯⋯⋯⋯⋯⋯⋯⋯⋯⋯⋯⋯⋯⋯⋯⋯⋯

Try to sketch a graph of the *distance* the car has traveled from the beginning of the story to the end. The horizontal axis should be *time*. In other words, the graph should show distance as a function of time. How would a graph of the *speed* of the car look over the same interval?

There are all sorts of situations involving time, rate, and distance. People walk and run at different rates and encounter various obstacles. They go up and down in buildings on stairs, elevators, and escalators. They climb hills and slide down them on sleds. Airplanes not only travel at different rates but also at different heights. The following activity could be done after children have sketched graphs for a variety of time and distance situations.

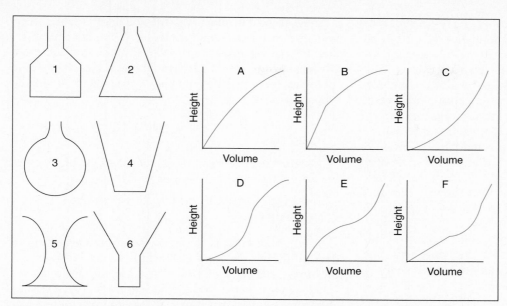

●**FIGURE 21.18** If the bottles are filled at a constant rate, match the graphs with the bottles.

────────── ACTIVITY ──────────

21.8 Create a Journey Story

Suppose that a student has created the time-distance graphs shown in Figure 21.19. Each is supposed to represent the journey of a single vehicle or person. Some of them are impossible and could not represent any journey. First identify the impossible graphs. Then make up a plausible journey story for each of the remaining graphs.

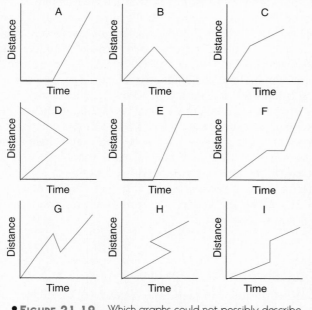

●**FIGURE 21.19** Which graphs could not possibly describe a journey? Why? Invent a journey story for each of the possible graphs.

Students could share their stories without telling which graph each story was supposed to match. The class could then discuss which graph best fits each tale.

VARIABLES

One of the most powerful ways we have of expressing the pattern and order of mathematics is with variables. With variables we can begin to use mathematical symbolism as a tool to think with, in addition to physical objects and drawings. But if variables are to be included with "thinker toys" and are to become powerful means of expressing ideas, it is important to help children construct clear ideas of what variables are all about.

We have actually been using variables extensively in this chapter without making a big fuss over that fact. Perhaps that is the way we should help children understand variables—simply use them in meaningful ways and discuss what we are doing as we go. The problem is not quite so simple, however. As teachers, we should be aware of some of the difficulties students have with variables and be ready with some ideas for dealing with them.

Misunderstandings

Even though students are exposed throughout the elementary years to boxes and letters in arithmetic expressions, studies indicate that most children have a very narrow understanding of the concept of "variable" (e.g., Booth, 1988; Chalouh & Herscovics, 1988; Wagner, 1983).

Wagner (1981) found that many 12- to 17-year-old students believe that $7w + 22 = 109$ and $7n + 22 = 109$ will have different solutions. Some students readily accept L for length but have difficulty using the letter r instead.

The L-for-length example suggests another confusion that arises because we frequently select variable names that help us in our thinking. Some students assume that the letter represents an object rather than a numeric value. For example, one child explained that $8y$ could possibly mean "8 yachts or 8 yams" (Booth, 1988). Converting the expression "John has three times as many apples as Mary" to symbolism, we might use $3a$ to represent John's apples. Here a is meant to stand not for *apples* but for *number of apples,* the specific number of apples that Mary has.

Notation used with variables only compounds the difficulties. For example, in algebra, $3n$ means "three times the value of n" or "the product of 3 and n," but in arithmetic, 37 means "3 tens and 7 ones." In the expression $5n$, if n is 2, many students will interpret the result as 52.

With numbers, $^-6$ stands for the number "negative 6," a distinctly negative quantity. With variables, the literal symbol ^-x stands for the opposite of whatever x is. If x is negative, ^-x is a positive quantity. This misinterpretation has confounded many students, especially in trying to understand the definition of absolute value:

$$|x| = x \text{ if } x \geq 0 \text{ (if } x \text{ is positive or zero)}$$

$$|x| = {}^-x \text{ if } x < 0 \text{ (if } x \text{ is negative)}$$

Because absolute value is always positive, students are confused by the second case. With numbers, they learn to "just take the sign off." For example, $|5 - 8| = |{}^-3| = 3$ (taking the sign off the 3). If x has the value $^-3$, confusion enters when considering $|{}^-x|$ and $|x|$.

That these and other difficulties with variables exist suggests that we should take extra care to help students develop appropriate meanings for variable as a readiness for algebra and the many places in mathematics where variables are commonly used.

Meanings and Uses of Variables

A *variable* is a symbol that can stand for any one of a set of numbers or other objects. This definition appears in a popular middle school textbook (Usiskin, 1992), and similar ones are found in other texts. What is significant about the definition is that variables are always associated with a referent set. In some contexts or for some uses, that referent set may have only one value, the value that makes an expression true. In other instances, the referent set may have many or even an infinite number of values, and the variable represents each of them. To define and explain variables in this manner does not alleviate the misconceptions students have.

Some of the difficulties with the notion of variables stems from the fact that variables are used in different ways. Meanings of variables change with the way they are used. Usiskin (1988) identified three uses and corresponding meanings for *variable* commonly encountered in middle school mathematics:

1. A specific yet unknown quantity: If $3x + 2 = 4x - 1$, solve for x.

2. A representative from a range of values on which other values depend: $y = 3x - 4$ or $p = \frac{1}{t}$.

3. As a pattern generalizer: For all real numbers, $a \times b = b \times a$ or $N + 0 = N$.

The first meaning is closest to the one students tend to develop during the early elementary school years. In expressions such as $3 + \square = 8$, the $\square$ has a single correct value. When moving to the other two meanings, the variables are not unknowns but may take on or represent any value from among a specified domain of values. In the second meaning, the variables are used to express relationships. In the equation $A = L \times W$, there are no numbers at all, but we can talk about what happens to the area, for example, as the length doubles, then triples, and so on. Here, as Usiskin puts it, the "variables vary." This is the use of variables that we have been making in our discussion of functions. In the third meaning, the letters again represent any value in a domain, but the purpose is to illustrate a property or pattern. Things that are known from arithmetic are generalized.

Students need to have experiences with these different meanings and uses of variables and become comfortable with them in different contexts. It is neither necessary nor appropriate to expect students to articulate different meanings or definitions of *variable*. At the same time, it is also not appropriate to offer definitions that are inaccurate or incomplete. For example, it is overly narrow to say "a variable is an unknown quantity" or "a variable stands for a number." These "definitions" relate almost exclusively to the first use of a variable as representing an unknown quantity but hinder the understanding of the variable as used in the second meaning. In the equation $y = f(x) = 3x + 2$, the y and the x represent numbers, but not specific ones, and there is no unknown to be found. When we used variables to create the equations for the growing patterns in this chapter, the referent set was positive whole numbers. In the equation $y = 3x + 2$, the referent set is all real numbers, positive and negative, rational and irrational.

Expressions as Quantities

Consider the following expressions involving variables:

$$3B + 7 \qquad 3B + 7 = B - C$$

The first is an expression of a quantity. It may be a specific quantity, or it may be a whole range of quantities related to a range of values of *B*. In the second expression, the same quantity is set equal to another quantity involving variables. The equal sign means that the quantity on the left is the same as the quantity on the right, even though they are expressed with different letters and different operations. To interpret these expressions in this way, students must also interpret similar arithmetic expressions with only numbers in the same way. Expressions such as 3 + 5 or 4 × 87 must be understood as single quantities, and the equal sign (=) must be understood as a means of showing that two quantities represented are the same.

Unfortunately, though we use both of these ideas and assume all through elementary school that students understand them, a large majority of students do not completely comprehend them (Behr, Erlwanger, & Nichols, 1976; Herscovics & Kieran, 1980; Kieran, 1988). Students tend to look on expressions such as 3 + 5 and 4 × 87 as commands or things to do. The + tells you to add, and students think of adding as a verb. The idea that 5 + 2 is another way of writing 7 is not considered. The equal sign is commonly thought of as an operator button, something like pressing ☐ on a calculator. As students read left to right in an equation, the = tells them, "Now give the answer." In a similar sense, students think of = as a symbol that is used to separate the question or problem from the answer.

The following simple activities are suggested as ways to help students with these basic concepts. They each initially use only numbers but can easily be extended to include variables.

Activities 21.9 and 21.10 are clearly related. To understand the balance or equation idea requires an understanding that the expressions in each pan or side of the equation represent quantities.

ACTIVITY

21.9 Names for Numbers

Challenge students to find different ways to express a particular number, say, 10. To introduce the idea, first suggest that they use only + or only − expressions, such as 5 + 5 or 12 − 2. Quickly, devise more challenging tasks such as "How many names for 8 can you find using only numbers less than 10 and using at least three operations?" One solution is (5 × 6 + 2) ÷ 4. Make it a point to emphasize that each expression is a way of representing a number. Restrictions on which operations and how many and which numbers can be used can produce real challenges. Groups can compete for the most expressions in a specified time.

ACTIVITY

21.10 Tilt or Balance

On the board, draw a simple two-pan balance. In each pan, write a numeric expression and ask which pan will go down or whether the two will balance (see Figure 21.20). Challenge students to write expressions for each side of the scale that will make it balance. For each, write a corresponding equation or inequality. Soon the scale feature can be abandoned, and students can simply write equations according to the directions given—for example, "Use at least three operations on each side, and do not use any number twice."

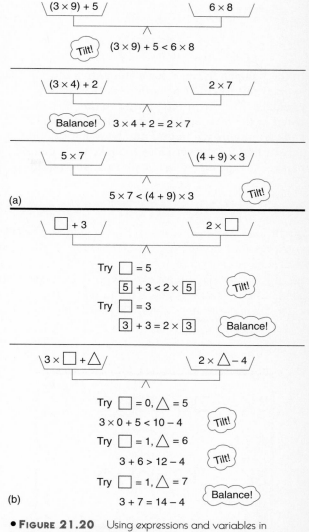

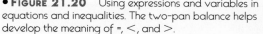

● **FIGURE 21.20** Using expressions and variables in equations and inequalities. The two-pan balance helps develop the meaning of =, <, and >.

After a short time with these two activities, variables can be added to each. Instead of names for numbers, have students write expressions for quantities such as the following (an example is given for each):

Two more than three times a number $2 + 3\square$ or
  $2 + 3N$

Any odd number $2N + 1$

The average age in this class; use S for the sum of our ages $\left(\frac{S}{23}\right)$

The average age of the students in *any* class $\left(\frac{S}{n}\right)$

A number cubed less another number squared $(A^3 - B^2)$

Notice in these examples that variables are used as both specific unknowns and as unspecified quantities.

The graphing calculator can be used in a similar manner to the two-pan balance and may be a more "sophisticated"

---ACTIVITY---

21.11 Variables in the Balance

In the two-pan balance, have students write expressions in either or both pans that include variables. Use directions similar to the ones just listed in the text. Students may then use a trial-and-error approach to find numbers that can be substituted for the variables to make the equation balance (a true equation) or tilt (a false equation).

approach for middle grade students. On graphing calculators, expressions involving signs such as $=$, $\neq$, $>$, or $\geq$ are evaluated as either true or false by the calculator. For example, if you enter $3 + 2 = 6$ and press Enter, the calculator responds with 0, meaning "false." If you enter a true expression, the calculator responds with a 1, indicating "true." Any

letter can be a variable and can be assigned a value with the STO or "store" key. Once an expression is entered, the values of the variables can be changed, and the expression can be recalled and tested again. An example is shown in Figure 21.21.

Evaluating Expressions and Formulas

Examples of charts are shown in Figure 21.22. Each chart has a separate column for the variable, and the variable expressions across the top of the chart are all related. Students can evaluate the expressions and fill in the charts. In this type of activity, several important ideas about notation and properties of the number systems can be explored informally. For example, $4n$ and $4 \times n$ can be placed in separate columns to help students see this convention for expressing multiplication. Other ideas include

$8x - 3x$ with $5x$ (many students think $8x - 3x$ is 5)

$b(3 + b)$ with $3b$, b^2, and $3b + b^2$

$(3 + 2x) - x$ with $3 + x$

$\frac{y}{5}$ and $y/5$ with $y \div 5$ (students may not realize these mean the same thing)

^-x and $(^-1)x$ (include both positive and negative values for x)

$3k + \frac{1}{k}$ with $(3k + 1)$ and $\dfrac{3k + 1}{k}$

The entries in the charts can also be expressions that appear in geometric formulas or formulas from other areas such as science. For example, while reviewing volume and surface area formulas, you might have students help you build a chart for a right circular cylinder with the following expressions:

$$r \qquad h \qquad \pi \qquad 2\pi r^2 \qquad \pi r^2 h \qquad 2h\pi r$$

With two variables, you may want to have students hold one variable fixed for several values of the other. In the pre-

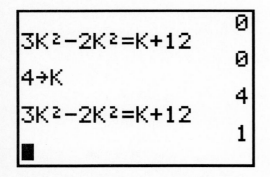

●FIGURE 21.21 Testing expressions with variables on a graphing calculator.

n	$(n + 2)$	$3(n + 2)$	$3n + 6$	b	$2b$	$6b$	$6b \div 2b$
0				0			
2				1			
−1				2			
−2				3			

x	y	$x + y$	$3x$	$(x + y)/3x$	$1 + y$	$(1 + y)/3$
0	0					
−1	1					
2	2					
−2	−1					

●FIGURE 21.22   Fill in these charts. What ideas can you discover?

ceding example, observe the values of the various columns as *r* changes (varies) from 1 to 5 and *h* remains fixed at 10. Then change *h* to 20 and repeat.

For a similar activity with tables like these, enter values in the columns, and have students determine the value of each variable. Notice that two different uses of variable are now included in the same example: letting the value of the variable vary and also solving for a fixed value.

As noted earlier, the graphing calculator stores values "in" a variable. As with a computer, the calculator has a memory position that is labeled with the name of a variable (a letter). For example, if you press 6 STO *X* (store 6 in *X*) and then enter $3(X + 2)$, the result will be 24. If you have also stored 4 in *A*, then $5X - 2A$ will be evaluated as 22. The values stored in variables remain until they are changed.

Solving Equations

Students can learn appropriate techniques for solving simple linear equations before they reach a formal algebra class. A good technique is to capitalize on the two-pan balance approach that was suggested earlier. With the balance, the idea of doing to one side what you do to the other can be developed meaningfully.

In Figure 21.23, a balance scale is set up with two numeric expressions. A box is drawn around both of the 5s. The task is to manipulate the numbers so that there is only one boxed 5 on the left. You can operate on numbers or on boxed 5s, but you may not combine the 5 in the box with any other numbers. Obviously, to keep the scale balanced, you must do the same things to both sides of the balance. At each step along the way, the balance can be confirmed.

After one or two similar examples, put variable expressions in the balance pans, and have students decide how to

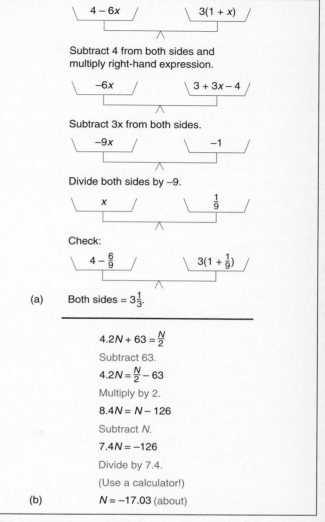

• **FIGURE 21.24** Using a balance scale to think about solving equations.

isolate the variable on one side. The other side should be all numeric.

Even after you have stopped drawing the balance, it is a good idea to refer to the scale or pan-balance concept of "equation" and the idea of keeping the two sides balanced. Operations on both sides of the equation should be done as illustrated in Figure 21.24. Division of both sides by a constant is best done with fraction notation.

A goal in these activities is to promote the use of inverse operations to solve an equation. Teachers are frequently frustrated when students prefer to solve simple equations such as $3N + 2 = 11$ by inspection or trial and error. One effective tactic is to use large numbers and avoid nice whole-number answers. For all computations, have students use a calculator to avoid tedium. For example, the *process* for solving $3.68N + 47.5 = 16$ is the same as for solving $3N + 2 = 11$.

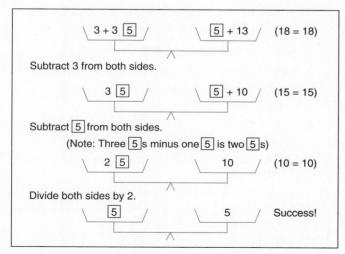

• **FIGURE 21.23** Learning how to solve an equation.

ASSESSMENT NOTES

The main thrust of the ideas in this chapter is that students should begin to see functional relationships in a variety of situations—relationships where the change in one quantity has a predictable effect on the change in another. Finding these relationships is intimately tied to the notion of mathematics as a science of pattern and order.

An equally important idea is related to the notion of communication of these functional relationships. Functions can be expressed in terms of context, language, tables, graphs, and equations. What is most important is that students see these different representations as just that, different but related methods of telling about a function.

With these big ideas in mind, your assessment plans should be focused accordingly.

Patterns.   Ask yourself these kinds of questions:

- What kinds of strategies do students use to search for patterns and generalizations? (Do they use the differences from one frame to the next, look for regularities in the physical patterns, coordinate frame numbers with different aspects of the physical pattern, exhibit flexible thinking in the search for patterns?)

- Do students distinguish between a rule that gives the next frame in a pattern from a functional rule that will produce the frame value for any frame?

- Are students able to assess their ideas independently, especially to determine if a potential function rule is correct for the given pattern?

- Do students understand the use of variables in generalizing a growing-pattern rule?

- Do students communicate pattern relationships with words, with pictures, and with symbolic expressions?

Functions in Real Contexts.   The kinds of things you should be looking for here are very similar to those listed for patterns. In real-world contexts, there is potential for a greater emphasis on communication.

- Do students effectively translate the real situation into functional language, graphs, symbols, tables?

- Are students able to demonstrate the way these various representations of a function are connected?

- When gathered data only approximate a function rule (scatter plots), do students indicate an understanding of the difference between the real data and the best-fit line or the constructed function rule?

Variables.   Variables are an important means of communicating ideas in mathematics. They form a significant part of the symbolic language that begins to be more and more prominent from the middle grades forward.

Your assessment should look to see that students seem to use variables in ways that make sense. If a student is making errors when using variables, it may be a good place to do some diagnostic work and find out what ideas the student has about the letters he or she uses in symbolic expressions. Be very aware of the kinds of misconceptions that students are likely to develop around variables. Rather than penalize or grade down students who have these misconceptions, find out specifically what the problems are and plan activities that help them confront their inappropriate ideas.

REFLECTIONS ON CHAPTER 21: WRITING TO LEARN

1. Describe in your own words the five different representations of a function and how they are related or actually represent the same thing. Use an example of your own (not one from the book) to explain.

2. Describe in general terms how you might develop function concepts with students through the use of growing patterns, a real-world situation, and an experiment. Indicate how the five representations are examined or created in each method.

3. The following growing pattern consists of square borders. The elements of each frame are the number of squares shaded in the border. Draw the fifth frame and the tenth frame. Make and complete a chart showing the number of elements in the first ten frames. What patterns can you discover? Try to use the pictures you have drawn to help you find a general formula for the number of squares in the *n*th frame.

4. Make up a real-world situation that defines a functional relationship. Use your example to do the following:

   a. Sketch a graph illustrating the relationship.

   b. State the relationship using the language of functions.

   c. Build a chart with numbers that might go with your relationship.

   d. Explain the graph and the chart as ways of presenting the same information in different forms.

   e. Explain how your example meets the formal definition of a function.

5. The table of values used to create a scatter plot, as in the height–versus–arm span example, is not a function table. Explain why not. How do you get a function out of a scatter plot?

6. Regarding graphs without equations, one activity in the text has students sketch graphs for situations, another

has students match graphs to a collection of situations, and a third has them make up stories to go with graph sketches. What is the value of these exercises? Are there any differences in what students learn or think about in these different exercises?

7. Explain what a variable is, and differentiate the three uses described by Usiskin.

8. Fill in the charts in Figure 21.22 if you have not done so. Explain what students are supposed to be learning by doing this exercise.

9. Explain how to solve the equation $4X + 3 = X + 12$ using a pan balance. To understand this idea, students need to be able to think of expressions such as $3 + 12$ or $X + 3$ as objects instead of operations or something to do. Explain why this understanding is important to the notion of solving equations.

10. Provide at least one example of how a graphing calculator can be used to help students with meanings of variables.

FOR DISCUSSION AND EXPLORATION

1. Some people feel that graphing calculators are too expensive for use in the middle grades. Others argue that students need to know the "basics" before they should be allowed to use these devices. What is your position? Can you defend it?

2. If your instructor or library has a copy of the NCTM videotape *Algebra for Everyone* (Mathematics Education Trust Committee, 1991), view it. The 19-minute tape demonstrates useful classroom techniques for helping students develop abstract algebraic ideas. Discuss your reaction to the video with a group, or write a short reaction paper.

SUGGESTED READINGS

Highly Recommended

Algebraic thinking [Focus issue]. (1997). *Teaching Children Mathematics, 3* (6).

Algebraic thinking [Focus issue]. (1997). *Mathematics Teaching in the Middle School, 2* (4).

Algebraic thinking [Focus issue]. (1997). *Mathematics Teacher, 90* (2).

These three issues of MCTM's popular journals provide an excellent resource for concepts of algebra across the K–12 curriculum. In the *Teaching Children Mathematics* issue, teachers of young children can read about algebraic ideas without being threatened. The articles provide appropriate activities and also help teachers begin to get a feel for what "algebraic thinking" might look and sound like in the early years. The middle-grades journal continues this same theme with challenging activities and explorations. What is interesting about the articles in the *Mathematics Teacher* is that they really are offering no new algerbraic ideas although the sophistication has been appropriately stepped up. All three issues include excellent use of technology and real-world examples to generate explorations of ideas. That NCTM chose to devote three issues to this theme of algebraic thinking speaks volumes about the importance of this strand in the K–12 curriculum. Algebra is no longer reserved for high school.

Arcidiacono, M. J., & Maier, E. (1993). *Picturing algebra: Unit 9, Math in the mind's eye.* Salem, OR: Math Learning Center.

This is one of the best examples of activities in which patterns lead to equations and functions. Like all *Math in the Mind's Eye* units, this series of lessons actively involves students and provides extensive teacher direction and blackline masters for materials and record sheets. Some of the patterns in Figure 21.8 were adapted from these materials. Unique to these materials are tiles of unspecified length or dimension that are used to develop a general formula or function.

Edwards, E. L. (Ed.). (1990). *Algebra for everyone.* Reston, VA: National Council of Teachers of Mathematics.

This little book is worth reading by anyone contemplating teaching concepts discussed in this chapter. Short chapters address such issues as change in focus, the transition from arithmetic to algebra, and the use of technology. The annotated list of resources is another plus.

Fey, J. T., & Heid, M. K. (1995). *Concepts in algebra: A technological approach.* Dedham, MA: Janson.

This is a full-year text for beginning algebra that was originally developed under a National Science Foundation grant to illustrate how technology could be used to teach algebra. The authors strongly believe that algebra should be tightly connected to real-world examples, not simply as applications at the ends of a unit but as the springboard of every idea. The emphasis is on functions and graphs. Symbol manipulation is minimal. Factoring is not included as a skill anywhere in the book. Many of the ideas in this book are embedded in the current chapter. This is a highly recommended resource for teachers if not a text for a middle grade algebra course.

Phillips, E. (1991). *Patterns and functions: Addenda series, grades 5–8.* Reston, VA: National Council of Teachers of Mathematics.

It is hard to improve on this book for ideas related to function development. The first section involves students with a wide variety of functions in real contexts, including exponential-decay, linear, quadratic, and cubic functions. Throughout the book, the concept of function grows out of pattern development in a variety of creative and interesting activities that connect many middle school mathematics topics to a development of functions. This is an important contribution to the development of function concepts prior to algebra.

Other Suggestions

Barrett, G., & Goebel, J. (1992). The impact of graphing calculators on the teaching and learning of mathematics. In T. J. Cooney (Ed.), *Teaching and learning mathematics in the 1990s* (pp. 205–211). Reston, VA: National Council of Teachers of Mathematics.

Bell, A. (1995). Purpose in school algebra. *Journal of Mathematical Behavior, 14,* 41–73.

Blubaugh, W. L. (1988). Why cancel? *Mathematics Teacher, 81,* 300–302.

Brueningsen, C., Bower, B., Antinone, L., & Brueningsen, E. (1994). *Real-world math with the CBL system: 25 activities using the CBL and TI-82.* Dallas: Texas Instruments.

Burrill, G., Burrill, J. C., Coffield, P., Davis, G., de Lange, J., Resnick, D., & Siegel, M. (1992). *Data analysis and statistics across the curriculum: Addenda series, grades 9–12.* Reston, VA: National Council of Teachers of Mathematics.

Coxford, A. F. (Ed.). (1988). *The ideas of algebra.* Reston, VA: National Council of Teachers of Mathematics.

Day, R. P. (1995). Using functions to make mathematical connections. In P. A. House (Ed.), *Connecting mathematics across the*

This section provides practical suggestions and will help you develop a professional perspective on important issues that pervade the teaching of mathematics in grades K–8.

Chapter 22 offers two suggestions for planning a lesson. Both are designed to encourage classroom discourse and are based on the constructivist views presented in Chapters 3 and 4. The chapter contains tips for dealing with a diverse classroom, detailed ideas for creating and using cooperative learning groups, and suggestions for incorporating writing into your mathematics program. You will also find a discussion of review and practice issues and ways to use homework effectively. The chapter ends with a look at traditional textbooks and how they can be used to best advantage in a developmental classroom.

Chapter 23 offers suggestions and perspective on reaching all children in the teaching of mathematics. Separate discussions deal with children with special learning problems, including learning disabilities and mental disabilities. Multicultural issues and social disparity are examined, as are problems of gender equity. The segment on gifted students provides a detailed look at Renzulli's model for integrating gifted programs into the regular programs of the school. The entire chapter is based on current research and the perspectives of experts working specifically in these important areas of mathematics education.

Chapter 24 looks at the role of the calculator and the computer in teaching mathematics. Here you will find NCTM's position on the use of these powerful aids and a framework that will guide your use and selection of technology as you teach. Included are ideas for profitable use of the Internet and a more detailed look at the computer programming language Logo.

CHAPTER

PLANNING FOR EFFECTIVE INSTRUCTION

This chapter describes some basic structures for lessons and other instructional strategies (cooperative groups, writing in mathematics, homework, and the use of textbooks). These are practical, rather than theoretical, suggestions but they are consistent with the developmental perspective of this text. Consider the ideas as suggestions, as food for thought. You must create a classroom that works for you.

There is one principle that should remain constant regardless of the style and structure of your instruction: *Children learn only when they are mentally active*—reasoning, sense making, problem solving, decision making, conjecturing, evaluating, and otherwise using their intellect. The implication of this basic tenet is to view all planning from the perspective of the students. Will the children's minds be *actively* involved?

STUDENT-CENTERED LESSONS

A student-centered lesson revolves around ideas that are generated by the students during the lesson. The teacher remains involved in directing the focus of student activities but turns responsibility over to the students, expecting *them* to develop their own ideas and solutions during the lesson. A student-centered model is in keeping with a constructivist view of learning.

Three-Part Structure

A good student-centered, constructivist lesson has three simple components: (1) a task, situation, or problem presented to the students for consideration; (2) an opportunity for students to work on the task; and (3) an opportunity for discussion and reflection on the work done by the students after working on the task. These three components of a lesson coincide with the before, during, and after teacher actions described in Chapter 4.

Presentation of the Task

A good lesson must begin with a good task that engages students. The selection of the task is based on the big ideas of the unit, your reflection on the needs and demonstrated understandings of your students, and the probability that the task will permit your students to "bump into" the big ideas you have in mind.

Chapter 4 discusses a wide variety of types of tasks that may be effective, from simple word problems to open-ended investigations. In the same chapter, you will see how tasks can be presented so that students understand what the goal is and are ready to go to work.

After selecting a task, consider what will be required for your students to understand the task and become involved in it. A truly artful teaching trick is to get students invested in the task or to make the problem theirs rather than yours.

Opportunity for Student Work

Once the students understand the problem or task, the next step is the one that distinguishes child-centered teachers from traditional teachers. It is time to let go! It is at this point that authority shifts from the teacher to the student. The students are now in charge of deciding how to proceed, how to solve the problem. If they are simply following your directions, they are not solving the problem you presented; you are!

Many teachers find it very difficult to relinquish control over their students' activities and ideas. They fear that students will come up with ideas they do not understand or go in unplanned directions. Stepping back is hard! It is an act of letting go in the same way a parent lets loose of the bike as the child first learns to ride without training wheels. If you don't let go, students will not be working with their own ideas. Letting go is a major key to student-centered lessons.

Your lesson plans should specify the organizational structure for the student work portion of your lesson. Depending on the task, you might plan for small cooperative groups, pairs working together, independent student work (probably the least effective), workstations (students exploring in predetermined areas of the room), computer work, or library work.

Chapter 4 provides suggestions for teacher actions during this time when students are working. In simple terms, you need to be an active listener and perhaps even a participant in the solution or the discussion. This is a time when you should gather information about the ideas students are developing. Use this information when conducting the discussion to follow and in planning tomorrow's lesson.

Your plans for this time may also include specific actions for gathering assessment data. On which groups or students are you going to focus? Are there group behaviors you want to assess? Refer to Chapter 5 for assessment options you may wish to consider. If assessment is not built into your plans, it may not happen.

Discussion and Reflection

Classroom discourse enters your lesson during the third phase. This is the time when the class becomes a community of learners as they debrief the ideas they have been considering or the solutions and methods they have been working on.

As discussed in the "After Actions" section of Chapter 4, you want to focus on the ideas and reasoning of your students and not just the answers to problems. Most important, you do not want to be seen as evaluating students' ideas and responses. You certainly have an obligation to maintain control and to direct the discussion in ways that are useful to your curricular agendas. The trick is to accept responses, help students respect others in the class, and make students responsible for judging the validity of ideas.

Allow sufficient class time for this third phase. Don't rush at the end of a period, or you will find yourself simply checking answers. In some instances, the student work portion of a plan may take more than a single period. If so, simply expand the three-part structure to span two or more days.

Written Work

The student-centered model just described does not preclude students' completing a worksheet or writing explanations. In fact, written work and a well-planned worksheet can be very helpful in focusing attention during student work. The problem or task may be written on a page you prepare or taken from a textbook activity. Tables, charts and graphs, drawings, and computations can all be part of the work students do in groups or independently.

Some teachers like to give each group a transparency on which to prepare solutions. This helps students present their ideas, focuses on the need for written expression, adds importance to written work, and saves time in getting ideas before the class during discussions. Younger children may prepare reports on large sheets of newsprint and present their work in a similar manner.

Written work in a fill-in-the-blanks format diverts the focus to getting answers rather than thinking and sense making. By contrast, a worksheet with questions and plenty of space to show work, answers, and rationale will promote productive student activity.

Minilessons

Many tasks do not require the full period for student work and reflection. The three-part approach can be collapsed to as little as 10 minutes. You might plan two or three cycles in a single lesson.

For example, consider any of the following tasks:

Grades K–1: Make up two questions that we can answer using the information in our graph.

Grade 2:   Suppose you did not know the answer to problem 14. What is a good way to help figure it out?

Grades 4–5: On your geoboard, make a figure that has line symmetry but not rotational symmetry. Make a second figure that has rotational symmetry but not line symmetry.

Grades 6–7: Margie has this drawing of the first floor of her house. (Pass out drawing.) She wants to reduce it on the photocopy machine so that it will have a scale of 1 cm to the foot. By what percentage should she reduce it?

These are worthwhile tasks but probably would not require a full period to do and discuss.

A profitable strategy for short tasks is *think-pair-share*. Students are first directed to spend a minute developing their own thoughts and ideas on how to approach the task or even what they think may be a good solution. Then they pair with a classmate and discuss each other's ideas. This provides an opportunity to test out ideas with someone and practice articulating them before trying to explain to the class. The last step is to share the idea with the rest of the class. The pair may actually have two ideas or can be told to come to a single decision to share. The entire process, including some discussion, may take less than 15 minutes.

TEACHER-DIRECTED LESSONS

In a teacher-directed (not teacher-*centered*) lesson, the teacher retains a greater degree of control than in the student-centered model. With the increasing popularity of constructivism and the belief that children must create their own ideas, direct instruction is viewed by some as inappropriate. However, the bad reputation of the teacher-directed approach may be due to a confusion between teacher-directed lessons and teaching by telling. The two are not the same.

As you were reminded at the outset of this chapter, *children learn only when they are mentally active*. Can children be mentally active in a teacher-directed activity? Absolutely. The main difference between teacher-directed lessons and student-centered lessons is that in the latter there is a clear shift of control from teacher to student. In a teacher-directed lesson, the teacher maintains control while directing the full development. The construction of ideas takes place in a tighter framework where teachers ask questions requiring students to think about a problem or situation on the spot. Students are not "set loose" to explore or solve on their own.

Two-Part Structure

A simple model for a teacher-directed lesson has only two main parts: development and consolidation.

Development

In the development portion of a teacher-directed lesson, the teacher presents a task or a small portion of a task and entertains discussion with the whole class. The main idea or concept to be learned should still emerge from the students but is generally the result of Socratic questioning and probing. The think-pair-share approach can be used multiple times throughout this questioning and development and is very useful in getting all children to participate. Ideas are solicited from the class through discussion. This part of the lesson should never be an explain-and-model type of presentation where students blindly mimic what the teacher has demonstrated.

The directed portion of the lesson, like a good student-centered lesson, should frequently involve physical models and students actively doing things. Students can do a quick activity with the materials and discuss immediately what they did and why. For example, students may all be told to set out on their desks a brown Cuisenaire rod (the 8 rod) and then find the single rod that is $\frac{3}{4}$ of brown. As students offer their solutions, the teacher can help students see how unit fractions—in this case, fourths—can be used to find any fraction with the same denominator. The big idea that the top number in a fraction counts and the bottom number tells what is being counted can easily emerge from discussing solutions to a few similar tasks.

The skillful teacher can direct discussion so that students will see themselves as developing nearly every idea. This requires listening to all ideas, good and not so good, and directing attention to the correct responses. The class community must be seen as the source of ideas.

A significant problem in the teacher-directed approach is keeping all students actively participating. Because the teacher is in control, the questions or problems are clearly those of the teacher. There is less student ownership of the investigations. This tends to cause the less motivated students to tune out or minimize their participation. Students who are not contributing or are unable to contribute can be called on to explain an idea already presented by a classmate or to make a judgment about a good idea on the floor. "Pat, what do you think about what Juanita just said? Does that seem to make sense to you? Why? How would you explain what she said in your own words?"

Consolidation

As just noted, a potential difficulty with a teacher-directed lesson is keeping all students actively involved. Because there is no extended period of working in pairs or groups prior to sharing ideas, the more reluctant student is very likely to be silent. Nor is there always time to involve all children. Furthermore, offering an idea or answering a well-formed question is not nearly the same as truly interacting with a task as in the student-centered approach, so that even the interested student must be an observer for a large percentage of the development portion of the lesson. Therefore, a consolidation period must always be planned where students have an opportunity to explore more fully the ideas developed in the first part of the lesson. Here students try out the ideas just developed and make sure that their discussions really made sense. You will find some students who were not tuned in at all in the directed segment and only now are attending to the activity.

The activity in this part of the lesson should be somewhat parallel to the tasks in the development portion. This is not a practice session where students simply mimic the procedure just explained. Rather, the activity should continue the exploration begun in the first portion. Now all students have a well-defined task to work on. Students may work in pairs, groups, or individually as suits the needs of the task. If models were used as part of the thinking process of the development portion, models should continue to play a part in the consolidation.

For example, if the development portion involved two or three examples of finding the fractional part of a designated Cuisenaire rod, the consolidation portion could have a series of similar questions that students could work on using the rods. The questions could be prepared on a worksheet with space for explanations or drawings. There could be an added dimension to the activity that was not included in the original development. In this example, the students might be given a rod that represents a fractional amount and asked to find the whole: "Suppose that dark green is $\frac{3}{4}$. What rod is the whole? Draw a picture to explain." Another type of variation is to change models. In this way, the concept remains the same, but students are not as likely to follow blindly a procedure seen in the development. In the fraction example, they could be asked to use sets of counters or draw rectangles for the fractions instead of using rods.

Variations

No lesson model is entirely prescriptive and applicable to all situations. There are a number of things you might consider that provide some flexibility to the consolidation portion of a lesson.

Worksheets with Manipulatives

One of the best ways to approach the consolidation portion of a lesson is to design a worksheet that requires the use of physical models. Such worksheets guide the specifics of a manipulative activity to be done at a desk or table. Students can draw simple pictures to show what they have done or record numeric results of a manipulative activity.

Figure 22.1 is a worksheet for number combinations that might be used in first grade. Counters are placed in the area at the top of the page and separated into two parts, and dots are drawn in the small versions at the bottom. Many textbooks incorporate physical models into first- and second-grade lessons in this way.

Activities that involve base 10 materials can include recording either with a drawing or with numerals. The worksheet in Figure 22.2 is designed to follow a full-class activity involving trading with base 10 models. Students draw small dots, sticks, and squares to represent the base 10 materials that they worked with to do the exercise.

The seventh-grade example in Figure 22.3 involves percentages approximated by familiar fractions. The students could use pie pieces and the hundredths disk (see Figure 14.1, p. 275) to determine the approximate equivalencies without doing any computation. Several examples of the worksheet activity could be explored as part of the developmental portion of the lesson.

Workstations

A workstation approach is another alternative for the consolidation portion of a lesson. It can be adapted to any level,

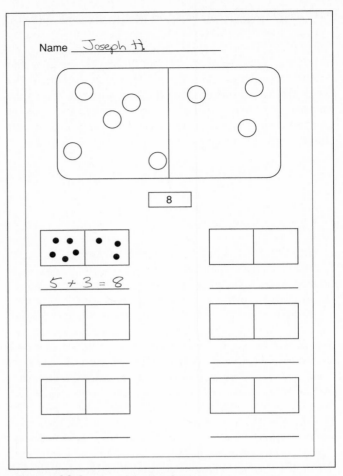

• **FIGURE 22.1**   A worksheet with counters.

including the middle school. Stations allow you to vary the task difficulty as well as the materials and yet keep all students on the same concept. Materials that go with a particular activity are placed in separate tubs or boxes. These materials might include special manipulatives, work cards or worksheets to help guide the activity, and, if required, such things as scissors, paper, or paste. For children at the K–2 level, the activities must be taught and practiced in groups or with the full class before being placed in a tub. Older children can be quickly told about an activity, or written directions can guide the activity at the station.

For a given topic, you might prepare as many as eight or ten related activities to be placed in workstations. At the primary level, these are carefully introduced over several days. Some activities may be games to be played by two or three children. Activities may be duplicated at more than one station, perhaps with slightly different levels of difficulty.

The workstation approach is useful even in middle school. The idea is simply to get all students involved independently or in small groups with familiar activities. For example, during a unit on percentage in the seventh grade, a number of different models and conceptual activities may be introduced during the first week. In the second week, the consolidation portion of each period can be devoted to

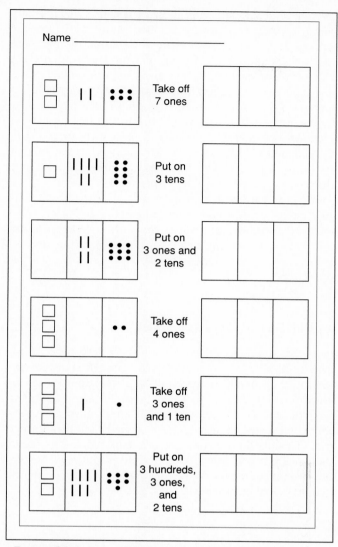

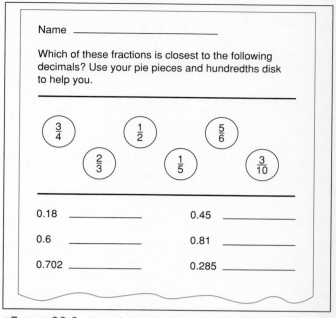

●**FIGURE 22.2**   A worksheet with base 10 materials.

●**FIGURE 22.3**   A worksheet for decimal-to-fraction estimation.

countability and thereby lends an air of responsibility and importance to the activity. Recording is a form of communication of mathematical ideas. Finally, the records are lasting. They provide an opportunity for assessment. They can be displayed on bulletin boards, sent home for parents, or placed in students' portfolios.

PLANNING FOR DIVERSITY

Classrooms are increasingly heterogeneous. While the benefits of broadly inclusive or heterogeneous classrooms far outweigh the problems they cause, there are problems. Not all students are ready to tackle the same problem at the same level of sophistication at the same time. Brighter students are more verbal and can dominate class discussions. The student-centered approach offers a number of possibilities for dealing with a wide range of student levels.

Involve Students in Collaborative Activities

Avoid ability grouping! Plan pairs and groups so that students with different skills and abilities work together. Too often, teachers feel that lower-level students are not able to do the regular work of the classroom. But the fact that students have not mastered computational skills does not mean that they are unable to participate in projects that involve reasoning or creative ideas. In fact, the perspective of lower-level students often can be a positive factor in a mixed group

working on activities involving these models. If not enough materials are available, different materials can serve different activities. Students simply get materials and return with them to their seats.

If you use workstations regularly, design an organizational scheme that makes the use of stations quick and easy. Use the same containers for activities throughout the year. In K–3 classrooms, label the containers, and assign each to an area of the room: a space on a carpet, a table, or a collection of desks shoved together. A sign or label at each area indicates which tub belongs there. Helpers can set out the tubs at the appropriate places in the room and return them at the end of the period. This procedure can remain the same throughout the year, with the activities within the tubs changing as they are taught to the class.

Some form of recording of the activity should be included when possible. This may involve drawing pictures, pasting down paper counters, or recording symbolically what was done manipulatively. The recording represents ac-of students working on a problem. Help skill-deficient students become proficient with calculators. Expect students to have calculators available at all times.

A mixed-grouping approach is also useful for accommodating students who are performing above grade level. Although certain students at the extreme upper end of the spectrum should be assigned projects and activities for the gifted (see Chapter 23), it is generally inadvisable to separate the more capable children from the rest of the class. Highly skilled students are not necessarily the most creative or even those with the best conceptual backgrounds. Interaction with a mixed group is good for all.

Plan Differentiated Tasks

Many tasks can be modified up or down in ability level by making small adjustments in the numbers or the requirements involved. A general task can be discussed at the beginning of a lesson. This can be followed by passing out paper with the task written out. Numbers or other variations can be prepared ahead of time for two or three different levels.

For example, in one second-grade class, the teacher regularly has students work on word problems that she prepares ahead of time. Two or three problems are on the page, with space for students to show their reasoning and their work. A problem may look like this:

Eduardo had _____ marbles. He gave Erica _____ marbles. How many marbles does Eduardo now have?

Before class, numbers are written in the blanks so that the same problem serves three different levels. For this example, Eduardo may have 121 marbles, 60 marbles, or 12 marbles and correspondingly give Erica 46, 15, or 5. Thus the same word problem involves $121 - 46$, $60 - 15$, and $12 - 5$, all at the same time.

A similar approach is to put three sets of numbers or three variations of the same task on the board or on the paper itself. Rather than assign students a particular task variation, students select the numbers or variation with which they are comfortable. This student-choice approach puts some control in the hands of the students. It tells students at the lower levels that it is OK to work on easier problems but that they are free to challenge or stretch themselves. It is a form of student self-assessment in the sense that students are telling you what they feel comfortable with. You can compare a student's choice with your sense of his or her abilities. And finally, the idea that there are several alternatives provides a ready task for those who finish quickly.

Use Workstations

Another way to modify the level of a task is to create variants of the task at different stations around the room. For example, if a fourth-grade task involved comparison of fractions, a variety of related tasks could be selected and presented at the same time and then placed in different stations. Several stations could be created with different materials (pie pieces, paper for folding, counters, Cuisenaire rods) to find common names for $\frac{2}{3}$. Of these, the pie piece approach is probably least challenging and counters the most challenging and open-ended. Other stations could have students find names for fractions by working with rectangles on a geoboard. Another station might involve slicing squares to develop a procedure for finding equivalent fractions. Yet another station could have students trying to find different ways to compare two fractions, an activity that frequently has equivalent fractions embedded in it. (These activities are all discussed in Chapter 12.)

Students can be assigned to a station that best suits their needs, or you may want students to self-select. Two students with different abilities can work together at a station that is challenging to the slower student but not demeaning to the more able student. Each can write a separate report.

Avoid Skill-Oriented Tasks

Tasks that simply practice textbook skills need never be assigned uniformly to the entire class. Though skills are important, they should be practiced at a level appropriate for the individual student. For students who are beyond the need for practice in a particular skill, an assigned practice is boring busywork. For students not ready for the practice level of a skill, the assigned practice reinforces their sense of inadequacy. If a task involves a lot of computation, be certain that all students have calculators. Avoid tasks in which computational proficiency is the objective.

COOPERATIVE LEARNING GROUPS

As has been frequently noted, having students work in groups is an extremely effective technique for getting students actively involved in doing mathematics. Group work can be a regular feature of both student-centered and teacher-directed models of instruction. Here you will find some suggestions for establishing effective groups and using them in the mathematics classroom.

Size and Composition

There is no magic number for the size of a group. Johnson, Johnson, and Holubec (1993) point out that the more members in a group, the more possible interactions need to be accommodated. In a group of three, there are three possible student-student interactions. With four students, that number jumps to six. With five students, there are ten different pairs that must be able to interact and get along, and the result is generally disappointing. If students have not worked in groups before, it may be good to begin with groups of two. In pairs, students can attend more easily to this new idea of working with someone. Later, you will probably want to shift to groups of three or at most four.

Some accommodation in the physical arrangement of the room is required for groups. Desks can be shoved together or tables arranged to allow students to work together. It is not necessary that the students remain in their group arrangement throughout the day or period, although most teachers prefer this.

A strong case can be made for forming heterogeneous groups, with a range of ability levels in each group. This permits less able students the chance to hear ideas expressed by others and thus learn from them. At the same time, more capable students can benefit from explaining their ideas to the group. Ability grouping quickly creates a sense of inferiority for the children in the slower groups. Slow groups begin to feel left out, and top groups become bored or aloof.

Random assignment of students to groups on a daily or weekly basis is one method of easily obtaining heterogeneous groups. If group composition changes at least weekly, quarrels over who gets to be with whom can be minimized. Tomorrow it will be different. Burns (1990) suggests dealing out playing cards, using all four suits of as many numbers (ace, two, three, and so on) as are required to allow one card for each class member. The ace group, the two group, and so on, are thereby quickly and randomly established.

For groups to be most effective, students must develop interpersonal skills of cooperation, sharing, listening, and responsibility. The group must view itself as a unit, not as individuals sitting at the same table. These skills are best developed by having groups remain intact for at least several weeks or even several months. If you use a fixed-group approach, spend considerable time composing groups. Work on more than balance in abilities. Try also to mix boys and girls, to spread out both the leaders and the followers, to blend troublemakers with those who are cooperative. Avoid putting your problem children all in one group.

Developing Productive Group Behavior

Working cooperatively and productively in groups is not something that children do automatically or easily. You cannot simply place students in groups and expect to see all of the benefits of group work magically happen. Students must explicitly be taught how to work cooperatively with their fellow students.

Specific Group Skills and Responsibilities

Some teachers like to assign special roles to students, such as encourager, recorder, and monitor. Role assignment places specific responsibilities on individual students and can help make a group function effectively. Before assigning roles—and even if you do not—all students should understand what behaviors make a group function effectively. The following are among the most important group behaviors for students to understand.

1. *Share ideas and opinions.* Groups must learn to operate as a group, not as a collection of individuals. Students need to understand that the entire group will "sink or swim together." Therefore, it is imperative that the members all share their ideas and contribute their best thoughts to the task. Sharing is a two-way street. Each student is responsible for getting his or her ideas to the group and also listening to and accepting the ideas of other members. Sharing is not dominating.

2. *Ask and answer questions.* Each group member is responsible for his or her understanding of the ideas the group generates. It is therefore a responsibility of every member to use the group to get information. If a student lacks some information or does not understand an idea being discussed, he or she has an obligation to ask other group members to explain the idea or task. All group members must be willing to help those who ask. Groups should come to realize that when they work together to share ideas and answer questions, they operate more effectively.

3. *Keep the group on task.* It is easy for students working alone (without teacher direction) to stray from the task at hand and begin to play, argue, or discuss things not related to the task. Students in a group need to learn to help each other attend to the job at hand. This can be done by reminding the group that there is only so much time, restating the purpose of the activity, or suggesting a direction for the task.

4. *Encourage participation.* Despite rules 1 and 2, there will be students who are reluctant to speak up in a group and who will sit and watch passively. Students in the group must not permit any member to be passive. When they notice a group member not participating, they need to bring him or her into the process. This can be done by asking, "What do you think, Nancy?" or "Mark, do you think this is a good idea? What do you think we should try?"

These are only four specific group skills taken from a much longer list suggested by Johnson, Johnson, and Holubec (1993). However, these four will go a long way to getting your groups to work productively. If you decide to assign roles or have groups select roles for their members, the most important roles should reflect these group skills or rules. For example, an "encourager" can be sure that all participate. A "director" can be assigned to keep the group on task. A "monitor" can be sure that all understand and are sharing ideas.

Teaching Group Skills

For students to understand and acquire the necessary skills for effective groups requires more than a simple explanation. The first thing that must be done is for students to understand and appreciate the values and benefits of working in a group.

- Everyone has two or three helpers.
- Everyone gets to talk and have his or her ideas heard.
- A collection of ideas is always better than just one idea.
- It is more fun to work with a partner than to work alone.

However, to reap these benefits, the group must learn how to work together.

Don't try to introduce all the group skills at once. Select one or two ideas at a time, and discuss them with the class. Make a poster for the skill being discussed, with space to record students' ideas about what the skill looks and sounds like. Simply telling students to "share ideas" or to "encourage others" is generally a waste of time. Arrange students in temporary groups and have them model one skill such as asking questions. Talk about how the skill sounded and discuss possible ways to ask for information politely. Practice how to use materials and talk about sharing.

When you have discussed a group skill, select three or four students to model the skill in a pretend group while all observe. Ask the students to comment on what they saw that was a good example of the skill and what they saw that could be improved.

Maintaining Group Skills

Each time you set students to work in groups, there should be two types of objectives that all groups understand. The first objective is the academic task or problem that is the goal of your lesson. The second objective is one or more group skills or general group behavior. In the beginning, have students focus on one particular skill at a time. After assigning the group task for the day, you might say, "Today I want you to work especially hard at helping each other in the group." You might write "Helping each other" on the board or quickly discuss the poster you made that describes that group skill. At the end of the period, have each group assess its performance on the designated group skill. Each student can be asked to respond to a statement such as "Today I offered help in my group: (a) not at all, (b) sometimes, (c) a lot." Also ask the group to respond to a similar statement: "Today our group's members helped each other: (a) really well, (b) sometimes, (c) not as well as we could have." Have the students add one or two sentences that describe their behavior and what they will do to improve.

Items for a self-rating scale are suggested in Figure 22.4. Collison (1992) suggests that the completed checklist be shared with the other members of the group, who are given the chance to disagree with that member's self-evaluation. After hearing the group's response, changes can be made, if desired, and comments can be added. The important idea is to involve students in reflecting on and evaluating their own and their group's behavior and effectiveness. Pride in the quality functioning of a group can easily result.

Continue to have groups work on their group skills throughout the year. Like other skills, these can be improved with practice and periodic evaluation. Group skills can also deteriorate if students forget to work on them.

Group Recording and Reporting

Most of the time when you have students work in groups, time should be left in the lesson to discuss as a class the results of the group work. Students should understand that when they report their group's work, they are sharing the ideas and the work of the group and not their own individual ideas. This is part of the "sink or swim together" idea of group interdependence. Groups should always be prepared to share ideas orally or in written form. Preparation for reporting can help groups work together more effectively.

Oral Reporting

One approach to group reporting is to make it very clear that every member of the group must be prepared to tell about the group's work. Let the students know that you may call on any member of the group to share or explain what the group did. In this way, students can be taught to be sure that every group member understands the ideas developed in the group. You may find it useful to stop students just before your class discussion and suggest that the groups make sure that each member understands what was done and is prepared to report if asked to do so.

Another approach is to have a designated reporter for each group. You can appoint a reporter for each group, or students can select a reporter themselves. The reporter should be selected before the group begins work. All group members must then make sure that the reporter is keeping up with the group's ideas.

Written Reports

If you use a record sheet or worksheet, it is a good idea to have only one sheet per group. All group members should put their names at the top of the paper to emphasize that it is group work and that what is written on the page represents the ideas of the group. The recorder or person responsible for the writing or recording must be designated in the same way as the reporter. Recorder and reporter are usually different roles within the group. If you give all students a worksheet, group cooperation tends to break down as students become absorbed in completing their own papers. Thus assigning a record sheet or worksheet to every student defeats the purpose of working in a group.

Assessment of Group Work

The main reason for having students work in groups is to promote interaction and therefore learning. In that sense, cooperative groups are an instructional device. Many teachers

GROUP PERFORMANCE RATING FORM

A. Group Participation

1. Participated in group discussion without prompting
2. Did his or her fair share of the work
3. Tried to dominate the group, interrupted others, spoke too much
4. Participated in the group's activities

B. Staying on the Topic

5. Paid attention, listened to what was being said and done
6. Made comments aimed at getting the group back on the topic
7. Got off the topic or changed the subject
8. Stayed on the topic

C. Offering Useful Ideas

9. Gave ideas and suggestions that helped the group
10. Offered helpful criticism and comments
11. Influenced the group's decisions and plans
12. Offered useful ideas

D. Consideration

13. Made positive, encouraging remarks about group members and their ideas
14. Gave recognition and credit to others for their ideas
15. Made inconsiderate or hostile comments about a group member
16. Was considerate of others

E. Involving Others

17. Got others involved by asking questions, requesting input, or challenging others
18. Tried to get the group working together to reach group agreements
19. Seriously considered the ideas of others
20. Involved others

F. Communicating

21. Spoke clearly, was easy to hear and understand
22. Expressed ideas clearly and effectively
23. Communicated clearly

G. Overall Experience

24. This group helped me to improve my understanding of the problems and the ways of solving them more than if I had worked alone.
25. Working with the group was an enjoyable experience.

●FIGURE 22.4   A group performance rating scale. Students respond to each item with "almost always," "often," "sometimes," or "rarely."

Source: Collison (1992, p. 44). Used with permission.

are concerned that they don't know how to evaluate the work done in groups. With the proper perspective, groups actually make assessment easier and more effective.

Value of Using Group Work for Assessment Purposes

As noted in Chapter 5, much assessment data can and should be gathered from observations. These observations may take the form of anecdotal notes, observation checklists, or an observation rubric. Group work makes gathering this type of information much easier and can ensure that data are gathered from all students, not just the vocal minority. If observation schemes are structured around groups, you will be able to focus your attention on the two or three groups you select for that day. Over a few days, all groups and thus all students will have been observed.

Group work provides you with much more information in any given period than you could possibly gather without groups. When six or eight groups are working at the same time, you have six to eight times as much student activity and talk to observe and listen to than in a full-class environment. It is easy to stand near as many as four groups at once and listen in on all four conversations or watch how all four groups are working.

Having each group submit a single written report substantially reduces the amount of paper you must review for assessment. The smaller amount of written data makes it considerably easier to make instructional decisions and provide feedback than having to face a stack of papers submitted by all students individually.

Uses of Group Assessment Data

The first purpose of assessment outlined in NCTM's *Assessment Standards* is to provide feedback to students in order to promote learning. By examining a group report, your feedback goes to the full group. The group is there to help its members if improvement is necessary. When the group has done well, you should value the members' achievement and also their group skills. Students need to see that their efforts in making the group function produce positive personal results.

Assessment should inform your instruction. When thinking about the performance of groups, it is much easier to examine or reflect on the work of seven or eight groups than on 25 individuals. Group tasks can be modified to match the needs of individual groups. During instruction, you can much more easily get to and work with several groups and thus nearly half of your class than when you have all students working independently.

The third reason for assessment is evaluation and grading. Many teachers find it difficult to assign grades to a group product when they do not feel comfortable that all members merit the same grade for the work done. Parents are apt to complain that their child was unfairly graded because of being assigned to work with a slower student. There are several ways to handle these problems.

Remember that you want to evaluate by finding out what students *can* do rather than simply testing them to find out what they *cannot* do. Students will show you many more things in groups than you will ever find out from tests alone. You can share these things—positive and negative—with parents in your evaluation. If you use rubrics that indicate the quality of performance rather than a grade based on the number correct, the rubric scores can be assigned to all members of a group for their group work. Keep group evaluations separate from individual evaluations when you record them in your grade book. When you make up your evaluation for the marking period, take both group composition and work within the group into account. Group work should not be your only source of data.

Evaluation of programs, the fourth purpose of assessment, is also served well by data gathered from groups. Since evaluation of programs should be based on the performance of the class, data from groups are generally going to be more stable and reflective of the class as a whole. Group work will be much easier to think about when you try to consider if a unit, a book, or a curriculum was effective in meeting your objectives.

WRITING IN THE MATHEMATICS CLASSROOM

Writing in the mathematics classroom is an extremely important instructional technique. It is entirely possible that you were never asked to write during your own mathematics learning experiences and wonder why you should have children write and how to go about it. Here are some ideas to get you started.

Value of Writing in Mathematics

Writing is very different from oral communication. When you write, you express your own ideas and use your own words and language. It is personal. In contrast, oral communication in the classroom is very public. Ideas "pop out" without editing or revision. Meaning is negotiated or elaborated on by the class as a whole. The individual reflective quality of writing as compared to classroom discourse is an important factor in considering the value of writing in mathematics.

Writing as a Learning Tool

The process of writing requires gathering, organizing, and clarifying thoughts. It demands finding out what you know and don't know. It calls for thinking clearly. Similarly, doing mathematics depends on gathering, organizing, and clarifying thoughts, finding out what you know and don't know, and thinking clearly. Although the final representation of a mathematical pursuit looks very different from the final product of a writing effort, the mental journey is, at its base, the same—making sense of an idea and presenting it effectively. (Burns, 1995b, p. 3)

When students write, they are able to stop first and think. They can incorporate drawings and symbolism to help convey their ideas. If needed, they can research an idea or look back on related work to help put ideas together. All of this is much more than learning to communicate in mathematics. It is very powerful and deliberate reflective thinking. No doubt you have heard or even said, "I never really understood such-and-such until I taught it." Writing is much like teaching in the sense of collecting ideas and having to explain them using only the tools you presently have. In that sense, writing is very much like constructing ideas. Writing is a way to learn. Rarely will someone not grow or change mentally by expressing ideas in writing.

Because writing is so powerful as a learning device, opportunities for writing should be built into your lesson plans. Writing fits nicely into both models of instruction. In the student-centered model, it can replace or be part of the student work portion of the lesson. In the teacher-directed model, it fits perfectly with the consolidation portion of the lesson. Writing can be an independent activity or can be done within a group. Group authoring is a bit more difficult for students but has many of the same advantages.

Writing as an Assessment Tool

Writing provides a unique window to students' thoughts that simply cannot be had in any other form. The personal nature of writing reflects uniquely the way a student is thinking about an idea. Even a kindergarten child can express ideas in drawings or other markings on paper and begin to explain what he or she is thinking.

Oral communication, valuable as it may be, is gone at the end of the day. No notes you might take can account for all that is said in your class. And oral discourse is less personal. When you are able to sit down with students' journals or other writing, you can reflect on each one individually as well as on the class as a whole. You can use writing to target feedback and design special work for individual students. Written work helps you assess the progress you are making with the current unit. Finally, student writing is an excellent form of communication with parents during conferences. Writing shows students' thinking to their parents in the same way it shows you, telling them much more than any grade or test score.

For writing to be effective, students need to feel free to tell you what they know and show you how they know it. To grade writing in the sense of grading a test will prevent the writing from being a learning opportunity for the students and a true assessment opportunity for you. You should,

however, provide feedback to students: point out serious errors that need attention, comment on interesting ideas, ask for further clarification. If you can find time to talk with students about their writing, that may be best. Not responding tells students you do not value what they have written. Help students see that their writing is important to you. Writing should never be busywork for students. Do not allow students to get that idea by your not responding.

A particular writing task may on occasion be used for evaluation. You can have students do the same kind of writing on a test that they do in their journals or other writings. Because you have had them write outside of these evaluations, they will have learned how to put their ideas on paper, and the evaluation will be much more effective.

Types of Writing Activities

Journal Writing

This has become the most popular form of writing in the mathematics classroom but is also the most loosely defined. Two teachers can have their students write in journals, and yet the kind of writing that occurs may be entirely different. As described in Chapter 5, journals are vehicles for communication. They can be thought of as private, to be read only by you unless permission is granted to show a parent or to share with the class.

The journal can be used to have students explain a concept or an idea you have been working on (*What does percent mean?*), to reflect on the day's lesson (*What did you learn today? What was easy to understand today? What was hard?*), or to show how a problem is solved. In fact, practically any writing activity can be done in a journal. It is the private-communication format of a journal that makes it unique. (The physical format of journals and suggestions for writing prompts are discussed in Chapter 5.)

Problem Solving

When a problem is solved, students should learn to write much more than answers. Written explanations of the reasoning and processes students used should convey to others why the solutions are correct. This means that students need to convince themselves that they are correct as well, an important part of doing mathematics. A single problem can be printed at the top of a page or copied down by the students. Encourage students to include drawings or any form of explanation that helps the reader understand the solution. By focusing on a single problem and its solution as a writing task, you are communicating that you value the process as much as the answer.

Explaining an Idea

Somewhat different from solving a problem is the process of explaining an idea. This is prompted by straightforward requests such as, "Explain to me what three-fourths means" or

"Show me what you know about the number 10" or "Why does the area formula 'one-half base times height' give the area of a triangle?" Usually, these writing tasks would closely follow the development of the idea in class. You might want to plan for a unit by first having students write about one of the big ideas in the chapter you are about to cover.

Reflective Writing

Sometimes it is useful to get a general feel for students' perspective on a unit, how well they think they understand something, or what they like or dislike about mathematics or a topic in mathematics. You may want this type of writing to go in journals, where the element of privacy is useful. But if you set aside a special time and make the writing task something a bit more special, you are more likely to get true reflective thinking from your students. Here are a few suggestions for this type of writing assignment:

If mathematics were an animal, it would be . . .

The thing I like best about mathematics is . . .

The hardest part of this chapter on subtraction is . . .

I need help with _____ because . . .

To me, geometry means . . .

Practical Suggestions

Writing in mathematics is not easy for most students. Many will complain that they don't know what to write or how to write about mathematics. They need some guidance. Here are some tips that might help.

Help in Getting Started

Before offering a writing prompt, have a class discussion concerning the same topic as the prompt. As students suggest ideas, write them on the board in shortened phrases. Make lists of key words that are used in the students' discussion. Do not impose your language, but rather, record ideas using the terminology of your students. To help writing about a particular concept in mathematics, you might have students brainstorm and draw a mind map on the board showing how one idea is connected to another. These notes on the board can now be used by students if they wish.

Nearly all of Marilyn Burns's books include examples of children's writing. She recommends the following formulation:

I (we) think the answer is _____.

I (we) think this because . . .

This simple formula can also be used in oral presentations and become a regular feature in your classroom. It is not necessary that children follow the exact wording, but these two lines are a nice way to suggest connecting an answer with its justification.

Many children will tell you they are stuck or don't know what to write. Have them tell you about the problem or the question in the prompt. "Why do you think that is the answer? What did you do to get this? Tell me something you know about this shape you made (this measurement you did, this graph you made, the estimate you made)." Try to get several ideas before returning to the writing task. Get the student thinking about his or her ideas rather than what to put on paper. Then have the child repeat some of those ideas. "What did you just tell me about how you got that answer?" Now he or she is ready to write. "What you just said to me are the same things you can write. Just pretend you are talking to me, and let those ideas go right through your hand and onto the paper."

Huinker and Laughlin (1996) suggest changing the think-pair-share idea to think-talk-write. The thinking part is the same—a short time for students to get their thoughts together. The talk part is done with a partner or a small group. For the writing part, students are told to use the same ideas and words they just talked about and heard in their conversation. They can add drawings or pictures to help. Think-talk-write can be a regular approach to writing in your classroom.

Write Often

One thing is certain: If you have your students write regularly—at least three times every week—they will get better at it. Try sharing some of the writing that has been done by students in the class or by students in another class so that students will have some models of what it means to write. Soon they will be their own good models as it becomes less of a chore and more of a learning experience.

If you have computers in your room, take advantage of the word processors and the ease of writing they provide. Suggest leaving a blank space for a drawing where necessary. The big advantage of the computer is ease of revision. For young students, the physical act of writing is difficult. That effort is much diminished with the computer.

Model Writing

Students need to see that writing is a useful and natural way to record and communicate ideas, not just an assignment to be done. By making a special effort to model writing in class on the board or overhead, you demonstrate to your students the value of writing. A good place to model writing is to record thoughts that are contributed during a discussion. Then step back and reflect aloud about the ideas that have been contributed. Now, with the help of the class, write a brief summary of the ideas in a separate paragraph. If appropriate, add a drawing or an equation to illustrate an idea. Talk about what has been written from a critical perspective to make sure that it conveys the ideas intended. Make revisions to demonstrate that the first ideas put on paper are not always in the best form.

Another modeling technique is to write a brief paragraph about an idea in preparation for class. The paragraph can be presented as a springboard for discussion. Be clear that the writing is based only on your ideas and that students may want to disagree or add their own ideas. Writing represents a personal understanding of the idea written about. There is never a "right" thing to write.

Provide Purpose and Audience

All writers need to have a sense of their audience and the purpose of the writing. For every writing prompt or assignment, make these two points clear. Often you will be the audience. Tell that to the students. "You are writing to me. I want to know what you understand about subtraction. Give me your best understanding so that what I read will let me know what you know."

Other useful audiences include class members (real or fictitious) who may have missed a class. The purpose is to explain the ideas of the day's lesson. In a similar manner, students can write to explain an idea for a student in a lower grade. This has the advantage of putting them in a position of confidence. Writing a letter to another class, to the principal, to parents, or to a public figure such as the mayor is useful when the purpose is to exhibit the results of a project.

Be very clear when writing is to be kept private between you and the student. If you tell students that writing, as in a journal, is to be confidential, you must honor that trust. If you want to share the writing with a parent, get permission from the student first.

Help the Prewriter and Early Writer

Writing is just as important for children who do not yet have writing skills. They need to begin the process of recording and communicating their ideas. When we look at pictures and drawings made by young children, we should understand that they are most concerned with communicating to themselves. They do not really have a sense of audience. Burns (1995b) suggests telling young children that what they put on their paper should remind them of what they were thinking. Suggest that they should think about using words, numbers, and pictures to show their ideas. The result will not always make sense at first glance. Be sure to talk to the students about their writing and have them explain what they have written. At this early level, personal expression of ideas is more important than correct symbolism, spelling, or communication.

When time permits, you can have students dictate what they want to write so that their words are on the paper. Be sensitive when using this technique; some children do not like having the teacher write for them.

In Chapter 5, there is an illustration of how one kindergarten teacher uses a large flipchart as a "big journal." She writes ideas taken from the class during discussion. This is good modeling and a useful practice, but it does not replace the students' own private writing and formulation of ideas in written form.

REVIEW AND PRACTICE

The emphasis throughout this text is largely on getting students to do mathematics, to engage in the science of pattern and order. Though it has not been stressed, there is a place for review and practice in a developmental program of this sort.

Drill and Practice

In the past, drill and practice were the mainstays of the mathematics classroom. Today the amount of drill should be drastically diminished because our needs are quite different. Practice does have its place, however. The key is for the practice to be effective and not the predominant feature of the instructional program.

What Should Be Practiced

There are many procedural skills in mathematics that are worth practicing. Practice is not how the skill is learned but rather how the skill becomes automatic after it is learned. A few examples may clarify this point.

Basic Facts. Mastery of basic facts is as important today as ever, perhaps even more so. But mindless drill will do little to help students to this end. What needs to become more automatic is the use of an effective strategy. As a good way of thinking about a fact is used over and over, it soon becomes so automatic that it is an unconscious process. Practice without an efficient strategy relies on rote memory and simply does not work very well.

Computation. Children who learn computational procedures without any understanding tend to practice what they think they should be doing rather than what they understand. This inevitably leads to *errors* that get practiced and strengthened. If students practice doing computations in their own invented ways, they are forced to focus on the ideas of what they are doing. There is no collection of rules to follow. By doing many computations with attention to the supporting ideas, students are free to invent shortcuts and mental strategies that they would never think of if blindly following a rule. It soon becomes second nature for students to focus on a collection of relationships and ideas rather than a prescribed procedure.

Proportion and Percent Problems. The argument for practicing flexible and conceptual approaches to these two related areas is similar to the argument just made for computation. Proportion problems can be solved using a variety of algorithms. Efficient strategies tend to vary from one problem to the next, depending on the numbers involved. Sometimes a simple mental multiplication is all that is necessary. Often a little sketch of the situation helps clarify what the two ratios are and the necessary operation to use. In a similar manner, percent problems can frequently be solved in many ways. The fraction $\frac{1}{4}$ is a useful substitute for 25 percent, and thus dividing by 4 is useful in figuring a 25 percent discount. At other times, the use of 10 percent or 1 percent of the whole can be easily found by shifting a decimal point. What is most important is to be able to think about all of these situations meaningfully and not get totally absorbed by a prescribed procedural maneuver.

These examples are intended to help you focus on the idea that practice should help students become comfortable and flexible with an idea. Lengthy drills of algorithmic skills tend to diminish flexibility and reflective thought. Often teachers want to drill skills in preparation for a standardized test. The result is that when students confront a computation on the test, they respond as they have been drilled to do: They begin immediately to perform the indicated algorithm. Often a mental computation, an estimation, or a non-standard approach would be twice as fast, especially when the format is multiple-choice. The distracter choices on standardized tests are designed to match the typical errors that students make in mindless application of the algorithms. Students who have practiced thinking are much less likely to make these errors and will actually be able to complete these tests more quickly.

Suggestions for Practice

The main suggestion for practice has already been made implicitly: Practice the use of flexible conceptual approaches, not isolated and meaningless procedures learned by rote. Having made this overarching suggestion, here are some additional thoughts:

- Keep practice short. Fifteen minutes three or four times per week is much better than any full period of practice.

- Individualize practice so that students are actually practicing the things they need to practice. Nothing is more pointless than repetitive drill of a mastered skill.

- Provide conceptual help. Students who are experiencing difficulty in a practice setting are not going to be aided by more practice. A conceptual deficit is nearly always the root cause of a skill deficiency.

- Help students understand why they are practicing. The purpose of practice is to become quick yet flexible. Practice of meaningful skills allows them to be used with greater ease. With this in mind, try to avoid practice of things students will never need to use, such as long division with three-digit divisors.

Periodic Review

As much as we would like it to be otherwise, our students do forget things they have learned and can benefit from occasional review of previously covered topics. Traditionally, publishers have designed early chapters of textbooks to be a review of last year's skills. This practice is questionable in that it delays the start of new ideas. It is better to begin the year with new and exciting material and build necessary reviews into that material as needed.

Textbooks frequently offer review pages as a unit feature throughout the book. Unfortunately, these reviews focus primarily on algorithmic skills and almost never on concepts. The most important review is the review of the big ideas that have been covered—the concepts *as well as* the skills.

Rather than rely on your textbook to provide review, set aside a "looking-back day" every two or three weeks to review ideas covered earlier. Do not start these days with drills, but consider doing one or more of the conceptual activities that you used in the unit being reviewed. If there is a related skill, that can be included as a short segment at the end of the lesson. A writing prompt that has students explain the idea can give you some indication of how well it has been retained.

HOMEWORK

Homework can be a useful instructional tool, but it must be coordinated with your instructional objectives.

Homework Used for Conceptual Development

We have traditionally used homework as a means of providing extra drill and practice on the procedures that have been taught that day. Drill-oriented homework is an obvious extension of lessons that end with a procedural "how to" recipe. In a developmental approach to instruction, most lessons do not have this mechanical goal. Rather, the instruction requires reflection and students justifying their results through the use of models or other methods. Drill-oriented homework is not an appropriate follow-up to these lessons.

When drill and practice are not appropriate, does it follow that no homework can be assigned? Certainly not! Homework can serve the same purpose as working on a task or a new idea in class. A homework assignment may involve a task similar to one done in class that day. This will provide an opportunity for students to apply again the ideas that were discussed in class.

Homework is also an effective way to communicate the importance of conceptual understanding to both students and parents. If only drill lessons are followed by homework, students may well infer that drill is more important than understanding. When students take work home that involves models, writing, or data gathering, parents can see that their children are doing more than drill. Homework is a parent's window to your classroom. Students may discuss homework with their parents, and most parents will see that it is done. If developmental lessons are not followed by similar homework assignments, parents will not see a problem-solving approach to your instruction.

Homework also builds self-reliance as students are forced to grapple with ideas apart from the teacher's guidance. In this sense, homework is a way of communicating to students, "I know you are able to do this on your own."

Homework Used for Drill

As already noted, practice is an important part of learning and requires time. When you have activities that require practice, from basic-fact drill to solving verbal percent problems, homework is one appropriate place to provide that practice. Be sure to follow the suggestions in the preceding paragraphs. Keep drills short, and when possible, individualize them, providing practice only when needed. Avoid drill-oriented homework just because you feel compelled to give a homework assignment.

A good idea is to provide an answer key along with the drill. As part of the assignment, have students check their own drills against the key or have them use a calculator to check answers. Encourage them to mark the ones they get wrong and redo these. Then they should write you a note about why they think they got these exercises wrong the first time. Was the error carelessness, or is there something they need help with? If you let students see that the purpose of a drill is to improve their skill, there is no reason they cannot help you assess this. With the offer of help when needed, the drill homework becomes an opportunity rather than an irksome chore.

Drill homework should never be graded, especially when you have directed students to check their own work with an answer key. You can certainly check that it was done, and you must respond to the self-assessments that are written. But do not penalize a student for wrong answers if he or she is aware of them and either knows why they are wrong or is asking for help.

Using Homework in the Classroom

How you attend or do not attend to what was done for homework sends a clear value message to your students. However, checking homework in class can easily become a major time-consuming burden. It is important to find ways of dealing with homework that are quick yet effective.

First, be sure that assigned homework was done, and acknowledge the effort! This does not mean that it is necessary to grade or evaluate it. Checking that homework was completed can usually be accomplished by simply asking students to place it on their desks for you to see. Make it obvious that you do keep a daily record of homework done and not done.

Checking answers on homework is probably a waste of time. For drill and practice, the self-assessment approach just described is much more effective and requires no class time. When homework is a task or problem, discussing the homework should be just the same as the discussion or discourse portion of a lesson. Students can share ideas developed in their homework and interact with the ideas of others just as would be done in a student-centered lesson. Homework with drawings and written explanations should be out on desks during the discussion. Instead of having all students share their work, ask students to compare what they did with what was shown first. "Martha, I see a different drawing on your paper. Can you tell us about that part?" "Pete, it looks like you may have done about the same thing. Is that right, or did you do something differently?" In this approach, homework is an extension or continuation of the learning process. The responsibility to do the homework is the same as the responsibility to work in class.

THE ROLE OF THE TEXTBOOK

The basal textbook has been by far the most significant factor influencing instruction in the elementary and middle school classroom. To make decisions about the use of the textbook, it is good to have an objective view of textbooks and the role they can serve in instruction. When you realize that textbooks are not necessarily the best guide to instruction, you can make wiser choices in using them.

How Are Textbooks Developed?

It is worthwhile to remember that publishing textbooks is a business. If the very best ideas from mathematics educators were incorporated into a textbook that did not sell, those excellent books sitting in warehouses would be of no value to students and would cost the publisher millions of dollars.

Most publishers enlist as authors mathematics educators and teachers who are quite knowledgeable about teaching mathematics. They also do extensive market research to determine what will sell and what teachers think they want in a book. There is frequently a significant gap between what the authors think would be good and what the publisher thinks will sell. Compromise between author and market becomes the rule. Rather than be forward with new ideas for content or pedagogy, publishers make a serious attempt to offend no one. As a consequence, there is frequently a significant time lapse between state-of-the-art mathematics education and what appears in textbooks.

Experience has demonstrated to publishers that if the text requires the teacher to provide additional materials or models, there is an increased likelihood that the text will not sell. As a result, authors are somewhat limited in writing textbooks that incorporate all the principles of learning mathematics they know to be effective or that include ideas on the cutting edge of curriculum reform. Since 1990, there has finally been enough demand for the use of manipulative models that publishers have tried to respond. Punch-out cardboard models come with many books. Kits of materials, a high-cost item for publishers, are made available as a purchase option or are built into the base price of the books.

Textbook authors are also limited by other factors. The textbook is a printed medium. Pictures can be put on pages, but manipulative models cannot. To illustrate movement and relationships, such as grouping 10 ones to make a single ten, requires a lot of page space. Young children have a great deal of difficulty following time-lapse-sequence drawings that show materials in several stages of an activity. To use more pages simply creates a book that is too expensive and too heavy. The result is frequently a simple illustration followed by symbolic exercises that require less space.

Another serious limitation of the textbook is that it cannot conduct good discussions or discourse in your classroom. The best suggestions for explorations and tasks that naturally lead to classroom discourse are more likely to be found in the teacher notes. The most recent mainstream books remain very close to the "teach by telling" model. The type of instructional model encouraged in this text and in much recent literature demands a quality teacher who can be flexible, who values understanding, and who believes that necessary skills will emerge from a highly conceptual approach. The mainstream textbook is designed for a teacher who believes that the best teaching is done by following the text and who values a high proportion of drill and practice.

It should be noted that there is a growing market for "alternative" textbooks. Nearly every publisher has for many years had a special or optional program for grades K–2. These programs generally include lots of hands-on activities, suggestions for activity centers, and a lot of children's literature. A few companies have begun to publish programs that have been developed through grants at various universities or educational development centers. There are a number of middle grades programs of this type that are relatively new on the market and a few that span the entire K–8 range. Generally, these programs are more constructivist, involve real-world projects and explorations, and attend only minimally or not at all to traditional computational skills. It remains to be seen if the market for these programs will expand beyond the small 5 to 10 percent they had in the mid-1990s.

Teacher's Editions

The teacher's editions provide considerably more author freedom. Many publishers now provide two extra teacher pages for each lesson as well as additional pages with ideas, explanations, and hints in the front and back of each chapter. The teacher's editions nearly always suggest ways to teach the content of the lesson completely apart from doing the activity presented on the student pages. Teachers should take advantage of this information, especially the suggestions for activities. Too many teachers interpret the textbook curriculum as "getting students through the student pages" when, in fact, the real objectives require the much broader scope presented in the teacher's editions. Pupil pages are just one tool for instruction. Pupil pages are not the objective, nor are they the curriculum.

Two-Page Lesson Format

The usual textbook lesson in the pupil book is presented on two pages. An observable pattern to these lessons can be seen in almost all popular textbook series. A portion of the first page consists of pictures and illustrations that depict the concepts for that lesson. The teacher is to use this section of the page to discuss the concepts with the students. Next are well-explained examples for the students to follow or an exercise guided by the text. Finally, the lesson has a series of exercises or practice activities. Thus many lessons move from conceptual development to symbolic or procedural activities rather than having a unit or chapter move gradually over a period of days from concepts to procedures.

This three-part characterization of a textbook lesson is unfairly oversimplified. At the K–2 level, where the children write directly in consumable workbooks, what the student writes for all or most of the two pages may be closely tied to meaningful pictures or even simple hands-on models. The clear adherence to the two-page lesson is not always evident in seventh- and eighth-grade texts. As noted earlier, there is a definite movement in the textbook industry to develop pupil pages that require some form of hands-on models.

The traditional two-page format sends a clear message to students that the pictures, concepts, and discussion part of a lesson can be ignored. They begin to tune out until the teacher begins to explain how to do the exercises. Following page by page and assigning procedural exercises from every lesson can easily negate all other efforts to communicate the importance of reasoning, of making and testing conjectures, of justifying results—in short, of doing mathematics.

Suggestions for Textbook Use

Our task as teachers is to help children construct relationships and ideas, not to get them to "do pages." We should look on the textbook as simply one of a variety of teaching tools available in the classroom. The textbook is not the object of instruction.

If one considers the limitations of the print medium and understands that the authors and publishers had to make compromises, the textbook can be a source of ideas for designing lessons rather than prescriptions for what each lesson will be. Here are some suggestions:

- Teach to the big ideas, not the pages. Consider chapter objectives rather than lesson activities. The chapter or unit viewpoint will help focus on the big ideas rather than the activity required to complete a page.

- Let the pace of your lessons through a unit be determined by student performance and understanding rather than the artificial norm of two pages per day.

- Use the ideas in the teacher's edition.

- Consider the conceptual portions of lessons as ideas or inspirations for planning more manipulative, interactive, and reflective activities, even if the students do not actually do the page.

- Think about how the practice exercises could be modified if students were to use models, write explanations, or discuss outcomes or approaches. The exercises are there for your use. Use them wisely, but do not let them rule how you teach.

- Remember that there is no law saying every page must be done or every exercise completed. Select activities that suit your instructional goals rather than designing instruction to suit the text. Feel free to omit pages and activities you believe to be inappropriate for the needs of your students and your instructional goals.

- If the general approach in the text for a particular unit is not the same as the approach you prefer, omit its use for that unit altogether, or select only exercises that provide appropriate practice after you have developed the concepts with your method.

- When drill and practice at the symbolic level are desired, look to the textbook as one source of such activity. Why write a drill if an acceptable one is there in the book?

The text is usually a good general guide for scope and sequence. There is no reason that you as a teacher should be required to be a curriculum designer. If exercises are selected from pages covering the objective you are teaching, you can be reasonably sure that they have been designed to work well for that objective. It is not easy to make up good exercises for all activities. Take advantage of the text.

Textbooks and other supplementary materials (ancillaries) supplied by publishers usually include evaluation instruments that may be of use for diagnosis, for guiding the pace of your instruction, or for evaluation. At present, such tests are more likely to assess computational skills than conceptual understanding, problem solving, or other process objectives. However, there is a definite effort on the part of publishers to develop better assessments for these higher-order skills.

REFLECTIONS ON CHAPTER 22: WRITING TO LEARN

1. Describe briefly the structure of a student-centered lesson and a teacher-directed lesson. How are the two alike? How are they different? What do you see as the benefits of each? Why is neither the same as "teaching by telling"?

2. How can differences in student abilities be dealt with in the classroom?

3. With respect to cooperative learning groups:

   a. Why are larger groups not likely to work as well as groups of two or three?

   b. What are some of the most important group skills for students to develop for cooperative groups to work effectively? How can students be helped to learn them?

   c. Why are heterogeneous groups better than homogeneous groups?

4. Describe several ways to include writing in mathematics classes.

5. "Practice is not how the skill is learned but rather how the skill becomes more automatic." What does this mean? Provide an example to explain your answer.

6. When and how should homework be used for conceptual development? When and how should it be used for drill and practice? Explain how to use a self-check method of practice for drill-oriented homework.

7. Describe briefly what is meant by the "two-page lesson format" that is often adhered to in traditional basal textbooks. Why is this format generally not in keeping with a chapter or unit perspective for a lesson? What can the teacher do if using a standard text of this sort?

FOR DISCUSSION AND EXPLORATION

1. Examine a textbook for any grade level. Look at a topic for a whole chapter, and determine the two or three main objectives or big ideas covered in the chapter. Restrict yourself to no more than three, and be sure that nearly all topics in the chapter can be built into these big ideas. Now look at the individual lessons. Are the lessons really aimed at the big ideas you have identified? Will the lessons effectively develop the big ideas for this chapter? Try to find two or three tasks or explorations related to the big ideas you have described. If students work on these explorations, how many of the individual lesson objectives will be met?

2. Select a lesson or several related lessons from a textbook. Design both a student-centered and a teacher-directed lesson that is aimed at the objectives of this lesson. Contrast the lesson in the book with each of the

lessons you have designed. Which do you think will be most effective and why? If possible, try the lesson you like the best, and reflect on the effectiveness of your plan.

3. What homework would you design for the lessons you designed in question 2? What would you do with this homework on the following day when it was due?

SUGGESTED READINGS

Highly Recommended

Hart, L. C., Schultz, K., Najee-ullah, D., & Nash, L. (1992). The role of reflection in teaching. *Arithmetic Teacher, 1,* 40–42.

Schroeder, M. L. (1996). Lesson design and reflection. *Mathematics Teaching in the Middle School, 1,* 649–652.

Each of these articles makes the suggestion that to become a better teacher, it is important to reflect on what you actually do as a teacher. Both articles are recommended as a guide for looking at your own teaching, whether you are a novice or an experienced teacher.

Johnson, D. W., Johnson, R. T., & Holubec, E. J. (1993). *Circles of learning: Cooperation in the classroom* (4th ed.). Alexandria, VA: Association for Supervision and Curriculum Development.

This is simply the best available guide for making cooperative learning work in your classroom.

Scheibelhut, C. (1994). I do and I understand, I reflect and I improve. *Teaching Children Mathematics, 1,* 242–246.

The author writes about beginning teachers' learning to incorporate writing into their teaching. In addition to providing useful examples of ways to bring writing into the elementary classroom, Scheibelhut emphasizes the value of reflecting on teaching. In that sense, the article is a good companion to the first two on this list.

Other Suggestions

Artzt, A. F., & Newman, C. M. (1990). *How to use cooperative learning in the mathematics class.* Reston, VA: National Council of Teachers of Mathematics.

Azzolino, A. (1990). Writing as a tool for teaching mathematics: The silent revolution. In T. J. Cooney (Ed.), *Teaching and learning mathematics in the 1990s* (pp. 92–100). Reston, VA: National Council of Teachers of Mathematics.

Behounek, K. J., Rosenbaum, L. J., Brown, L., & Burcalow, J. V. (1988). Our class has twenty-five teachers. *Arithmetic Teacher, 36*(4), 10–13.

Borasi, R., Sheedy, J. R., & Siegel, M. (1990). The power of stories in learning mathematics. *Language Arts, 67,* 174–189.

Davidson, N. (Ed.). (1990). *Cooperative learning in mathematics: A handbook for teachers.* Menlo Park, CA: AWL Supplemental.

Davidson, N. (1990). Small-group cooperative learning in mathematics. In T. J. Cooney (Ed.), *Teaching and learning mathematics in the 1990s* (pp. 52–61). Reston, VA: National Council of Teachers of Mathematics.

Ellis, A. K. (1992). Planning for mathematics instruction. In T. R. Post (Ed.), *Teaching mathematics in grades K–8: Research-based methods* (2nd ed.) (pp. 23–48). Needham Heights, MA: Allyn & Bacon.

Fitzgerald, W. M., & Bouck, M. K. (1993). Models of instruction. In D. T. Owens (Ed.), *Research ideas for the classroom: Middle grades mathematics* (pp. 244–258). Old Tappan NJ: Macmillan.

Helton, S. M. (1995). I thik the citanre will hoder lase: Journal keeping in mathematics class. *Teaching Children Mathematics, 1,* 336–340.

Hill, S., & Hill, T. (1990). *The collaborative classroom: A guide to cooperative learning.* Portsmouth, NH: Heinemann.

Huinker, D., & Laughlin, C. (1996). Talk your way into writing. In P. C. Elliott (Ed.), *Communication in mathematics, K–12 and beyond* (pp. 81–88). Reston, VA: National Council of Teachers of Mathematics.

Johnson, D. W., & Johnson, R. T. (1989). Cooperative learning in mathematics education. In P. R. Trafton (Ed.), *New directions for elementary school mathematics* (pp. 234–245). Reston, VA: National Council of Teachers of Mathematics.

Johnson, D. W., Johnson, R. T., & Holubec, E. J. (1994). *Cooperative learning in the classroom.* Alexandria, VA: Association for Supervision and Curriculum Development.

Keedy, M. L. (1989). Textbooks and curriculum: Whose dilemma? *Arithmetic Teacher, 36*(7), 6.

Leinhardt, G. (1989). Math lessons: A contrast of novice and expert competence. *Journal for Research in Mathematics Education, 20,* 52–75.

Madsen, A. L., & Baker, K. (1993). Planning and organizing the middle grades mathematics curriculum. In D. T. Owens (Ed.), *Research ideas for the classroom: Middle grades mathematics* (pp. 285–302). Old Tappan, NJ: Macmillan.

Newman, V. (1994). *Math journals: Tools for authentic assessment.* San Leandro, CA: Teaching Resource Center.

Norwood, K. S., & Carter, G. (1994). Journal writing: An insight into students' understanding. *Teaching Children Mathematics, 1,* 146–148.

Rowan, T. E., & Cetorelli, N. D. (1990). An eclectic model for teaching elementary school mathematics. In T. J. Cooney (Ed.), *Teaching and learning mathematics in the 1990s* (pp. nnn–nnn). Reston, VA: National Council of Teachers of Mathematics.

Sutton, G. O. (1992). Cooperative learning works in mathematics. *Mathematics Teacher, 85,* 63–66.

Suydam, M. N. (1990). Planning for mathematics instruction. In J. N. Payne (Ed.), *Mathematics for the young child* (pp. 285–302). Reston, VA: National Council of Teachers of Mathematics.

Thornton, C. A. (1991). Think, tell, share: Success for students. *Arithmetic Teacher, 38*(6), 22–23.

Thornton, C. A., & Wilson, S. J. (1993). Classroom organization and models of instruction. In R. J. Jensen (Ed.), *Research ideas for the classroom: Early childhood mathematics* (pp. 269–293). Old Tappan, NJ: Macmillan.

CHAPTER

TEACHING ALL CHILDREN MATHEMATICS

The vision of the NCTM *Standards* is a vision for *all* children, not just the mathematically adept. As noted in the introduction to the *Curriculum and Evaluation Standards for School Mathematics*, a societal goal is opportunity for *all*, not just capable white males. This vision of mathematics for all is clarified in the *Professional Standards for Teaching Mathematics*. One of the four assumptions on which the Teaching Standards are based states:

All students can learn to think mathematically. The goals described in the *Curriculum and Evaluation Standards for School Mathematics* are goals for all students. Goals such as learning to make conjecture, to argue about mathematics using mathematical evidence, to formulate and solve problems—even perplexing ones—and to make sense of mathematical ideas are not just for some group thought to be "bright" or "mathematically able." Every student can—and should—learn to reason and solve problems, to make connections across a rich web of topics and experiences, and to communicate mathematical ideas. By "every student" we mean specifically—

- students who have been denied access in any way to educational opportunities as well as those who have not;

- students who are African-American, Hispanic, American Indian, and other minorities as well as those who are considered to be part of the majority;

- students who are female as well as those who are male;

- students who have not been successful as well as those who have been successful in school and mathematics. (NCTM, 1991, pp. 21–22)

MATHEMATICS FOR ALL CHILDREN

Stop and think for a minute. Do you personally believe the quoted statement? Children with learning disabilities, children from broken and impoverished homes, children with handicaps, minority children—can all of these children learn to think mathematically? The reality is that they most certainly can. It is largely the responsibility of the regular classroom teacher to make that vision a reality.

Diversity in Today's Classroom

It is no longer reasonable to talk about "regular education." It is even difficult to talk about the "average child." In recent years, the range of abilities, handicaps, and socioeconomic circumstances in the regular classroom has posed a significant challenge to teachers. Addressing the needs of *all* children means being sensitive to and providing opportunity for any or all of the following:

- *Students with learning problems.* These may be students who are identified as having a specific learning disability, such as a problem with visual or auditory perception. The range and types of specific learning problems are quite varied. Other children have difficulties learning because they are slow learners or mildly handicapped.

- *Students from different cultural backgrounds.* America is becoming an increasingly multicultural society. Education policymakers have reached no consensus concerning what to do about our multiethnic classrooms. Education remains mostly "mainstream," oriented toward the white middle class, and is not necessarily congruent with other cultures. Yet those are the cultures of the children in our classrooms, the very ones we want to teach.

- *Students who are female.* Girls present the caring teacher with another concern. Traditionally, after about the seventh grade, girls begin to fall behind boys in mathematics, although the difference has decreased in recent years. More troubling is that girls exhibit more hesitancy about mathematics and have poorer self-concepts concerning mathematics than boys do.

- *Students who are mathematically talented.* Nearly every class has at least one child who finds the standard mathematics fairly trivial. These talented children are either bored or constantly providing the answers before others can think. A continued diet of traditional mathematics instruction is not serving this group of students well.

Challenging Traditional Beliefs

Meeting the needs of all children requires that we challenge and perhaps change many of our long-held assumptions about the mathematics curriculum and about how children learn mathematics.

Change Beliefs About the Mathematics Curriculum

Our concept of mathematics as a rule-driven, computation-dominated curriculum actually creates much of the difficulty we have in coping with the range of children's talents and abilities. When every child is required to master each algorithm and memorize every basic fact before being permitted to move on to the next procedure or rule, the more able children in the room are quickly bored. Children at the other extreme begin to doubt that they have any mathematical ability.

Computation can be accomplished through invented procedures or with the aid of technology. Geometry, measurement, probability, statistics, and algebra can all be accessed with minimal computational proficiency. There is neither evidence nor any logical argument for the position that demands computational proficiency as a prerequisite for really important and meaningful mathematics. Furthermore, the computational curriculum of the past is no longer necessary for the daily lives of citizens once they leave school. What is critically important, however, is the ability to reason and solve problems.

Change Beliefs About How Children Learn Mathematics

Traditionally, mathematics instruction has broken content into small, bite-sized increments. Each bit is explained, demonstrated, and then practiced until mastery is achieved and then the next bit is introduced. The belief is that somehow essentially passive children will put the bits together into some sort of cohesive whole. In classrooms for learning-disabled or low-average students, this approach has been even more pronounced and resistant to change. The unfortunate truth is that much of the instruction for children experiencing mathematical difficulties is replete with worksheets and rote drill focused on "basic skills." What we know about how children learn would suggest a quite different approach.

All students should have the opportunity to construct their own mathematical understandings, connecting them uniquely to their own individual knowledge base. Children learn and build understanding of new ideas by integrating meaningful experiences with existing knowledge and understanding. It is their current knowledge that in fact gives meaning to new ideas. Linkages between old and new content are best created through problem-solving experiences that include the new ideas. There is no reason to believe that children with special needs, regardless of the nature of those needs, should learn any differently (Baroody & Hume, 1991; Carey, Fennema, Carpenter, & Franke, 1995; Poplin, 1988a, 1988b; Trafton & Claus, 1994).

When skills rather than problem solving and concepts dominate, teachers find it useful to form ability groups. The results of creating ability groups are usually not as good as teachers believe. The degree of skill variability within each of two or three subgroups is not likely to be significantly less than that for the whole class. Furthermore, children in the lower groups are typically denied opportunities for interacting with their peers in situations involving higher-order thinking or reasoning. The mathematics in the bottom group is generally relegated to skill remediation and isolated practice. There is little or no evidence to support the homogeneous grouping of children within classrooms or the creation of special homogeneous classes (Davidson & Hammerman, 1993; Oakes, 1990; Usiskin, 1993).

> Approaches that appeal to *all* students of mathematics nurture the building of intuitions or sense making and encourage students to attach their own idiosyncratic meanings to the content. Such approaches will be most readily employed by establishing a student-centered classroom environment and by acknowledging, as well as accepting, the loss of some control of the direction of a lesson. To do so requires that the teacher be flexible and willing to take some risks. (Speer & Brahier, 1994, p. 49)

CHILDREN WITH LEARNING PROBLEMS

The federal law that guarantees access to appropriate education for all children is the Individuals with Disabilities Education Act (IDEA, also known as PL 101-476), which was passed in 1990. IDEA amended the 1975 law (Education of the Handicapped Act, PL 94-142) and gave preference to the term *disabled* instead of *handicapped*. The general thrust of these laws is to meet the educational needs of children with special needs in the "least restrictive environment."

Categories of Disabilities

Children bring to the classroom an enormous array of difficulties and differences based on both environmental and psychological factors. Each child is unique in his or her own way and should be regarded as such. IDEA provides legal definitions for a wide range of disabilities, including autism, mental disability (mental retardation, or MR), specific learning disabilities (LD), and various physical disabilities such as hearing or vision impairment and orthopedic handicaps. In 1991, the law was clarified to include children with attention deficit disorder (ADD) and attention-deficit hyperactivity disorder (ADHD). It is not necessary to examine these definitions of disability in this text.

The IDEA definitions of disabilities are used to determine which children are eligible for special services. A wide range of support is available to eligible students, including placement in specialized self-contained classrooms; time with a specialist such as an LD resource teacher, vision teacher, or speech teacher; or access to specialized equipment (e.g., desks for the orthopedically disabled, talking calculators for the visually impaired).

Regular classroom teachers need not be expert in all of the potential disabilities they may confront. However, any given class is likely to have a variety of children with special learning problems.

Inclusion or Referral?

Although IDEA provides special services for eligible students, the "least restrictive environment" is increasingly the regular classroom. Moreover, there are many children with special learning needs that are not eligible under the law, and they will also require the special attention of the regular classroom teacher (Downs, Matthew, & McKinney, 1994).

With the practice of placement in special classes or resource pull-out programs seen as less and less desirable, the regular classroom teacher faces increasing problems. This is not to say that help is not available. Every classroom teacher should become very familiar with the special resources available. Referral to the school's instructional support or consultation team should always be considered. The objective should be to secure assistance and, most important, information about the child. The more a teacher knows about the nature of a child's learning difficulties, the better prepared that teacher will be to help.

Inclusion or collaborative models where the resource or special education teacher works full or part time in the regular classroom as a teaching partner with the regular teacher are becoming more and more popular. Help for the regular teacher may also come in the form of ideas for instructional modifications or adaptations, and special equipment, manipulatives, computer programs, or supplementary curriculum materials may be available through the various specialists in the school.

As more and more children with special needs are included in regular classrooms, "the distinction between special and regular education will soon become obsolete" (Greenes, Garfunkel, & De Bussey, 1994, p. 133). The loud and clear message should be, "Get help." Find out about how the special children in your classroom learn.

Rather than be defeated by the reality of a diverse class of children, consider the real benefits of an inclusion model (Borasi, 1994):

- Regular students serve as learning models for special students.
- Special students frequently offer unique alternative solutions to challenging problems encountered by the full class or in small cooperative groups.
- All students develop an awareness of and respect for individual differences.
- All students, not just the "regular" students, are exposed to good mathematics and challenging experiences.

SPECIFIC LEARNING DISABILITIES

The predominant instructional model for learning-disabled students has historically viewed the learner as essentially passive, with the mastery of skills taking precedence over understanding (Poplin, 1988a). It is this thinking that led to pull-out and self-contained classroom approaches because the tight control over content and a mastery-learning approach to atomized content demanded methods difficult to deliver in the regular classroom. As we have already noted, these skills-oriented models have proved to produce very limited results.

Poplin's conclusion is that constructivist theory, not behaviorism, provides the best directions for teachers of special students. That same suggestion is made either implicitly or explicitly by nearly every author in NCTM's excellent book *Windows of Opportunity: Mathematics for Students with Special Needs* (Thornton & Bley, 1994). Put simply, there is no need to change the content of the curriculum for students with learning disabilities. There are real benefits to including special children in the regular classroom—benefits not just for the special students but for all students. It is clear that these children can learn. What must be done is to do what all good constructivist teachers do, and that is pay careful attention to the child and how he or she learns and design instruction (not content) that maximizes the strengths of the child while minimizing the impact of weaknesses.

A Perspective on Learning Disabilities

Students with learning disabilities have very specific problems with perceptual or cognitive processing. These problems may affect memory or the ability to speak or express ideas in writing, perceive auditory or written information, or integrate abstract ideas. It is insufficient simply to label a child "LD." The following insights offered by Borasi (1994) are an important point of departure for teachers who have learning-disabled children in their classes:

• Learning-disabled students are mentally capable; they are not slow or retarded.

• Specific learning disabilities are many and varied. The classification of LD is not useful to the classroom teacher without a clear understanding of the child's specific learning problem.

• Learning disabilities are not easily remediated and perhaps cannot be remediated.

• Learning disabilities should be compensated for by helping students use their strengths.

• Instructional modifications will be needed to accommodate the specific needs of children with specific learning disabilities.

Borasi suggests that teachers accept the fact that learning disabilities are real in the same sense that being blind or deaf is a real disability. You would not ask a blind person to "look more closely" or a deaf person to "listen more carefully." Hence we should never ask a learning-disabled child to do things that depend heavily on his or her area of deficit.

Adaptations for Specific Learning Difficulties

Table 23.1 identifies specific disabilities and gives a few examples of the mathematical problems that each might cause. Note that deficits or disabilities may be present as auditory problems, visual problems, or sometimes both. It is important that the teacher have as much detailed information as possible about children who have specific learning difficulties. The school psychologist is the principal source of information. If the child has already been evaluated by the psychologist, test information will be available to help pinpoint specific weaknesses and also strengths. Working with the psychologist, you can find ways to adapt instructional strategies to avoid weaknesses and capitalize on strengths *without major modification of the curriculum.*

Adaptations for Perceptual Deficits

There are many variations of perceptual problems; some are visual and others auditory. All involve confusion of input in one way or another. Children with *figure-ground* difficulties have trouble sorting out or recognizing component parts of what they see or hear. *Discrimination* difficulties refer to the inability to discern differences in things seen or heard. Children with *reversal* problems have difficulty with left-right perceptions and tend to see things in mirror images of what they really are. *Spatial* organization deficits affect children's ability to interpret or implement the positions and arrangements of things. Spatially challenged children have difficulty not only with geometric models and drawings but also with organizing their own writing on paper.

The entire area of perceptual problems is perhaps the clearest area where the maxim "avoid weaknesses and capitalize on strengths" is best observed. The following are simply a few specific suggestions:

• Seat the child near you and the chalkboard.

• Keep the child's desk or workspace free of clutter.

• Maintain a moderate voice. Repeat main ideas.

• Structure text or worksheet pages for the child. Provide templates to block out all but one problem or exercise at a time. (Cut a rectangle in the center of a half-sheet of tagboard. Make several templates with different-sized holes, and have the child keep them in his or her text.)

• Help design methods of organizing written work. Have computations done on centimeter grid paper writing one number per square. Provide paper with columns or drawn templates such as those found in the Blackline Masters for traditional algorithms.

• Use a tape recorder (headphones) with instructions explaining what may be difficult to discern from the available visual materials.

• Provide real geometric models whenever possible instead of relying on pictures in the text. Use geoboards and tiles such as pattern blocks for constructions so that drawing will be kept to a minimum.

• Assign a buddy to help read, explain, or repeat directions.

Adaptations for Memory Deficits

Memory deficits can also be specifically visual or auditory. Some children may have more difficulty recalling things seen than things heard, or vice versa. Children with *short-term memory* deficits can have trouble recalling things for even a few seconds, as when copying from the board or recalling information in a word problem. Lengthy directions are also a problem. *Long-term memory* deficits are quite different. Children with this disability may show no difficulty with material when presented but appear to have not learned at all a day or a week later. Mastery of basic facts is a hallmark problem for children with this disability. *Sequential memory* problems refer to the inability to retain an order to a sequence of events or a series of steps in directions or procedures. These children are likely to ask, "What do I do next?" when working on a computation or extending a pattern. It is important to distinguish this inability to retain order from a lack of understanding.

TABLE **23.1**   EXAMPLES OF SPECIFIC LEARNING DISABILITIES
AND THEIR POSSIBLE EFFECTS ON PERFORMANCE IN MATHEMATICS

DISABILITY	VISUAL DEFICIT	AUDITORY DEFICIT
Perceptual Figure-ground	• May not finish page or loses place • Has difficulty reading multidigit number	• Has trouble hearing patterns in counting • Has difficulty attending to classroom discourse
Discrimination	• Has difficulty differentiating coins • Has difficulty with numeral identification such as 2 for 5 or 3 for 8 • Mixes operation symbols	• Has trouble distinguishing between similar-sounding words, such as *thirty* and *thirteen*
Reversal	• Reverses digits in numbers • Has difficulty in regrouping	
Spatial	• Has trouble writing on lined paper • Fails to notice size differences in shapes (fractions or geometry) • Has difficulty writing numbers, especially fractions and decimals	
Memory Short-term	• Has difficulty retaining newly presented material • Has difficulty copying problems from the board. • Has difficulty remembering facts in a word problem	• Has difficulty with oral drills • Has trouble with dictated assignments
Long-term	• Has difficulty retaining basic facts or procedures over long period • Has difficulty solving multioperational computation (written or mental)	
Sequential	• Has difficulty following through a long or multistep procedure such as computational algorithms • Has difficulty solving multistep word problems	• Cannot retain story problems that are dictated
Integrative Closure	• Has difficulty visualizing groups • Has difficulty with missing addends and missing factors • Is unable to draw conclusions and so has trouble noticing and continuing patterns • Has difficulty with word problems • Has trouble continuing counting patterns from within a sequence	• Has difficulty counting on from within a sequence
Expressive language	• Finds rapid oral skills difficult	• Has difficulty counting on • Has difficulty with explanations
Receptive language	• Has difficulty relating words to meaning • Has difficulty with words having multiple meanings	• Has difficulty relating words to meanings • Has difficulty writing numbers from dictation
Abstract reasoning	• Is unable to solve word problems • Is unable to compare numbers in symbolic form • Cannot understand problems	

Source: Adapted from Bley & Thornton (1995, pp. 8–9).

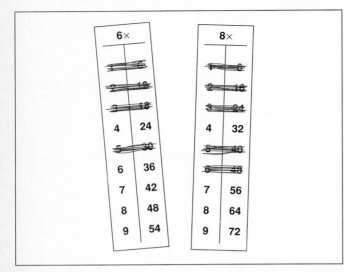

● **FIGURE 23.1**   *Permit the use of fact charts, but encourage memorization.*

You can diminish the load on short-term memory by breaking tasks and directions into small steps and providing a buddy to help with recall. Long-term memory problems require overlearning, frequent practice, and as many associations with other ideas as possible. The following more specific suggestions may be useful:

- Rather than a series of instructions, provide only one at a time. With good planning, sequenced instructions can be written out ahead of time.
- When teaching a specific procedure such as an algorithm, create a model exercise showing each step. Work with the student to create the model and the labels for each step.
- For basic facts, use strategies and number relationships (see Chapter 8). Provide fact charts as shown in Figure 23.1, crossing out facts that are mastered.
- Provide complete freedom to use a calculator at all times.

Memory deficits tend to be exhibited in procedural work. Remember that no routine procedural knowledge, including mastery of basic facts, should prevent a student from progress in mathematical ideas. Exploration of new concepts is never dependent on mastery of skills.

Adaptations for Integrative Deficits

Children with integrative problems seem to have difficulty with abstract ideas and conceptualization. Remember that these children are not slow or retarded, but they have difficulty making the cognitive connections that others may find easy. Children with an integrative disorder may do quite well at rote procedures such as computational algorithms, but these are no longer the focus of the mathematics curriculum. A general principle for helping these children integrate concepts and develop understanding is similar to a whole-language approach and is not unlike the methods espoused for a good constructivist classroom. In short, help

students use experiences and ideas most familiar to them: their own invented procedures for solving problems, familiar models or personal drawings that make sense to them, and their own words in either written or oral form to express their ideas. As noted, these are good approaches for all children. The following more specific approaches may be helpful for children with integrative difficulties:

- Use familiar physical models for longer than the usual period of time.
- Have students verbalize what they do as often as possible. Use both written and oral expression.
- Frequently require explanations and justifications. This self-monitoring can heighten the children's awareness of new ideas, and the verbalization can aid in making connections.
- Allow for repetition or practice of new conceptual ideas.

Adaptations for Attention Deficits

Many (not all) students with learning disabilities also are identified as having attention deficit disorder (ADD) or attention-deficit hyperactivity disorder (ADHD). These children have chronic difficulties with attention span, impulse control, and sometimes hyperactivity. The symptoms can begin early and extend through adulthood. Teachers should be careful to distinguish these true disorders from the behavior of children who are discipline problems for other reasons. The following are a few strategies that have proved useful:

- Establish clear routines, and discuss them with the child. Make expectations and consequences clear.
- Design learning activities that are active and involved rather than tedious or requiring lengthy periods of silent seatwork.
- Plan for the child to do independent work in an environment free of visual and auditory distractions (a seat near a blank wall, away from classmates, for example).
- Use highlighters to attract attention to important key ideas in textual material.
- Keep assignments short. Shorten exercise lists. Plan smaller subtasks within larger explorations or projects.
- Assign a buddy, and impress on both that the agenda is to stay on task.
- Instead of placing the child in a cooperative group of three or four, use a buddy to form a separate group of two. Larger groups have more distractions and require more patience while others talk.

MENTAL DISABILITIES

All of us possess different mental capacities in addition to our individual strengths and weaknesses or learning styles. Children with mental disabilities (generally with IQ scores between 50 and 70) will be limited in the kind and degree of mathematical reasoning they can perform. Other children not as severely limited are sometimes labeled *slow learners.* Although severely disabled children are generally best served in a special classroom, a wide range of mental disabilities are likely to be present in the regular classroom.

Modifications in Instruction

Limited cognitive abilities do not in any way alter the way that children learn. However, those with mental disabilities will learn much more slowly than children with normal intelligence and will much more quickly reach a plateau with respect to the mathematical ideas they can work with (Bley, 1994; Callahan & MacMillan, 1981). These children are likely to have limited memory, attention, and language abilities to assist them in the development of new ideas.

Though a fast-paced, highly interactive classroom may be somewhat overwhelming for slower children, they can benefit from many of the same experiences as the rest of the class. They can and should participate in projects and hands-on activities with their peer group. They can participate in cooperative groups by taking on less demanding roles, such as materials organizer or encourager. They can learn to perform calculations on a calculator and can serve as the person in a group who performs this activity. Many disabled children are good at drawing or making graphs. These helping roles are consistent with the kinds of jobs they are likely to have in the adult world.

Making expectations clear, simple, and appropriate for the child is another important consideration. Within any activity planned for the class, find subtasks or related activities appropriate for the disabled child. Clearly explain these expectations using simple directions. Have the child repeat the expectations in his or her own words.

Partner the disabled child with different students periodically, and have the partner help the child with the same task or idea. In this way, there is opportunity for needed repeated exposure or "overlearning," and other students also will gain from serving as the explainer. It is important for all children in the room to involve slower-learning children in activities and projects. The slow child gains from the richer ideas and interactions and will frequently contribute alternative solutions or ideas. All children gain an appreciation for and acceptance of human differences.

Modifications in Curriculum

Since mentally disabled children learn much more slowly than other children, it follows that less content can be learned during the years they are in school. It makes sense to focus the available instructional time on those areas that are going to be of the most value to these students as adults. Computational skill is the most obvious area where changes

in curricular expectations should be made. There is no reason to be obsessive about fact mastery. Traditional computational algorithms can be eliminated from their curriculum altogether.

Students should be taught to have a calculator handy for all mathematics work. The disabled child should be given careful instruction and lots of practice in using the calculator. A calculator with a printer is useful because it creates a printed record of work done. These students can do the same exercises that others are doing but do them with a calculator.

An area that should be stressed is the relationship of number to the real world. Whereas calculations can be mastered via the calculator, the meanings of numbers in the real world cannot. Do not confuse number meaning with place-value concepts. What is important here is to realize that a bag of flour weighs 5 pounds, that $100 buys a pair of fancy sneakers, or that it takes about 20 minutes to walk a mile. Numbers in the abstract will be of little use.

MULTICULTURAL AND SOCIAL EQUITY

Traditionally, we have assumed that of all the subjects in the curriculum, mathematics was the most likely to be culturally neutral. After all, 2 + 2 = 4 is a logical fact having little to do with ethnicity or poverty. At the same time, there is clear evidence that African-American, Hispanic, and Native American children and children from homes with low socioeconomic status (SES) do poorly in mathematics (Hilliard, 1995; Oakes, 1990, 1995). Do children belonging to these groups not have the same mathematical or even general academic ability as their white, middle-class suburban counterparts? There is no evidence to support such a view, yet discrepancies in achievement levels in mathematics remain a fact.

A Question of Access

Students in at-risk populations (non-Asian ethnicities and low SES) are simply not getting the same access to quality teachers, to adequate resources and technology, or to quality curriculum as their middle- and upper-class suburban counterparts.

Access to Quality Teachers

According to Oakes (1990, 1995), low-income and minority students are not being taught mathematics or science by high-quality teachers. It is more difficult to convince quality teachers to accept jobs in predominantly minority schools, and turnover is greater because these schools are seen as less desirable places in which to teach. Tracking (to be discussed shortly) is also a source of teacher quality discrepancies.

Nearly all schools tend to place their least qualified teachers in low-ability classes. In fact, Oakes (1990) reports that "low-track students in the most advantaged schools are likely to have better-qualified teachers than high-track students in the least-advantaged schools" (p. 67).

Teachers do exist who are able to help traditionally at-risk students achieve at the highest levels without any special "minority training," without special technology, and without special texts or materials.

> For some teachers, the surprising reality is that the low achievers change not because of the invention of some culturally specific exotic new method, but because many of them are exposed to regular high-quality instruction, to which many of the traditionally low performers had not been previously exposed. (Hilliard, 1995, p. 109)

Access to Resources

The disparity in school spending between schools located in areas with low- versus high-income families is increasing. Most low-income and minority children attend schools where fewer dollars have been spent (Oakes, 1995). The result is felt in terms of inadequate facilities, larger class size, inadequate equipment such as computers and CD-ROMs, and fewer materials. There are examples where huge sums of money have been lavished on disadvantaged schools with little success. These counterexamples notwithstanding, the lack of resources has to have some effect on instruction, if only in terms of teacher and student attitudes toward school. Computers, the Internet, and the World Wide Web are now such important assets in everyday life that access to these technologies is becoming a must rather than a desirable option.

Access to Curriculum

Evidence suggests that teachers in minority schools tend to place less emphasis on curricular goals such as inquiry and problem solving. Differences apparently occur in both pace or coverage of content as well as emphasis on lower-level skills instead of higher-order thinking and engaging, meaningful explorations. Beginning in the junior high school, the curriculum access issue can be told in terms of available courses. Fewer algebra courses, for example, are taught in low-SES and predominantly minority schools, making access to higher-level mathematics courses in the secondary schools more difficult. In elementary schools, the differences have to be caused primarily by choices of emphasis that teachers make within the standard curricular materials and by the outside resources that are available to enrich the curriculum.

Expectations

It remains true that students will rise or fall to the level of our expectations. Two related factors seem to be working against minority and low-SES students: teachers' beliefs in their abilities and the effects of tracking or homogeneous grouping.

Teacher Expectations

Among teachers of at-risk children, there is a striking difference between those who believe in the abilities of their students and those who expect very little. The latter group of teachers have found it easy to blame the performance of their students on the myriad factors that exist outside the classroom. *It's the neighborhood. They don't have two parents making them work. The parents are not educated. These kids come from an environment infested with drugs.* Teachers who voice such laments are using real facts as excuses for not making a difference. "They are allowing the students' circumstances to define their possibilities" (Ladson-Billings, 1995, p. 139). If the excuses were valid, no teachers would believe in their students, yet many do and achieve outstanding results.

Experts believe that one of the most important factors for success with disadvantaged or minority students is to develop in them a strong sense of self-esteem, helping children believe in themselves. This is an incredibly difficult task for the teacher whose expectations are low to begin with.

Negative Effects of Tracking and Homogeneous Grouping

Teachers' assessments of students' abilities play a key role in deciding what types of educational experiences a student may receive. Tracking, curricular access, and belief systems are interrelated. Once students are placed in a lower-level track or in a "slow" class, expectations decline accordingly. Students in low tracks are frequently denied access to challenging material and high-quality mathematics (Silver, Smith, & Nelson, 1995). The mathematics for the lower tracks or classes is almost totally oriented toward remedial skills. The result is day after day of drill with minimal success and no excitement. Teachers become reinforced in their low expectations because students are not encouraged to think, nor are they engaged in activities and interactions that would encourage thinking.

To highlight the negative effects of tracking, Usiskin (1993) described a process of placing students in "special" classes beginning in the early grades of his own child's elementary school. Placements in the "high" class were made on the basis of tests of traditional skills given at the end of the previous year. During the year, the high class spent less time reviewing old material and more time on problem-solving experiences. With more time, they covered more material. At the end of each year, testing was repeated for all students and new placements made. To the surprise of no one, the students in the high class were predominantly the ones who placed into the high class each subsequent year. Usiskin argues that the experiences in the high class were not exceptional and were appropriate for all of the students. Expectations based on the grouping process simply provided greater access to good mathematics. That very first simple skill test, not at all based on higher-order thinking or mathematics, preempted the majority of students from quality experiences from which all could benefit. The reverse phenomenon occurs when students are placed in low or remedial groups. Lower expectations restrict access to quality mathematics and lead to instruction actually targeted at lower achievement.

In addition to the effect on expectations, tracking severely diminishes the potential for valuable interactions in the classroom. Based on their experiences in a small but very diverse school, Davidson and Hammerman (1993) argue that heterogeneity enriches experiences for all students. Different viewpoints and problem solutions from an array of ability levels provide opportunities for all to learn. In their school, class discussions tend to focus a bit above the middle of the group, keeping work challenging for top and midrange children. Students at the lower end get to see and experience what higher-level interactions are like. Many times, expectations are turned upside down as children usually perceived as less able come to understand and work meaningfully with concepts to which they would never be exposed in a low-track homogeneous class. Furthermore, exposing all students to higher-level thinking and quality mathematics avoids accentuating differences from year to year caused by low-track expectations.

Examples of What Works

What we have learned over the years from massive federal programs that have failed is that narrow, skill-focused, highly prescriptive approaches do not work. We have also seen that programs within schools or school systems that target disadvantaged kids by grouping them in special classrooms do not work. We can point to some recent examples of programs and the efforts of individual teachers that have worked exceptionally well with urban, minority, low-SES children. The common factors in these programs are not money, curriculum, materials, technology, or tracking. What makes them succeed is a constructivist approach to instruction and a positive belief in the children.

The three examples described here are just that—examples. Many more success stories could be told, but most exhibit the same instructional characteristics of these examples.

Project IMPACT: CGI in an Urban Setting

Cognitively Guided Instruction (CGI) is a program developed at the University of Wisconsin in the mid-1980s. It is based on the belief that if "teachers had research-based knowledge about children's thinking in general, they would be more able to focus on individual children" (Carey et al., 1995, p. 101). The program is not a curriculum. It focuses on helping teachers listen to how children think and determine what they know and understand. Based on this knowledge of individual children, teachers try to build mathematics ideas on the considerable mathematical understanding that all children naturally bring to school.

Beginning in 1990, the CGI philosophy and approach were brought to three predominantly minority urban public schools outside of Washington, D.C. The schools were quite diverse in their ethnic makeup and included students speaking a wide variety of languages. Project IMPACT (Increasing the Mathematical Power of All Children and Teachers) began in grades K–3 and later extended to grade 5. The teachers were trained in CGI techniques during the summer and were supported by a specialist in the schools during the year. Teachers in the project came to recognize that every child, regardless of background or SES, has mathematical knowledge.

The CGI method is essentially a constructivist approach based on the theory that ideas grow as children solve problems using their existing knowledge. IMPACT teachers would frequently propose a task, problem, or investigation; provide an opportunity to work on or consider the task; and then ask questions: *What do you see? Tell us something else about this problem. What do you know? What else do you know? Tell us your thinking. What could we try? Does anyone have a different idea or notice something else about this problem?* All responses were valued by being listened to without judgment or evaluation. All children were expected to be active listeners, and all were called on to participate. When a child was reluctant, students and teacher would be patient until a response was made. IMPACT schools used no tracking, and there was no grouping in the classrooms (Campbell, P. F., 1993).

Students in IMPACT were not taught traditional algorithms, nor was there any stress on basic facts and skills. On standardized tests, children excelled at problem solving and concepts and were about average in skill development. A striking effect is the confidence in being able to do mathematics that the children displayed. Teachers also became true believers that all children could do mathematics and could think mathematically (Campbell, P. F., 1996).

The QUASAR Project

QUASAR (Quantitative Understanding: Amplifying Student Achievement and Reasoning), begun in 1989, was a large reform project for middle schools. It was aimed strictly at schools in economically disadvantaged communities and attempted to improve the participation and performance in mathematics of females, ethnic minorities, and the poor. The belief was that these groups have traditionally failed due primarily to a lack of "access to meaningful, high-quality experiences with mathematics learning" (Silver, Smith, & Nelson, 1995, p. 10). QUASAR believed that virtually all students can learn middle school mathematics and move on to a challenging program at the secondary level.

The instruction in QUASAR schools was aimed at improving thinking, reasoning, and problem solving. Tasks were designed with multiple entry points and multiple paths to solutions, allowing for heterogeneous classrooms to participate fully in developing solutions. There was an emphasis on communication and discourse in the creation of classroom communities where thinking and reasoning are valued and risk takers are made to feel safe.

One change that QUASAR made in each of its sites was nearly to eliminate the entrenched practice of academic tracking. Teachers came to recognize that tracking tends to work to the detriment of the students. A teacher at one site noted that "a lot of the kids that are classified as lost, or turned off, or unintelligent, or whatever, really have some powerful ideas and some powerful ways of thinking, and exposing the other kids to that and them to the ways the other kids think is just too powerful to overlook" (Silver et al., 1995, p. 28). To aid in handling the diversity of the classroom, many teachers used heterogeneous cooperative groups. In one classroom, test scores on a standardized test ranged from the 15th to the 98th percentile. Posters in the room suggested phrases that all students were to use: *Good answer. You can do it! You're on the right track. Give it a try. We'll help you through it.* Trust and mutual respect were key features of the program. Fear of giving wrong answers eventually disappears in this kind of atmosphere as students learn that there is no such thing as a "dumb question" or a "bad answer." Communication and sense making are the focus more than getting correct answers.

Teachers began to call the QUASAR project the "revolution of the possible."

Impact of a Single Teacher

For an individual teacher, there is comfort and value in being part of a project that promotes the kind of teaching described in each of the preceding projects. There are colleagues with whom to discuss troubles and fears. But for the majority of teachers, the only project will be the one they initiate in their own rooms.

Ms. Rossi is a veteran sixth-grade teacher in a low-SES, predominantly African-American school. She is one of eight teachers studied by Ladson-Billings (1995) who are effective working with African-American students. In one lesson, Ladson-Billings notes that Rossi made a point of involving all students individually, continually assuring them that they were capable of mastering the problems. Students cheered one another and celebrated explanations. Students were pushed to explain "How do you know?" The textbook curriculum may have been followed, but the text was generally not used. Rossi would help students see that what they had been doing was the same as what was in the text. The point was always that mathematics was not threatening and that the students were capable of good mathematics and quality thinking.

Based on her study of effective teachers, Ladson-Billings lists five guidelines or principles for the successful teaching of students who are traditionally at risk of failing:

1. *Have high expectations for all students, letting them know that you believe in them.* If you treat students as competent, they are likely to demonstrate competence.

2. *Use "instructional scaffolding."* Instead of worrying about what students do not know, work from what they do know toward what they do not know.

3. *Make instruction the focus of each class.* Avoid busywork. Confront restlessness with an adjustment in instruction rather than a focus on misbehavior.

4. *Extend students' thinking and abilities beyond what they already know.* Instead of attempting to maintain students' low levels of performance, provide challenging mathematics for all students.

5. *Work at gaining in-depth knowledge of your students as well as knowledge of the subject matter.* Develop a positive identification with all students. Learn to see students of different ethnicities as being like you rather than trying to make minority children "fit in."

Again you notice principles of developmental or constructivist teaching, belief in students, and challenging curriculum. The fifth principle applies to multicultural student populations. It dictates respect for culture, without which the other suggestions may well fail.

FROM GENDER BIAS TO GENDER EQUITY

Most elementary and middle school teachers work with both boys and girls, and most are aware of few, if any, differences between the sexes. Yet when careful comparisons were made over the years, real differences between boys and girls emerged. Elementary school girls have traditionally outperformed boys on standardized tests, although their lead disappears around the seventh grade. By the time of entry to college, many more boys than girls are entering fields of study that include heavy emphases on mathematics and science. Furthermore, there persists a common belief in our society that boys are better than girls at mathematics, or what Damarin (1995) refers to as the "maleness of mathematics." In an age in which the ability to reason and solve problems, a knowledge of technology, and competence with general mathematical ideas are all demanded for an ever-increasing majority of jobs, it is more vital than ever that teachers address the issues surrounding gender inequity in mathematics.

Defining the Problem of Gender Inequity

Three possible areas of inequity can be examined: differences in achievement, differences in beliefs and attitudes, and differences in representation in mathematics, science, and related careers.

Achievement

Twenty-five years ago, concern over differences in mathematics achievement between males and females led some observers to suggest that girls were perhaps not as "capable" of doing mathematics as boys. As noted, research indicated that girls tended to outperform boys until the junior high years, equaled them in early algebra, and began to lag well behind in geometry and beyond. When the range of performance was examined (instead of the average), the top and bottom levels were about the same for males and females. Thus it was not true that girls were outperformed but rather that more boys than girls did well (Burton, 1995).

Further study has indicated that a large part of the differences noted earlier could be attributed to fewer girls taking mathematics courses in the high school years. When courses taken is factored into the data, differences diminish. In recent years, gender differences in mathematics achievement have almost disappeared.

Despite that development, two facts remain. First, differences among girls are significantly greater than differences among boys. There are still many girls who for one reason or another are not achieving well. Second, the perception that boys are better at mathematics remains a seemingly intractable trait of our society.

There is no convincing evidence of a biological or genetic basis for gender differences in mathematics achievement.

Beliefs and Attitudes

The educational system does seem to have an effect on how girls view mathematics. As girls move into the upper grades, they report they like mathematics less and have more self-doubts concerning their personal abilities than boys do. Self-doubts and poor self-concepts concerning mathematics lead to further problems. For example, girls are less likely to persist on challenging tasks than boys are. Weak self-concepts are likely to diminish participation in classroom interactions and group problem solving (Leder, 1995).

Societal norms of the past have another lingering negative effect. In a 1988 study of 9-year-olds, girls were just as likely as boys to say that they were good at mathematics. However, the girls were much less likely to say that mathematics would be useful in their future careers. In general, girls are much more ambivalent concerning the value of mathematics as an occupational prerequisite (Burton, 1995; Leder, 1995). If, as early as age 9, you regard the study of mathematics as irrelevant to your future, this will undoubtedly have an effect on your cognitive efforts and the courses you select at the secondary and college levels.

Underreprezsentation

Choices that students make in terms of coursework and career decisions continue to reflect real differences between the sexes. While it is true girls are taking more mathematics courses, "differences in favor of male enrollments continue

to be reported for higher-level and more intensive mathematics courses, related applied fields, and occupations that require mathematical sophistication" (Leder, 1995, p. 213). By opting out of advanced courses in high school, females are effectively excluded from a wide range of college options. Even when the actual mathematics knowledge is not the real issue, mathematics is often used as a filter for entrance into certain demanding career paths. "Equating intelligence with [mathematics] achievement keeps women out of well-paid, high status fields which they would find interesting and exciting and for which they have the talent" (Tyrrell et al., 1994, p. 332). The result has been a substantially unequal distribution of the sexes across careers.

The serious gender gap in upper-level mathematics courses and in career patterns is perhaps the most serious issue in the entire gender equity discussion. With evidence ruling out a genetic difference or the existence of a "math gene," women are still not embarking on career paths that are among the most valuable in today's economy.

Possible Causes of Gender Inequity

If the problem is not genetic, we should look to the educational system for the causes of gender inequity. The discussions that follow offer some insights.

Teacher Interactions and Gender

Observations of teachers' gender-specific interactions in the classroom indicate that boys get more attention and different kinds of attention than girls do. Boys receive more criticism as well as more praise for correct answers. Boys also tend to be more involved in discipline-related attention and have their work monitored more carefully (Campbell, P. B., 1995; Leder, 1995). The increased attention that teachers unconsciously provide males, both positive and negative, contributes to the impression of mathematics as a male domain. Attention is interpreted as value, with a predictable effect on both sexes.

Research has found that teachers wait longer for responses from boys than from girls (Leder, 1995). In one study, females received more wait time on low-level questions concerning facts and procedures, whereas males received longer wait times on more difficult, more challenging, and higher-cognitive questions. Over time, these subtle but real differences suggest to girls that they are not perceived as capable of quality thinking and eventually adopt this belief themselves.

Belief Systems Related to Gender

The belief that mathematics is a male domain persists in our society and is held by both sexes. The "maleness of mathematics" as viewed by males can have negative effects in school. In adolescent years, when girls are significantly interested in and influenced by boys, many girls are afraid to act "too smart" for fear of alienating boys. P. B. Campbell (1995) points out that "unless boys as well as girls are convinced that 'real women do math,' efforts toward gender equity in mathematics will encounter obstacles based on stereotyped social roles" (p. 229).

There is evidence that teachers' and parents' erroneous belief that girls can't do math has a transfer effect on girls. It is easy for a mother to reinforce this belief in her daughter and to suggest that it is not important to excel at mathematics "because you're a girl." Teachers and counselors make similar subtle and sometimes not so subtle comments that cumulatively convince girls that they are not good at mathematics or that mathematics and science are male domains.

Working Toward Gender Equity: What Can Be Done?

P. B. Campbell (1995) makes a compelling argument that we have tended to address gender inequity as a "girl problem." This places the focus of our solution efforts on girls—to make them somehow like mathematics more, to take more courses in mathematics. This approach, she says, makes it seem that there really is something wrong with girls that needs to be fixed. "If you change a girl so that she 'loves math,' but then you put her back into the same environment and situations that caused her to hate mathematics in the first place, she will revert to hating mathematics" (p. 226). As already noted, the causes of girls' perceptions of themselves vis-à-vis mathematics is largely a function of the educational environment. That is where we should look for solutions.

Become Aware

Few, if any teachers, purposely engage in gender-specific actions that would have a negative effect on girls, and yet many teachers do report that even as early as the first grade, if a boy is good at mathematics, it is taken as a reflection of mathematical ability, whereas if a girl excels, it is seen as the result of personal efforts. This differential belief system can be transmitted in the manner that praise is given: "Wow, Mark! You really are showing how smart you are" versus "Margie, I am glad to see how hard you worked on this problem" (Fennema, Peterson, Carpenter, & Lubinski, 1990).

As a teacher, you need to be aware if you treat boys and girls differently and work at ensuring equal treatment. Balance the number of questions and overall interactions between boys and girls. A simple approach is to keep a mental tally of girls and boys asked questions. If discipline problems tend to draw more attention to boys, work at being less preoccupied with the boys' disturbances. Instead of reacting to the boys causing trouble, increase your attention to the girls.

Being aware of your gender-specific actions is more difficult than it may sound. To receive feedback, try tape-recording a class or two on a periodic basis. Tally the number of questions asked of boys and girls. Also note which students ask questions and what kind of questions are being asked. At first, you will be surprised at how gender-biased your interaction is. Awareness takes effort.

Focus on Higher-Level Questioning

Shift from telling to asking. Focus your student interactions on higher-level questioning and problem-solving activities instead of lecture followed by practice. Be certain to be equally interested in the ideas of all students. It requires extra time, especially at the upper grades, to increase questioning and deemphasize telling. When teachers feel this pressure of time and the need to "cover the material," girls are more likely to sense this pressure and avoid asking questions.

Stress understanding for all students. Move from questions that focus on the answer to questions that probe thinking and understanding. Ask, "How did you get that?" instead of "What answer did you get?" Help all children understand, not just those (mostly males) who seek clarification. Instead of asking, "Are there any questions?" address individuals, especially girls: "Sally, do you have any questions?" The latter approach shows interest in the individual addressed and emphasizes your value of understanding over coverage.

Involve All Students

Find ways to involve all students in your class, not just those who seem eager. Girls tend to shy away from involvement and are not as quick to seek help. The use of physical materials can be a way for all students to be active at the same time and to develop self-confidence and for you to observe the thinking of each student. Cooperative learning groups are another way to encourage involvement. Use mixed-gender groups to avoid gender-oriented competition between groups and to increase boy-girl interactions. Neither suggestion is an automatic solution, however. With physical materials, all students must be required to be active. Similarly, cooperative groups must be continually monitored and evaluated to ensure that all students are participating.

Other assistance can be found from the EQUALS program (Lawrence Hall of Science, University of California, Berkeley, CA 94705) and GESA (Gender Ethnic Expectations/Student Achievement) (GESA, Graymill Foundation, Rt. 1, Box 45, Earlham, IA 50072).

MATHEMATICS FOR THE GIFTED AND TALENTED

Children who are typically known as "gifted" no doubt deserve special consideration in the educational decisions required to provide *all* children the best possible education. Considerable literature and research are available on the education of the gifted but offer little consensus. Alternative views surround two major questions: What does it mean to be gifted, and should the program for gifted children focus on acceleration or enrichment?

In addition to these two basic questions, there are practical considerations, not the least of which is how to deliver an appropriate program. Alternatives include pull-out designs, after-school models, and in-class programs. There are also questions of time, teachers, and materials.

Identification of the Mathematically Gifted

Legal definitions of gifted children exist but vary considerably from one state to the next and are not useful for general purposes. Theoretical definitions also abound. In 1978, Joseph S. Renzulli proposed a definition that is often referred to or recommended for use (Downs et al., 1994). The Renzulli three-ring conception of giftedness (see Figure 23.2) requires the presence of all three distinct characteristics illustrated in the diagram. In addition to the traits described by the Renzulli definition, the *mathematically gifted* student will exhibit specific characteristics in mathematics. These will include a clearly demonstrated interest in things mathematical, mastery of mathematical skills at an early age, an ability to reason analytically, and an ability to perceive mathematical patterns and generalizations (House, 1987; Ridge & Renzulli, 1981).

In 1995, NCTM convened a Task Force on the Mathematically Promising to prepare recommendations and a draft policy statement concerning the mathematically talented. The report stopped short of establishing a firm definition but favored definitions that recognize "mathematical promise as a function of ability, motivation, belief, and experience or opportunity" (NCTM, 1995, p. 2). The report repeatedly calls for programs to be more inclusive rather than exclusive, noting that a wide variety of measures should be used in identification, including such things as student essays, peer recommendation, performance in mathematics contests, and tests of abstract reasoning ability. Efforts should be made to include males and females from a range of cultural and socioeconomic backgrounds.

Acceleration or Enrichment

Debate continues over the relative merits of acceleration versus enrichment as the appropriate general model for providing mathematics education for gifted children. *Acceleration* can occur in either of two forms. One approach places students ahead of those in their normal age grouping (starting kindergarten early, skipping a grade, attending class for part of the day with a higher grade level). Another form of acceleration involves speeding the pace at which instruction in the regular curriculum occurs. *Enrichment* refers to the expansion of the regular curriculum. In some instances, this includes completely different content that would not normally be encountered in the regular curriculum. Another view, one that generally is more appealing, is an examination of topics in the regular curriculum but at some greater depth, involving a higher level of abstraction or reasoning (Schiever & Maker, 1991). Enrichment should be challenging and have a purpose. In contrast to acceleration, enrichment should broaden the understanding and coverage of the standard curriculum.

NCTM's Task Force on the Mathematically Promising chose not to endorse either an enrichment or an acceleration model. Instead, the Task Force suggested that whatever model is designed, school systems need to be clear about the ramifications of the design. In discussing this issue, the need to be nonexclusionary and to include the greatest number of promising students continued to be their utmost concern.

A Model for Instruction

Most elementary and middle schools that have a program for the gifted in the same building employ some form of pull-out model: Students leave the room for one or more periods during the week to work with a special teacher of the gifted. Without such a program, most teachers face the dilemma of trying to accommodate a small number of talented children within the regular class. This is a difficult task for a single teacher working alone. Often the result is one or two children working independently on "enrichment" activities consisting of clever puzzles, computer games, or various independent explorations that fail to fit together in a cohesive way or to challenge the child's true abilities.

Another equally unsatisfactory alternative is to permit gifted students to engage in self-directed acceleration, perhaps by working alone in next year's text. Independent acceleration can be dangerous. Without the guidance of a skilled teacher and the benefit of directed discourse and exploration, students frequently focus on the procedural aspects of the mathematics found in textbooks. The result can be a very rule-oriented or instrumental form of mathematics learn

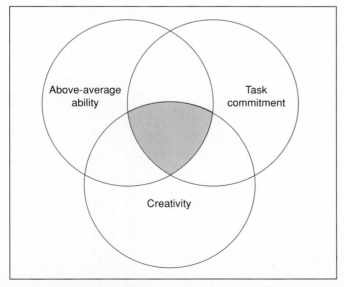

● **Figure 23.2** Renzulli's three-ring conception of giftedness.

Schoolwide Enrichment Model

One of the most popular and best-researched models for working with the gifted is the Schoolwide Enrichment Model (SEM) developed by Renzulli and Reis (1985), an outgrowth of the earlier enrichment triad model (Renzulli, 1977). SEM involves the classroom teacher in a variety of roles but integrates these roles with other teachers and personnel in the school. Goals of the model are to expand "advanced learning" beyond the small percentage of students usually served by gifted programs, to integrate special programs with the regular curriculum, to minimize the elitism often associated with gifted programs, and to expand the enrichment opportunities for all students (Renzulli & Reis, 1991).

SEM is essentially an enrichment approach. However, plans are made for top students to shorten their study of the regular curriculum through such approaches as eliminating review work, reducing practice exercises, or pretesting when unit ideas seem already present. The "compacting of the curriculum" is a unit-by-unit acceleration that provides extra time for students to engage in enrichment or acceleration in the same or in a different subject area.

Another interesting feature of SEM is the method of selecting students. SEM begins with a large (approximately 20 percent) talent pool for all activities. Students in the pool are all eligible for the first two levels of activities. A few students may opt into the third level of activities, depending on interest, motivation, and desire. In this way, a wide range of students has access to enrichment or acceleration as may be appropriate. This avoids the labeling and segregation of a small group of "gifted" students and opens quality enrichment to more students.

Triad Model of Enrichment

The dominant feature of SEM is a sequence of three types of activities that build and develop a particular area of content.

Type I: Exploratory Experiences. The initial experiences are designed to expose students to new ideas, special topics, or even whole fields of knowledge not generally covered by the regular curriculum. These initial experiences are planned by teachers, parents, principals, and others who may have interest or expertise in the school. Frequently, Type I experiences involve a guest speaker, a field trip, or a special video or CD-ROM. Type I experiences are open to the full class and thus serve to enrich all students, not just a select few.

Type II: Group Training Activities. Type II experiences are designed to provide interested students with specific process skills and knowledge related to the area of study. These activities are developed by a team of teachers and are frequently based on published materials. The full talent pool is eligible for these activities. Type II experiences may take place in the classroom, or the planning team may decide that some form of pull-out arrangement will best suit a group opting to work on these activities. Recall that curriculum "compacting" is also an SEM feature that helps free up time for such explorations.

Type III: Investigations of Real Problems. In Type III experiences, students assume the role of inquirer. The purpose is to have students act as "practicing professionals." To engage in these activities, students must display a high level of interest and ability growing out of the Type II experience. Renzulli and Reis describe a detailed selection procedure for entry to the Type III experience, with typically only a small percentage of students being selected. Again, note that this small group may be quite different for different projects and in different curricular areas. The objectives of the Type III experience include opportunities to apply interest and knowledge, use higher-level thinking and processes, and create a product that goes well beyond the typical encyclopedia-based report. Products are to be addressed to a well-defined audience—the class, the school, the PTA, an outside group, and so on. These projects thus incorporate student responsibility, commitment, planning, organization, and elements of self-direction. Classroom teachers and other resource teachers help students plan Type III activities.

A Triad Example

The Logo programming language provides a simple example of how the SEM triad model might work. A Type I experience with Logo might be conducted by a specialist with computers either in the school or brought in from outside. There also are videos and structured approaches to the Logo language that could be set up in the school computer lab. Based on this initial exposure, eligible students could opt to spend several class periods as well as out-of-class time exploring Logo through activity books and project cards that are readily available from the major mathematics resource companies. The level of independence or teacher guidance would vary with the age of the students, the resources, and the number of students involved.

With some initial knowledge of Logo, appropriately motivated students would apply to work on a Type III exploration. Logo provides such a wide range of possibilities that it is easy to conceive of many different projects at a given grade level. Some may wish to explore an aspect of geometry with Logo. Others may be interested in the possibilities of robotics using LEGO/Logo. Some may be more interested in the logic of Logo programming and perhaps explore the intricacies of recursion. Applications to physics, music, or art are possible. These are just a few of the possible avenues that a teacher might suggest, based on the expressed interest of the students. Depending on the project, an audience for the product should be determined in advance. For example, the goal of an exploration of recursion could be preparation of a guest presentation to a high school class. A Logo and art exploration might develop into a schoolwide contest. A game for first graders could be designed and tested with the first grade in the school. The presentation of the product is an important feature. It removes the project from the realm of superficiality and provides a sense of real worth.

Ideas and Beginnings

SEM is not the only way to provide appropriate learning experiences for exceptionally capable students. It has been described here because of its adaptability to the classroom. It is designed to blend with or augment the regular curriculum. It provides opportunities for all students to be exposed to special content and to experience exciting enrichment. Providing for gifted students will usually be a school or system decision and will involve many more people than the single classroom teacher. But every teacher will have a group of students that he or she would like to provide with extra opportunities. The following features of SEM can be integrated into a single-room model of providing for talented children:

- Collapse the regular curriculum within selected units of study to provide time.

- Provide activities for the full class that would be classified as Type I experiences.

- Work with other grade-level teachers to design Type II explorations that a small class of students could work on. Decide how to allocate time and space across classrooms to maximize planning time and resources.

- Consider engaging your best students in more independent projects that meet the criteria of Type III explorations. Avoid the typical "write a report on . . ." assignment, and focus student attention on investigations that go beyond the typical school library resources. Include the notion of a product and an audience to present it to.

REFLECTIONS ON CHAPTER 23: WRITING TO LEARN

1. What traditional ideas about curriculum and teaching children must be changed so that the NCTM vision of all children learning mathematics can be realized?

2. How would you argue for the values of a diverse class that includes children with learning problems? That is, what are some of the benefits of including these students in the regular classroom?

3. Briefly describe each of the following specific learning disabilities, and give some indication of how the disability may affect mathematics learning or ability. For each disability, also list at least two ideas that can be used by the classroom teacher to help the child.

    a. Perceptual deficits (figure-ground, discrimination, reversal, spatial)

    b. Memory deficits (short-term and long-term)

    c. Integrative deficits

    d. Attention deficits

4. For children with mental deficits (low-ability students, slow learners), how should content and instruction each be modified?

5. Explain how teacher expectations and tracking have detrimental effects on minorities and low-SES children.

6. Describe in general terms one or more of the most significant ideas that should guide the teacher who is working with students from a cultural minority.

7. What are some factors that contribute to gender inequity, and what are the long-term effects of that inequity?

8. How can teachers in the elementary or middle school work to erase gender inequity?

9. Describe and contrast the approaches of acceleration and enrichment for talented students.

10. What ideas from the Renzulli and Reis Schoolwide Enrichment Model (SEM) could a classroom teacher modify and adapt profitably for his or her own classroom?

FOR DISCUSSION AND EXPLORATION

1. Two common threads in this chapter are the beliefs that all children will benefit from a developmental or constructivist approach to teaching and that there is real value in teaching children in diverse, heterogeneous classrooms. Some teachers may argue with this position, contending that it is best for the majority of children if "special-needs" students are isolated. And besides, the argument continues, their special needs are best met by special teachers in classes with fewer students. Pick a position in this argument, and articulate it in writing or in a classroom discussion.

2. In the discussion of multicultural equity, there was no mention of two ideas that are sometimes discussed in the literature. One is that students should be exposed to mathematics topics that reflect and honor the cultural heritage of ethnic students. This is a matter of *cultural infusion*. For example, examine the African strategy game of Kalah or the geometry of Native American art. The other idea is that instruction for African-Americans should be modified to reflect their particular cognitive learning styles, usually described as "field-dependent" and "global." The learning style argument is also applied to gender differences. How do you feel about either or both of these positions? (You may wish to consult Carey, Fennema, Carpenter & Franke (1995), Downs, Matthew & McKinney (1994), or Marolda & Davidson (1994) for some perspective on these issues.)

3. Based on your personal experiences, do you believe there is a gender problem in mathematics education? Cite some experiences that support your position. What do you think the situation is like today?

4. What would you do if you found yourself teaching a class with one exceptionally talented child who had no equal in the room? Assume that acceleration to the next grade has been ruled out due to social adjustment factors.

SUGGESTED READINGS

Highly Recommended

Cuevas G., & Driscol, M. (Eds.). (1993). *Reaching all students with mathematics.* Reston, VA: National Council of Teachers of Mathematics.

This 244-page book contains stories and visions about the teaching of mathematics to all students. The focus is on cultural minorities, and contributors are some of the best-known authors in the field and successful educators sharing their experiences. It is very readable and very worthwhile.

Hilliard, A. G., III. (1995). Mathematics excellence for cultural "minority" students: What is the problem? In I. M. Carl (Ed.), *Seventy-five years of progress: Prospects for school mathematics* (pp. 99–114). Reston, VA: National Council of Teachers of Mathematics.

This is one of four chapters in this superb book from NCTM that address issues of gender and cultural equity. Hilliard provides objective perspective on the history and nature of the problem of inequities for minorities and heads us in the proper direction.

Secada, W. G., Fennema, E., & Adajian, L. B. (Eds.). (1995). *New directions for equity in mathematics education.* New York: Cambridge University Press.

The editors, long known for their research in this field, have assembled one of the best collections of essays to date on the issues of equity in this extremely readable book.

Thornton, C. A., & Bley, N. S. (Eds.). (1994). *Windows of opportunity: Mathematics for students with special needs.* Reston, VA: National Council of Teachers of Mathematics.

There are very few books that even attempt to address the issues of special-needs children and mathematics. NCTM's last effort was in 1981. Thornton and Bley have put together an excellent book that could be a methods text or a resource for the classroom teacher, consisting of seven chapters on issues, eight that address content through perspective and vignettes, and six that look at promising practices. This book is indispensable.

Other Suggestions

Bley, N. S. (1994). Accommodating special needs. In C. A. Thornton & N. S. Bley (Eds.), *Windows of opportunity: Mathematics for students with special needs* (pp. 137–163). Reston, VA: National Council of Teachers of Mathematics.

Bley, N. S., & Thornton, C. A. (1995). *Teaching mathematics to students with learning disabilities* (3rd ed.). Austin, TX: Pro-Ed.

Campbell, P. B. (1995). Redefining the "girl problem in mathematics." In W. G. Secada, E. Fennema, & L. B. Adajian (Eds.), *New directions for equity in mathematics education* (pp. 225–241). New York: Cambridge University Press.

Campbell, P. F. (1993). Making equity a reality in classrooms. *Arithmetic Teacher, 41,* 110–113.

Campbell, P. F. (1996). Empowering children and teachers in the elementary mathematics classrooms of urban schools. *Urban Education, 30,* 449–475.

Cawley, J. F. (1985). *Cognitive strategies and mathematics for the learning disabled.* Austin, TX: Pro-Ed.

Cuevas, G. (1990). Increasing the achievement and participation of language minority students in mathematics education. In T. J. Cooney (Ed.), *Teaching and learning mathematics in the 1990s* (pp. 159–165). Reston, VA: National Council of Teachers of Mathematics.

Davidson, E., & Hammerman, J. (1993). Homogenized is only better for milk. In G. Cuevas & M. Driscol (Eds.), *Reaching all students with mathematics* (pp. 197–212). Reston, VA: National Council of Teachers of Mathematics.

Education Development Center. (1995). *Equity in education series: Gender-fair math.* Newton, MA: Author.

House, P. A. (Ed.). (1987). *Providing opportunities for the mathematically gifted, K–12.* Reston, VA: National Council of Teachers of Mathematics.

Lamon, W. E. (Ed.) (1984). Educating mathematically gifted and talented children [Special issue]. *Focus on Learning Problems in Mathematics, 6.*

Oakes, J. (1995). Opportunity to learn: Can standards-based reform be equity-based reform? In I. M. Carl (Ed.), *Seventy-five years of progress: Prospects for school mathematics* (pp. 78–98). Reston, VA: National Council of Teachers of Mathematics.

Renzulli, J. S., & Reis, S. M. (1991). The schoolwide enrichment model: A comprehensive plan for the development of creative productivity. In N. Coangelo & G. A. Davis (Eds.), *Handbook of gifted education* (pp. 111–141). Needham Heights, MA: Allyn & Bacon.

Rowser, J. F., & Koontz, T. Y. (1995). Inclusion of African-American students in mathematics classrooms: Issues of style, curriculum, and expectations. *Mathematics Teacher, 88,* 448–453.

Silver, E. A., & Stein, M. K. (1996). The QUASAR Project: The "revolution of the possible" in mathematics instructional reform in urban middle schools. *Urban Education, 30,* 476–521.

Steen, L. A. (1990). Mathematics for all Americans. In T. J. Cooney (Ed.), *Teaching and learning mathematics in the 1990s* (pp. 130–134). Reston, VA: National Council of Teachers of Mathematics.

Stiff, L. V. (1990). African-American students and the promise of the *Curriculum and Evaluation Standards.* In T. J. Cooney (Ed.), *Teaching and learning mathematics in the 1990s* (pp. 152–158). Reston, VA: National Council of Teachers of Mathematics.

Trafton, P. R., & Claus, A. S. (1994). A changing curriculum for a changing age. In C. A. Thornton & N. S. Bley (Eds.), *Windows of opportunity: Mathematics for students with special needs* (pp. 19–39). Reston, VA: National Council of Teachers of Mathematics.

Vaac, N. N. (1993). Questioning in the mathematics classroom. *Arithmetic Teacher, 41,* 88–91.

Wilmot, B., & Thornton, C. A. (1989). Mathematics teaching and learning: Meeting the needs of special learners. In P. R. Trafton (Ed.), *New directions for elementary school mathematics* (pp. 212–222). Reston, VA: National Council of Teachers of Mathematics.

CHAPTER

TECHNOLOGY AND SCHOOL MATHEMATICS

Technology is a common feature of our day-to-day living. Calculators, computers, CD-ROMs, videodisks, the Internet, and the World Wide Web are all technologies that we see, use, or hear about every day. The continually growing capabilities of even the "ordinary" technologies available through retail stores and catalogs are astounding.

In schools, a serious problem of this cutting-edge technology is the matter of ready access and availability. However, as technology continues to improve and become commonplace in society at large, it also becomes more necessary and more affordable for ordinary classrooms. Problems of access and availability will undoubtedly fade in the near future, and useful technology will become as common in schools as chalkboards and textbooks.

TECHNOLOGY AND MATHEMATICS EDUCATION: A GENERAL PERSPECTIVE

Most readers of this book will have had limited or perhaps no experience with technology in school mathematics. It may be difficult to envision the proper role of calculators and computers in the mathematics classroom without any firsthand exposure. When the use of technology is finally commonplace in the classroom, there will be no more need for this chapter than there is for one on how to use chalk. In the meantime, some perspective may be helpful.

NCTM's Position on the Use of Technology

The National Council of Teachers of Mathematics has for many years been very clear in its support of technology in the mathematics classroom. Various position statements on the use of computers and calculators have been adopted by the council, beginning well over a decade ago. In February 1994, NCTM adopted a single comprehensive position on the use of technology in the learning and teaching of mathematics. The statement encompasses the use of all technologies, including calculators and computers. Excerpts from that position statement follow.

It is the position of the National Council of Teachers of Mathematics that the use of the tools of technology is integral to the learning and teaching of mathematics. Continual improvement is needed in mathematics curricula, instructional and assessment methods, access to hardware and software, and teacher education.

- Teachers should plan for students' use of technology in both learning and doing mathematics. A development of ideas is to be made with the transition from concrete experiences to abstract mathematical ideas, focusing on the exploration and discovery of new mathematical concepts and problem-solving processes. Students are to learn how to use technology as a tool for processing information, visualizing and solving problems, exploring and testing conjectures, accessing data, and verifying their solutions. Students' ability to recognize when and how to use technology effectively is dependent on their continued study of appropriate mathematics content. In a mathematics setting, technology must be an instructional tool that is integrated into daily teaching practices, including the assessment of what students know and are able to do. In a mathematics class, technology ought not be the object of instruction.

- Every student is to have access to a calculator appropriate to his or her level. Every classroom where mathematics is taught should have at least one computer for demonstrations, data acquisition, and other student use at all times. Every school mathematics program should provide additional computers and other types of technology for individual, small-group, and whole class use.

The National Council of Teachers of Mathematics recommends the appropriate use of technology to enhance mathematics programs at all levels. Keeping pace with the advances in technology is a necessity for the entire mathematics community, particularly teachers who are responsible for designing day-to-day instructional experiences for students. (NCTM, 1996, p. 24)

NCTM makes it clear in this statement that technology is not an add-on or a frill but should be an integral part of doing mathematics every day. In the last sentence, the need to keep pace with advancements in technology is highlighted with particular emphasis on the classroom teacher. Teachers serious about their profession cannot ignore these statements.

Five years prior to the adoption of this position, NCTM gave considerable attention to the use of technology in the *Curriculum Standards*. Two statements in the introduction (NCTM, 1989, p. 8) are reflective of the theme of this chapter:

The new technology not only has made calculations and graphing easier, it has changed the very nature of problems important to mathematics and the methods mathematicians use to investigate them.

Access to this technology is no guarantee that any student will become mathematically literate. Calculators and computers for users of mathematics, like word processors for writers, are tools that simplify, but do not accomplish, the work at hand. Thus, our vision of school mathematics is based on the fundamental mathematics students will need, not just on the technological training that will facilitate the use of that mathematics.

Technology's Threefold Impact on Mathematics Education

Calculators and computers are having a profound impact on what mathematics we teach to students as well as the manner in which it is taught. Some mathematics we used to teach is now essentially obsolete because technology has made it so. Much of what we teach we can teach better with technology. And many topics that we were unable to teach before can now be made accessible to students in meaningful ways.

Less Important or Obsolete Mathematics

Much of the mathematics that we used to teach is far less important today than in the days before technology. The most obvious case in point is pencil-and-paper computation, which has been almost entirely superseded by the ready availability of calculators. Some attention to these skills is probably defensible, but certainly not the large percentage of time that was typically devoted to them in the past. Nor is there a need for any skill with exceedingly tedious computations, such as long division with a three-digit divisor.

Another area where less time need be spent is in the techniques of constructing various graphs. For example, in the past, a sixth-grade student wishing to construct a pie graph would first have to use long division to determine each percentage involved, determine the size of the central angle of the circle needed to show that percentage, and finally use a protractor to measure the angle. None of these activities contributes anything to the analysis of data or an understanding of how the pie graph shows data differently than a bar graph or a line plot. Today, software is available for students at all grade levels that allows the instant conversion of data to pie graphs and other forms of statistical representations. The student emphasis can be placed on interpretation and presentation of the relationships found in the data rather than the tedium of graph construction.

At the level of algebra and above, technology has made even larger chunks of the established curriculum less important or perhaps even obsolete.

Mathematics Taught Better

At the elementary level, one of the most striking changes due to technology is the ability to examine real problems with real numbers. This takes problem solving into the real world without the use of artificial constructs. There is no need for the answers to "come out even" or to use unrealistic numbers just to ensure that students can compute.

The connections between decimals and common fractions is clearly enhanced by calculators that illustrate fractions and permit changing easily from fraction to decimal and back again. Computer geometry tools bring an analysis of shapes to the classroom that was never possible before. Students can begin to make conjectures about the properties of shapes and explore their thinking without having to check the text.

Many manipulative materials, including base 10 blocks, fraction models, and pattern blocks, are now available as computer models. The computer has the potential of offering the same advantages as the physical models and more. Computer models provide greater flexibility, attached symbolism, linked representations (two or more models tied to the same symbolism), individualization, and records of what students have done.

More Accessible Mathematics

Whereas some topics can be removed from or reduced in the curriculum, others are much more possible for students to access and can now receive greater emphasis. Data analysis is a striking case in point. Real data and measurements can be collected and analyzed with ease so that students can begin to explore the meaning of simple statistics and statistical representations. With the help of a computer or graphing calculator to perform random chance experiments, probability can now be explored in a meaningful way without the need for abstract formulas or theories. Experiments involving chance can be simulated thousands of times in less than a minute. Graphs of functions are easily drawn and analyzed without the need for point-by-point plotting. Functions can represent real phenomena because it is as easy to graph $y = 345.39x^2 - 72.3$ as it is to graph $y = 3x + 2$. The computer or graphing calculator can be used to find approximating functions to fit scatter plots of real data.

The mathematical concepts in these topics are accessible to students. Now technology makes the formerly difficult procedures accessible as well.

CALCULATORS IN THE MATHEMATICS CLASSROOM

NCTM has officially advocated the use of calculators in the classroom since 1976, when it published a special issue of *The Arithmetic Teacher* devoted to the topic. Since then, there have been other focus issues, other position statements (NCTM, 1996), the *Curriculum Standards,* and a yearbook, *Calculators in Mathematics Education* (Fey, 1992), all advocating the regular use of calculators in the teaching of mathematics at all grade levels. The following are excerpts from NCTM's position statement, *Calculators and the Education of Youth.*

> Instruction with calculators will extend the understanding of mathematics and will allow all students access to rich, problem-solving experiences. This instruction must develop students' ability to know how and when to use a calculator. Skill in estimation and the ability to decide if the solution to a problem is reasonable are essential adjuncts to the effective use of the calculator.
>
> Evaluation must be in alignment with normal everyday use of calculators in the classroom. Testing instruments that measure students' understanding of mathematics and its applications must include calculator use. As the availability of calculators increases and the technology improves, testing instruments and evaluation practices must be continually upgraded to reflect these changes.
>
> Research and experience have clearly demonstrated the potential of calculators to enhance students' learning in mathematics. The cognitive gain in number sense, conceptual development, and visualization can empower and motivate students to engage in true mathematical problem solving at a level previously denied to all but the most talented. The calculator is an essential tool for all students of mathematics.(NCTM, 1996, p. 18)

The popular everyday use of calculators in society, along with the lengthy history of professional support for calculators in schools, has had a less than spectacular impact on the mathematics classroom, especially at the elementary level. It is finally safe to say that resistance to the use of calculators has diminished. The public at large is beginning to understand and accept that mathematics is more than computation and that thinking is more important than long division. It remains difficult for many, however, to accept that the calculator is not going to prevent Johnny from learning something basic about mathematics. Nothing could be further from the truth.

Reasons for Using Calculators

Perhaps when the next edition of this book is published, this discussion will be unnecessary. (Unfortunately, that sentence appeared in the previous edition also.) If you need some ammunition to talk to parents or principals, or just to help convince yourself, here are some reasons why calculators should be an everyday part of every classroom at every grade level, K–12.

Enhanced Instruction

The wide availability of calculators has made it difficult to defend spending significant portions of the school curriculum teaching pencil-and-paper computation. The calculator is now as much a teaching tool as the chalkboard or the overhead projector. In truth, not only does the calculator eliminate much of the tedious computation required in school, but it can also be used to help develop concepts and skills in other areas of mathematics. Activities for teaching with the calculator have been suggested throughout the book, but a few additional activities are presented here as examples of teaching concepts.

---ACTIVITY---

 24.1 And the Remainder Is . . .

Consider a division problem such as 796 ÷ 42. Have students find a method for determining the whole-number remainder using only a simple four-function calculator. This task requires that students understand the decimal part of a quotient, the meaning of division, and, in most instances, how the calculator truncates the extended decimal quotient. Discussion of why various solutions do or do not make sense helps develop a clearer understanding of division.

ACTIVITY

24.2 Fold and Divide

Give students a strip of paper exactly 22 cm long and a centimeter ruler. Have them measure and record the length. Next, carefully fold the paper in half, and measure the result as accurately as possible. On the calculator, divide 22 by 2, and compare this result with the measurement. Fold the paper in half one more time, and again measure carefully. Divide the last result on the calculator by 2, and compare. Go through this fold, measure, and divide sequence several more times. How do the results of the measurement compare with the results of dividing by 2 on the calculator? Try this with other lengths. (This activity, suggested by a second-grade teacher, is reported by Shumway, 1992.)

Activity 24.2 provides a vivid contrast between symbolic manipulation and physical reality. What happens if after the first division by 2, you press $=$ over and over? Is this the same thing that happens in physical reality? That mathematical models and physical reality do not always match is a good discussion for students to have. What other ideas might develop at least informally from that exploration?

Almost any problem-solving activity that involves computation is enhanced by letting students use a calculator. Besides encouraging trial and error or exploration of different approaches to a solution, students also learn the value of recording intermediate results as they go along. Many interesting explorations arise from the use of the calculator itself. The following are examples.

ACTIVITY

24.3 Too Hard for the Calculator?

Find a way to use the calculator to compute the product of two numbers such as 3456 and 88,888. (The standard method of entering this product on the calculator causes an overload.)

ACTIVITY

24.4 Keypad Partner Numbers

For the purpose of this activity (there is no practical purpose), define a *keypad partner number* (KPN) as a two-digit number that can be entered on a calculator by pressing two adjacent keys, either vertically, horizontally, or diagonally in any direction. Examples of KPNs are 48, 63, 12, and 21. The numbers 73 and 28 are not KPNs. The initial task is to find two different pairs of KPNs that have the same sum (for example, 32 + 65 = 62 + 35). Once the idea of pairs of KPNs with the same sum is established, try to find some sort of pattern or generalization about KPNs with like sums. When a pattern has been found that seems exciting or interesting, challenge students to figure out an explanation for why the pattern works. You might suggest looking at differences of KPNs instead of sums. Patterns also exist in products of KPNs, but these are a bit more difficult to discover.

The KPN activity is an interesting exercise in searching for patterns and reasons. It is surprising how many different ideas students can discover, especially if they work in groups to share ideas. Ideas that rely on place value include looking at the sum of the digits or examination of the addition algorithm. Students have drawn pictures of the keypad and discovered geometric patterns of various sorts. These then have interesting descriptions as well as explanations. Is the activity valuable? This is a good example of doing mathematics: searching for patterns, communicating ideas, justifying results.

The following activity is adapted from Goldenberg (1991). It is useful for children in grades 2 to 5 who have limited concepts of decimals.

ACTIVITY

24.5 Numbers in Between

First, examine the idea that a number can be quickly multiplied by itself by pressing the number followed by $\times$ $=$. For example, 4 $\times$ $=$ produces 16. What number can be multiplied by itself to get 43? After some discussion around 6 being too little and 7 too large, introduce the idea that there are numbers *between* 6 and 7. (Children do not think of fractions as numbers at this age.) List in a column the numbers 6.1, 6.2, . . . , 6.9, and explain simply that these are numbers that are more than 6 and less than 7. Have students use their calculators to multiply each of these by itself. This will show that 6.5 is too small and 6.6 is too large to produce 43. Next, suggest that there are numbers between 6.5 and 6.6, and list these in a column: 6.51, 6.52, . . . , 6.59. Repeat the exercise of squaring each of these, and list all of the results. The process can be repeated again if students show interest.

The "Numbers in Between" activity is not the only way to discuss decimals and not even the best way. But it does introduce ideas in a meaningful way that adds to student understanding of decimal numbers in a powerful manner.

Many books and resources for calculator activities are available with excellent ideas. The CAMP-LA books (Pagni, 1991), for example, have literally hundreds of excellent activities organized by content and grade level. Almost every chapter in this text features calculator activities as well.

Affective and Indirect Benefits

The overwhelming conclusion of numerous research studies is that students' attitudes toward mathematics are better in classrooms where calculators are used than where they are not (Hembree & Dessart, 1986; Reys & Reys, 1987). Students using calculators tend to be enthusiastic and are more confident and persistent in solving problems. (These studies are quite old. Is there any reason to believe they would be less valid today?)

In addition to positive affective results, students using calculators discover a wide variety of interesting ideas that might otherwise remain unnoticed. For example, decimal numbers and negative numbers are almost inescapable, and children learn to explore these ideas at an early age. The number of digits that result in some computations is very different than in others. For example, $2 \div 7$ fills up the display, but $1245 \div 5$ has only three digits. Students quickly find that it is easy to make errors on a calculator and so develop a real appreciation for estimation. Students also learn that it is frequently easier to do a mental computation than to search for a calculator and press buttons. All of these outcomes are positive benefits that can result without any direct instruction. They can happen just by having calculators in every school, on every desk, every day, all of the time, at every grade.

Common Usage in Society

The fact is, almost everyone uses calculators in almost every facet of life that involves any sort of exact computation—except schoolchildren. The traditional reasons for teaching pencil-and-paper computation, especially with numbers involving more than two or three digits, have all but evaporated. It is more than a little hypocritical to forbid the use of calculators.

It also makes good sense that students should know how to use this popular tool effectively. Many adults have not learned how to use the memory keys, how to do a chain of mixed operations, how to use the automatic constant feature, or how to recognize if a gross error has been made. These are important practical skills that can easily be learned over the school years if the calculator is simply there for open, everyday use.

Time Savings

Pencil-and-paper computation is time-consuming, especially for young students who have not developed a high degree of mastery. Why should time be wasted having students add numbers to find the perimeter of a polygon when the lesson is about geometry? Why compute averages, find percents, convert fractions to decimals, or solve problems of any sort with pencil-and-paper methods when such skills are not the objective of the lesson? Defending laborious and time-consuming computations in noncomputational lessons is indeed difficult.

It really comes down to this: *Why teach children to do inefficiently what a $5.00 machine can do efficiently?*

Practical Considerations Concerning Calculators

Like other tools in the classroom, there are things to consider about calculators after you have decided you want them. There are different types of calculators with different features. Which ones should you use?

Automatic Constant Feature

Simple four-function calculators are all that are necessary through the third grade and are adequate even through the fifth or sixth grade if nothing else is available. The one important feature that is not on all simple calculators is the automatic constant for addition and subtraction. (That is the one that allows you to enter $+$ 1 $=$ $=$ $=$ ... and have the calculator count.) Almost all calculators have this feature for multiplication and division. It is also important to note that automatic constant features do not operate exactly the same on all calculators.

Algebraic Logic

Demana and Osborne (1988) made a strong case for the use of calculators that include algebraic logic. In essence, that means that expressions are evaluated according to the correct order-of-operations rules rather than as they are entered. On a standard four-function calculator, if 5 $+$ 3 $\times$ 4 $=$ is keyed in, the result will be 32. The rules concerning order of operations dictate that multiplication and division precede addition and subtraction. Thus the correct result of 5 $+$ 3 $\times$ 4 $=$ is 17. At the very least, you should be aware of these differences. In 1990, Texas Instruments introduced MathMate, a four-function calculator for young children that has algebraic logic and keys for left and right parentheses. The TI Explorer Plus, the Casio fx-55, and the Sharp EL-E300 all have these features, as do scientific calculators. (For a more detailed discussion of algebraic logic, see Chapter 20, p. 440.)

Fractions and Other Capabilities

Several inexpensive calculators now allow for common fractions to be entered, with operation results displayed in fraction form. In addition to being able to enter and operate on fractions, it is possible to simplify a fraction using any appropriate factor (e.g., $\frac{12}{16}$ can be simplified to $\frac{6}{8}$ or $\frac{3}{4}$). Displays can be switched back and forth between fraction and decimal forms and between mixed and improper forms. (Several activities have been suggested for this feature in Chapters 12, 13, and 14.) The Explorer Plus, the Casio fx-55, and the Sharp EL-E300 have these features.

Most of the calculators designed to display fractions have several other capabilities that make them attractive tools for the upper grades. Often available is a key that will produce a random number (useful for probability experiments), the ability to round a number to a specified number of places, and an integer division function that results in whole-number quotients with a remainder. A few calculators display full multioperation expressions that are not evaluated until the $\boxed{=}$ key is pressed. Some can store data on which single-variable statistics can be performed.

Overhead Projector Versions

Several suppliers make transparent versions of calculators that can be placed on the overhead projector. These allow you to show students exactly what keys you are pressing for demonstrating calculator usage. The overhead calculator is especially useful for showing young children how to use the calculator or for illustrating new features for older children. Overhead calculators permit many good activities to be conducted with the full class instead of having every child pressing buttons. There are many times when this approach has definite advantages.

Graphing Calculators

The graphing calculator is on a higher level of sophistication than the calculators discussed so far. At the high school level, they are changing what can be taught and how it is taught. It is a mistake, however, to reserve these amazing machines for high school when valuable use can be made of them beginning in about the sixth grade. Vonder Embse (1992) suggests the following values for the middle grades:

- The large-screen display permits compound expressions such as $3 + 4(5 - 6/7)$ to be displayed completely before being evaluated. Further, the expressions are easily modified (e.g., adding or removing parentheses), with corresponding results displayed. This can aid in understanding notation and order of operations.

- The large screen allows students to construct tables of values by inserting different numbers into formulas or equations. The table of values that a student might develop this way can also be stored in the calculator for further analysis.

- The ability to enter different values in a formula or an expression is a way to get at the idea of a variable as "something that varies."

- Students can plot points on a coordinate screen and begin to appreciate the relationships among tables of values, equations, and graphs.

These points are all included in the discussion of function and variable found in Chapter 21. The argument for the graphing calculator at the middle school level is actually stronger than that. The ideas mentioned so far are the ones that are most obvious to anyone who first picks up one of these tools and plays around with it. But these calculators have many more features, some of which could be quite useful to middle grade students. Here are just a few more points that should be considered:

- The built-in statistical functions allow students to examine mean, median, and standard deviation of reasonably large sets of realistic numbers. There is no reason not to use real data with large numbers for any exploration. With a simple calculator, lists of numbers cannot be stored, ordered, added to, or changed.

- Box-and-whisker plots and histograms are readily plotted to take the tedium away from statistical inferences based on graphs.

- Scatter plots of ordered pairs of data allow students to examine trends in data and to begin to understand fairly sophisticated ideas of statistical inference without requiring fancy symbolic mathematics.

- Random-number generators (also on some simpler calculators) allow for the simulation of a wide variety of probability experiments that would never be possible without this device. A few simple examples are included in Chapter 19.

- The graphing calculator is programmable. Programs are very easily written and can be understood at the middle grade level. For example, a program to compute the quadratic formula adds another dimension to the discussion of the Pythagorean theorem.

- The calculator can be connected to your computer to store programs and data and to print calculator information on your printer.

Besides all of these specific reasons, there is the overriding notion of opening up real mathematics to young children, a way to excite them and provide them with opportunities to explore well beyond the lessons you may have planned.

It is clear that there are considerable advantages to the use of the graphing calculator beginning at about the sixth grade. What are the disadvantages? Cost is the obvious issue to be raised. In response, the cost of these "computer-calculators" continues to drop. At the time this is being written, at least three different brands of graphing calculators can be purchased for under $75—the cost of a moderately priced pair of "must-have" sneakers or a few CDs. A calculator purchased in the sixth grade is the last calculator that will be needed through high school and perhaps college. A classroom set can be purchased by the school for less than the cost of a single computer. The cost is very cheap from this perspective.

Most of the other arguments are similar to those against any calculator: "Won't it keep my students from learning the basics?" Many teachers sputter, "It is OK for students to use one of those things *next* year, but *this* year we are going to learn the *real* way to do math." These arguments are hollow and unsupported by research data.

The graphing calculator is not yet part of the standard set of tools for the middle grades, but it is probably only a matter of time. In your classroom, the time should be now.

When and Where to Use Calculators

Calculators should be in or on students' desks at all times from kindergarten through high school! This position may seem radical to some educators. It is time to give this proposition, supported by the *Standards* in 1989, some serious thought.

Calculators for All Students at All Times

Here are a few arguments to support immediate availability of calculators at all times:

- The need to make a special effort to use calculators for any activity is diminished. If you have to stop the flow of your lessons to pass out calculators, you are likely not to take the time. Instead there is a tendency to save calculators for special "calculator lessons" or perhaps not even use them at all. Many excellent calculator explorations will happen spontaneously and will take up only a few minutes of class time. These activities simply will not get done if you have to stop to distribute and collect calculators.

- Ready availability of calculators allows students on their own to choose when it seems appropriate to use them. There are many times when it is much easier or quicker to use a mental computation or estimation or even to use the pencil that happens to be in our hands rather than to reach for the calculator. How can students ever learn to make these choices if you decide for them by keeping calculators out of sight unless otherwise directed? The call for calculators to be ever present does not suggest that all computation will be done on calculators or that the various methods of computation will not be taught.

- It simply does no harm to have calculators available! This is very difficult for many teachers, prospective teachers, and parents to accept. But the fact of the matter is that there is virtually no research to suggest that students fail to develop basic skills when taught in the presence of a calculator. Even basic facts and pencil-and-paper skills will still be learned with the calculator on the desk.

Middle school teachers sometimes complain that their students will use calculators for every possible computation including 3 + 5 if they are permitted. Their reaction is to forbid free use of calculators. A better solution is to ignore

this trivial use rather than reinforce students' mistaken belief that they are "getting away with something" by using the calculator. In those few instances where a student is not sure of his or her basic facts at the seventh or eighth grade, the calculator makes important mathematics accessible and provides an opportunity for practicing unknown facts with immediate feedback. An eighth grader who does not know basic facts will not learn them by enduring yet another year of stumbling through computations and feeling inadequate.

Equitable Access to Calculators

The price of a calculator is now so low that it is entirely reasonable to require that each of your students obtain one at the start of the year, just as pencils, notebooks, and other supplies are required. Be sure to provide parents with a short list of particular calculators that you recommend. Include both brand and model number when appropriate. In this way, you can be assured that every student has a calculator with the features you desire and that all of the calculators in the room operate the same way. Nothing is more frustrating than having to stop in the middle of an activity to provide special directions to one or two students with a nonconforming calculator. Another good idea is to have a few extra calculators available to fill in when one breaks or is left at home.

By the time students reach the fourth or fifth grade, they should be aware that all calculators are not alike and do not even use the same logic. Having some calculators around that perform differently may provide some interesting opportunities for learning. For example, if some calculators employ algebraic logic, as discussed earlier, the results on that calculator could be contrasted with the results on a simple four-function calculator. The need for a rule concerning order of operations will become apparent in this context.

In some school districts, classroom sets of calculators are being purchased by the schools. Some book publishers have also provided calculators at reduced prices as part of their sales promotions. Major manufacturers have designed calculators specifically for this market and sell them at reasonable prices in large quantities. There is no need, however, to wait for someone else to supply your room with calculators.

THE COMPUTER AS A TOOL IN MATHEMATICS

Using the computer as a *tool* for teaching mathematics is perhaps one of the most exciting uses of the computer, albeit one that has only recently been tapped at the elementary and middle school levels. *Tool software* is a generic term for software that performs a function that makes doing something easier. The most common computer tool is the word processor, followed closely by database software and spreadsheets. Now there are numerous software tools for doing mathematics at all levels. In contrast with instructional software, tool software does not teach. What it does is put power into the hands of the user in much the same way that the calculator provides power.

Computer Manipulatives as Tools

More and more programs are becoming available that permit students to have free use or control of screen versions of popular manipulative models. These models include pattern blocks (geometric shapes in various colors), tiles such as Color Tiles, geoboards, attribute materials, base 10 blocks, simple counters, connecting blocks, and various fraction models. Thus if a teacher was well equipped with software, in theory it would be possible to have most popular manipulatives available to students on the computer.

The obvious question is, "Why not simply use the actual physical models?" In fact, this is the key question that should always be asked when selecting software that offers computer manipulatives. There should be some clear advantage to the screen versions.

The most important advantage offered by the computer is the potential of linking symbolic forms directly with the visual model. Changes made in the display can cause corresponding changes in the symbolism. Similarly, a change in the symbolism can cause changes in the display. Some programs permit the symbolic form to be turned on or off either by the teacher or the student. Perhaps two different arrangements of base 10 blocks will permit separate numerals for each set. A geoboard figure can have area or perimeter computed and displayed.

A good program can also link two or more representations of the same concept—for example, circular pie pieces, number lines, and set models for fractions. Some fraction models are much more flexible in the computer version. For example, fraction strips may be adjusted to virtually any length, and circular pie pieces may be cut into fractional parts that are quite unlikely in the physical versions. Fraction models may be connected to decimal or percent symbolism as well as common fractions.

A computer program with models will generally provide more guidance, materials availability, flexibility, and chances for individualization than traditional materials. However, at present, no single program offers all of the positive features noted here. Sometimes added guidance becomes overly directive and prevents students from exploring or using their own approaches. Often the program is designed so that the models can only be used for the particular task that the program presents. For example, a base 10 models program might be used for addition when addition is the task but cannot be used in a completely free form. In some cases, manipulation of the screen models is actually more tedious than in physical form.

As computers become more and more commonplace in the elementary classroom, it is likely that more tool programs that offer completely open use of models with many of the added benefits described here will appear.

A few examples of software in this general category are listed here. (No list in this chapter is intended to be exhaustive, nor should listing of a program be taken as a recommendation.)

Hands-On Math: Learning with Computers and Math Manipulatives, Vols. 1, 2, and 3 (Ventura Educational Systems)

Exploring Mathematics with Manipulatives: Levels I, II, and III (EduQuest)

MathKeys (MECC/Houghton Mifflin)

Probability Constructor (Logal)

Some programs focus on only a single manipulative. Generally, these are more generic, with little or no attempt to include problem tasks or instruction:

Unifix Software (Didax)

The Manipulative Math Series (Learning Box)

Elastic Lines (Sunburst)

Shape Up! (Sunburst)

Polynomials and Rational Functions Investigations				
First X value:		−4		
Increment for X:		0.5		
X	X^2	X^3	X^3–X^2	(X^3 + 2X)/(3+X)
−4.0	16	−64	−80	72
−3.5	12.25	−42.875	−55.125	99.75
−3.0	9	−27	−36	#DIV/0!
−2.5	6.25	−15.625	−21.875	−41.25
−2.0	4	−8	−12	−12
−1.5	2.25	−3.375	−5.625	−4.25
−1.0	1	−1	−2	−1.5
−0.5	0.25	−0.125	−0.375	−0.45
0.0	0	0	0	0
0.5	0.25	0.125	−0.125	0.321428571
1.0	1	1	0	0.75
1.5	2.25	3.375	1.125	1.416666667
2.0	4	8	4	2.4
2.5	6.25	15.625	9.375	3.75
3.0	9	27	18	5.5
3.5	12.25	42.875	30.625	7.673076923
4.0	16	64	48	10.28571429
4.5	20.25	91.125	70.875	13.35
5.0	25	125	100	16.875

● **FIGURE 24.1** A typical spreadsheet program can be used to investigate functions in table form.

Professional Information

Many professional organizations have established Web sites on which they provide information about their organization, conferences, current events, publications, and more. Often these sites provide useful links to related resources or provide publications and resources that can be downloaded and then printed for more leisurely use. Periodic visits to these sites is a good way to stay current with professional information. Here are some suggested sites:

National Council of Teachers of Mathematics
<http://www.nctm.org>

NCTM's home page provides up-to-date news information, information found in current journals, conference information, job information, and more. There are links to pages for each of the four journals published by the council. Surprisingly, the most useful journal site is the *Journal for Research in Mathematics Education* This site has links to a wonderful list of curriculum materials, databases, and other professional organizations.

American Association for the Advancement of Science
<http://www.aaas.org>

This is the association responsible for *Project 2061,* a national science standards document. Access to this and other information concerning science education is available.

Association for Supervision and Curriculum Development
<http://www.ascd.org>

ASCD is an international, nonprofit educational association that is committed to successful teaching and learning for all. It publishes an excellent journal and many other worthwhile publications.

EQUALS at the Lawrence Hall of Science
<http://128.32.86.301>

The EQUALS program is dedicated to equal opportunity for women in mathematics and science. It publishes *Family Math* and other valuable resources for elementary teachers.

AIMS Education Foundation
<http://204.161.33.100/AIMS.html>

AIMS stands for Activities Integrating Mathematics and Science. The AIMS materials are widely recognized as among the best sources of activities to involve children in good mathematics and science, especially ones that integrate the disciplines.

Eisenhower National Clearinghouse
<http://www.enc.org>

This site contains links to a variety of curriculum materials and programs for K–12 mathematics and science education. The site has made available a complete version of NCTM's *Curriculum Standards.*

Lessons and Curriculum

The Internet is a surprising source of creative and useful lesson ideas. It is also a good way to find out about curriculum materials and software. Some sites list curricular materials and software and provide links to appropriate places to receive information. Many publishers of educational materials have home pages where their products are described along with purchase information. Occasionally, software publishers will provide demonstration versions of their products that can be downloaded and tested out.

The suggested sites that follow were selected because of the quantity of information available and because they are most likely to continue to be around while this volume is in print.

Mathematics Archives: K12 Internet Sites
<http://archives.math.utk.edu/k12.html>

This page contains a very large collection of links to lessons, software information (both public domain and commercial), and curriculum materials. This is a good place to begin a search for materials.

The Math Forum
<http://forum.swarthmore.edu>

This site grew out of one devoted to geometry and the use of *The Geometer's Sketchpad,* which was developed at Swarthmore College. Now it covers a wide range of mathematics with links to unusual lessons and projects. For example, one site, MathMagic! is intended to motivate students K–12 to use technology, problem-solving skills, and communication. Problems are regularly posted, and solutions can be entered via the Internet.

MegaMath!
<http://www.c3.lanl.gov/mega-math/>

This is a project of the Computer Research and Applications Group at Los Alamos National Laboratory intended to develop curriculum materials that bring unusual and important mathematical ideas to elementary classrooms.

EdWeb Home Page
<http://k12.cnidr.org:90>

This Web site, sponsored by the Corporation for Public Broadcasting, explores issues of educational reform technologies. The site contains links to on-line educational resources around the world.

AskERIC Home Page
<http://ericir.syr.edu>

The Educational Resources Information Center (ERIC) is a national information system supported by the U.S. Department of Education. The site contains links to ERIC's reference databases, lesson plans, and other collections.

Databases

With technology facilitating the analysis of real data and statistics, it is extremely useful to have a way to access up-to-date statistical information for your students and for their projects. The Internet is a big help in this regard. For example, from the *Journal for Research in Mathematics* home page, you can link to sites with data from the Bureau of Labor Statistics, census data from the Lawrence Berkeley Laboratory, demography and population studies, and weather information.

LEARNING THROUGH PROGRAMMING

When computers first became popular in schools, there was a heavy emphasis on teaching programming. Most often this was (and is) done in the interest of "computer literacy." Computer literacy refers to practical knowledge about computers that every person in our society should have. As such, it is not so much a topic of mathematics as one of social studies. Today, fortunately, the emphasis has shifted from teaching students to use computers to using computers for learning. From a practical standpoint, very few people in society need to know how to program a computer. Is there any value, then, in teaching elementary or middle school children to program? How much programming knowledge do children need to have? What can be learned by learning to program other than a social utility knowledge of how computers work? These questions do not have simple answers. What does seem to be true is that less programming is being taught in schools, perhaps due to the time constraints on the curriculum demanded by an increasing number of topics.

Programming to Learn Mathematics

Some mathematics educators believe that students can learn mathematics through the process of programming (Shumway, 1987, 1992; Smith, 1984). If students are asked to program a computer to perform some task, they (not the computer) must understand any mathematics that might be involved. For example, a student who must write a program that will accept any number as input and will output the absolute value of that number must understand the definition of absolute value. In the process, he or she will confront the symbolism ^{-}N as representing a positive quantity if the value of N is negative.

For those who may be interested in how BASIC programming projects can enhance the learning of mathematical concepts, see Shumway (1992). As Shumway points out, programming graphing calculators is very similar to using BASIC. Much programming that used to require a computer can now be done on the graphing calculator. The absolute value example is a case in point.

Programming and Problem-Solving Skills

Another possible benefit of having students learn to program computers involves the mental processes that are involved rather than the mathematics. Programming involves many of the process skills that are desired in a good problem solver. The issue is whether or not these skills, which do develop as students engage in programming, actually transfer to other environments.

Research evidence supporting transfer of computer problem-solving skills is at this time inconclusive and sketchy. The methods of instruction used in teaching programming, the amount of time required to develop transferable skills (months or even years), and the ability to detect effects in controlled research settings are all factors that make it difficult to be definitive about the possible effects of programming.

Problem Solving and the Logo Language

The most vocal proponents of the programming-for-problem-solving position are the advocates of Logo (e.g., Au, Horton, & Ryba, 1987; Campbell & Clements, 1990; Clements, 1985a, 1985b, 1985c, 1986; Clements & Meredith, 1993; Papert, 1980). Unlike BASIC, Logo permits students to design relatively powerful programs using user-defined words. The turtle graphics feature, only one aspect of the Logo language, can be used to create complex designs, draw pictures, and produce geometric shapes. The graphics mode also provides immediate visual feedback to the programmer. The power of Logo is accessible to very young children, is captivating in its graphics capabilities, and yet is powerful enough to be used in high school and college.

Originally developed at MIT by Seymour Papert, Logo has been the object of numerous research efforts. Much of this interest is due to the claims of Papert (1980) and his followers for the cognitive gains and problem-solving capabilities of children who have had experience with Logo programming. Papert's basic thesis is that the computer is a tool to think with. By exploring or analyzing an idea on the computer, a learner has an object that can be manipulated, viewed, modified, combined, expanded, and, in a sense, played with. In fact, Papert's original explorations during the development of Logo were with a robot turtle that moved around on the floor and could draw pictures with a marker pointing down from its body. Several robot floor turtles are now available that are controlled with Logo. Screen versions of Logo use a small triangular shape about 1 cm tall called a "turtle" or else a small picture of a turtle. It is controlled the same way that the floor turtle would be. The computer thus adds a personal reality to a child's experimentation and should, according to Papert, enhance logical reasoning abilities.

Papert's arguments are so inviting and the Logo language is so captivating and powerful that troops of teachers and mathematics educators have been on a headlong and enthusiastic pursuit of Logo. What have been the results? In a review of early Logo-related research, Clements (1985c) made these observations:

- Programming appears to facilitate the development of specific problem-solving behaviors.
- Younger students may benefit more than older students.
- Logo may enhance social interaction, positive self-images, positive attitudes toward learning, and independent work habits.

Researchers are very cautious about making definitive claims for Logo. Barron and Hynes (1996) note that "the conflicting results may be due to inappropriate research designs, lack of random assignment to groups, lack of control groups, and incomplete documentation of the studies" (pp. 134–135). Exactly what the teacher and students are doing in a Logo experience is not clear in many of the studies that have been conducted. The transfer of thinking processes to situations that do not involve Logo is not always well supported. After nearly two decades of Logo in the classroom, much of the interest in Logo continues to emanate from Logo enthusiasts who are convinced of the values of Logo more by their intuition than by careful research. Sawyer (1995), based on experiences in England with children from age 5 through middle school, is more definitive:

The benefits for children are:

- increased understanding and use of mathematical vocabulary;
- in the linking of the strands of the mathematics curriculum, so that children can use knowledge and understanding acquired in one area, for example number, or shape, or space, use and apply it within measure, and extend their knowledge and understanding of algebra through further investigation. This can lead to accelerated learning in the particular areas of the mathematics curriculum included;
- the development of problem-solving strategies;
- the development of personal qualities through the need for children to collaborate, to persevere and to talk about their work. (p. 70)

A Brief Look at Logo

It is difficult to appreciate the enthusiasm that Logo tends to generate without some firsthand experience. If you have never played around with Logo, you are strongly encouraged to give it an honest try. Even if you have had a negative experience with programming in another language such as BASIC, you owe it to yourself at least to try Logo. It is a truly different way to work with computers, and almost everyone has fun.

One minimal approach is to work through the examples and explorations provided in the following paragraphs while actually sitting at a computer. A better idea is to get one of the many books about Logo and teaching Logo and work through some of it on your own or with a friend. A few such books are suggested at the end of the chapter.

If you have never experienced Logo, this is where to start. First, you will need a computer with some version of Logo installed. This text will not provide you with all of the details of getting the language booted up, correcting typos, or other nuances. A good idea is to find someone who knows a little about Logo to help you get started. If you are using Terrapin Logo, you will be able to follow the directions given here exactly. If you are using Logo Writer or some other dialect of Logo, there are a few minor differences. Where these differences occur, you will be directed to check a manual.

Simple Turtle Commands

To get Logo to show a screen where the turtle draws pictures, type DRAW and press Return. (This command varies with different Logo versions.) There are a few commands the turtle understands without being taught. Here are some of them.

FD Short for FORWARD. You must also say how far forward you want the turtle to go. For example, FD 100 or FD 30 will make the turtle go forward. Notice the space between FD and 100. Spaces are important in Logo.

BK Short for BACK. BK works like FD and needs an "input" or a number that tells how far, like BK 140.

RT Short for RIGHT. The turtle can turn, but you have to tell it how much, like RT 30 or RT 90 or RT 200. You will soon discover that those turn numbers are degrees.

LT LEFT. Works the same as RT.

Try these commands, and make the turtle scribble around. You have to press the Return key before it will do anything. When you want to start all over with a clean screen, type DRAW. (In other versions, this may be CLEARSCREEN or CS.) The turtle has a "pen" that is usually down, causing the line to be drawn when it moves. If you want the turtle to move without drawing a line, type PU for PENUP (and press Return). To draw again, type PD for PENDOWN.

Before going any further, play with these commands. Try to draw something: your initials, a rectangle, or a triangle. What happens if you send the turtle really far, like FD 2000? Try that when the turtle is turned just a little from "north." Can you figure out what happens when the turtle goes off the side of the screen?

At this point, try to draw a simple house like the one in Figure 24.4. All of the distances should be the same. Plan on paper the list of turtle commands you want to use. Test out your list, and revise it as necessary.

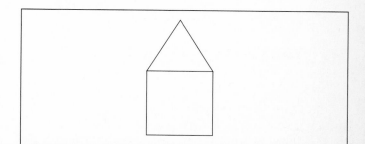

●**FIGURE 24.4** A typical house drawn with Logo.

Teaching the Turtle

One of the nice things about Logo is that there are very few words to remember. You can define the language as you go along, using your own words for whatever you want them to mean. This is called *defining procedures*. Young children might call it "teaching the turtle."

By way of illustration, teach the turtle how to do some simple little squiggle—for example, FD 60 LT 45 BK 20. Since this is just two lines at an angle, you can call it anything you want, like GEORGE, CHECK, SQUIGGLE, YZR, or S3.

Suppose you decide on SQUIGGLE. Type TO SQUIG-GLE and press Return. (Look up *defining procedures* in other versions.) The word TO tells Logo you want to define the word that follows it. In Terrapin Logo Plus, a new window is opened, the Edit window. This is the place where procedures are defined. Now type each of the three commands FD 60, LT 45, and BK 20. It is a good idea to press Return after each. Then type END for the end of the procedure. If you made any mistakes, you can use the mouse or arrow keys to edit as you would on a word processor. When you are done, press Ctrl-C (hold down Control and press C). Logo returns you to the text window and responds, SQUIGGLE DEFINED. Now the turtle knows the word SQUIGGLE.

Now try out your new word. Type SQUIGGLE. Try it again (or you can place the cursor on any line that says SQUIGGLE and press Return). Use SQUIGGLE along with the other commands. Figure 24.5 shows some experiments with SQUIGGLE.

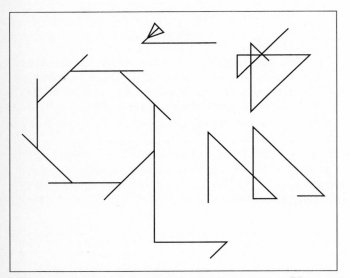

● **FIGURE 24.5**   Playing with Logo and the SQUIGGLE procedure.

SQUIGGLE is an example of a procedure that you defined. It is actually a little Logo program. Define some other words. Define your initial or a dashed line or some simple shape. If you try to define a word that Logo already knows, Logo will tell you. Just change the word a bit. If you want to change SQUIGGLE, just type TO SQUIGGLE, or click in the Edit window to make changes. Remember Ctrl-C to finish or "define the procedure."

Before you go any further, try to define two more procedures. Call them BOX and TRI. Define BOX to be a square and TRI to be a triangle so that all of the sides of BOX and TRI are the same length.

Putting Procedures Together

Once you have defined a procedure, that word can be used just like any other Logo word. That means that it can be used inside another procedure. For example, here are four procedures. CANE and CORNER are used inside RECTS, and RECTS is used in DOWNTOWN. With a pencil and paper to draw a path, pretend you are the turtle. See if you can predict what each procedure will do by itself. Then define these procedures on the computer and try them out.

TO CANE	TO RECTS	TO DOWNTOWN
FD 60	CANE	RECTS
RT 90	LT 90	BK 50
FD 20	CORNER	RT 90
END	RT 90	RECTS
	CORNER	BK 50
TO CORNER	LT 90	RT 90
FD 30	CANE	CANE
RT 90	END	RT 90
FD 30		CANE
END		END

If you were successful, your DOWNTOWN procedure should draw what looks a little like a building. Try putting the building in different places on the screen. Use CANE, CORNER, and RECTS to make other procedures. Add some ideas of your own.

Finally, before you continue, can you use your BOX and TRI procedures to make HOUSE as in Figure 24.4 (p. 531)? Try to make a single procedure that draws three houses in a row.

This has been a very limited exposure to Logo. You should not generalize or make major conclusions about Logo from this experience. If you are at all intrigued by this little exercise, or if you just had fun, there is much, much more that Logo has to offer you. Your next explorations should involve the REPEAT command and also variables. Middle school students can use Logo to investigate the concept of recursion. Much can be done without turtle graphics, as Logo can be used to manipulate words and perform operations on numbers as well. Get a book and a friend. Take a course or go to a workshop.

REFLECTIONS ON CHAPTER 24: WRITING TO LEARN

1. Technology has affected the mathematics curriculum and how it is taught in three ways. Explain each, and give an example to support your explanation.

2. Review the arguments for using calculators in elementary school. Select two that are most appealing to you, and describe them as if you were arguing before your principal or grade-level committee to allow calculators in your class or school.

3. Explain briefly these features of calculators and why they may be important:

   a. Automatic constant feature

   b. Algebraic logic

   c. Fraction capability

4. Give two reasons for promoting the use of graphing calculators in grades 6–8. Describe and defend your own opinion about this.

5. Briefly describe at least three different categories or types of computer tool software. How are these tools used in teaching mathematics?

6. If you were to select computer software that involved a computer version of a physical manipulative, it should have some advantages over the physical version of the same manipulative. What advantages might a computer manipulative have that would make it different from or perhaps better than the physical version?

7. How does instructional software differ from tool software?

8. What are some different types of mathematics education information you can expect to find on the Internet?

9. Describe the general arguments that are used to defend the teaching of Logo (or any programming). Why are researchers still undecided about these arguments?

FOR DISCUSSION AND EXPLORATION

1. Talk with some teachers about their use or nonuse of calculators in the classroom. How do the teachers who use them go about doing so? What are the main reasons for not using them among the teachers who do not? The *Standards,* the NCTM position statements on calculators and technology, and this book all strongly favor the use of calculators in schools. If you or any of the teachers you talked with do not accept this position, what arguments would you bring to bear against these various authors?

2. Among the software kept at your school, find one example of drill-and-practice software and one example of some other form of instructional software for mathemat-

ics. Try to find new titles that are most representative of recent developments in technology. Try each, and decide how it would be used in your classroom (if at all). Be sure to check the documentation for suggested grade levels. In trying to use the software, do not forget that a teacher would be there to help students learn how to use it.

3. Find two or three sites on the Internet that provide you with useful information that could be used in your classroom.

4. Read the short article "My Turn: A Talk with the Logo Turtle" (Clements & Meredith, 1993). Find a computer where you can explore Logo, at least doing the activities suggested at the end of this chapter, and see if you agree with the authors. Can you use Logo to draw the figures in the article? What would the issues be for a second grader? What about for a seventh- or eighth-grade student?

SUGGESTED READINGS

Highly Recommended

Battista, M. T. (1994). Calculators and computers: Tools for mathematical exploration and empowerment. *Arithmetic Teacher, 41,* 412–417.

In this article, Battista shares children's explorations with calculators, Logo, and a geometry tool. The ideas remain timely and give a quick view of what can actually be done if we take advantage of the power of these tools.

Dockterman, D. A. (1991). *Great teaching in the one-computer classroom* (3rd ed.). Watertown, MA: Tom Snyder.

Though not about teaching mathematics, this little book is written in a very teacher-friendly style about practical uses of a single computer in the classroom. Topics include cooperative learning, interactive video, and using the computer to make your classroom life easier.

Fey, J. T. (Ed.). (1992). *Calculators in mathematics education.* Reston, VA: National Council of Teachers of Mathematics.

This is one of the best perspectives on the impact of calculators in mathematics that has been written. It remains timely, offering both vision and practical ideas for teachers at all grade levels. Included are sections on calculators in assessment and strategies for implementation of calculators. Every teacher will find much of value here.

Other Suggestions

Aieta, J. F. (1985). Microworlds: Options for learning and teaching geometry. *Mathematics Teacher, 78,* 473–480.

Barrett, G., & Goebel, J. (1990). The impact of graphing calculators on the teaching and learning of mathematics. In T. J. Cooney (Ed.), *Teaching and learning mathematics in the 1990s* (pp. 205–211). Reston, VA: National Council of Teachers of Mathematics.

Barron, A. E., & Hynes, M. C. (1996). Using technology to enhance communication in mathematics. In P. C. Elliott (Ed.), *Communication in mathematics, K–12 and beyond* (pp. 126–136). Reston, VA: National Council of Teachers of Mathematics.

Battista, M. T., & Clements, D. H. (1988). A case for a Logo-based elementary school geometry curriculum. *Arithmetic Teacher, 36*(3), 11–17.

Bayliffe, J., Brie, R., & Oliver, B. (1994). Using technology to enhance "My Travels with Gulliver." *Teaching Children Mathematics, 1,* 188–191.

Calculator-Enhanced Mathematics Instruction Steering Committee. (1992). *Calculators for classrooms* [Video and guidebook]. Reston, VA: National Council of Teachers of Mathematics.

Campbell, P. F., & Clements, D. H. (1990). Using microcomputers for mathematics learning. In J. N. Payne (Ed.), *Mathematics for the young child.* Reston, VA: National Council of Teachers of Mathematics.

Campbell, P. B., & Stewart, E. L. (1993). Calculators and computers. In R. J. Jensen (Ed.), *Research ideas for the classroom: Early childhood mathematics* (pp. 251–268). Old Tappan, NJ: Macmillan.

Charischak, I., & Berkman, R. (1995). Looking at random events with Logo software. *Mathematics Teaching in the Middle School, 1,* 318–322.

Clements, D. H. (1989). *Computers in elementary mathematics education.* Upper Saddle River, NJ: Prentice Hall.

Clements, D. H., & Meredith, J. S. (1993). My turn: A talk with the Logo turtle. *Arithmetic Teacher, 41,* 189–191.

Coburn, T. (1987). *How to teach mathematics using a calculator.* Reston, VA: National Council of Teachers of Mathematics.

Demana, F., & Waits, B. K. (1990). Enhancing mathematics teaching and learning through technology. In T. J. Cooney (Ed.), *Teaching and learning mathematics in the 1990s* (pp. 212–222). Reston, VA: National Council of Teachers of Mathematics.

Drosdeck, C. C. (1995). Promoting calculator use in elementary classrooms. *Teaching Children Mathematics, 1,* 300–305.

Hembree, R., & Dessart, D. J. (1992). Research on calculators in mathematics education. In J. T. Fey (Ed.), *Calculators in mathematics education* (pp. 23–32). Reston, VA: National Council of Teachers of Mathematics.

Jensen, R. J., & Williams, B. S. (1993). Technology: Implications for the middle grades. In D. T. Owens (Ed.), *Research ideas for the classroom: Middle grades mathematics* (pp. 225–243). Old Tappan, NJ: Macmillan.

Lilly, M. W. (Ed.). (1987). Calculators [Special issue]. *Arithmetic Teacher, 34*(6).

McDonald, J. L. (1988). Integrating spreadsheets into the mathematics classroom. *Mathematics Teacher, 81,* 615–622.

Niess, M. L. (1993). Forecast: Changing mathematics curriculum and increasing pressure for higher-level thinking skills. *Arithmetic Teacher, 41,* 129–135.

Owens, J. E. (1995). Playing green globs on a TI-81. *Mathematics Teaching in the Middle School, 1,* 370–374.

Pagni, D. (Ed.). (1991). *Calculators and Mathematics Project, Los Angeles (CAMP-LA)* (4 vols.: K–2, 3–4, 5–6, 7–8). Fullerton, CA: Cal State Fullerton Press.

Papert, S. (1980). *Mindstorms: Children, computers, and powerful ideas.* New York: Basic Books.

Reys, B. J. (1989). The calculator as a tool for instruction and learning. In P. R. Trafton (Ed.), *New directions for elementary school mathematics* (pp. 168–173). Reston, VA: National Council of Teachers of Mathematics.

Reys, B. J., & Smith, N. (1994). Integrating calculators: How far have we come? *Teaching Children Mathematics, 1,* 206–207.

Russell, J. C. (1992). *Spreadsheet activities in middle school mathematics.* Reston, VA: National Council of Teachers of Mathematics.

Sawyer, A. E. (1995). *Developments in elementary mathematics teaching.* Portsmouth, NH: Heinemann.

Shumway, R. J. (1992). Calculators and computers. In T. R. Post (Ed.), *Teaching mathematics in grades K–8: Research-based methods* (2nd ed.) (pp. 363–419). Needham Heights, MA: Allyn & Bacon.

Taylor, L. J. C., & Nichols, J. A. (1994). Graphing calculators aren't just for high school students. *Mathematics Teaching in the Middle School, 1,* 190–196.

Vonder Embse, C. (1992). Concept development and problem solving using graphing calculators in the middle school. In J. T. Fey (Ed.), *Calculators in mathematics education* (pp. 65–78). Reston, VA: National Council of Teachers of Mathematics.

Wheatley, G. H., & Shumway, R. J. (1992). The potential for calculators to transform elementary school mathematics. In J. T. Fey (Ed.), *Calculators in mathematics education* (pp. 1–8). Reston, VA: National Council of Teachers of Mathematics.

Zech, L., Vye, N. J., Bransford, J. D., Swink, J., Mayfield-Stewart, C., Goldman, S. R., & the Cognition and Technology Group at Vanderbilt. (1994). Bringing geometry into the classroom with videodisc technology. *Mathematics Teaching in the Middle School, 1,* 228–233.

Appendix A

Curriculum and Evaluation Standards for School Mathematics

CURRICULUM STANDARDS FOR GRADES K–4
Summary of Changes in Content and Emphasis in K–4 Mathematics

Increased Attention

Number

Number sense
Place-value concepts
Meaning of fractions and decimals
Estimation of quantities

Operations and Computation

Meaning of operations
Operation sense
Mental computation
Estimation and the reasonableness of answers
Selection of an appropriate computational method
Use of calculators for complex computation
Thinking strategies for basic facts

Geometry and Measurement

Properties of geometric figures
Geometric relationships
Spatial sense
Process of measuring
Concepts related to units of measurement
Actual measuring
Estimation of measurements
Use of measurement and geometry ideas throughout the
  curriculum

Decreased Attention

Number

Early attention to reading, writing, and ordering numbers
  symbolically

Operations and Computation

Complex paper-and-pencil computations
Isolated treatment of paper-and-pencil computations
Addition and subtraction without renaming
Isolated treatment of division facts
Long division
Long division without remainders
Paper-and-pencil fraction computation
Use of rounding to estimate

Geometry and Measurement

Primary focus on naming geometric figures
Memorization of equivalencies between units of measurement

Source: From *Curriculum and Evaluation Standards for School Mathematics* (NCTM, 1989). The changes in emphasis are from pages 20–21 and 70–73. The standards are quoted from the front of each standard in the K–4 and 5–8 sections of the document. Used by permission.

Probability and Statistics

Collection and organization of data
Exploration of chance

Patterns and Relationships

Pattern recognition and description
Use of variables to express relationships

Problem Solving

Word problems with a variety of structures
Use of everyday problems
Applications
Study of patterns and relationships
Problem-solving strategies

Problem Solving

Use of clue words to determine which operation to use

Instructional Practices

Use of manipulative materials
Cooperative work
Discussion of mathematics
Questioning
Justification of thinking
Writing about mathematics
Problem-solving approach to instruction
Content integration
Use of calculators and computers

Instructional Practices

Rote practice
Rote memorization of rules
One answer and one method
Use of worksheets
Written practice
Teaching by telling

Standards for Grades K–4

1. Mathematics as Problem Solving

In grades K–4, the study of mathematics should emphasize problem solving so that students can

- Use problem-solving approaches to investigate and understand mathematical content
- Formulate problems from everyday and mathematical situations
- Develop and apply strategies to solve a wide variety of problems
- Verify and interpret results with respect to the original problem
- Acquire confidence in using mathematics meaningfully

2. Mathematics as Communication

In grades K–4, the study of mathematics should include numerous opportunities for communication so that students can

- Relate physical materials, pictures, and diagrams to mathematical ideas
- Reflect on and clarify their thinking about mathematical ideas and situations
- Relate their everyday language to mathematical language and symbols
- Realize that representing, discussing, reading, writing, and listening to mathematics are a vital part of learning and using mathematics

3. Mathematics as Reasoning

In grades K–4, the study of mathematics should emphasize reasoning so that students can

- Draw logical conclusions about mathematics
- Use models, known facts, properties, and relationships to explain their thinking
- Justify their answers and solution processes
- Use patterns and relationships to analyze mathematical situations
- Believe that mathematics makes sense

4. Mathematical Connections

In grades K–4, the study of mathematics should include opportunities to make connections so that students can

- Link conceptual and procedural knowledge
- Relate various representations of concepts or procedures to one another
- Recognize relationships among different topics in mathematics
- Use mathematics in other curriculum areas
- Use mathematics in their daily lives

5. Estimation

In grades K–4, the curriculum should include estimation so students can

- Explore estimation strategies
- Recognize when an estimate is appropriate
- Determine the reasonableness of results
- Apply estimation in working with quantities, measurement, computation, and problem solving

6. Number Sense and Numeration

In grades K–4, the mathematics curriculum should include whole-number concepts and skills so that students can

- Construct number meanings through real-world experiences and the use of physical materials
- Understand our numeration system by relating counting, grouping, and place-value concepts
- Develop number sense
- Interpret the multiple uses of numbers encountered in the real world

7. Concepts of Whole-Number Operations

In grades K–4, the mathematics curriculum should include concepts of addition, subtraction, multiplication, and division of whole numbers so that students can

- Develop meaning for the operations by modeling and discussing a rich variety of problem situations
- Relate the mathematical language and symbolism of operations to problem situations and informal language
- Recognize that a wide variety of problem structures can be represented by a single operation
- Develop operation sense

8. Whole-Number Computation

In grades K–4, the mathematics curriculum should develop whole-number computation so that students can

- Model, explain, and develop reasonable proficiency with basic facts and algorithms
- Use a variety of mental computation and estimation techniques
- Use calculators in appropriate computational situations
- Select and use computation techniques appropriate to specific problems and determine whether the results are reasonable

9. Geometry and Spatial Sense

In grades K–4, the mathematics curriculum should include two- and three-dimensional geometry so that students can

- Describe, model, draw, and classify shapes
- Investigate and predict the results of combining, subdividing, and changing shapes
- Develop spatial sense
- Relate geometric ideas to number and measurement ideas
- Recognize and appreciate geometry in their world

10. Measurement

In grades K–4, the mathematics curriculum should include measurement so that students can

- Understand the attributes of length, capacity, weight, mass, area, volume, time, temperature, and angle
- Develop the process of measuring and concepts related to units of measurement
- Make and use estimates of measurement
- Make and use measurements in problem and everyday situations

11. Statistics and Probability

In grades K–4, the mathematics curriculum should include experiences with data analysis and probability so that students can

- Collect, organize, and describe data
- Construct, read, and interpret displays of data
- Formulate and solve problems that involve collecting and analyzing data
- Explore concepts of chance

12. Fractions and Decimals

In grades K–4, the mathematics curriculum should include fractions and decimals so that students can

- Develop concepts of fractions, mixed numbers, and decimals
- Develop number sense for fractions and decimals
- Use models to relate fractions to decimals and to find equivalent fractions
- Use models to explore operations on fractions and decimals
- Apply fractions and decimals to problem situations

13. Patterns and Relationships

In grades K–4, the mathematics curriculum should include the study of patterns and relationships so that students can

- Recognize, describe, extend, and create a wide variety of patterns
- Represent and describe mathematical relationships
- Explore the use of variables and open sentences to express relationships

CURRICULUM STANDARDS FOR GRADES 5–8
Summary of Changes in Content and Emphasis in 5–8 Mathematics

Increased Attention

Problem Solving

Pursuing open-ended problems and extended problem-solving projects

Investigating and formulating questions from problem situations

Representing situations verbally, numerically, graphically, geometrically, or symbolically

Communication

Discussing, writing, reading, and listening to mathematical ideas

Reasoning

Reasoning in spatial contexts

Reasoning with proportions

Reasoning from graphs

Reasoning inductively and deductively

Connections

Connecting mathematics to other subjects and to the world outside the classroom

Connecting topics within mathematics

Applying mathematics

Number/Operations/Computation

Developing number sense

Developing operation sense

Creating algorithms and procedures

Using estimation both in solving problems and in checking the reasonableness of results

Exploring relationships among representations of, and operations on, whole numbers, fractions, decimals, integers, and rational numbers

Developing an understanding of ratio, proportion, and percent

Patterns and Functions

Identifying and using functional relationships

Developing and using tables, graphs, and rules to describe situations

Interpreting among different mathematical representations

Algebra

Developing an understanding of variables, expressions, and equations

Using a variety of methods to solve linear equations and informally investigate inequalities and nonlinear equations

Decreased Attention

Problem Solving

Practicing routine, one-step problems

Practicing problems categorized by types (e.g., coin problems, age problems)

Communication

Doing fill-in-the-blank worksheets

Answering questions that require only yes, no, or a number as responses

Reasoning

Relying on outside authority (teacher or an answer key)

Connections

Learning isolated topics

Developing skills out of context

Number/Operations/Computations

Memorizing rules and algorithms

Practicing tedious paper-and-pencil computations

Finding exact forms of answers

Memorizing procedures, such as cross-multiplication, without understanding

Practicing rounding numbers out of context

Patterns and Functions

Topics seldom in the current curriculum

Algebra

Manipulating symbols

Memorizing procedures and drilling on equation solving

Statistics

Using statistical methods to describe, analyze, evaluate, and make a decision

Probability

Creating experimental and theoretical modes of situations involving probabilities

Geometry

Developing an understanding of geometric objects and relationships
Using geometry in solving problems

Measurement

Estimating and using measurement to solve problems

Instructional Practices

Actively involving students individually and in groups in exploring, conjecturing, analyzing, and applying mathematics in both a mathematical and a real-world context
Using appropriate technology for computation and exploration
Using concrete materials
Being a facilitator of learning
Assessing learning as an integral part of instruction

Statistics

Memorizing formulas

Probability

Memorizing formulas

Geometry

Memorizing geometric vocabulary
Memorizing facts and relationships

Measurement

Memorizing and manipulating formulas
Converting within and between measurement systems

Instructional Practices

Teaching computations out of context
Drilling on paper-and-pencil algorithms
Teaching topics in isolation
Stressing memorization
Being the dispenser of knowledge
Testing for the sole purpose of assigning grades

Standards for Grades 5–8

1. Mathematics as Problem Solving

In grades 5–8, the mathematics curriculum should include numerous and varied experiences with problem solving as a method of inquiry and application so that students can

- Use problem-solving approaches to investigate and understand mathematical content
- Formulate problems from situations within and outside mathematics
- Develop and apply a variety of strategies to solve problems, with emphasis on multistep and nonroutine problems
- Verify and interpret results with respect to the original problem situation
- Generalize solutions and strategies to new problem situations
- Acquire confidence in using mathematics meaningfully

2. Mathematics as Communication

In grades 5–8, the study of mathematics should include opportunities to communicate so that students can

- Model situations using oral, written, concrete, pictorial, graphical, and algebraic methods

- Reflect on and clarify their own thinking about mathematical ideas and situations
- Develop common understandings of mathematical ideas, including the role of definitions
- Use the skills of reading, listening, and viewing to interpret and evaluate mathematical ideas
- Discuss mathematical ideas and make conjectures and convincing arguments
- Appreciate the value of mathematical notation and its role in the development of mathematical ideas

3. Mathematics as Reasoning

In grades 5–8, reasoning shall permeate the mathematics curriculum so that students can

- Recognize and apply deductive and inductive reasoning
- Understand and apply reasoning processes, with special attention to spatial reasoning and reasoning with proportions and graphs
- Make and evaluate mathematical conjectures and arguments
- Validate their own thinking
- Appreciate the pervasive use and power of reasoning as a part of mathematics

4. Mathematical Connections

In grades 5–8, the mathematics curriculum should include the investigation of mathematical connections so that students can

- See mathematics as an integrated whole
- Explore problems and describe results using graphical, numerical, physical, algebraic, and verbal mathematical models or representations
- Use a mathematical idea to further their understanding of other mathematical ideas
- Apply mathematical thinking and modeling to solve problems that arise in other disciplines, such as art, music, psychology, science, and business
- Value the role of mathematics in our culture and society

5. Number and Number Relationships

In grades 5–8, the mathematics curriculum should include the continued development of number and number relationships so that students can

- Understand, represent, and use numbers in a variety of equivalent forms (integer, fraction, decimal, percent, exponential, and scientific notation) in real-world and mathematical problem situations
- Develop number sense for whole numbers, fractions, decimals, integers, and rational numbers
- Understand and apply ratios, proportions, and percents in a wide variety of situations
- Investigate relationships among fractions, decimals, and percents
- Represent numerical relationships in one- and two-dimensional graphs

6. Number Systems and Number Theory

In grades 5–8, the mathematics curriculum should include the study of number systems and number theory so that students can

- Understand and appreciate the need for numbers beyond the whole numbers
- Develop and use order relations for whole numbers, fractions, decimals, integers, and rational numbers
- Extend their understanding of whole number operations to fractions, decimals, integers, and rational numbers
- Understand how the basic arithmetic operations are related to one another
- Develop and apply number theory concepts (e.g., primes, factors, and multiples) in real-world and mathematical problem situations

7. Computation and Estimation

In grades 5–8, the mathematics curriculum should develop the concepts underlying computation and estimation in various contexts so that students can

- Compute with whole numbers, fractions, decimals, integers, and rational numbers
- Develop, analyze, and explain procedures for computation and techniques for estimation
- Develop, analyze, and explain methods for solving proportions
- Select and use an appropriate method for computing from among mental arithmetic, paper-and-pencil, calculator, and computer methods
- Use computation, estimation, and proportions to solve problems
- Use estimation to check the reasonableness of results

8. Patterns and Functions

In grades 5–8, the mathematics curriculum should include explorations of patterns and functions so that students can

- Describe, extend, analyze, and create a wide variety of patterns
- Describe and represent relationships with tables, graphs, and rules
- Analyze functional relationships to explain how a change in one quantity results in a change in another
- Use patterns and functions to represent and solve problems

9. Algebra

In grades 5–8, the mathematics curriculum should include explorations of algebraic concepts and processes so that students can

- Understand the concepts of variable, expression, and equation
- Represent situations and number patterns with tables, graphs, verbal rules, and equations and explore the interrelationships of these representations
- Analyze tables and graphs to identify properties and relationships
- Develop confidence in solving linear equations using concrete, informal, and formal methods
- Investigate inequalities and nonlinear equations informally
- Apply algebraic methods to solve a variety of real-world and mathematical problems

10. Statistics

In grades 5–8, the mathematics curriculum should include exploration of statistics in real-world situations so that students can

- Systematically collect, organize, and describe data
- Construct, read, and interpret tables, charts, and graphs
- Make inferences and convincing arguments that are based on data analysis
- Evaluate arguments that are based on data analysis
- Develop an appreciation for statistical methods as powerful means for decision making

11. Probability

In grades 5–8, the mathematics curriculum should include explorations of probability in real-world situations so that students can

- Model situations by devising and carrying out experiments or simulations to determine probabilities
- Model situations by constructing a sample space to determine probabilities
- Appreciate the power of using a probability model by comparing experimental results with mathematical expectations
- Make predictions that are based on experimental or theoretical probabilities
- Develop an appreciation for the pervasive use of probability in the real world

12. Geometry

In grades 5–8, the mathematics curriculum should include the study of geometry of one, two, and three dimensions in a variety of situations so that students can

- Identify, describe, compare, and classify geometric figures
- Visualize and represent geometric figures with special attention to developing spatial sense
- Explore transformations of geometric figures
- Represent and solve problems using geometric models
- Understand and apply geometric properties and relationships
- Develop an appreciation of geometry as a means of describing the physical world

13. Measurement

In grades 5–8, the mathematics curriculum should include extensive concrete experiences using measurement so that students can

- Extend their understanding of the process of measurement
- Estimate, make, and use measurements to describe and compare phenomena
- Select appropriate units and tools to measure to the degree of accuracy required in a particular situation
- Understand the structure and use of systems of measurement
- Extend their understanding of the concepts of perimeter, area, volume, angle measure, capacity, and weight and mass
- Develop the concepts of rates and other derived and indirect measurements
- Develop formulas and procedures for determining measures to solve problems

APPENDIX B

PROFESSIONAL STANDARDS
FOR TEACHING MATHEMATICS

STANDARDS FOR TEACHING MATHEMATICS

1. Worthwhile Mathematical Tasks

The teacher of mathematics should pose tasks that are based on

- Sound and significant mathematics
- Knowledge of students' understandings, interests, and experiences
- Knowledge of the range of ways that diverse students learn mathematics

and that

- Engage students' intellect
- Develop students' mathematical understandings and skills
- Stimulate students to make connections and develop a coherent framework for mathematical ideas
- Call for problem formulation, problem solving, and mathematical reasoning
- Promote communication about mathematics
- Represent mathematics as an ongoing human activity
- Display sensitivity to, and draw on, students' diverse background experiences and dispositions
- Promote the development of all students' dispositions to do mathematics

2. Teacher's Role in Discourse

The teacher of mathematics should orchestrate discourse by

- Posing questions and tasks that elicit, engage, and challenge each student's thinking
- Listening carefully to students' ideas

- Asking students to clarify and justify their ideas orally and in writing
- Deciding what to pursue in depth from among the ideas that students bring up during a discussion
- Deciding when and how to attach mathematical notation and language to students' ideas
- Deciding when to provide information, when to clarify an issue, when to model, when to lead, and when to let a student struggle with a difficulty
- Monitoring students' participation in discussions and deciding when and how to encourage each student to participate

3. Students' Role in Discourse

The teacher of mathematics should promote classroom discourse in which students

- Listen to, respond to, and question the teacher and one another
- Use a variety of tools to reason, make connections, solve problems, and communicate
- Initiate problems and questions
- Make conjectures and present solutions
- Explore examples and counterexamples to investigate a conjecture
- Try to convince themselves and one another of the validity of particular representations, solutions, conjectures, and answers
- Rely on mathematical evidence and argument to determine validity

---

Source: From *Professional Standards for Teaching Mathematics* (NCTM, 1991). The standards are quoted from the front of each of the six standards for teaching mathematics in the document. Used by permission.

4. Tools for Enhancing Discourse

The teacher of mathematics, in order to enhance discourse, should encourage and accept the use of

- Computers, calculators, and other technology
- Concrete materials used as models
- Pictures, diagrams, tables, and graphs
- Invented and conventional terms and symbols
- Metaphors, analogies, and stories
- Written hypotheses, explanations, and arguments
- Oral presentations and dramatizations

5. Learning Environment

The teacher of mathematics should create a learning environment that fosters the development of each student's mathematical power by

- Providing and structuring the time necessary to explore sound mathematics and grapple with significant ideas and problems
- Using the physical space and materials in ways that facilitate students' learning of mathematics
- Providing a context that encourages the development of mathematical skill and proficiency
- Respecting and valuing students' ideas, ways of thinking, and mathematical dispositions

and by consistently expecting and encouraging students to

- Work independently or collaboratively to make sense of mathematics
- Take intellectual risks by raising questions and formulating conjectures
- Display a sense of mathematical competence by validating and supporting ideas with mathematical argument

6. Analysis of Teaching and Learning

The teacher of mathematics should engage in ongoing analysis of teaching and learning by

- Observing, listening to, and gathering other information about students to assess what they are learning
- Examining effects of the tasks, discourse, and learning environment on students' mathematical knowledge, skills, and dispositions

in order to

- Ensure that every student is learning sound and significant mathematics and is developing a positive disposition toward mathematics
- Challenge and extend students' ideas
- Adapt or change activities while teaching
- Make plans, both short- and long-range
- Describe and comment on each student's learning to parents and administrators, as well as to the students themselves

REFERENCES

Ann Arbor Public Schools. (1993). *Alternative assessment: Evaluating student performance in elementary mathematics.* Palo Alto, CA: Dale Seymour.

Armstrong, R. D. (1981). An area model for solving probability problems. In A. P. Shulte (Ed.), *Teaching statistics and probability* (pp. 135–142). Reston, VA: National Council of Teachers of Mathematics.

Au, W. K., Horton, J., & Ryba, K. (1987). Logo, teacher intervention, and the development of thinking skills. *Computing Teacher, 15*(3), 12–16.

Azzolino, A. (1990). Writing as a tool for teaching mathematics: The silent revolution. In T. J. Cooney (Ed.), *Teaching and learning mathematics in the 1990s* (pp. 92–100). Reston, VA: National Council of Teachers of Mathematics.

Backhouse, J., Haggarty, L., Pirie, S., & Stratton, J. (1992). *Improving the learning of mathematics.* Portsmouth, NH: Heinemann.

Baker, A., & Baker, J. (1991). *Maths in the mind: A process approach to mental strategies.* Portsmouth, NH: Heinemann.

Baker, J., & Baker, A. (1990). *Mathematics in process.* Portsmouth, NH: Heinemann.

Ball, D. L. (1992). Magical hopes: Manipulatives and the reform of math education. *American Educator 16* (2), 14–18, 46–47.

Baratta-Lorton, M. (1976). *Mathematics their way.* Menlo Park, CA: AWL Supplemental.

Baratta-Lorton, M. (1979). *Workjobs II.* Menlo Park, CA: AWL Supplemental.

Baroody, A. J. (1985). Mastery of the basic number combinations: Internalization of relationships or facts? *Journal for Research in Mathematics Education, 16,* 83–98.

Baroody, A. J. (1987). *Children's mathematical thinking: A developmental framework for preschool, primary, and special education teachers.* New York: Teachers College Press.

Baroody, A. J., & Hume, J. (1991). Meaningful mathematics instruction: The case of fractions. *Remedial and Special Education, 12,* 54–68.

Barron, A. E., & Hynes, M. C. (1996). Using technology to enhance communication in mathematics. In P. C. Elliott (Ed.), *Communication in mathematics, K–12 and beyond* (pp. 126–136). Reston, VA: National Council of Teachers of Mathematics.

Behr, M. J., Erlwanger, S., & Nichols, E. (1976). *How children view equality sentences.* PMDC Technical Report No. 3. Tallahassee: Florida State University.

Behr, M. J., Lesh, R. A., Post, T. R., & Silver, E. A. (1983). Rational-number concepts. In R. A. Lesh & M. Landau (Eds.), *Acquisition of mathematics concepts and processes* (pp. 91–126). Orlando, FL: Academic Press.

Bennett, A., Jr. (1982). *Decimal squares: Step-by-step teachers guide, readiness to advanced levels in decimals.* Fort Collins, CO: Scott Scientific.

Bennett, D. (1992). *Exploring geometry with* The Geometer's Sketchpad. Berkeley, CA: Key Curriculum Press.

Bezuszka, S. J., Kenney, M., & Silvey, L. (1977). *Tessellations: The geometry of patterns.* Palo Alto, CA: Creative Publications.

Bley, N. S. (1994). Accommodating special needs. In C. A. Thornton & N. S. Bley (Eds.), *Windows of opportunity: Mathematics for students with special needs* (pp. 137–163). Reston, VA: National Council of Teachers of Mathematics.

Bley, N. S., & Thornton, C. A. (1995). *Teaching mathematics to students with learning disabilities* (3rd ed.). Austin, TX: Pro-Ed.

Board gives *Standards* project green light for 21st century. (1996, July-August). *NCTM News Bulletin, 7.*

Bolster, L. C., et al. (1988). *Invitation to mathematics Gr. 2.* Glenview, IL: Scott, Foresman.

Booth, L. R. (1988). Children's difficulties in beginning algebra. In A. F. Coxford (Ed.), *The ideas of algebra, K–12* (pp. 20–32). Reston, VA: National Council of Teachers of Mathematics.

Borasi, R. (1992). *Learning mathematics through inquiry.* Portsmouth, NH: Heinemann.

Borasi, R. (1994, April). Implementing the NCTM *Standards* in "inclusive" mainstream classrooms. Presented at the annual meeting of the National Council of Teachers of Mathematics, Indianapolis, IN.

Bresser, R. (1995). *Math and literature (grades 4–6).* White Plains, NY: Cuisenaire (distributor).

Bright, G. W., Behr, M. J., Post, T. R., & Wachsmuth, I. (1988). Identifying fractions on number lines. *Journal for Research in Mathematics Education, 19,* 215–232.

Brooks, J. G., & Brooks, M. G. (1993). *In search of understanding: The case for the constructivist classroom.* Alexandria, VA: Association for Supervision and Curriculum Development.

Brownell, W., & Chazal, C. (1935). The effects of premature drill in third grade arithmetic. *Journal of Educational Research, 29,* 17–28.

Brueningsen, C., Bower, B., Antinone, L., & Brueningsen, E. (1994). *Real-world math with the CBL system: 25 activities using the CBL and TI-82.* Dallas: Texas Instruments.

Bruni, J. V. (1977). *Experiencing geometry.* Belmont, CA: Wadsworth.

Burger, W. F. (1985). Geometry. *Arithmetic Teacher, 32*(6), 52–56.

Burger, W. F., & Shaughnessy, J. M. (1986). Characterizing the van Hiele levels of development in geometry. *Journal for Research in Mathematics Education, 17,* 13–48.

Burk, D., Snider, A., & Symonds, P. (1988). *Box it or bag it mathematics: Teachers resource guide (K, 1–2).* Salem, OR: Math Learning Center.

Burns, M. (1982). *Math for smarty pants*. New York: Little, Brown.

Burns, M. (1987). *A collection of math lessons from grades 3 through 6*. White Plains, NY: Cuisenaire (distributor).

Burns, M. (1990). The math solution: Using groups of four. In N. Davidson (Ed.), *Cooperative learning in mathematics: A handbook for teachers* (pp. 21–46). Menlo Park, CA: AWL Supplemental.

Burns, M. (1992a). *About teaching mathematics: A K–8 resource*. White Plains, NY: Cuisenaire (distributor).

Burns, M. (1992b). *Math and literature (K–3)*. White Plains, NY: Cuisenaire (distributor).

Burns, M. (1995a). Timed tests. *Teaching Children Mathematics, 1*, 408–409.

Burns, M. (1995b). *Writing in math class*. White Plains, NY: Cuisenaire (distributor).

Burns, M. (1996). *50 problem-solving lessons: Grades 1–6*. White Plains, NY: Cuisenaire (distributor).

Burns, M., & Tank, B. (1988). *A collection of math lessons from grades 1 through 3*. White Plains, NY: Cuisenaire (distributor).

Burton, N. (1995). Trends in mathematics achievement for young men and women. In I. M. Carl (Ed.), *Prospects for school mathematics* (pp. 115–130). Reston, VA: National Council of Teachers of Mathematics.

Callahan, L. G., & Glennon, V. (1975). *Elementary school mathematics: A guide to current research* (4th ed.). Washington, DC: Association for Supervision and Curriculum Development.

Callahan, L. G., & MacMillan, D. L. (1981). Teaching mathematics to slow-learning and mentally retarded children. In V. J. Glennon (Ed.), *The mathematical education of exceptional children and youth: An interdisciplinary approach*. Reston, VA: National Council of Teachers of Mathematics.

Campbell, P. B. (1995). Redefining the "girl problem in mathematics." In W. G. Secada, E. Fennema, & L. B. Adajian (Eds.), *New directions for equity in mathematics education* (pp. 225–241). New York: Cambridge University Press.

Campbell, P. F. (1988). Microcomputers in the primary mathematics classroom. *Arithmetic Teacher, 35*(6), 22–30.

Campbell, P. F. (1993). Making equity a reality in classrooms. *Arithmetic Teacher, 41*, 110–113.

Campbell, P. F. (1996). Empowering children and teachers in the elementary mathematics classrooms of urban schools. *Urban Education, 30*, 449–475.

Campbell, P. F., & Clements, D. H. (1990). Using microcomputers for mathematics learning. In J. N. Payne (Ed.), *Mathematics for the young child* (pp. 265–283). Reston, VA: National Council of Teachers of Mathematics.

Campbell, P. F., & Johnson, M. L. (1995). How primary students think and learn. In I. M. Carl (Ed.), *Prospects for school mathematics* (pp. 21–42). Reston, VA: National Council of Teachers of Mathematics.

Campione, J. C., Brown, A. L., & Connell, M. L. (1989). Metacognition: On the importance of understanding what you are doing. In R. I. Charles & E. A. Silver (Eds.), *The teaching and assessing of mathematical problem solving* (pp. 93–114). Reston, VA: National Council of Teachers of Mathematics.

Carey, D. A., Fennema, E., Carpenter, T. P., & Franke, M. L. (1995). Equity and mathematics education. In W. G. Secada, E. Fennema, & L. B. Adajian (Eds.), *New directions for equity in mathematics education* (pp. 93–125). New York: Cambridge University Press.

Carpenter, T. P., Carey, D. A., & Kouba, V. L. (1990). A problem-solving approach to the operations. In J. N. Payne (Ed.), *Mathematics for the young child* (pp. 111–131). Reston, VA: National Council of Teachers of Mathematics.

Carpenter, T. P., & Moser, J. M. (1983). The acquisition of addition and subtraction concepts. In R. A. Lesh & M. Landau (Eds.), *Acquisition of mathematics concepts and processes* (pp. 7–44). Orlando, FL: Academic Press.

Carrier, C., Post, T. R., & Heck, W. (1985). Using microcomputers with fourth-grade students to reinforce arithmetic skills. *Journal for Research in Mathematics Education, 16*, 45–51.

Carroll, W. M. (1988). Cross sections of clay solids. *Arithmetic Teacher, 35*(7), 6–11.

Cauley, K. M. (1988). Construction of logical knowledge: Study of borrowing in subtraction. *Journal of Educational Psychology, 80*, 202–205.

Chalouh, L., & Herscovics, N. (1988). Teaching algebraic expressions in a meaningful way. In A. F. Coxford (Ed.), *The ideas of algebra, K–12* (pp. 33–42). Reston, VA: National Council of Teachers of Mathematics.

Chambers, D. L. (1994). Cognitively guided instruction. *Teaching Children Mathematics, 1*, 116.

Charles, R. I., et al. (1985). *Problem-solving experiences in mathematics* (Series for grades 1–8). Menlo Park, CA: AWL Supplemental.

Charles, R. I., & Lester, F. K., Jr. (1982). *Teaching problem solving: What, why & how*. Palo Alto, CA: Dale Seymour.

Charles, R. I., Lester, F. K., Jr., & O'Daffer, P. (1987). *How to Evaluate progress in problem solving*. Reston, VA: National Council of Teachers of Mathematics.

Clark, F. B., & Kamii, C. (1996). Identification of multiplicative thinking in children in grades 1–5. *Journal for Research in Mathematics Education, 27*, 41–51.

Clements, D. H. (1985a). *Computers in early and primary education*. Upper Saddle River, NJ: Prentice Hall.

Clements, D. H. (1985b). Logo programming: Can it change how children think? *Electronic Learning, 4*(4), 28, 74–75.

Clements, D. H. (1985c). Research on Logo in education: Is the turtle slow but steady, or not even in the race? *Logo in the Schools, 2*(2/3), 55–71.

Clements, D. H. (1986). Early studies on Logo and problem solving. *Logo Exchange, 5*(2), 23–25.

Clements, D. H., & Battista, M. T. (1989). Learning of geometric concepts in a Logo environment. *Journal for Research in School Mathematics, 20*, 450–467.

Clements, D. H., & Battista, M. T. (1990). Constructivist learning and teaching. *Arithmetic Teacher, 38*(1), 34–35.

Clements, D. H., & Meredith, J. S. (1993). My turn: A talk with the Logo turtle. *Arithmetic Teacher, 41*, 189–191.

Clements, D. H., & Meredith, J. S. (1994). *Turtle math* [Computer software]. Montreal: Logo Computer Systems.

Cobb, P. (1988). The tension between theories of learning and instruction in mathematics education. *Educational Psychologist, 23*, 87–103.

Collison, J. (1992). Using performance assessment to determine mathematical dispositions. *Arithmetic Teacher, 39*(6), 40–47.

Coombs, B., & Harcourt, L. (1986). *Explorations 1*. Don Mills, Ontario: Addison Wesley Longman.

Corwin, R. B. (1996). *Talking mathematics: Supporting children's voices*. Portsmouth, NH: Heinemann.

Countryman, J. (1992). *Writing to learn mathematics: Strategies that work, K–12*. Portsmouth, NH: Heinemann.

Crowley, M. L. (1987). The van Hiele model of the development of geometric thought. In M. M. Lindquist (Ed.), *Learning and teaching geometry, K–12* (pp. 1–16). Reston, VA: National Council of Teachers of Mathematics.

Damarin, S. K. (1995). Gender and mathematics from a feminist standpoint. In W. G. Secada, E. Fennema, & L. B. Adajian (Eds.), *New directions for equity in mathematics education* (pp. 242–257). New York: Cambridge University Press.

Davidson, E., & Hammerman, J. (1993). Homogenized is only better for milk. In G. Cuevas & M. Driscol (Eds.), *Reaching all students with mathematics* (pp. 197–212). Reston, VA: National Council of Teachers of Mathematics.

Davidson, P. S. (1975). *Chip trading activities: Teacher's guide.* Fort Collins, CO: Scott Scientific.

Davis, R. B. (1986). *Learning mathematics: The cognitive science approach to mathematics education.* Norwood, NJ: Ablex.

Demana, F., & Osborne, A. (1988). Choosing a calculator: Four-function foul-ups. *Arithmetic Teacher, 35*(7), 2–3.

Dossey, J. A., Mullis, I. V. S., Lindquist, M. M., & Chambers, D. L. (1988). *The mathematics report card: Are we measuring up?* Princeton, NJ: Educational Testing Service.

Downs, R. E., Matthew, J. L., & McKinney, M. L. (1994). Issues of identification. In C. A. Thornton & N. S. Bley (Eds.), *Windows of opportunity: Mathematics for students with special needs* (pp. 61–81). Reston, VA: National Council of Teachers of Mathematics.

Education Development Center. (1991). *My travels with Gulliver.* Scotts Valley, CA: Wings for Learning.

EduQuest. (1993). *Exploring math with manipulatives: Patterns and shapes* [Computer software]. Atlanta, GA: Author.

Elementary Science Study. (1966). *Teacher's guide for attribute games and problems.* Nashua, NH: Delta Education.

Fair, J. (1987). *Tangram treasury (Books A, B, and C).* White Plains, NY: Cuisenaire (distributor).

Fennema, E., Carpenter, T. P., Franke, M. L., & Carey, D. A. (1993). Learning to use children's mathematics thinking: A case study. In R. B. Davis & C. A. Maher (Eds.), *School, mathematics, and the world of reality* (pp. 93–117). Boston: Allyn and Bacon

Fennema, E., Peterson, P. L., Carpenter, T. P., & Lubinski, C. (1990). Teacher attributes and beliefs about girls, boys, and mathematics. *Educational Studies in Mathematics, 21,* 55–69.

Fey, J. T. (Ed.). (1992). *Calculators in mathematics education.* Reston, VA: National Council of Teachers of Mathematics.

Fischer, F. E. (1990). A part-part-whole curriculum for teaching number in the kindergarten. *Journal for Research in Mathematics Education, 21,* 207–215.

Fortunato, I., Hecht, D., Tittle, C. K., & Alvarez, L. (1991). Metacognition and problem solving. *Arithmetic Teacher, 39*(4), 38–40.

Fosnaugh, L. S., & Harrell, M. E. (1996). Covering the plane with rep-tiles. *Mathematics Teaching in the Middle School, 1,* 666–670.

Fuson, K. C. (1984). More complexities in subtraction. *Journal for Research in Mathematics Education, 15,* 214–225.

Fuson, K. C. (1992). Research on whole number addition and subtraction. In D. A. Grouws (Ed.), *Handbook of research on teaching and learning* (pp. 243–275). Old Tappan, NJ: Macmillan.

Fuson, K. C., & Brinko, K. T. (1985). The comparative effectiveness of microcomputers and flash cards in the drill and practice of basic mathematics facts. *Journal for Research in Mathematics Education, 16,* 225–232.

Fuson, K. C., & Hall, J. W. (1983). The acquisition of early number word meanings: A conceptual analysis and review. In

H. P. Ginsburg (Ed.), *The development of mathematical thinking* (pp. 49–107). Orlando, FL: Academic Press.

Fuson, K. C., Secada, W. G., & Hall, J. W. (1983). Matching, counting, and conservation of numerical equivalence. *Child Development, 54,* 91–97.

Fuys, D., Geddes, D., & Tischler, R. (1988). The van Hiele model of thinking in geometry among adolescents. *Journal for Research in Mathematics Education Monograph, 3.*

Garland, T. H. (1987). *Fascinating Fibonaccis: Mystery and magic in numbers.* Palo Alto, CA: Dale Seymour.

Garofalo, J. (1987). Metacognition and school mathematics. *Arithmetic Teacher, 34*(9), 22–23.

Gelman, R., & Gallistel, C. R. (1978). *The child's understanding of number.* Cambridge, MA: Harvard University Press.

Gelman, R., & Meck, E. (1986). The notion of principle: The case of counting. In J. Hiebert (Ed.), *Conceptual and procedural knowledge: The case of mathematics* (pp. 29–57). Hillsdale, NJ: Erlbaum.

Gerver, R. (1990). Discovering pi: Two approaches. *Arithmetic Teacher, 37*(8), 18–22.

Ginsburg, H. P. (1977). *Children's arithmetic: The learning process.* New York: Van Nostrand.

Gnanadesikan, M., Schaeffer, R. L., & Swift, J. (1987). *The art and techniques of simulation: Quantitative literacy series.* Palo Alto, CA: Dale Seymour.

Goldenberg, E. P. (1991). A mathematical conversation with fourth graders. *Arithmetic Teacher, 38*(8), 38–43.

Goodnow, J., Hoogeboom, S., Moretti, G., Stephens, M., & Scanlin, A. (1987). *The problem solver: Activities for learning problem solving strategies.* Palo Alto, CA: Creative Publications.

Greenes, C., Garfunkel, F., & De Bussey, M. (1994). Planning for instruction: The individualized education plan and the mathematics individualized learning plan. In C. A. Thornton & N. S. Bley (Eds.), *Windows of opportunity: Mathematics for students with special needs* (pp. 115–135). Reston, VA: National Council of Teachers of Mathematics.

Greer, B. (1992). Multiplication and division as models of situations. In D. A. Grouws (Ed.), *Handbook of research on mathematics teaching and learning* (pp. 276–295). Old Tappan, NJ: Macmillan.

Groff, P. (1996). It is time to question fraction teaching. *Mathematics Teaching in the Middle School, 1,* 604–607.

Gutstein, E., & Romberg, T. A. (1995). Teaching children to add and subtract. *Journal of Mathematical Behavior, 14,* 283–324.

Hankes, J. E. (1996). An alternative to basic-skills remediation. *Teaching Children Mathematics, 2,* 452–457.

Harvey, W., McHugh, R., & McGlathery, D. (1989). *Elastic lines* [Computer software]. Pleasantville, NY: Sunburst Communications.

Hazekamp, D. W. (1986). Components of mental multiplying. In H. L. Schoen (Ed.), *Estimation and mental computation* (pp. 116–126). Reston, VA: National Council of Teachers of Mathematics.

Hembree, R., & Dessart, D. D. (1986). Effects of hand-held calculators in precollege mathematics education: A meta-analysis. *Journal for Research in Mathematics Education, 17,* 83–99.

Herscovics, N., & Kieran, C. (1980). Constructing meaning for the concept of equation. *Mathematics Teacher, 73,* 573–580.

Hiebert, J. (1990). The role of routine procedures in the development of mathematical competence. In T. J. Cooney (Ed.), *Teaching and learning mathematics in the 1990s* (pp. 31–40). Reston, VA: National Council of Teachers of Mathematics.

Hiebert, J., & Carpenter, T. P. (1992). Learning and teaching with understanding. In D. A. Grouws (Ed.), *Handbook of research on mathematics teaching and learning* (pp. 65–97). Old Tappan, NJ: Macmillan.

Hiebert, J., & Lefevre, P. (1986). Conceptual and procedural knowledge in mathematics: An introductory analysis. In J. Hiebert (Ed.), *Conceptual and procedural knowledge: The case of mathematics* (pp. 1–27). Old Tappan, NJ: Macmillan.

Hiebert, J., & Lindquist, M. M. (1990). Developing mathematical knowledge in the young child. In J. N. Payne (Ed.), *Mathematics for the young child* (pp. 17–36). Reston, VA: National Council of Teachers of Mathematics.

Hiebert, J., & Wearne, D. (1986). Procedures over concepts: The acquisition of decimal number knowledge. In J. Hiebert (Ed.), *Conceptual and procedural knowledge: The case of mathematics* (pp. 199–223). Old Tappan, NJ: Macmillan.

Hilliard, A. G., III. (1995). Mathematics excellence for cultural "minority" students: What is the problem? In I. M. Carl (Ed.), *Prospects for school mathematics* (pp. 99–114). Reston, VA: National Council of Teachers of Mathematics.

Hoffer, A. R. (1983). Van Hiele–based research. In R. A. Lesh & M. Landau (Eds.), *Acquisition of mathematics concepts and processes* (pp. 205–227). Orlando, FL: Academic Press.

Hoffer, A. R., & Hoffer, S. A. K. (1992a). Geometry and visual thinking. In T. R. Post (Ed.), *Teaching mathematics in grades K–8: Research-based methods* (2nd ed.) (pp. 249–277). Needham Heights, MA: Allyn & Bacon.

Hoffer, A. R., & Hoffer, S. A. K. (1992b). Ratios and proportional thinking. In T. R. Post (Ed.), *Teaching mathematics in grades K–8: Research-based methods* (2nd ed.) (pp. 303–330). Needham Heights, MA: Allyn & Bacon.

Holden, L. (1986). *The fraction factory*. Palo Alto, CA: Creative Publications.

Hope, J. A. (1986). Mental calculation: Anachronism or basic skill? In H. Schoen (Ed.), *Estimation and mental computation* (pp. 45–54). Reston, VA: National Council of Teachers of Mathematics.

Hope, J. A., Leutzinger, L. P., Reys, B. J., & Reys, R. E. (1988). *Mental math in the primary grades*. Palo Alto, CA: Dale Seymour.

Hope, J. A., Reys, B. J., & Reys, R. E. (1987). *Mental math in the middle grades*. Palo Alto, CA: Dale Seymour.

Hope, J. A., Reys, B. J., & Reys, R. E. (1988). *Mental math in the junior high school*. Palo Alto, CA: Dale Seymour.

House, P. A. (Ed.). (1987). *Providing opportunities for the mathematically gifted, K–12*. Reston, VA: National Council of Teachers of Mathematics.

Howden, H. (1989). Teaching number sense. *Arithmetic Teacher, 36*(6), 6–11.

Huinker, D. (1994, April). Multi-step word problems: A strategy for empowering students. Presented at the annual meeting of the National Council of Teachers of Mathematics, Indianapolis, IN.

Huinker, D., & Laughlin, C. (1996). Talk your way into writing. In P. C. Elliott (Ed.), *Communication in mathematics, K–12 and beyond* (pp. 81–88). Reston, VA: National Council of Teachers of Mathematics.

Janvier, C. (Ed.). (1987). *Problems of representation in the teaching and learning of mathematics*. Hillsdale, NJ: Erlbaum.

Johnson, D. W., Johnson, R. T., & Holubec, E. J. (1993). *Circles of learning: Cooperation in the classroom* (4th ed.). Alexandria, VA: Association for Supervision and Curriculum Development.

Kamii, C. K. (1985). *Young children reinvent arithmetic*. New York: Teachers College Press.

Kamii, C. K. (1989). *Young children continue to reinvent arithmetic: 2nd grade*. New York: Teachers College Press.

Kamii, C. K., & Joseph, L. (1988). Teaching place value and double-column addition. *Arithmetic Teacher, 36*(6), 48–52.

Kamii, C. K., & Lewis, B. A. (1990). Constructivism and first-grade arithmetic. *Arithmetic Teacher, 38*(1), 36–37.

Karplus, E. F., Karplus, R., & Wollman, W. (1974). Intellectual development beyond elementary school (Vol. 4): Ratio, the influence of cognitive style. *School Science and Mathematics, 74*, 476–482.

Karplus, R., Pulos, S., & Stage, E. K. (1983). Proportional reasoning of early adolescents. In R. A. Lesh & M. Landau (Eds.), *Acquisition of mathematics concepts and processes* (pp. 45–90). Orlando, FL: Academic Press.

Key Curriculum Press. (1995). *The geometer's sketchpad* (Version 3.0) [Computer software]. Berkeley, CA: Author.

Kieran, C. (1988). Two different approaches among algebra learners. In A. F. Coxford & A. P. Shulte (Eds.), *The ideas of algebra, K–12* (pp. 91–96). Reston, VA: National Council of Teachers of Mathematics.

Kouba, V. L. (1989). Children's solution strategies for equivalent set multiplication and division word problems. *Journal for Research in Mathematics Education, 20*, 147–158.

Kouba, V. L., Brown, C. A., Carpenter, T. P., Lindquist, M. M., Silver, E. A., & Swafford, J. O. (1988a). Results of the fourth NAEP assessment of mathematics: Number, operations, and word problems. *Arithmetic Teacher, 35*(8), 14–19.

Kouba, V. L., Brown, C. A., Carpenter, T. P., Lindquist, M. M., Silver, E. A., & Swafford, J. O. (1988b). Results of the fourth NAEP assessment of mathematics: Measurement, geometry, data interpretation, attitudes, and other topics. *Arithmetic Teacher, 35*(9), 10–16.

Kroll, D. L., Masingila, J. O., & Mau, S. T. (1992). Cooperative problem solving: But what about grades? *Arithmetic Teacher, 39*(6), 17–23.

Kulm, G. (1994). *Mathematics and assessment: What works in the classroom*. San Francisco: Jossey-Bass.

Labinowicz, E. (1980). *Piaget primer: Thinking, learning, teaching*. Menlo Park, CA: AWL Supplemental.

Labinowicz, E. (1985). *Learning from children: New beginnings for teaching numerical thinking*. Menlo Park, CA: AWL Supplemental.

Labinowicz, E. (1987). Assessing for learning: The interview method. *Arithmetic Teacher, 35*(3), 22–24.

Ladson-Billings, G. (1995). Making mathematics meaningful in multicultural contexts. In W. G. Secada, E. Fennema, & L. B. Adajian (Eds.), *New directions for equity in mathematics education* (pp. 126–145). New York: Cambridge University Press.

Lamon, S. J. (1993). Ratio and proportion: Connecting content and children's thinking. *Journal for Research in Mathematics Education, 24*, 41–61.

Lampert, M. (1990). When the problem is not the question and the solution is not the answer: Mathematical knowing and teaching. *American Educational Research Journal, 27*, 29–63.

Landwehr, J. M., Swift, J., & Watkins, A. E. (1987). *Exploring surveys and information from samples: Quantitative literacy series*. Palo Alto, CA: Dale Seymour.

Landwehr, J. M., & Watkins, A. E. (1987). *Exploring data: Quantitative literacy series*. Palo Alto, CA: Dale Seymour.

Lappan, G., & Briars, D. (1995). How should mathematics be taught? In I. M. Carl (Ed.), *Prospects for school mathematics* (pp. 115–156). Reston, VA: National Council of Teachers of Mathematics.

Lappan, G. & Even, R. (1989). *Learning to teach: Constructing meaningful understanding of mathematical content* (Craft Paper 89-3). East Lansing: Michigan State University.

Leder, G. C. (1995). Equity inside the mathematics classroom: Fact or artifact? In W. G. Secada, E. Fennema, & L. B. Adajian (Eds.), *New directions for equity in mathematics education* (pp. 209–224). New York: Cambridge University Press.

Lesh, R. A., Post, T. R., & Behr, M. J. (1987). Representations and translations among representations in mathematics learning and problem solving. In C. Janvier (Ed.), *Problems of representation in the teaching and learning of mathematics* (pp. 33–40). Hillsdale, NJ: Erlbaum.

Lester, F. K., Jr. (1989). Reflections about mathematical problem-solving research. In R. I. Charles & E. A. Silver (Eds.), *The teaching and assessing of mathematical problem solving* (pp. 115–124). Reston, VA: National Council of Teachers of Mathematics.

Lester, F. K., Jr. (1994). Musings about mathematical problem-solving research, 1970–1994. *Journal for Research in Mathematics Education, 25,* 660–675.

Leutzinger, L., Rathmell, E. C., & Urbatsch, T. D. (1986). Developing estimation skills in the primary grades. In H. L. Schoen (Ed.), *Estimation and mental computation* (pp. 82–92). Reston, VA: National Council of Teachers of Mathematics.

Liedtke, W. (1988). Diagnosis in mathematics: The advantages of an interview. *Arithmetic Teacher, 36*(3), 26–29.

Lindquist, M. M. (1987a). Estimation and mental computation: Measurement. *Arithmetic Teacher, 34*(5), 16–17.

Lindquist, M. M. (1987b). Problem solving with five easy pieces. In J. M. Hill (Ed.), *Geometry for grades K–6: Readings from* The Arithmetic Teacher (pp. 152–156). Reston, VA: National Council of Teachers of Mathematics.

LOGAL Educational Software and Systems. (1994). *Geometry Inventor* [Computer software]. Cambridge, MA: Author.

Lubinski, C. A., & Thiessen, D. (1996). Exploring measurement through literature. *Teaching Children Mathematics, 2,* 260–263.

Madell, R. (1985). Children's natural processes. *Arithmetic Teacher, 32*(7), 20–22.

Marolda, M. R., & Davidson, P. S. (1994). Assessing mathematical abilities and learning approaches. In C. A. Thornton & N. S. Bley (Eds.), *Windows of opportunity: Mathematics for students with special needs* (pp. 83–113). Reston, VA: National Council of Teachers of Mathematics.

Markovits, Z., Eylon, B. S., & Bruckheimer, M. (1988). Difficulties students have with the function concept. In A. F. Coxford (Ed.), *The ideas of algebra, K–12* (pp. 43–60). Reston, VA: National Council of Teachers of Mathematics.

Mathematics Education Trust Committee. (1991). *Algebra for everyone: Videotape and discussion guide.* Reston, VA: National Council of Teachers of Mathematics.

Mathematical Sciences Education Board, National Research Council. (1989). *Everybody counts: A report to the nation on the future of mathematics education.* Washington, DC: National Academy of Sciences Press.

Mathematical Sciences Education Board, National Research Council. (1993). *Measuring what counts: A policy brief.* Washington, DC: National Academy of Sciences Press.

Michigan State Board of Education (1988). *Michigan essential goals and objectives for mathematics education.* Lansing: Michigan Department of Education.

Milauskas, G. A. (1987). Creative geometry problems can lead to creative problem solvers. In M. M. Lindquist (Ed.), *Learning and teaching geometry, K–12* (pp. 69–84). Reston, VA: National Council of Teachers of Mathematics.

Minnesota Educational Computing Consortium. (1990). *Estimation: Quick solve I* [Computer software]. St. Paul, MN: Author.

Minnesota Educational Computing Consortium. (1994). *TesselMania!* [Computer software]. Minneapolis, MN: Author.

Mullis, I. V. S., Dossey, J. A., Owen, E. H., & Phillips, G. W. (1991). *The state of mathematics achievement: NAEP's 1990 assessment of the nation and the trial assessment of the states.* Washington, DC: U. S. Department of Education.

National Council of Supervisors of Mathematics. (1987). Position paper on basic mathematics skills. *Arithmetic Teacher, 37*(1), 18–22.

National Council of Teachers of Mathematics. (1986). *A position statement: Provisions for mathematically talented and gifted students.* Reston, VA: Author.

National Council of Teachers of Mathematics. (1989). *Curriculum and evaluation standards for school mathematics.* Reston, VA: Author.

National Council of Teachers of Mathematics. (1991). *Professional standards for teaching mathematics.* Reston, VA: Author.

National Council of Teachers of Mathematics. (1995). *Assessment standards for school mathematics.* Reston, VA: Author.

National Council of Teachers of Mathematics. (1996). *1996–97 Handbook: NCTM goals, leaders, and positions.* Reston, VA: Author.

Noelting, G. (1980). The development of proportional reasoning and the ratio concept: 1. Differentiation of stages. *Educational Studies in Mathematics, 11,* 217–253.

Oakes, J. (1990). *Multiplying inequalities: The effects of race, social class, and tracking opportunities to learn mathematics and science.* Santa Monica, CA: Rand.

Oakes, J. (1995). Opportunity to learn: Can standards-based reform be equity-based reform? In I. M. Carl (Ed.), *Prospects for school mathematics* (pp. 78–98). Reston, VA: National Council of Teachers of Mathematics.

Oppedal, D. C. (1995). Mathematics is something good. *Teaching Children Mathematics, 1,* 36–40.

Pagni, E. (Ed.). (1991). *Calculators and Mathematics Project, Los Angeles (CAMP-LA)* (4 vols.: K–2, 3–4, 5–6, 7–8). Fullerton, CA: Cal State Fullerton Press.

Papert, S. (1980). *Mindstorms: Children, computers, and powerful ideas.* New York: Basic Books.

Payne, J. N. (1976). Review of research on fractions. In R. A. Lesh & D. A. Bradbard (Eds.), *Number and measurement: Papers from a research workshop* (pp. 145–187). Columbus, OH: ERIC/SMEAC.

Payne, J. N. (Ed.). (1990). *Mathematics for the young child.* Reston, VA: National Council of Teachers of Mathematics.

Pólya, G. (1957). *How to solve it: A new aspect of mathematical method.* Princeton, NJ: Princeton University Press. (Originally published 1945.)

Poplin, M. S. (1988a). Holistic/constructivist principles of the teaching/learning process: Implications for the field of learning disabilities. *Journal of Learning Disabilities, 21,* 401–416.

Poplin, M. S. (1988b). The reductionistic fallacy in learning disabilities: Replicating the past by reducing the present. *Journal of Learning Disabilities, 21,* 389–398.

Post, T. R. (1981). Fractions: Results and implications from the national assessment. *Arithmetic Teacher, 28*(9), 26–31.

Post, T. R., Behr, M. J., & Lesh, R. A. (1988). Proportionality and the development of prealgebra understandings. In A. F. Coxford (Ed.), *The ideas of algebra, K–12* (pp. 78–90). Reston, VA: National Council of Teachers of Mathematics.

Post, T. R., Wachsmuth, I., Lesh, R. A., & Behr, M. J. (1985). Order and equivalence of rational numbers: A cognitive analysis. *Journal for Research in Mathematics Education, 16,* 18–36.

Pothier, Y., & Sawada, D. (1983). Partitioning: The emergence of rational number ideas in young children. *Journal for Research in Mathematics Education, 14,* 307–317.

Prentice, G. (1989). Flexible straws. *Arithmetic Teacher, 37*(3), 34–37.

Problem of the day. (1992). Glenview, IL: Scott, Foresman.

Quintero, A. H. (1986). Children's conceptual understanding of situations involving multiplication. *Arithmetic Teacher, 33*(5), 34–37.

Ranucci, E. R., & Teeters, J. L. (1977). *Creating Escher-type drawings.* Palo Alto, CA: Creative Publications.

Rathmell, E. C. (1978). Using thinking strategies to teach the basic skills. In M. N. Suydam (Ed.), *Developing computational skills* (pp. 13–38). Reston, VA: National Council of Teachers of Mathematics.

Renzulli, J. S. (1977). *The enrichment triad model: A guide for developing defensible programs for the gifted and talented.* Mansfield Center, CT: Creative Learning Press.

Renzulli, J. S., & Reis, S. M. (1985). *The schoolwide enrichment model: A comprehensive plan for educational excellence.* Mansfield Center, CT: Creative Learning Press.

Renzulli, J. S., & Reis, S. M. (1991). The schoolwide enrichment model: A comprehensive plan for the development of creative productivity. In N. Coangelo & G. A. Davis (Eds.), *Handbook of gifted education* (pp. 111–141). Needham Heights, MA: Allyn & Bacon.

Resnick, L. B. (1983). A developmental theory of number understanding. In H. P. Ginsburg (Ed.), *The development of mathematical thinking* (pp. 109–151). Orlando, FL: Academic Press.

Resnick, L. B. (1988). Treating mathematics as an ill-structured discipline. In R. I. Charles & E. A. Silver (Eds.), *The teaching and assessing of mathematical problem solving* (pp. 32–60). Reston, VA: National Council of Teachers of Mathematics.

Reys, B. J., & Reys, R. E. (1983). *Guide to using estimation skills and strategies (GUESS)* (Boxes I and II). Palo Alto, CA: Dale Seymour.

Reys, B. J., & Reys, R. E. (1987). Calculators in the classroom: How can we make it happen? *Arithmetic Teacher, 34*(6), 12–14.

Reys, B. J., & Reys, R. E. (1995). Japanese mathematics education: What makes it work. *Teaching Children Mathematics, 1,* 474–475.

Reys, R. E., Trafton, P. R., Reys, B. J., & Zawojewski, J. S. (1987). *Computational estimation (grades 6, 7, 8).* Palo Alto, CA: Dale Seymour.

Ridge, H., & Renzulli, J. S. (1981). Teaching mathematics to the talented and gifted. In V. J. Glennon (Ed.)., *The mathematical education of exceptional children and youth: An interdisciplinary approach* (pp. 191–266). Reston, VA: National Council of Teachers of Mathematics.

Romberg, T. (1992). Perspectives on scholarship and research methods. In D. A. Grouws (Ed.), *Handbook of research on teaching and learning* (pp. 49–64). Old Tappan, NJ: Macmillan.

Ross, S. H. (1986). *The development of children's place-value numeration concepts in grades two through five.* Presented at the annual meeting of the American Educational Research Association, San Francisco. (ERIC Document Reproduction Service No. ED 2773 482)

Ross, S. H. (1989). Parts, wholes, and place value: A developmental perspective. *Arithmetic Teacher, 36*(6), 47–51.

Rowan, T. E. (1995, March). Helping children construct mathematical understanding with IMPACT. Presented at the regional meeting of the National Council of Teachers of Mathematics, Chicago, IL.

Rowan, T. E., & Bourne, B. (1994). *Thinking like mathematicians: Putting the K–4 standards into practice.* Portsmouth, NH: Heinemann.

Runion, G. E. (1990). *The golden section.* Palo Alto, CA: Dale Seymour.

Sawyer, A. E. (1995). *Developments in elementary mathematics teaching.* Portsmouth, NH: Heinemann.

Scheer, J. K. (1980). The etiquette of diagnosis. *Arithmetic Teacher, 27*(9), 18–19.

Schiever, S. W., & Maker, C. J. (1991). Enrichment and acceleration: An overview and new directions. In N. Colangelo & G. A. Davis (Eds.), *Handbook of gifted education* (pp. 99–110). Needham Heights, MA: Allyn & Bacon.

Schifter, D., & Fosnot, C. T. (1993). *Reconstructing mathematics education: Stories of teachers meeting the challenge of reform.* New York: Teachers College Press.

Schoenfeld, A. H. (1987). A brief and biased history of problem solving. In F. R. Curcio (Ed.), *Teaching and learning: A problem-solving focus* (pp. 27–46). Reston, VA: National Council of Teachers of Mathematics.

Schoenfeld, A. H. (1988). What's all the fuss about metacognition? In A. H. Schoenfeld (Ed.), *Cognitive science and mathematics education* (pp. 189–215). Hillsdale, NJ: Erlbaum.

Schoenfeld, A. H. (1992). Learning to think mathematically: Problem solving, metacognition, and sense making in mathematics. In D. A. Grouws (Ed.), *Handbook of research on teaching and learning* (pp. 334–370). Old Tappan, NJ: Macmillan.

Schroeder, T. L., & Lester, F. K., Jr. (1989). Developing understanding in mathematics via problem solving. In P. R. Trafton (Ed.), *New directions for elementary school mathematics* (pp. 31–42). Reston, VA: National Council of Teachers of Mathematics.

Schwartz, J., & Yerushalmy, M. (1985). *The geometric supposers.* Cambridge, MA: Educational Development Center. (Distributed by Sunburst Communications.)

Schwartz, S. L. (1996). Hidden messages in teacher talk: Praise and empowerment. *Teaching Children Mathematics, 2,* 396–403.

Sconyers, J. M. (1995). Proof and the middle school mathematics student. *Mathematics Teaching in the Middle School, 1,* 516–518.

Seymour, D. (1971). *Tangramath.* Palo Alto, CA: Creative Publications.

Sheffield, S. (1995). *Math and literature (K–3)* (Vol. 2). White Plains, NY: Cuisenaire (distributor).

Shumway, R. J. (1987). *101 ways to learn mathematics using BASIC (K–8).* Upper Saddle River, NJ: Prentice Hall.

Shumway, R. J. (1992). Calculators and computers. In T. R. Post (Ed.), *Teaching mathematics in grades K–8: Research-based methods* (2nd ed.) (pp. 363–419). Needham Heights, MA: Allyn & Bacon.

Silver, E. A. (1986). Using conceptual and procedural knowledge: A focus on relationships. In J. Hiebert (Ed.), *Conceptual and procedural knowledge: The case of mathematics* (pp. 181–198). Hillsdale, NJ: Erlbaum.

Silver, E. A., Smith, M. S., & Nelson, B. S. (1995). The QUASAR project: Equity concerns meet mathematics education reform in the middle school. In W. G. Secada, E. Fennema, & L. B. Adajian (Eds.), *New directions for equity in mathematics education* (pp. 9–56). New York: Cambridge University Press.

Silver, E. A., & Stein, M. K. (1996). The QUASAR project: The "revolution of the possible" in mathematics instructional reform in urban middle schools. *Urban Education, 30,* 476–521.

Skemp, R. (1978). Relational understanding and instrumental understanding. *Arithmetic Teacher, 26*(3), 9–15.

Smith, J. P., III. (1996). Efficacy and teaching mathematics by telling: A challenge for reform. *Journal for Research in Mathematics Education, 27,* 387–402.

Smith, S. (1984). Microcomputers in the middle school. In V. P. Hansen (Ed.), *Computers in mathematics education* (pp. 135–145). Reston, VA: National Council of Teachers of Mathematics.

Speer, W. R., & Brahier, D. J. (1994). Rethinking the teaching and learning of mathematics. In C. A. Thornton & N. S. Bley (Eds.), *Windows of opportunity: Mathematics for students with special needs* (pp. 41–59). Reston, VA: National Council of Teachers of Mathematics.

Steffe, L. (1988). Children's construction of number sequences and multiplying schemes. In J. Hiebert & M. J. Behr (Eds.), *Number concepts and operations in the middle grades* (pp. 119–140). Hillsdale, NJ: Erlbaum.

Steinberg, R. M. (1985). Instruction on derived facts strategies in addition and subtraction. *Journal for Research in Mathematics Education, 16,* 337–355.

Stenmark, J. K. (1989). *Assessment alternatives in mathematics: An overview of assessment techniques that promote learning.* Berkeley: EQUALS, University of California.

Stenmark, J. K. (Ed.). (1991). *Mathematics assessment: Myths, models, good questions, and practical suggestions.* Reston, VA: National Council of Teachers of Mathematics.

Stenmark, J. K., Beck, P., & Asturias, H. (1994). A room with more than one view. *Mathematics Teaching in the Middle School, 1,* 44–49.

Stoessiger, R., & Edmunds, J. (1992). *Natural learning and mathematics.* Portsmouth, NH: Heinemann.

Suydam, M. N. (1984). Microcomputers in mathematics instruction. *Arithmetic Teacher, 32*(2), 35.

Task Force on the Mathematically Promising. (1995). *Report: Task force on the mathematically promising.* Reston, VA: National Council of Teachers of Mathematics.

Terrapin. (1994). *Crystal rain forest* [Computer software]. Portland, ME: Author.

Texas Instruments. (1994). *Cabri geometry II* [Computer software]. Dallas: Author.

Thompson, C. S. (1990). Place value and larger numbers. In J. N. Payne (Ed.), *Mathematics for the young child* (pp. 89–108). Reston, VA: National Council of Teachers of Mathematics.

Thompson, C. S., & Hendrickson, A. D. (1986). Verbal addition and subtraction problems: Some difficulties and some solutions. *Arithmetic Teacher, 33* (7), 21–25.

Thompson, C. S., & Van de Walle, J. A. (1984a). Modeling subtraction situations. *Arithmetic Teacher, 32*(2), 8–12.

Thompson, C. S., & Van de Walle, J. A. (1984b). The power of 10. *Arithmetic Teacher, 32*(3), 6–11.

Thompson, P. W. (1994). Concrete materials and teaching for mathematical understanding. *Arithmetic Teacher, 41,* 556–558.

Thompson, P. W., & Thompson, A. G. (1994). Talking about rates conceptually, part 1: A teacher's struggle. *Journal for Research in Mathematics Education, 25,* 279–303.

Thornton, C. A. (1982). Doubles up—easy! *Arithmetic Teacher, 29*(8), 20.

Thornton, C. A. (1990). Strategies for the basic facts. In J. N. Payne (Ed.), *Mathematics for the young child* (pp. 133–151). Reston, VA: National Council of Teachers of Mathematics.

Thornton, C. A., & Bley, N. S. (Eds.). (1994). *Windows of opportunity: Mathematics for students with special needs.* Reston, VA: National Council of Teachers of Mathematics.

Thornton, C. A., & Noxon, C. (1977). *Look into the facts: (Addition, subtraction, multiplication, division).* Palo Alto, CA: Creative Publications.

Thornton, C. A., & Toohey, M. A. (1984). *A matter of facts: (Addition, subtraction, multiplication, division).* Palo Alto, CA: Creative Publications.

Tom Snyder. (1993). *The graph club* [Computer software]. Watertown, MA: Author.

Trafton, P. R., & Claus, A. S. (1994). A changing curriculum for a changing age. In C. A. Thornton & N. S. Bley (Eds.), *Windows of opportunity: Mathematics for students with special needs* (pp. 19–39). Reston, VA: National Council of Teachers of Mathematics.

Tsuruda, G. (1994). *Putting it together: Middle school math in transition.* Portsmouth, NH: Heinemann.

Tyrrell, J., Brown, C., Ellis, J., Fox, R., Kinley, R., & Reilly, B. (1994). Gender and mathematics: Equal access to successful learning. In J. Neyland (Ed.), *Mathematics education: A handbook for teachers* (Vol. 1) (pp. 330–347). Wellington, New Zealand: Wellington College of Education.

Usiskin, Z. (1987). Why elementary algebra can, should, and must be an eighth-grade course for average students. *Mathematics Teacher, 80,* 428–438.

Usiskin, Z. (1988). Conceptions of school algebra and uses of variables. In A. F. Coxford (Ed.), *The ideas of algebra, K–12* (pp. 8–19). Reston, VA: National Council of Teachers of Mathematics.

Usiskin, Z. (1992). *University of Chicago School Mathematics Project: Transition mathematics.* Glenview, IL: Scott, Foresman.

Usiskin, Z. (1993). If everybody counts, why do so few survive? In G. Cuevas & M. Driscol (Eds.), *Reaching all students with mathematics* (pp. 7–22). Reston, VA: National Council of Teachers of Mathematics.

Ventura Educational Systems. (1995). *Hands-on math* (Vol. 1) [Computer software]. Newbury Park, CA: Author.

Vonder Embse, C. (1992). Concept development and problem solving using graphing calculators in the middle school. In J. T. Fey (Ed.), *Calculators in mathematics education* (pp. 65–78). Reston, VA: National Council of Teachers of Mathematics.

von Glasersfeld, E., (1990). An exposition of constructivism: Why some like it radical. In R. B. Davis, C. A. Maher, & N. Noddings (Eds.), *Constructivist views on the teaching and learning of mathematics* (pp. 19–29). Reston, VA: National Council of Teachers of Mathematics.

Wagner, S. (1981). Conservation of equation and function under transformations of variable. *Journal for Research in Mathematics Education, 12,* 107–118.

Wagner, S. (1983). What are these things called variables? *Mathematics Teacher, 76,* 474–479.

Watt, D. (1983). *Learning with Logo.* New York: McGraw-Hill.

Welchman-Tischler, R. (1992). *How to use children's literature to teach mathematics*. Reston, VA: National Council of Teachers of Mathematics.

Wheatley, G. H., & Hersberger, J. (1986). A calculator estimation activity. In H. Schoen (Ed.), *Estimation and mental computation* (pp. 182–185). Reston, VA: National Council of Teachers of Mathematics.

Whitin, D. J., & Wilde, S. (1992). *Read any good math lately? Children's books for mathematical learning, K–6*. Portsmouth, NH: Heinemann.

Whitin, D. J., & Wilde, S. (1995). *It's the story that counts: More children's books for mathematical learning, K–6*. Portsmouth, NH: Heinemann.

Winter, M. J., Lappan, G., Phillips, E., & Fitzgerald, W. (1986). *Middle grades mathematics project: Spatial visualization*. Menlo Park, CA: AWL Supplemental.

Wirtz, R. (1974). *Mathematics for everyone*. Washington, DC: Curriculum Development Associates.

Wood, T. (1995). An emerging practice of teaching. In P. Cobb & H. Bauersfeld (Eds.), *The emergence of mathematical meaning: Interaction in classroom cultures* (pp. 203–227). Hillsdale, NJ: Erlbaum.

Wood, T., Cobb, P., Yackel, E., & Dillon, D. (Eds.). (1993). *Rethinking elementary school mathematics: Insights and issues* (*Journal for Research in Mathematics Education* Monograph No. 6). Reston, VA: National Council of Teachers of Mathematics.

Yackel, E., Cobb, P., Wood, T., Wheatley, G. H., & Merkel, G. (1990). The importance of social interaction in children's construction of mathematical knowledge. In T. J. Cooney (Ed.), *Teaching and learning mathematics in the 1990s* (pp. 12–21). Reston, VA: National Council of Teachers of Mathematics.

Children's Literature

Anno, M. (1982). *Anno's counting house*. New York: Philomel Books.

Anno, M., & Anno, M. (1983). *Anno's mysterious multiplying jar*. New York: Philomel Books.

Briggs, R. (1970). *Jim and the beanstalk*. New York: Coward-McCann.

Carle, E. (1969). *The very hungry caterpillar*. New York: Putnam.

Chalmers, M. (1986). *Six dogs, twenty-three cats, forty-five mice, and one hundred sixteen spiders*. New York: HarperCollins.

Clement, R. (1991). *Counting on Frank*. Milwaukee: Gareth Stevens Children's Books.

Dee, R. (1988). *Two ways to count to ten*. New York: Holt.

Friedman, A. (1994). *The king's commissioners*. New York: Scholastic.

Gag, W. (1928). *Millions of cats*. New York: Coward-McCann.

Giganti, P. (1988). *How many snails? A counting book*. New York: Greenwillow.

Giganti, P. (1992). *Each orange had 8 slices*. New York: Greenwillow.

Hoban, T. (1981). *More than one*. New York: Greenwillow.

Hutchins, P. (1986). *The doorbell rang*. New York: Greenwillow.

Jaspersohn, W. (1993). *Cookies*. Old Tappan, NJ: Macmillan.

Juster, N. (1961). *The phantom tollbooth*. New York: Random House.

Lobal, A. (1970). *Frog and Toad are friends*. New York: HarperCollins.

Mathews, L. (1979). *Gator pie*. New York: Dodd, Mead.

McKissack, P. C. (1992). *A million fish . . . more or less*. New York: Knopf.

Munsch, R. (1987). *Moira's birthday*. Toronto: Annick Press.

Myller, R. (1990). *How big is a foot?* New York: Dell.

Norton, M. (1953). *The borrowers*. New York: Harcourt Brace.

Parker, T. (1984). *In one day*. Boston: Houghton Mifflin.

Pluckrose, H. (1988). *Pattern*. New York: Franklin Watts.

St. John, G. (1975). *How to count like a Martian*. New York: Walck.

Schwartz, D. (1985). *How much is a million?* New York: Lothrop, Lee & Shepard.

Schwartz, D. (1989). *If you made a million*. New York: Lothrop, Lee & Shepard.

Scieszka, J., & Smith, L. (1995). *Math curse*. New York: Viking Penguin.

Sharmat, M. W. (1979). *The 329th friend*. New York: Four Winds Press.

Silverstein, S. (1974). One inch tall. In *Where the sidewalk ends* (p. 55). New York: Harper & Row.

Tahan, M. (1993). *The man who counted: A collection of mathematical adventures*.

Waverly, B. (1990). *How big? How fast? How hungry?* Milwaukee, WI: Raintree.

Wells, R. E. (1993). *Is a blue whale the biggest thing there is?* Morton Grove, IL: Whitman.

Wolkstein, D. (1972). *8,000 stones*. New York: Doubleday.

INDEX

Abstract reasoning difficulties, 505
Abundant numbers, 438
Acceleration, 513
Access, educational, 507–508
Accommodation; 22
Acting out, 54
Active involvement, 483, 485
Active listening, 35
Activities, evaluation/selection of, 35–37
Acute triangles, 361
Addition
    algorithms, 217–219, 261–263
    of decimals, 288
    facts, strategies for, 143–149
    of fractions, 261–265
    front-end, 195, 202
    of integer, 446–449
    mental, 194–196
    models for, 122–126
    pencil-and-paper, 217–219
    repeated, 127, 222–223, 227–228
    rounding, 203–204
    word problems for, 119–122
Add one more set, 156–157
Affective factors, 30, 50–51, 83
Affective goals, 52, 58–59, 393
African-American students, 507
Algebra, 11, 272
    and functions, 457, 461–462
    and number theory, 436, 440, 444,
        454–455
Algebraic logic, 521
Algorithms
    addition, 217–219, 261–263
    cross-product, 304–305
    defined, 23, 192
    division, 228–235, 271–272
    equivalent-fraction, 256–257
    fraction, 260–263, 265–269, 271–272
    invented, 214, 217–218, 220–223,
        228–229
    mental, 192–193, 213–215
    multiplication, 221–228, 265–269
    pencil-and-paper, 192–193, 213–215
    subtraction, 220–221, 261–263
Alignment, and grading, 87
American Statistical Association, 408
Analysis, 346
Analytic scales, 74–75
Anchors of five and ten, 100, 103–104
Anecdotal notes, for observations, 75

Angles
    measurement of, 325–327, 374–375
    of triangles, 361
Angstroms, 443
Answer books, 18
Answers
    for estimations, 200–201
    looking back at, 41
Approximate numbers, 178–180
Approximation
    fractions to decimals, 282
    measurement, 314
Area, 44, 332, 377
    measurement of, 310–311, 318–322,
        381
    and ratio, 302–303
    simple plane shapes, 333–335
    standard units of, 328–329
Area models
    fractions, 238–239, 253–254, 256, 262
    pencil-and-paper computations,
        221–222, 227–228
    probability, 415–416
Arithmetic, fundamental theorem of, 437
Arrays, 131–134
Assessment
    combined with instruction, 66–71
    and decimals, 290
    defined, 62, 64
    and estimation, 209–210
    and functions, 478
    and geometry, 387–389
    goals reflected by, 59
    and grading, 86–88
    of group work, 490, 492
    and interviews, 85–86
    and measurement, 338–339
    and mental computation, 209–210
    and number theory, 454–455
    and observations, 75–76
    and operation meaning, 136–137
    and pencil-and-paper computation, 234
    and percents, 290
    and place value, 186–188
    of portfolios, 83–85
    and probability, 433
    and proportions, 307–308
    purposes of, 63–65
    questioning, 76–78
    and ratios, 308
    and rubrics, 71–75

    self-, student, 80, 82
    and statistics, 433
    and tests, 82–83
    and variables, 478
    what should be assessed, 65–66
    of writing, 78–81
Assessment standards, 7, 62–65
Assessment Standards for School Mathematics,
    5, 7–8, 11–13, 47, 62–64, 162, 209,
    333, 348, 492, 501
Assessment tasks, 66–67
Assimilation, 22
Attention deficit disorders, 503, 506
Attention deficit hyperactivity disorders,
    503, 506
Attention span difficulties, 506
Attitudes
    about gender, 511–512
    improvement of 30
    and logical reasoning, 393
    and problem solving, 50–51
Attribute activities
    classification schemes, 395–396
    difference games, 398
    logic problems, 396–398
    materials, 393–394
    objectives, 392–393
Attribute materials, 393–394
Attributes
    defined, 393
    measurement, 310–312
Autism, 503
Automatic constant features, 521
Averages, 425
Averaging techniques, 204–205
Axis of symmetry, 372–373

Backward trades, 215
Backward trading games, 215–216
Balls, 323, 336
Bar graphs, 420–424, 429
Bases, 332–333, 364–365
Base 10, 31, 164–167, 214, 218, 221,
    224–227, 284
Base 10 fractions, 275–276, 279, 283
BASIC, 530
Basic facts
    addition, 143–149
    defined, 140
    division, 157

Basic facts (*continued*)
  mastery of, 140–143, 157–160
  multiplication, 153–157
  subtraction, 149–153
Basic meanings. *See* Operation meanings
Beliefs
  about gender, 511–512
  improvement of, 30
  and logical reasoning, 393
  and problem solving, 50–51
Benchmarks for units of measure, 330
Best-fact practice, 527
Best-fit lines, 430–432
Bilateral symmetry, 370–372
Billion, 184
Blocks, geometric, 383
Borrowing, 215
Bottom numbers, in fractions, 243–244
Box-and-whisker plots, 425–427
Brainstorming, 43, 80
Bring-down method of division, 231–233
Building solids, 355–357
Burns, Marilyn, 70

Calculators, 35
  classroom use of, 122, 130, 133
  for computation, 190, 205–207, 233
  for decimals, 280
  for exponents, 440–441, 443
  for fractions, 245, 521–522
  for functions, 462–463, 470–471
  as graphical tools, 419–420, 427–428,
    431–433, 522
  impact on mathematics education, 4,
    518–519
  and mastery of basic facts, 140, 154, 159
  models, 31–32
  for numeral recognition, 97
  patterns with, 403–406
  permitted for tests, 82
  practical considerations, 521–522
  for primes, 437
  reasons for using, 519–521
  for scaling activities, 299
  for signed numbers, 444–445
  for variables, 476–477
  when/where to use, 523
Calculators and the Education of Youth, 519
Calculators in Mathematics Education, 519
California Mathematics Council, 73
Capacity. *See* Volume
Cardinality principle, 94
Carrying, 215
Cartesian products, 126–127
Chance, 31, 411
Charles, R., 40
Charts, 4, 55, 175–176, 180–181, 420,
  438
Checklists
  for mental computations, 209
  for observations, 75–76
Children. *See* Students
Children's literature, 50, 112–114,
    137–138, 185–186, 208–209, 257,
    289, 307, 339–340, 406, 454
Chunking of units of measure, 330

Circle graphs, 424–425
Circles, 334–335, 375–376
Circumference, 334, 375–376
Classification schemes, 395–396
Classifying activities, for shapes, 349–350,
    362–365
Classroom environment, shifts in, 6–7,
    19–20
Classrooms
  diversity in, 487–488, 501–502
  for doing mathematics, 13
  homework used in, 497
  models used in, 33
  reviews, 495–496
  traditional, 10–11, 502
  writing in, 492–495
Clay, modeling, 367–369
Clock reading skills, 336–338
Closure difficulties, 505
Cognitively Guided Education program,
    509
Coherence standard, 63
Collaborative activities, 487–488
Combinations problems, 127–129
Common denominator method, 252,
    261–263, 271–272
Common-factor approach, 256
Common multiples of denominators, 263
Communication, mathematics as, 6, 12
Commutative property, 125, 133
Compare models, 124–125
Compare problems, 120–121
Comparisons, measurement, 312, 315,
    318–320, 322–325
Compatible numbers, 196, 203–205, 269
Composite numbers, 437
Computation, 11, 48, 137, 162, 180–183
  alternative forms of, 190–192
  with calculators, 190, 205–207
  with decimals, 287–289
  with fractions, 260–272
  mental, 190, 192–200
  methods, construction of, 23–24
  pencil-and-paper, 190, 192–193,
    213–235
  student-invented methods, 214
Computational estimation, 190–193,
    200–209
Computational form, 121
Computer-assisted instruction, 526
Computers. *See also* Software
  for computation, 207
  for functions, 463
  as graphical tools, 419–420, 428, 433
  impact on mathematics education, 4,
    518–519
  informal geometry on, 383–397
  Internet access, 528–529
  programming, 529–532
  spreadsheets, 428, 523–526
  as tools, 523–524
Concave curves, 361
Conceptual knowledge, 25, 66
  of mathematics, 25–26
  models for, 30–33
  new concepts, 29–30, 33
  understanding, 27–28

Cones, 336–337, 364–365, 367–368
Confidence, need for, 12
Connections, mathematical, 6, 111–112,
    176–177
Consecutive numbers, 18
Consolidation, lesson, 485–486
Construction
  activities, 300–303
  of shapes, 352–356, 364–370, 382
Constructivism, 22, 25, 39
Constructivist view of learning, 22
  for algorithms, 215
  and knowledge, 23–25
  and mathematics, 32
  principles, 25
  and understanding, 22–23
Contextual representations of functions,
    458, 462
Continuous data graphs, 423–424
Conversions, between units of measure,
    329–330
Convex curves, 361
Cooperative learning groups, 35, 488–492
Cores, of repeating patterns, 399–400
Counters, 131–132, 445–446
Counting, 94–95, 97–98, 164, 187
Counting back, 99
Counting books, 112–114
Counting fractional parts, 242–243
Counting on, 99, 148
Counting sets, 98–99
Countryman, J., 35
Created problems, 49
Credits/debits, 444
Cross-multiplication, 303–304
Cross-product algorithm, 304–305
Cube roots, 453–454
Cubes, 323, 335, 356, 364, 369, 372–373
Cultural equity, 507–510
Curriculum, for teaching problem solving,
    52–53
*Curriculum and Evaluation Standards for
    School Mathematics*, 3–8, 10–13, 33,
    47, 52, 57, 62–63, 65, 87, 162,
    190–191, 209, 213–214, 260, 287,
    292, 333, 348, 388–389, 418, 501,
    518–519
Curriculum standards, 5
Curves, 361
Customary system, 327–330
Cylinders, 333, 335–337, 363–364,
    367–368

Data
  collection/presentation of, 49, 71–76,
    418–419
  extremes of, 426
  graphical representations, 419–425
  range of, 426
Data analysis, 4
Databases, 523, 529
Database software, 523
Data graphing software, 525
Dealing with Data and Chance, 409
Debits/credits, 444
Decimal points, 276–278, 288

Decimals
addition of, 288
and assessment, 290
computation with, 287–289
division of, 288–289
estimating with, 208, 287–288
models, 278–279
multiplication of, 288–289
names for, 275–276
number sense, 280–283
ordering of, 282–283
as rational numbers, 452–453
relation to fractions, 274–275, 279–280, 283
for simple fractions, 281–282
subtraction of, 288
Decisions, instructional, 64
Deduction, 346–347
Deficient numbers, 438
Definitions, of shapes, 379
Degrees, of angles, 325–327
Denominators, 244, 252, 261–263, 265, 271–272
Density of rational numbers, 453–454
Dependent events, 415–417
Descriptive statistics, 425–428
Development, lesson, 485
Developmental approaches, 33
foundations of, 33–34
proportional reasoning, 294–295
strategies, 34–35
student activities, 35–37
Diagnostic interviews, 85–86, 210
Diagonals, of quadrilaterals, 373–374
Diameter, 334, 376
Difference games, 398
Difference realtionships, 120–121, 124–125
Differentiated tasks, 488
Digit correspondence, 187–188
Directed distances, 445
Disabilities
categories, 503
learning, 503–506
mental, 506–507
Disadvantaged students, 502, 507–510
Discrimination difficulties, 504–505
Discussions, 46–47, 484
Disequilibrium, 22, 24
Dissonance, 22
Distributive property, 134
Diversity, classroom, 487–488, 501–502
Dividends, 230, 232, 288
Divisibility, tests for, 439
Division
algorithms, 228–235, 271–272
of decimals, 288–289
facts, strategies for, 157
of fractions, 269–272
fractions as, 450–452
front-end, 202
of integers, 449–450
mental, 198–200
models for, 131–134
pencil-and-paper, 228–235
rounding, 203
word problems for, 126–130

Divisors
decimal, 289
one-digit, 228
proper, 437
same as factors, 126, 133–134, 265–268, 437–438
two-digit, 228, 233–234
whole number, for decimals, 288–289
Dodecahedrons, 382
Doing mathematics, 12–13, 40, 72, 214, 455
Domains, of functions, 463
Domalik, Laura, 32n
Dot card activities, 108–109
Dot paper, 354–355, 370
Double and double again, 156
Double-and-halve approach, 156–157, 198
Double and one more set, 156
Double relationships, 110
Doubles facts, 145–146, 150
Doubles-plus-two facts, 148
Drills, 142, 159, 495–497, 527
Dynamic geometry software, 525, 527

Edges, 363
Efficient strategies, 141–142, 158
Eights, multiplying factors with, 198
Electronic random number devices, 412–413
Elements, 363–365, 401
Enjoyment in problem solving, 393
Enrichment, 513–515
Environment, for doing mathematics, 13, 19–20, 34
Equal-groups problems, 127
Equal shares, 241
Equation representations of functions, 460–462
Equations, 56, 123, 477
Equilateral triangles, 361
Equity standard, 63
Equivalent-fraction concepts, 253–257
Equivalent fractions, as proportions, 305–306
Equivalent groupings, 164
Equivalent ratios, 297–303
Equivalent representations, 164
Error analyses, 50
Escher, M. C., 377–378
Estimation, 111, 162, 179–180, 185, 527
and assessment, 209–210
with compatible numbers, 204–205
computational, 190–193, 200–201
with decimals, 208, 287–288
exercises, 205–208
with fractions, 208, 252–253, 268–269, 272
front-end methods, 202
language of, 200
measurement, 313–314, 330–331
with percents, 208, 286–287
rounding, 202–203, 234
strategies for, 201–205
Evaluation
defined, 64
of portfolios, 85
of programs, 65

standards of, 6
of student achievent, 64
Events
defined, 410
dependent, 415–417
independent, 413–414
Everybody Counts, 3, 11
Expectations, educational, 43–44, 508–509
Experimental probability, 409–410
Explanations, 50, 82, 493–494
Explicit-trade method of division, 231–233
Exponents, 440–441, 443
Expressive language difficulties, 505
Extensions, 45, 114
Extremes of data, 426

Face cards, 350–352
Faces, 363
Fact families, 124
Factor-of-change approach, 296
Factors, 126, 133–134, 265–268, 437–438
Facts. *See* Basic facts
Fair shares, 241
Fair-sharing problems, 127
Female students, 502, 510–512
Fibonacci sequence, 402–403, 438
Figure-ground difficulties, 504–505
Flash cards, 144, 147–148, 157
Flips, 355, 371–372
"Floating strands," 193
Formulas
development of, 24–25
functions from, 468–470
measurement, 331–337, 339, 381
variables from, 476–477
Forward trades, 215
Forward trading games, 215–216
Fosnot, C. T., 39
Fractional parts, 240
connecting concepts with symbolism, 243–245
constructing, 241–243
counting, 242–243
exercises, 245–248
flexibility with, 248–249
Fractional parts of units of measure, 316–317
Fractional parts of whole, 241
Fractions, 43, 237, 521–522
addition of, 261–265
algorithms for, 260–263, 265–269, 271–272
base 10, 275–276, 279, 283
comparisons of, 250–252
computation with, 260–272
in curriculum, 237–238
division of, 269–272
equivalent, 253–257, 305–306
estimating with, 208, 252–253, 268–269, 272
improper, 244–245
as indicated division, 450–452
models, 238–240, 245–246, 275, 279
multiplication of, 265–269
names for, 253–256, 275–276
number sense, 248–253

Fractions (*continued*)
  as rational numbers, 452–453
  as ratios, 293
  relation to decimals, 274–275, 279–280, 283
  simple, for decimals, 281–282
  subtraction of, 261–265
  unit, 246
  written in simplest terms, 256
Frame numbers, 465–466
Frames, 401, 463–466
Free-form quadrilaterals, 362
Front-end methods, 195, 197–198, 202
Function graphers, 526
Function machines, 463
Functions, 432, 457
  and assessment, 478
  concept of, 457–458
  for development in classrooms, 461–463
  from formulas, 468–470
  graphs without equations, 471–473
  from patterns, 463–467
  and proportion, 468
  from real world, 467–473
  representations of, 458–462
  from scatter plot data, 470–471
Fundamental theorem of arithmetic, 437

Gender equity, 502, 510–512
General rubrics, 71–72, 75
Geoboards, 353–354, 359–360, 383–384
Geometric blocks, 383
Geometric models, computer versions of, 383
Geometric puzzles, 357–359
Geometric thinking, 345–349
Geometric tools, computer versions of, 383–385
Geometry, 294, 302, 342
  and assessment, 387–389
  exploratory activities, 342–344, 348, 383–385
  informal, 344–345, 349–387
  objectives, 387–388
  problem-solving activities, 356–36, 376–377
  reasons for studying, 345
Geometry software, 525, 527
"Giant journals," 79–80
Gifted students, 502, 512–515
Goals
  affective, 52, 58–59, 393
  for attribute/pattern activities, 392–393
  for mental algorithms, 193
  metacognitive, 52, 58, 393
  new, 10–12
  problem-solving, 52–59
  process, 52
  reflected by assessment, 59
  strategy, 52–58, 392–393
  teaching, understanding of, 41–42
Goldbach, Christian, 437
Golden ratio, 402
Golden rectangle, 402
Grading, 86
  issues, 87–88

myths about, 86–87
Grading scales, 88
Graphical representations of functions, 459–460, 462
Graphing calculators. *See* Calculators
Graphing software, 526
Graphs, 4, 112, 300–301, 419–425, 429, 466–467, 471–473
Grid paper, 354–355, 357, 360
Grids, 18, 301–303, 321–322, 355, 370
Groupable base 10 models, 166–167
Group behavior, 489–490
Grouping activities, 168–172
Groupings of ten, 164–167, 169–171, 188
Group performance rating scale, 490–491
Group reporting, 490
Group responsibilities, 489
Groups, cooperative learning, 35, 488–492
Group skills, 489–491
Growing patterns, 401–402, 463–464
Guess-and-check strategies, 56–57

Halve-and-double approach, 156–157, 198
Hearing impairment, 503
Heaviness, 324
Height, 332–333
Helping facts, 156–157
Heuristics, 40, 51
Hexahedrons, 382
Hex grids, 354
Hexominoes, 358
Higher-decade facts, 194–195
Hints, use of, 45
Hispanic students, 507
Histograms, 423–424
Holistic scales, 73
Homework, 496–497
Hours, 337–338
"How many ways" problems, 359–360
Hundred, 171
Hundreds, computation with, 180–182, 194
Hundreds charts, 438
Hundredths, 284
Hundredths disks, 275
Hyperactivity difficulties, 506

Icosahedrons, 382
IMPACT project, 509
Improper fractions, 244–245
Impulse control difficulties, 506
Inclusion, 503
Independent events, 413–414
Individuals with Disabilities Education Act, 502–503
Inferences standard, 63
Informal deduction, 346
Informal geometry
  on computers, 383–387
  defined, 344–345
  level 0, 349–361
  level 1, 361–378
  level 2, 378–387
Informal proofs, 379–382
Informal units of measure, 313, 315, 320, 323–324

Instruction, combined with assessment, 66–71
Instructional decisions, 64
Instructional software, 526–528
Instrumental understanding, 27–29
Instruments, measuring, 312–313
Integers, 31, 444–450
Integrative deficits, 505–506
Interactions, appropriate, 45–46
Internet, 528–529
Interviews, diagnostic, 85–86, 210
Invented algorithms, 214, 217–218, 220–223, 228–229
Inverse ratios, 301
Invert-and-multiply method, 271–272
Irrational numbers, 283, 453–454
Isoceles trapezoids, 361
Isoceles triangles, 361
Isometric grids, 321, 354–355
Iteration of units of measure, 330

Japan, mathematics education in, 122
Join problems, 120
Journals, 78–81, 493
Jump numbers, 13–14

Kentucky Mathematics Portfolio Holistic Scoring Guide, 65, 74
Keypad partner numbers, 520
Kites, 361
Knowledge
  conceptual, 25–26
  construction of, 23–25
  procedural, 25–27

Ladson-Billings, G., 510
Language expressions for functions, 459, 462
Large numbers, 130, 134–135, 184–185, 442–443
Learning disabilities, 503–506
Learning opportunities, 40
Learning problems, students with, 501–507
Learning standard, 63
Least squares regression line, 430
"Left-hand" computational algorithms, 214
Length, 31
  measurement of, 310–311, 315–318
  and ratio, 302–303
  standard units of, 327, 329
Length models, 239–240, 254–255
Less, concept of, 95–96, 110
Lessons, 529
  student-centered, 483–485
  teacher-directed, 485–487
  textbook, 498
Lester, Frank, 40, 53
Light-years, 442
Like denominators, 263
Line graphs, 423–424
Line plots, 423
Lines, 315–316, 374–375
Line symmetry, 370–372

Lists, organized, 57
Literature. *See* Children's literature
Logical reasoning, 57, 392–406
Logic problems, 396–398
Logic problem software, 528
Logo, 385–387, 514, 530–532
Long division, 228–235
Long-term memory deficits, 504–506
Looking-back processes, 41, 51
Looking-back strategies, 57–58
Loops, 395–396
Lower extreme, 426
Lower quartile, 426
Lowest terms, writing fractions in, 256–257

McPhillips, Mary, 39
Make-10 facts, 147–148
Making Sense of Data, 409
Male students, 502, 510–512
Manipulative tasks, 49
Mass. *See* Weight
Mastery of basic facts
    defined, 140
    development of efficient strategies, 141
    drill of efficient methods, 142
    making it work, 157–159
    overview of approach, 142–143
    remediation, 159–160
    role of number/operation concepts, 141
Matching activities, for shapes, 350–352
Mathematical connections, 6
Mathematical environment, 13, 19–20, 34
Mathematical power, 65–66, 388–389
Mathematical Sciences Education Board, 3
Mathematical tasks, worthwhile, 34–35, 40
Mathematics
    for all students, 7, 501–502
    and basic facts, 159
    as communication, 6, 12
    conceptual knowledge of, 25–26
    construction of, 32
    doing, 12–13, 40, 72, 214, 455
    forces driving revolution in, 4–5
    newness of mental computation, 192–193
    as problem solving, 6
    procedural knowledge of, 25–27
    as reasoning, 6, 12
    revolution in teaching of, 3–4
    role of models, 30–33
    as science of pattern/order, 11
    teaching, 3, 7–8
    and technology, 517–519
    traditional views of, 10–11, 502
    understandability of, 12
    understanding, 27–30
    valuing, 11–12
    writing in, 492–495
Mathematics Assessment, 83
Mathematics standard, 62–63
Mathematics Teaching in the Middle School, 48
Mean, 425, 427–429
Meanings. *See* Operation meanings
Measurement, 111, 310

activities, 300–303, 314–315, 318–320, 322–325, 331
    of angles, 325–327
    of area, 310–311, 318–322
    and assessment, 338–339
    concepts, 311–314
    defined, 310–311
    estimation of, 313–314, 330–331
    formulas, 331–337, 339
    informal units of, 313, 315, 320, 323–324
    of length, 310–311, 315–318
    models, 239–240, 253–256, 312
    problems, 127
    process, 310–311
    of shapes, 364–370
    skills, 311–314
    standard units of, 313, 326–330, 339
    of volume, 310–311, 322–323
    of weight, 310–311, 323–325
Measurement concept for division, 270–271
Measures of covering, 321
Measuring cups, 323
Measuring instruments, 312–313, 317–318, 323–327
Median, 425
Median-median line, 430–432
Median point, 431
Memory, enhancement of, 29
Memory deficits, 504–506
Mental algorithms, 192–193, 213–215
Mental computation, 115, 190, 192–193, 527
    addition, 194–196
    and assessment, 209–210
    division, 198–200
    multiplication, 197–198
    subtraction, 194–196
Mental disabilities, 506–507
Mental retardation, 503
Metacognition, and problem solving, 50–51
Metacognitive goals, 52, 58, 393
Methods, discovery of, 393
Metric system, 278–279, 327–330
Michigan State Board of Education, 228
Million, 184
Minilessons, 484–485
Minority students, 502, 507–510
Minutes, 337–338
Mirror symmetry, 370–372
Missing-factor approach, 199–200
Missing numbers, 152–153
Missing-part activities, 106–108
Mixed numbers, 244–245, 264–266, 268
Mode, 425
Models, 30, 35, 54
    for addition, 122–126
    base 10, 165–167
    base 10 fractions, 275, 279
    for computational algorithms, 218, 220–222, 227–228, 230
    and constructing mathematics, 32
    decimals, 278–279
    for division, 131–134
    of equivalent ratios, 300–303

examples of, 30–32
    expansion of idea of, 32
    fractions, 238–240, 245–246, 254–256, 261–262, 269, 275, 279
    geometric, computer versions of, 383
    incorrect use of, 33
    for instruction of gifted students, 513–515
    integers, 445–446
    for mathematical concepts, 30–32
    for multiplication, 131–134
    operation meanings from, 118
    percents, 284
    physical, 16
    for probability, 415–416
    for subtraction, 122–126
    of units of measure, 312
    used in classrooms, 33
    used on tests, 82
Money, 168, 179, 278–279
Monitoring student progress, 64
More, concept of, 95–96, 110
Multicultural equity, 502, 507–510
Multiples, 263, 437
Multiplicand, 126
Multiplication
    algorithms, 221–228, 265–269
    of decimals, 288–289
    facts, strategies for, 153–157
    of fractions, 265–269
    front-end, 197–198, 202
    of integers, 449–450
    mental, 197–198
    models for, 131–134
    pencil-and-paper, 221–228
    problems, 16–17
    and repeated addition, 222–223, 227–228
    rounding, 203
    to solve proportion, 303–304
    word problems for, 126–130
Multiplicative comparison problems, 127
Multipliers, 126
    one-digit, 223–226
    two-digit, 226–227
Multiply-by-one method, 256–257
Music, compared to mathematics, 12–13, 19–20

Names
    for decimals, 275–276
    for fractions, 253–256, 275–276
    for numbers, 172–173
National Assessment of Educational Programs, 28, 30, 244, 281–282, 312, 332
National Council of Teachers of Mathematics, 3–8, 10–13, 20, 48, 83, 408–409, 513, 517–519
Native American students, 507
Near-double relationships, 110
Near doubles facts, 145–146, 150
Near facts, 157
Negative exponents, 443
Negative integers, 31, 444–446
Nets, 357

New concepts, 48
"Nice" fractions, 282–283
"Nice" numbers, 178–180, 196, 200, 282–283, 285–286
Nifty nines, 155–156
Nines
    multiplying factors with, 198
    nifty, 155–156
Nonisoceles trapezoids, 362
Nonproportional materials, 168
Nonregular polygons, 361
Nonsymmetrical shapes, 361
nth root, 453
Number, concept of, 93
Number concepts, 93–94, 141, 162–163
    counting, 94–95
    more/less/same, 95–96
Number lines, 122–123, 177–178, 317–318, 445–446
Number names, 172–174
Number relationships
    numbers 1 to 10, 99–109
    numbers 10 to 20, 109–110
    numbers to 100, 114–116
Numbers
    approximate, 178–180
    compatible, 196, 203–205, 269
    composite, 437
    consecutive, 18
    on homemade rulers, 317
    integers, 31, 444–446
    irrational, 283, 453–454
    large, 130, 134–135, 184–185, 442–443
    missing, 152–153
    mixed, 244–245, 264–266, 268
    models for, 30–31
    more than 1000, 183–185
    negative, 31, 444–446
    "nice," 178–180, 196, 200, 282–283, 285–286
    prime, 437–438
    procedural knowledge of, 97–99
    random, 412–413
    rational, 237n, 283, 450–453
    real, 453–454
    small, 443
    start/jump, 13–14
    top/bottom, in fractions, 243–244
Number sense, 4, 137, 162
    decimals, 280–283
    defined, 93–94
    development of, 177–183
    fractions, 248–253, 260–261
    and real world, 111–112
Number strings, 23
Number theory
    and assessment, 454–455
    defined, 436
    divisibility, 439
    exponents, 440–441, 443
    factors, 437–438
    integers, 444–450
    large numbers, 442–443
    primes, 437–438
    rational numbers, 450–453
    real numbers, 453–454
    small numbers, 443

Numeral writing/recognition, 97
Numerators, 244, 265, 271
Numeric patterns, 403

Oblique cylinders, 363–364
Observation rubric, 75–76
Observations, of performance tasks, 75–76
Obtuse triangles, 361
Octahedrons, 382
One, role in multiplication, 134, 154–155
One and two more/less facts, 143–144, 150
One and two more/less relationships, 100–103
One-digit divisors, 228
One-digit multipliers, 223–226
Ones, counting by, 164
Open-ended problems, 70
Open exploration, 50
Openness standard, 63, 72
Open questioning, 77–78
Open sentences, 56
Operation meanings, 117, 141
    and assessment, 136–137
    from models, 118, 122–126, 131–134
    and translations, 118–119
    from word stories, 117, 134–136
    from word problems, 117–122, 126–130
Operations, order of, 440–441
Opposites, 445
Oral counting, 97–98
Oral names for numbers, 172–174
Oral responses/reports, 35, 78, 490
Order, 11, 18
Order-of-operations rules, 440–441
Order property, 125, 133
Organized lists, 57
Orthopedic handicaps, 503
Outcomes, 410
Overhead projectors, 207–208, 338, 522

Pairs, 127–129
Papert, Seymour, 32n, 530
Parallel faces, 363
Parallelograms, 319, 333–334, 361–362
Parentheses, operations with, 440
Partition concept for division, 269–270
Partition problems, 127
Part-part-whole activities, 105–106
Part-part-whole models, 122–124
Part-part-whole problems, 120
Part-part-whole relationships, 100, 104–108
Parts, 241–243, 245–248, 265
Part-to-part ratios, 293–294
Part-to-whole ratios, 293–294
Pattern activities
    with calculators, 403–406
    Fibonacci sequence, 402–403
    growing patterns, 401–402
    materials, 399
    numeric patterns, 403
    objectives, 392–393
    repeating patterns, 399–401
    two-dimensional patterns, 401
Pattern blocks, 383

Patterns, 11, 18, 54–55
    construction of, 23
    Fibonacci sequence, 402–403
    functions from, 463–467
    growing, 401–402, 463–464
    on hundreds charts, 438
    numeric, 403
    repeating, 399–401
    searching for, 13–14
    tiling, 343
    two-dimensional, 401
    on 0–99 chart, 176
Pencil-and-paper algorithms, 192–193, 213–215
Pencil-and-paper computation, 190, 192–193, 213–215
    addition, 217–219
    and assessment, 234
    division, 228–235
    multiplication, 221–228
    readiness activities, 215–217
    subtraction, 220–221
Pentominoes, 357–359
Percents, 284–285
    and assessment, 290
    defined, 284
    estimating with, 208, 286–287
    models, 284
    problems, 285–287, 306–307
    as proportions, 305–306
    realistic problems, 285–287
Perceptions, changes in, 10–12
Perceptual deficits, 504–505
Perfect numbers, 438
Performance assessment tasks, 66–67
Performance indicators
    defined, 71
    self-rating scales, 490–491
    written after lessons, 72
    written before lessons, 71–72
Performance tasks
    collecting data from, 71–76
    defined, 39–40, 66–67
    examples, 67–71
    observation of, 75–76
    and questioning, 76–78
    and rubrics, 71–75
    student assessment of, 80, 82
    and tests, 82–83
    and writing, 78–81
Perimeter, 44, 332, 370
Periodic reviews, 496
Perseverance, 393
Personal abilities, faith in, 393
Physical models, 16
Pi π, 334–335, 375–376
Piaget, Jean, 22, 25, 294, 318, 347
Picture graphs, 420
Pictures, 54, 79, 82
Pie graphs, 424–425
"Pizza fallacy," 251, 261
Place value, 162
    and assessment, 186–188
    basic ideas, 163–165, 276
    development of concepts/procedures, 168–177
    grouping activities, 168–172

models for, 165–168
number ideas before, 163
and number sense development,
177–183
for numbers more than 1000, 183–185
oral names for numbers, 172–174
written symbols, 174–177
Place-value development, 162–177
Place-value language, 172
Place-value mats, 174–175
Plan-and-carry-out strategies, 54–57
Planes, 374–375
Planes of symmetry, 372–373
Plans/planning
assistance in, 44
for diversity, 487–488
devising/carrying out, 41
implementation of, 42
Platonic solids, 376, 381–382
Pólya, George, 40–41, 53, 64
Polygons
classification of, 361–362
measuring angles in, 326, 374
two from one, 380
Polyhedrons, regular, 381–382
Portfolios
content suggestions, 83–85
defined, 83
management of, 85
Positive integers, 31
Practice, 495–496, 527
Praise, use of, 46, 59
"Preanswered" tests, 83
Predictions, 411–412
Pregrouped base 10 models, 166–167
Premature drills, 142
Pre-place-value relationship, 109–110, 163
Prime numbers, 437–438
Prisms, 335–336, 364
Probability, 4, 408–409
and assessment, 433
concepts of chance, 411
experimental, 409–410
random numbers, 412–413
for simple events, 411–412
and simulations, 417–418
theoretical, 409–410
two or more independent events,
413–414
using area models, 415
Problems
defined, 39–40
looking back at, 41
plans for, 41
process, 53
types of, 47–50
understanding, 40–41
Problem solving, 4, 12, 39, 137, 527–528
and beliefs/attitudes, 50–51
enhancing abilities, 30
general framework for, 39–41
geometry activities, 344, 357–361,
376–377
goals of, 52–59
integers, 446–450
mathematics as, 6
and metacognition, 50–51

phases of, 40–41
processes for, 50–51, 53–58
and programming, 530–532
strategies for, 50–51, 53–58
teacher actions, 42–47
teaching about, 41–42, 50–53
as writing task, 493
Procedural knowledge, 25, 66
of mathematics, 26–27
new procedures, 29–30
of numbers, 97–99
role of, 27
understanding, 28–29
Processes
looking back at, 41
problem-solving, 50–51
Process goals, 52
Process problems, 53
Product, 127, 265
Product-of-measures problems, 129
Professional organizations, 528–529
Professional Standards for Teaching Mathematics, 5–8, 11–13, 20, 34, 47, 162,
209, 333, 348, 501
Programming, 529–532
Programs, evaluation of, 65
Proofs, informal, 379–382
Proper divisors, 437
Properties, of shapes, 349–352, 362–365,
370–376, 379
Proportional reasoning, 292–293
and children, 294–296
construction activities, 300–303
defined, 294
measurement activities, 300–303
and proportions, 294
and ratios, 293–294
scaling activities, 298–300
selection of equivalent ratios, 297–298
Proportions, 292
and assessment, 308
in base 10 models, 166
defined, 294
as equivalent fractions, 305–306
and functions, 468
as percents, 305–306
solving, 303–307
Protractors, 325–327
Pyramids, 336–337, 364–365, 373
Pythagorean theorem, 381

Quadrilaterals, 361–362, 373–374
Quartiles, 426
QUASAR project, 509–510
Questions
for assessment of performance tasks,
76–78
to clarify tasks/problems, 42–43
Quick graphs, 420–421
Quotients, 288–289

Radius, 375–376
Random numbers, 412–413
Range of data, 426
Ranges of functions, 463

Rate problems, 127
Rates, 293–294
Rational numbers, 237n, 283, 450–453
Ratios, 28, 292, 302
and assessment, 308
in circles, 375–376
defined, 293
equivalent, 297–303
examples, 293–294
as expressions of rates, 293–294
as fractions, 293
inverse, 301
within/between, 298–299
Rays, of angles, 325, 327
"Real" graphs, 420
Real numbers, 453–454
Real-world situations, 11, 70, 178,
191–192, 200–201, 213–214,
285–287, 293–294, 417–418, 444,
467–473
Reasoning, 4
logical, 57, 392–406
mathematics as, 6, 12
proportional, 292–303
Receptive language difficulties, 505
Rectangles, 31, 318–320, 333–334, 361,
437
Rectangular prisms, 335, 364
Rectangular solids, 364
"Reducing fractions," 256
Referents for units of measure, 330
Referral, 503
Reflections, 371
Reflective writing, 494
Region models. See Area models
Regular polygons, 361
Reis, S. M., 514
Relational understanding, 27–30
Relationships
anchors of five and ten, 100, 103–104
construction of, 23
difference, 120–121, 124–125
double/near-double, 110
functions from patterns, 464–467
more/less, 95–96, 110
number, 99–110
one and two more/less, 100–103
part-part-whole, 100, 104–108
pre-place-value, 109–110
real-world, 11, 178
of shapes, 370–376
spatial, 100–101, 348
ten-to-one, 276–277
Relative magnitude, 177–178
Remainders, 129–130
Remediation, fact, 159–160
Renzulli, Joseph S., 513–514
Repeated addition, and multiplication,
222–223, 227–228
Repeated-addition problems, 127
Repeated-subtraction problems, 127
Repeating patterns, 399–401
Rep-tiles, 377
Resnick, Lauren, 19, 104–105
Reversal difficulties, 504–505
Reviews, 495–496
Rewards, intrinsic, 29

Rewriting of problem, 263
Rhombuses, 361–362
Right cylinders, 363–364
"Right-hand" computational algorithms, 214
Right prisms, 335
Right triangles, 361, 381
Rigor, 347
Romberg, T., 12, 19
Roots, 453–454
Rotational symmetry, 372–373
Rounding, 178–180, 202–203, 233–234, 283
Rubrics
    defined, 71
    examples, 72–75
    general, 71–72, 75
    observation, 75–76
    and performance indicators, 71–72
    student involvement with, 72
    used by teachers, 71–72
Rulers, 317–318
Rules, 11, 261

Same, concept of, 95–96
Sample space, 410
Scale drawings, 302
Scalene triangles, 361
Scales
    group performance rating, 490–491
    for measuring weight, 324–325
    for rubrics, 71–75
Scaling activities, 299–300
Scatter plots, 428–433, 470–471
Schifter, D., 39
Schoenfeld, A. H., 34
Schoolwide Enrichment Model, 514–515
Scientific notation, 442–443
Second methods, 45–46
Self-assessment, student, 80, 82
Self-confidence, 393
Self-monitoring, student, 58
Separate problems, 120
Sequences, 401
Sequential memory problems, 504–505
Set models, 240, 254–255
Shape hunts, 352
Shapes, 26, 318–322, 332–336, 342–343, 348
    constructing, 352–356, 364–370, 382
    definitions of, 379
    exploring, 349–352
    in Logo, 385–386
    matching, 350–352
    measuring, 364–370
    properties of, 349–352, 361–364, 370–376, 379
    sorting/classifying, 349–350, 361–364
    special properties of, 370–376
Shares, 241
Sheered prisms, 336
Short-term memory deficits, 504–506
Sides, 332–333, 361
Signed numbers, 444–446
Similar figures, 374–375
Similarity, 302

Simple versions, 44, 55–56, 135
Simplest terms, writing fractions in, 256
Simulations, 417–418
Situational problems, 70
Size, 318, 322
Skemp, Richard, 27, 30
Skill-oriented tasks, avoidance of, 488
Skills, group, 489–491
Slides, 355
Slow learners, 507
Small numbers, 443
Social equity, 502, 507–510
Society, demands of, 4
Socioeconomic status, low, 507–508
Software
    for concept instruction, 528
    databases, 523
    for data graphing, 525
    drill-and-practice, 527
    for dynamic geometry, 525, 527
    for function graphers, 526
    instructional, 526–528
    for problem solving, 527–528
    for spreadsheets, 428, 523–526
    tools, 523–524
Solids
    building, 355–357
    Platonic, 376, 381–382
    volumes of, 335–337
Solutions
    differing, 15–16
    none given, 18
    working backwards from, 57
Sorting activities, for shapes, 349–350
Spatial organization deficits, 504–505
Spatial relationships, 100–101
Spatial sense, 4, 348, 387–388
Special students, 59, 501–502
Speed tests, 158
Spelling, 80
Spheres, 323, 336
Spinners, 415–416
Spread, 325
Spreadsheets, 428, 523–526
Square/diagonal grids, 354
Square grids, 321–322, 354
Square roots, 453–454
Squares, 319–320, 361–362, 381
Standard deviation, 427
Standard units of measure, 313, 326–330, 339
Standards. *See Assessment Standards for School Mathematics*; *Curriculum and Evaluation Standards for School Mathematics*; *Professional Standards for Teaching Mathematics*
Start numbers, 13–14
Statement of problem, 263
Statistics, 408–409
    and assessment, 433
    collection of data, 418–419
    defined, 425
    descriptive, 425–428
    graphical representations, 419–425
    scatter plots, 428–433
Stem-and-leaf plots, 422–423
Story problems, 48, 117, 134–136
Story problem software, 527–528

Strategies, 40, 50–51, 53–54
    acting out, 54
    computational estimation, 201–205
    development of, 141, 158
    drawing pictures, 54
    drills for, 142, 159
    efficient, 141–142, 158
    equations, 56
    guess-and-check, 56–57
    individualized, 143
    introduction of, 142–143
    logical reasoning, 57
    looking-back, 57–58
    looking for patterns, 54–55
    models, 54
    new, 143
    open sentences, 56
    organized lists, 57
    plan-and-carry-out, 54–57
    practice with, 143
    simple versions of problems, 55–56
    tables/charts, 55
    think-pair-share, 484–485
    try-and-adjust, 56–57
    understanding-the-task, 54
    working backwards from solutions, 57
Strategy goals, 52–58, 392–393
Strategy retrieval, 142, 158
Strategy selection process, 51, 142–143, 158
String cylinders/cones, 367–368
Structured attribute materials, 393
Student-centered lessons, 483–485
Students
    activities of, 35–37
    computation methods invented by, 214, 217–218, 220–223, 228–229
    cultural/social backgrounds, 502, 507–510
    doing mathematics, 13
    evaluating achievement of, 64
    gender, 502, 510–512
    gifted/talented, 502, 512–515
    involved with rubrics, 72
    with learning problems, 501–507
    monitoring progress of, 64
    new goals for, 11–12
    perceptions of, 11
    and proportional reasoning, 294–296
    responses of, 35
    self-assessment, 80, 82
    self-monitoring, 58
    special, 59, 501–502
    thinking processes of, 33
Student work, opportunities for, 484
Subdivisions
    of shapes, 354
    of units of measure, 330
Subtraction, 28
    algorithms, 220–221, 261–263
    of decimals, 288
    facts, strategies for, 149–153
    of fractions, 261–265
    front-end, 202
    of integers, 446–449
    mental, 194–196
    models for, 122–126
    pencil-and-paper, 220–221

repeated, 127
rounding, 203–204
word problems for, 119–122
Suggestions, use of, 45
Surfaces, 363
Surveys, 418–419
Symbolic graphs, 420
Symbols/symbolism, 26
exponents, 440
fractions, 243–245
and models, 33
operation meanings, 118–119, 129
pencil-and-paper computations, 214,
218–219, 221, 226, 231, 234–235
percents, 284
place value, 174–177
Symmetry, 361
axis of, 372–373
line, 370–372
rotational, 372–373
in solids, 372–373

Table representations of functions,
458–459, 462
Tables, 55
Talented students, 502, 512–515
Tallies, 414
Tally charts, 420
Tangrams, 319–320, 357, 359
Tape measures, 317–318
Tasks
differentiated, 488
performance, 39–40, 66–76
planning, 42
presentation of, 483
questions to clarify, 42–43
short, 484–485
simple versions, 44, 55–56, 135
types of, 47–50
worthwhile, 34–35, 40
Teacher-directed lessons, 485–487
Teachers
and algorithms, 218–221, 223,
230–232
choices of questions, 18
developmental approaches, 33–37
doing mathematics, 13
expectations of, 508
impact of, 510
new role of, 19–20
and problem solving, 42–47
rubrics used by, 71–72
traditional role, 10–11
Teacher's editions of textbooks, 498
Teaching, as problem-solving endeavor,
41–42, 50–53
Teaching Children Mathematics, 48, 528
Teaching standards, 7
Technology, 4, 517–519. See also Calculators; Computers
Ten, 170–171
Ten-frame facts, 148–150
Ten-frames, 103–104, 147–148, 151
Ten-makes-one relationship, 166–167
Tens
computation with, 180–182, 194

groupings of, 164–167, 169–171, 188
Ten-to-one relationships, 276–277
Tessellations, 360–361, 377–378
Testing of ideas, encouragement of, 45
Tests, 82–83, 158–159
Tetrahedrons, 382
Textbooks, 497–499
Theoretical probability, 409–410
Think-addition, 149–153
Think-multiplication, 152
Think-pair-share strategy, 484–485
Thousand, 184
Three-digit number names, 174
Tiles, shapes made from, 352–353, 360,
377–378
Tiling patterns, 343
Time, measurement of, 336–338
Timed tests, 158–159
Tool software, 523–524
Top numbers, in fractions, 243–244
Trades/trading, 215
Trading activities, 215–217
Trading base 10 models, 166–167
Trading games
forward/backward, 215–216
recording in, 216–217
variations, 215–217
Traditional algorithms, 192–193,
213–215
Traditional classrooms, 10–11, 502
Translation problems, 48
Translations, 48–49, 118–119
Trapezoids, 19, 25, 333–334, 361–362
Tree diagrams, 17–18, 414–416
Triangles, 318–320, 333–334, 342, 344,
356, 361, 365, 381
Try-and-adjust strategies, 56–57
Tsuruda, Gary, 24–25
Turns, 355
Two-apart facts, 148
Two-digit divisors, 228, 233–234
Two-digit multipliers, 226–227
Two-digit number names, 173–174
Two-step problems, 135–136

Understanding, 27
conceptual knowledge, 27–28
construction of, 22–23
individual nature of, 29
instrumental, 27–29
models for, 30–33
problems, 40–41
procedural knowledge, 28–29
relational, 27–30
strategies for, 51
Understanding-the-task strategies, 54
Unit fractions, 246
Unit position, designated by decimal point,
277–278
Unit-rate method, 296
Units of measure, 310–313
informal, 313, 315, 320, 323–324
standard, 313, 326–330, 339
for time, 336–338
Unlike denominators, 263
Unstructured attribute materials, 393

Upper extreme, 426
Upper quartile, 426

Values
defined, 393
and grading, 87
Van Hiele, Pierre, 345–348, 388
Van Hiele-Geldof, Dina, 345–348, 388
Variables, 432, 457, 466, 473
and assessment, 478
defined, 474
expressions as quantities, 474–476
from formulas, 476–477
misunderstandings about, 473–474
solving equations, 477
uses of, 474
Variance, 427
Verbs, for doing mathematics, 13
Vertices, 363, 365
Video, 528
Vision impairment, 503
Visualization, 346
Volume
common solid shapes, 335–337
measurement of, 310–311, 322–323, 381
and ratio, 302–303
standard units of, 327–329
Web sites, 528–529
Wedges, of angles, 326–327
Weight
measurement of, 310–311, 323–325
standard units of, 328–329
Whole, 126, 241–243, 245–248, 265
Whole-number exponents, 440
Willingness to try, 393
Windows of Opportunity, 503
Word problems, 40, 48
for addition, 119–122
for division, 126–130
for multiplication, 126–130
operation meanings from, 117–118
for subtraction, 119–122
Word processors, 523
Word stories, 48, 117, 134–136
Working backwards from solutions, 57
Worksheets, 216–217, 486–487
Workstations, 486–488
Writing, in mathematics, 492
practical suggestions, 494–495
types of, 493–494
value of, 492–493
Written responses/reports, 35, 78–81, 137,
484, 490, 492
Written symbols, for place value, 174–177

Zero
role in division, 134
role in multiplication, 134, 154–155
Zero facts, 144–145, 150, 154–155
Zero property, 125, 134
Zeros
difficulties in subtraction, 221
dividing factors with, 199
multiplying factors with, 197
0–99 chart, 175–176, 180–181

BLACKLINE MASTERS AND MATERIALS CONSTRUCTION TIPS

BLACKLINE MASTERS

Permission is given to reproduce any of the Blackline Masters for classroom use. Pages are perforated.

Dot cards   1–6
10 × 10 multiplication array   7
Missing-part blanks   8
Base 10 materials grid   9
10 × 10 bean chart   10
Hundreds master for bean stick base 10 pieces   11
Little base-ten-frames   12–13
Place-value mat (with ten-frames)   14
Base 10 grid paper   15
Addition and subtraction record blanks   16
Multiplication and division record blanks   17
Blank hundreds or 0–99 chart (10 × 10 square)   18
0–99 chart   19
Four 0–99 charts   20
Circular fraction pieces   21–23
10 × 10 grids   24
Hundredths disk   25
10,000 grid   26
2-cm square grid   27
1-cm square grid   28
0.5-cm square grid   29
1-cm square dot grid   30
2-cm isometric grid   31
1-cm isometric dot grid   32
1-cm square/diagonal grid   33
1-cm hex grid   34
Geoboard pattern   35
Geoboard recording sheets   36
Tangrams and Five Easy Pieces   37
Woozle Cards   38

SUGGESTIONS FOR USE AND CONSTRUCTION OF MATERIALS

Card Stock Materials

A good way to have many materials made quickly and easily for students is to have them duplicated on *card stock* at a photocopy store. Card stock is a heavy paper, not quite as heavy as tagboard, that comes in a variety of colors. It is also called *cover stock* or *index stock*. The copy stores use it for report covers, and it can be printed on, just as paper can be. The price is about twice that of paper.

Card stock can be laminated and then cut into smaller pieces, if desired, and the laminate adheres very well. Laminate first, and then cut into pieces afterward. Otherwise you will need to cut each piece twice.

Materials are best kept in plastic bags with zip-type closures. Freezer bags are recommended for durability. Punch a hole near the top of the bag so that you do not store air. Lots of small bags can be stuffed into the largest bags. You can always see what you have stored in the bags.

The following list is a suggestion for materials that can be made from card stock using the masters in this section. Quantity suggestions are also given.

Dot Cards

First make a duplicate of the first page. This is so that there will be adequate cards with 1, 2, and 3 dots. One complete set of cards will serve four to six children. Duplicate each set in a different color so that mixed sets can be separated easily. Laminate and then cut with a paper cutter.

10 × 10 Multiplication Array

Make one per student in any color. Lamination is suggested. Provide each student with an L-shaped piece of tagboard.

Base 10 Pieces (Centimeter Grid)

Use the grid (number 9), and make a master as directed. Run copies on white card stock. One sheet will make 4 hundreds and

10 tens or 4 hundreds and a lot of ones. Mount the printed card stock on white poster board using either a dry-mount press or permanent spray adhesive. (Spray adhesive can be purchased in art supply stores. It is very effective but messy to handle.) Cut into pieces with a paper cutter. For the tens and ones pieces, it is recommended that you mount the index stock onto *mount board* or *illustration board,* also available in art supply stores. This material is thicker and will make the pieces easier to handle. It is recommended that you *not* laminate the base 10 pieces. A kit consisting of 10 hundreds, 30 tens, and 30 ones is adequate for each student or pair of students.

Bean Stick Base 10 Pieces

Use dried beans (great northern, pinto, etc.) to make bean sticks. Craft sticks can be purchased in craft stores in boxes of 500. Use white glue (such as Elmer's) or a glue gun. Also dribble a row of glue over the beans to keep them from splitting off the sticks. (The white glue dries clear.) For hundreds, use the master mounted on poster board as described for the grids.

Little Base-Ten-Frames

There are two masters for these materials. One has full ten-frames and the other has 1 to 9 dots, including two with 5 dots. Copy the 1-to-9 master on one color of card stock and the full ten-frames on another. Cut off most of the excess stock (do not trim) and then laminate. Cut into little ten-frames. Each set consists of 20 pieces: 10 full ten-frames and 10 of the 1-to-9 pieces, including 2 fives. Make a set for each child.

Place-Value Mat (with Ten-Frames)

Mats can be duplicated on any pastel card stock. It is recommended that you not laminate these because they tend to curl and counters like beans slide around too much. Make one for every child.

One way to make a three-place place-value mat is simply to tape a half sheet of blank card stock to the left edge of a two-place mat. Use strapping tape (filament tape used for packages). The tape will act as a hinge and permit the extra piece to be folded under for storage.

Circular Fraction Pieces

First make three copies of each page of the master. Cut the disks apart and tape onto blank pages with three of the same type on a page. You will then have a separate master for each size with three full circles per master. Duplicate each master on a different color card stock. Laminate and then cut the circles out. A kit for one or two students should have two circles of each size piece.

Hundredths Disk

These disks can be made on paper but are much more satisfying on card stock. Duplicate the master on two contrasting colors. Laminate and cut the circles and also the slot on the dotted line. The smiley face is used as a decimal point on the desktop. Make a set for each student. It's easy and worthwhile.

Tangrams and Five Easy Pieces

Both tangrams and Five Easy Pieces should be copied on card stock and then laminated. Especially for younger children, the card stock should first be mounted on poster board to make the pieces a bit thicker and easier to put together in puzzles. You will want one set of each per student. Keep individual sets in plastic bags.

Woozle Cards

Copy the Woozle Card master on white or off-white card stock. You need two copies per set. Before laminating, color one set one color and the other a different color. An easy way to color the cards is to make one pass around the inside of each Woozle, leaving the rest of the creature white. If you color the entire Woozle, the dots may not show up. Make one set for every four students.

Transparencies

A copy of any page can be made into a transparency with thermal transparency masters and a transparency machine. Masters come in various colors on a clear background and in blackline on various colored backgrounds. Follow the directions on the box. (Check with your media specialist.) Photocopiers can also be used to make transparencies.

Some masters make fine transparency mats to use for demonstration purposes on the overhead. The 10×10 array and the large geoboard are examples. The place-value mat can be used with strips and squares or with counters and cups directly on the overhead. The 10×10 bean chart is a useful hundreds board, as is the blank hundreds board. The missing-part blank and the record blanks for the four algorithms are pages that you may wish to use as write-on transparencies. Of course, you will want to copy these and many other pages on paper for your students to write on.

A transparency of the 10,000 grid is the easiest way there is to show 10,000 or to model four-place decimal numbers. You will need to be careful in making the transparency. If too dark, the squares run together, and if too light, you will find that some squares do not reproduce. It can be done! If you pull the overhead away from the screen until the square is as large as possible, each tiny square can be seen across the average room and individual squares or strips of squares can be colored with a pen.

All of the line and dot grids are useful to have available as transparencies. You may find it a good idea to make several copies of each and keep them in a folder where you can get to them easily.

For the Woozle Cards, dot cards, and little base-ten-frames, make a reduction of the master on a photocopy machine. Then make transparencies of the small cards, cut them apart, and use them on the overhead. The dot cards and little base-ten-frames are best on a colored transparency. Use two colors for the little base-ten-frames. The Woozle Cards are best on a clear transparency. Color them with a permanent transparency marker.

Making Geoboards

It is possible to mass-produce geoboards so that large numbers of them can be made quickly and clearly. The master (number 35) is for a $7\frac{1}{2}$-inch board. Seventy-two boards this size can be made for about $20. Get one or two other teachers to go in on them with you to share the cost.

Use $\frac{5}{8}$-inch particle board. This can be found at lumber stores or home supply stores and is very inexpensive, especially if purchased in a 4-by-8-foot sheet. Have someone with a table saw cut the board into $7\frac{1}{2}$-inch squares. These squares should be cut fairly accurately. (Go to the shop teacher at the junior or senior high school for help.) Purchase 1-inch #16 wire brads. These have no heads. The #16 refers to the thickness. You want the nails as thick as possible so that they will not bend. Buy nails in bulk at a hardware store. You will want about a pound of nails to make 25 boards.

Make a "geoboard maker" out of a piece of $\frac{1}{2}$-inch-thick plywood or similar lumber. You will need about a 1-foot square. Tape a copy of the geoboard master in the center of the board. Nail strips of wood (about 1 inch by 6 inches) around all four sides of the master. These strips should be about $\frac{1}{16}$ of an inch outside of the outline of the geoboard. This will allow the squares of particle board to fit snugly but allow for minor errors in cutting them out. Now drill small holes through each dot on the master. The holes should be just barely large enough for one of the brads to be pulled through. Be certain that the holes are drilled perpendicular to the board.

Now you are ready to make geoboards. Put the geoboard maker over one of the squares of particle board. Place a nail in each hole, and hammer it flush. Then with a screwdriver, gently pry the geoboard maker off the board. The nails will each be a uniform $\frac{1}{2}$ inch in height and all perfectly arranged. Try not to bang on the geoboard maker because it will eventually suffer from overuse. However, one maker should serve for the production of several hundred geoboards.

You may want to paint your geoboards a dark color before nailing in the nails (or spray-paint them afterward). This makes it easier to see brown rubber bands on the boards.

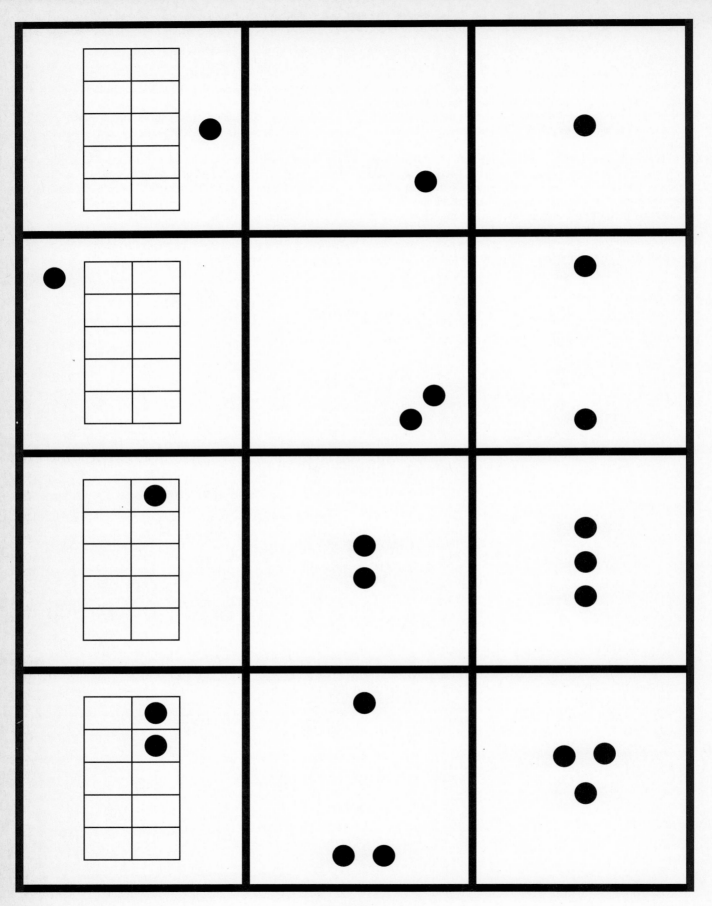

Dot cards—1

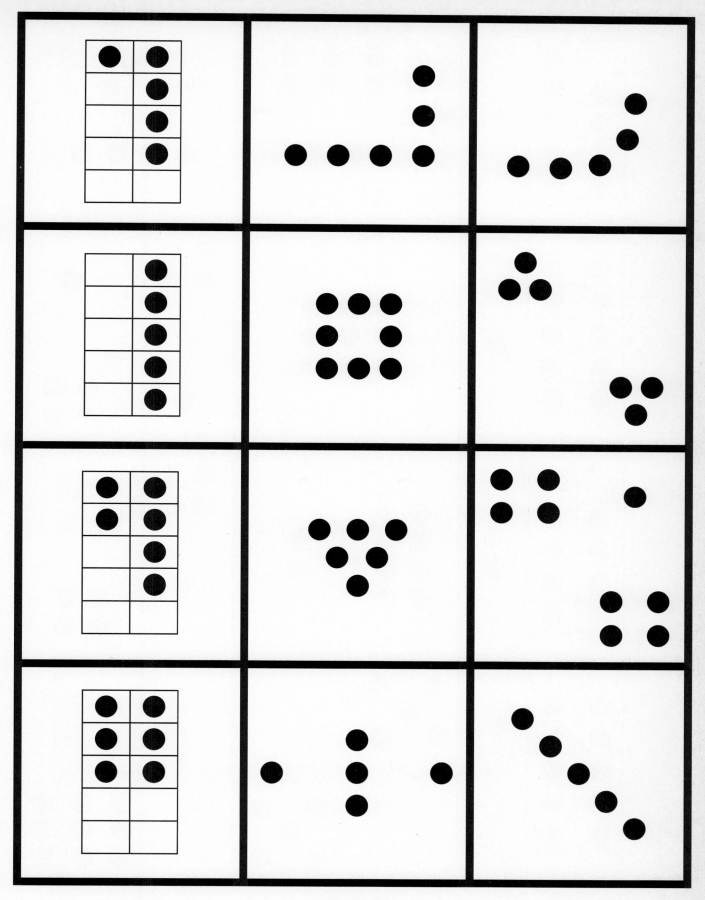

Dot cards—2

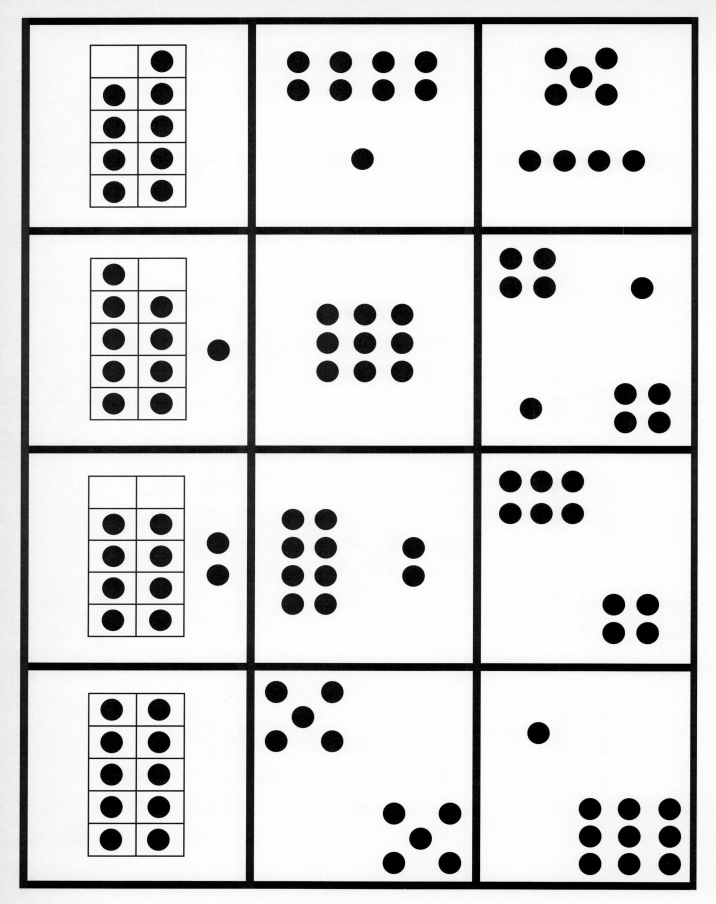

Dot cards—3

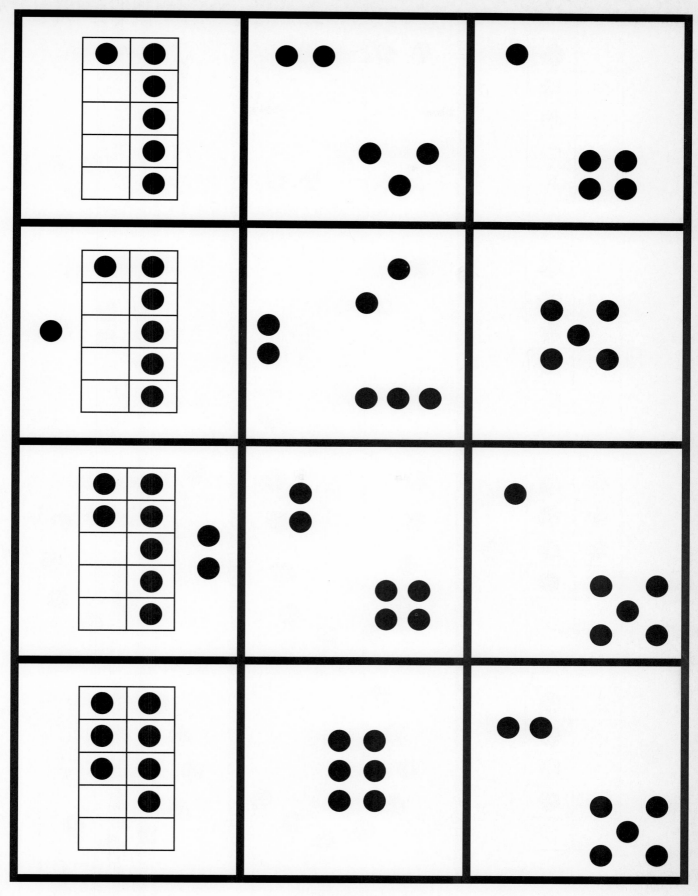

Dot cards—4

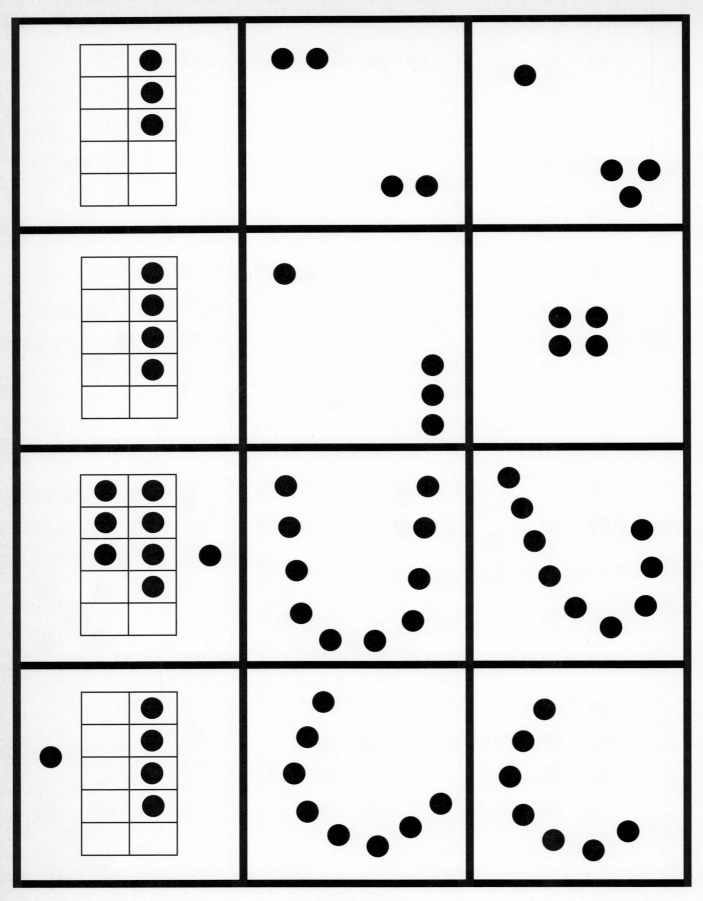

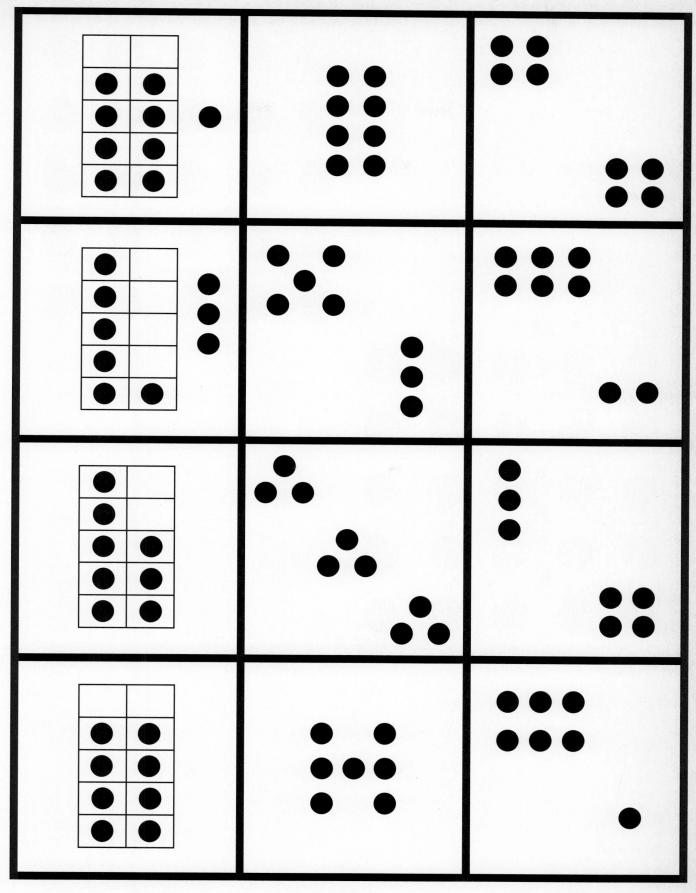

Dot cards—6

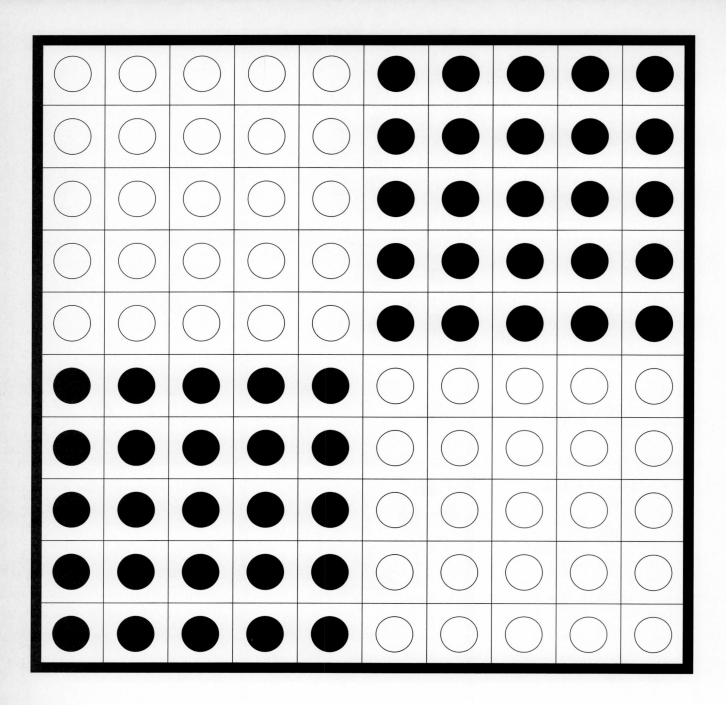

Missing-part blanks—8

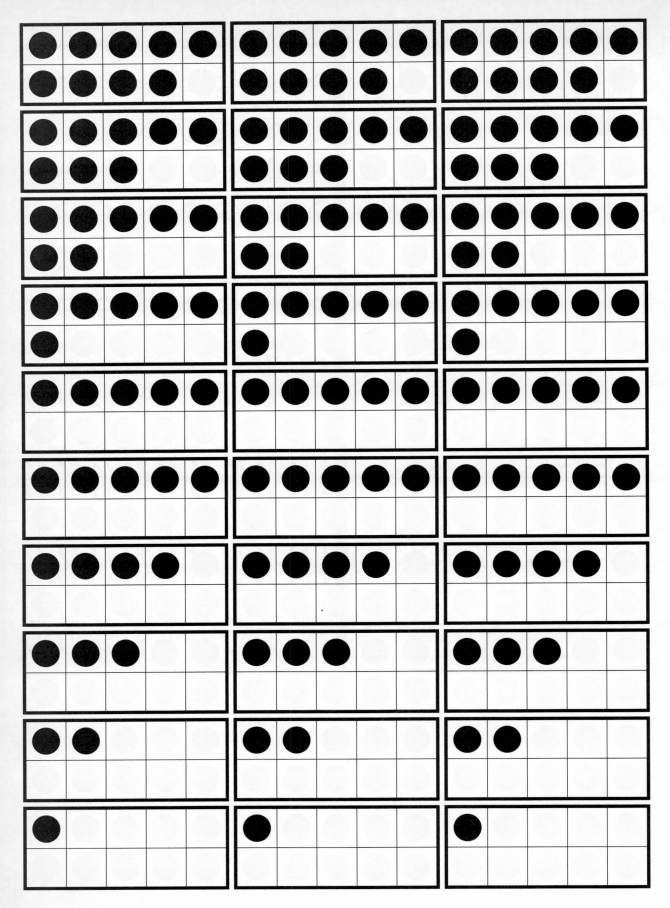

Place-value mat (with ten-frames)—14

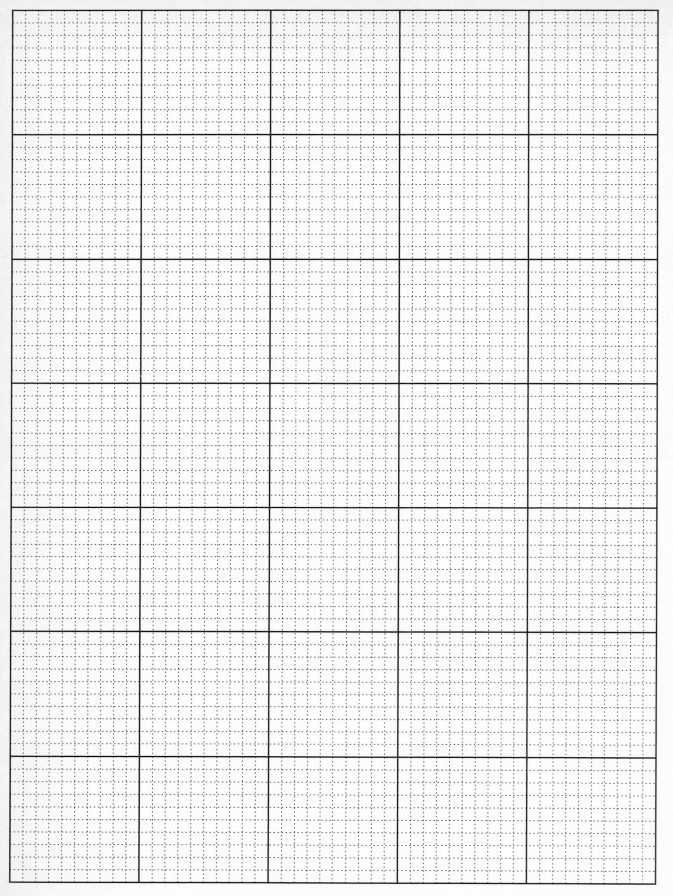

Base 10 grid paper—15

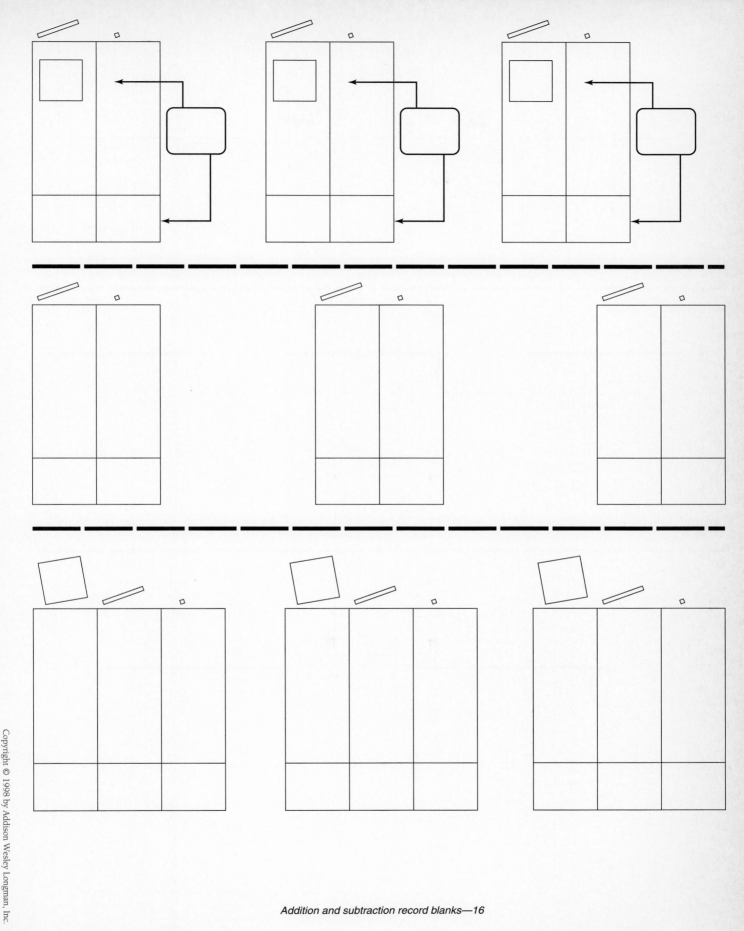

Addition and subtraction record blanks—16

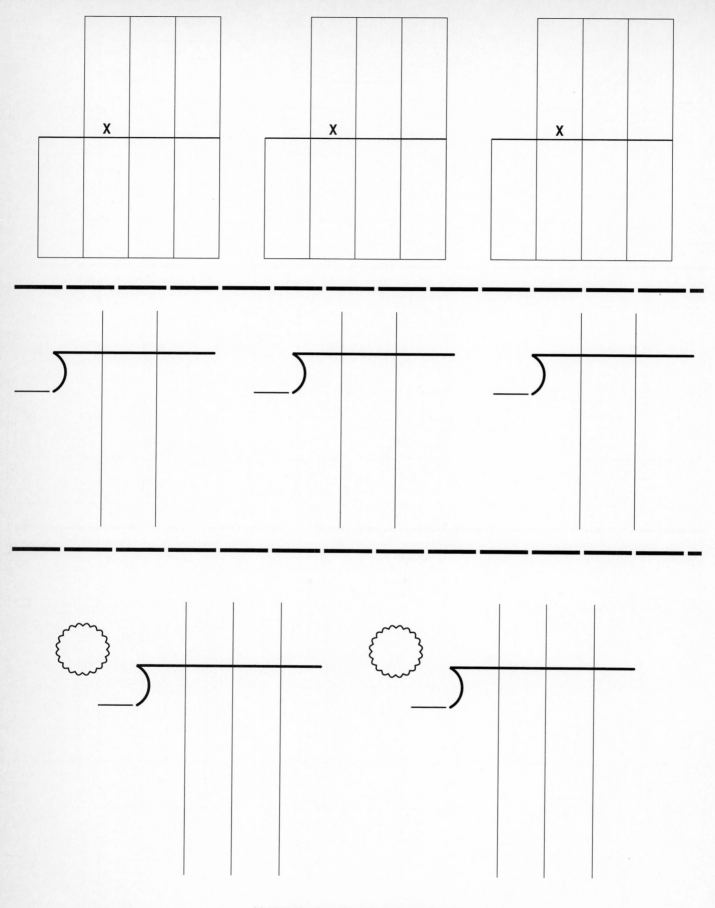

Multiplication and division record blanks—17

Blank hundreds or 0–99 chart (10 × 10 square)—18

0	1	2	3	4	5	6	7	8	9
10	11	12	13	14	15	16	17	18	19
20	21	22	23	24	25	26	27	28	29
30	31	32	33	34	35	36	37	38	39
40	41	42	43	44	45	46	47	48	49
50	51	52	53	54	55	56	57	58	59
60	61	62	63	64	65	66	67	68	69
70	71	72	73	74	75	76	77	78	79
80	81	82	83	84	85	86	87	88	89
90	91	92	93	94	95	96	97	98	99

0	1	2	3	4	5	6	7	8	9
10	11	12	13	14	15	16	17	18	19
20	21	22	23	24	25	26	27	28	29
30	31	32	33	34	35	36	37	38	39
40	41	42	43	44	45	46	47	48	49
50	51	52	53	54	55	56	57	58	59
60	61	62	63	64	65	66	67	68	69
70	71	72	73	74	75	76	77	78	79
80	81	82	83	84	85	86	87	88	89
90	91	92	93	94	95	96	97	98	99

0	1	2	3	4	5	6	7	8	9
10	11	12	13	14	15	16	17	18	19
20	21	22	23	24	25	26	27	28	29
30	31	32	33	34	35	36	37	38	39
40	41	42	43	44	45	46	47	48	49
50	51	52	53	54	55	56	57	58	59
60	61	62	63	64	65	66	67	68	69
70	71	72	73	74	75	76	77	78	79
80	81	82	83	84	85	86	87	88	89
90	91	92	93	94	95	96	97	98	99

0	1	2	3	4	5	6	7	8	9
10	11	12	13	14	15	16	17	18	19
20	21	22	23	24	25	26	27	28	29
30	31	32	33	34	35	36	37	38	39
40	41	42	43	44	45	46	47·	48	49
50	51	52	53	54	55	56	57	58	59
60	61	62	63	64	65	66	67	68	69
70	71	72	73	74	75	76	77	78	79
80	81	82	83	84	85	86	87	88	89
90	91	92	93	94	95	96	97	98	99

0	1	2	3	4	5	6	7	8	9
10	11	12	13	14	15	16	17	18	19
20	21	22	23	24	25	26	27	28	29
30	31	32	33	34	35	36	37	38	39
40	41	42	43	44	45	46	47	48	49
50	51	52	53	54	55	56	57	58	59
60	61	62	63	64	65	66	67	68	69
70	71	72	73	74	75	76	77	78	79
80	81	82	83	84	85	86	87	88	89
90	91	92	93	94	95	96	97	98	99

Circular fraction pieces—21

Circular fraction pieces—22

Circular fraction pieces—23

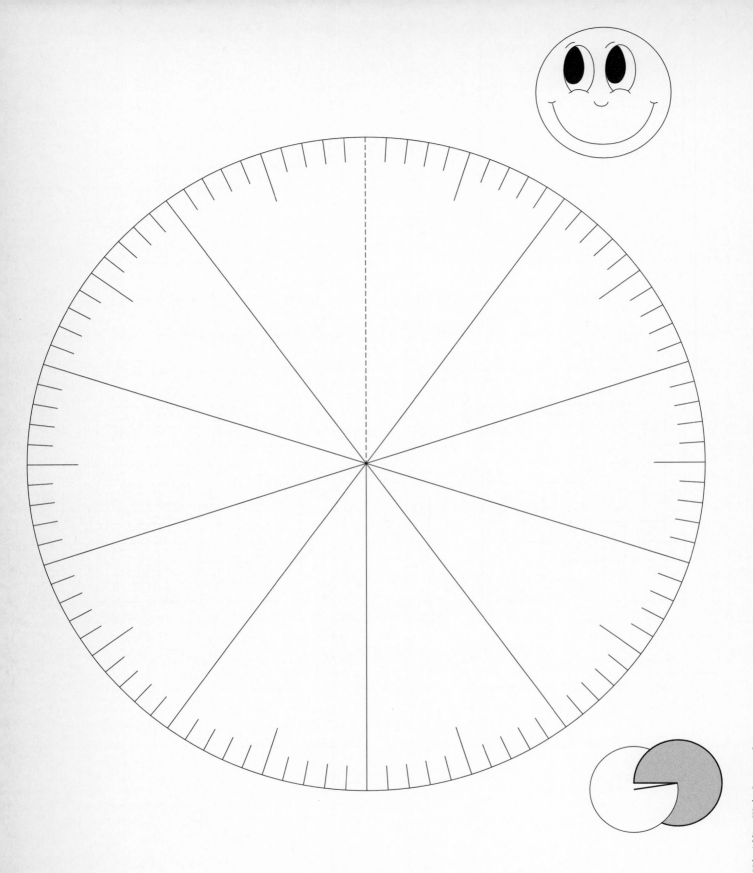

Hundredths disk—25

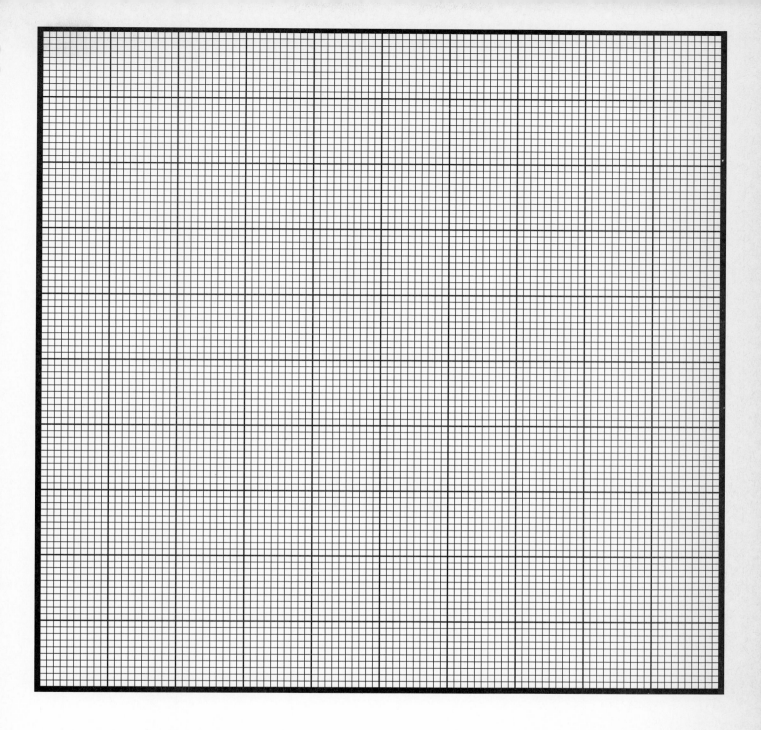

2-cm square grid—27

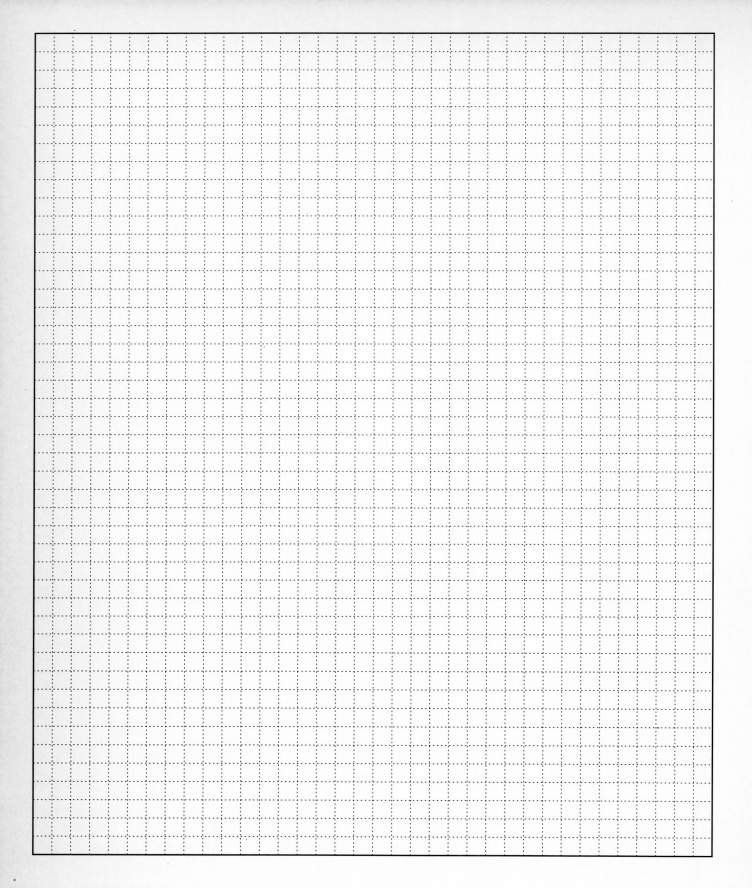

0.5-cm square grid—29

1-cm square dot grid—30

2-cm isometric grid—31

1-cm isometric dot grid—32

1-cm square/diagonal grid—33

1-cm hex grid—34

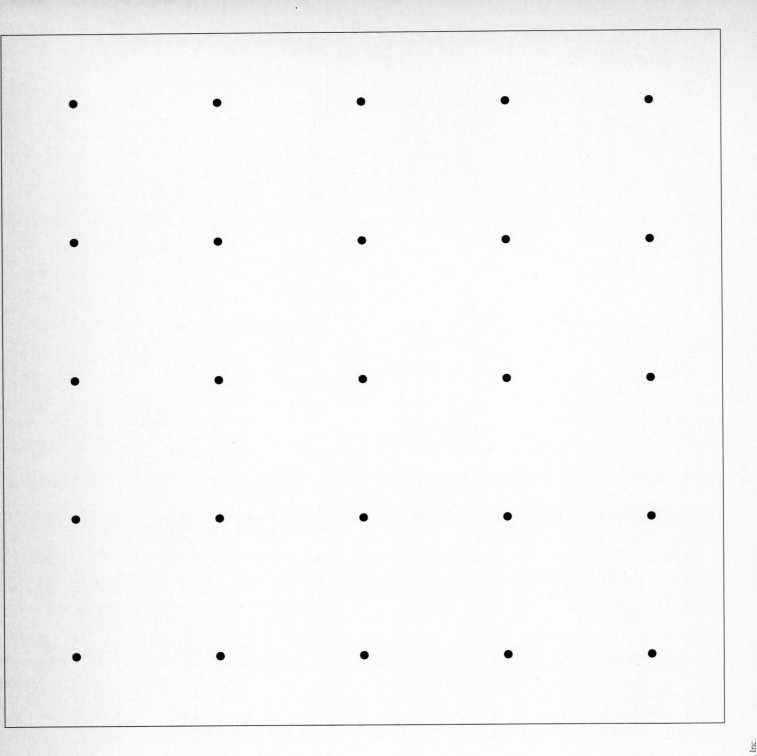

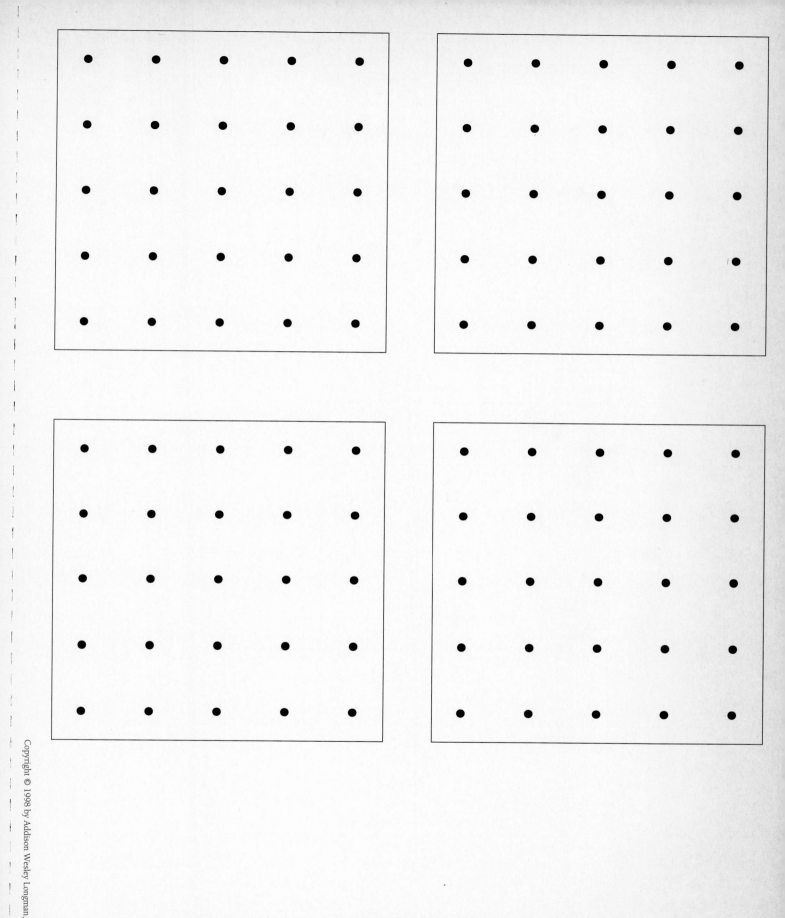

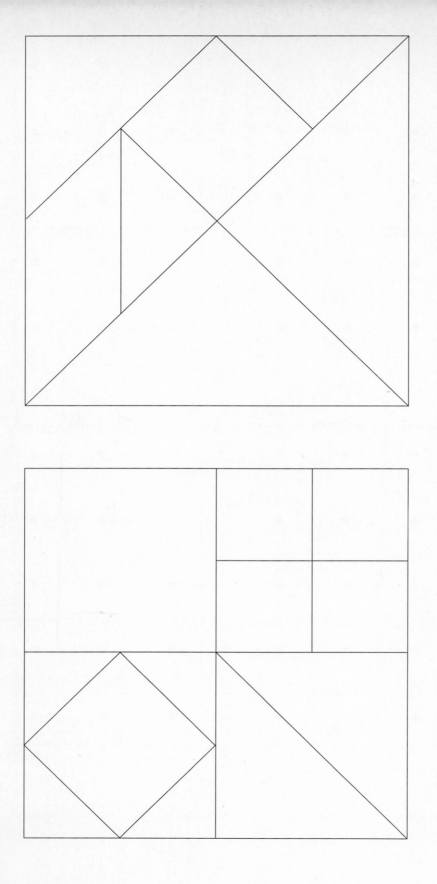